# On Signs

*A Semiotics Reader*

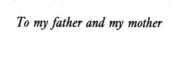

*To my father and my mother*

# On Signs

EDITED BY
## MARSHALL BLONSKY

Basil Blackwell

© Marshall Blonsky 1985

First published 1985
Reprinted 1986

Basil Blackwell Ltd
108 Cowley Road, Oxford OX4 1JF, UK

**British Library Cataloguing in Publication Data**

On signs: a semiotics reader
1. Semiotics
I. Blonsky, Marshall
001.51     P99

ISBN 0–631–10261–2
ISBN 0–631–10271–X

Typeset by Oxford Publishing Services
Printed in Great Britain by T. J. Press, Padstow

# Contents

# Preface

A consciousness about signs, semiotics, now pervades social life from the most abstruse of academic pursuits to the most tough-minded of commercial enterprises. Most publications about signs and meanings do not recognize the broad and sweeping nature of the semiotic concern. I have tried to gather the various strands of semiotic inquiry and arrange them so that they will serve the diverse publics and permit even practitioners in the field to recognize and acquaint themselves with the more arcane and difficult pursuits that are part of this discipline.

This, among other reasons, accounts for the fact that you will find highly theoretical and learned articles side by side with much more everyday and popular types of discourse – both of which partake equally of the semiotic impetus. This collection will therefore aid the student, provoke the scholar, be of value to the businessman or woman, be of interest to people in politics, educate those in the media and please and amuse the general reader.

There are three parts to this book: 'Seeing Signs' is an entrée to a mode of consciousness that still, today, after twenty and more years of semiotic activity, disturbs and wounds many people. This semiotic "head", or eye, sees the world as an immense message, replete with signs that can and do deceive us and lie about the world's condition. This is because signs are entirely independent of the objective, natural properties of the entities towards which they point. The arbitrary is a fundamental concept of semiotics. In the seventies, in the heady days, professors enjoyed citing Mallarmé, finding in his work subtle theories of the sign and its arbitrary nature. The line of verse plays at being nature, poems set up structures within which the arbitrary acts as if it were suspended. But it is only that: an *act*. Literary language isn't based on sensation, the referent of "wood" isn't the sensation of wood. The "horror of the forest" (Mallarmé's reference to forest-symbolism) isn't the thing itself. The text can at most suggest the sentiment associated to the thing. The word doesn't evoke the sentiment of an object, but rather, its having been put down on paper, put into writing (see Mallarmé, *Oeuvres complètes*, Paris, Gallimard, 1945, 365–6).

So if the sign isn't the thing, we can use the sign to lie. Buy a copy of the *The Name of the Rose*. Skip over the compendia of heretical movements. Speed read the language of theological disputation. Jump over all the Latin. In fact, we need never even read the heart of the story. Fingering the embossed, cowled monk on the American paperback cover as we ride the bus, shop, entertain friends, we can tell the absolute fiction of our erudition and complicity with the Establishment's fascination for signs and detection, mediaevalism and apocalypse. And on Saturday night, when the code requires a film not a book as entertainment, we can watch *The [Evil] Empire Strikes Back*, a film about the Soviet Union which never refers to the Soviet Union.

Signs are not related to the things or states of the world they appear to designate, *but they stand for, they stand in front of, quieter intents, words and deeds*. Having read their surfaces, we can know the secrets in lying signs. *Whether* to know them, whether to jump from the sign to the silent agents of material existence, from the lie to its concealed, distant masters, from the signifier to what is forcing it to signify, this is a crisis of what has been until now tranquil, domesticated semiotics.

'Understanding the Meaning of Signs' enables the reader to attain a historical perspective, presenting key lectures, seminars and conference papers by the leaders in the field. Delivered principally in French, a few in English and one in Russian, in the main in the seventies, they are didactic. Their utterers were pedagogic – etymologically, *pais-agagos*: they were leaders of children.

Probably it will be difficult for the reader to form a concept of those heady days in Paris, Milan or in the European countryside, or at Yale, Berkeley and Oxford, when (I am not mythifying it) adults acted like eager children, listening to the Word from scholars and authors who were in love with felt discovery, whose discourse and minds were young and generous. It is to give the reader the flavour of this past intentionality that I asked Kristeva, Marin, Jakobson (while he lived), De Certeau and others here for their *pièces de résistance*, keys to unlock a necessary past.

The articles have been arranged – Lacan with Eco, Ivanov with Derrida – to create a "global utterer"; a thinker of good will who in his/her search for method doesn't make a fetish of any end as a privileged place to arrive at, to the detriment of any other end. The reader is presented, finally, with Non-Method, or if he/she wants, the *paideia*, the eccentric tracing of possibility. The texts giving concepts, and those applying them, enable the reader to *experiment*.

'Signs of Life' opens semiotics to the world today, and initiates a *vita nuova*. In this part, the authors attempt to bring the discipline to life, carrying its clean theory into turbulent application. Today, the discourse on signs has splintered into adversarial schools speaking impenetrable languages (deconstruction, Lacanian psychoanalysis, and so on), each with a living or dead king of its castle (celebrity professor, international specialist). As if the schools had taken vows of abstinence, they talk of past cultural artefacts or present canonized objects – not of government, or business, or the busyness of the world.

"The middle of my life is nothing other than the moment when I discover death as real", Roland Barthes said in his 1978 lecture, "Proust and Me". He continued:

> And then all of a sudden is produced this evidence, on the one hand, that I no longer have time to try several lives. I have to choose my last life, my new life, my *vita nuova*; and on the other hand, I must leave this tenebrous state where the wear and tear of repeated work and mourning have conducted me.

Now he is dead, as are Foucault, Lacan and Jakobson. Semiotics has suffered a catastrophe. The desire for a new life for semiotics comes from these events.

The reader will find here several founders of the discipline as well as the probing ideas of unexpected people who are exploring it. Sebeok is a consultant to the Bechtel Group, fathering "Atomicsemiotics"; Franco is thinking her way into Latin American ruling circles as they "recode" women; Weintraub is using semiotics to facilitate entry into the marketplace. Some of the writers here are ill at ease. Jameson shows that Flaubert's *Coeur Simple* doesn't reflect social reality or class relations; it programs its reader, trains him/her to live within the joyless cubicles that have become the modern home. But other writing here is sunny of disposition. Klein tells with aplomb why the face one "puts on" – and photographs – must be blank save for this message: "I'm fine, hope you are." Radicals, technocrats, aspirers to the ruling circle, the writers here attempt to destroy and recreate semiotics, to broaden its themes and topics, to reach out to affairs of the world.

America gave its signs to Europeans to decipher to make semiotics. Part III brings the system of ideas called semiotics back to America and into the polemic of the Third World.

No anthology of this sort can claim to be exhaustive and to be fully representative of a field that is vast and beyond the mastery of a single individual. Besides this general disclaimer, I wish to draw attention to two areas in particular which have been given shorter shrift than one might have expected. First, there is a large variety of semiotic practices in film analysis today. To select among them would be to adjudicate current polemics, battles much too big to warrant insertion in a book of this kind. I felt it preferable to choose a relatively early mode of doing film semiotics on a classical film; an article that shows the potential of a relationship between film and semiotics, but which is far from exhaustive. Second, it is a fact that semiotics was fundamentally initiated and adumbrated by men who were unaware they were putting forward a methodology that would have the effect of loosening their stranglehold on modes of social analysis. This book is a record of what did happen and a glimpse into the future, and surely can point to new paths for those who wish to learn from, and exceed, the patriarchs.

In the various schools of our knowledge and in our practices, it has become a cliché to speak of forms of crisis. Many of these crises have to do with our inability to discover the meanings of objects, of artefacts, of processes now under way. In this book are gathered essays by individuals who propose the ways of dealing with this problem of meaning and thus, perhaps, propose also a way of living with the crises.

*Marshall Blonsky*

# Friends

This book was several years in the making. The process began when practitioners in this field serenely thought they were explicators of the world's sense. It ended when several began to suspect they had all along been complicit with a system that they thought they had been denouncing.

Over the course of these years, commissions had to be given out, fulfilled; permissions granted – interests and egos colliding; translations accomplished – the translators all the while cursing: "But this isn't French *in the original*!" Several of the articles here speak of "the system", the Establishment. Had it not smiled (key people saying "yes", permitting, writing, translating, designing), this book would not exist.

I have all of my authors to thank, of course. But special thanks go to a little cortège of friends who, each in a different way, brought this book into existence. Here they are.

Umberto Eco, Richard Howard and Wlad Godzich remind me of Lacan talking of bliss, *jouissance*: it is there when you are *not* parcelling out pleasure, it is the opposite of the usufruct, that legal word that tells you to have so much enjoyment and no more. During the planning moments of this book, Eco, Howard and Godzich spent their knowledge and intellectual pleasure without thought of limit.

If a book could have a *consigliere*, this book's was Wendy Schacher. She was really my godmother. She put her political and literary savvy into sensitive decision points. Arthur Wang intervened at a delicate moment as did Jean Franco and Geoffrey Hartman and I thank them for it. Michel de Certeau and Susan Meiselas gave enormously of their precious work. And Bernard Whalen gave his journalistic support when such propping was rare; the discipline owes him thanks. Matthew Ward and Edward Schneider often felt like Sisyphus, rolling stones; but they translated what sought to be science into what I believe is literature. Richard Miller performed the wonder of turning what many have termed hermetic language into elegant, if not plain, English. And my friend Richard Howard, quite simply, taught me the meaning of the words "brilliant man" and translator. John Shepley, translating from the Italian, put his years of literary know-how into this book. Barbara Spackman, Stephen Rudy and Stuart Schneiderman must also be recognized for their translational skills.

Near the end, I come to the editorially cunning Holly Keith, my personal assistant, and to Harriet Barry, Patricia Connolly and Valery Rose, very wise editors. Pages like these often bore readers (who may have disappeared by now), but I hope that at least a few will know that I thank Bill Sisler, John Davey and Eric Halpern, my publishers, for a patience beyond professionalism. And thank also Ronald Weintraub, Milton Glaser and Ino and Annamaria Cassini, adamantine supporters of this project and of the discipline.

M.B.

MARSHALL BLONSKY

# Introduction
# The Agony of Semiotics:
# Reassessing the Discipline

> I have never kept a diary. History, as far as I am concerned, is just a byproduct of action.
>
> Fidel Castro

> HOEDERER: . . . Purity is an idea for a yogi or a monk. You intellectuals and bourgeois anarchists use it as a pretext for doing nothing. To do nothing, to remain motionless, arms at your sides, wearing kid gloves. Well, I have dirty hands. Right up to the elbows. I've plunged them in filth and blood.
>
> Jean-Paul Sartre,
> *Dirty Hands*

## Semiotics: A Crisis of Theory

I was in the audience at New York University in the autumn of 1978 when Roland Barthes gave the season's James Lecture, "Proust and Me". When it was over, I saw, as Barthes and his entourage made their slow way up the theatre to the exits, shaking hands, that the faces were peculiar. None in that obsequious procession had the look required by the code of the evening: jubilatorily intellectual, smug in the Presence. It was a funereal cortège that I was seeing. And for good reason. Here is a fragment of what Barthes delivered:

> A moment comes when what one has done, what one writes, one's work, one's practices, all of it seems a little like an endlessly repeated substance doomed to repetition. . . . And then suddenly you see the future that remains to you, the future of writing, the future of work, as a kind of foreclosure of everything new . . .

... the subject who sees his life foreclosed of any possible novelty ... is quite simply in jail. That is the definition of jail, isn't it, when there is nothing new possible?[1]

As Barthes' friend Richard Howard said (as he translated this discourse of halts, fadings, sighs, strewn in French with the untranslatable "n'est-ce pas"): "There is nothing didactic about it, there is a ceaseless, conscious, self-questioning speaker."[2] Barthes goes on:

This is part of all intellectual work. At a specific moment, the future appears to you as denying, rejecting any possibility of risk, as doomed to repetition. And you see the future, your future of working until your death, as a kind of routine. You *know*, as they say.

Barthes had turned his semiotic instrument from texts onto life, onto his own life. He had applied Jacques Lacan's idea of the fading self (Lacan, 1973, ch. 16) to his productive life. Given Lacan's intentional unreadability, it is best to find this fading self in the literature that prefigured Lacan. Rousseau gives the example of party talk, of telling anecdotes, which the speaker calls "the babble of conversation":

Its progress, more rapid than my ideas, forcing me almost always to speak before thinking, has often suggested to me stupidities and ineptitudes that my reason disapproved and my heart disavowed at the moment they escaped from my mouth, but which, preceding my own judgement, could not be reformed by its censure. (Rousseau, 1959, p. 1033 – editor's translation)

Rousseau is writing about a syntax of narrative that governs us (just as in conversation, you always speak faster than you think). To speak faster than you think means, for Rousseau as he converses, and for his listeners, that *ideas are going to be lacking*. The discourse goes on at the party, but sense or meaning will sometimes be missing.[3]

Richard Howard was saying that he saw his friend Roland regressing, fading in the very lecture *delivery* – his friend's social prosthesis, syntax, was failing. Lacan taught that there can be an uttering that doesn't utter anything, an

[1] "Proust and Me", delivered 6 November 1978, has not yet been published in English.
[2] Howard translated the text orally in a public conversation with me, called "Residual Barthes", at a New York University Department of French symposium, 11 May 1983.
[3] Rousseau is saying that, conversing, we tell the pure contingency of what happens to come into our "heads". We are dominated by rapidity, by a pressure to come up with something as we try to fill in the gaps. This leaves a very considerable site open for "slug" language, brute signifiers without signifieds. If, as Rousseau suggests, our texts obey a logic of keeping going, then they are not willed by the self. A failure to issue in meaning is built into them. Sense can always be lacking, and it is made to be lacking – religion uses repetition to an enormous extent to make sense flee, to make utterers into believers.

uttering without statement – what speaks when we sigh. Richard Howard thought he heard Barthes sigh (I would say fade) that night as he talked of fading.

Barthes thought that as sense can go from our words, departing like soap bubbles from a child's blow-toy, so sense can depart a whole life. You feel a panic suspension of language *as* you write, talk to students, etc.; a blank by no means agreeable.

Language in its sense-making function is a veil of Maya. The fabrications of signs – symbols and reasoning, metaphors and syllogisms – carry us away from the sentiment of being a body. Producing vital meaning, we articulate not according to the body's beat but according to a civilized (rhetorical, linguistic) organization that removes any possibility of delirium. The body lives (in haste, desire, anxiety, mounting pleasure, and so on) when language ceases (see Barthes, 1975b), or ceases to make sense.

A close friend of Barthes told me that Roland hated his body as he lived. Dying, in the hospital, a respirator tube in his throat, Barthes said (I was told[4]) that he felt decapitated, as if he were only a head. He told his semiotic followers in New York that he was feeling himself to be flesh, a body without vital spirit or breath, just meat. It was an unendurable condition.

Barthes turned the Lacanian instrument onto a teaching, writing life – his own. The time unfortunately has come to turn it onto the movement that is partially his – modern semiotics. His recounted experience, his fading, is the experience of modern semiotics. At present this semiotic instrument, like that life, is doomed to repetition, because of failure of theory, because of abstracting, ahistorical discourse, because of a language with little responsibility towards the real.

## In the Beginning

Saussure and a mélange of his pupils founded modern linguistics by a series of separations. *I shall study you and not you, this and not that* (Saussure, 1974, ch. 3). Linguistics must have an object, an entity separate from the knowing subject. It must be founded in a project of coherence and systematicity; and a systematic point of view wants to describe nothing that cannot be systematized. From Saussure's perspective, the only object to justify such a conceptual framework is *la langue*, the national tongue. This is what we call natural language and it is supposed to characterize "human nature", all the while transcending the individuals who use it.

In the Saussurian dichotomy, speech, *parole*, is immediately opposed to natural language; not in order to be defined in itself, but to circumscribe the notion of *langue* – the sole object, for Saussure, of linguistics. Speech is the act

---

[4] This is hearsay, to be sure, but semiotics refuses nothing. It sifts everything, even the supposed refuse of social life.

of uttering, the individual realization of the language in an instance of discourse. Saussure refuses any linguistics of speech, will have nothing to do with the process of appropriating the formal apparatus by an individual act. This individuality, the empirical, he regards as a dust cloud, comprised of the contingent features in the speech act (like tone), which cannot be scientific objects. But some of this "dust", namely the instance of discourse – the intermediary state between natural language and individual speech – is what French semiotics called the uttering, or *énonciation*, enunciation. As Louis Marin shows in his article on Racinian uttering (p. 267), the appropriation of the language can indeed be studied: necessary and permanent features can be found in the dust of speech.

This entity, which Marin studies and which the French call *langage*, Saussure refused. *Langage* designates the social function of language, language as a means of communication. But since communication tends towards the formal in our societies, *langage* comes to designate a particular, professionally defined language, such as that of law, politics or medicine. From the beginning Saussure spoke of *le langage*, of a unity where none exists. Social life knows idioms, *langages*, a diversity of discourse dependent on the situations requiring speech and documentation – all were mingled, then excluded, to found modern linguistics. By a process of rarefaction, the world is excluded at the origin.

The magisterial Word seemed to promise a *general* semiotics: "One can thus conceive of *a science which studies the life of signs in the heart of social life.* ... It would teach us of what signs consist, what laws rule them" (Saussure, 1974, p. 33 – editor's translation). What ensued developed within the narrow framework of the *linguistic* sign, which was in its turn narrowly conceived.[5]

What Saussurian semiotics made possible was this: The sign is not substance, it is the correlation of two sets of differences (see Godzich, p. 440). It is a recognition marker, an expression, a signifier. It is correlated by a culture (and this correlation is a code) to items of the culture's contents (the signified, the form of the content). A theory of codes results and also a theory of sign production; that is, a theory of signification systems, of ideological functioning, even of population control devices (see Eco, p. 164).

What is missing is the concept that language itself is *not* pure sign, it is also a thing. Language is tied to voice, to materiality. The word is thus partly object, partly sign.

One can think of Kafka. When Gregor leaves his bedroom guided by the vibrato of his sister's violin, when he leaves his gaol, it is the bad vibrato that

---

[5] Semiotics held that speech sounds are not heard as gross, raw phonic matter, but are artefacts fabricated so that we may abstract from, leave behind their concrete substance. We formalize the expression /d/, hearing it as *not* the unvoiced /t/. By analogy, a culture is held to make its world pertinent by negation, dissimilarity: a mouse is not a rat, Holland is not Germany; neither expression nor content is grasped as itself, only in opposition to other places in a system of sounds, ideas, images (see Jackobson, 1978, p.66, and Eco, pp. 170–1).

summons him, not composed music, semiotically formed, but pure sonorous matter (see Deleuze and Guattari, 1975, ch. 1). Thus there can be a semiotics of the concrete, of the material; the signifier doesn't always engender sense, but sometimes desire, the sentiment of animal spirits, the return to the happiness of childhood; this was an impossible concept in a semiotics devoted to a formed expression transforming itself unproblematically into a formed signified. "We speak in order to be heard . . . for it is in order to be understood that we seek to be heard" (Jakobson, 1978, p. 25). This is logocentrism. The signifier is in the service of the signified. There is nothing left over, nothing fails along the way. A concept is always signified, always easily present to thought (see Derrida, 1972, pp. 29–31).

Modern semiotics was founded to enable myth to be read *easily*, to enable ideology to be read *simply*. But quasi-mechanically, modern semiotics applied the model of the composed, formed sign; that is, the linguistic sign triumphed over all others. For semiotics postulated that natural language mediated the process of decoding the world; only that which can be verbalized has been thought; only that which can be translated into words has meaning.

Starting in 1953 with Barthes' *Degré zéro de l'écriture*, and his *Mythologies* (1957), and with the immense productivity of his, Eco's and their colleagues' journal *Communications*, these Europeans used the linguistic sign to analyse social symbols, collective representations. Mingling Saussure with Marx and Sartre, they discovered the power to grasp unassertive objects as signs, as the bearers of accepted opinion and ideological trickery. The first semiology was a vast project of ideological criticism aimed at spying out the wheelworks of idea and content production. Everything non-linguistic, images, objects, comportment, was treated as if it were language, fabricating content (or, in the jargon of the time, the signified).

Once elaborated (by the early seventies), the semiological instrument lost interest in the social sign. Americanized, gaudy, the collective representation was no longer a respectable object for a new science eager to become the lay saint, Method, eager to transmit a knowledge capital, deliver the secrets of a technique, and thereby become the guru of a Movement of Ideas. Thus was born the second semiology, and the heady days of seeing the functioning of the (respectable) world's semantic organization; of catching not the meaning, but the production of meaning, the *signification*, the decisive statements of architecture, urban studies, painting, poetry, narrative, cinema, gestures, rites – their deep being, their truth, their official meaning.

Semiotics in anxiety was a third stage, a divergence (dating also from the early seventies). Semiotics was worried it had become a positive science. It had, in fact, become a potential law, misunderstanding the symbol whose formal functioning it pretended to observe from outside. It was so preoccupied with the manufacture of meaning that it failed to take into account that concepts, themes, signifieds might be undone, that within the obvious or unobvious statements made by an utterance are murmured meanings from "between the words", words under words.

Were we to engage this third semiotics with language on our very theme, signs:

> . . . Folly vice,
> Extravagance in gesture, mien, and dress,
> And all the strife of singularity,
> Lies to the ear, and lies to every sense –
> Of these, and of the living shapes they wear,
> There is no end. Such candidates for regard,
> Although well pleased to be where they were found,
> I did not hunt after, or greatly prize,
> Nor made unto myself a secret boast
> Of reading them with quick and curious eye;
> But, as a common produce, things that are
> To-day, to-morrow will be. . . .
>
> (Wordsworth, *Prelude*,
> 1805, VIII, 571–82)

we could remark how casual the language is – thus seizing not the representation, or meaning, but the way the meaning is announced. It is not a fully intended message we search out, we read *in spite of* the message, fastening onto tenuous details, traits of the text. Reading these lines of Wordsworth, we hear that the semiotic narrator is not involved. It is a text of modernity, of alienation. We read states of desire (or lack of it) carried by the passage of words succeeding one another. We are searching for the repressed marks of the enunciator.

Such are the three moments of semiotics, lingering still.

## Semiotics at the Crossroads

To make the semiotic instrument stronger, we must stop using only the linguistic sign as our glasses to see the world. We need to, and can do things other than watch signs make and *un*make their meanings. If we pass beyond the sign to its production, to codes, then we can spy out primary codes rather than supporting ones. We can do other than content ourselves with seeming to have reached a profound meaning, a transcendentally stable content, or signified. Reading the chain of signs, the so-called text, we can follow the successivity of its meanings (see Eco, p. 182). We can read not only what the language is saying, its content, signified, cause, or philosophy; we can also read what the language is doing, its material deployment, the social intervention being accomplished by its signifying elements, its signifiers (see Marin, p. 267).

We can also leave the text. First, by reasoning our way from it to its implicit, or model reader (Eco, p. 289), or, by reasoning to the place of its signifiers – their position in a strategic intentionality or a configuration of power (Jameson, p. 373). The authors in this collection show us how to respond to an admonition recently haunting the literary and philosophical student: Beware, you are not taking in evidence from the page.

We can devise strategies for investigating the empirical, no longer the implicit reader (see Franco, p. 414, Desnoes, p. 390); also the sender of messages (Blonsky, pp. 505–11). We can rise up, as it were, to understand immense constructs such as modern cities, whose driving force may be rhetoric, like that of language, and which keeps us microbian, scurrying creatures, blind to the city's logic (see De Certeau, p. 122). And for how one people suffer a mutation in this logic – and what they do about it – we can look at Susan Meiselas' portfolio of Central American photographs (p. 43).

Passing to everyday life, we can learn how we ourselves, by decoding, govern ourselves. We can grasp this self-government in the supposedly most free, most animal life we experience – our sexual life (see Foucault, p. 365). We govern ourselves, but great men *and* women govern us also, and we can approach the royals and the greats, their acts, words, images, presence even, to find intent, meaning (see Sebeok, p. 448, Desnoes, p. 12, Dayan and Katz, p. 16). In short, we can try to grasp the culture's bloodstream as sign *and* secret practices, as the language of our rationality and also silent, infinitesimal procedures. Semiotics must not weigh on a part (whether literature, politics, commerce or social life) without awareness of the flow of the process in which that part was immersed and within which it lived.

In this collection, the authors have turned their intelligence onto the body, onto laughter, onto space and land, the intentionality of the right and left, the machinery of success and failure, the apparatus of governing and selling – onto objects that a semiotics of the first three moments never addressed. The articles assembled for this book are probes, early attempts to push semiotics off its repetitive path. All the authors, the orthodox and the more outré alike, have travelled roads leaving markers, signs of their search. Above all, they have recorded stages of the search and pointed towards other possible roads, other bloodstreams. We can read their signs, not as finished discourse, achieved, closed residues from which the creators have left in self-satisfaction, but rather as individual recitals, stories of will sparking with the effort not to repeat its prior work.

## Ivory Tower Semiotics

In the fall of 1977, the Establishment review *Daedalus* commissioned ten divergent and distinguished scholars to sum up the limits to progress and the conceptual advances in their fields of research. Semiotics was given the honour of being among the fields to be judged, and Jonathan Culler was given the privilege of taking stock of semiotics:

> It is a commonplace of historiography that decisive events are difficult to perceive, except retrospectively.... Such an event was the first

congress of the International Association of Semiotic Studies, held in Milan in 1974. . . . [T]he presence of about 650 committed or bemused scholars at a congress of this sort made it an event and testified to a new articulation of scholarly activity. . . . Semiotics, the science of signs, became something to be reckoned with, even for those who reject it as a Gallic or a technological obfuscation. And of course when a discipline establishes an organization with committees, officers, publications, when it distributes titles and responsibilities to its adepts, it imposes itself on the scholarly world in symbolic fashion. (Culler, 1981, pp. 95–6)

We are interested only in the enunciation, the implicit utterer of this statement – a self writing three years after the event and still basking in its afterglow. An index, let us say, of almost any of the 650 (myself included) whose hopes were so high, and who were unaware that "symbolic fashion" can mean semiotic fashion, a *sign* of imposition, a lie. A birth, a "new arrival", "an [a blessed] event", is announced. Semiotics is being grasped as discourse, an instrument of action as well as the bearer of messages.

Far from being *infans*, this new arrival has claimed a past for itself, constructed unheard-of questions and flexed its ambition by announcing a bright future. The enunciator captures very well the spirit of the Milan birthplace, but what the enunciation depicts isn't the birth of a discipline; and, by no means is it certain that what is being depicted is a decisive event. The enunciator is describing the production of a narrative. For the science of signs envisioned by Saussure does not yet exist. What exists is a *story* about such a science, told in universities and from time to time in the councils of letters. The discipline of signs is still a narrative of a discipline of signs.

First, because looking for the logic of culture, semiotics proposes "*structural* explanation in place of *historical* and causal reconstruction, making explicit the interdependence of social phenomena on one another by analyzing them in terms of systems of relations . . . " (Culler, 1981, 110, my emphasis). At the heart of the discourse is a belief only in the present. In this respect, semiotics is the scientific descendant of Paul Valéry, who identified the present with sensation ("Now, whatever is sensation is essentially *present*. There is no other definition of the present except sensation itself. . . .") and wrote of past and future (called memory, anticipation, sentiment, desire, planning) as a *production of absent things* ("Poésie et pensée abstraite", Valéry, 1332). A past, for semiotics, is a point merely *seen from a present* (therefore *distortedly* seen, since it is already gone). A future, like a past, is a present *imaginarily* projected elsewhere. Structurally, semiotics denounces the possibility of recovering history or planning the future.

Next, because it finds hidden clarity in poems, plays, pages of philosophy, in canonized and *discrete* signs, and endlessly analyses them, semiotics tells us that the discourse that envelops us makes no responsible pronouncements about the nature of the world (although creating the opposite illusion). Semiotics insists on the failure of the sign's referential power. The sign-receiving, sign-using self, therefore, cannot know the world or itself; it cannot enunciate any kind of truth about the world.

Yes, signs lie, make no responsible pronouncements, but they *act on people*. And from inside the institutions that manage these pronouncements, the councils of law, medicine, government and business, doubtless has come, on first inspection of semiotics, a shrug, an indifference, a feeling that it is frivolous. Semiotics has been impertinent to an Establishment steeped in history, engineering the future of peoples.

On the other side of the divide, semiotics has been content with its university role, resisting use by commerce and politics, fearing that otherwise it would become a soiled instrument.

Such "soiling" befell psychoanalysis when, after Freud's 1905 *Three Essays on the Theory of Sexuality*, it had weight in the world. Freud had the first inkling his mental child (as Jones called it) would pass into the world when, en route for America to give the Clark Lectures, he saw his cabin steward reading the *Psychopathology of Everyday Life* (Jones, 1955, 2, p. 55). He was by then the monarch, the totalitarian power; like the primitive ego rejecting, denying, spitting out, refusing what wasn't good for him – Adler, Jung and so forth. (In this, Freud was like Saussure.) Psychoanalysis was the "motherland"; mythology, semiology (which Jones urged on Freud) and so on had to be "colonies" (1955, 2, pp. 68–9, 140).

In short, as with the Racine the reader will find in Louis Marin's essay (p. 267), the internal requirement of totalitarian power entails its totalizing narrative leaving no remainder: what doesn't have to be spat out can be laughed at, as Freud did when telling with gusto this tale of the vulgar Americans. Psychoanalysis has become a totalitarian power so great and its subjects so vulgar that at last, one of them, Samuel Goldwyn, offers Freud $100,000 to collaborate on "Great Love Stories Through The Ages" (Jones, 1955, 3, p. 114).

Freud armoured himself and his disciples well; what he said of psychoanalytic writing applied to the entirety of the psychoanalytic discourse:

> One has to become a bad fellow, transcend the rules, sacrifice oneself, betray; and behave like the artist who buys paints with his wife's household money, or burns the furniture to warm the room for his model. Without some such criminality there is no real achievement. (Jones, 1955, 2, p. 139)

An early, Marxist, version of semiotics in fact did become criminal. It is that of Georg Lukács who in Budapest, in 1919, participating in an insurrection, conceived as follows: that labouring selves are made never to have contact or form a community; these subjects are made fragments, objectified into hands, eyes, legs, back, whatever the boss wants, the remainder (intellect, affects, desire) thrown away; these body pieces are calculated, a monetary number (wages) is assigned to them, another number (square feet) is given for rest and recovery; and the mind helplessly watches (Lukács, 1971, p. 90) until such intellect burns with the vigilance that it is a leftover, spat out of culture. This is an idea of such terror (if you are a worker), and it generates such rage, that it had to come from a crucible like revolutionary Budapest.

Lukács was revolted by the first, helpless consciousness that formed him – he sought to overthrow its objective forms. But within Lukács' student, Lucien Goldmann, the concept became *peaceful*. In 1966 at the Johns Hopkins University symposium establishing structuralism, Goldmann lectured on Jansenism and Racine. Racine, the self that knows, found a structure Jansenism had elaborated. As a child, a toy, Racine manipulated this "world view" working out his personal problems. Lukács' actor was emotional: disturbed, strong, violent, strained, phallic. He was a worker. Goldmann's actor is tranquil. He is content, consistent, an artist who expresses the "vision du monde", the tendencies, the aspirations of his privileged group. He writes what the group felt and thought "without knowing it", and revealing this, becomes its leader, "so that [for the group] life becomes more acceptable" (Goldmann, 1970, pp. 108–10, 334). In 1966 in Baltimore, in an originating moment for semiotics, nothing is left over in this perfect expression; gone is the dis-ease, Lukács' twitch of consciousness.

In spring 1970 Goldmann, lecturing at Cambridge, met Raymond Williams, who had only recently studied his writing and that of Lukács. A year later, Williams wrote of Goldmann's impact on him:

> In humane studies, at least, and with mixed results, British thinkers and writers are continually pulled back towards ordinary language: . . . in a manner of exposition which can be called unsystematic but which also represents an unusual consciousness of an immediate audience: a sharing and equal-standing community, to which it is equally possible to defer or reach out. . . . the negative aspects are serious: a willingness to share, or at least not too explicitly to challenge, the consciousness of the group of which the thinker and writer . . . is willingly or unwillingly but still practically a member. And while this group, for so long, and of course especially in places like Cambridge, was in effect and in detail a privileged and at times a ruling class, this pull towards ordinary language was often, is often, a pull towards current consciousness: a framing of ideas within certain polite but definite limits. (Williams, 1980, p. 12)

The actor in the theory we are tracking – thanks to Edward Said's contribution – is now the intellectual/professor *resisting* the tendencies towards non-theory of a privileged group, in order to call a crisis in the university.

By 1984 here is what our semiotic concept has become under the pen of Williams: an extended musing, an unhappiness (replete with historiography) over the narrowness of English studies, their particularization to canonized authors and works. The canon is literature's protector shield, saving it from the dirt of the world. And against this shield perhaps will triumph a new actor, radical semiotics, which may crack open English studies (Williams, 1984, pp. 194, 208–9). A crisis of *English* studies. A crisis of English *studies*. The triumph of the part.

Yet, because Williams is at Cambridge safe from turbulent affairs, he can be a critic, can put action into crisis. He is able to understand that if social power turns humans into discontinuous blocks; that if power presents itself as a transcendent authority; that if it wishes only to rule over morsels which surround it at a distance; and wishes for one human-thing to be at a distance from another; that if the apparatuses that rule us can truly enact this astronomic law of life, then obviously *they will have anticipated and protected themselves* from disquietudes ranging from insurrection to chafing to radical semiotics.

Silent social agents have kept semiotics in the tower,[6] while, in the meantime, power disconnects our lives, making totality impossible. In the first three months of 1980, Mobil Oil created its own television network, composed of fifty-three stations in the largest markets in the US. The Mobil Showcase Network had as its first function to present Mobil's production of "Edward and Mrs Simpson", and second, to deliver an audience to the sponsor. Mobil created six "Fables For Now" – each a three-minute public relations film, each employing a different, major US dance company. Two of the "Fables" won awards. The intelligible body was rare in these two films; the gross body commanded them. In *The Misunderstood Elephant*, ostriches strut across our foreground. Being ostriches, they have tail feathers, arched prettily. Being worn by women, these feathers reveal a tail, as we say in vulgar English (tail for buttock). Perhaps this small lingusitic (therefore intelligible) play is one of the effects experienced. But it is minor, absorbed in the sensual partial object of the female dancer's curvaceous buttock (see figure 1). The camera zooms in, an instruction to us to cut the buttock out imaginarily. These are women who say: "Look but don't touch. Don't touch and die with desire." The message is lost in

[6] Look at "Sects Again" in "Day By Day with Roland Barthes" (p. 98). Barthes gives us the code of suicide (it is for one – two at the most), broken in Guyana; he tells us why he couldn't do a semiotics of Guyana: excess stops thought, stops sense and semiotics; tells one of the world's power modalities (the world will not tolerate a loss of sense, as graceful an explication of "logocentrism" as ever there was); even gives a gentle nudge to semiotics itself, to its Lacan-inspired version, which absorbed attention onto the Imaginery (away from ideology, content): it's a miniature plea for a conservation of the semiotics of the signified, that of *Mythologies*.

It was to chronicle in minute detail the media-octopus sucking his weak life into its fierce events that Barthes wrote *in his apartment, sitting perhaps with his mother, watching, Day 3, the news of Jim Jones in Guyana.* Read what he wrote as conclusion, seeking to bring us back to the semiotics of ideology. "I am embarrassed . . . not to know more about what these poor bastards believed." But it would have been easy to find out what those poor bastards thought about in Guyana – but to do so, one would have had to go outside, ask the survivors (use one's semiotic technique to interpret their language and behaviour), and in doing so, one would be a journalist. The implicit image of the utterer, the semiotic actor in "Day By Day" is that of a sequestered apartment dweller, behind doors, assigned a place, accepting it. What place? A grey space of small extension; and living within it, Roland Barthes, a diaphanous self convening imaginary characters let loose by a screen.

Figure 1    *She combines elegant head attire and intricate costume with the*
*snap of hip . . .*

Figure 2    *. . . and snarl of mouth that cuts her body into lips, hip, nylon, the partial object said to*
*engage our drive.*

the actual vector towards them of the driven viewer's body. Her body in (good) pieces – mouth, buttock and so on – calls upon *my* body. Here are sights whose naturalness, to use Hegelian language, retains the mind, encumbering it. To speak in a current idiom, it is difficult to pass from the expression, the signifying substance, to the content, the signified; indeed, it is difficult to leave the substance of expression. The woman's flesh massively obtrudes in our interiority. The ostrich shows very much buttock, very much hip and thigh. She struts, making these partial objects surge. Male and female viewer alike are as if in a blind vector in her direction.

But into our staring lives comes a trouble. This *animation* elephant (see figure 3). Who walks up a hill that looks like an orb – behind which is the immense orb of the moon. This lumbering elephant looks as if he walks on the moon in his search for "water" (figure 4). (The animals are dancing at their "watering hole" – when it suddenly becomes dry, hence the elephant trip.) This is a real message. Our sensual identification is disturbed. We are no longer perfectly mired in substance.

He left without fanfare (it was an incident, like a leaf that blows away). *I* could never be so light and light-footed. I could never escape my naturalness: that is why the elephant looks at *me* sadly (figure 5). I could never achieve the discipline of the multinational, the transnational executive.

Figure 3    *I don't know* how he can be so gracious. *I couldn't* stop myself *from demand and histrionics.*

Figure 4    *I couldn't stop myself from* wanting too much. *He tells me, "Shame on you for leading a dionysiac life . . ."*

Figure 5    *". . . while every day you have orgies, we have been transnational (transcendental), flying around the world doing good things for peoples."*

When onto the scene of the erotic identification comes the animation, its function is to call, but not take, me from my erotic self. Power is abstract while the powerless are sensual, says power to the people. It does not say: "Rise and join me." The message of Mobil is: "Live, mired in sensuality. But be ashamed of it and respect me." This is how a citizenry is made to say yes to the transnational's request: "Let me go my way around the world. No need to comprehend me."

This is how a life is pleasure-splintered into parts. And if the law of our lives is fragmentation, logically it will not only be the *worker's* life that is fragmented. The professor of semiotics will also be given fragments, never the whole, not the code, to study and teach.

## Out of the Tower . . .

Seeing the world as signs able to deceive, semiotics should teach the necessity to fix onto *every* fact, even the most mundane, and ask, "What do you mean?" as if, as the Greeks thought, meaning was in every tree and brook, as it is in our packages, ads, political slogans, the artefacts that for us have replaced nature (De Certeau, p. 152). But these narratives don't talk candidly or explicitly. They talk out of the side of the mouth, saying something else. In the key word of the discipline: they "naturalize" their messages.

Wordsworth wrote of "mimic sights that ape/ The absolute presence of reality" (*Prelude*, 1805, VII, pp. 232–3); that is, a referential presence produced by signs. Nietzsche wrote of the *Natürlichkeit*, the naturalness of speech. Language, spectrally, says that it is the referent, and the receiver believes. There is nothing new then in the semiotic idea, *except for its force*. I would like to bring the reader nearer to that force, to dramatize the social intervention accomplished by the authors here. Read Jakobson on the table talk of Turgenev (p. 303); semiotics is the study of words felt as words, not simple substitutes for the objects named. Language is perceived in itself, not as a transparent, transitive mediator of a different thing. A semiotics of poetry pursues the transformation of *verbal* material, it finds the *phonic* sources of semantic features. Semiotics in general is the study of signs as signifiers (not content, not signifieds). The semiotic mind asks not what signs mean but how they mean. Semiotics is a forced march into the form of meaning, a form felt to constrain one perhaps totally. The Poe article (p. 84) shows that the life the reader of Poe might think he/she is in touch with *isn't*. It is not a life; life is out of reach. What the receiver gets access to is a mélange of common opinion, half-wisdom and worn information. Language (semiotics keeps saying) doesn't bear a responsibility to conduct its recipient to anything real. Rhetorically speaking, all language is figurative; it doesn't lead to a proper sense, an essence. But we as readers/listeners keep forgetting this. Why do we let signs ape the absolute presence of reality? Some theoreticians here believe in a referential longing or urge that wants signs to make things *be*. Others here look to culture, believe that a fundamental use of power is to *make* us believe that signs can be transparent, true, natural, free of any determinations save those of the object they designate. Whichever position we choose, we understand that it's either we ourselves or the culture (finally the two conflate) making everything normal, fine, okay, and semiotics has work to do to force away the transparency.

It would be misleading to seek to present a semiotics untempted by immediacy. Semiotics can address immediacy, not in order to valorize the present but, instead, to sift it for what within it partakes of the typical. In our present there is a convergence of modes of signification. What occurs in one supposedly autonomous sphere is being reinforced and is operating in another. Here the semiotic perspective is particularly useful, insofar as we are accustomed to thinking of these spheres as detached from one another (fashion as separate from advertising, in its turn separated from drama, and so forth).

I pass a poster in the subway, an ad for a pleasure product (figure 6). It shows a man in uniform on a ship coming towards me. Again on the street seeing that poster, I several times mistook the man for a military, not a merchant marine officer. The mistake was intended; the intent was to add the value of pleasure to

Figure 6

current militarism. Only in the Reagan Age in America the Bland could a uniform, after Vietnam, be popular again. Not only so popular that Merit (Philip Morris) constructed a major campaign upon submerged militarism, but so popular also that *People* magazine, during the 1984 presidential race, reprinted this four-year-old photo of *candidate* Ronald Reagan (figure 7) to join a three-year-old photo of Christie Brinkley on its cover (figure 8) to tell that "America Sends A Message." These are *People's* words, the title of its cover (16 July 1984); its message is of an America at once enormously and narrowly semiotic. It is sending a message the way an admiral sends a shot over the bows. *People* is telling us that life imitates art, that Reagan imitates the Merit Man (or the Merit Man, Reagan), that militarism is as sexy now as the pleasure miss whose pose was originally purely sexual – intended for a summer 1981 cover for *New York* magazine (its title: "Summer Pleasures").[7]

Ten years after the end of the war, America buried its unknown soldier from Vietnam. Bob Simon of CBS News, reporting on television (28 May 1984), called it pomp and circumstance, as the cameras showed, behind the procession, uninvited to the *image* opportunity, the hobbling, crutch-walking, wheelchairing, ragtag Vietnam veterans *punching a hole in the pomp* (Simon's words – "reality punching through"). The veterans wanted to sicken the pomp with their presence (they had decoded it) in order to be remembered.

Here is a moment to pause for theory, that of Lacan's image realm, the Imaginary. Sometimes it is translated into English as the Image-repertoire. One can read Lacan directly, although as always he will be elliptic (see pp. 206–9). One can also read this popularization by Barthes:

> What is a filmic image (including the sound)? A *lure*. This word must be taken in its analytic sense. I am shut up with the image as though I were taken in by the famous dual relation which establishes the Image-repertoire, the Imaginary. The image is there before me, *for* me: coalescent (its signifier and its signified nicely blended), analogical, total, suggestive; it is the perfect lure: I hurl myself at it like an animal at a "lifelike" rag waved in front of it; and of course the image perpetuates in the subject I believe I am the misunderstanding attached to the self and to the Imaginary. In the movie theater, no matter how far back I sit, I press my nose, to the point of flattening it, right up against the mirror of the screen, against this Imaginary "Other" with which I narcissistically identify (they say that the people who prefer to sit as close to the screen as possible are children and film buffs): the image captivates me, captures me: I am glued to the picture on the screen, and it is this bond, this glue which establishes the *naturalness* (the pseudo-nature) of the filmed scene (a glue prepared with all the ingredients of "technique"): whereas the Real knows only distances, the Symbolic knows only masks: only the image (the Imaginary) is *close*, only the image is *true* (able to produce the ring of truth). (1975a, p. 106)

[7] The Christie Brinkley photo was an "out-take", not sexy enough for summery New York "yuppies", now wonderfully appropriate for a septuagenarian Captain.

Figure 7

But *what* is close and why do we "press our nose"? The category of the Imaginary is an attempt to think the experience of *absencing*: a fascinating presence absents itself, what I thought there to my body escapes it. This is why the model in the *Harper's Bazaar* layout, "Flying Down to Havana" (p. 391), is truly Imaginary. Gloves on, mannekin face, astonishingly slender next to the ragged campesinos, she is *unrealized*. Something seems to be holding itself in suspense.

The Imaginary is not at first a state of signification, but a condition of possession, from light hypnosis all the way to stupefaction. It is a suspended state, a staring life. Look at the little girl (a third of the way in from the right) in Meiselas' photo of the coffins laid up in the churchyard (p. 48). Her head is through the bars in front of these corpses that the authorities refused to allow to be buried. Death unburied: it is a prevalent object, a first, a natural symbol drawing her towards itself. The Imaginary is this coaptation (see pp. 207–8).

That little girl reminds us that the origin of the Imaginary is another prevalent object, the mother. When we are infants, *infans*, unable to move the body as a whole, we cannot form the concept of a whole. We are not some body, *somebody*. Yet, in the period six to eighteen months, blessed with ocular maturity and perceptive passion, we are said to see our mirror image, propped up by the mother (or whoever serves her function). Jubilatorily, it is said, we mistake ourselves for that wholeness: we forget the bits and pieces we have felt ourselves to be. The "I", or ego, is the residue of this mistake in the moment

Figure 8

Lacan called the mirror stage (1966, pp. 93–100). It is the moment when the child decides that what is next to it resembles it. The mother and it become part of the same concept. This is when the child invents the word "Man", when the ego is born. The image today, by its prevalence and refinement, possesses all the characteristics of the mother in the mirror stage. Images regress us, carry us away to the infant inside that we remain.

But Lacan also thought of this identification through the mirror as an archaic experience of death. From the moment we imagine ourselves, we can only imagine ourselves *contingently*, as mortal. Hence the *béance*, the gaping of the image. It is as if a gaping hole had opened in it. Images fail, they dissipate. We can grasp the *gaping* concept empirically in the experience of amorous crisis, the state in which we say "I" all the time – I suffer, I need, I demand. The pronoun *I* is the very pronoun of the imaginary; and the anguish of the love-wounded I always goes away. Because it was *Imaginary*.

We return to *our* image, Reaganism – American Ideology/Imaginary. Neither the veterans in the requiem nor CBS News waited for this image to collapse. The United States, in Sartre's metaphor, is a beast with many heads. Cautiously, one of them answered Reagan back. Not so other heads. On 19 May 1984 the *New York Times* reported dutifully on the newly *à la page* medal (figure 9). The page will turn, be forgotten, *and that is fashion's function.* Forgetting, the citizenry forgets to criticize. *What had a meaning that I may not have been vigilant enough to notice, I now certainly forget.* The blandness machine enforces blandness.

Such ideas on forgetting/naturalizing, impressive twenty years ago at the birth of modern semiotics, are a commonplace now in responsible circles. Anthony Lewis writes:

> America is a land without memory . . . Those of us who are middle-aged or older have all had the experience of talking to people in their twenties about some central part of our experience and finding an utter lack of recognition. In college clases today even a reference to Vietnam is likely to produce blank stares. (*New York Times*, 28 May 1984)

Figure 9

He is writing of an amnesia nourished by pleasure and pleasure products in this land that has perfected the friendliness of signs. Craig Claiborne (*New York Times* Food Editor and the voice of the present American gastronomic revolution) writes of food and conviviality: "At table, I like to discuss current events that give one pleasure, like the theater, film, books. No weighty matters like politics. No global, no national, no local politics" (Claiborne, forthcoming). In the idiom of Eco, Claiborne has been reformulating the American pleasure content (see p. 164–5). He writes of a Marvin Davis, a New York executive. "Seven years ago, his idea of heaven was a piece of beef with spaghetti and tomato sauce." Now:

> He is the embodiment of the American gastronomic revolution over the last decade. This man, who had never cooked a day in his life, has suddenly, through his own reading, discovered the joy of eating, the joy of cooking. He has a penthouse apartment with 11,000 feet, fantastic things like snow peas, romaine lettuce, thyme, sage, tarragon, parsley, peppers, Japanese eggplant, cucumbers, basil, oregano, four kinds of tomato, eggplant, Portuguese peppers, Japanese eggplant, cucumbers.

Producing more refined categorizations, Claiborne has proliferated signs, made an extravaganza of the culinary code.

The safe and selfish pleasure of the eighties has a relentless unity of intent and performance, from President Reagan:

> We saw the signs all around us. Years ago, pornography, while available, was mostly sold "under the counter". By the mid-70's it was available in virtually every drugstore in the land. Drug abuse used to be confined to limited numbers of adults. During the 60's and 70's it spread through the nation like a fever, affecting children as well as adults. [. . . Like a toxic pill from the pharmacy, pornography made the nation and its children sick.] Liberal attitudes viewed promiscuity as acceptable, even stylish. Indeed, the word itself was replaced by the term "sexually active". . . . But the Almighty [Antidote] who gave us this great land also gave us free will – the power, under God, to choose our own destiny. The American people decided to put a stop to that long decline, and today our country is seeing a rebirth of freedom and faith – a great national renewal.
>
> Ronald Reagan, National Association
> of Evangelicals (6 March 1984)

to *Cuisine* magazine (see figure 10). After the socially oriented sixties and early seventies, pleasure products feed a basic shift: from the future into the present (from there, looking with nostalgia at the past); from world politics to America the Beautiful and soon perhaps, America the Great. The fantasy of changing the world and confronting society has been turned into the urge to accept society and live within its values. Sex and politics have become romance and knowledgeable eating and drinking. Pleasure is the great naturalizer – food, drink and no analysis.

Figure 10

Anthony Lewis is near the ruling circle. Nourished by America's Newspaper, bathed by admiration, he seems to make sense of, and for, our society. His discourse is theoretic, panoptic. But save for the top, the strata of America are comprised of men and women more like a curious kind of peasant than lords. These men's and women's former glimpse of world history has been transformed into private lives – instantiated by the image factory of American film, journalism, advertising and television. Preparing the scattered pleasure bits of life, imbibing them, most people live "mouse lives", unable ever to see systems, general social plans or the ideological and political laws revealed by the scattered fragments that make up their land and lives. Will semiotics appeal to them? Probably not, because it tears away the veil of pleasure; and often those who cleave to semiotics spring to it because of their marginality *vis-à-vis* pleasure. Nevertheless what *can* semiotics offer a population of mainline pleasure seekers? It offers a way to understand that all signs are related to what individuals and their leaders want, rather than to the referents these signs appear to designate: words, images, *signs* – things which appear but are not; and secrets – things which are but do not appear. Reading the unobvious meanings borne by signs, the community inside the covers of this book teaches how to pass from the evident signs to *other, spectral* presences; how to discern the difference between appearance and the secret beyond that appearance.

### . . . Uninvited into the World

A European friend, significant in the field of semiotics, told me in 1980, "You know, I could never love a woman with a body like a Rubens." In a café, lots of laughter between us, he spoke a learned, perverse little discourse that all my experience and theory confirm. Just the flavour of it: "*Playboy* is in my head. I can't help it. I decode, a centerfold, say, and it's sex between two autarchies. There *I* am, learned before the class, connotation, ideology, blah blah, flush with my students' praise. And *she's there too.* She subsists, I want her – all the while I'm decoding. I never dismantled anything."

*Playboy* is a code, a type of beauty, pneumatic flesh, intelligent physiognomy, painterly lighting that are close to us; we are *sticky with Playboy.* It is a key code for understanding America, the pleasure land that has extended its code of beauty over most of the western world.

Were there more space we could offer more evidence of the power of the pleasure image in America. And not only a national image, but an image spreading through the world, often to contradictory conditions where (in Europe and Latin America) there isn't the wealth to support the *Playboy* imagery of American pleasure. In Desnoes' film *Memories of Underdevelopment*, the hero Sergio lives in Havana, in the south, with the image faces coming from the north, America. By comparison, his own nation's women appear as overripe fruits to him. He is estranged by their too solid flesh. Unable to obtain the referent of a pleasure image ("Look and die with desire", it says), what you *can* have appears sickly and denigratory.

We could make the case for *Playboy*, together with *Time*, as revolutionary instruments of America. *Time* is the magazine for the political and executive cadres. Its formula suffuses the social life and bloodstream of the world. The world is digested for us. The information is synthetic, and there is just enough background to give us the sense of being informed about the events of the world. But it's impossible, we can't be thus informed by a weekly magazine as if we were Renaissance princes – or Henry Kissinger. And it is impossible because *Time* is a magazine with a profound bias – Luce didn't want the person living the experience he/she reports to do the final writing. Everything had to be rewritten back in New York, to respond to Luce's, and the American, ideology. The pleasure and power of America: *Playboy* and *Time*: both equal America, USA power.

Semiotics has been a futile gaze at the world's seeming pleasures, its drunken stupidities; and it may all the while have been imaginary, the way in which we, semiotic intellectuals, have wanted to be loved and respected. No, a critic will answer me, semiotics can also be *un*political, *un*ideological. It can yield up a renewed joy every time we see the functioning of the world's semantic organization. Studying poetry, painting, narrative and so on, we learn that the world is an immense message, we enjoy all the intelligence of everything that is intelligible. To which we can respond: but spying out the world's meanings, you have spied out its misery once more. Meaning is an instrument, a conduit of power. Today, advanced thinkers pivot from the literature, history, philosophy or art they read or watch to the power effects induced by it, or apparatuses subtending it. (See Jameson reading Flaubert, or Marin on Racine, or Foucault on St Augustine.) Let us say that this discourse (semiotics in the widest sense: an intense interest in signs) has been a look at the world's misery in more fineness by far than the ways in which the misery-makers conceive their handicraft. Then who wants it? What is it worth? The discourse you will read teaches hidden things to a world organization that feels it cannot/should not tolerate semiotic knowledge.

The reason the discourse has never "taken" – never become, itself, an ideology, ideas that insist – is that action would be threatened by it. For example, photography today is no longer content with a facsimile of persons, landscapes and objects. It wants to transform these images, to give them personality in a depersonalized world. Photography wants to do it easily, without attracting too much attention, to surprise the "decisive moment". While words now are accepted as lies, as signs, not so the still photograph – *it* tells the truth. This is a Playmate, this is Somoza, says the photo – a slice of reality (see box 1). That a photo could be used to topple Somoza is unthinkable. Photography is an instrument of such power over people (who are not to see it as sign) that *of course* semiotics is the devil to it. (Read Desnoes, mediating between the devil and Meiselas, p. 39.)

Then veil semiotics, sequester it, teach it in the university, limit it to literature, philosophy or film studies. Limit it further to minute particulars, a few poems, a passage in a short story, a folktale, a fetish. There is no need then to worry about disturbance to the population at large.

The clientele of Marin, de Certeau *et al.* comprise an élite who, by empirical contingency, aren't "equipped" with, "hooked up to" the "zombie invaders" (Félix Guattari's term) – the commentators, actors, models, the media figures who appear to be persons, appear to intend me well, but who enter my life to alienate me, to cause me to mistake myself for them; to cause the image, the Imaginary, to sweep me away. They enter my life, then, to subject me: make me the subject, the self I believe, mistakenly, I am. Also, they enter my life to play on my perceptive, sensitive, affective behaviour (Guattari, 1975, 1977). The population at large is structurally incapable of wanting, of being able to tolerate that presumptively quite different piece of equipment – semiotics.

But what about the masters? What impression has semiotics made on great men (and women) or lesser ones, on office holders who impress their intent on us? One must answer, not only in the abstract, logically, as I have already, but empirically, with finality. Semiotic intellectuals are thus far market jesters; they amuse, merely grazing the lives of the lawyers, politicians, entertainers and journalists they occasionally encounter. Everyone who has been in the situation

## Uncovering Photographic Signs

Look at figure 11. There is P.J. She has a last name that I never have been able to remember in the silliness of her first – *pajamas*. To look at this innocent triptych you have already turned over the first page of a *Playboy* centerfold – P.J., back to you, pushing her pants off, almost nude, a signal. To see the result, to see her frontally, said the signal, then grab the page, turn it left, disclosing the under-page, figure 11, which you must turn right if you want to disclose P.J., fully nude. What is figure 11? An undergarment. *Playboy* made textual life mimic the sensual.

Above: P. J. gets plenty of fresh air and exercise hiking in the Colorado high country. At right: She relaxes during the scenic—and strenuous—walk. "It's at times like this that I feel really lucky to be living in such beautiful surroundings. It's too bad that everyone can't." Below: She and her companions reach the top and set up for an afternoon of food and conversation.

Figure 11

You stripped her as *she* stripped. If you strip further – turn figure 11 over – you throw away a derisory exterior (the black-and-white quarter-page photos/the signifier) for a precious (colourful) interior: P.J. pink, P.J. big before you, P.J. on knees and elbows. You'll literally go down (deep, you'll think).

Also, P.J. is stupid, has been made stupid by the captions/signs. It is Vietnam wartime (the issue is February 1972) and she "gets plenty of fresh air and exercise hiking in the Colorado high country. . . . She relaxes during the scenic – and strenuous – walk." (Look at her beneath you, sexually beneath also, top left photo. Look at her meditative body, right photo.) This is of course the period of marches on Washington. "It's at times like this that I feel really lucky to be living in such beautiful surroundings." February 1972 – this was still a moment of the look at the world. Five months later, Jane Fonda will be militantly in North Vietnam. *How can she be so stupid!* escapes our lips. But stupidity (mythically) is sexy. Hoist by his own semiotically formed sexuality, the playboy/reader has no mind left over with which to criticize.

See them at the top of the hill (photo of the foursome, bottom left): "She and her companions reach the top [continues the mendacious caption] and set up for an afternoon of food and conversation." After what (if you are a man) you have just seen/done (nudity/stripping) *you know* it's not talk they'll soon be having. That affective knowledge is but one more procedure of this natural code that makes the playboy grunt "yes" to the figure.

When *The New York Times Magazine* (30 July 1978) printed this Susan Meiselas photograph of Somoza bald as an insert in its Meiselas-photographed cover story (figure 12), we who saw it tended to think it was Somoza's baldness that made necessary the photo from on high. The photograph seemed to be sticky with its model, accounting to it and nothing but it. However, it is a code, a rule play that makes us learn, then forget, that Somoza is being photographed from above to deride him, baldness being a sign of marginality more than of virility. Without a frame of hair, you are not manufactured – you are still animal, not civil. Hair makes a face, establishes one of its limits. This photograph/page was a derisory act, entering the lives of Americans at the most sensitive moment in Somoza's career. The American support he rested on would shortly be kicked away. For his was not a "viable democracy", a concept worked out by professional teams from the State Department in the last stage of the Ford Administration. Subordinating everything to the demands of military logic and national security, a repressive state could hardly be expected to remain in power permanently. The violent overthrow of a strong-arm Nicaragua might drag US interests down with it. Therefore the United States must foster, country by country, a transition towards gradual and realistic democratic formulas, identifying the civilian sectors best suited to lead the process of change to make the military leave the political scene.

To make Somoza leave, the *New York Times* did its part, shaping the conscience of the so-called upper middle class. There, in black and white – like sepia, a sign of the past – is Somoza's son. He is of the past, he is history, never to be active, at

not going and I won't be run out," vows General Somoza (above, with sash), is grooming his son (inset) to succeed him. But the number and intensity of onstrations against the regime (like the one at top near Masaya) are increasing.

## NATIONAL MUTINY IN NICARAGUA

The revolution taking place throughout Nicaragua today is no ordinary political movement pitting left against right or civilians against the military.

Figure 12

the margin of the page, flat like a postcard, a nothing amidst the presencing motorcyclist revolutionaries behind him (in colour). Revolutionary Parousia.

Such is an unveiling of the nonoriginary nature of seeing Somoza from above, bald. It is not because of his essence at all that you saw him that way (Meiselas told me that, in terms of manners, he was charming). The photograph isn't "true" – it's because of a political, "democratic" code that you saw him this way; a code shared, not reflected upon, by newspaper and government. Semiotics dis-covers this truth and naturalness of signs.

of "explaining" semiotics knows: They give you your five minutes, then politely turn away.[8]

The world doesn't want to see itself. It doesn't *want* semiotics.


## To What End? . . .

The US is an image country in which image is much more important than social or economic facts. Reagan has been the epitome of this image power. He is the pleasure president in a consumer pleasureland. He is in the White House but he acts as if he were not. He lives a short workday and has a long fun day. He is the man of the moment, standing for American resurgence. He may indeed be relying too heavily on the power of his image and too little on the power of economic and world issues. The interest rate harms the country; the cold war, the world; and Europe, the victim of both, suffers crises. America seems too powerful and too dangerous to Europeans.

If we remove their anger from our semiotics, it is capable of revealing the ghostly presences taking the form of evident signs and imagery. Reagan's 1984 presidential campaign, showing slices of Americana, often did not include his physical presence. He is not individual, he is America as De Gaulle was France. De Gaulle was accused of suffering from a Joan of Arc complex; Ronald Reagan suffers from a High Noon complex. He comes from the (famous) people and when his Americana work is done, he will return to the (powerful) people. Ronald Reagan . . . I have to pause, for I almost slipped and wrote Donald Duck. Eco caused it. It was he who suggested that Ronald Reagan is like Ronald McDonald in the American unconscious (or, God forbid, conscious). "Where's the beef?" Eco asked, parodying the 1984 Wendy's commercial attacking McDonald's. "It doesn't exist", he answered. "Because presidents, like McDonald's, are a pure *sign*" (*Vanity Fair,* June 1984). Ronald

---

[8] I am with Eco. I have just seen Fellini's *City of Women*, the part where the boy climbs the stairs, enters the prostitute's room, sees monstrously large buttocks. I dream an idea. Even when we are caught up in the erotic drive, even then the buttock – the real thing, the referent – eludes us. The real is never there for you. You never see (touch, hear) it "straight." Your signs of it are always in the way.

Could Eco introduce me to Fellini? Who perhaps will write for this book on the referent gliding away. Eco tells me his duty is *not* to introduce me, since Fellini's duty as artist is not to know nor talk of what he is doing.

A friend in advertising, who has developed a signaletic theory of commercial life, is telling me why his firm won't allow him to write an article for this book: "A few years ago, an insider wrote a book called *I Can Sell You Anything*. He broke the code. In business, we tell the public we only listen to their needs. When we advertise, we're only telling the product's benefits. We sidle up next to the brain and get those circuits in there to light up to our benefit. When we face the public, we put our bland face on. 'Hi, I'm just a working stiff like you, doing my honest day for honest pay.' But that guy [who wrote *I Can Sell*. . .) *told*. He's in Pittsburgh now!" In the United States, going to Pittsburgh would be a little like going to hell.

Reagan is like Ronald McDonald, like Donald Duck, like Mickey at Disneyland. All of them are icons, all are interchangeable in the Fun House this country has become. For an instant, Eco and I shared an unconscious, a kind of delirium in which Ronald (Mc)Donald produces Donald and the RR of our president makes for the DD of the Donald Duck that, for once at least, Reagan himself thought he was like:

Figure 13    *President Reagan celebrating the Duck's fiftieth birthday in the White House before a gathering of "senior citizens".*

Ronald Reagan is passing through the White House – while Ralph Lauren is passing by his competitors. What has Reaganism to do with Lauren's marketing of skin-care products (see figure 16)? By means of a hypothesis, a guess at an ideological law, one can transfer a past experience to the present and understand something of the present's determinations. Reaganism transferred to skin care.

Look at Charles of the Ritz (in figure 14). A material object, a jar and a realistic face. But there is drama here, of light and darkness, and an anxiety

THE
IMPROVEMENT
LASTS

Expect to see improvement
within one week. And the
improvement won't fade
overnight. Your skin is soothed,
moisturized—actually protected.
Moisture Balancing Daycare
acts as a barrier against
moisture loss to help restore
the natural balance of oil
and water in your skin.
Even dry, flaky skin will look
and feel smooth, supple, soft.
Wear it every day. Under
makeup or alone. Fragrance-
free.

MOISTURE BALANCING
DAYCARE
Better skin in just seven days.

Charles of the Ritz
BEAUTIFUL SKIN NOW AND FOREVER

Figure 14

created by the diagonal, which creates instability. The light is a metaphysical light. Now there is a darkness taking her over. You see it bulging towards the figure like night coming on her face. She looks towards the black zone – I am tempted to say dead zone. Black in our symbology signifies death, night, and night is not a good god.

Here we have Montecatini (figure 15). Waiting for God in the mud. It is a piece of sculpture in the making. The product cakes you, leaves your body firm as marble. One has the impression that the product is "gooey", it is uncomfortable, it is complicated to apply, it is dirty, it is European. It is old, old as the Roman Empire. Now anyone who is able to let American ideas and images resonate within him or herself can feel the relief of looking at the Ralph Lauren image (figure 16) after the magic, anxiety, historicity and miracle of the skin-care discourse. The simplicity of skin. American simplicity. The *myth* of America the Simple.

You are looking at an image of American resurgence; almost a slap at the

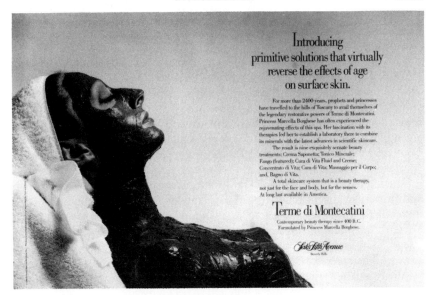

Figure 15

Figure 16    *No jar here, no "goo", no metamorphosis, no unpleasant procedure that is good for you, no French culture and "funny" ways to use one's mouth like the "respiratoire" of Chanel.*

Europeanness and medicinal quality of the competitive images. No culture, no dermatologist, simply good old American health and lots of skin and the infinite (American) sky is before you.

This triumphal meaning is read in this image because of *other experience*, Reagan, Christie Brinkley, Craig Claiborne; we could go on. Had Lauren created the image in the late sixties or early seventies, we would have found it a contradiction to the times, or an irony, because we would simultaneously be seeing the students trampling flags. And taken to the fifties, it would have been a commonplace. But in the eighties, it is a loaded, almost revolutionary image. You only *think* you see a blue sky (in the original). You see "America", you see "perfection", you see "cleanliness" – you see the ideal.

The United States, because of its advanced capitalism, its enormity, its youth and ahistoricity, the degeneration of the extended family – for many reasons – is increasingly the Image Country. Images unify, make avid consumers, form an effective substitute for history and family. But why is pleasure a content of this image? Why is America a content? Why (we can ask of Reagan) is this man *smiling?* The answers are conjunctural.

America, after Vietnam (a first defeat), after the Ayatollah (a monstrous snubbing sign), had to become adult, and so become *less its proper self.* American culture is so large it doesn't daily, regularly suffer challenge from foreign cultures, a fact normal for European nations. It suffers no challenge from the entirety of Europe – subdued now culturally as formerly it was militarily and economically.

Unmindful even of Europe, America's *tendency* resurges; towards ignorance of other cultures, of the Other and its factual specificity. Ignorance is bliss, we say. Ignorance is being returned to us by the pleasure ego. We have been turned to it to forget the frustration of two decades of social change and dangerous world involvement. Change and involvement continue, but Americans avoid these pages of the *Times* to uncork a bottle of Chardonnay. The global way of ignorance: Self-Love, the Pleasure of the Mirror. The United Sates is no longer a primary economy, its industries are mainly "clean". Latin America and Europe no longer are *needed*. It is not for its coffee beans that we are "saving" El Salvador – it is for an Idea: America the Beautiful. That idea – suffused with imagery – *makes for, it fabricates* forgetfulness of facts, of Europe, et cetera.

Let us watch our technocrats fashion signs that make reality. For example, the Bell System discovered that it wasn't because of thrift or stinginess that children didn't call out-of-state parents, or vice versa. Bell's market research told it that Americans didn't like each other that much – true of relatives as of "mere" friends. To manufacture affection (in order to enlarge its long-distance market) Bell commissioned its celebrated "reach out" approach (see figure 17). Bell is doing more than fattening the market. It is doing more than "riding" a preexistent wave of sentimentality. It is doing its share, along with other institutions, to *produce* romance, sentimentality in order to reinstall more firmly, to root, the family as the matrix of productive labour – and the wife/woman as the family's hearth and guarantor. (See Derrida, 1974, pp. 161–71 on the

Figure 17    *On the phone to Parent, subtracted from the sexual moment, she reestablishes familial connections. She is already on the way to being . . .*

"woman's role".) America the Beautiful is also America the Familial – an *actual* answer to a partly imaginary US decline (see figure 18).

Reagan (that is, the apparatus for which he fronts) also has another historic function to fulfil. Reagan is a pupil of Thatcher who, using the new wave inside the Conservative party, convinced voters that *she* would carry out what they wanted but had no courage to perform – production of a freer market, the partial dismantling of state welfare. The spirit of the eighties is characterized by

---

[9] A bit of evidence taken at random: artificial heart recipient William Schroeder received a phone call from President Reagan in his Louisville bed, testily tells the president he hasn't received his social security benefits, that he's been getting the runaround. The president promises to look into it. *The next day*, two officials from Social Security arrive bedside with his check. "Do you want to feel my heart?" Schroeder says to them in thanks. Ending his report on it for CBS TV News, Bruce Morton says: "Problems with the bureaucracy? Call the nice man at the White House."

When millions of Americans
sit down to dinner, go on a picnic, play tennis, or watch football,
our family is right there along with their families.

Stokely's Finest fruits and vegetables. Van Camps' pork and beans. Gatorade thirst quencher.

Figure 18... *the diaphanous Keeper of the Family, Cradle for the Worker/Husband.*

this free-market mind, hateful of bureaucracy. Reagan is fun, as bureaucrats are not.[9] Once a "libertarian" pupil, Yankee Doodle now leads the way.

Images *do* things, operate for real interests although they are, themselves, struck with unreality. Informed by an image, formed from within by an image/Jodie Foster, an image that went haywire and did too much, John Hinckley found himself in productive space, "photo opportunity" space – on the wrong side of the image. That wasn't an image gun he was pointing – that is not what the image machine is to accomplish. Corporality shall be *un*done, animal transformations hunted down. Image power is to be exercised over souls, or subjects, but there Hinckley was, like an animal searching – a hunter.

Hinckley could not stop face, landscape, photo and film from *resonating* with one another. The face of Foster – its chubby cheeks and bedroom eyes – never stopped referring to other things; to a fragment of Yale, the White House, the gun De Niro straps to himself as he shaves his head in *Taxi Driver*, about to search out his victim. This signifying arrangement prepared for the next

Figure 19

moment, subjective and passionate, in which the jealousy, quarrelsomeness and
erotomania of Hinckley developed (calls to Yale, violence with father, descent
into subjectivity with his psychotherapist). The Foster face, the despot
everywhere, was seen head on by a subject who was snapped up by the eyes.
Hinckley in Love – with a ready-made object seeming to have subjectivity.

A different way to live with image faces is to make them *a*signifying,
*a*subjective, and know that it is only an image, you are not in love, that above all,
this face – Jodie Foster's, say – will never love you. You must pierce through the
wall of the face, emerge from the hole of the eye, the face is something you
must escape (see Deleuze and Guattari, 1980, pp. 227–8) – into music as
Swann escaped Odette's face, into art like Proust, or into politics, action.
Hinckley crawled into life with the image, the face, all stuck to him.

He teaches us this lesson about the subjected: the image is their sustenance,
they are sick with images. To hasten through a fashion magazine, to see the

Figure 20

latest film, to visit a department store and search among its images for *my* image
has become a distracting, exhausting research.

Back at home, stuffed with armchair, television, magazines, food, fashion,
children and spouse, are master images, the Manufactured Man, the
Manufactured Woman. The male in America, a vestige of nature still, has not
yet been fully commodified. Not so the woman whose image gives "fun" for the

man, but anxiety (she is an unreachable image) for the woman, who watches. Look at Lauren Hutton for Ultima (figure 19). Once, the little space between her teeth was her signature of subjectivity. Now, there are no teeth. You see a subjectivity being stilled, flowers, lace; there is an aspect of the grave to her.

The fictive days of Henry Miller are ending, days when one might look into "the full face gleaming like calcium" (1961, p. 342), when one might "think of nothing but the face, the strange, womblike quality of the smile, the engulfing immediacy of it", "the whole being ... concentrated in the face" (p. 341). Modern intersubjectivity is today being founded on a void faciality, on a blind face-to-face between two vapid looks.

## And What Beginnings?

The power élite is *reading*. In the cadres of the powerful, in commerce, entertainment, journalism and government, there are reports, scripts, discussions, decisions – language, *langage*, for the powerful. It is uttered in quiet rooms, decorated, to be sure, but in such ways that the figuration (pictures, television sets, secretaries, magazines, art) is sublimated, displaced far from the foreground of the view.

These circles are the constituency of the Pleasure Sign. A real constituency, the most important of the late twentieth century (see Lyotard, 1984). Their quiet lives, however, are not ours. Most of us are playthings of sign and image. Moral reaction, with the understanding gained through semiotics, is up to us now. We must read, understand the sign, the discourse of images, and react.

Read "Cuba Made Me So" (p. 384). The author, at 24, was disciplined by a *Harper's Bazaar* image. Latin America was then (and still is) disciplined by a mass of American images. Cuba, in the South with the face of the North, reacted. Here (figure 20) is one instance, an image not intended just to take the place of chastising northern imagery, but also to be hurled back up north and as far over the world as possible. This poster was designed by a group that understood the machinery of the Imaginary: the face presencing (lower left quadrant), making itself absent (sliding off lower right edge), disappearing (middle right), reappearing (center top). A fascinating presence absents itself. The very words, "Hasta la victoria siempre", are the words with which Che ended his letter to Fidel Castro shortly before he left Cuba for Bolivia (see Desnoes, 1971).

Cuba was and is a small nation *attempting* a world project, seeking to make stronger images than those of America. In a cauldron of such fierce intentionality, anything is possible, semiotics cooked with Marxism included. The Cuban designers did not ask their people's permission to fabricate this image. The Cuban revolution was a radical reordering of a society, the leadership trying to yank its people from consumerist ways and imagery. It got its hands dirty making this Imaginary – and many others. It was, in Freud's sense, criminal.

Semiotics up north is not part of the bloodstream, it is something added to the world, an afterthought from a monastery playing its part in leadership, in a power élite that has created an image – America the Beautifully Bland. Yet semiotics should be part of society, it should be tuned in. So long as it remains something added, it will be small. Hands have to get soiled, Sartre said.

Semiotics is operable, analytically and creatively. It can be applied in the world. But one has to crack it out of its present uses and override refusals to abuse it. It is not a corruption of the semiotic enterprise to use it politically, or commercially. Quite the contrary: isolation will be the destruction of semiotics.

No one has tried to turn semiotics 180 degrees around to deal with the living present and the possible future. Meanwhile, Reagan acts on Europe, Fellini is kept safe from theory, and so on. Semiotics is refused by those who act because it shows that what you thought bland is the beast, it shows the forces that form and move the body, making it buy, read, watch, mourn, remember, contribute.

The disciplines I grazed in my brief test of semiotics – religious, philanthropic, revolutionary, artistic, commercial and political – want nothing to do with any force or discourse that interferes with their disciplinary power. They want to keep the machinery hidden. Semiotics dissects what is supposed to be spontaneous and living, and shows it to be contrived. It reveals that you will find little in America today that isn't a substance manifesting some one, or apparatus, or code *intending* you.

I believe this is the moment for semiotics, given the maturity of the West. In Hegel's metaphor, the owl of Minerva takes flight at sunset. Hegel believed that one can only understand a culture when a period is ending. We have reached such a point.

## References

Barthes, Roland, *Le Degré zéro de l'écriture*, Paris, Seuil, 1953 (trans. A. Lavers and C. Smith as *Writing Degree Zero*, New York, Hill and Wang, 1972)
—, *Mythologies*, Paris, Seuil, 1957 (selection, trans. A. Lavers as *Mythologies*, New York, Hill and Wang, 1972)
—, "En sortant du cinéma", in *Communications* 23, Paris, Seuil, 1975a
—, "Rasch", in *Langue, discours, société*, ed. J. Kristeva, *et al.*, Paris, Seuil, 1975b (trans. R. Howard as "Rasch" in *The Responsibility of Forms*, New York, Hill and Wang, 1985)
Claiborne, Craig, "Vodka, Caviar and Silence", in *The Market Stops to Think*, ed. M. Blonsky (forthcoming)
Culler, Jonathan, "In Pursuit of Signs", in *Daedalus*, v. II, Fall 1977 (reprinted in Culler, *The Pursuit of Signs*, Ithaca, N.Y., Cornell University Press, 1981)
Deleuze, Gilles and Guattari, Félix, *Kafka*, Paris, Minuit, 1975
—, *Mille Plateaux*, Paris, Minuit, 1980
Derrida, Jacques, *Positions*, Paris, Minuit, 1972 (trans. A. Bass as *Positions*, University of Chicago Press, 1981)
—, *Glas*, Paris, Galilée, 1974
Desnoes, Edmundo, "From Consumerism to Social Conscience", intro. to *Cubaanse Affiches*, catalogue of Stedelijk Museum Amsterdam, 1971

Freud, Sigmund, *The Standard Edition of the Complete Psychological Works of Sigmund Freud*, 24 vols., ed. J. Strachey, London, Hogarth and The Institute of Psycho-Analysis, 1953–

Goldmann, Lucien, "Structure: Human Reality and Methodological Concept", in *The Languages of Criticism and the Sciences of Man: The Structuralist Controversy*, ed. R. Macksey and E. Donato, Baltimore, Md., Johns Hopkins University Press, 1970

Guattari, Félix, "Le divan du pauvre", in *Communications* 23, Paris, Seuil, 1975

—, *La révolution moléculaire*, Paris, 10/18, 1977 (trans. R. Sheed as *Molecular Revolution*, New York, Penguin, 1984)

Jakobson, Roman, *Six leçons sur le son et le sens*, Paris, Minuit, 1976 (trans. J. Mepham as *Six Lectures on Sound and Meaning*, Cambridge, Mass., MIT, 1978)

Jones, Ernest, *The Life and Work of Sigmund Freud*, vols 2, 3, New York, Basic Books, 1955

Lacan, Jacques, *Écrits*, Paris, Seuil, 1966 (trans. A. Sheridan as *Écrits: A Selection*, New York, Norton, 1977)

—, *Le Séminaire. XI: Les quatres concepts fondamentaux de la psychanalyse*, ed. J.-A. Miller, Paris, Seuil, 1973 (trans. A. Sheridan as *The Four Fundamental Concepts of Psychoanalysis*, New York, Norton, 1978)

Lukács, Georg, *History and Class Consciousness*, Cambridge, Mass., MIT, 1971

Lyotard, Jean-François, *La condition post-moderne: rapport sur le savoir*, Paris, Minuit, 1979 (trans. G. Bennington and B. Massumi as *The Postmodern Condition: A Report On Knowledge*, Minneapolis, Minn., University of Minnesota Press, 1984)

Miller, Henry, *Tropic of Capricorn*, New York, Grove, 1961

Rousseau, J.-J., *Oeuvres complètes*, ed. B. Gagnebin and M. Raymond, Paris, Pléiade, 1959

Said, Edward W., "Travelling Theory", in *Raritan* Vol. 1, no. 3, 1982, pp. 53-4

Saussure, F. de, *Cours de linguistique générale*, ed. T. de Mauro, Paris, Payot, 1974 (trans. W. Baskin as *Course in General Linguistics*, New York, McGraw-Hill, 1959)

Valéry, Paul, *Oeuvres*, 1, ed. J. Hytrer, Paris, Pléiade, 1957

Williams, Raymond, *Problems in Materialism and Culture*, London, Verso, 1980, reprinted from "Literature and Society: in Memory of Lucien Goldmann", in *New Left Review*, 67, May–June 1971, based on a lecture given at Cambridge University, April 1971.

—, *Writing in Society*, London, Verso, 1984

Wordsworth, William, *The Prelude*, ed. E. de Selincourt, 2nd edn., Oxford, Oxford University Press, 1959

# Part I
# Seeing Signs

UMBERTO ECO

# Strategies of Lying

## Cardinal Mazarin Tells How to Simulate a Self

Let's face it. What we know about Cardinal Mazzarino (beyond a name
glimpsed in the pages of textbooks towards the end of the Thirty Years War) we
learned from Dumas's *Vingt ans après*. An odious cardinal – whose name
popular tradition has spelled with a single "z" – a squalid swindler and
impostor as compared to his famous predecessor, the great Richelieu, who
knew how to strike down his enemies and give captains' commissions to
deserving musketeers. Mazarin lies, breaks his promises, is late in paying his
debts, and poisons the Duc de Beaufort's dog, which had been trained not to
jump in his honour. He is a third-rate Italian actor, whom Beaufort caricatures
in charcoal and calls the "illustrissimo facchino Mazarini", the illustrious
scoundrel. He is cowardly, base, a perjurer, and worms his way by night into the
bed of Anne of Austria, who in better times had been capable of loving men of
the stature of Buckingham. But can Mazarin really have been such a bastard?
On the other hand, we knew that Dumas, when he spoke of historical figures,
did not invent: he embellished and dramatized, yes, but he paid attention to
sources, chroniclers, and memorialists, even when dealing with fictional
characters – just imagine him with a man of Mazarin's importance. And so we
trusted him.

I do not know whether Dumas knew the *Politician's Breviary*. He may have,
since the short treatise was issued in Latin in 1684, by an unlikely publisher in
Cologne, but was widely translated and circulated in subsequent centuries.
Probably Dumas had only heard of it. For what emerges from a superficial
reading of the book is a Mazarin *à la* Dumas, a hack Machiavellian who
contrives to arrange his outer appearance and his reception, his words and
actions in such a way as to ingratiate himself with his patrons and embroil his
enemies, while concealing the hand that casts the stone. But a close reading

reveals a figure who, though still the one Dumas had divined, at least appals us by the complexity, consciousness, and lofty theoretical rigour of his calculated and eminently human knavery.

It will be said that the book is not his, but a collection of his maxims, whether uttered or practised. So why not read it as a satire, as many have read and interpreted Machiavelli, as the work of a crafty moralist who, while pretending to advise the Prince, "strips him of his laurels and bares him to the people", in Ugo Foscolo's words? But the fact is that whoever wrote this pamphlet, if not Mazarin, was at least someone who took seriously what he wrote, for in the seventeenth century – as Croce reminded us in his *Storia dell'età barocca in Italia* – "the art of simulation and dissimulation, of cunning and hypocrisy, was, because of the intolerant conditions of the society of the time, widely practised and furnished material for innumerable treatises on politics and prudence".

Machiavelli's text was in that case a treatise on imprudence, in its loud and bold proclamation of what the Prince ought to do for the common good. But the Counter-Reformation and the casuistry of the Jesuits intervene between Machiavelli and Mazarin: these short treatises of the seventeenth century accordingly tell how to defend oneself in a world of treacherous princes, who by now are all too consciously Machiavellian, in order to preserve one's inner dignity or physical well-being or advance one's career.

Two other better-known manuals had appeared prior to Mazarin's: *The Manual Oracle or Art of Prudence* (1647) by Baltasar Gracián, and *On Honest Dissimulation* (1641) by Torquato Accetto. They could well have provided inspiration, but Mazarin's treatise seems original in its shameless intentions. Gracián and Accetto were not men of power, and their doleful reflections concern the techniques by which, in a difficult age, one might defend oneself against the powerful. For Gracián the problem was how to live in harmony with one's fellows, undergoing the least possible harm (and he underwent a good deal of it in his lifetime, for he was not as prudent as his preachings). For Accetto it was not a question of simulating what is not (which would have been deceit), but of dissimulating what one is in order to avoid irritating others with one's own virtues (his problem was not how to cause harm, but how not to suffer it). Not Mazarin: he sets forth the programme of a man who, by learning the ways to win favour with the powerful, to gain the love of his subjects, and to eliminate his enemies, uses techniques of simulation to keep the reins of power firmly in hand.

Simulation, not dissimulation. Mazarin (or whoever wrote this handbook) has nothing to dissimulate: he has nothing because he is only what he produces as his own external image. The first chapter, simulatingly entitled "Know Thyself", thus begins with an aphorism on the necessity of examining oneself carefully to see if one has any passions in one's soul (yet even here the question is not "Who am I?" but "How do I appear to myself?"), and immediately proceeds, by other maxims, to sketch a self that is nothing but an artfully constructed mask. Mazarin is what he succeeds in appearing to be to others: he has a clear notion of the subject as a semiotic product. Erving Goffman ought to have read this book; it is a manual for the total theatricalization of the "self". It sets forth an idea of psychic depth made up entirely of surfaces.

We have here a model of "democratic" strategy (in the age of absolutism!), since its instructions for gaining power through violence are very few and carefully circumscribed; in any case, the use of violence is never direct, but always through an intermediary. Mazarin gives us a splendid image of how to obtain power through the sheer manipulation of consensus. How to please not only your boss (a fundamental precept) and not only your friends, but also your enemies, who are to be praised, flattered, persuaded of your benevolence and good faith, in such a way that they die while at the same time blessing you.

There is not, in this first fundamental chapter, a single maxim that does not contain a verb having to do with appearance: to show signs, to give the impression, to reveal, to look, to observe, to pass for. . . . Even the maxims that concern others are directed towards symptoms and revealing signs, whether these have to do with friends and enemies or countries, cities and landscapes. How to find out if someone is a liar, if he loves or hates someone else. The instructions are quite subtle and of this kind: speak ill of your interlocutor's enemy and observe his behaviour and how he reacts. Or the techniques for discovering whether someone is able to keep a secret: sending him another who will provoke him, making it clear that he is in the know, to see whether the first lets the cat out of the bag or meets the challenge with an imperturbable mask. A mask like the one Mazarin contrives for himself when he goes so far as to suggest the way to write a letter in the presence of others so that they will be unable to read it or how to conceal whatever one is reading oneself, and then how to pass for a serious man ("Don't stare at others, don't twitch your nose or wrinkle it. . . . Let your gestures be few, your head held straight, offer few words, allow no spectators at your table").

And always make sure that your adversary does willingly what you intend him to do. "If you have a competitor for a position to which you aspire, secretly send him someone who, in the name of friendship, will dissuade him by exaggerating the difficulties he would encounter." Be aware of all possible snares, and prepared to counter them: "Set aside certain hours of the day to ponder by yourself what decision you should make should this or that mishap befall you." (This, by the way, is the modern theory of "scenarios" of war and peace, except that the Pentagon does them with computers.) Mazarin even gives instructions on how to stay out of prison (since anything can happen to a man of power) and how to call forth panegyrics in one's own honour that will be brief and inexpensive and force everyone to take note. And how to dissimulate wealth ("Always grumble about your lean purse"; here Dumas had caught his man), yet not always, for unexpectedly our author surprises us with a description of the right sort of banquet to astound one's guests, a description that cannot be summarized here – it is a piece of High Baroque theatre.

But enough admiration; one reads books of this sort to extract a lesson. But do not think you can use it to become a man of power. It is not that its maxims are not good ones, quite the contrary. It is that this book describes what the man of power already knows, perhaps by instinct. In this sense it is not only a portrait of Mazarin; you can use it as a catalogue of mug shots in your daily life. In it you will find many people you know, whether seen on TV or met at the office. At each page, you can say, "But I know this man!" Of course. The Mazarins of the world become famous and never fade away. There is an Italian proverb that says "Power consumes". The Italian politician Giulio Andreotti has said: "That is incorrect. Power consumes only those who have none." Mazarin was right: Power consumes only those who do not already know such things.

## The Leader of the Free World Tried, But . . .[1]

The televised speech of 30 April 1973, in which Richard Nixon sought to justify himself in the eyes of public opinion, represents one of the highest and one of the lowest points of American behaviour. What seems positive (and could never happen in Italy) is that, faced with pressure from the media, which as yet had no specific proof, the President of the United States, unable to resist the rising tide of mere suspicion, should have to justify himself before 200 million citizens, by baring his own weaknesses and (a highly dramatic characteristic of televised speeches) his own fears and anguish.

What sets limits to such a conspicuous democratic relationship is that the way in which Nixon, at least temporarily, got himself out of his predicament follows the traditional patterns of the mass media. In other words, put with his back to the wall by a story staged with the skill of Hitchcock by the press, Nixon tried to regain public trust by staging a counter-story. If the press had succeeded in organizing a detective story, or better a Western, which could hardly fail to elicit the approval of the masses, Nixon proceeded to fish other and older stories from the narrative unconscious of his audience, and on these examples constructed the undeniable masterpiece of rhetoric that was his speech. We shall see how and to what extent it failed to work. The fact remains that the choice of narrative was calculated, and one might say that Nixon, given the desperate situation in which he found himself, resolved it in the best possible way.

The following remarks refer to table 1. I shall examine three types of exemplary stories: "Little Red Riding Hood", the epic of the Second World War (as recounted in movies like *Tora! Tora! Tora!* or in old war films like *Iwo Jima*), and the classical Western. And I shall develop a simplified pattern to render these different kinds of stories comparable: there is a "hero" who asserts a "value" to be pursued; in order to secure and protect this value, an "interdiction" must be respected; the interdiction is violated, either by the hero

---

[1] In the light of Nixon's successful attempt to stage a surreptitious come-back, it is illuminating to recall the method of his madness and media downfall. This article was written in 1973, while Eco was a visiting professor at the Graduate Center of the City University of New York. It is witness to the technical development and concerns of semiotics at a precise moment in the discipline's modern history [Editor's note].

*Table 1*

| Functions | Little Red Riding Hood | Pearl Harbor | The Press's "Western" | Nixon's Speech |
|---|---|---|---|---|
| *Hero* | Little Red Riding Hood | The Americans | The Americans | The President |
| *Value* | Security | Security and strength | Controllable government | The American way of life |
| *Interdiction* | Do not stop in the woods | Be alert | Do not corrupt; do not spy | Supervise one's collaborators |
| *Villain* | The Wolf | The Japanese | The President | Careless collaborators |
| *Violation of Interdiction* | Little Red Riding Hood talks to Wolf | Too much confidence | Watergate | Distractions in China and Vietnam |
| *Misfortune* | Little Red Riding Hood is devoured | Pearl Harbor | Abuse of power | Loss of credibility |
| *Rescuer* | The Woodcutter | The Americans | The press and the courts | The President |
| *Struggle* | Pursuit of Wolf | Second World War | Investigation and reporting | Governmental investigation |
| *Victory* | The Wolf is killed | Japan surrenders | White House under investigation | Bad collaborators fired |
| *Value Re-established* | Security | Security and strength | Controllable government | The American way of life |
| *Evaluation of Facts* | The hero was imprudent, but someone saved him | The hero was imprudent, but managed to redeem himself on his own | The villain attempted to lie to the community, but the community's heroes punished him | The hero was imprudent, but managed to redeem himself on his own |

under the influence of a "villain", or by the villain himself to the detriment of the hero, and a "misfortune" results; at this point a "rescuer" intervenes and engages in a struggle with the villain until victory is attained; the defeat of the villain re-establishes the compromised value.

As we see from the table, in "Little Red Riding Hood" the hero(ine) commits an imprudence by violating the interdiction and the misfortune involves her directly; the rescuer helps the hero and defeats the villain. In the story of the Second World War, on the other hand, the hero who commits the imprudence (the entire epic reminds us that if the American command had been more vigilant, the attack on Pearl Harbor could have been prevented) is then able to become his own rescuer, to redeem himself on his own by defeating the villain (in this case, the Japanese). The pattern of the Western film is somewhat different: the interdiction concerns everyone, and it is the villain who violates it to the detriment of the hero; but the hero brings forth an elected representative (usually the sheriff) who punishes the villain and restores peace to the community.

The Western staged by the press was exactly of this type: Americans want a government accountable for its actions and which can be controlled by public opinion; the villain (here, the President) has instead committed a series of interdicted acts that have led to excessive and covert power in the White House, to a real abuse of power at the expense of civil liberties. The press and the courts then intervene, and, through a series of inquiries and accusations, succeed in placing the White House and the President under investigation; the goal is thus accomplished, and government cannot evade the control of the citizens.

What did Nixon do when faced with the narrative perfection of this mechanism contrived by the press? He constructed his speech in legendary terms and rearranged the pieces on the chess board. The President, who in the tale told by the press was the villain, became the hero. Nixon's entire speech was centred on the confession of a man, himself, struck down by great misfortune and nevertheless capable of rising up again for the common good. Indeed, in his speech the hero is a president who must guarantee the continuity of the American way of life to all Americans who place their trust in him (figures 1–3). This president has undoubtedly committed an imprudence: he should have been more careful not to choose rash collaborators ("who did wrong thinking they were doing the right thing"), but he was too busy securing the triumph of the American cause in his international negotiations (China and Vietnam), and he could not personally oversee the electoral campaign. He knows that he has been imprudent and in fact does not try to justify himself: "I assume all responsibility," he said, "I should have paid attention and I was distracted." What is the result? Here Nixon's speech is truly masterful, for the mishap to which he has directed the public's attention is not the series of crimes known as "Watergate"; Watergate, if anything, is seen as a passing incident for which moreover the "bad collaborators" were responsible. The real mishap was the risk that the President might lose credibility and that Americans begin to doubt the value of the system.

With this substitution of chess pieces, Nixon accomplished yet another skilful operation: in the end, those who have made him risk loss of credibility are precisely the reporters. He did not dare to cast the reporters in the role of "villains"; rather, he reserved them a place among the rescuer's helpers (the value of the system, he said, is reaffirmed the moment that the President succeeds in rendering justice, aided by a courageous press and courts of the

Figures 1–3    *Nixon's speech of 30 April 1973*

Figures 4–6    *Nixon's speech of 8 August 1974*

utmost integrity), but imperceptibly he laid the weight of responsibility for the misfortune upon their shoulders.

How did he react to this misfortune? Up to this point, Nixon had played the part of Little Red Riding Hood, imprudent but good; now in his speech, he switches to the pattern of the Second World War. The President is, in fact, the imprudent hero but he is also the rescuer of the American way of life. He orders a rigorous investigation, discovers that several of his collaborators may have erred (or at least exposed themselves to suspicion), and has the courage to fire them, sparing no one, not even his best friends. Once justice is re-established, who can doubt the worth of the system?

With the identification of hero and rescuer, the displacement of the President from the role of villain to that of hero, and the substitution of the misfortune (from the Watergate scandal to the loss of credibility), Nixon undoubtedly accomplished a masterpiece of rhetorical manipulation. He reckoned on having before him a public accustomed to the narratives of the mass media, and replaced one story with another, equally spellbinding one. And a series of polls conducted by the American press showed that many listeners accepted the game, which also restored a human, emotional dimension to the events.

All the same, what happened? Before the televised speech, a small percentage of Americans distrusted Nixon, yet after it the figure increased enormously and exceeded fifty per cent. Why?

The narrative construction would have been perfect had the discourse been a written text. But it was "spoken". And every muscle of Nixon's face betrayed embarrassment, fear, tension. Such a fine story, with the benefit of a happy ending, was told by a frightened man. Frightened from start to finish. Nixon's speech was the visual representation of insecurity, acted out by the "guarantor of security". It was this fear that Americans perceived on their television screens. Thus they suspected that this Little Red Riding Hood was actually a Big Bad Wolf caught with his pants down. The press won the first round.[2]

---

[2] The second round is almost over now. Nixon is projecting himself as the elder statesman: sagging face (the fright lines gone), pondered or ponderous declarations and the visits to China to remind his audience of the main success of his administration. The media is going along, on another American myth: "Don't step on the fallen", or "Give the man a break". [Editor's note]

EDMUNDO DESNOES

# "Will You Ever Shave Your Beard?"

Fidel Castro's beard, blurred and alive, first appeared on the front page of the *New York Times* on 24 February 1957. Herbert L. Matthews, a foreign correspondent for the newspaper, had "discovered" the guerrillas in the dense forests of the Sierra Maestra. Matthews had interviewed the young man and, above all, photographed himself with the Cuban rebel leader. A ghost had appeared in battle fatigues, although the Batista Government and United Press International had pronounced him dead.

Since then, gradually but relentlessly, the media in the United States has created and perpetuated the bearded double exposure of a Frankenstein/Robespierre image. Fidel Castro has become an American obsession. A Frankenstein because in trying to portray, discredit and destroy him they have created a mechanical monster. And a Robespierre because in spite of time and numerous attempts on his life – because he actually exists in flesh and blood – he has proved to be an obdurate and uncorruptible figure.

The media in the United States – especially since television has become a household authority – has accomplished one of the major goals of the Surrealist movement: the destruction of the gap separating fantasy and dreams from the reality principle of bourgeois society. A photo, a news item, a film or a television programme can and often does substitute social awareness in a predominantly ahistorical, manipulative system. (The schizoid behaviour of John W. Hinckley, in his attempt to assassinate President Reagan, is an exacerbated proof of how the realm of fiction overlaps the implacable non-fiction event.)

This is why and how Castro's beard has become Castro. The symbol has replaced the man and his political reality. The most absurd and expensive and ludicrous example is the CIA plot – acknowledged before Congress – to deprive the Cuban leader of his copious beard through a chemical introduced in his cigars or some other equally outlandish device. A costly and delicate assignment in which an agent would risk years in prison or even his own life.

The premise was that without his beard Fidel Castro would become politically impotent. Samson Castro and Delilah Cia. He would no longer have any authority or prestige – in other words, he would become a stage comedian in a gag, the laughing stock of his Cuban and Third-World audience. Yet Castro is, ultimately, what he has done and does in a social and political context and not what he looks like, the image projected by the media.

In the case of Castro one must not confuse the signifier with the signified.

Matthews, a pre-TV era man, in his political biography of Castro, gives us the best historical account of the birth of the symbol:

> There was a picturesque flowering to be noted at that time [just after landing in Oriente province in 1956]. The famous beards of the guerrillas, which led them to be called *los barbudos*, was an early and natural development. . . . The photograph of Fidel that was taken when I saw him in the Sierra shows him with the same kind of beard and short haircut that he has worn to this day. Aside from its being a convenience not to shave in the Sierra, Fidel shrewdly realized that it was a picturesque trademark for the rebels. Besides, he knew he looked better since when he was much younger, and in spite of his superb physical condition, he had a little double chin that the beard hides.

So it was first practical, then glamorous and finally symbolic.

What was born as a practical development, a by-product of armed rebellion in the mountains of Eastern Cuba, became a fashion during the early sixties among the beatnik poets and the movement people – a rebellious defiance of the traditional image of the "silent generation" of the fifties. Soon, a few years later, long hair, also projected by the guerrilla fighters, epitomized by Che Guevara, was added to the beard. It was eventually watered down and co-opted by the system, losing most political or radical connotations. It became a youth fashion.

Nearly thirty years after the appearance of Fidel Castro's beard, the US media continue to be obsessed with his facial hair. No longer to discredit or destroy his political identity – but maybe to tame the Caribbean crocodile; to subdue the unpredictable Cuban leader and, once beardless, deal with an average-looking (and acting?) Castro.

When Barbara Walters interviewed Castro in 1977 for the ABC network news she might have thought that by questioning once more the existence of his beard her audience back North would be impressed and amused with her attempt to bring Castro down to the size of a beardless Southern leader. (Her question showed gross disrespect for one of the most outstanding world leaders alive today. Would she have asked Mrs Thatcher if she went every morning to the hairdresser or Ronald Reagan why he left Washington so often to go horseback riding on his California ranch?)

But when Ms Walters thrust the question, she probably felt entitled, from her own ethnocentric US world view, to violate the privacy of a second-rate leader, a Third-World dictator.

"I have one final question. Will you ever shave your beard?"

Castro's answer, after drawing on his cigar, showed his awareness of the media's disproportionate fixation with his beard:

"As an exchange for what? The ceasing of the blockade?"

Ms Walters was forced to face the facts:

"If we stop the blockade you shave off your beard, eh? I don't think that would make America do it, but. . . ."

Castro had brought her down to factual issues; then felt he could proceed candidly:

"We would be importing Gillette razor blades, right? Do you know why we left our beard? Because we did not have razor blades. But as time passed, the guerrillas were known by their beards. It was more difficult to introduce a spy. They had to wait many months for the beard to grow. So that is why the beard became a useful thing. And finally, it became a symbol.

"After the Revolution, many people started shaving. Then some regulations appeared in the Army: people had to shave. And little by little, I was left as one of the very few with a beard. Well, I continue with the beard.

"But what happens? When grey hair comes, it starts to appear precisely in the beard. And you can notice them more. That is why my idea now is to wait until I have a totally white beard. And then I will make a decision, whether I tint it or shave it."

Barbara tried again to turn her crude and ludicrous question to her advantage:

"And the country can vote?"

"The country? That's a personal matter! Don't forget about human rights!"

Fidel Castro scored an obvious political point by placing his beard in an objective context – it would change nothing in US–Cuban relations – then went into giving some candid, revealing information and ended by returning to the original media fantasy and commercial break: maybe he would tint it with Clairol or shave with Gillette.

More sinister and serious was Anastasio Somoza Debayle's request, as the contingent of Cuban counter-revolutionary forces left Nicaragua in 1961 headed for the Bay of Pigs: "Bring me back the hair of Fidel Castro's beard." A modest proposal given what it implied.

Latin American revolutions are serious affairs and people put their lives on the line. The Bay of Pigs invasion failed and almost twenty years later, in 1979, Somoza had to flee Nicaragua – although he had claimed: "*Ni me voy ni me van*" (I'm not leaving nor can you force me to leave). Shortly after, during his exile in Asunción, Paraguay, Somoza was blown to pieces in his white Mercedes Benz. No one requested any part of his anatomy. The dethroned heir of Nicaragua's forty years' dynasty was forced to leave defeated by the Sandinistas – but his death was probably linked to jealousy, a fight for love not glory.

On 19 July 1980, when Fidel Castro spoke at a mass rally in Managua, Nicaragua, to celebrate the first anniversary of the Sandinista revolution, he referred to his beard for the first time in a public address: "Nor can we forget our arrival in Nicaragua, right in the territory of Puerto Cabezas, from where the mercenary invasion of Girón (Bay of Pigs) was launched. It is said that the tyrant Somoza, in bidding farewell to the troops, asked them to bring back at least one hair from Castro's beard. I have come with my entire beard, to offer it, if only symbolically, to the victorious people of Nicaragua."

"History" (with all its surprises and symbols) – as Fidel Castro once told Saul Landau in an interview – "is a subproduct of action." Man, as a symbolic animal, operates and is moved to believe and act, in highly industrialized societies, under the spell of the mass media industry. Socratic dialogue – the most powerful means of clarifying the world around us – has been substituted by media monologue. A manipulated and mediated vision is confusing our construction of reality.

DANIEL DAYAN and ELIHU KATZ

# Electronic Ceremonies: Television Performs a Royal Wedding

Walter Benjamin asks[1] what becomes of the audience's relationship to works of art, when these works become copies diffused through mechanical reproduction. We raise a similar question: what happens to ceremonies when, instead of being attended, they are delivered to each of us at home?

Anthropology may throw some light on this problem, by proposing concepts in terms of which one can examine different forms of participation appropriate to different forms of occasions. Following Don Handelman and John MacAloon in their independent but converging attempts at constituting an ethnology of audiences[2] we shall propose here a schematic typology of such occasions by stressing three exemplary types: cinema, as an extreme form of spectacle; festival as another polar extreme, almost entirely free of spectacle; ceremony as a ground between "pure" festival and "untainted" spectacle. We suggest that these forms differ along dimensions of focus, specificity of response, and interaction between audience and performers.

Film, and spectacles in general, such as sports or theatre, share a narrowness of focus, a limited set of appropriate responses and (at least when one does not include modern rediscoveries of "*théâtre total*") a minimal level of interaction. What there is to see is very clearly exhibited: spectacle implies a distinction between the roles of performers and audience. Performers are set apart and audiences asked to respond cognitively and emotionally in predefined categories of approval, disapproval, arousal or passivity. Audience interaction with the performance may enhance it, but it is not meant nor allowed to become

[1] Walter Benjamin, "The Work of Art in the Age of Mechanical Reproduction", in *Mass Media and Society*, ed. Gurevitch, Curran and Woolacott (Beverly Hills, Calif.: Sage, 1978).
[2] Don Handelman, "Towards an Analytic Model for Public Ceremonies" (unpublished) and John MacAloon, "Olympic Games and the Theory of Spectacles in Modern Societies" (Annenberg School, seminar on media events, July 1979).

part of its definition. (In the case of cinema, such an interaction becomes so irrelevant that audience responses are almost entirely internalized.)

Festival, on the contrary, is diffuse in focus. No simple picture or pageant imposes itself monopolistically on participants. Appropriate responses may be many and varied. Indeed, creative responses are quite often welcome. Interaction is obviously called for since roles of performers and spectators are neither fixed nor irreversible. Equally obvious is the observation that the nature of the resultant "performance" is altogether dependent on audience "responses".

Ceremony shares features with both spectacle and festival in that, on the one hand, it offers a clear focus, a definite distinction between performers and respondents – the latter being expected to respond in specific (and usually traditional) ways – while, on the other hand, its existence consists of an interaction between audience and performers. Audience response is one of the constitutive features of ceremony. Without it, a ceremony might become empty.

This typology of forms of participation makes it possible to examine the role of television in an event such as the royal wedding. To do so, let us propose an artificial distinction between the event as organized and the event as broadcast.

The event as organized contains elements of both spectacle and festival. It would be reasonable to assume that the event as televised would only be a spectacle, since its focus is irremediably narrowed, since reactions are highly limited and can in no way affect the performance. But is this really so?

## Participation in the "Original" Event

Consider the royal wedding from the point of view of spectators who were present (ignoring for the moment that these spectators, despite their overwhelming numbers, might have become props). The event clearly combined festival with spectacle aspects.

As a spectacle, it allowed its audience a very circumscribed repertoire of responses. Ceremonial space stressed the distinction between performers and spectators by clearly isolating a performance "stage" – the processional itinerary enclosed on each side by policemen and guards – from the reaction "floor" extending on both sides. Within this setting, public behaviour was to be one of emotional reactions, spontaneous (as in cheers or acclamations) but strictly defined. The behaviour of the principals was very highly ritualized and displayed an impersonal aspect which ideally precluded any show of emotion (figure 1). It consisted of a performance, either of commitment or authority, in the case of, respectively, the newlyweds and the clerics. Each of the principals was consciously enacting a "persona". The public, on the other hand, was in no way expected to perform (unless one defines the very act of responding as a performance). The royal wedding displayed a striking but asymmetric consumption of symbols. To the performers, all the symbolic wealth of centuries of history was made available with a prodigality which invited quantitative evaluation rather

Figure 1

than discrete interpretations. Respondents, however, had access to a very small set of accessories such as balloons, small Union Jacks, little party hats painted in Union-Jack patterns or imitating the headgear of policemen, emblazoned T-shirts. The symbols worn by the principals affected the whole of their persons. The symbols available to spectators were discrete, detachable decorations, relatively independent of the rest of their attire: dressing up event-style was restricted to performers (figure 2). Besides being smaller and detachable, the symbols available to the responding crowds had a "secondary" quality, describable in Walter Benjamin's terms. Not only were they symbols, they were symbols of symbols: not real flags (inasmuch as a "real" flag exists), but paper images of flags; not real police hats, but plastic copies of these hats. While the performers carried or wore authentic or "original" symbols, the public was provided with mass-produced, stereotyped copies (figure 3) and, for their part, when the principals wanted to manifest their closeness to the public, they made use of this impoverished repertoire (thus allowing balloons to be facetiously attached to their carriage) (figure 4).

Figure 2

Figure 3

Figure 4

But beyond this spectacle dimension, the festival aspect was very clearly in evidence. Waiting along the lines of the parade, people developed relationships with each other, invented new forms of response which trespassed on the formal division of roles between themselves and performers. While television (and, to some extent, the police) eventually censored such violations, it is clear that the public in attendance at the event developed its festival aspect as its own contribution to the day. Spectators painted Union Jacks on their faces (figure 5), pinned hundreds of small emblems all over themselves or draped themselves entirely in flags. Their symbols were often appropriate – flag waving is a legitimate response to the display of royal and historical symbols – but their overzealousness cast them as usurping performers, as show-stealers (figure 6); threatened to turn the event into a carnival which it sometimes became when members of the public went further in departing from the strict boundaries of their assigned roles and assumed an active rather than reactive stance, attempting to enlist the reaction of others to themselves. Such was the case in Trafalgar Square where a group of skinheads and punks choreographed a mock splashing fight in the fountains (figure 7). When the police arrived, the *Dolce Vita*-inspired performers draped themselves in English flags and resumed their place in the cheering crowd, thus acknowledging the "spectacle" dimension of an event which required their participation, but within precise limits. This was not simply a festival.

This was not a simple spectacle either, and many an attempt at "carnivaliz-ing" the occasion may be explained by the frustration of the attendants who had paradoxically so little access to the "spectacle" aspect of the ceremony. Indeed different spaces were provided for the general public and the invited elite. Some could participate by struggling to watch the carriages fly past (figure 8),

Figure 5

Figure 6

Figure 7

while others could see the mass from a pew inside the church. However, the moments of highest tension were clearly distinct from those which provided the best spectacular conditions, and it was not inside St Paul's Cathedral, but on its threshold or on Buckingham Palace's balcony that the event realized its *ceremonial* vocation. Attendants who could not see the principals and had to guess their presence and identity by the nature of the surrounding murmurs or cheers were meant to reconfirm the contract between themselves and the performers, between the people of England and its monarchs.[3] This interaction constituted the core of the event. Spectacle was amply provided, but often remained invisible. Festival was in the air, but it had to be subdued: crowds were willing to canalize their reactions into appropriate responses to a given focus, a focus whose physical splendour many would discover only later, on television's evening recorded highlights.

The success of the royal wedding thus points to the nature of a ceremonial

[3] Inspiration for this point, and many others in this article, is drawn from Edward Shils and Michael Young, "The Meaning of the Coronation", *Sociological Review*, vol. I, no. I (1953) 68–81. Further support for the Shils thesis is presented in J. G. Blumler *et al.*, "Attitudes to the Monarchy: their Structure and Development During a Ceremonial Occasion", *Political Studies*, vol. XIX, no. 2 (1971) 143–171.

Figure 8

event which shares common features with both spectacle and festival, but depends on a specific mode of interaction between performers and audience. This interaction offers a *charismatic legitimation* of the proposed event. It *legitimizes* by being a "proper" reaction, and thus safe from the risks of "wrong" reaction – illustrated by the short-lived attempts to turn the royal wedding into a carnival; of "over-reaction" – a constant concern of the organizers of Pope John Paul's first visit to Poland, since it would have transposed his pilgrimage from the sphere of the religious to that of the political, and provoked the risk of repression; of "counter-reaction" – an active rejection to which the organizers of President Sadat's funeral did not want to provide a focus. It is *charismatic* in that the presence of the crowds can be opposed to the possibility of non-reaction, of indifference. Equally feared in the case of President Sadat's funeral, the non-attendance of crowds represents definitional failure for such events.

The meaning of the royal wedding had less to do with the fact of marriage than with the attendance of crowds (figure 9).

All these examples stress how much the very nature of each of our events depends on attendance, and on a channelled but indispensable participation. One can then wonder what happens to such an event when it is broadcast on television and thus turns into a spectacle, making very little provision for audience response and, *a fortiori*, for audience interaction.

By turning into a spectacle, an interactive ceremony undergoes an obvious impoverishment. The surprise is that, while television *represents* an occasion, and therefore flattens it into a spectacle, it gives itself a new mission: that of

Figure 9

offering an equivalent to the lost participatory dimension. Thus, while destroying interaction by its very similarity to cinema, television *performs* (or simulates) it anew. How does it attempt to reinject it?

## Participation in the Media Event: Diasporic Celebrations

A spectacle of a ceremony is not a ceremony. The live broadcast of an occasion is distinct from that occasion even though it may serve as a focus for another occasion. In attempting to maintain the interactive value of the ceremonies it broadcasts, television faces an apparently original problem. This problem is only apparently original, since it has been haunting, among others, Jewish liturgy: how can one create a communality of celebration when the members of the concerned community are physically separated? In reference to their dispersed audiences, our media events could be defined as diasporic celebrations. At least diasporic celebrations they wish to be, rather than mass-available spectacles about *a* celebration. Such a wish determines a number of features of the broadcasts. Some of these features may be nothing more than symptoms, compensatory behaviours, ritual affirmations that the ceremony is all there, that "nothing is missing". Some of these features may, however, be more than rhetorical fetishes. Do they succeed in achieving interaction?

## Reinjecting Unequal Access

By orchestrating the passage from a qualitative, selective participation in the ceremony to a quantitative, global one, television has created a remarkable historical or cultural artefact: the notion that one can attend the "whole of an event". The experience of anybody who tries to attend a public event or ceremony constantly proves that "attending" means attending *part* of the event. One cannot view a procession from all vantage points unless one moves along with the procession (and therefore one loses one's place), or unless one is part of the procession (and therefore totally unable to focus on it as a spectacle). You see an event from a given place, from a given distance and this place and distance tell you (and tell the others) who you are. In the case of the royal wedding, either you are in the church (that is, a guest of the royal family), or you are outside the church, and the conquest of a place with good visibility has to be paid for, in terms of waking up before dawn or sleeping on the pavement. As in the theatre, your distance from stage, your placement in regard to the centre of the event, is a very clear reminder of your place in society. (To use Benjamin's notion, your distance from the event constitutes its "aura".)

What happens with the introduction of television is that, in accordance with narrative structures and the exigency of continuity they introduce, everybody attends the whole of the event. Everybody attends, at least, something which is called "the whole of the event". What seems new to us is this very notion of a totality of the event,[4] a notion which seems inherited from the domain of a spectacle.

An event such as the royal wedding indeed presents itself as a string of smaller ceremonial units, featuring the same actors (the royal family, the newlyweds) but different audiences, and the dramaturgy of each of these units is an answer to the nature of the audience. What happens with television is that the distinctive self-presentations of the royalty to the different constituents of the British public are no longer conceptualized on the mode of "either/or", but become available on the mode of "and/and". The different groups now form one audience. The different sub-events now form one narrative (and one of the tasks of the broadcasters is to organize the rhythmic continuity, the unity of the performance). By turning the event into one spectacle, TV acts as a class equalizer: only the attendant audiences maintain the privilege of seeing only part of the event, thus experiencing their deprivation as its aura. However, the equi-distance introduced between the various segments of the public is compensated by a television-performed reintroduction of distance.

This distance is that which now separates members of the television

---

[4] Consider in comparison Clifford Geertz's analysis of the coronation of Elizabeth I: C. Geertz, "Center, Kings and Charisma", in J. Ben David and T. Clark (eds), *Culture and its Creators* (Chicago: University of Chicago Press, 1980). Also A. Burnett, "Wedding Thoughts – Royal Occasions of the Past and Relationship between Monarchy and the Media", *Independent Broadcasting*, no. 30 (November 1981).

personnel involved in the event. A clear distinction is made between those television people who were part of the event (for example, Tom Fleming for the BBC) and those television people who were out of the event (for example, Angela Rippon, also for the BBC). To be "in" and not, as Angela Rippon, "out", in the desolate limbos of television studios, is a mark of added prestige, of seniority, of participation in the event's mana, as evidenced by Rippon's interview of Fleming.

While, on the one hand, destroying the event's "aura", television tries to reinject it through strategies which seem to repeat themselves from media event to media event. When President Sadat left on his historical visit from Cairo to Jerusalem, many of the stars of the American channels were with him on the plane: Walters, Cronkite, Chancellor. From the tarmac they were observed by special correspondents of the respective channels. The less elevated status of these envoys meant not only that they were out with the crowds, while their prestigious colleagues were "in" with the actors, but also that they saw less of what was taking place than the telespectators or the studio anchors at home.

Being pressed in the crowd, with no monitors at their disposal, they had to guess a large part of what was happening from audio clues or visual deductions, and their commentaries seemed to corroborate the images on screen by a constantly renewed miracle.[5] In such an extreme case, one might wonder why special or local correspondents are used at all, since they both know less than the stars accompanying the principals and see less than their studio counterparts. One might answer that, precisely, their function is to know less and to see but little, to be pressed in a crowd, elbowed, pushed around, frantically trying to perceive, see or guess (figure 10). Their function is an aesthetic function (even though it is probably not planned that way). They are there to compensate for the spectacular display of the whole of the event, to re-establish the sense of distance, of specific involvement in this or that partial aspect of the ceremony. They are there, finally, to reinject in the event, by their frantic and futile attempts to see and know, its lost aura. They are performing that archaic dimension of events which is specific to audience participation and which disappears when a ceremony is flattened, ironed out, indifferently offered to equi-distant glances, evenly soaked in a banalized knowledge. It is within this framework that one can understand the importance of rumours in so many media events: rumours reinject depth into the displayed event, suggest a distinction between those who share a given knowledge and those who do not share it yet, suggest the existence of a distance within the event, counter-balance its pedagogic utilitarianism.

---

[5] Of course the local correspondent is able to identify people and places with which his seniors are unfamiliar, and he may cue them from his specialist knowledge of the local scene concerning aspects of the larger picture. However, here we are speculating on the aesthetic function he performs, which distances him from his own panoramic expertise.

Figure 10

## Ostentatious Unobtrusiveness

A characteristic of a media event is that the television narrator's voice be unobtrusive. This voice and what it tells are clearly defined as secondary to the event itself. The voice must be quiet, hushed, reverent, the statements concise, sparse and grammatically simple in order to be easily interrupted at any point. Visual continuity has clear precedence over that of narration. When an event is given "media event" treatment, one can expect the editorializing function to be performed inside the event and not by the narrator's voice. That voice provides clarifications, information, footnotes, but its status is essentially discontinuous. It grafts itself on to the continuity of the event, and its presence must not prevent spectators from "flowing with" this event. This is because most media events, if not all of them, are expressive occasions. Most media events, in both their verbal and non-verbal aspects, are intended as acts of communication. Television communicators are therefore required to avoid superimposing their own act of communication over the one provided by the event. If the event itself is speech, then television as "mere" mediator, which it proclaims itself to be, is supposed to connect this speech to its audience without superimposing its own speech over it. Television is thus entrusted with, and appears to restrict itself to, the "phatic" function of communication: insuring that there is a contact between partners, that the channel for communication is free. This explains why the narrator's performance steps aside, so to speak, as often as possible in order to leave precedence to the communication acts within the event. It also explains why, when the narrator does not step aside, the producers' policy often consists of drowning the narrative with the cheers and rumours of the crowd, and this to the point of depriving the commentary of any intelligibility.

The narrator's unobtrusiveness is not only physical, it may also be semantic: the narrator speaks the values of the event, echoes them, prolongs them. Within the semantic domain, unobtrusiveness reaches beyond denotation, even connotation: it affects the narrator's voice, its tone, accent, everything in it referring to a given generation or social group. This last, and apparently secondary, feature was given quite some prominence in what looked to foreigners like a hair-splitting exercise: that of justifying the existence of a double television broadcast of the royal wedding (by both BBC and ITV) by pointing to differences in the respective styles of narrators Alastair Burnett (ITV) and Tom Fleming (BBC). Both their narratives were reverent. Both remained ancilliary to the event. Both echoed its main values. How, then, did they differ?

It was less, we were told, a question of attitude (slightly more journalistic in the one case, slightly more celebrational in the other) than of vocabulary, cadence, tone of voice. Youngsters and members of groups less attached to establishment values seemed to find Tom Fleming's voice irritating, comical or pretentious. Such aesthetic distaste did not prevent them from being quite interested in attending the event on television. Distaste with Fleming's voice was not synonymous with rejecting the wedding. Quite the contrary: Fleming's voice was cumbersome to its non-establishment receivers; alien to their own socio-cultural values, it stood between them and the event, prevented them from "flowing with it", making it theirs. It acted as a reminder of distance, preventing them from immersing themselves in the occasion. It produced a desire for contact.

This created the condition for Alastair Burnett. His voice, as alternative to Fleming's performance, was a means of granting the desired contact. For the non-establishment, this vocal existence was a second logical moment, a switch of the dial, a means of enjoying – after a moment of being unable to enjoy – the narrator's invisibility. Television – here, the BBC and ITV in combination – proclaims it is (merely) phatic. Television says it is like a street, a piazza, a communicative space. It calls itself an electronic ceremony ground.


## The Model of Contagion

The point was to deny that there was any discontinuity between the celebration in London and the audiences who were receiving it; to ignore the transformation of celebration into spectacle. In order to achieve this, an image was proposed: that of an epidemic, of a contagion of celebrations which progressively merged into each other until one was plunged into a vast party involving the whole of England.

Such tactics seem to become permanent features of media events. On the day of the investiture of President Mitterand, French television's second channel (Antenne 2) chose to transport its studio to a village away from the Paris-based ceremonies. Within this bucolic setting (possibly chosen for its affinity with the Rousseauist ethos of the festivals that followed the French Revolution), local ceremonies and celebrations transformed the reception of the broadcast into an event in its own right. The spectacle of a celebration was immediately converted into a focus of another celebration. Similar tactics were used for the royal wedding, with similarly unconvincing results – differences in celebrating styles tend to act as cruel reminders of the importance of props and pageantry – but a slightly different *mise-en-scène*. Instead of two celebrations, three were offered. The original celebration (the wedding) was viewed from a studio where it became the occasion for a party-like talk show which, in turn included a feature on a village celebration during which ice-cream-stuffed children waved little flags in the direction of majestically displayed TV sets. Despite the ice cream and flag waving, TV sets, however, remained TV sets, and the model of contagion remained a wish.

This model had been made explicit the night before the wedding in the broadcast devoted to the fireworks in Hyde Park, a broadcast which started by a sequence showing fire signals travelling over countryside, from hilltop to hilltop, from beacon to beacon, until the last of them came in actual view of the royal party, allowing Prince Charles to start the fireworks. The use of beacons suggested a progressive unification of England, a string of parties situated at eye's distance from each other, a physical contagion of the party mood modelled on that of forest fires. It is, of course, ironic that the beacons' progression had to be conveyed by television, but the metaphor of the beacon was precisely that by which television tried to absolve itself from the sin of "representing" a celebration rather than diffusing it. Again, television displayed itself as a phatic channel, the instrument of a spatial continuity rather than the locus of semiotic exercises. This was particularly manifest in apparently secondary features of the event, such as the breakfast menu, or the dress of Lady Diana. Not only was the British public informed that the Queen would offer her guests a breakfast party, but the menu of the breakfast was widely advertised, and advertised as one which included no specially "fancy" items: anyone who so wished could, in other words, buy the food and enjoy a breakfast similar in composition (if not in culinary expertise) to that served in Buckingham Palace's dining rooms. The suggestion, however, was only implicit. It became quite explicit with the huge publicity given to the copying of Lady Diana's dress. Organized as a suspense story, the reproduction of the dress became one of the threads which helped to unify the wedding day into a continuous event. By the end of the day, the copy was to be displayed in a London window (figure 11). A few days later, it would be mass reproduced and on sale. Before the end of the day, a number of young ladies were interviewed saying they would buy copies for their own weddings. It is clear here that both the breakfast menu and the dress served as unifiers of dispersed celebrations into one celebration. Symbolically, all England was served the same breakfast. Symbolically also, television served a continuation of

Figure 11

the tradition which requires that a young bride, on her wedding day, distribute to the brides-to-be around her, to the unmarried maids, fragments of what she wears, in order to associate them, by some sort of magical contagion, to the "mana" which inhabits her on that day. Instead of (metonymic) fragments of veil, Lady D. circulated, via television, (metaphoric) images of the dress, thus offering to share her good luck with all the maids of England; thus also characterizing television as a means of physical continuity, of contagion. Television is that which abolishes distance.

Television is that also which reinstates it in the very process of abolishing it. The breakfast menu was publicized, but the recipe of the wedding cake emphatically kept secret. So was the wedding dress until the last minute, and all sorts of stratagems were used to maintain this secrecy, including that of announcing that many dresses had been prepared and that any leak would lead to the choice of a new dress. Characteristically, the lady who busied herself with the copying of the dress, had no access to it, except by television. She had to infer all the decisions that went into making it from whatever she could see on screen (with the help of an instant-replay videotape). On both ends of a broadcast stood two dresses, presented as – almost – identical. But one was "original" and destined to remain that, and that only. The other was the matrix for mass-reproduction. Copies were *almost* those of the original dress, but in an emphatically *mediated* way (figure 12). One could have imagined the authors of the dress selling their sketches to the copyist (with, of course, all due financial arrangements). This was not done. The activity of copying was both allowed, encouraged, publicized and submitted to an intricate *mise-en-scène*, the point of which was to assert the aura of Lady Diana's dress, as opposed to the availability of its master copy. Thus television was reasserted as an instrument

Figure 12

of distance, dismissed as a means of participation. Participation was a simulation benevolently looked upon as long as it did not infringe on what distinguishes royalty from movie stars: their aura. As soon as it did, television was sent back to its true realm: that of copies, of images; that of "lesser realities". Less lucky than Cinderella, the would-be extended, diasporic celebration was reverted to its true status: that of a spectacle.

The strategies we have just analysed have been revealed as elements in the spectacle, rather than means of transforming its nature. An electronically connected agora was what television meant to achieve but not what it succeeded in bringing into existence. And somehow, while television acted as a "wedding photographer", it also proposed a self-portrait where it chose to play the unassuming role devoted by Jakobson to the "phatic" function of communicative acts.[6]

This self-portrait of television has, in and by itself, theoretical importance. It corresponds precisely to the dimension of all narrative structures which, following Benveniste's reflection on certain universally found grammatical features, semioticians agreed to call *discourse*.[7] Opposing itself to a *story*, *histoire* (the subject matter of a given story, that aspect of the story concerning itself with the portrayed referent, here the wedding), *discourse* consists of the way in which any given text exhibits to its readers or viewers the very process of its

[6] Roman Jakobson, "Linguistics and Poetics", in Thomas Sebeok (ed.), *Style in Language* (New York: Wiley, 1960).
[7] Emile Benveniste, "Man and Language", in his *Problems in General Linguistics* (Coral Gables, Fla.: University of Miami Press, 1976).

being communicated to them. Discourse, in a text, is a dramaturgy, the subject of which is the communication of the text: its emission, its reception, its nature. But, while offered as a comment upon a given text, this dramaturgy is, in fact, immanent to it. Thus television only proclaimed itself a phatic channel and the receivers of the ceremony's broadcast are only claimed to be participants in that ceremony.

## The Electronic Ceremony

Public events have no fixed form and, throughout history, they may be expected to adapt themselves to prevailing modes of making an event public – publicness, in our own neologism. Television, in our time, has become the dominant form of publicness, and we are witnessing the gradual replacement of what could be called a "theatrical" mode of publicness, an actual meeting of performers and public in such places as parliament houses, churches, convention floors, by a new mode of publicness based on the potential separation of performers and audiences, and on the rhetoric of narrative rather than the virtue of contact.

This mode is justifiably mistrusted since its dynamics lead to substitute simulation for representation, and since simulation, when endowed with authority, may turn into what Austin called "performative", and thus constitute a social reality. Our era, as Baudrillard pointed out,[8] after Benjamin, might be that of simulacre; of images without originals, of images whose effectiveness is not in the least impoverished by such a lack. On the day of his presidential investiture, François Mitterand paid a visit to the Panthéon, France's mausoleum to its great men, and rendered a specific homage to a few graves, including that of Socialist leader Jean Jaurès. Providing the day's ceremonial climax, his visit was broadcast live and he was seen entering the Panthéon, holding in his hand what had become the Socialist party's emblem during the presidential campaign: a single red rose. Once in the mausoleum, Mitterand, who of course had only one rose, was seen placing flowers on three graves. As a socialist winner, he had to enter the Panthéon with one rose only. As heir to many French traditions, he had to pay homage to many graves. In order to meet these distinct symbolic requirements, some editing was needed and the "realistic" character of live broadcasting necessarily tampered with. More fundamentally, the time theoretically spent by the President in silent communion with his spiritual mentors had to be, at least partly, devoted to replenishing his provision of flowers. Thus this dignified and almost eerie consultation with the dead existed for the broadcast. The Panthéon had been turned into a studio. Through the miracle – or hocus-pocus – of the multiplication of roses, another of France's great men found himself celebrated on that day: Georges Méliès.

[8] Jean Baudrillard, "La précession des simulacres", in Le Simulacre. Traverses, no. 10 (Paris: Minuit, 1978).

ROLAND BARTHES

# The Shape I'm In: Interview with French *Playboy*

BARTHES: I had a *super skinny* morphology throughout my youth, I was even rejected by the draft because I did not make the regulation weight. And at that time I always lived with the idea that I would be skinny, forever. But, in fact, after my illness – tuberculosis – when I had been cured (or stabilized), my morphology started to change. I remember very well, I can still see myself, it happened in the bed at the clinic, at Leysin, in Switzerland, where I ended up after my operation (a pneumothorax). I started to swell up. And I let it happen: at that time the mythology of "slimming down" was not as strong as it is now. And then one day, while being examined for something completely different, I was being told, "You have to slim down". So I started to do it: not for reasons of aesthetics or of "youth", but with a scientific and medical alibi.

There is a book to be written about all the problems of losing weight. Not so much about "recipes" for reducing, since there are so many of them, as about the phenomenon and its mythology. I talk about it a lot because there is something very "mobilizing" about it, as they say. You understand, it is a religious phenomenon, a "religious neurosis". Going on a diet has all the characteristics of a conversion. With all the same problems of lapsing, and then returning to the conversion. With certain books that are like gospels, etc. A diet mobilizes an acute sense of wrongdoing, something which threatens, which is there every minute of the day. It is only when you sleep that you are sure of not doing something wrong. From the moment you accept the rules of the diet, whether it is "low calorie" or "sugar free", since the rules are very strict, there are . . . a thousand failures.

Very quickly, when you are in the frame of mind to diet, you end up "hallucinating" your body. By that I mean that if you take in ten grams of sugar, which absolutely cannot make you get materially fatter – in any case not for twenty-four or forty-eight hours – well, within the next hour you "feel" your body getting fat.

Losing weight is a question of deliberate choice, of struggle. That is not the most difficult thing: you are aware of fighting, you mobilize yourself. But the whole question is one of *maintenance*. This consists of finding a way of eating that you will not think about any more. It takes a lot of time.

PLAYBOY: *The trouble is that the forbidden is always desirable by definition.*

BARTHES: The very fact that you would set up a strictly "metrical" rule makes you cheat a little: you set up systems of compensation for yourself. You say to yourself: oh, well, since I have denied myself that, I shall make up for it with this, etc. They tell you that quitting smoking makes you gain weight, so you take advantage of this – non-scientific – assertion so as not to add a cure for tobacco detoxification to a cure for losing weight.

PLAYBOY: *Your problem is sugar?*

BARTHES: For me, yes. But that is not the case for everybody. And then you know, there are fads. Take Atkins, for example. He maintains that if you get rid of all sugars, fruits included, you can eat as much as you want of everything else. In reality, it is an ideology that is tailor-made for Americans, in so far as, on the one hand, it frustrates them enormously (they are the people who eat the most sugar): therefore it gives them the energy to struggle over an important point (no more sundaes, no more ice cream, no more Cokes, etc.). On the other hand, the Atkins diet gives Americans an enormous compensation: breakfast! It recurs on every page of Atkins like a kind of description of the golden age: all is not lost because with Atkins, in the morning, you are entitled to eat anything you want, bacon, sausage, eggs, poached, fried, etc.

PLAYBOY: *Another compensation: it gives them a guru. Part of the "religious" aspect of dieting.*

BARTHES: It is better to "add up" diets. And then in the end there is only one system for losing weight: do not eat. Do you know what I spoke about with the administrator of the Collège de France, during my first visit for candidature? The American statistics on the percentage of successful weight-loss diets. Barely 5 per cent last – the others last a while, then they give up. In the modern world, there is a social dialectic which keeps you from sticking to a diet: if you eat something with someone, you are immediately subjected to the other's attention, which keeps you from respecting your diet in one way or another.

I am forced to compensate for my meals in restaurants by eating ascetically when I am at home. A salad. A grilled steak – I don't like meat. But it is the food best suited to keeping you from getting fat.

PLAYBOY: *And cheese?*

BARTHES: I like it enormously. I often have some between meals. I should not but . . .

UMBERTO ECO

# *Casablanca*, or the Clichés Are Having a Ball

When people in their fifties sit down before their television sets for a rerun of *Casablanca*, it is an ordinary matter of nostalgia. However, when the film is shown in American universities, the boys and girls greet each scene and canonical line of dialogue ("Round up the usual suspects", "Was that cannon fire, or is it my heart pounding?" – or even every time that Bogey says "kid") with ovations usually reserved for football games. And I have seen the youthful audience in an Italian art cinema react in the same way. What then is the fascination of *Casablanca*?

The question is a legitimate one, for aesthetically speaking (or by any strict critical standards) *Casablanca* is a very mediocre film. It is a comic strip, a hotch-potch, low on psychological credibility, and with little continuity in its dramatic effects. And we know the reason for this: the film was made up as the shooting went along, and it was not until the last moment that the director and scriptwriters knew whether Ilse would leave with Victor or with Rick. So all those moments of inspired direction that wring bursts of applause for their unexpected boldness actually represent decisions taken out of desperation. What then accounts for the success of this chain of accidents, a film that even today, seen for a second, third or fourth time, draws forth the applause reserved for the operatic aria we love to hear repeated, or the enthusiasm we accord to an exciting discovery? There is a cast of formidable hams. But that is not enough.

Here are the romantic lovers – he bitter, she tender – but both have been seen to better advantage. And *Casablanca* is not *Stagecoach*, another film periodically revived. *Stagecoach* is a masterpiece in every respect. Every element is in its proper place, the characters are consistent from one moment to the next, and the plot (this too is important) comes from Maupassant – at least the first part of it. And so? So one is tempted to read *Casablanca* the way T. S. Eliot reread *Hamlet*. He attributed its fascination not to its being a successful work (actually he considered it one of Shakespeare's less fortunate plays) but to something quite the opposite: *Hamlet* was the result of an unsuccessful fusion of several earlier Hamlets, one in which the theme was revenge (with madness as only a stratagem), and another whose theme was the crisis brought on by the mother's sin, with the consequent discrepancy between Hamlet's nervous excitation and the vagueness and implausibility of Gertrude's crime. So critics and public alike find *Hamlet* beautiful because it is interesting, and believe it to be interesting because it is beautiful.

On a smaller scale, the same thing happened to *Casablanca*. Forced to improvise a plot, the authors mixed in a little of everything, and everything they chose came from a repertoire of the tried and true. When the choice of the tried and true is limited, the result is a trite or mass-produced film, or simply kitsch. But when the tried and true repertoire is used wholesale, the result is an architecture like Gaudi's Sagrada Familia in Barcelona. There is a sense of dizziness, a stroke of brilliance.

But now let us forget how the film was made and see what it has to show us. It opens in a place already magical in itself – Morocco, the Exotic – and begins with a hint of Arab music that fades into "La Marseillaise". Then as we enter Rick's Place we hear Gershwin. Africa, France, America. At once a tangle of Eternal Archetypes comes into play. These are situations that have presided over stories throughout the ages. But usually to make a good story a single archetypal situation is enough. More than enough. Unhappy Love, for example, or Flight. But *Casablanca* is not satisfied with that: it uses them all. The city is the setting for a Passage, the passage to the Promised Land (or a Northwest Passage, if you like). But to make the passage one must submit to a test, the Wait ("they wait and wait and wait", says the off-screen voice at the beginning). The passage from the waiting room to the Promised Land requires a Magic Key, the visa. It is around the winning of this Key that passions are unleashed. Money (which appears at various points, usually in the form of the Fatal Game, roulette) would seem to be the means for obtaining the Key. But eventually we discover that the Key can be obtained only through a Gift – the gift of the visa, but also the gift Rick makes of his Desire by sacrificing himself. For this is also the story of a round of Desires, only two of which are satisfied: that of Victor Laszlo, the purest of heroes, and that of the Bulgarian couple. All those whose passions are impure fail.

Thus, we have another archetype: the Triumph of Purity. The impure do not reach the Promised Land; we lose sight of them before that. But they do achieve purity through sacrifice – and this means Redemption. Rick is redeemed and so is the French police captain. We come to realize that underneath it all there are two Promised Lands: one is America (though for many it is a false goal), and the other is the Resistance – the Holy War. That is where Victor has come from, and that is where Rick and the captain are going, to join de Gaulle. And if the recurring symbol of the aeroplane seems every so often to emphasize the flight to America, the Cross of Lorraine, which appears only once, anticipates the other symbolic gesture of the captain, when at the end he throws away the bottle of Vichy water as the plane is leaving. On the other hand the myth of sacrifice runs through the whole film: Ilse's sacrifice in Paris when she abandons the man she loves to return to the wounded hero, the Bulgarian bride's sacrifice when she is ready to yield herself to help her husband, Victor's sacrifice when he is prepared to let Ilse go with Rick so long as she is saved.

Into this orgy of sacrificial archetypes (accompanied by the Faithful Servant theme in the relationship of Bogey and the black man Dooley Wilson) is inserted the theme of Unhappy Love: unhappy for Rick, who loves Ilse and cannot have her; unhappy for Ilse, who loves Rick and cannot leave with him; unhappy for Victor, who understands that he has not really kept Ilse. The interplay of unhappy loves produces various twists and turns: in the beginning Rick is unhappy because he does not understand why Ilse leaves him; then Victor is unhappy because he does not understand why Ilse is attracted to Rick; finally Ilse is unhappy because she does not understand why Rick makes her leave with her husband. These three unhappy (or Impossible) loves take the form of a Triangle. But in the archetypal love-triangle there is a Betrayed Husband and a Victorious Lover. Here instead both men are betrayed and suffer a loss, but, in this defeat (and over and above it) an additional element plays a part, so subtly that one is hardly aware of it. It is that, quite subliminally, a hint of male or Socratic love is established. Rick admires Victor, Victor is ambiguously attracted to Rick, and it almost seems at a certain point as if each of the two were playing out the duel of sacrifice in order to please the other. In any case, as in Rousseau's *Confessions*, the woman places herself as Intermediary between the two men. She herself is not a bearer of positive values; only the men are.

Against the background of these intertwined ambiguities, the characters are stock figures, either all good or all bad. Victor plays a double role, as an agent of ambiguity in the love story, and an agent of clarity in the political intrigue – he is Beauty against the Nazi Beast. This theme of Civilization against Barbarism becomes entangled with the others, and to the melancholy of an Odyssean Return is added the warlike daring of an *Iliad* on open ground.

Surrounding this dance of eternal myths, we see the historical myths, or rather the myths of the movies, duly served up again. Bogart himself embodies at least three: the Ambiguous Adventurer, compounded of cynicism and generosity; the Lovelorn Ascetic; and at the same time the Redeemed Drunkard (he has to be made a drunkard so that all of a sudden he can be redeemed, while he was already an ascetic, disappointed in love). Ingrid Bergman is the Enigmatic Woman, or *Femme Fatale*. Then such myths as: They're Playing Our Song; the Last Day in Paris; America, Africa, Lisbon as a Free Port; and the Border Station or Last Outpost on the Edge of the Desert. There is the Foreign Legion (each character has a different nationality and a different story to tell), and finally there is the Grand Hotel (people coming and going). Rick's Place is a magic circle where everything can (and does) happen: love, death, pursuit, espionage, games of chance, seductions, music, patriotism. (The theatrical origin of the plot, and its poverty of means, led to an admirable condensation of events in a single setting.) This place is *Hong Kong, Macao, l'Enfer du Jeu,* an anticipation of *Lisbon,* and even *Showboat.*

But precisely because *all* the archetypes are here, precisely because *Casablanca* cites countless other films, and each actor repeats a part played on other occasions, the resonance of intertextuality plays upon the spectator. *Casablanca* brings with it, like a trail of perfume, other situations that the viewer brings to bear on it quite readily, taking them without realizing it from films that only appeared later, such as *To Have and Have Not,* where Bogart actually plays a Hemingway hero, while here in *Casablanca* he already attracts Hemingway-esque connotations by the simple fact that Rick, so we are told, fought in Spain (and, like Malraux, helped the Chinese Revolution). Peter Lorre drags in reminiscences of Fritz Lang; Conrad Veidt envelops his German officer in a faint aroma of *The Cabinet of Dr Caligari* – he is not a ruthless, technological Nazi, but a nocturnal and diabolical Caesar.

Thus *Casablanca* is not just one film. It is many films, an anthology. Made haphazardly, it probably made itself, if not actually against the will of its authors and actors, then at least beyond their control. And this is the reason it works, in spite of aesthetic theories and theories of film making. For in it there unfolds with almost telluric force the power of Narrative in its natural state, without Art intervening to discipline it. And so we can accept it when characters change mood, morality and psychology from one moment to the next, when conspirators cough to interrupt the conversation if a spy is approaching, when whores weep at the sound of "La Marseillaise". When all the archetypes burst in shamelessly, we reach Homeric depths. Two clichés make us laugh. A hundred clichés move us. For we sense dimly that the clichés are talking *among themselves,* and celebrating a reunion. Just as the height of pain may encounter sensual pleasure, and the height of perversion border on mystical energy, so too the height of banality allows us to catch a glimpse of the sublime. Something has spoken in place of the director. If nothing else, it is a phenomenon worthy of awe.

EDMUNDO DESNOES

# The Death System

> We might say that the timid hero
> procures a restricted life for men,
> whereas the brazen hero brings them a
> promise of resurrection.
>
> (Claude Lévi-Strauss)

Susan Meiselas did not go South looking for dead bodies; she found them. When Susan left New York in 1977 to see and understand Nicaragua, she was anxious to live and live radically, to discover herself in the world.

In Nicaragua she saw herself as a product made in the United States of America. Opposites – as Gide used to say – touch in me:

> I think as an American. One thing became very clear to me in Nicaragua. Coming from the States I've never had to stand on one side of the line or the other side. Even in the sixties that could easily be avoided. One participated as an activist, but that did not fundamentally affect everything about one's life. One could still masquerade, to some extent. Very, very early in Nicaragua I was confronted with the meaning of people's actions. They took certain risks, and those risks became obvious, so obvious that they could lead to: actual death, isolation or exile. The people had a capacity to determine what was public and what was private in a way that I didn't. I realized that everything about the way I dressed, the way I walked, the way I talked to people, was indicative of my culture and my condition and my consciousness.

The photographer discovered one of the keys to understanding Latin America: a different context creates a different discourse. What she saw and what she shot in Nicaragua could not be plucked away and packaged in New York.

The United States is a fragmented society, a society where people are encouraged to live centrifugally. The parts never make a whole. The whole is removed by the subtle mechanisms of advanced capitalism and its multiple ways of escape and dispersion. In Latin America everything is centripetal, everything is striving after unity and an axis. These discourses are in conflict due to economic and political differences; it is not a matter of temperament.

The abundance and diversity of the United States economy encourages fragmentation and dispersion. The scarcity and contradictions of most Latin American economies lead to class consciousness and confrontation. The nature of the state in the North is organic, accepted by most citizens; most people see the state as representing, including them or able to include them with some minor adjustments. Only blacks feel outside the system, are against a state that fails to represent or include them in its dreams and material shares. In Latin America the state is an arbitrary entity, imposed on the people and the country and unable to satisfy their needs. The state, the system is alien and oppressive. These two factors – economic development and the state – are at the root of the centrifugal and centripetal nature of social forces in America the continent.

The images of Central America sliced out of the flow of events by Susan Meiselas belong to southern discourse and yet are printed and distributed mostly for a northern audience with a different way of decoding messages. Her work is prey to a whole range of distortions and ideological readings.

The bodies may stand as metaphors, as epiphanies of war in Central America (see pp. 43–53). The bodies are testimonies of how the people of El Salvador are willing and able to put their lives on the line, are willing to risk everything to improve their lot and mean something more than blood, something more than inert matter, something that transcends horror and calls for solidarity and a future.

They are not over: they are beginning to mean. There are two kinds of bodies in Central America: the bodies that are against history and the bodies that are on the side of history. Susan Meiselas has deliberately photographed only the bodies of those that want to change things, to improve the lot of the poor; I have never seen a photo of a dead government soldier taken by Susan. Her bodies are infused with the meaning of the New Testament read in Latin America today: *El que pierda su vida se salvará.*

Bodies have an effect and a meaning. They are practical weapons; they challenge the system. They resist the system; they fight the system. It is an absolute message: death or country. My death or my country. A country, a nation that I feel belongs to me, a state that reflects my needs and does everything to feed, educate and give meaning to my existence.

The terrified dignity of the woman being questioned by government troops, who knows she can easily become a dead body. Bodies are obstinate signs; they are dragged by their feet on a dusty road, and each humiliation leads the onlooker to feel more indignant than fearful. In the North these bodies, for example, could lead to pity, horror, empathy or indifference. The two discourses are at odds.

Contact bombs explode in children's hands, and the bleeding stumps of their fingers are recorded. How should we decode this image? I would rather see his fingers blown away than his hand outstretched and begging in the streets of Managua or San Salvador. He does not know what he is doing, he is only a child; it is pure fanaticism. Or is it: the government that breeds such courage in a child should be abandoned by the people, defeated, destroyed.

The men and women that mourn their dead are not castrated, they cry and pray and then fight back. Death does not engender fear and passivity, it breeds rebellion, hope in the future – the right to decide the shape of that future.

The meaning of these bodies is not in the photo but outside. There are many possibilities, many angles from which to photograph a dead body. It is static. They are frozen images and you can move around these women, children, men. They were moving, alive, when they were shot by a bullet; they are immobile now that they are shot with a camera. The difficulty is in being there, in El Salvador, in being there as a photographer who knows how to read the signs of death. Everything is happening around, outside these photos. The repressive state could appear at any minute. The photographer is shooting the statement made by a body that defied the government. The risk, though much less than if you are a native, is taken by an *American* who hopes her photos will not lose too much of their original meaning. That is the agony of Susan Meiselas. The agony of her work. Images trapped in two discourses.

Most photos taken in the North are self-referential, rely heavily on what is happening inside the frame. They are images constructed or acted out for the camera. And they are often author referent. The photos of Susan Meiselas have a historical, social, political and moral referent. And so the author wishes to banish, to lose her face. For safety reasons as well as respect for a moral cause she only purports to witness.

"You go to discover the nature of something, rather than to prove something", Susan told the *Soho News* (20 May 1981). "When I see repression on the scale that I do, I respond humanly, but I try to document how the people respond, not how I respond. As a photographer you witness and document what happens. If people end up thinking simply that these are my pictures, I've failed in terms of what was important." The photo that illustrates this interview is not the standard photo of the smiling or intense face of the author. Susan refuses to lend her image, a face you can recognize and identify with, to any media promotion of her work. The photo she gave shows her walking away from the camera, her head bowed in respect or meditation; she is walking away from the camera and into the dense landscape of Central America. The only tender note that brings back to me the face of the moral photographer that Susan is is her blond braided hair between her frail shoulder blades.

There is a tragic element in the work and the way Susan Meiselas positions herself. In the West it is difficult to decode photography within an alien code, it is almost impossible not to be author referential, and even more difficult to let form remain in the background. I do not wish to talk about her technical abilities, her warm detachment, the simple rigour of her composition, the deep cultural richness of her images: it is there to make her message more transparent, deeper and as direct as a photographer can make a statement in the second half of the century.

These photos are not in art, these photos are in history. These images are not saved by Susan Meiselas; these bodies are rescued – if such a monstrous survival is possible – by society. "If we do not believe in God," as José Martí wrote and lived, "we believe in history."

I do not wish to proceed any further. My words cannot add anything to these bodies, cannot give meaning to the Central American war photos of Susan Meiselas. You can, *hypocrite lecteur! – mon semblable – mon frère!* It is too trite, too trivial, to continue decoding these bodies thrown at us by Susan. And it is also too easy to feel guilty for being alive, for surviving, for looking and writing about *mis hermanos muertos* in relative safety.

SUSAN MEISELAS

# A Portfolio on Central America

Figure 1

Figure 2

Figure 3

Figure 4

Figure 5

Figure 6

Figure 7

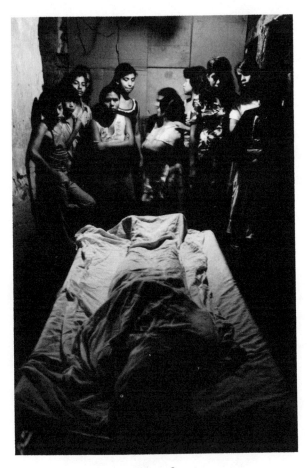

Figure 8

Figure 9

Figure 10

Figure 11

Figure 12

Figure 13

Figure 14

Figure 15

Figure 16

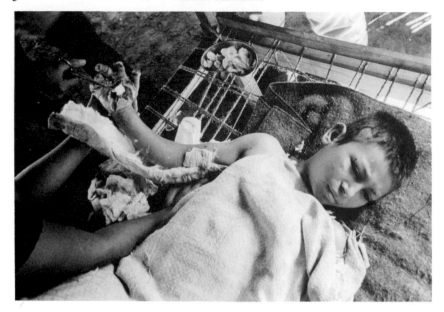

Figure 17

Figure 18

Figure 19

Figure 20

# ROLAND BARTHES

# I Hear and I Obey . . .

Repeat after me: I belong to both of you.
I will be everything both of you want me
to be.

. . . is what each of the minor characters (slaves and genii) says to everything
throughout *The Arabian Nights*. It is also what O says. It is all she says, and it is
this unfailing response which Guido Crepax had to vary in 160 images (see pp.
56–60). Even so: a single signified, but dozens of signifiers: here once again is
the Great, the Unique Metaphor which says tirelessly, "I love you", and thus
establishes the lyric discourse.

What is a sign? It is a piece of an image, a fragment of something murmured
which I can recognize: without recognition there is no sign. As in every readable
sequence, the signs formed by Crepax are of two kinds: those recognized as
existing (in the world of men): a whip, a hat, buttocks, a position, a scene; those
recognized as persisting (in O's world): the identity of a face, of a grin, of a type,
of a garment, of a style. Along these sign-embankments, *The Story of O*
proceeds, travels, and travels well, skilfully kept on the tracks of an anecdote
recounted with all the explosive art of the cartoon strip (of a cartoon that strips).
Crepax is a very good narrator: he knows that the image must be brought to life,
captured in a flash (the merest detail or a large, action-packed composition), in
order to keep up the suspense; he knows that everything must be recognized at
once (characters, objects, intentions, actions) so as to enable the voluptuous
logic of the narration to unfold immediately, effortlessly within the reader. This
is Crepax's art, as it were. His genius, however, lies elsewhere. Where? In his
way of *insisting* on a unique sign, co-extensive with all the anecdotal signs of the
story, and which brands (as O is branded) each of Crepax's panels: this is where
we discover our Great Metaphor.

When all is said and done, it may be that eroticism (i.e., desire meeting an
object) is never found in representation (the analogical image), nor even in
description (the evoked image). When all is said and done, it may be that the
eroticism in *The Story of O* (as illustrated by Crepax) occurs neither in what one
sees nor in what one reads; it occurs in the universal picture, immanent in all

language, which does not result from either image or discourse – the *interlocution*: it is because others speak words to O that she in turn speaks to them. It is because we are given this particular sort of thrust and counter-thrust to look at that the eroticism "takes" and spreads. The order which O's partners continually give her and to which the book's erotic provocation confines itself, the ideal form of the phantasmatic interlocution, is this: *that the other be nullified except as he listens and obeys*. Represented, placed before our eyes, under our nose, O's erotic organ is most certainly not her sex (or her breasts or her buttocks), it is – a bizarre thing to say – *her ear*. And Crepax has understood just that: he has drawn (in many different ways, it is true, none of which is auricular) only one ear: O is depicted, in a great number of positions and through many parts of her body, only as she listens. Listen to what she hears: "Get up and sit down . . . . I want to see you completely naked . . . . Now, take off your skirt . . . . " etc.; that is when desire is passed (the desire of the reader, the voyeur). The drowned eyes, the face's oval, the nipples of her breasts, the little hat, the twenties dress, the high heels, are all saturated with listening. Where does this voice of subjection come from? From everywhere: less from a pair of lips than from a hand, fingernails, a cigarette, naked feet, a knot in a bathrobe, a flower somewhere in the room. Crepax has reconstituted the paths of sado-masochistic interlocution. But do not let this figure from the psychoanalytic vulgate put you off: what is recounted and illustrated is maybe simply the story of two human subjects speaking to each other.

# GUIDO CREPAX
from
# The Story of O

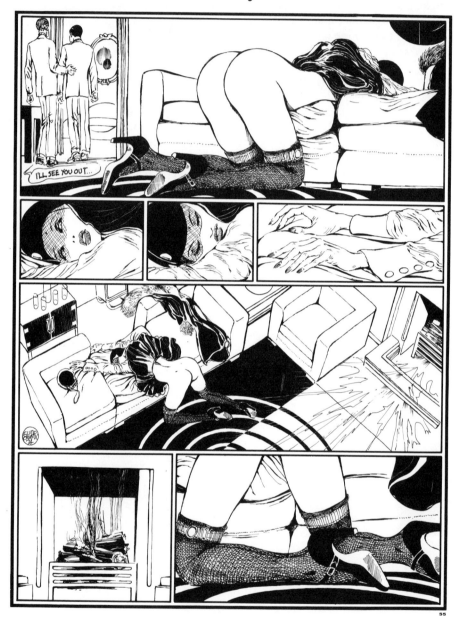

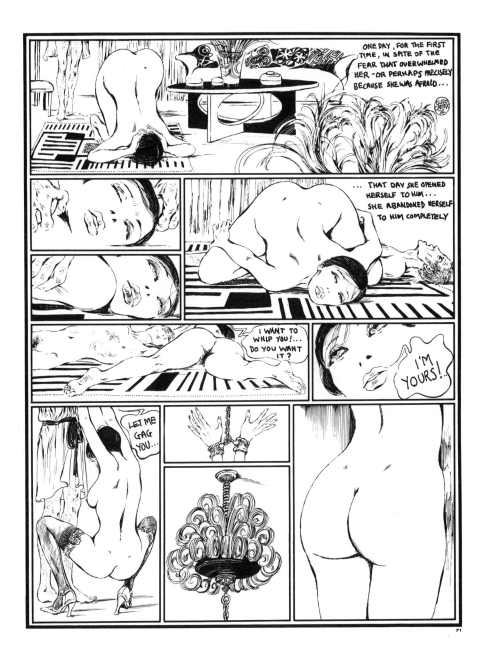

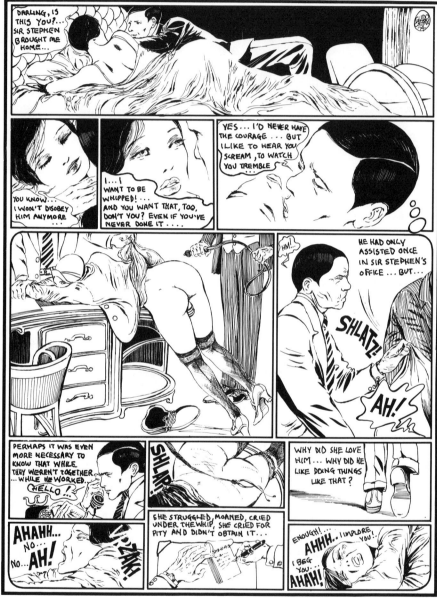

ROLAND BARTHES

# Reading Brillat-Savarin

## Degrees

Brillat-Savarin (whom we shall henceforth call BS) maintains that champagne is exciting in its first effects and stupefying in those which follow (I am not so sure of this: I myself would say this rather of whisky). Here, set forth *à propos* of nothing (but taste implies a philosophy of nothing) is one of modernity's most important formal categories: the *tiering* of phenomena. What we are dealing with is a form of time, much less familiar than rhythm, but present in so great a number of human productions that it would not be going too far to designate it with a neologism: "bathmology". Bathmology would be the field of discourses subject to a play of *degrees*. Certain languages are like champagne: they develop a signification subsequent to their first hearing, and it is in this recoil of meaning that literature is born. The tiering of the effects of champagne is a crude one, entirely physiological, leading from stimulation to stupefaction; but it is clearly this same principle of uncoupling, now refined, which governs the quality of taste: taste is that sense which experiences and practises multiple and successive apprehensions – beginnings, recurrences, overlappings, a whole counterpoint of sensation: to the arrayed arrangement of the sense of sight (in great panoramic delights) corresponds the *tiering* of taste. This is how BS decomposes the gustatory sensation *in time* (for it is not a matter of simple analysis):

1 *direct* (when the flavour is still acting on the front of the tongue);
2 *complete* (when the taste moves to the back of the mouth);
3 *reflective* (at the final moment of judgement).

All the *luxury* of taste is found in this scale; submitting the gustatory sensation to time actually allows it to develop somewhat in the manner of a narrative, or of a language: temporalized, taste experiences surprises and subtleties: these are flavours and fragrance, constituted beforehand, as it were, as memories: nothing would have kept Proust's madeleine from being analysed by BS.

## Need/Desire

Had BS written his book today, he most certainly would have considered this taste for food which he defended and illustrated as a perversion. Perversion, one might say, is the exercise of a desire which serves no purpose, such as that of the body given to lovemaking with no idea of procreation. Now BS always pointed out, on the level of food, the distinction between need and desire: "The pleasure of eating requires if not hunger, at least appetite; the pleasure of the table is most often independent of both." In an age when the bourgeoisie felt no social culpability, BS makes use of a cynical opposition: there is, on the one hand, *natural appetite*, which is of the order of need, and, on the other, *luxurious appetite*, which is of the order of desire. Everything is there, in fact: the species *needs* to procreate in order to survive, the individual *needs* to eat in order to subsist; and yet the satisfaction of these two needs is not enough for man: he must stage for himself, as it were, the luxury of desire, amorous or gastronomic. An enigmatic, useless supplement, the desired food – the one BS describes – is an unconditional loss, a kind of ethnographic ceremony whereby man celebrates his power, his freedom to burn his energy "for nothing". In this sense, BS's book is, from beginning to end, a "proper study", for it is desire (as spoken) which distinguishes man. This anthropological basis gives a paradox-ical cast to the *Physiology of Taste*: for what is expressed through the felicities of its style, the worldly tone of its anecdotes and the trifling grace of its description, is the great adventure of desire. The question, however, remains entirely one of knowing why the social subject (at least in our societies) should assume sexual perversion in a dark, wild, accursed style, as the purest form of transgression, while gastronomic perversion, described by BS (and on the whole it is difficult to see how it could be described otherwise), always implies a sort of friendly and gently obliging avowal which never departs from *good manners*.

## The Gastronome's Body

Food provokes an *internal* pleasure: inside the body, enclosed in it, not just beneath the skin, but in that deep, central zone, all the more primordial because it is soft, tangled, permeable, and called, in a very general sense, the intestines. Although taste is one of the five acknowledged classified senses of man, and although this sense is localized (on the tongue, and as BS describes so well, throughout the mouth), gustatory delight is pervasive, spread over the entire secret lining of the mucous membranes; it arises from what should be considered our sixth sense – if BS had not reserved precisely this place for the *genesic* sense – coenaesthesia, the overall sensation of our internal body. BS, like everyone else, of course, recognized this diffuse arrangement of the pleasure of food: it is a feeling of *well-being* which follows a good meal; but curiously, he does not analyse, he does not detail, nor does he "poeticize" this internal sensation. When he wants to grasp the voluptuous effects of food, it is on the adverse body that he is going to look for them; these effects are signs, as it were, taken from an interlocution: one deciphers the pleasure of the other; sometimes, if the other is a woman, one spies on it, *surprises* it as if one were involved in a little erotic rape; conviviality, the pleasure of eating well with others, is thus less innocent a value than it appears. There is in the staging of a good meal something other than the exercise of a worldly code, even one of a very old historical origin: a vague scopic drive hovers about the table: one sees (spies?) the food's effects on the other, one grasps how the body is worked from within; like those sadists who "come" with the mounting excitement on their partner's face, one observes the changes in the body eating well. The index of this mounting pleasure, according to BS, is a very precise thematic quality: *glow*: the physiognomy glows, colour heightens, the eyes sparkle, while the brain cools down and a gentle warmth penetrates the entire body. This glow is obviously an erotic attribute: it refers to a state of matter at once inflamed and moistened, desire giving the body its brightness, ecstasy its radiance (the word is BS's), and pleasure its lubrication. The gourmand's body is thus seen as a softly radiant painting, illuminated *from within*. This sublime condition, however, carries a subtle grain of triviality; one readily perceives this unexpected supplement in the scene of "la belle gourmande" ("a lovely gourmande armed for the fray", BS says): her eyes sparkle, her lips glisten, and she is biting into a partridge wing; beneath the amiable hedonism, which is the obligatory genre of descriptions of conviviality, another index must then be read in this glow: that of carnivoral aggression, of which the woman is, paradoxically, the bearer here: she is not devouring the food, she is biting into it, and this bite is radiant. Perhaps, in this rather brutal light, we must detect an anthropological notion: by fits and starts, desire returns to its origin and becomes its converse, need; gluttony becomes appetite (in the realm of the amorous, this reversal would lead humanity back to the simple practice of coupling). The strange thing about the excessively civilized tableau BS continually gives of gastronomic practices, is that the strident note of Nature – of our natural being – is struck by a woman. We know that in the immense mythology men have elaborated around the feminine ideal, food is systematically omitted; one commonly sees a woman in a state of amorousness or innocence; she is never seen eating: hers is a glorious body, purified of all need. Mythologically, food is the business of men; a woman only takes part in it as either cook or servant; it is she who prepares or serves, but does not eat. On a lighter note, BS undermines two taboos: that of a woman innocent of all digestive activity, and that of a gastronomy which would be pure repletion: he puts food into the Woman, and into the Woman appetite (appetites).

## The Antidrug

Baudelaire held a grudge against BS for not having spoken well of wine. For

Baudelaire, wine is remembering and forgetting, joy and melancholy; it enables the subject to be transported outside himself, to yield up the consistency of his ego in favour of alien and strange states of being; it is a path of deviance; in short, a drug.

Now for BS, wine is not at all a conductor of ecstasy. The reason for this is clear: wine is a part of food, and food, for BS, is itself essentially convivial, therefore wine cannot derive from a solitary protocol. One drinks while one eats and one always eats with others; a narrow sociality oversees the pleasure of food; hash smokers can certainly gather together, as do the guests at a good meal, but in principle they do so that each may more efficiently "go off" into his singular dream; now this departure is forbidden to those gathered round the table, because as they eat they submit themselves to a rigorous communal practice: conversation. Conversation (with others) is the law, as it were, which guards culinary pleasure against all psychotic risk and keeps the gourmand within a "sane" rationality: by speaking – by chatting – while eating, the person at the table confirms his ego and is protected from any subjective flight by the image-repertoire of discourse. Wine holds no particular privilege for BS: like food and with it, wine lightly amplifies the body (makes it "brilliant") but does not mute it. It is an antidrug.

## Cosmogonies

Concerned with substances that can be transformed, culinary practice naturally leads the writer who speaks of it to deal with a general thematics of matter. Just as ancient philosophies assigned great importance to fundamental states of matter (earth, air, fire, water) and derived from these states kinds of generic attributes (the aerial, the liquid, the burning, etc.) which could pass into all forms of discourse, beginning with poetic discourse, so food, through the treatment of its substances, takes on a cosmogonic dimension. The *true* state of food, what determines the *human* future of the aliment, thinks BS, is the liquid state: taste results from a chemical operation which is always performed by means of humidity and "there is nothing sapid except what is already dissolved or soon to be soluble". Here food merges with the great maternal and thalassal theme: water is nourishing; fundamentally, food is an integral bath, and this bath – BS is very precise about this – is not only vital, but is also happy, paradisical; for it is what taste depends upon, i.e. the joy of eating.

The liquid is the prior or the subsequent state of the aliment, its total history, and hence, its truth. But in its solid, dry state, alimentary matter experiences differences of value. Take whole coffee beans: one can crush them or grind them. BS greatly prefers the first method of reduction, for which he honours the Turks (does not one pay a lot for the wooden mortar and pestle which has long served to triturate grains?). Playing the scientist, BS gives experimental and theoretical proofs of the superiority of the one means of manipulation over the other. But it is not difficult to guess the "poetics" of this difference: what is ground depends on a mechanism; the hand is applied to the mill as a force, not as an art (witness the fact that the hand grinder is quite naturally converted into an electric grinder); what the grinder thus produces – abstractly, as it were – is a coffee dust, a dry and depersonalized substance. On the other hand, what is crushed comes from a series of bodily gestures (pressing, turning in various ways), and these gestures are transmitted directly through the most noble, the most human of all materials, wood; what comes out of the mortar is not a simple dust, but a powder, a substance whose alchemical vocation is attested to by an entire mythology, which is to unite with water in order to produce magic brews: powdered coffee is, one might say, closer therefore to the great state of alimentary matter – the liquid. In the little conflict which opposes the ground to the crushed, one must read a reflection of the great myth at work today, more than ever, on technological humanity: the excellence of the tool (as opposed to the machine), the precedence which the artisanal takes over the industrial – in short, nostalgia for the Natural.

## The Search for Essence

Scientifically speaking, the mechanism of digestion had been nearly elucidated by the end of the eighteenth century: it was understood then how the most varied list and the most heteroclite of aliments one can imagine (all those which humanity, since the dawn of life, has been able to discover and ingest) produce a single vital substance, by which man survives. With a slight historical lag, from 1825 on, chemistry discovers the elements. BS's entire culinary ideology is armed by a notion which is simultaneously medical, chemical and metaphysical: that of a simple essence, the nutritive (or gustative, since for BS the only food is that which is *tasted*) *juice*. The consummate state of the aliment is therefore the juice, the liquid and rarefied essence of a piece of food. Reducing something to its essence, or quintessence, the old alchemical dream, greatly impressed BS: he delighted in it as a surprising spectacle – did not the Prince de Soubise's cook, like a magician in the *Arabian Nights*, conceive of enclosing fifty hams in one crystal flagon no bigger than his thumb? Miraculous equations: the ham exists in its juice and this juice is itself reducible to an essence – and this essence alone is worthy of crystal. Alimentary essence thus considered takes on a divine *aura*; the proof of which is that, like the Promethean fire, outside the laws of humanity, it can be stolen: while the English are cooking a leg of mutton at an inn, BS steals the juice (in order to make eggs in meat juice): he pierces into the rotating meat and robs it of its quintessence by "breaking and entering" (moreover, an Anglophobic characteristic).

## Ethics

It has been possible to discern the physical aspect of amorous pleasure (tension/relaxation), but gustatory pleasure escapes all reduction, and consequently, all science (witness the heteroclite nature of tastes and distastes throughout history and the world). BS speaks like a scientist, and his book is a physiology; but (does he know?) his science is a mere irony of science. All gustatory bliss arises from the opposition of two values: the *agreeable* and the *disagreeable*, and these are quite simply tautological values – the *agreeable* is that which agrees and the *disagreeable* that which disagrees. BS can go no further: taste comes from the "ability to appreciate", exactly as in Molière where sleep comes from a dormitive virtue. The science of taste thus turns back into an ethos (the habitual fate of science). BS immediately associates physiology with moral qualities (what else could he do if he sought to continue his discourse?), of which there are two principal ones. The first is legal, castrating: it is *exactitude* ("Of all the qualities of a good cook, the most indispensable is exactitude"); here we find the classical rule: no art without constraints, no pleasure without order. The second is familiar from the ethics of sin: it is *discernment* which allows one to make a fine distinction between Good and Bad; there exists a casuistry of taste: taste must always be on the alert, practising subtlety and meticulousness. BS respectfully cites the gourmands of Rome who could distinguish the taste of fish caught between the bridges of the city and those caught further downstream, or the hunters who were able to perceive the particular flavour of the thigh on which a partridge rested while sleeping.

## The Tongue

Cadmus, who brought writing to Greece, had been cook for the King of Sidon. Let us give this mythological reference as apologue to the relation which unites language and gastronomy. Do not these two powers share the same organ and more broadly, the same apparatus, productive or appreciative: the cheeks, the palate, the nasal cavities, whose gustatory role BS reminds us of and which produce beautiful singing? Eating, speaking, singing (need one add kissing?) are all operations which originate in the same bodily place: cut out the tongue and you have neither taste nor speech.

Plato had pointed out the similarity (in a bad sense, it is true) between rhetoric and cuisine. BS does not explicitly benefit from this precedent: he has no philosophy of language. Since the symbolic is not his strong point, we must look for whatever interest this gastronome takes in language, or more exactly, in *tongues* (in the Latin sense of the term) in his empirical remarks. He takes a great deal of interest in them. BS, it will be remembered, knew five languages; thus he possessed an immense repertory of words of every sort, which he took for his own use, in different pigeonholes of his brain, shamelessly. In this respect, BS is very modern: he is convinced that French is a poor language, and that it is therefore permissible to borrow or to steal words from elsewhere; in the same way, he appreciates the charm of marginal languages, such as popular language; he derives pleasure from transcribing and citing the patois of his region, Bugey. Finally, whenever he gets the chance, as far removed as it may be from his gastronomical discourse, he notes linguistic curiosities: "to make with the arms" means to play the piano with elbows raised, as if overcome with feeling; "to make eyes" means to raise them towards the sky as if about to swoon; "to make brioches" (a metaphor which must have pleased him) means to lack a feature, an intonation. His attention to language is, therefore, meticulous, as the culinary art itself should be.

We must, however, go beyond these contingent proofs of interest. BS is most certainly tied to language – as he was to food – by an amorous relation: he desires words, in their very materiality. Did he not come up with the shocking invention of classifying the movements of the tongue, when it participates in manducation, with the help of strangely erudite words, such as *spication* (when the tongue assumes the shape of a spathe), and *verriculation* (when it sweeps around the mouth)? Double bliss? BS becomes a linguist; he treats food as a phonetician would treat (and will treat later on) vocality, and he fits this scientific discourse into a radically – might one say brazenly? – neological style. Neologisms (or extremely rare words) abound in BS; he uses them unrestrainedly and each of these unexpected words (*irrorative, garrulity, esculent, gulturation, soporous, comessation,* etc.) is the trace of a deep pleasure, which refers to the desire for a language (a "tongue"). BS desires the word as he desires truffles, a tuna omelette, a *matelote*; like all neologues, he has a fetishistic relation to the solitary word, hemmed in by its very singularity. And since these fetishized words remain drawn from a very pure syntax, which restores to neological pleasure the framework of a classical art, made up of constraints, of protocols, it can be said that BS's language is, literally, *gourmand*: gourmand with the words it handles and the dishes to which it refers; fusion or ambiguity, of which BS takes note when he sympathetically evokes those gourmands in whom can be recognized the passion and the competence merely in the way – the *gourmand* way – that they pronounce the word "good".

We know how much modernity has insisted on unveiling the sexuality which lay hidden in the exercise of language: to speak, under certain censures or certain alibis (one of which is pure "communication"), is an erotic act. A new concept permitted this extension from the sexual to the verbal: the concept of *orality*. Here BS provides what his brother-in-law Fourier had called a *transition*: that of taste, oral like language, libidinal like Eros.

## Death

And death? How does it enter into the discourse of an author whose subject and style designate him as the very model of the "bon vivant"? One suspects it enters in a completely trivial manner. Beginning with the domestic fact that sugar preserves foods and allows them to be conserved, BS asks why sugar has not been used in the embalmer's art: an exquisite corpse – crystallized, candied, "preserved"! (A preposterous imagining not unlike Fourier's.)

(While the bliss of love is always associated – by many mythologies – with death, nothing of the kind is true of the bliss of food; metaphysically – or anthropologically – it is a *matte* bliss.)


## Obesity

The most recent issue of a weekly magazine attracts attention by announcing that a doctor has just discovered the secret of losing weight, from all parts of the body, at will. This announcement would have interested BS, who good-naturedly described himself as stricken by truncal obesity, "which confines itself to the belly" and which does not occur in women – what BS calls *gastrophoria*; those who suffer from it are gastrophores (they appear as if carrying their bellies before them): "I am among their number," says BS, "but though bearing a rather prominent belly, my lower legs are still lean, and my nerves steady as an Arabian horse."

The tremendous fortune of this theme in our mass culture is well known: not a week goes by without an article appearing in the press on the need and the ways to lose weight. This mania for reducing no doubt goes back, from one stage to another, to the end of the eighteenth century; under the influence of Rousseau and the Swiss doctors Tronchin and Tissot, a new idea of hygiene took shape. Its principle was *reduction* (and no longer repletion); abstinence replaced universal bleeding; the ideal diet consisted of milk, fruits, fresh water. When BS devotes a chapter of his book to obesity and how to fight it, he is thus conforming to the direction of this mythological History, whose importance we are only just beginning to understand. However, as a gastronome, BS is unable to accentuate the Rousseauian aspect of this myth: how could he defend a rural nature (milk and fruits) when at the same time he defends the culinary art which produces truffled quail *à la moelle* and meringue pyramids *à la vanille et à la rose*? The philosophical alibi – originating with Rousseau – fades away in favour of a strictly aesthetic rationale: of course, we have not yet arrived at that moment in history (our own) when *it goes without saying* that to be thin is more beautiful than to be fat (a proposition whose relativity is attested to by both history and ethnology); the aesthetic of the body evoked by BS is not directly erotic; it is pictorial: the principal harm done by obesity is "to fill cavities which nature intended to be empty", and "to make very distinct physiognomies nearly insignificant"; the model for the body is, then, the life drawing, and dietetics is a sort of plastic art.

What is BS's idea of a weight-reducing plan? Nearly the same as ours. To begin with, he understood very well the differences in the caloric levels of foods; he knew that fish, especially shellfish, oysters, are low in calories, and that starches, for example flour, are high; he advises against soups, sugary pastries and beer; he recommends green vegetables, veal, poultry (but also chocolate!); he suggests that one weigh oneself often, eat and sleep sparingly, get plenty of exercise, and he sets straight this or that misconception along the way (like the one which led to the death of a young girl who believed she would lose weight if she drank large amounts of vinegar); add to this an anti-obesity belt and some chinchona, and there you have it.

BS's participation in the myth of reducing, so powerful nowadays, is not without importance; he sketched out a very modern synthesis of dietetics and gastronomy, postulating that it was possible for cooking to retain the prestige of a complex art, while thinking of it with a more functional view in mind. A somewhat specious synthesis, for a weight-reducing diet remains a genuine ascesis (and it is at this *psychological* cost that it succeeds); a literature has been founded: that of cookbooks elaborated according to a certain *reason* of the body.

## Osmazome

We know that during the Middle Ages culinary technique always required that all meat be boiled (because of its poor quality) before being fried. This technique was repugnant to BS. First, because he had, as it were, an exalted idea of frying, the secret of which – and thus its thematic sense – is to *surprise* (with intense heat) the food which is submitted to it: what we like about the crust of something fried (what Americans call "crispy"), is, as it were, the "rape" of which the substance has been the object; and secondly, and above all, because BS condemns boiling (with the exception of *bouillon*): boiled meat in fact loses (according to the views of the chemistry of the time) a precious substance (through its sapidity), naturally associated with red and mature meats. This substance is osmazome.

True to his philosophy of essence, BS attributes to osmazome a sort of spiritual power – it is the very absolute of taste, a sort of meat alcohol, as it were; as a universal (demoniacal?) principle, it takes on sundry and seductive appearances; it is osmazome that produces the *roux* of meats, the browning of roasts, the gamey scent of venison; most importantly it makes the juice and the *bouillon*, direct forms of quintessence (the word's etymology refers to the joint notion of smell and *bouillon*).

Chemically, osmazome is a carnal principle; but the symbolic does not respect chemical identity; by metonymy, osmazome lends its value to anything browned, caramelized, grilled: to coffee, for example. BS's chemistry (however outdated) helps us to understand the present vogue of grilling: beyond the functionalist alibi (it is a quick way of preparing a dish), there is a philosophical reason for the use of the grill: grilling combines two mythical principles: fire and rawness, both transcended in the figure of the *grilled*, the solid form of the vital juice.

## Pleasure

Here is what BS writes about pleasure:

Only a few months ago, I experienced while sleeping an altogether extraordinary sensation of pleasure. It consisted of a kind of delicious quivering in every particle of my being. It was a thoroughly charmed kind of tingling which, starting in my skin, then running from my feet to my head, thrilled me to the marrow of my bones. I saw what appeared to be a violet flame dancing about my forehead.

This lyrical description gives a good account of the ambiguity of the notion of pleasure. BS most often describes gastronomic pleasure as a refined and reasonable sense of well-being; certainly, it does give the body a brightness (a *glow*), but it does not depersonalize the body: neither food nor wine has the power of a drug. But on the other hand, what is put forth here is a sort of limit of pleasure; pleasure about to topple over into bliss, into ecstasy: it alters the body, which feels as if it is in a state of electric dispersal. This excess is no doubt accounted for as a dream; however, it points to something very important: the incommensurate nature of pleasure. Consequently, all that is needed to produce a utopia (once again we find Fourier) is to socialize the *unknown* in pleasure. BS says it very well: "The limits of pleasure are yet neither known nor posited, and no one knows the point to which the body may be beatified." It is surprising to read this in an author whose style of thinking is generally epicurean: it introduces into his thinking the feeling of a sort of historical limitlessness of sensation, of an unheard-of plasticity in the human body, which one finds in only the most marginal philosophies: it postulates a sort of mysticism of pleasure.

## Questions

The intended object of a sign is called a referant. Whenever I speak of food, I give out (linguistic) signs which refer to a particular aliment or to an alimentary quality. The implications of this banal situation are poorly understood when the intended object of my utterance is a desirable object. This is clearly the case with the *Physiology of Taste*. BS speaks and I desire that about which he speaks (especially if I have an appetite). Because the desire it arouses is an apparently simple one, the gastronomic utterance presents the power of language in all its ambiguity: the sign calls forth the delights of its referent at the very moment it traces its absence (which we know very well is what every word does, ever since Mallarmé spoke of the flower "absent from every bouquet"). Language creates and excludes. Hence, the gastronomic style raises for us a whole series of questions: what does it mean to represent? to figure? to project? to say something? What does it mean to desire? What does it mean to desire and to speak at the same time?

## The First Hour

Like all hedonistic subjects, BS seems to have a vivid acquaintance with boredom. And as always, boredom, linked to what philosophy and psychoanalysis have denoted under the name *repetition*, implies, *a contrario* (which is the opposition of meaning), the excellence of novelty. Everything which arises from an initial temporality is endowed with a sort of enchantment: the first moment, the first time, the newness of a dish, of a ritual, in short the *beginning* refers to a sort of pure state of pleasure: where everything that goes into making us happy is mingled together. Thus, of the pleasure of the table BS says, "The table is the only place one is not bored for the first hour." This first hour is marked by the appearance of new dishes, the discovery of their originality, the *élan* of the conversation – in a word which BS applies to the excellence of good frying: *surprise.*

## The Dream

Appetite partakes of the dream, for it is at once memory and hallucination, which is why, moreover, it would perhaps be better to say it is akin to fantasy. When I have an appetite for a particular food, do I not imagine myself eating it, is there not in this predictive imagination the memory of our past pleasures? I am clearly the constituted subject of a scene about to take place in which I am the sole actor.

BS reflected on the nature of the dream as "a life apart, a kind of extended novel". He clearly grasped the paradox of the dream, which can be an intense pleasure, yet one exempt from all sensual reality: in the dream, neither smell nor taste exist. Dreams are memories or combinations of memories: "dreams are but the memory of the senses". Like a language that will elaborate itself only from certain chosen signs, the scattered remains of another language, the dream is a ramshackle narrative built out of the ruins of memory. BS compares it to a melody vaguely remembered, of which one can play only a few notes, without harmony. The discontinuity of the dream opposes itself to the continuity of sleep, and this opposition is reflected in the very way foods are organized; some are sleep-inducing: milk, chicken, lettuce, orange blossom, pippin apples (when eaten before going to bed); others induce dreams: brown meats, rabbit, asparagus, celery, truffles, vanilla: these are strong foods, aromatic or aphrodisiac. BS makes the dream into a marked, one could almost say, a virile state.

## Science

"Thirst" says BS, "is the internal feeling of the need to drink." We might have guessed as much, and the interest of such phrases certainly does not lie in the information they provide (which here is, frankly, nil). Through these tautologies BS is, visibly, trying his hand at science, or at least at scientific discourse; he produces utterances without surprise, which have no *value* other than to present a pure image of the scientific proposition (definition, postulate, axiom, equation): and is there a science more rigorous than the one which defines the same by the same? No risk of error here; BS is safe from that evil power which is the ruin of science: paradox. His audacity is in his style: using a scientific tone to speak of a reputedly pointless (because flatly sensual) sense – taste.

Science is the great superego of the *Physiology*. The book, we are told, was edited under the guidance of an official biologist, and BS sprinkles his discourse with scientific solemnities. He thus imagines himself to be subjecting food to experimental measurements: "Each time one serves a dish having a well-known flavour, we shall observe closely those at the gathering, and we shall note as unworthy all those whose physiognomy does not show delight." As outrageous as the idea might be, BS, through the use of these "gastronomic tests", takes into account two very serious and very modern factors: sociality and language. The dishes he presents for his subjects to try vary according to the subject's social class (income); a fillet of veal or eggs *à la neige* if one is poor, a fillet of beef or a boiled turbot if one is comfortable, truffled quail *à la moelle*, meringues flavoured with rose water if one is rich, etc. – which is to let it be understood that taste is modelled by culture, i.e. by social class. Then, a surprising method, in order to *read* gustatory pleasure (since that is the purpose of the experiment), BS suggests that one examine not the mimicry (which is probably universal), but the language, a socialized object if ever there was one: the expression of approval changes according to the speaker's social class; seated before his eggs *à la neige*, the poor man will say, "God damn!", while the ortolans *à la provençale* elicit from the rich man, "What an admirable fellow your cook is, my lord!"

These observations, which mix together different sorts of true intuitions, bespeak quite well the way BS took science: seriously and ironically at the same time. His project to establish a science of taste, to wrest from culinary pleasure its habitual marks of triviality, was certainly heartfelt; but he carries it out rhetorically, i.e. ironically; he is like a writer who puts the truths he utters in quotation marks, not out of scientific prudence, but out of fear of appearing naïve (where one can see that the irony is still timid).


## Sex


There are, we are told, five senses. From the opening of his book, BS postulates a sixth sense: the *genesic*, or physical love. This sense cannot be reduced to touch; it implies a complete apparatus of sensations. "Let us", says BS, "give the genesic the *sensual* place it cannot be denied, and let us bestow on our descendants the scruple of assigning it its rightful position." (We, who are those descendants, have not been unworthy of that scruple.)

BS's intent is obviously to suggest a sort of metonymic exchange between the first of sensual pleasures (even if censured) and the sense he undertakes to defend and illustrate, i.e. taste; from the point of view of sensuality, it signifies taste to assign it sexual pleasure as fellow-in-arms. BS thus insists, when he can, on the aphrodisiac virtue of certain foods: truffles, for example, or fish; he was amazed (a little anti-clerical irony) that monks, vowed to chastity, nourished themselves on fish during Lent. Yet to no avail, for there is little analogy between lust and gastronomy; between these two pleasures there is a capital difference: orgasm, i.e. the very rhythm of excitation and its relaxation. The pleasure of the table involves neither rapture, nor transport, nor ecstasy – nor aggression; its climax, if there is one, is not paroxysmal: no rise in pleasure, no crisis, no outburst; nothing but duration; one could say that the only critical element of gastronomic joy is its expectation; as soon as satisfaction begins, the body enters the insignificance of repletion (even if it assumes the aspect of a gluttonous compunction).

## Sociality

It would no doubt be quite easy for general ethnology to demonstrate that at all times and in all places taking food is a social act. One eats with others, that is the universal law. This alimentary sociality may assume many forms, many alibis, many nuances, depending on the society and the time. For BS, the gastronomic collectivity is essentially worldly, and its ritual figure is conversation. The table is the geometric locus, as it were, of all topics of conversation. It is as if alimentary pleasure vivified them, gave them new life; the celebration of a food is laicized in the form of a new mode of gathering together (and participating): the convivium. Added to good cheer, the convivium produces what Fourier (whom we always find close to BS) called a *composite* pleasure. A vigilant hedonism inspired the two brothers-in-law with the thought that pleasure should be *overdetermined*, that it would have several simultaneous causes, among which there are no grounds for distinguishing which one is responsible for bliss; for compound pleasure does not stem from a simple compatibility of excitations: it represents a complex space in which the subject no longer knows where he comes from or what he wants – only to experience bliss. The convivium – so important in BS's ethic – is therefore not a sociological fact; it requires us to consider communication (which the human sciences have scarcely done up to now) as a bliss – and no longer as a function.

## Social Classes

We have seen that in the game (or experiment) of gastronomic tests, BS linked differences in taste to differences in income. What is original about this is not the acknowledgement of monetary classes (average, well-off, wealthy), it is the concept that taste itself (i.e. culture) is socialized: if there is an affinity between eggs *à la neige* and a modest income, it is not only because this dish is not very costly, it is also, it seems, due to the social formation of taste, the values of which are established not in an absolute but in a determined field. Hence it is always through the relay of culture – and not through that of needs – that BS socializes food. Also, when he proceeds from incomes to professional classes (what have been called "states" or "conditions"), establishing the fact that the great gourmands of society are principally financiers, doctors, men of letters, and the devout, what he is considering is a certain profile of habits, i.e. a social psychology. In his eyes gastronomic taste seems linked by privilege either to a positivism of the profession (financiers, doctors), or to a particular aptitude for displacing, sublimating, or intimizing bliss (writers, the devout).

In this culinary sociology, modest as it is, the purely social is none the less present: there precisely where it is missing from the discourse. It is in what he does not say (in what he hides from view) that BS most surely points to social condition, in its nakedness: and what is repressed, pitilessly, is popular food. What did this food principally consist of? Bread and, in the country, boiled beef – the cook there using a grain she herself ground on a "grindstone" which kept her from having to submit to the monopoly of the mills and communal ovens; honey, but not sugar. The staple food of the poor was the potato; boiled potatoes were sold on the streets (as one still sees in Morocco), in the same way as chestnuts; long snubbed by people "of a certain standing", who relegated its use "to animals and the very poor", the potato owes nothing of its social ascent to Parmentier, the military pharmacist who wanted above all to substitute potato starch for the flour used in bread. During BS's own time, the potato, while beginning its redemption, still carried the mark of discredit attached to anything "boiled". Look at the menus of that period: nothing but separate, plain dishes, the mixed belonging only to sauces.

## Topic

BS understood very well that as a subject of discourse food was a sort of grid (of *topic*, the classical rhetorician would have said), through which one could successfully pass all the sciences that we today call social and human. His book tends toward the encyclopaedic, even if he only made a vague outline of it. In other words, discourse is empowered to attack food from several angles: it is, in short, a total social fact around which a variety of metalanguages can be gathered: physiology, chemistry, geography, history, economics, sociology, and politics (today we would add the symbolic). For BS, it is this encyclopaedism – this "humanism" – which covers the term *gastronomy*: "Gastronomy is the knowledge of everything related to man in so far as he nourishes himself." This scientific opening clearly corresponds to what BS himself was in his own life: he was essentially a polymorphous subject – jurist, diplomat, musician, man of the world, well known both abroad and in the provinces; food was not a mania for him, but rather a sort of universal operator of discourse.

In conclusion, we must perhaps meditate a little on dates. BS lived from 1755 to 1826. He was nearly the exact contemporary of, for instance, Goethe

(1749–1832). Goethe and Brillat-Savarin: these two names, alongside one another, are an enigma. Certainly, Werther did deign to cook some buttered peas for himself at his retreat at Wahlheim; but do we see him take an interest in the aphrodisiac virtues of truffles and the flashes of desire which cross the faces of beautiful *gourmandes*? The fact is that the nineteenth century is embarking on its double voyage, positivist and romantic (and perhaps the *one* because of the *other*). Around 1825, the year the *Physiology of Taste* was published, a double postulation of history, or at least of ideology, was effected, from which it is not certain we have yet emerged: on the one hand a sort of rehabilitation of earthly joys, a sensualism, linked to the progressivist sense of history, and on the other hand, a grandiose explosion of the *mal de vivre* linked to an entirely new culture of the symbol. Occidental humanity thus established a double repertory of its conquests, its values – on the one side chemical discoveries (which guaranteed a rise in industry and the transformation of society) and on the other a very great symbolic adventure: was it not the year 1825, BS's year, when Schubert composed his quartet *Death and the Maiden*? BS, who has taught us the concomitance of sensual pleasures, also represents for us (indirectly, as befits a good witness) the still undervalued importance of cultures and of *composite* histories.

JAN KOTT

# The Infarct

We all know the world contracts when we leave childhood. Lazienki Park is still impossible for me to cross and full of secrets. As a child I was left alone there, and lost my way chasing a boy in a sailor suit riding a tricycle. I pursued him along a path, then found myself stranded before a satyr with a chipped nose. The world, shrunken and tamed once childhood is left behind, stretches when old age begins. But not horizontally, only vertically. What was level is level no more. What was flat suddenly becomes steep. Houses without elevators suddenly acquire storeys they never had before. For ten years, Quaker Path where I live in Stony Brook seemed as flat as a board. But two years ago, as I was carrying a heavy briefcase from the campus (it had never been heavy before), I noticed that midway home my street rises to a hill. Halfway up, I had to stop and set down my briefcase.

The pain was dull. Really quite mild, but there was something strange about it. It started at the breast-bone, but did not end anywhere. The pain was mild but it was in the whole body. I felt I had to lie down immediately. I was dining at the Journalists' Club, and asked to be taken back to Nabielak Street. I did not finish my coffee, and put out a half-smoked cigarette. It was not until a week later, when once again I craved nicotine, that I recalled the half-smoked cigarette, felt its taste in my throat and regretted not finishing it.

Back in my room I lay down but the pain persisted. It was still mild, but curiously I did not feel like getting up or even talking. I had promised to attend a party that afternoon. First I sent a message that I had been detained, later my

This essay is for Dr Halina Kotlicka.

regrets. I was supposed to leave for Cracow at 6.oo a.m. the following morning. Otherwise, I would never have called Doctor K. "Strange pains", I said.

Half an hour later an ambulance arrived. They carried me out on a stretcher. Quite a ritual, I thought. In the emergency room on Stepinska Street they asked if I could walk to the ECG. The question seemed laughable; it was only thirty or forty steps. I returned to the waiting room on my own. A moment later, the doctor on duty entered and said it was an infarction. So, I would not be leaving. I phoned S., asked her to let Cracow know I would not be coming, and that it was an infarct. "Where are you? Are you in ICU?" I did not yet know what ICU [intensive-care unit] was, but her voice told me that something had happened. To me. I realized I should call K. at once. "Let me talk to the doctor", K. ordered. She must have yelled terribly at him, for I heard in the depths of my body that I am to lie down immediately and that she is sending an ambulance. And only when I was again lying on a stretcher did it finally strike me: I was having a heart attack. Until then it was always others who had heart attacks. About heart attacks I knew only that one dies of them.

The pain was still dull. Only it seemed to be everywhere. Or rather, it was as if I were beyond this pain. That is, I felt I was walking off, leaving myself and the pain behind; as on marijuana, when one can for a moment leave oneself and, with some effort, simply go away. And, as if on marijuana, time slows and is different at the core. At this very core the same pain persisted. I do not know how long I waited for the ambulance, an hour or a day.

In the ambulance I held someone's hand, probably one of the nurses from Miedzylesie. I was not scared. Later I was told that I had asked her not to be scared and insisted that I was merely pretending to be in pain. And that none of this was real. But it really hurt when they put the I.V. in my arm. It was in the vein of my right wrist which had been immobilized. Perhaps the veins were too frail. It seemed needles were continuously being injected and withdrawn.

I knew I was being saved. There were three or four heads around me. I myself was laid out, as in an exhausting dream. The right hand, detached as if severed, was connected to an i.v., the chief source of pain. The left hand was sheathed and constricted to measure the pulse. Also completely detached were the lips pressed to a rubber oxygen tube. I was still not scared. I must have lost and regained consciousness several times. Of those many hours of alien time (I was told later that I was not left alone even for a moment until 3 a.m.), I remember only the sting of needles and the proximity of eyes. I knew I was drifting away. I remember someone saying "You're not going to drift off again, not today." But who, and when? By then I was already longing to drift and for the pain in my right hand to cease. And I thought to myself that I am drifting away so cleanly, without blood, without suffocation. I am only discarding this pain which is so lightly left behind. I am drifting away in whiteness.

"You were pretty far gone last night", said the nurse bringing the waterbasin the next morning. "That was quite a ruckus you made last night", the patient next to me rejoined. I could not reply as the oxygen tube was still taped to my mouth. Neither could I lift myself, for it seemed that soft tubes, like snake skins, were coiled all around me. Only later did I discover that they were attached to the five metal discs on my chest.

So this was ICU. I was in the recovery room of the Railroad Union's Hospital, Miedzylesie. There were two other heart patients in the room, one across from me, one to my left. This was the morning after the attack. After my attack. A heart attack always has its day and hour, its beginning and end. In itself it is brief. One is either in the time before the heart attack, or in the time after.

Because of its brevity, dying of a heart attack is unlike dying of cancer. This is true for the patient and to some extent for his family and friends. By dying I do not mean the progress of a disease, the body's struggle with a foe. I mean the fear of death, its dread – the patient's and his companions'. In my experience, dying was drifting. For other infarct patients, dying was a piercing pain in the chest. For family and friends, a heart attack is a series of late-night phone-calls to the doctor on duty. For family and for victim, the dramaturgy of a heart attack is hurried.

Dying from cancer takes weeks, months, sometimes years. It begins long before diagnosis, and often continues even after the verdict has been reversed and the tumour is pronounced benign. I experienced the agony of expectation when, nearly twenty years ago, I underwent surgery for the removal of what on an X-ray looked like a dark stain the size of a walnut in the upper lobe of my right lung. For weeks I watched the fear in the eyes of my wife.

The infarct experience is different. Once the attack is over, one is cured. Another attack is of course possible, a second, a third or a fourth. But with coronary disease, the prognosis of death has nevertheless a different character than with cancer. And not only does it have a different character, but – I cannot call it by a different name – it has a different metaphysic. Five years of remission is called a cure for cancer. Yet one continues to die from the incurable fear of a relapse. Dying from cancer, whether slow or fast, is continuous and gradual, and always without respite. Cancer, the terminal disease, is a suspended death sentence. Dying is this very suspension of death. The dread and torture of cancer, described in Susan Sontag's moving *Illness as Metaphor*, is this intransgressible *terminus adquem*, which gives the disease the horrifying shape of a verdict, of destiny, of *fatum*, as if it were the work of dark forces. A heart attack has no *terminus* and there are no dark forces. There is only a heart which failed.

The heart is a sack which pumps blood. The blood from the veins enters the heart through the auricles, and then is expelled through the arteries and the aorta. An infarct is a wound to the heart. A part of the coronary muscle atrophies and blocks the passage of blood. An infarct means atrophy in the heart, the heart's partial death if one survives, and death if one does not. A wound to the heart heals like all wounds, and like every wound, leaves a scar. A trace remains until death. The ECG is a most exact record of the heart's wounds. It is the graphic image of the infarct, the underside of a wave, a valley instead of a peak among a mass of trajectories on cardiographic paper. The lines on our fingertips do not change from birth to death, and they are the only infallible record of our identity. The broken lines of an electrocardiogram, forming hills and valleys, chronicle the history of a heart.

Whenever I lifted my head I saw a box about the size of a small television above the bed of the patient lying across from me. A light, like a needle of the electrocardiograph, relayed a continuously pulsating message to his screen. Once I was able to prop myself up in bed, I discovered that the five metal amplifiers on my chest were sending messages to an identical luminous screen above me. On the third or fourth day of my stay in ICU, M. visited me. When I lifted myself to embrace her, she froze. She was not looking at me; she was staring at the screen. I remembered her in so many roles, frozen on stage with her widened almost transparent bovine eyes – a Pallas Athena with a tiny silvery head precariously poised on a long and fragile neck. In none of her roles had she ever been so frozen with horror. As I moved to greet her, two of the discs above my nipple slipped off. The iridescent notation on the green screen stopped vibrating, and stretched out into a broad flat stripe. The nurse on duty instantly rushed to my bedside. The flat line signifies the cessation of the heart, or fallen discs. The nurse instantly reattached them. Many weeks later M. told me that the flat line above my bed, over my tousled hair, had recurred in her dreams. And I remembered the lines from Miekiewicz:

> But look, oh, look upon his heart
> Like a scarlet ribbon hung
> Or corals on a necklace strung.
> A bleeding stripe there takes its start
> And stretches down from breast to feet.
>                          (trans. M. B. Peacock)

As I gained strength I would lift myself out of the pillows and stare intently into the screen above my bed, into my beating heart. With every vigorous movement, the luminous lines jumped as though startled. "Look how my heart beats", she would say, placing my hand on her breast. "Look how my heart beats", I said and put her hand on my chest. "Look! Only our fingers can see the heart beating beneath warm and naked flesh." For the first time I was actually seeing the graph of a beating heart.

During the third week, when I was already allowed to walk around, I slipped off to the nurses' observation room at night. Above an enormous table, luminous zigzags beamed from eight little screens. On each one, a patient's heart was projected. If permitted, I would have spent hours staring into those beating hearts. Every heart beat differently, forming jagged or blunt teeth, as though traced by the fine stitching of a sewing machine, or by the sweeping strokes of a pen. But all hearts were pulsating, and their luminous signals fascinated me. I was spying at night on other people's hearts. There was something disturbingly erotic in this experience, as though the heart's pulse during those hospital nights had become the pulse of sex.

A hospital is always a separate time and a separate place. But still more thorough is the separation in time and in place during the weeks of immobilization in the intensive care unit. Sartre wrote that in Faulkner, characters and events escape into the past, like the landscape and road viewed through a car's rear window. They are at once already in the past. Before they are, they already were.

During our healthy life we move through time like passengers on an escalator. While we remain stationary, everything around us imperceptibly shifts into what has been. It is others who grow older. We age only in the mirror, and in the eyes of others. During healthy life time is continuous, recorded on a watch or calendar, passing outside us but never through us. The past is yesterday, the future tomorrow, and yesterday and tomorrow belong to the same continuum. A heart attack has not only its hour of day or night. It is an incision into time, the scission of time. The before, the pre-infarct, is severed from the after, the post-infarct.

During the weeks of immobilization only the pre-infarct is present, and the incision is perceived with exceptional sharpness. Immobilization is that separate time and place, hollow in itself, where the future, the post-infarct, is a desperate, almost maniacal wish to repeat the pre-infarct. Time's continuity and sequence are violated, if not totally destroyed. In more technical, studied terms, the diachrony of events is broken and the pre-infarct is given as a synchronic memory. The trauma, the past events, the past desires are always going through the process of hibernization in memory. The memory as the vast refrigerator hiding goods from different shopping sprees is always synchronic.

But the pre-infarct memory is different. The story line was cut off, the desires were not fulfilled, the events were not naturally exhausted. The ICU is no man's time. The pre-infarct is now an agony of desire asking for fulfilment and continuation. All desires, all stories, every non-fulfilment as one boiling stream is present in the ICU room. You make the impossible love climax with all the women of your pre-infarct.

The emergency room around you, within you, is a wall-less place, a bottomless basket for this synchrony of all desires not exhausted, not fulfilled. They are projected into the future.

And the future in the emergency room is also synchronic. It is the past's projection, as in Beckett's *Happy Days* and perhaps even more saliently in

*Rockaby*. The experience of time is destruction of time and hence the dramatic analogies to the infarct experience. Hospital time is filled with static trivia, like almost everything that happens on stage in Chekhov. The real drama occurs off-stage. Like dialogues between Chekhov's characters, conversations between patients are only about the past, although the future tense is used. Because theatre dramatizes time such analogies help, though only partially, to describe the post-infarct experience of time.

The last work, the last painting or musical score is read in two distinct configurations simultaneously: in the regular course of succession, simply as the latest work in the bio-bibliographical chronology, and also, in terms of the phenomenology of the end, as the last work before the author's death. The last work is never intended as the last, but sometimes, as in Barthes' *Camera Lucida*, consciousness of imminent death seems to infuse the writing. In the phenomenology of the end, death transforms the final work into the last will and testament. Probably the falsest readings of Shakespeare's *Tempest* have been produced this way. Yet that is exactly how the last events before the heart attack, the last landscapes and people, those accidental affinities preceding that moment when time was severed, become elective ones. Accident becomes fate; *fate* as Hegel understood it.

A week before the attack I spent a few days in Cracow. On my last evening there I saw Wajda's *Hamlet* at the Wawel, the palace of Poland's monarchs. We waited that June night in front of the upper gate to the courtyard until almost 11.00 p.m. People were tossing garlands into the Vistula. It was Saint Wanda's Day. In the fireworks, as if in a dream, gigantic spires appeared. It was as cold as in the real Elsinore. We sat in the courtyard, wrapped in blankets and coats, warming each other's hands. A Hamlet from Wyspianski's vision paced through the galleries with a book in hand. Gertrude was thoroughly prescient. She knew every stone of the Wawel. Ophelia also divined everything, but what could she do? She was an ugly old maid. Hamlet mocked her but he was the first man to desire her. Like Wanda, she threw herself into the Vistula that night. These were only the bare elements of the tragedy. The walls also performed, rising up in the light and falling away into darkness. They were impenetrable. Usually confined within artificial canvas drops, *Hamlet* is carved out of impenetrability of walls. I departed with T. through the deserted public gardens. It was my first night walk through Cracow in seventeen or eighteen years. The last I remember had been with W. a year or two before I moved away. We had taken another walk together through the streets of Rome a few months before his death. On Via Gulia we had promised each other a long night ramble through Cracow, from church to church, from bar to bar, from the Market to the Pilsudcki Mound. This time I was to return to Cracow within a week. I did not return. I had a ticket for the 6.00 a.m. express. That night I had the heart attack.

On the third day in the hospital I asked S. for Proust's *Remembrance of Things Past* and *Tristan and Isolde*. Initially I could not read more than a few pages a day. But for the first time I was reading Proust as if it were my own history.

Albertine fled. Everything before the infarct suddenly took on significance. The irreversible had occurred. Until then it seemed that tomorrow would always be like yesterday. Albertine would come for the evening caresses, as Marcel's mother came with goodnight kisses. Then Albertine crashed into a tree. And was gone forever. I wept when I read of Albertine's death. For the first time since childhood I was crying over a book. I was crying for myself. My mother had died. I had lost Albertine.

I read Proust three times: twice from beginning to end, and once desultorily. But in the intensive care unit, in the hospital bed next to an enormous oxygen tank, under a screen of my own beating heart, I read Proust differently. I did not need a madeleine to recover things past. With the pre-infarct still in me, I was reading Proust not to recall past time, but to search for a way to repeat the unrepeatable. For a way to live, when the pre-infarct past, the imperfect, had, after the attack become the past perfect.

The *Hamlet* at the Wawel was one of the scores of *Hamlets* I have seen. The walk through the empty public gardens and the conversation with T. were among many walks and talks. I knew that I could return in a week and once again cross that dark park. But as I lay in the post-infarct in my hospital bed in Miedzylesie, the *Hamlet* of a week ago became the last *Hamlet*, and the walk through the public gardens, the last walk. And if I ever see *Hamlet* again, or walk from the Wawel across the public gardens, it will be the first *Hamlet* and the first walk. Like death, or even its shadow, a heart attack endows people, and events from the before with symbolic meanings and signs of necessity.

After Albertine's death I put Proust aside and read *Tristan and Isolde*. King Mark sent the faithful Tristan over the sea to bring back Isolde to be his wife. On the barge, Tristan and Isolde shared a bed separated by a sword. One evening as a storm was approaching, Isolde's maid brought them golden goblets containing a love potion for the duly wed. That evening Tristan and Isolde transgressed the sword and slept together as man and wife. Later Isolde married King Mark, and Tristan was exiled. But perhaps the real story was quite different. Tristan and Isolde laid a sword between them, but were lovers from the start. As the barge approached the shore where the impatient king was waiting, they suddenly realized what they had done. Overcome with shame, they demanded from Brangane the potion of eternal love. Thus the fornicators became the tragic lovers and entered the legend.

"My heart, my physical heart, / Is the object of medical inquiry", wrote Broniewski in one of his more lyrical poems. "My heart, my aching heart, / Is the object of sorrow, / There is one person too few in this empty room." The underside of the wave on the rising and falling lines of the electrocardiogram is until death the sign of a wound to the heart. Even after it has healed. But the heart has still another memory and still other scars. A heart attack, like perhaps every other brush with death, activates this memory. Death does not shelter us from love, nor love from death. The Albertine that is, is no more. There is only dying in love (*la petite mort*), the dying of love, and one's own death. That is how I read Proust in intensive care at the hospital in Miedzylesie.

"Be careful, it's fragile", said Theresa. I called her "clairvoyant" because she worked in the X-ray department. "There is a catheter inside of you." It was not necessary to tell me. I felt as if the thing inside me were made of glass. Particularly, when after two weeks I was "mobilized". The first time out of bed is almost a ritual. The doctor leads you by the hand as the other patients watch from their beds. He releases you. The bed and the window are very far apart. The thing inside beats. Your hand is dressed. The doctor meticulously measures your pulse.

On the first day I received "nitros", twenty tablets of nitroglycerin in a tiny vial. There were some on every nightstand. When the pain hits, you quickly place a tablet under your tongue, the blood vessels expand, and the fear passes. Heart patients never go anywhere without "nitros", carrying them about like a life-belt in the breast pocket. In the sanatorium I received a small furry purse for my "nitros", and I still carry it today. Like a fetish.

You carry "nitros" because you carry your heart. After the infarct, the heart is constantly present. Although in you, it is a thing apart. You listen to it as though it belonged to someone else. But it is yours. It trembles. You feel a cramp. "Doctor, my heart hurt last night."

And only in saying so, did I realize that the heart really aches, and that I can feel in me everything language says about the heart. I have a heart. I am lighthearted or heavyhearted. My heart is in the right place. I pour out my heart. And what it means to break someone's heart. And what a blow to the heart is. "My bowels, my bowels!" Jeremiah IV: 19 – "I am pained at my very heart; my heart maketh a noise in me; I cannot hold my peace."


In the entrance hall and on all three floors of the Railroad Union's Sanatorium in Naleczow hang small posters with the caption "Save the Heart". A perfectly symmetrical red heart is portrayed on them. But on these posters at the sanatorium for heart patients, unexpectedly growing from the beautiful symbolic heart, are an aorta and pulmonary artery, copied from an anatomical atlas. The mild Naleczow lies at the bottom of a steep-sided valley. It has a micro-climate, with damp mornings and evenings, and nights that are chilly even during heat spells. It rarely has storms. There are five sanatoriums for heart patients in Naleczow. Each one is shown on the town map posted at the main intersection near the bus station and the small marketplace, where only apples are sold. Above the map is a sign: "Naleczow cures the heart". Hearts have been carved with jacknives and nail files into the wooden map and also into the pole that supports it. They are not perfectly symmetrical like those hearts on the posters at the sanatorium. They are crooked. Like the ones on school-desks or on the benches in Lazienki Park. Round these hearts, sometimes pierced by arrows, are faded letters.

ROLAND BARTHES

# Textual Analysis of a Tale of Poe

Textual analysis does not attempt to *describe* the structure of a work; it is not a matter of recording a structure, but rather of producing a mobile structuration of the text (a structuration which shifts from reader to reader throughout history), of staying within the signifying volume of the work, within its *significance*. Textual analysis does not seek to know what it is that determines the text (i.e. what gathers it together as the end term of a causal sequence), but rather how it bursts forth and is dispersed. So we are going to take a text, a narrative, and we are going to read it, as slowly as is necessary, stopping as often as we must (*ease* is a most important dimension of our work), trying to locate and to classify as *loosely as possible* not all the meanings of the text (this would be impossible for the text is open *ad infinitum*: no reader, no subject, no science can exhaust the text), but the forms, the codes which make meanings possible.

We are going to locate the *avenues* of meaning. Our goal is not to discover *the* meaning, or even *a* meaning for the text, and our work is not akin to a hermeneutic type of literary criticism (whose aim is to interpret the text according to the truth it believes is hidden within), such as, for example, Marxist or psychoanalytic criticism. Our goal is ultimately to conceive, to imagine, to live the plurality of the text, the open-endedness of its significance. It would seem then that what is at stake in our work is not limited to the university treatment of the text (albeit overtly methodological) not even to literature in general; it borders on a theory, a practice, a choice caught up in the struggle between men and signs.

In order to move on to the textual analysis of a narrative, we are going to follow a certain number of operating procedures (let us say a certain number of elementary rules of manipulation, rather than methodological principles; which would be too ambitious and above all ideologically questionable in so far as the word "method" too often postulates a positivistic result). We can reduce these procedures to four measurements laid out in summary fashion, preferring to let the theory run its course within the analysis of the text itself. For the time being, we shall say only what is necessary in order to *begin* as quickly as possible the analysis of the tale we have chosen.

1. We shall cut up the text I am proposing for our study into contiguous and generally very short segments (a sentence, a phrase, at most a group of three or four sentences); we shall number these fragments starting from one (in some ten pages there are 150 segments). These segments are units of reading, which is why I have proposed they be called "lexias".[1] A lexia is obviously a textual signifier; but as our aim here is not to observe signifiers (our work is not stylistic), but meanings, it is not necessary that the segmentation be theoretically founded (since we are in *discourse* and not in *language*, we must not expect there to be an easily perceived homology between the signifier and the signified; we do not know how one corresponds to the other, and consequently, we must be willing to cut up the signifier without being guided by the underlying segmentation of the signified). In short, breaking up the narrative text into lexias is purely empirical, dictated by a concern for convenience: the lexia is an arbitrary product, it is simply a segment within which we observe the distribution of meaning, what surgeons would call an operating field. A useful lexia is one in which only one, two or three meanings occur (superimposed within the *volume* of a bit of text).

2. For each lexia, we shall observe those meanings which emerge from it. By *meaning*, we understand not the meanings of words or groups of words which a dictionary or a grammar, i.e. knowledge of the French language, could adequately account for, but the *connotations* of the lexia, the secondary meanings. These connotative meanings can be *associations* (for example, the physical description of a character, drawn out over several phrases, may have only one signified of connotation, that particular character's "nervousness", though the word does not figure at the level of denotation); they may also be *relations*, resulting from the bringing together of two loci in the text, sometimes quite far apart (an action further on). Our lexias will be, if I may say so, the finest filters possible, thanks to which we shall "skim off" the meanings, the connotations.

3. Our analysis will be progressive: we shall proceed step by step along the path of the text, at least postulatively, since for reasons of space we can only give one fragment of analysis here. This means that we shall not attempt to extract the large (rhetorical) sections of the text; we shall not construct a map of the text and we shall not be seeking out its thematics; in a word, we shall not be doing an *explication de texte*, unless we give the word "explication" its etymological sense, in so far as we shall unfold (*ex-plicare*) the text, the foliation of the text. We shall allow our analysis to follow the text exactly *as read*; simply put, this reading shall be *filmed in slow motion*, as it were. This manner of proceeding is theoretically

---

[1] For a closer analysis of the notion of *lexia*, as for the operating procedures that will follow, I am obliged to refer to my book *S/Z* (Paris: Seuil, 1970; New York: Hill and Wang, 1974).

important: it signifies that our aim is not to reconstitute the structure of the text, but to follow its structuration of reading, more important than that of composition (a rhetorical and classical notion).

4. Finally, we shall not concern ourselves unduly if, in our notation, we "forget" some meanings. The forgetting of meaning is, in a certain way, part of reading: what matters to us is to show *departures*, not arrivals, of meanings (basically, is not meaning merely a departure?). What founds the text is not an internal, closed meaning that can be accounted for, but the *opening* of the text onto other texts, other codes, other signs: what makes the text is the intertextual. We are beginning to glimpse (through other sciences) that research must little by little get used to the conjunction of two ideas which for a very long time have been considered contradictory: the idea of structure and the idea of combinative infinity; the conciliation of these two postulations is forced upon us now because language, which we are getting to know better, is both infinite and structured at once.

These remarks are, I believe, sufficient for us to begin the analysis of the text (we must always yield to the text's impatience, never forgetting that, whatever the demands of the study, the *pleasure* of the text is our law). The text which has been chosen is a short narrative by Edgar Allan Poe, "The Facts in the Case of M. Valdemar", which I have read in Baudelaire's translation: "*La vérité sur le cas de M. Valdemar*".[2] My choice – at least consciously, for in fact it might be my unconscious which made the choice – has been dictated by two didactic considerations: I needed a text that was very short, in order to be able to master entirely its signifying surface (the sequence of lexias), and that was very dense symbolically, in order that the text being analysed touched us continuously beyond all particularism: who would not be touched by a text whose declared "subject" is death?

I should, for frankness's sake, add this: in analysing the text's significance, we shall voluntarily refrain from dealing with certain problems; we shall not speak of the author, Edgar Allan Poe, nor of the literary history of which he is part; we shall not take into account the fact that the work is going to be carried out on a translation: we shall take the text as is, as we read it, without having to know whether in a university it would belong to students of English rather than to students of French or to philosophers. This does not necessarily mean that these problems will not pass into our analysis; on the contrary, they will *pass*, in the proper sense of the term: the analysis is a *crossing* of the text; these problems can be located as cultural *citations*, departures of codes, not of determinations.

A final word, which is perhaps in the way of conjuration, exorcism: the text we are about to analyse is neither lyrical nor political, it speaks neither of love nor of society, it speaks of death. That is to say that we shall have to lift a particular censorship: that attached to the *sinister*. We shall do so with the conviction that any censorship stands for all others: to speak of death outside

[2] *Histoires extraordinaires*, trans. by Baudelaire (Paris: NRF, 1969; Livre de poche edn) pp. 329–45.

all religion is to lift both the religious and the rationalist prohibition simultaneously.

## Analysis of Lexias 1 – 10

### (*1*) *"The Facts in the Case of M. Valdemar"*

(2) Of course I shall not pretend to consider it any matter for wonder, that the extraordinary case of M. Valdemar has excited discussion. It would have been a miracle had it not – especially under the circumstances. (3) Through the desire of all parties concerned, to keep the affair from the public, at least for the present, or until we had farther opportunities for investigation – through our endeavours to effect this – (4) a garbled or exaggerated account made its way into society, and became the source of many unpleasant misrepresentations, and, very naturally, of a great deal of disbelief.

(5) It is now rendered necessary that I give the *facts* – as far as I comprehend them myself. (6) They are, succinctly, these:

(7) My attention, for the last three years, had been repeatedly drawn to the subject of Mesmerism, (8) and, about nine months ago, it occurred to me, quite suddenly, that in the series of experiments made hitherto, (9) there had been a very remarkable and most unaccountable omission: (10) – no person had as yet been mesmerized *in articulo mortis*.

(1) *"The facts [la vérité sur, the truth about, in Baudelaire's translation] in the Case of M. Valdemar"*

The function of the title has not been well studied, at least from a structural point of view. What can be said immediately is that society, for commercial motives, needing to assimilate the text to a product, a commodity, must have *markers*: the function of the title is to mark the beginning of the text, i.e. to constitute the text as a commodity. Thus all titles have several simultaneous meanings, at least two of which are: (1) what it utters, linked to the contingency of what follows it; and (2) the announcement itself that a piece of literature is going to follow (i.e., in fact, a commodity); in other words, the title always has a double function: as utterance and as deixis.

(a) To announce a truth is to stipulate the existence of an enigma. The posing or positioning of the enigma (on the plane of the signifiers) results from the word "truth"; from the word "case" (that which is exceptional, therefore marked, therefore significant, and whose meaning must consequently be found); from the definite article *the* (there is only one truth, thus all the work of the text will be needed to make it through this narrow gate); from the cataphoric form implied by the title: what follows is going to bring about what is announced, the resolution of the enigma is already announced; we note that the English says: "The facts in the case ..." Poe's intended signified is of an empirical order, whereas that intended by the French translator (Baudelaire) is hermeneutic: the truth then refers to the exact facts, but also perhaps to their meaning. However this may be, we shall code this first sense of the lexia: *enigma, position* (*enigma* is the general name of a code, the *position* is merely one of its terms).

(b) The truth could be spoken without being announced beforehand, without any reference being made of the word. If one speaks of what one is going to say, if one doubles the language into two layers, the first of which tops off as it were the second, one is merely resorting to a metalanguage. Here, therefore, we have the presence of the metalinguistic code.

(c) This metalinguistic announcement has an aperitive function: it is a matter of whetting the reader's appetite (a process akin to "suspense"). The narrative is a commodity, the proposition of which is preceded by a "sales pitch". This "appetizer" is a term of the narrative code (the rhetoric of narration).

(d) A proper name should always be examined carefully, for the proper name is, one might say, the prince of signifiers; its connotations are rich, social and symbolic. In the name Valdemar, one can read at least the two following connotations: (1) the presence of a socio-ethnic code: is it a German name? Slavic? In any case, it is not Anglo-Saxon; this little enigma, formulated implicitly here, will be resolved in no. 19 (Valdemar is Polish); (2) "Valdemar" is "the vale of the sea"; the oceanic abyss, the underwater depths is a theme dear to Poe: the gulf refers to that which is twice outside nature, subaqueous and subterranean. Thus, from the point of view of the analysis there is the trace of two codes here: a socio-ethnic code and a (or the) symbolic code (we shall return to these codes a little later).

(e) Saying "M(onsieur) Valdemar" is not the same thing as saying "Valdemar". In many tales, Poe uses simple first names (Ligeia, Eleonora, Morella). The presence of this "Monsieur" carries with it an effect of social reality, of the historically real; the hero is socialized, made part of a defined society, in which he is provided with a civil title. We must therefore note: social code.

(2) *Of course I shall not pretend to consider it any matter for wonder, that the extraordinary case of M. Valdemar has excited discussion. It would have been a miracle had it not – especially under the circumstances.*

(a) The obvious function of this sentence (and those immediately following) is to arouse the reader's expectations and this is why they are apparently insignificant: what one wants is the solution to the enigma posed in the title (the "truth"), but even the exposition of this enigma is put off. So we must code: delay in positioning the enigma.

(b) Same connotation as in (1)c: it is a matter of whetting the reader's appetite (the narrative code).

(c) The word "extraordinary" is ambiguous: it refers to that which departs from the norm, but not necessarily from nature (if the case remains "medical"), but it can also refer to the supernatural, to that which has become a transgression (that is the "fantastic" – i.e. the "extraordinary" – element in the stories Poe tells). The word's ambiguity is significant here: a horrible story (outside the limits of nature) and yet covered by the alibi of science (here connoted by the "discussion", which is a scientist's word). This blending is in fact cultural: the blend of the strange with the scientific reached its peak in that part of the nineteenth century to which Poe, broadly speaking, belongs: it excited people to observe the supernatural (mesmerism, spiritualism, telepathy, etc.) scientifically; the supernatural takes the rationalist, scientific alibi; this, then, is the *cri du coeur* of that positivist age: if only one could believe *scientifically* in immortality! This cultural code which for simplicity's sake we shall call the scientific code, will be of great importance throughout the narrative.

(3) *Through the desire of all parties concerned, to keep the affair from the public, at least for the present, or until we had farther opportunities for investigation – through our endeavours to effect this –*
(a) Here is the same scientific code, taken up again by the word "investigation" (which is also a police word: the fate of the detective novel in the second half of the nineteenth century – precisely from Poe on – is well known; what is important, ideologically and structurally, is the conjunction of the code of the police mystery and the code of science – of the scientific discourse – which proves that structural analysis can work together with ideological analysis quite well).
(b) We are not told the motives for the secret; they may proceed from two different codes, both present together in the reading (to read is also to imagine, silently, what is not said). (1) The scientific deontological code: Poe and the doctors, out of loyalty and prudence, do not want to make public a phenomenon which has not been clarified scientifically; (2) the symbolic code: there is a taboo on living Death – we do not speak of it because it is horrible. It must be said here (even though we shall have to return to it and insist on it later) that these two codes are *undecidable* (we cannot choose one over the other), and it is this very undecidability which makes for a good narrative.
(c) From the point of view of narrative *actions* (this is the first one we come upon), a sequence is here started up in effect "to keep hidden" logically (or pseudo-logically) implies consequent operations (e.g. to unveil). Here then we must posit the first term of an actional sequence: *to keep hidden*, and we shall find what follows it later on.

(4) *a garbled or exaggerated account made its way into society, and became the source of many unpleasant misrepresentations, and, very naturally, of a great deal of disbelief.*
(a) The demand for truth, i.e. the enigma, has already been made twice (by the word "truth" and by the expression "extraordinary case"). The enigma is "posed" here a third time (to pose an enigma, in structural terms, means: to utter – *there is an enigma*), by the error it gave rise to: the error posited here, retroactively justifies the title by anaphora ("*La vérité sur . . .*"). The redundance which reflects the *position* of the enigma (the fact that there is an

enigma is repeated in several ways) has an operative value: it is a matter of exciting the reader, of procuring clients for the narrative.

(b) A second term appears within the actional sequence "to hide": the effect of the secret, distortion, mistaken opinion, the accusation of mystification.

(5) *It is now rendered necessary that I give the facts – as far as I comprehend them myself.*

(a) The emphasis placed on "the facts" assumes the intrication of two codes, between which, as in (3)b, it is impossible to decide: (1) the law, the scientific deontology enslaves the scientist, the observer to the *fact*; the opposition between fact and rumour is an old mythical theme; when *fact* is invoked in a fiction (and invoked emphatically, by a word in italics), its structural function (for the actual scope of this artifice does not fool anyone) is to authenticate the story, not to make the reader believe it happened, but to pursue the discourse of the real, and not that of the fable. The fact then becomes part of a paradigm in which it is placed in opposition to *mystification* (Poe admitted in a private letter that the story of M. Valdemar was a pure mystification: "it is a mere hoax"). The code which structures the reference to the fact is the scientific code which we have already come across. (2) However, any more or less grand recourse to the Fact can also be considered as the symptom of the subject's quarrel with the symbolic; to argue aggressively in favour of the "Facts alone", to claim victory for the referent is to cast suspicion on signification, to mutilate the real's symbolic supplement. It is an act of censorship against the signifier which *displaces* the fact – it is a refusal of the *other scene*, that of the unconscious. By pushing aside the symbolic supplement, the narrator takes on an imaginary role (even if to our eyes he does so by a narrative trick), that of the scientist; the lexia's signified is thus the *asymbolism* of the subject of the utterance: *I* passes itself off as being asymbolic; the denial of the symbolic is obviously part of the symbolic code itself.

(b) The actional sequence "to hide" is further developed: the third term announces the necessity of rectifying the deformation pointed out in (4)b; this rectification stands for: *wanting to unveil* (what was hidden). This narrative sequence "to hide" clearly constitutes an excitation "as" the narrative; in a sense, it justifies it, and thereby points to its *value* (its *worth-for*), making a commodity of it: I tell the story, says the narrator, *in exchange* for a demand for counter-error, for truth (we live in a civilization in which truth is a value, i.e. a commodity). It is always quite interesting to try to pick out the worth-for of a narrative: in exchange for what is the story told? In the *Arabian Nights*, each story stands for one day's survival. Here we are warned that the story of M. Valdemar stands for the truth (first presented as a counter-distortion).

(c) The *I* appears explicitly in the French for the first time – it was already present in the *we* of "our effort" (3). The utterance is in fact made up of three *I*s, i.e. three imaginary roles (to say *I* is to enter into the imaginary): (1) a narrator, artist-*I*, whose motive is the search for effect; to this *I* then corresponds a *You* which is that of the literary reader, he who is reading "a fantastic tale by the great writer Edgar Allan Poe"; a witness-*I*, who has the power to bear witness to a scientific experiment; the corresponding *You* is that of a jury of scientists, of serious opinion, of the scientific reader; (3) an actor, experimenter-*I*, he who is going to mesmerize Valdemar; the *You* is then Valdemar himself; in these last two cases the motive for the imaginary role is the "truth". We have here the three terms of a code we shall call, perhaps provisionally, the code of *communication*. Between these three roles there is doubtless another language, the language of the unconscious, which is uttered neither *in* science nor *in* literature; but this language which is literally the language of *interdiction* does not say *I*: our grammar with its three persons is never directly that of the unconscious.

(6) *They are, succinctly, these:*
    (a) Announcing what follows depends on metalanguage (and the rhetorical code); it is the signpost marking the start of a story within the story.
    (b) "Succinctly" carries three mixed and undecidable connotations: (1) "Don't be afraid, this won't take too long." Within the narrative code, this is the phatic mode (pointed out by Jakobson), the function of which is to hold the attention, to maintain contact; (2) "It will be brief because I shall stick strictly to the facts"; this is the scientific code, which allows for the utterance of the scientist's "paring down", the superiority of the authority of the fact over the authority of the discourse; (3) to pride oneself on speaking briefly is in a certain sense to lay a claim against speech, to limit the *supplement* of the discourse, i.e. the symbolic; it is to speak the code of the asymbolic.

(7) *My attention, for the last three years, had been repeatedly drawn to the subject of Mesmerism,*
    (a) The *chronological code* must be closely observed in any narrative; here in this code ("the last three years") two values are mixed together; the first is naïve, as it were; one of the temporal elements of the experiment to be conducted is noted: its preparation time; the second does not have a diegetical, operative function (the commutation test makes this quite clear; if the narrator had said *seven years* instead of *three*, it would not have had any effect on the story); it is therefore a matter of pure *effet de réel*: the number emphatically connoted the truth of the fact – that which is *precise* is reputedly *real* (an illusion moreover, since there exists a well-known delirium of figures). Let us note that linguistically the word "last" is a "shifter", it refers to the placement of the one who utters in time; it thus reinforces the *presence* of the account which is to follow.
    (b) A long actional sequence begins here, or at the very least a sequence well stocked with terms; its object is to get an experiment under way (we are under the alibi of experimental science); structurally, this getting things under way is not the experiment itself; it is an experimental *programme*. This sequence in fact stands for the *formulation* of the enigma, which has already been posited several times ("there is an enigma"), but which has not yet been formulated. So as not to weigh down the reporting of the analysis, we shall code the programme

separately, it being understood that through procuration the entire sequence stands for a term of the code of the enigma. Here we have the first term of this "programme" sequence: the posing of the scientific field of the experiment.

(c) The reference to magnetism is drawn from a cultural code, a code recurrent throughout this part of the nineteenth century. Following Mesmer (in English "magnetism" can be called "mesmerism") and the Marquis Armand de Puységur, who had discovered that magnetism could induce somnambulism, the number of magnetizers and magnetist societies had multiplied in France (around 1820); it appears that in 1829 it had been possible to carry out the painless excision of a tumour under hypnosis; in 1845, the year of our tale, Braid, in Manchester, codified hypnotism by inducing nervous fatigue through the contemplation of a shiny object; in 1850, at the Mesmeric Hospital of Calcutta, painless births were achieved. We know that Charcot thereafter classified hypnotic states and circumscribed hypnosis to hysteria (1882), but since then hysteria has disappeared from hospitals as a clinical entity (from the moment it was no longer observed). The year 1845 marks the high point of scientific illusion: there was belief in a physiological reality to hypnosis (though Poe, pointing out Valdemar's "nervousness", may lead one to believe that the subject was hysterically predisposed).

(d) Thematically, magnetism connotes (at least during that period) an idea of *fluid*: something passes from one subject to another; there is an interchange (an interdiction) between the narrator and Valdemar: this is the code of communication.

(8) *and, about nine months ago, it occurred to me, quite suddenly, that in the series of experiments made hitherto,*

(a) The chronological code ("nine months") calls for the same remarks as those that have been made in (7)a.

(b) Here we have the second term of the sequence "programme": a domain was chosen in (7)b, that of magnetism; it is now cut up into segments; a particular problem is going to be isolated.

(9) *there had been a very remarkable and most unaccountable omission:*

(a) The structure of the "programme" continues to be uttered; here is the third term: the experiment which has not yet been done and therefore, for any scientist concerned about research, which remains to be done.

(b) This experimental lack is not a simple "omission" or at least this omission is strongly significant: it is quite simply the omission of Death; there has been a taboo (which is going to be lifted, in the furthest depths of horror); the connotation belongs to the symbolic code.

(10) *– no person had as yet been mesmerized* in articulo mortis.

(a) Fourth term of the "programme" sequence: the contents of the lacuna (there is clearly a falling off in the relation between the assertion of the lacuna and its definition in the rhetorical code: to announce/to specify).

(b) Latin (*in articulo mortis*), a juridical and medical language, produces an effect of scientificity (the scientific code), but through the intermediary of a euphemism (saying in a little-known language something one dare not say in everyday language), it also designates a taboo (the symbolic code). It seems clear that what is essentially taboo in Death is the passage, the threshhold, the "dying" itself; life and death are relatively classified states, moreover, they enter into paradigmatic opposition, they are taken over by meaning, which is always pacifying; but the transition between the two states, or more exactly, as will be the case here, their *encroachment*, frustrates meaning, and engenders horror: an antithesis, a classification is transgressed.

Before moving on to methodological conclusions, I shall recall, on a purely andecdotal plane, the end of the story: Valdemar remains dead under hypnosis for seven months; with the agreement of the doctors, P. then decides to wake him; the passes succeed and a little colour returns to Valdemar's cheeks; but while P. tries to activate the subject's awakening by intensifying the passes, the ejaculations of "Dead! Dead!" explode on his tongue, and all at once, his whole body caves in, crumbles away, rots beneath the experimenter's hands, leaving nothing but a "nearly liquid mass of loathsome – of detestable putridity".

## Methodological Conclusions

The remarks that will serve as conclusion to this analytical fragment will not necessarily be "theoretical"; theory is not abstract, speculative: the analysis itself, although dealing with a contingent text, was already theoretical, in the sense that it observed (which was its aim) a language in the process of formation. Which is to say – or recall – that we have not carried out an explication of the text; we have simply tried to grasp the narrative as it was constructing itself (which implies both structure and movement, system and infinity at once). Our structuration does not go beyond that spontaneously achieved by reading. Thus in concluding, it is not a matter of delivering the "structure" of Poe's tale, still less that of all narratives, but simply of returning, in a freer, less attached manner, to the progressive unrolling of the text, to the principal codes we have identified.

The word *code* itself should not be taken here in the rigorous, scientific sense of the term. The codes are merely associative fields, a supra-textual organization of notations imposing a certain idea of structure; the authority of the code is, for us, essentially cultural: the codes are certain types of *déjà-vu*, *déjà-lu* and *déjà-fait*: the code is the form this *déjà* takes, constitutive of all the writing in the world.

Although all the codes are in fact cultural, there is, however, one, among those we have come across, which we shall privilege by calling it the *cultural code*: it is the code of knowledge, or rather of human knowledge, public opinion, of culture as transmitted through books, education, and in a more general, more diffuse way, though all sociality; the referent of this code is knowledge, as a body of rules elaborated by society. We have come across several of these cultural codes (or several sub-codes of the general cultural code): the scientific code, which (in our tale) is supported at once by both the precepts of experimentation and by the principles of medical deontology; the rhetorical code, which brings together all the social rules of what is *said*: coded forms of narrative, coded forms of discourse (the announcement, the résumé, etc.); the metalinguistic (the discourse speaks of itself) is part of this code; the chronological code: "dating" the discourse, which seems natural and objective to us today, is in fact a very cultural practice – which is to be expected since it implies a certain ideology of time ("historical" time is not the same as "mythical" time); the entire set of chronological reference points therefore constitutes a strong cultural code (an historical way of segmenting time for purposes of dramatization, of scientific appearance, of giving the effect of reality); the socio-historical code permits the mobilizing, within the utterance, of all the inbred knowledge we have about our time, our society, our country (the fact of saying *M. Valdemar* – and not *Valdemar* – it will be remembered, is part of this). We must not be worried by the fact that extremely banal notations can be constituted into a code; on the contrary, it is their banality, their apparent insignificance which predisposes them to codification, as we have defined it; a body of rules so widely used that we take them as natural features; but if the narrative departed from these rules, it would very quickly become *unreadable*.

The code of communication could also be called the code of destination. *Communication* should be understood in a restricted sense; it does not cover all *signification* in a text, still less its *significances*; it designates only those relations in the text which are uttered as forms of *address* (as in the case of the "phatic" code, responsible for accentuating the relationship between narrator and reader), or *exchange* (the narrative is exchanged for truth, for life). In short, *communication* should here be understood in an economic sense (the communication, the circulation of goods).

The symbolic field (here "field" is less rigid than "code") is, to be sure, quite vast; the more so in that here we are taking the word "symbol" in the most general sense possible, without bothering about any of its usual connotations. The sense to which we are referring is close to that of psychoanalysis: in short, the symbol is that feature of language which *displaces* the body and gives a "glimpse" of a scene other than that of the utterance, such as we believe we read it. The symbolic armature in Poe's tale is obviously the transgression of the taboo of Death, the classificatory disturbance, what Baudelaire translated (very well) by the "*empiétement*" (encroachment) of Life on Death (and not, banally, of Death on Life); the tale's subtlety comes in part from the fact that the utterance seems to issue from an asymbolic narrator, who has assumed the role of the objective scientist, tied to the facts alone, a stranger to symbols (which do not fail to recur in force in the story).

What we have called the code of actions upholds the anecdotal armature of the narrative; the actions, or the utterances which denote them, are organized in sequences; the sequence has an *approximate* identity (its contour cannot be determined either rigorously or irrecusably). It is justified in two ways: first because one is led spontaneously to give it a generic name (for example, a certain number of notations – poor health, deterioration, agony, the mortification of the body, its liquefaction – are naturally grouped under one stereotyped idea, that of "Medical Death"), and second because the terms of the actional sequence are linked to each other (from one to the next, since they follow one another along the narrative) by an apparent logic; whereby we mean that the logic which institutes the actional sequence is very impure from a scientific point of view; it is only the appearance of logic which comes not from the laws of formal reasoning but from our habits of reasoning and observing: an endoxal, cultural logic (it seems logical to us that a severe diagnosis would follow the determination of a poor state of health). Furthermore this logic becomes confused with chronology: what comes *after* appears to us as *caused by*. Temporality and causality, though never pure in any narrative, seem to us to found a kind of *naturalness*, intelligibility, readability for the anecdote: they allow us, for example, to *resume* it (what the ancients called the *argument*, a word at once logical and narrative).

One last code has (from the outset) run throughout our tale: that of the Enigma. We have not had a chance to see it at work because we have analysed only a very small part of Poe's tale. The code of the Enigma brings together the terms through whose linkage (like a narrative sentence) an enigma is posited, posed, and after a few "delays", which give the narration all its piquancy, the solution is unveiled. The terms of the enigmatic (or hermeneutic) code are well differentiated; a distinction must be made, for example, between the *positing* of the enigma (every notation whose meaning is "there is an enigma") and the *formulation* of the enigma (the question is exposed in its contingency). In our story the enigma is posited in the French title itself (the "truth" (*vérité*) is announced but we do not yet know about what question), formulated from the outset (i.e. the scientific account of the problems linked to the planned experiment) and even, from the outset, delayed. Every narrative obviously has an interest in delaying the solution to the enigma it posits, since this solution will toll its own death knell as a narrative: we have seen that the narrator uses an entire paragraph to delay the account of the case, under the pretext of scientific precautions. As for the solution to the enigma, it is not of a mathematical order here; it is, in sum, the entire narrative which answers the question posed at the outset, the question of the truth (this truth can, however, be condensed into two points: the uttering of "I am dead" and the sudden liquefaction of the dead man at the moment he awakes from hypnosis); the truth here is not the object of a *revelation*, but of a *revulsion*.

Such are the codes which have run throughout the fragments we have analysed. It is a deliberate choice we make not to structure them further, not to try to distribute the terms within each code according to a logical or semiological schema; because for us the codes are merely *departures* from *déjà-lu*, the starting points of intertextuality: the *unravelled* quality of the codes is not what contradicts structure (as life, imagination, intuition, disorder are thought to contradict system and rationality), but on the contrary (and this is the fundamental affirmation of textual analysis), it is *an integral part of structuration*. It is this "fraying" of the text which distinguishes structure (strictly speaking, the object of structural analysis) from structuration – the object of the textual analysis we have attempted to practise here.

The textile metaphor we have just used is not fortuitous. Textual analysis in fact demands that the text be represented as a *tissue* (this is moreover its etymological sense), as a skein of different voices, of multiple codes, at once interwoven and incomplete. A narrative is not a tabular space, a flat structure; it is a volume, a stereophony (Eisenstein repeatedly insisted on the *counterpoint* of his stagings, thus instigating an identity between film and text). There is a *field of listening* in a written narrative; meaning's mode of presence (except perhaps for actional sequences) is not development, but *bursting-forth*: calls for contact and communication, the positing of contracts and exchanges, outbursts of references, glimmerings of knowledge, and heavier, more penetrating blows all coming from "the other (the symbolic) scene", that of the symbolic, the discontinuity of actions attached to the same sequence, but in a loose way, ceaselessly interrupted.

All this "volume" is pulled forward (toward the end of the narrative), thus provoking the impatience of reading, through the effect of two structural dispositions. (a) *Distortion*: the terms of a sequence or of a code are separated, threaded with heterogeneous elements; a sequence seems to have been abandoned (for example, the deterioration in Valdemar's health), but there is a *reprise* further on, sometimes much further; an expectation is created; we can even define the sequence now: this floating micro-structure which constructs not a logical object, but an expectation and its resolution. (b) *Irreversibility*: despite the floating nature of structure, in the classical, readable narrative (like Poe's tale), there are two codes which maintain a vectorized order, the actional code (based on a logico-temporal order) and the code of the Enigma (the question is brought to its knees by its solution); thus a narrative irreversibility is created. It is clearly on this point that the modern subversion will be carried out: the avant-garde (to keep a convenient label) attempts to make the text reversible from one part to the other, to expel the logico-temporal residue, to make an attack on *empiricism* (the logic of behaviour, the actional code) and on the *truth* (the code of the Enigma).

We must not, however, exaggerate the distance which separates the modern text from the classical narrative. Very often in Poe's story we have seen the same sentence refer to two codes simultaneously, without being able to choose which is "true" (for example, the scientific code and the symbolic code): the characteristic of the narrative, once it attains the quality of a *text*, is to constrain us to the *undecidability* of the codes. In whose name could we decide? In the author's name? But the narrative only gives us the one who utters, a performer caught up in his own production. In the name of such and such criticism? All can be challenged, carried off by history (which does not mean they are useless: each one participates, but as one voice only, in the volume of text). Undecidability is not a weakness, but a structural condition of narration: there is no univocal determination of the utterance: in an utterance, several codes, several voices *are there*, without pre-eminence. Writing is precisely this loss of origin, this loss of "motives" to the benefit of a volume of indeterminations or overdeterminations: this volume is precisely the *significance*. Writing occurs exactly at the moment when speech ceases, that is, at the instant when one cannot locate *who is speaking* and when one can establish only that *speaking has begun*.

ROLAND BARTHES

# Day by Day with Roland Barthes

### Leni

I have been reading (belatedly) Glenn Infield's book on Leni Riefenstahl and the Third Reich. Over and over again the author asks: was she a Nazi or wasn't she? Or rather: to what degree? (The degrees of complicity stick in the craw of political justice.) But this point, though taken as central, is of no interest to me. What fascinates me is what happens, indirectly but massively, during the trial: the horror of Nazism. Now this horror, here, is all the more dreadful in that it is in some way casual, distilled by trivia: for instance that conversation between Goering and Goebbels on allowing Jews on trains, or again, made current by Darquier's arguments, Goebbels' project for entrusting to Gerron the production of a propaganda film to show how well the Jews were treated by the "nice Nazis": the ghetto city of Theresienstadt "given" by Hitler to the Jews, cleaned and polished, the sick removed, the houses decorated with flowers and flags, prisoners in the nearby camps dressed in new clothes, invited to a sumptuous banquet which they were not entitled to touch, then Gerron and his team, once the film was made, sent to Auschwitz and gassed. Here we reach a point of horror which exceeds, if we dare say it, death and torture. The fear such a world inspires is so strong that even the sight of German typography terrifies me (there are several letters from Leni here), with its thick black exclamation points.

"Curiosity is a beautiful virtue and Roland Barthes is without doubt the most famous on-looker of his time", wrote *Le Nouvel Observateur*. Barthes wrote a column for the *Observateur* from December 1978 to April 1979.

## At the Barber's

In the chair next to mine a handsome fellow with a beard *à la François premier* sprawls between the barber who is working on his head and the manicurist holding his limp hands. The conversation is general, everyone in the shop participates. All of a sudden I hear a sentence very distinctly – elaborated as clearly as a maxim. "I use the same method for training dogs and women – but it is harder with women." The manicurist and the cashier seem enchanted, either because they want to emphasize the fact that a witticism has been made or because they feel flattered at having more "character" than dogs – or just because they delight in the comfort of the stereotype. As a matter of fact the man has a dog, sitting sadly and rather uncomfortably on a chair behind him: "I got him when he was four months old, and he's been with me ever since for the last five years", he says with the satisfaction of the beloved master. (How is it that dogs, often so noble, fail to perceive the stupidity of their masters?) Several days later, I read in the personal columns of *Libération*: "You women! You run the world like a goddess while the rest of us get it up for you and all the same you're nothing but bitches! I dare anyone to prove that there's still such a thing as love!"

## Sects Again

The suicides in Guyana being all dead, or virtually all, there was no possible suspense except about their number which grew with each bulletin. All the pathos derived, as a matter of fact, from their exorbitant quantity. Suicide is usually a matter of solitary individuals or couples; over two begins excess, which always discourages explanations. Hence we have seen some people cheerfully turn from the difficulties of explanation to the convenience of projection; sects are used as a kind of a universal monster which is applied to whatever we do not like: for some, American society; for *Pravda*, the dissidents; for Devereux the psychoanalyst, right here, "fashionable" intellectuals. For me myself, I am embarrassed given the present state of my knowledge, not to know more about what these poor bastards believed, as if the attempts at interpretation today are so concerned with forms (such as fascination, possession, hypnosis, etc.) that we feel it is unnecessary to consider the contents.

## Rumour

Place Saint-Germain-des-Prés: we watch a few boys getting ready to perform some music in public; two policemen are there (without our knowing whether there is trouble ahead). X then tells me with assurance that Chirac wants to keep the musicians off the street and the boats off the river. No matter how often I tell myself that he may not be sure of what he is saying it makes an unpleasant effect on me. I realize that I am affected (sometimes even distressed) more readily by rumours than by news; for news immediately mobilizes a rationale to argue it out, while rumours affect me in that lower region of my body acted on by bile and by fear.

## Sirens

From time to time, on Thursday, around noon, you hear the sirens. Nothing more than a strange noise between the remote recollection of the phoney war and a vague future which would be horrible if one had any idea what it would be; but one does not: the French are no longer afraid of war – they are afraid of . . . burglars.

## The Trip-up

A lady has been mugged in a parking lot; her assailant tried to snatch her purse. Luckily her husband was there: "I shouted to my wife: 'Hit him with your umbrella!' The mugger let go and ran away: 'Stop thief! Stop thief!' " A co-operative bystander trips up the mugger who falls full length on the ground; after which it is easy enough to take him into custody. I look up from my newspaper and dream. I dream of the thousand and one nights where there are so many thieves but as far as I can remember not one gets tripped up. Then I think that the art of great storytelling, of master narratives – is perhaps incompatible with ignominy, the minor ignominy of the "co-operative bypasser": the tale has its own nobility which can narrate enormous betrayals but not the petty meannesses of "real citizens" (this is the *satisfecit* bestowed by the police commissioner on the cast of characters).

## Zouc Does More

The art of observing and imitating, of listening and reproducing, of criticizing by the mere fact of reproducing – all of which Zouc does with genius – is an art, after all, entirely classical (hence our interest in knowing – as I do not yet know – if Zouc is successful with a wide public, the audience at the Bobino, for instance, where she is playing now). But Zouc does more . . . than herself. In some of her sketches, we no longer know who is talking to whom: it is a language between two mirrors, hence infinite, without a brake. Besides, Zouc often shifts from one sketch to the next without warning. Is one number finishing or another beginning? In this way an endless fabric of language is created (the language of others) among which the speaker and what is spoken of are no longer discernible: a web, without a spider in the corner.

## Badge

This morning I received a badge in the mail: "I'm an intellectual, how about you?" My first thought is to wear another one, very prominently: "Don't worry about me."

## Nureyev and Berma

The other evening I saw my first performance by a great dancer – preceded, among my friends, by a reputation of genius. The first ballet was danced by a young man whom I regarded as quite ordinary. "That can't be him," I said to myself with some assurance: stars never come on at the beginning and, besides, his entrance would have been applauded. In the intermission a friend enlightened me: of course it was Nureyev I had been watching. I was astonished; but during the second ballet my eyes were opened and I saw how incomparable this dancer's quality was and that he justified the ovation of an electrified house. Then I realized that I had just reproduced in 1978 the scene where the Proustian Narrator goes to see Berma act. Everything was there, quite literally: the longing, the murmurs, the expectation, the disappointment, the conversion, the movements of the audience. I left the theatre amazed by the genius . . . of Proust: we never stop adding to the "Search" (as Proust kept adding to his manuscripts), we never stop writing it. And no doubt that is what reading is: rewriting the text of the work within the text of our lives.

## Japanese

Once again (although the afternoon is grey and cold to the point of darkness), an ageless Japanese is taking photographs of the Place de la Concorde, toward the distant neutral roofs of the grand Palais (actually there is not much to see). Do the Japanese ever look, and if so during what ceremonies, at the photographs we see them constantly taking? Obviously it is the action that excites them; who knows how they feel about the product. Which makes them, perhaps, very modern: to phase out the image for the sake of its capture.

## Cherries

In the Saint Germain marketplace, I found cherries (they had come from Australia). I hear that in the Buci market, which has an even more "popular" clientele, there are also, nowadays, out-of-season fruits. Even if such goods remain expensive – very expensive – all the same, it is as if Fauchon had opened a street stall. But it is not the economic riddle that fascinates me; but rather this: that technological progress (importing fruit in a few hours from the ends of the earth) dispossesses man of his sense of the seasons (of their *tempo*) and little by little – "with the best of intentions" – robs him of a delight, that of alternation; for perhaps there was a kind of delight in waiting for winter to end, in seeing lovely things bud, grow and vanish and regretting their loss even as they disappear and return: the greatest joy of all is over – that of the return. Henceforth, on the horizon, markets without seasons: the time of differences is past.

## Complexity

I went to a scientist's lecture on a problem of cellular biology. I was fascinated by this scientific language – euphoric for me precisely to the degree that I had no resistance to offer it. I did not resist but I distorted: as the speaker went on talking, I filtered out and grabbed hold of what, in such utterance, could make metaphors and, thenceforth, concern me. For instance, from the discontinuity of the nervous system (the subject of the lecture was the way the neurons communicate), I retained precisely the theme of the discontinuous, delighted that the most respected science of the day, biology, bestowed its warrant on a very contemporary sensibility, that of the flaw, the gap, the break, in a rationality which no longer operates by the image of a "constant" causality. I came up with this undoubtedly familiar notion but one whose scientific vulgarizations – however abundant in the press – never expand: that the main problem of modern epistemology is complexity. Whether in science, in economics, in linguistics, in sociology, the present task is less to be sure of the main principles than to be able to describe imbrications, relays, returns, additions, exceptions, paradoxes, ruses: a task which very quickly becomes a combative one, since it comes to grips with a henceforth reactionary force: *reduction*.

## Molière

The doctor has given me a complicated prescription: to take a spray four times a day for three weeks, to stop for one week, then to go on with two sprays a day for two weeks; to get one shot a week for six weeks then once a month for three months, etc. These figures produced the converse effect to the one the doctor might have expected. I had the overall euphoric sensation of a wild fantasy, of a magic pass, or of a game of lotto: in short a mixture of inspiration and chance. As everyone knows, as everyone says – or at least as everyone is beginning to say – medical discourse is intimidating but that is precisely why it is comical. Perhaps we should question the comic in its relations to power which it simultaneously jeopardizes and respects. For of course I shall scrupulously respect the programme of the sprays and shots. Laughter has allowed me to *fix* (as we say of an abscess) the laws of medicine and hence to submit to them.

## Power Failure

Late last Tuesday I saw the lightbulb in my kitchen flutter, fade, go out. Immediately I searched for the right name: a strike or a power failure. Other people, it appears, thought sabotage or war? Anything that makes a breach in the complicated equilibrium of our common life thus tends immediately to receive a name which sops it up: language fills gaps, plugs holes: that is its function. In the old days, the stop-gap was simple: god, the devil; today it is complex and rational; the event is immediately polysemic. We have entered the age of interpretation: a power failure is never a power failure, it is a government collapse.

## Very French

I saw on television (I had to wait till midnight) a very French film: "Vincent, François, Paul and the Rest". Why "very French"? We see a young woman take her dresses out of a closet and stuff them in her suitcase: she is leaving the conjugal bed and board – situation, adultery, crisis. Well, then it is a good dramatic film. Here is what makes it more French: the actors seem to spend their time in a café or at family meals. Here the stereotype is nationalized: it belongs to the setting, not to history: hence it has a meaning, not a function. Well, then it is a good realistic film. Finally, and above all, each actor has his fit of rage which terrorizes everyone else; after which comes the reconciliation. That is all because of Gabin. Yes, but where did Gabin himself come from? Doubtless he had realized that there is a kind of French delight in quarrelling and making up: starting a street fight, or one in the privacy of the home, and finishing it at the café, or in bed. In the first part, there is a display of oratorical qualification. One belongs to a rhetorical nation, one coins phrases, one delights in this or that superlative remark: the remark *in anger*. In the second part, one reveals a different qualification: one is good at pathos and shows as much, and simultaneously one shows that one can restrain it. It is always the same routine: first of all to signify that one is not deceived, and then that one is "after all", "deep down", a decent sort. Well, then it is a good psychological film.

## Badge II

*Grapus* has sent me another badge, the one I had suggested in these columns: "Don't worry about me." Now I can wear it, becoming the walking paradox who draws attention to his desire not to draw attention.

## Banal and Singular

A runaway car crashes against a wall on the Eastern Belt Parkway: the fact is (alas) banal. Neither the cause of the accident nor the five occupants of the car, all young, and almost all dead, can be identified: this is singular. Such singularity is that of what one might call a perfect death, in that it frustrates twice over what might appease the horror of dying: knowing who and from what. Everything comes down not to nothingness but to something even worse:

to *nullity*. This explains the kind of intense chronicling which our society elaborates around death: necrologies, annals, a history, everything that can name and explain, afford a purchase to memory and to meaning. How generous is Dante's *Inferno*, where the dead are called by their names and discussed according to their sins.

## The Imperative

It just so happens that I received three or four orders, one after the other in the guise of affectionate (and well-intentioned) jokes: "Stop smoking", "Don't be sad", "Don't forget your glasses", etc. Then I think: what if we got rid of the imperative? If men had the power to erase from the language all its repressive morphemes? I have always been fascinated by that story which a friend found for me in a geography textbook: certain Australian tribes when one of their members dies, eliminate a word from the vocabulary as a sign of mourning. This makes language equivalent to life, asserts that men are in control of what they say and that they give it orders rather than receive them from it.

– As always, you pin up utopias which, however, you have the bad faith to make up according to what science tells you (history, ethnology and even biology): look at what you have written right here on the discontinuity of the nervous system and the complexity of neuronal communication. If some order from the Barre government were to eliminate the imperative, what a spontaneous hue and cry there would be! And then this mode would immediately be replaced in common usage by a thousand other forms of command. Moreover this is what happens in at least two of our kinds of discourse: that of the law ("It is forbidden . . . " "No one may . . . ") and that of manners, which employs circumlocutions ("Would you be so good as to . . . ").

– In other words, you are a formalist. It is the imperative *form* that bothers you.

– Form is a clue, a residue. In the imperative there is a violence which is even more obvious when it is addressed to you "for your own good". Whatever one thinks, the imperative is the index of a manumission, it is a desire for power.

## Old Age Moves Me More Than Childhood

A little old woman, dressed very poorly, wanted to buy an orchid plant. It cost fifty francs. She offered five. I guessed what the misunderstanding was and followed the scene. Believing that she thought the plant too expensive, the young salesman suggested she take a pot of primroses which cost thirty. The same procedure. She did not know how to count in new francs (moreover she may have been a little deaf). When she was informed that the primroses cost 3000 francs, far from showing any outrage at the cost, she laughed and with difficulty pulled out of an old skinny wallet three crumpled bank notes. During this long deliberation, seeing that I was watching her sympathetically, she spoke to me and managed to share her whole life. She was eighty-five, she had a bad heart, she got winded easily, often she had to stop and lean against a wall: "I've worked and worked, you can't imagine. If I'm still alive it's because work doesn't kill you. It didn't used to be the way it is now, when you sit on a chair in an office." She was buying the pot of primroses as a present for a friend who had come to see her every week for the last fifty years. I resisted buying the flowers for her, being intimidated by the salesman. I was wrong.

– But that is a nice story, of respectable populism and all! Work, retirement, old people, the high cost of living . . .

– I could answer (making use of a famous revolutionary's remark) that "the facts are stubborn". But actually I have not told this story for political purposes; rather because it has taught me something: that I believe in facts only if they move me – and as for this one, I am well aware, in my heart of hearts, where the emotion came from.

## Limelight

In *Limelight* Chaplin energetically removes his make-up in front of a mirror. Out of the towel emerges then a strange, almost embarrassing face – young and feminine, the lines are so pure. The violence of this transformation has something magical about it: it is literally a metamorphosis, the kind that only mythology and entomology could speak of. The genius of the cinema then would be to *intensify* rational phenomena, so as to make them appear somehow *an additional purity*. Here we would connect up with the mythological basis of humanity, not by some grandiloquent appeal to the fabulous but simply by relying on the image. For after all, by removing his make-up "cinematographically" Chaplin merely takes literally the metaphor which commands us to "take off the mask" or "to reveal the old Adam".

## "No Smoking"

In the great days of tuberculosis, when the collectivity said "No spitting", it was merely protecting its members according to a classical principle of prophylaxis: prohibition implied a solidarity, a community. However, behind the "no smoking" ban imposed or recommended by the state looms the spectre of a non-contagious disease which affects only the individual: cancer. Then the society says: "I no longer need to be responsible for the community's health, hence I am free to be responsible for *your* health now, and I do so mercilessly. Be responsible for yourself. If need be, I will help you by regulations." Thus there occurs a return of the old voluntarist morality. The individual is limited no longer because he risks harming others, but because he depends on the Law (and not solely on the laws), which society henceforth assumes the right to incarnate. "I shall be responsible for you personally, in spite of yourself": such is the disturbing little light I see winking in the ban on smoking.

## Mao/Tao

Having broken with China, Albania has revised its judgements about Mao. According to Enver Hoxha, Mao was never a Marxist: his thought was only a revisionist variant: it actually had its roots in "the ancient philosophy of China". I remember that during our trip to that country (Mao was still alive) we tried to find out by asking people (though the quantity was limited) if there was still a living relation between the new ideology and the Tao (the question was all the more plausible in that the campaign against Confucius was at its height): no answer of course – the Tao did not belong among acceptable notions. Yet how fascinating it would be (and perhaps how useful) to be able to discern politics in the density of its text. Behind the rationalism of the great Western systems, such as Marxism, can loom certain logics, certain turns of thought, certain defences, certain ruses, which belong to quite another universe. Within the discourse of the politician, one can always re-establish *religious sources*.

## Manners

Someone to whom I had spoken hastily and banally about his manuscript wrote to me: "You talk to keep from saying anything." He does not know that "talking to keep from saying anything" means something. In this case it meant: "Right now I'm tired, I don't want to criticize you either favourably or otherwise and at the same time I don't want to hurt your feelings by suggesting to you that by my silence I have a poor opinion of your text."
   – Well, frankly I prefer frankness.
   – But the Neutral cannot be spoken frankly. Besides, ultimately manners are more generous than frankness, for they signify that one believes in the other's intelligence: one trusts him: he will understand.
   – And suppose he doesn't understand?
   – One writes this for one must always defend one's ethic.

## A Dreadful Life

I was astonished to read the life of Giordano Bruno (in the little book on Italian writers by J. M. Gardair). What a dreadful life! Persecuted the first time, he fled from Naples, then a second time from Rome. No sooner converted to Calvinism, and settled in Geneva, then he has to leave, rejected by his new co-religionists. Summoned to Paris by Henri III, Catholic reaction forces him to England (fourth escape). The Oxford authorities are hostile to him: he goes back to Paris, which he has to leave in order to escape from the Duc de Guise. He then takes refuge in Germany. Suspected of Calvinism by the Lutherans, he escapes a seventh time and returns to Italy. There, betrayed by his host, he is handed over to the Inquisition and imprisoned; after seven years of a virtually interminable trial, he is condemned: his tongue shackled by a bit to keep him from blaspheming, stripped naked, bound to a stake, he is burned alive. All this for having thought and written; after virtually four centuries (this happened around 1600), it matters little what; all that remains is what Michelet called the sad and savage history of man.

The major figure in this story is the hideous beast of dogmatism (which is what I call the functional collusion of idea and power). Bruno was tracked down by the simultaneous dogmatisms of his time: a heretic for Catholics, a liberal for Calvinists, a Calvinist for Lutherans: in each pigeon-hole on the chart, he was a loser. But what is perhaps still more perverse, the systematic nature of his woes, the regularity of their excesses endow his life with something melodramatic: Bruno becomes something of the Bread Bearer of the freedom of thought.

A better impression is made by one well-chosen disaster than an uninterrupted series of proscriptions. What my reading leaves me with is not so much the representation of a wandering, but the final image of that naked man, led in chains, to a hideous death, a bit in his mouth.

## Fluctuation

Again in Gardair's little book, I read the life of Aretino. After the death of his protector, Leo X, he travels from city to city seeking and perhaps combining (this is the interesting point) new protections. For example, he offers his services *simultaneously* to Frederico Gonzaga and to Cardinal Julius de Medici. "Thereby," Gardair says, "he is already concerned by *calculated* hesitations [my italics] to reverse in his own favour the traditional dependence of men of letters on princely patronage." How I should like to find a book (since I cannot write one myself) which would discuss (in the form of a great historical panorama) the writer's relation to money and power! Perhaps the writer is invariably *dependent* (on an authority, an economy, a morality, a collective superego, etc.)? Perhaps he writes, whatever the liberalism of his society, only by *deceiving* power? Perhaps writing is always politically *perverse*? The "Book of Ruses" would be the name of this new handbook of literature, if this title were not already taken.

## Understanding

An ageing writer may feel abandoned by his own age; but it is not his solitude which is the cause of his suffering; that comes from a supplementary power muffled by the racket of the world forgetting him which he none the less continues to discern with acuity. "I understand everything!" he exclaims with intoxication and bile.

## Kuznetzov

Intellectuals and writers have gathered together on the occasion of Kuznetzov's fortieth birthday to protest once again at his long, his very long imprisonment: already fifteen years in jail or in a camp, seven more to go. Such an evening, of homage and protest, cannot fail to provoke, in the very individuals who participate in it quite wholeheartedly, a secret doubt: are all these words really good for something? Yes: many words constitute public opinion; and public opinion can force the arbitrary actions of governments – we have several examples of this: "Rulers", says Joseph de Maistre, "effectively and lastingly rule only within the circle of matters acknowledged by public opinion; and it is not they who draw this circle."

But furthermore, in all the words provoked by the defence of Kuznetzov, one rises up and touches me, pierces me, individually wounds me, and then bears my feeling as no reason and no *general* image had yet been able to do. Of course I can adhere to positions of justice; of course I can identify myself with the woes of a man in prison. But to *rouse* me it takes this unpredictable detail which will bring me into the presence of a kind of personal horror (each of us has what might be called the list of his own horrors).

Already the image of that distant Russian separated from me by so many things (education, religion, language, courage itself) had gradually come to adapt itself to my own, when some mention was made of his mother, who was not allowed to visit him (Tolstoy mocks the French for constantly speaking of their mothers: but we must always defend that thing in us which is mocked). However, what struck me more intensely was the observation made by Marthe Robert that Kuznetzov could not have read Kafka's *The Trial*. To be a (Western) writer and never have read Kafka!

Of course it is not in the name of "culture" that something in me protested so harshly: I could not care less whether it is good or bad to have read Kafka. It is in the name of "literature": my name for that essential, vital link which certain men have made with the work of the language, and in this sense literature transcends culture – it is not of the same order. Hence, the fact that a writer like Kuznetzov, has been doomed to be ignorant of Kafka because of the country of his birth (Kafka, who conceived of literature in its tragic mode) distressed me as much as seeing an animal born blind. A caste reaction? Yes, but ultimately it seems to me fairer to experience the evils of society through the particular than through general principles. Do we not see today that "the human" is in a sense the infinite total of irreducible particularities?

## Mexico

In the course of this same evening, Kuznetzov's lawyer read out messages of solidarity. One came from Mexico. My eyes (because of television) were full of the Pope's trip, standing in his special car, covering the crowd with a gesture cunningly divided between greeting and blessing, so as to make everyone happy: the laity, the faithful and those out to see the show. So I was thinking that the message came from him. But no: merely from a writer, Octavio Paz.

## Writer

There is no reason to suppose that Kuznetzov is a "good" writer. I am more or less inclined to suppose that he is not – any more than Solzhenitsyn: not that our criteria are so different from theirs, but on the contrary because their literary culture, long since cut off from any avant-garde, is like the archaic residue of what ours was a hundred years ago. None the less, what matters is not the judgement we make of Kuznetzov's work. What matters is that his decision to write is of a vital nature: writing is what allows him not only to survive but even, within his humiliations, to live supremely – it is in this that he is a writer.

## "As Long as the Language Lasts"

– You know this remark of Flaubert's which I find very beautiful: "I write not for today's reader, but for every reader who might appear, as long as the language lasts."

– How banal. What nineteenth-century writer has not said he wrote not for his contemporaries but for posterity? It is an arrogant reasoning and its politics are stale: what difference does today make (whether we suffer or cause suffering), tomorrow will justify us.

– That is not what Flaubert is saying. His declaration is a modest one. He writes for an uncertain reader who may not even appear. And far from linking literature to great, triumphant doctrines, to revolutions in mentality, in short, to its content, he is attaching it to a form: the French language. And he does not conceive of this form as an eternal one.

– And he is right! After all, language for Flaubert is "style", a chiselled style, a cultural, artificial prose as *calculated* as the poetry of his period. And this language happens to be dying. Flaubert's days are numbered.

– You are simplifying. You are saying: language, for Flaubert, is only style. I should reverse the proposition: style for Flaubert is his whole language. For what he is "chiselling" are not figures of speech, turns of phrase, ornaments, rhetorical effects, but a purely linguistic object: the sentence. What he wants to find is an absolute sentence – perhaps, in fact, an eternal one?

– But the sentence itself is provisional. First of all, we really do not know where we are with regard to the French sentence. Do we speak in sentences? No one really knows. Listen to a conversation: it begins, it branches off, it stops, it overlaps, in short it never ends, and not to end a sentence is to destroy the very idea of it. Do we write in sentences? Yes, no doubt, since we punctuate our texts. But here and there, on the margins of normal (or normative) culture, the sentence frays out: for example, in poetry, in the avant-garde text – and in personals, some of which, and this is a new thing, now speak the language of affect.

– That is merely a surface movement. What is threatened is the stylistic sentence. But for the grammatical sentence, you know that certain American linguists regard it, following Chomsky, as a biological legacy: the sentence is actually innate in man and not acquired by learning.

– Hence what is alarming is not the destruction of the sentence. Rather, secured by the scientific hypotheses you have just mentioned, the advent throughout society of a standard, insipid sentence, a sentence without diversity or individuality: a monster-sentence of the communication-society.

– I am amazed that among the countless prospective speculations in which we indulge concerning society in the year 2000, this question has never come up: what language will we speak tomorrow? What language are they choosing for us, those great leaders who are imagining France?

– In other words (and here we will agree): the sentence is an absolutely political object.


## The Sacred

One day I was helping a student with his dissertation on legal history on Power and the Sacred. We were looking for examples from antiquity, comparing Rex and Basileus, etc. Was that the reason we received such a mediocre grade (10 out of 20)? Today the examples would be more direct. Khomeini (inexhaustible subject), having appointed his Prime Minister, has specified that those who resist him would be punished first of all by Allah and then because opposition is a blasphemy. This is to say aloud what the unconscious of power only whispers: *I am sacred and anyone who contests me is a blasphemer.*

This observation comes from neither the right nor the left. I hear it in President Carter's Christian moralism and in the outraged tone of the Communist leaders who are as offended as priests when they are attacked. The "sovereign", as the eighteenth century said, can only be sacred: legality, legitimacy, divinity shade into each other and become the same thing. Khomeini is neither old nor new, simply revealing; he puts the urge to dominate on the big screen. For what are to be enlarged in the "reasons adduced" for power, are not interests, struggles and stakes, but *theology*.

### First Record

A young singer, Patrick Fierry, asked me to listen to his first record. It was vehement, bitter, sensitive, with something sharp, imperious, implacable about it, and a little crazy too, in so far as the stories told by these songs do not follow the docile rules of narrative. I am convinced that this art expresses a whole new youth, the very one which has the singer's age. But I am no longer of that age: my models, my culture, my values, my wounds and my language are different. I am a little lost. So am I no longer modern? Am I *ageing*? But while I say this, and without my immediately realizing it, the text and its rhythm suggest intellectual questions which touch me deeply and constitute a burning immediacy (the intellect can be moved): the (difficult) relation between the French language and music, the elimination of stereotypes, the creation of a new style, the shift of syntax, neological inventions, and above all the energy of pulsions, scansions, breathing, spasms, music – these all serve as a link between the language and the body.

In short, where I cannot quite participate, I can at least try to understand what is happening on the formal level; where I cannot project myself I can experience the stimulus of the intellect. Intellectual? It keeps me from ageing badly.

### Superman

A father writes to me about his son. Franck Oswald has been jailed in Uruguay since 17 April 1974. Political suffering is today so normal that we can read it the way a doctor reads a disease. The words "Uruguay" and "prison" are simple symptoms. They suffice for us to guess a whole banal story. No need to tell it: we know that it concerns a political arrest, torture, degrading incarceration, futile protests.

What is to be done? Doubtless a constant denunciation, protest and an appeal to public opinion. For there is no magic power that with a single touch of a wand can open the doors of the Uruguay prisons. It is true that the American superman uses his fabulous powers to capture a wretched hotel thief with a bag full of jewels and two grotesque speculators, as if the moral goal of superpower were the defence of private property and not that of the rights of man.

### Friendship

We learn the bad things people say about us from our well-intentioned friends: "The other day, you know, I spoke up for you . . . " Which is how I learn that I have been attacked. At which point a kind of difference is established between the friends. All of them like me well enough, no doubt, but only some know the precise map of my wounds. The one who hurts me without knowing it, in order to show me his devotion, distresses me twice over: by the news he gives me and because I discover that he does not know me *subtly* (unless he is acting perversely?).

## Superman II

An American child jumps out of a seventh-story window because he wants to fly like Superman. One might say in the same manner that Mme Bovary died from having read books.

"Be careful, soon you will be justifying censorship."

## Napping

Doors closed, the telephone switched off, curtains drawn and the doorbell detached, flat on my bed, I know that for an hour nothing can disturb a peace which from now on is up to me. What I get from napping is the *suspension* of my image: nothing comes to feed it; I am resting, not from others nor from myself, but from myself seen, thought, questioned, required by others.

## Packaging

The hardest thing about the books one receives is not talking about them or even reading them but opening the package: you have to wage a real battle against the cardboard, and the little tab that is supposed to afford you a jiffy opening breaks off; you have to cut, and the wadding which pads the envelope spreads everywhere, sticks to the carpet and to the furniture. After which – the great pain of modern times – you have to *get rid* of all this packaging.

Perhaps unfairly, I have the impression that this excessive security measure is quite French; our packaging is always too heavy, too compact, too tightly sealed, as if it were meant to close up the merchandise as long as possible, not to make it available (aberration of those price tags which stick so fast to the object that once home with them, you cannot remove them except by scratching and spoiling forever what you so much enjoyed buying).

## *Perceval*

At the cinema, smoke risks bothering the spectators, which is why it is forbidden to smoke. But the laughter behind me which accompanies this film – a film I find moving, a film I love and admire – is forbidden by no regulations and yet it offends me. For that evening the public was laughing, as I think I realized, at those sensitive things which were precisely what I liked in Rohmer's film: an art of narrative, the savour of a different language though a distinct one, the charm of assonance in speech, the contrast of the characters, the very subtle relation between literature and image – in short, a kind of nobility, of friendliness, of goodness.

Of course there are deliberately funny moments in *Perceval*. But once the laughter proceeds from a mockery or from a kind of crudity of feeling, once people laugh at sensitivity or innocence, once they laugh at an author unaware of their laughter, barbarism appears.

It is one thing to laugh at "virgin", "kiss", "bitch", every schoolboy does that. But to laugh at the hero's "simplicity" (now Rohmer's film is precisely that: simple in every sense of the word), is to insist on the rejection of difference. Laughter means: I do not understand the other, I do not want the other, I want the same; all I want is a Middle Ages in which nothing is different from today but the costumes.

### Stylistics

Bronchitis, fever, the body suffers: and I try to read. Yet I cannot read *what is badly written*; the page blurs, the book drops on the blanket. Good writing (not necessarily high style) would be a kind of drug, a tranquillizer. In dealing with the written text, we are in a usual state of dyspnoea; style is oxygen. Let us re-examine all writing from this therapeutic angle.

### Co-ownership

If Balzac were writing a novel today, he would not fail to include in it a meeting of co-owners. The scene (a café), the characters, the faces, clothes, dialogue, the union speeches, the imperative of interests and images (the image the speaker wants to give of himself) – all this can only be seen and heard as already affected by literature: I mean pastiche and parody (such as Proust could have brought off). Thus we see here a strange dialectic: the present (for this meeting took place eight days ago) is actually *what has been written*. The absolute unwritten exists only in flashes, the sounds, breaks, incidents, the instants of meaning which suddenly disintegrate. Structure, the "scene", is always described in the past tense.

### Dinner

Invited to a "dinner", I happened to be among several unknown fellow guests. And I very quickly grew bored. I then tried to figure out why and managed to come up with this: it was not the others who bored me; if I could have made myself invisible I would have been interested in their remarks, styles, personalities, in the little conflict of social images, in short, in rules of differences. But I was paralysed by the fear that my own language (which I foresaw as "intellectual") would seem preposterous and (as I thought deep down) crazy. Whereupon I slid down the slope of silence; impossible to catch hold of anything: I grew bored because I look bored. In other words boredom is a kind of hysteria.

## Butter

In the metro, a huge advertisement: a man's hand with well-tended fingernails, carefully filed, clean, just the right length, holding a slice of bread, buttered. All very idyllic, but this is not how it comes out in the bar, where the bartender shoves the butter at you on the cigarette paper that he sells between two sandwiches.

## Fascinated

Another advertisement: the photograph of a Chinese family in the old days. It fascinates me. I would go into the metro just to see it again (aesthete, not a worker!). There they are: straight on, lined up, motionless, frozen, and as though painted; for us the Oriental countenance possesses a kind of greasepaint-vocation: smooth and stained as though a sheet of paper, a piece of silk; even the Chinese soldier which the *Nouvel Observateur* has just put on its cover seems to be drawn with a brush; and the "make-up" is invariably fascinating. And then, it is a kind of archetypical family – the father, the mother, the little boy, the daughter (or the daughter-in-law), the grown-up son (or the son-in-law): and the essence of a thing transfixes me. Why?

## Demystification

For a long time I supposed that an average intellectual like myself could and should join the struggle (even if it was only with regard to himself) against the tidal wave of collective images, the manipulation of affects. This was called *demystification*. I still struggle, now and then, but deep down I really do not believe in it any more. Now that power is everywhere (a great and sinister discovery – even if a naïve one – of people of my generation), in whose name are we to demystify? Denouncing manipulation itself becomes part of a manipulation-system: *recuperated*, such would be the definition of the contemporary *subject*. The only thing left to do would be to make heard a voice *to one side*, an *oblique voice*: a voice *unrelated*.

## Collectivization

In a text I come across by accident, Tretiakov optimistically describes the collectivization of literary work as a leftist process: the creation of *artels* in which the functions of writing are divided and distributed among distinct agents – collectors of raw material, arrangers, literary compositors, checkers, etc. What Tretiakov is describing here is quite simply the enterprise of *writing* in the mass media. The socialist dream and hope are returning as a parody in our technocratic societies.

## *Roberte ce soir*

I attended the private screening of the film by Pierre Klossowski and Pierre Zucca, *Roberte ce soir*. I was delighted. This film plays on many effects, each of which is very powerful (popular, melodramatic, novelistic, parodic, metaphysical, perverse) – starting with the incredible mussel lunch – but the sum total of which risks disconcerting everyone, from the mass public to the avant-garde: the work is untouched by fashion, high or low. Why? Perhaps because each scene has an imperious clarity – the dazzling obviousness of *tableaux vivants* – yet this clarity is put to no definitive purpose: it is not a "clarification", there is no *last word*. One might call it a comedy, but it is a Nietzschean comedy, as enigmatic as Nietzsche's last period, about which Klossowski has written so well.

## Tempo

Surprised by the radio: I tune in by accident to Schumann's *Abend*, which I have heard in unsatisfactory versions so many times, and I immediately realize that this was how it should be performed: "That's it, yes, that's it!" What is it that produces this quality of truth? Simply this, that the piece was played *more slowly* than usual; it then (finally) produced an impression of meditation, of dreamy slowness and of "diction" (Schumann's music is always a *quasi parlando*: it is not an accident that he is *the* musician of the voice). In music, the right tempo (the one which matches my inner demand) produces the enthusiasm of truth, just as the wrong one makes hideous the countenance of a piece one loves. I shall always be furious with Richter for playing much too slowly a certain minuet in a Beethoven sonata and always grateful to Homero Francesch (I think that is who it was) for the Schumannian *Abend*.

## Tempo II

Another surprise: the strike has obliged me to listen regularly to the news broadcasts on Europe I. The pace of the speakers seemed to me dizzying: faster, faster, always faster. This systematic rapidity refers slow delivery, by contrast, to a kind of static conformism; sometimes it is on the verge of the intelligible as if it were better to risk being obscure than being boring, for the great obsession is to not be "boring". The media are so frantically concerned to make their messages "lively" that we are obliged to deduce that ultimately in themselves, such messages seem to them entirely stultifying. In the same way, on the France-Musique radio station they must secretly consider "good music" as very boring to be so clever about breaking up works, programmes, stuffing them with jokes and familiarities (which do not exclude banalities), apparently limiting that piece of simple pleasure which used to be called the concert. In short, the right to slowness is an ecological problem.

### The Look in Your Eyes

Ran across an old friend: "You haven't aged." – "Neither have you." – "Because we still have the same look in our eyes." The look does not age. Those who age do so because they no longer have a look in their eyes.

### Pause

Since I must break off this chronicle for some time, I should like to take advantage of this pause to explain something of what it is for me (not knowing what it is for others): an experiment in writing, the search for a form (it is entirely to the honour of a newspaper like this one to give a writer the possibility of trying a form which interests him and which he wants to work on[1]).

The form sought for is a brief one, or, if you prefer, a *soft* form: neither the solemnity of the maxim nor the harshness of the epigram; something which, at least in tendency, might suggest the Japanese haiku, the Joycean epiphany, the fragment of the *journal intime*: a deliberately minor form, in short – recalling, with Borges, that the minor is not a lessening, but a genre like any other. Doubtless I myself am put out of countenance when my column appears, at seeing my little prose, my little (worked up) syntax, in short my little form, crushed and somehow annihiliated by the voltage of the writing surrounding us. But after all, there is a fight to be waged for softness: from the moment when softness is determined, does it not become a force? It is a moral decision to write small.

Yet how can such a form be *political?* Someone told me (the voice of rumour): "I don't read your chronicles; apparently they're just *Mythologies*, only not so good." No, they are not *Mythologies*; but rather the collecting of certain incidents which week by week star my sensibility as it receives certain stimuli or

[1] This essay was Barthes' column in the *Nouvel Observateur* chronicling fourteen weeks of his life from 18 December 1978 to 1 April 1979 [Editor's note].

discouragements from the world: my personal *scoops* which are not directly those of the present. Then why present them? Why give the tenuous, the futile, the insignificant, why risk the accusation of saying "trifles"? The thought of this effort is as follows.

The event which concerns the press seems a simple enough thing; I mean: it always appears obvious that there is an event, and that this event is an extreme one. But suppose there were also minor events whose tenuity none the less does not fail to involve meaning, to designate what is not well with the world? In short, suppose one were gradually and patiently to be concerned with transforming the grid of intensities? The mass media seem to me to deal with the event the way that painters under the Empire treated a famous battle; but painting has evolved only because it has agreed to change measurements: all of Nicolas de Staël, it is said, has come out of a few square inches of Cézanne. Perhaps, and in the press itself, we must try to resist the glamour of large proportions, so that we restrain the craving of the media (a new historical event) to create the event themselves. I know that my language is small. ("The limits of language", Wittgenstein used to say, "signify the limits of my world.") but this "smallness" may be useful; for with it I feel in my turn, sometimes, the limits of the other world, the world of others, of the "great" world, and it is to express this embarrassment, perhaps this suffering, that I write: ought we not to make heard today the greatest possible number of "little worlds"? To attack the gregarious "great world" by the tireless division of particularities?

As a writing experiment (I am speaking here of a certain practice, not of a value) these columns are for me a way of making the various roles which constitute me speak (without forewarning, of course). In a sense, it is not "I" who is writing them but a sometimes contradictory collection of voices: voices of beings I love and from whom I in passing borrow certain values, ideological voices proceeding from the bourgeois, the petty bourgeois or from the "Brechtian" being whom I can be at one moment or another, archaic, unfashionable voices, voices of stupidity. These voices also have various targets: sometimes one person, sometimes another who is very specific in my time, sometimes a group, sometimes another part of myself. They are like pieces of prose for a novel (voices of a character as yet unnamed), or for a play (a genre in which remarks are exchanged).

This last word allows me to designate what, in my eyes, constitutes their defect in principle (I am not discussing their success or failure in any particular instance, I am not here putting myself on the level of performance). The defect is that with each incident reported, I feel myself obliged (by what power – or what weakness?) to give it (a social, moral, aesthetic) meaning, to produce a final observation. In short these chronicles constantly risk being "moralities", and with that I am not happy, since for a long time now I have thought of writing as that power of language which pluralizes the meaning of things and, in short, suspends it. Here is an enterprise which is possible on the level of the book (literature testifies to that) but which seems to me very difficult within the context of a newspaper – which is why, also, it seems to me to be worthwhile trying. That is the point where I am now.

ROLAND BARTHES

# How to Spend a Week in Paris: 8–14 October 1979

## Monday, 8 October

*Jessye Norman*. Recital of lieder by Brahms, Poulenc, Gluck, Mahler. Pianist: Philipp Moll (Athénée).

ROLAND BARTHES. – This year I renewed my subscription to "Musical Mondays" at the Athénée, a formula which allows me to go to concerts under simple, calm conditions. So I will be hearing Jessye Norman for the first time. With that minor, sympathizing voyeurism one has in the presence of an artist. Voice and piano, everything I like is there. Of course, I always sit on the left side of the house to watch the pianist's hands – I play half an hour every day myself.

*The Normandy – The Île de France*. Auction of objects from these ocean liners (Drouot Rive Gauche, 8, 9, 10 and 11 October, at 10, 2.15 and 8.30 p.m.).

ROLAND BARTHES. – I discovered the skyscrapers of Manhattan from the decks of the "Île de France" and I must have eaten from those dishes. The auctioning of objects from the liner is even more sinister than the disappearance of the liner itself; it is like dismembering the dead.

*Direct from China*. China Day on Antenne 2. Notably the one o'clock news and "A Question of Time" at 8.35 p.m.

ROLAND BARTHES. – I recommend paying as little attention as possible to the

Nicole Boulanger, an editor with the *Nouvel Observateur*, met Roland Barthes, and she asked him to give his reactions to the events in a typical Parisian cultural week. Barthes agreed to do this, but added these caveats: that he did not have much use for television "except in the country, sometimes", that he was somewhat remote from the cinema ("I have a taste for the classics, pre-chosen"), and that he had decided to stay out of arguments and public life since "what I need for my evenings is my friends – my friends more than culture" – ed.

commentators; but look as closely as possible at the clothes and the faces. You can catch certain signs of development, focus on concrete details (the studio sets, the street . . .), observe whom you might find beautiful or feel the unexpected desire to seduce by our Western ways. To be dazzled by what is not ourselves.

## Tuesday, 9 October

*Merce Cunningham Dance Company* (Théâtre de la Ville, 8–14 October).
ROLAND BARTHES. – There remains with me from one of Cunningham's ballet evenings at the Opera a memory of great gentleness. It is rare to feel such a sensation with dance, which is the show of muscle, hysteria or hieratism. Delicacy then, but what affords me my memory also governs the arbitrariness of remembering.

*Les Frères Jacques.* ". . . Farewell to the Fans . . ." (Centre culturel de Sucy-en-Brie).
ROLAND BARTHES. – They stand at the beginning of a change in song. Now it is part of folklore history.

*Bob Wilson.* Première of *Edison*, performance-opera created at the Théâtre National de Paris, Villeurbanne (8–13 October, before its arrival in Paris on the 24th).
ROLAND BARTHES. – I have never been to one of Bob Wilson's performances, but I have a sincere, authentic, particular desire to see one. What I have been told about the new relations he creates between text and image attracts me. Like Robert Mapplethorpe's photograph of him: I am intrigued by his eyes, his face. And after all, that may be enough to make me go to the performance.

*César Franck. Les Béatitudes* with Hanna Schaer, Nadine Denize, Michel Piquemal, Philippe Dogan . . . (The Church of Saint-Germain-des-Prés, 8.30 p.m.).
ROLAND BARTHES. – Some things by this composer, like his "Symphony", are boring, others are quite lovely, like his "Sonata for violin and piano". So . . . as an adolescent I was forced to listen to the music of the Franck school, now in disfavour, but in need of re-evaluation.

*Point 2000.* To acquaint yourself with the great problems of modern science. (First in a series of six shows. Antenne 2, 5.20 p.m.).

## Wednesday, 10 October

*Opera Film Week. Aïda* and *Il Trovatore*, films by Pierre Jourdan, *Les Noces de Figaro* by Jean-Pierre Ponnelle (Tourcoing, Cinema ABC).
ROLAND BARTHES. – I have never seen a filmed opera I liked. I did not like

Bergman's *Magic Flute* and I am afraid that I will not like Losey's *Don Giovanni* (opening 14 November). The dark theatre blots out the filmgoer's body, whereas the opera, by nature, calls for immediate participation. During a stage performance, I am extremely aware of perfumes and there is the ostentation of the audience, the intermissions, the ceremony, the stage. . . .

## Thursday, 11 October

*Antique Cars.* A motorcade of Benz, Panhard, Rolls Royce, Talbot, and others (Hippodrome at Longchamp, 2.30 p.m.).

ROLAND BARTHES. – A Panhard! My grandmother had one and I will not be able to attend this retrospective with the ease of a simple spectator. The same thing happens with certain old films. Recently I went back to see *La Nuit du Carrefour* by Jean Renoir (1932) at the Cinémathèque. The young people in the audience burst out laughing at the sight of the clothes and hair-styles, laughter which hurt me since it fed on the natural surroundings of my adolescence. What bothers me is the flip way in which our civilization presents as amusing or quaint the sight of what will never be again.

## Friday, 12 October

*Théâtre de Marionnettes.* Twelve troops from around the world (Festival de Lille).

ROLAND BARTHES. – I am fascinated by the Bunraku, the otherness of peoples interests me and only because these puppets come from elsewhere does my curiosity remain aroused.

*The Opening of the Picasso Bequest.* A collection of eight hundred pieces, many of which have never been seen before.

ROLAND BARTHES. – I do not like openings, or private screenings, or theatre premières. I need the anonymity of the commercial theatre, like that of an unknown group of museum-goers. Moreover, Picasso's painting does not respond to my ethic. My deepest identification is with Pollock (at the Musée de la Ville de Paris) for his sumptuousness, his vigorous plenitude.

*Cambodia.* A report by Jérôme Kanapa for *Le Nouveau Vendredi* (France Radio 3, 8.30 p.m.).

ROLAND BARTHES. – I hope they show us more faces than temples. You can read a lot about what really happens in a country on the faces of its people.

## Saturday, 13 October

*Ready-to-Wear Show* (13–17 October, Parc des Expositions, Porte de Versailles).

ROLAND BARTHES. – Now this does concern me: as long as it goes on, the Café de Flore is jam-packed – there is not a single seat to be found. I am in the habit of having my coffee and reading my paper there, so. . . .

*The Moon.* A specialist in spatial mechanics gives an account of "lunar" research (Palais de la Découverte, 3.00 p.m.).

ROLAND BARTHES. – Do I ever need to hear this lecture! But my reflex is always to retreat from whatever everyone unanimously calls major. Perhaps out of anxiety or fear. It is very hard for me to mobilize myself about something that I have not discovered on my own. Bourgeois individualism? Ten years later, the event remains mythical all the same.

*The States-General of Philosophy.* To protest against the dismissal of seven professors of philosophy (Nantes).

ROLAND BARTHES. – A country which would limit, repress philosophy would become more vulnerable to anti-democratic enterprises.

*Paintings.* Mentally handicapped children from the studio at Bois-Mesmuls present their work. (Galerie Yves Brun, through 20 October).

ROLAND BARTHES. – Psychosis in the service of art.


## Sunday, 14 October

*The Hopi in Paris.* Ritual songs and dances (Chopin-Pleyel, 3.00 p.m.).

ROLAND BARTHES. – Can we Westerners really consume a fragment of civilization totally isolated from its context? The same problem with regard to radio which inundates us with traditional music.

*Le Palace.* Sister Sledge, disco-soul party (midnight).

ROLAND BARTHES. – Just as crowds frighten me, I feel excluded from the people who go to Le Palace, and I only go very late at night. I like it a little empty. I am not bothered by a deserted theatre, it gives me a feeling analogous to what you feel in a springtime city when you go there in summer. I found this out a long time ago in Marrakesh.

MICHEL DE CERTEAU

# Practices of Space

> Metaphor is the *transport* to one thing of
> a name which designates another.
> (Aristotle, *Poetics*)

## The Blind City

To *see* Manhattan from the 107th floor of the World Trade Center. Below the wind-stirred haze, the urban island, a sea upon the sea rises on the crested swell of Wall Street, falls into the trough of Greenwich Village, flows into the renewed crests of midtown and the calm of Central Park, before breaking into distant whitecaps up beyond Harlem. For a moment, the eye arrests the turbulence of this sea-swell of verticals; the vast mass freezes under our gaze. It is transformed into a texturology in which the extremes of defiance and poverty, the contrasts between races and styles, between yesterday's buildings already relegated to the past (New York, this anti-Rome, has never learned to age) and the new outcroppings that erect barriers to block space – all are conjoined. Paroxystic sites with monumental reliefs. The spectator can even read the fading urban universe. Inscribed upon it are the architectural figures of the *coincidatio oppositorum* sketched long ago in mystical miniatures and textures. On this concrete, steel and glass stage, bounded by the cold water of two oceans (the Atlantic and the American) the tallest letters in the world create this gigantesque rhetoric of excess in expenditure and production.[1]

To what erotics of knowledge can the ecstasy of reading such a cosmos be connected? Delighting in it as violently as I do, I speculate as to the origin of the pleasure of seeing such a world wrought by hubris "as a whole", the pleasure of looking down upon, of totalizing this vastest of human texts.

To be lifted to the summit of the World Trade Center is to be carried away by the city's hold. One's body is no longer criss-crossed by the streets that bind

---

[1] Consult "New York City" by Alain Médam, in *Les Temps modernes*, August–September 1976, pp. 15–33; and, by the same author, *New York Terminal* (Paris: Galilée, 1977).

and re-bind it following some law of their own; it is not possessed – either as user or used – by the sounds of all its many contrasts or by the frantic New York traffic. The person who ascends to that height leaves behind the mass that takes and incorporates into itself any sense of being either an author or spectator. Above these waters Icarus can ignore the tricks of Daedalus in his shifting and endless labyrinths. His altitude transforms him into a voyeur. It places him at a distance. It changes an enchanting world into a text. It allows him to read it; to become a solar Eye, a god's regard. The exaltation of a scopic or a gnostic drive. Just to be this seeing point creates the fiction of knowledge. Must one then redescend into the sombre space through which crowds of people move about, crowds that, visible from above, cannot see there below? The fall of Icarus. On the 107th floor, a poster poses like some sphinx, a riddle to the stroller who has been in an instant changed into a seer: "It's hard to be down when you're up" (see figure 1).

Figure 1

The desire to see the city preceded the means of fulfilling the desire. Medieval and Renaissance painting showed the city seen in perspective by an eye that did not yet exist.[2] They both invented flying over the city and the type of representation that made it possible. The panorama transformed the spectator into a celestial eye. It created gods. Since technical processes created an "omnivisual power", things are different.[3] The fiction invented by the painters of the past slowly became fact. The same scopic drive haunts the architectural (and no longer pictorial) productions that give materiality to Utopia today. The 1350-foot tower, Manhattan's prow, continues the construction of a fiction that creates its readers, that transforms the city's complexity into readability and that freezes its opaque mobility into a crystal-clear text. Can the vast texturology beneath our gaze be anything but a representation? An optical artefact. The analogue to the facsimile which, through a kind of distancing, produces the space planner, the city planner or the map-maker. The city-panorama is a "theoretical" (i.e. visual) simulacrum: in short, a picture, of which the preconditions for feasibility are forgetfulness and a misunderstanding of processes. The seeing god created by this fiction, who, like Schreber's, "knows only corpses",[4] must remove himself from the obscure interlacings of everyday behaviour and make himself a stranger to it.

On the contrary, it is below – "down" – on the threshold where visibility ends that the city's common practitioners dwell. The raw material of this experiment are the walkers, *Wandersmänner*, whose bodies follow the cursives and strokes of an urban "text" they write without reading. These practitioners employ spaces that are not self-aware; their knowledge of them is as blind as that of one body for another, beloved, body (figure 2). The paths that interconnect in this network, strange poems of which each body is an element down by and among many others, elude being read. Everything happens as though some blindness were the hallmark of the processes by which the inhabited city is organized.[5] The networks of these forward-moving, intercrossed writings form a multiple history, are without creator or spectator, made up of fragments of trajectories and alterations of spaces: with regard to representations, it remains daily, indefinitely, something other (figure 3).

Eluding the imaginary totalizations of the eye, there is a strangeness in the commonplace that creates no surface, or whose surface is only an advanced limit, an edge cut out of the visible. In this totality, I should like to indicate the processes that are foreign to the "geometric" or "geographic" space of visual,

---

[2] Cf. H. Lavedan, *Les Représentations des villes dans l'art du Moyen-Age* (Paris: Van Oest, 1942); R. Wittkower, *Architecturals: Principles in the Age of Humanism* (London: Tiranti, 1962); L. Marin, *Utopiques: jeux d'espaces* (Paris: Minuit, 1973).

[3] M. Foucault, "L'oeil du pouvoir", in J. Bentham, *Le Panoptique [Panopticon]* (1791) (Belfond, 1977) p. 16.

[4] D. P. Schreber, *Mémoires d'un nécropathe*, trans. (Paris: Seuil, 1975) pp. 41, 60, etc.

[5] In his *Regulae*, Descartes made the blind man the guarantor of the knowledge of things and places against the illusions and deceptions of sight.

Figure 2

Figure 3

panoptic or theoretical constructions (figure 4). Such spatial practices refer to a specific form of *operations* (ways of doing); they reflect "another spatiality"[6] (an "anthropological", *poïétik* and mystical spatial experiment); they send us to an opaque, blind domain of the inhabited city, or to a *transhuman city*, one that insinuates itself into the clear text of the planned, readable city.

## From Concept to Practices

The World Trade Center is the most monumental figure of a Western urbanism. The atopia-Utopia of optical science has long tried to surmount and articulate the contradictions created by the urban conglomeration. It is a question of working towards an increase in the human collection or accumulation. A perspective view or a prospective view, the dual projection of an opaque past and an unclear future on to an accommodating surface, it has (since the sixteenth century?) begun the transformation of the *urban reality* into the concept of *city*, and it has begun – long before the concept itself can become history – to make it part of an *urbanistic* ratio. The alliance of city and concept never makes them one; rather, it employs their progressive symbiosis: city planning is both to *give thought to the plurality* of the real and to *make effective* that notion of the plural – it is to know and to be able to articulate.

Figure 4

[6] M. Merleau-Ponty, *Phénoménologie de la perception* (Paris: Gallimard, 1976) pp. 332–3.

The "city" established by Utopian and urbanistic discourse[7] is defined by the possibility of a threefold operation: the creation of a *clean space* (rational organization should eliminate all physical, mental and political pollution); the substitution of a non-time or a synchronic system for the indiscernible, stubborn resistance of tradition (univocal strategies, made possible by the exhaustion of all data, should replace the tactics that cleverly play upon "opportunities", catch-occurrences, and the opacities of history); and finally the creation of a *universal and impersonal subject* (this is the city itself: as with its political model, the Hobbesian state, it is gradually possible to endow it with all the functions and predicates previously disseminated and allocated to many real subjects, groups, associations and individuals). Thus, the city enables us to conceive and construct a space on the basis of a finite number of stable and isolatable elements, each articulated to the other.

In this site organized by "speculative" and classifying operations,[8] management combines with elimination: on the one hand we have the differentiation and redistribution of the parts and function of the city through inversions, movements, accumulations, etc., and on the other hand we have the rejection of whatever is not treatable, and that thus constitutes the "garbage" of a functionalist administration (abnormality, deviance, sickness, death, etc.). Progress, of course, allows for the reintroduction of an increasing proportion of these wastes into the management network and the transformation of those very flaws (in health, security, etc.) into means for strengthening the system of order. In fact, however, it constantly produces effects that run counter to what it aims for: the profit system creates a *loss* which, with all the multifarious forms of poverty outside and waste inside, is constantly inverting production into "expenditure". Furthermore, rationalizing the city involves *mythifying* it through strategic modes of discourse. Lastly, by favouring progress (time), functionalist organization allows the condition of its feasibility – space itself – to be overlooked, and space then becomes the unanticipated factor in a scientific and political technology.[9] That is how the city concept functions, a site of transformations and appropriations, the object of interventions, but also a subject continually being enriched with new attributes: simultaneously the plant and the hero of modernity.

Whatever the past avatars of this concept, it must be noted that today, while in *discourse*, the city acts as a totalizing and almost mythic gauge of socio-economic and political strategies, *urban life* allows what has been

---

[7] Cf P. Choay, "Figures d'un discours inconnu", in *Critique*, April 1978, pp. 293–317.

[8] We cannot connect urbanistic techniques, which classify things spatially, with the tradition of the "art of memory" (cf. F. A. Yates, *L'Art de la mémoire* (Paris: Gallimard, 1975). The capacity to build a spatial organization of knowledge develops its procedures on the basis of that "art"; it determines Utopias; it was almost realized in Bentham's *Panopticon*. It is a stable form, despite the diversity of its content (past, future and present) and its plans (to conceive or to create) *vis-à-vis* successive modes of thought.

[9] Foucault, "L'oeil du pouvoir", p. 13.

excluded from it by the urbanistic plan to increase even further. The language of power is "urbanized", but the city is subjected to contradictory movements that offset each other and interact outside the purview of the panoptic power. The city becomes the dominant theme of political epic but it is no longer a theatre for programmed, controlled operations. Beneath the discourses ideologizing it, there is a proliferation of tricks and fusions of power that are devoid of legible identity, that lack any perceptible access and that are without rational clarity – impossible to manage.

The city-concept is deteriorating. Does that mean that the sickness of the mind that created it and its professionals is also the sickness of the urban population? Perhaps the cities are deteriorating together with the procedures that set them up. However, we must be wary of our analyses. Ministers of knowledge have always assumed that the changes that shake their ideologies and their positions are universe-threatening. They transform the evil of their theories into theories of evil. Transforming their aberrations into "catas-trophes" or trying to lock the people into the "panic" of their discourse, must they still be right?

Rather than staying within a discourse that maintains its privileged position by inverting its content (catastrophe, not progress), there is another way: analysing the microbial processes – both singular and plural – an urbanistic system should manage or eliminate and survive its decline; following the pullulation of those practices that, far from being controlled or eliminated by the panoptic administration, are abetted in their proliferating illegitimacy, developed and inserted into the networks of surveillance and combined according to strategies that, albeit unreadable, are stable to the extent that they constitute everyday rules and surreptitious creativities that serve only to conceal the frantic existing models and discourses of the observing organization. That path could be regarded as a continuation of – but also as the inverse of – Michel Foucault's analysis of power structures. Instead of focusing his analysis on localizable, dominant, repressive, legal centres, he turned it to bear on technical machinery and procedures, those "minor instrumentalities" that, through a mere organization of "details", can transform diverseness of humanity into a "disciplined" society, and manage, differentiate, classify and fit into a hierarchy every deviancy that can affect training, health, justice, the army or labour.[10] "The often tiny ploys of discipline", the "minor but flawless" machinery that has colonized and made uniform the institutions of the state, derive their effectiveness from a relationship between *procedures* and the *space* they redistribute to create an "operator". They set up an "analytic arrangement of space". From the standpoint of playing at (with) discipline, however, what spatial practices correspond to these disciplined space-creating apparatuses? In light of the current contradiction between the collective management mode and the individual mode of reappropriation, such a question is no less pressing – if we posit a society to be defined not only by its networks of technical

[10] M. Foucault, *Surveiller et punir* (Paris: Gallimard, 1975).

surveillance, and if we further recognize that in fact spatial usage creates the determining conditions of social life. I should like to review some of the procedures – many-sided, resilient, cunning and stubborn – that evade discipline, without thereby being outside its sphere, and that can lead to a theory of daily practices, to a theory of experienced *space* and of the disturbing familiarity of the *city*.

## Pedestrian Utterings

History begins at ground level, with footsteps. They are the number, but a number that does not form a series. They cannot be counted because each unit is qualitative in nature: a style of tactile apprehension and kinesic appropriation. They are replete with innumerable anomalies. The motions of walking are spatial creations. They link sites one to the other. Pedestrian motor functions thus create one of those "true systems whose existence actually makes the city", but which "have no physical receivability".[11] They cannot be localized: they spatialize. They are no more inscribed in a content than are the characters the Chinese sketch out on their hand with one finger.

Of course, the walking process can be marked out on urban maps in such a way as to translate its traces (*here* heavy, *there* very light) and its trajectories (*this* way, not *that*). However, these curves, ample or meagre, refer, like words, only to the lack of what has gone by. Traces of a journey lose what existed: *the act of going by* itself. The action of going, of wandering, or of "window shopping" – in other words, the activity of passers-by – is transposed into points that create a totalizing and reversible line on the map. It therefore allows for the apprehension of a mere relic set in the non-time of a projective surface. It is visible, but its effect is to make the operation that made it possible invisible. These fixations make up the procedures of forgetting. The hint is substituted for practice. It displays property (voracious) of the geographic system's ability to metamorphose actions into legibility, but it thereby causes one way of existing to be overlooked.

A comparison with the act of speaking enables us to go further[12] and not be restricted only to criticism of graphic representations as if we were aiming from the limits of legibility at some inaccessible Beyond. The act of walking is to the urban system what the act of speaking, the *Speech Act*, is to language or to spoken utterance.[13] On the most elementary level it has in effect a threefold

[11] C. Alexander, "La Cité semitreillis, mais non arbre", in *Architecture, Mouvement, Continuité* (1967).

[12] Cf. R. Barthes' remarks in *Architecture d'aujourd'hui*, no. 153, December 1970–January 1971, pp. 11–13 ("We speak our city . . . simply by living in it, by travelling through it, by looking at it"), and C. Soucy's comments in *L'Image du centre dans quatre romans contemporains* (Paris: CSU, 1971) pp. 6–15.

[13] Cf. the many studies on the subject since J. Searle's "What is a Speech Act?", in Max Black (ed.), *Philosophy in America* (London: Allen & Unwin, 1965; Ithaca, NY: Cornell University Press, 1965) pp. 221–39.

"uttering" function: it is a process of *appropriation* of the topographic system by the pedestrian (just as the speaker appropriates and assumes language); it is a spatial *realization* of the site (just as the act of speaking is a sonic realization of language): lastly, it implies relationships among distinct positions, i.e. pragmatic "*contracts*" in the form of movements (just as verbal utterance is "allocution", "places *the others*" before the speaker, and sets up contracts between fellow speakers[14]). A first definition of walking thus seems to be a space of uttering.

We can extend this problem to the relationships between the act of writing and writing, if we like, and even transpose it to relationships of "touch" (the brush and its gestures) to the finished picture (forms, colours, etc.). First isolated in the field of verbal communication, uttering is only one of its applications, and its linguistic modality is only the first indication of a far more general distinction between the forms employed in a system and the ways in which the system may be employed, i.e. between two "different worlds", because the "same things" are there viewed according to opposed formalities.

Considered from this angle, the pedestrian's uttering displays three characteristics that immediately distinguish it from the spatial system: the present, the discontinuous and the "phatic". First, it is true that a spatial order sets up a body of possibilities (e.g. by a place) and interdictions (e.g. by a wall); the walker then *actualizes* some of them. He thereby makes them be as well as appear. However, he also displaces them and invents others (see box 1), since the crossings, wanderings and improvisations of walking favour, alter or abandon spatial elements. Thus Charlie Chaplin multiplied the possibilities of his japes: out of one thing he made other things, and he went beyond the limits that the purposes and functions of the object impose upon its user. In the same way, the walker transforms every spatial signifier into something else. And while, on the one hand, he makes only a few of the possibilities set out by the established order effective (he goes only here – not there), on the other hand, he increases the number of possibilities (e.g. by making up shortcuts or detours) and the number of interdictions (e.g. by avoiding routes regarded as licit or obligatory). In short, he selects: "The user of the city takes up fragments of utterance in order in secret to actualize them."[15] Thus he creates *discontinuity*, either by choosing among the signifiers of the spatial language or by altering them through the use he makes of them. He dooms certain sites to inertia or to decay, and from others he forms "rare" ("fortuitous") or illegal spatial "shapes". However, this is already inherent in a rhetoric of walking.

Within the framework of uttering, the walker, in relation to his position, creates a near and a far, a *here* and a *there*. In verbal communication, the adverbs *here* and *there* are actually the indicators of the locutory fact[16] – a coincidence

---

[14] É. Benveniste, *Problèmes de linguistique générale*, vol. 2 (Paris: Gallimard, 1974) pp. 79–88.

[15] R. Barthes, quoted in C. Soucy, *L'Image du centre*, p. 10.

[16] "*Here* and *now* demarcate the spatial and temporal instance, which is coextensive and contemporary with the present source of a discourse containing *I*" (É. Benveniste, *Problèmes de linguistique générale*, vol. 1 (Paris: Gallimard, 1966) p. 253.

*Box 1*

## Passers-By

Like words, places are articulated by a thousand usages. They are thus transformed into "variations" – not verbal or musical, but spatial – of a question that is the mute *motif* of the interweavings of places and gestures: *where to live?* These dances of bodies haunted by the desire to live somewhere tell interminable stories of the Utopia we construct in the sites through which we pass. They form a rhetoric of space. They are "steps" (dance figures), glances (composing mobile geographies), intervals (practices of distinction) (figure 5), criss-crossings of solitary itineraries, insular embraces (figure 6). These gesturations are our everyday legends. They open up unpredictable spaces in an order of sites. They also play within the labyrinth of city signs (street names, advertising slogans, historic landmarks, commercial, political or academic identities), in the same way in which the voice wanders, delinquent, stubborn, through the networks of the linguistic system, tracing pathways foreign to the meaning of the sentences. Proliferant, these practices seem to repeat the mute experiment of the child, who invents a foreignness wherever he is in order to create for himself his own space – ecstasies in the window of the closed taxi (figure 7); dancing suspended on the sidewalk that is the shoreline of some story (figure 8); liminal astonishments (figure 9). Ceaselessly we have always to pass by in order to be able to inhabit.

*Michel de Certeau*

that reinforces the parallelism between linguistic uttering and the pedestrian uttering – and we must add that another function of this process of location (*here/there*) necessarily entailed by walking and indicative of an actual appropriation of space by an "I" is to set up *another* relative to that "I", and thereby establish a conjunctive and disjunctive articulation of places. Above all, I highlight the *"phatic"* aspect – if by that we understand, as Malinowski and Jakobson have noted, the function of terms that establish, maintain or interrupt contact: terms like "hello", "well, well", etc.[17] Walking, which now pursues and now invites pursuit, creates a mobile organicity of the environment, a succession of phatic *topoi*. And although the phatic function – the effort to set up communication – can characterize the language of talking birds as it does "the first verbal function acquired by children", it is not surprising that, anterior to or parallel with informative declamation, it also skips along, crawls

---

[17] R. Jakobson, *Essais de linguistique générale* (Paris: Seuil, 1970) p. 217.

Figure 5

on all fours, dances and strolls, heavily or lightly, like a series of "hellos" in an echoing labyrinth.

We can analyse the modalities of the pedestrian's uttering hereby freed from the mapped route, i.e. the types of relationship it entertains with routes (or "utterances"), by assigning to them a value of truth ("alethic" modalities of the necessary, the impossible, the possible or the contingent), a value of knowledge ("epistemic" modalities of the certain, the excluded, the plausible or the arguable), or finally, a value regarding obligation ("deontic" modalities of the obligatory, the forbidden, the permissible or the optional).[18] Walking affirms, suspects, guesses, transgresses, respects, etc., the trajectories it "speaks". All modalities play a part in it, changing from step to step and redistributed in proportions, successions, intensities that vary with the moment, the route, the stroller. The indefinable diversity of these operations of utterance. They cannot be reduced to any graphic tracing.

## Perambulatory Rhetorics

The paths taken by strollers consist of a series of turnings and returnings that can be likened to "turns of phrase" or "stylistic devices". A perambulatory rhetoric does exist. The art of "turning" a phrase has its counterpart in the art

[18] On modalities, see H. Parret, *La Pragmatique des modalités* (Urbino, 1975), or A. R. White, *Modal Thinking* (Ithaca, NY: Cornell University Press, 1975).

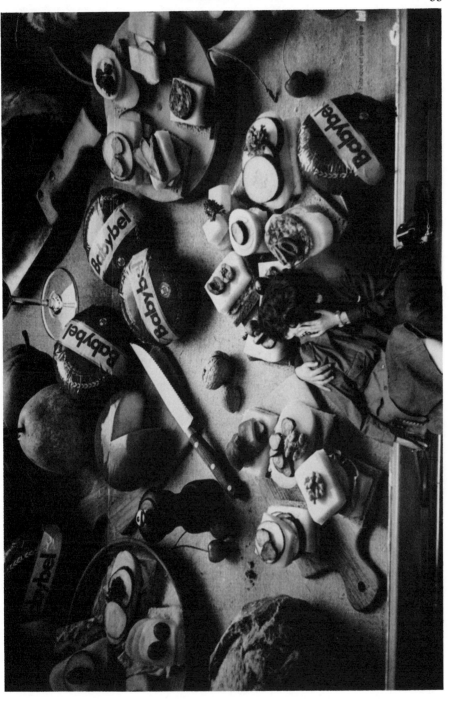

Figure 6

Figure 7

Figure 8

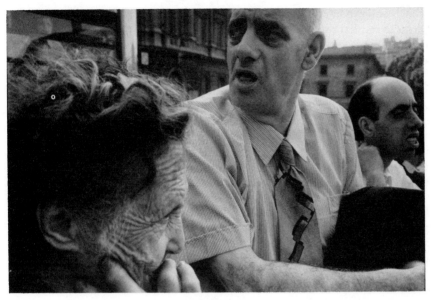

Figure 9

of "turning" course. As with everyday language,[19] this art entails and combines both *styles* and *usages*. Style specifies a "linguistic structure that can manifest on the symbolic level ... one man's basic way of existing in the world":[20] it connotes a singular. Usage defines the social phenomenon by which a system of communication is actually manifested: it refers to a norm. Both are aimed at a "way of doing" (speaking, walking, etc.), but one as a singular treatment of the symbolic and the other as an element of a code. They intersect to form a style of usage, a way of being and a way of doing.[21]

In introducing the notion of an "inhabitant rhetoric" – a fertile path indicated by A. Médam[22] and systematized by S. Ostrovesky[23] and J.-F. Augoyard[24] – it was posited that the "tropes" catalogued in rhetoric furnished

[19] See the analyses of P. Lemaire, *Les Signes sauvages: Philosophie du langage ordinaire* (Paris: duplicated thesis, 1972) pp. 11–13.

[20] A. J. Greimas, "Linguistique statistique et linguistique structurale", in *Le Français moderne*, October 1962, p. 245.

[21] In a related field – rhetoric and the poetic in the sign language of mutes – see E. S. Klima and U. Bellugi, "Poetry and Song in a Language without Sound" (San Diego, California, 1975), and E. S. Klima, "The Linguistic Symbol With and Without Sound", in J. Kavanagh and J. E. Cummings (eds), *The Role of Speech in Language* (Cambridge, Mass: MIT Press, 1975).

[22] A. Médam, *Conscience de la ville* (Paris: Anthropos, 1977).

[23] UER de sociologie, Aix-en-Provence, France.

[24] J.-F. Augoyard, *Le Pas. Approche de la vie quotidienne dans un habitat collectif à travers la pratique des cheminements* (Grenoble: duplicated thesis, 1976) pp. 163–255: "La rhétorique habitante".

models and hypotheses for the analysis of the methods for appropriating sites. It seems to me that two postulates condition the validity of that application: spatial practices also correspond to *manipulations* of the fundamental elements of a constructed order; like rhetorical tropes, they are *divergent* from a kind of "literal" meaning defined by the urban system. Verbal figures and "perambulant" figures may be homologous (the latter already stylized in dance steps), for both are "treatments" or operations that affect isolable units,[25] and "ambiguous arrangements" that divert and move meaning towards the equivocal,[26] as when a moving image blurs and multiplies the photographed object. Both these modes make for analogy. I would add that the geometric space of city-planners and architects appears to have the validity of the "literal meaning" *constructed* by grammarians and linguists in order to establish a normal and normative level to which the deviations of the "figured" can be referred. In fact, this "literal" (without figures) is not to be found in ordinary usage, whether verbal or pedestrian: it is only the fiction produced by a usage that is also special – the metalinguistic usage of science that makes itself unique through that very distinction.[27]

The perambulatory gesture plays with spatial organizations, however panoptic: it is not foreign to them (it does not eschew them), nor does it conform to them (it does not take its identity from them). It creates of them shadow and ambiguity. It insinuates into them its multifarious references and citations (social models, cultural usage, personal coefficients). It is in itself the effect of the successive encounters and occasions that are constantly altering it into the advertisement for the other, the agent of whatever may surprise, cross or seduce its route. These different aspects establish a rhetoric; they even define it.

In analysing by means of the narratives of spatial practices this "modest art of everyday expression",[28] J.-F. Augoyard singled out two basic stylistic figures: synecdoche and asyndeton. I believe that this predominance, based on two complementary poles, establishes a formalism for such practices. Synecdoche is "employing the word in a sense that is part of another sense of the same word";[29] in essence, it is naming a part for the whole in which it is included: hence, "head" for "man" in the expression "I know not the fate of so dear a head"; and thus, in the narrative of a route the stone colonnade or the knoll stands for a park. Asyndeton is the elimination of linking words, conjunctions,

---

[25] In his analysis of culinary practices, P. Bourdieu considers not the ingredients but their treatments to be decisive ("Le sens pratique", in *Actes de la recherche*, February 1976, p. 77).

[26] J. Sumpf, *Introduction à la stylistique du français* (Paris: Larousse, 1971) p. 87.

[27] On the "theory of the literal" see J. Derrida, *Marges* (Paris: Minuit, 1972) pp. 247–324: "La mythologie blanche".

[28] Augoyard, *Le pas*, p. 256.

[29] T. Todorov, "Synecdoques", in *Communications*, no. 16, 1970, p. 30. Cf. also P. Fontanier, *Les figures du discours* (Paris: Flammarion, 1968) pp. 87–97, and J. Dubois et al., *Rhétorique générale* (1970) pp. 102–12.

adverbs, within a sentence or between sentences; it jumps over linkages and it omits whole parts (from this point of view, any promenade jumps or skips like a child playing hopscotch).

These two perambulatory figures are mutually reflective. One enlarges one element of space in order to make it play the role of a "more" (of a totality) and substitute itself for that (the motorbike or the furniture for sale in a shop window stands for an entire street or neighbourhood); the other, through elision, creates a "less" and makes gaps in the spatial continuum, retaining only selections or relics from it. Wholes are replaced by fragments (less in place of more); the other dissolves them by eliminating the conjunctive and consecutive (nothing in place of something). One concentrates: it amplifies detail and miniaturizes the whole. The other cuts: it dismantles continuity and weakens its verisimilitude. Thus handled and shaped by practices, space forms itself into enlarged anomalies and separate islets.[30] Through such swellings, diminutions and fragmentations – the tasks of rhetoric – a spatial sentencing is created, a sentence-making of an anthological (composed of juxtaposed quotations) and an elliptical (made up of gaps, slips and allusions) kind. The perambulatory figures substitute journeys with the structure of a myth for the technological system of a coherent, totalizing space, a "linked" and simultaneous space, at least if by "myth" we understand a discourse regarding the site/non-site (or origin) of concrete existence, a narrative cooked up out of elements drawn from shared sites, an allusive, fragmented tale whose gaps fall into line with the social practices it symbolizes.

Figures are the gestures of this stylistic metamorphosis of space; or rather, as Rilke put it, "gesture trees" in motion. They even affect the rigid and preplanned territories of the special educational institutions in which mentally ill children dance and act out their "spatial histories" at play.[31] These gesture trees are in motion everywhere. Whole forests of them stroll in the streets. They alter the scene, but image cannot fix them in one place. If despite everything we must have an illustration, it would be in transit images, in the yellow-green and electric-blue calligraphy that silently screams as it striates the city's undergound – "embroideries" of letters and numbers, the perfect gestures of spray-painted acts of violence, handwritten Sivas, dancing graphics whose fleeting apparitions are accompanied by the roaring of subway trains: New York's graffiti (figure 10). Indeed, while it is true that the forests of gesture can have meaning, their progress cannot be fixed by a picture, nor can the meaning of their movements be confined within a text. Their rhetorical transhumance carries away and off the analytical and coherent, literal, meanings of urbanism; it is "semantic wandering"[32] produced by the masses that make the city in some of its

---

[30] On this space organized by practices into "islets", see P. Bourdieu, *Esquisse d'une théorie de la pratique* (Geneva: Droz, 1972) pp. 215 ff., and his "Le sens pratique", pp. 51–2.

[31] Cf. Anne Baldassari and Michel Joubert, *Pratiques relationnelles des enfants à l'espace et institution* (CRECELE, CORDES, 1976), and by the same authors, "Ce qui se trame", in *Paralleles*, no. 1, June 1976.

[32] Derrida, *Marges*, p. 287, concerning metaphor.

Figure 10

neighbourhoods disappear, that in others exaggerate it or infect it with a cancer; that twist it, break it up and divert it from its order, albeit immobile.

## The Mythics of the Proper

The figures for these movements (synecdoches, ellipses, etc.) characterize both "symbolics of the unconscious" and "certain procedures typical of the subjectivity manifested in discourse".[33] The likeness created between "discourse"[34] and "dream"[35] by the use of the same "stylistic procedures" thus includes pedestrian activities. The "old catalogue of tropes" that, from Freud to Benveniste, furnished a suitable inventory for the rhetoric of the first two levels of expression is equally valid for the third. If parallelism exists it is not only because utterance dominates in all three regions, but also because its discursive progress (verbalized, dreamed or paced off) is established as a relationship between the *site* from which it issues (an origin) and the *non-site* it creates (a way of *passage*).

From this point of view, having linked linguistic formations with the

[33] Benveniste, *Problèmes de linguistique générale*, vol. 1, pp. 86–7.
[34] For Benveniste, "discourse" "is language, as assumed by the speaking man and in a state of intersubjectivity" (ibid., p. 266).
[35] Cf., for example, S. Freud, *La Science des rêves* (PUF, 1973) pp. 240–300, on condensation and transfer, which are "procedures of figuration" belonging to the "dreamwork".

perambulatory processes, they can be approached from the standpoint of oneiric figurations, or at least one can glimpse on that other bank what, in spatial practice, is indissociable from the site dreamed. *To walk is to lack a site.* It is the indeterminate process of being both absent and in search of the proper, of one's own. Undoubtedly the errancy that multiplies and assembles the city makes of it a vast social experience in site deprivation – an experience, true, that is weakened by innumerable and minuscule deportations (displacements, walks); that is fleshed out by the relationships and intersections of such exoduses, which create interweavings (the solidarity of the urban fabric) and are set within the framework of what must ultimately have been the *site* (the City). However, the identity created by this site is all the more *figured* since, despite the inequality in titles and profits, there is here only a swarming mass of passers-by, a network of dwellings taken over by traffic, a strolling through the semblances of the real, a universe of places haunted by a non-site or by dreamed sites.

An indication of the relationship between the practices of space and this lack is provided by the ways in which they play with and upon "proper" names. The relationships between the "sense" of a stroll and the sense of words set up two kinds of apparently contrary movement: one exterior (to walk is to go outdoors) and the other interior (mobility within the stability of the signifier). Walking, in effect, is subject to semantic tropisms; it is drawn to or repelled by things named in the *obscure* sense, while the city itself largely becomes a desert in which the bizarre (see figure 11), not to mention the terrifying, no longer takes on shadowy shapes but rather, as in Genet's plays, that of the *light* itself, which technocratic power creates everywhere and which places the dweller under surveillance (of what? who knows?): "The eye of the city is upon us, we cannot bear it without growing dizzy", as one inhabitant of Rouen said.[36] In those white spaces of some foreign logic, proper nouns plumb the reserves of hidden and familiar meanings. They "make sense", i.e. they impel movements, like the vocations and appeals that turn or divert the itinerary by making it resound with still uncertain meanings. They create non-sites within sites; they change them into passages.

A friend who lives in Sèvres is drawn when in Paris to the rue des Saints-Pères and the rue de Sèvres when he is on his way to visit his mother in another part of town; the names articulate a sentence that his feet construct without his being aware of it. Numbers (112th Street, or 9, rue Saint-Charles) also draw us towards them just as they can haunt our dreams. Another friend unconsciously represses streets that have the names of famous or forgotten persons; she prefers routes without signatures. This is another way such proper nouns move us. What are they spelling out? Once they were arranged in constellations that gave a semantic hierarchy and order to the face of the city, creators of chronologies and historical justifications; such names have little by little lost their graven surface validity, like worn coins, but their capability to

[36] P. Dard, F. Desbons et al., *La Ville: symbolique et souffrance* (Paris: CEP, 1975) p. 200.

Figure 11

signify has outlived them. Saints-Pères, Corentin Celton, Place Rouge – they offer themselves to the polysemes with which passers-by endow them; they become things apart from the places they were intended to define and turn into imaginary meeting-places in the journeys they map out, having become metaphors, for reasons foreign to their original validity, however known/ unknown to the passers-by. A strange toponymy, detached from the sites, floating above the city like a misty geography of "suspended meaning" and from the heights directing physical displacements below: Place de l'Étoile, Concorde, Poissonnière. As Malaparte said, "The Place de la Concorde does not exist, it is a notion."[37]

It is more than a notion. We must multiply comparisons in order to talk of the magic powers of proper names, slipped to the stroller like jewels on to moving fingers, guiding them as they adorn them. They link gestures and steps, they open up meanings and directions; such words even act to empty and erode their primary function. They are liberated, occupiable spaces. Through semantic rarefaction, their rich vagueness earns them the *poetic* function of expressing an illogical geography: "With a lovely nave I shall fill this great empty space."[38] The relics of meaning, and sometimes their shells, the inverted leftovers of great ambitions, maybe for walking.[39] Nothings – or near-nothings – symbolize and direct our steps; names that have, precisely, ceased to be "proper".

[37] See also, for example, the epigraph of *Place de l'Étoile* by Patrick Modiano (Paris: Gallimard, 1968).
[38] Joachim du Bellay, *Regrets*, p. 189.
[39] For example, *Sarcelles* – the name of a vast urban experiment – has taken on a

Three distinct (but combined) functionings of the relationships between spatial practices and signifying practices are sketched in (and perhaps based on) these symbolizing nuclei: the *believable*, the *memorable* and the *primitive*. They indicate that which "authorizes" (or makes possible and believable) spatial appropriations, that which is repeated (or remembered) of a silent and convoluted memory, and that which is structured and still marked by an in-fantile (*in-fans*) origin. These three symbolic mechanisms arrange the *topoi* of the discourse on/of the city (legend, recollection and dream) in a way that is also beyond urbanistic systematicity. They can even be found in the functions of proper names: they make the place they clothe with a word habitable and believable (by calling their classifying power they put on authorization); they recall or evoke the phantoms (dead and supposedly gone) that still stir, lurking in gestures and walking bodies; and, as they name – i.e. as they impose a command issuing from the other (a history) – and as they alter functionalist identity by breaking off from it, they create in the site itself this erosion or non-site carved out by the law of the other.

### Believabilia and Memorabilia: Habitability

By an all-too-obvious paradox, the discourse that creates belief is the discourse that takes away that which it enjoins, or which never gives what it promises. Far indeed from expressing a vacuum, from describing emptiness, it creates one. It makes room for a vacuum. Thus it makes openings; it "permits" play within a system of defined sites. It "authorizes" a playing-space (*Spielraum*) to be produced on a checkerboard that analyses and classifies identities. It makes habitable. As such I call it a "local authority". It is a flaw in the system that saturates sites with meaning and reduces them to the point of making them unbearable, "stifling". A symptomatic tendency of functionalist totalitarianism (even when it programmes games and festivals) is that it thus seeks to eliminate local authorities, for these comprise the system's univocity. It challenges what it quite rightly calls *superstitions*: superfluous semantic coverings that insinuate themselves "more" or "too much"[40] and that in a past or in a poetics alienate a part of the territory the partisans of technological motives and financiers have reserved for themselves.

In the end these proper names are already "local authorities" or "superstitions". Therefore, they are replaced by numbers. It is the same for the stones and legends that haunt the urban space like so many additional or superfluous inhabitants. They are the targets of a witch-hunt, if only because of the logic of the technostructure. Their extermination, however (like that of the

---

symbolic value among the inhabitants of the city by becoming, for all of France, a benchmark of total failure. That extreme example ended up by lending its citizens an unexpected "prestige".

[40] *Superstare*: to be above, like *more* or *too much*.

trees, the woods and the dells where these legends live),[41] is turning the city into a "suffering symbol".[42] The habitable city is being wiped out. Thus, as a woman from Rouen says, here "there is no special place; except for my place, that's all. . . . There's nothing." Nothing "special", nothing unusual, nothing created by a memory or a tale, nothing made significant by someone else. The only thing that remains believable is the cave of one's own dwelling, for the present still permeable by legend, still touched with shadows. Aside from that, according to another city-dweller, there are only "places where you can no longer believe in anything".[43]

It is through the opportunity they afford of storing up pregnant silences and inarticulate stories – or rather through their ability to create cellars and attics everywhere – that local legends (*legenda*: that which must be read, but also that which can be read) create exits, ways of leaving and re-entering, and thus habitable spaces. The setting out and the journey complete and enlarge on departures, comings and goings that were once provided by a body of legend now lacking in sites. Physical movement has the itinerant function of yesterday's or today's "superstitions". And in the end what does travelling produce if not, through a sort of "going back", "an exploration of the deserts of my memory", a return to a close-by exoticism via far-off detours, the "invention" of relics and legends ("fleeting glimpses of the French countryside", "fragments of music and poetry"),[44] in short, a "total uprooting" (Heidegger)? This long peregrination leads directly to the body of legend that the close-by site now lacks; it is a fiction, one that also has, like the dream or the perambulatory rhetoric, the dual characteristic of being the result of movements and of condensations.[45] As a corollary, we can gauge the importance of such signifying practices as we do spatial practices.

From this viewpoint, their content is no less revealing, even more so their organizing principle. The narratives of sites are makeshift. They are made of fragments of world. Although literary form and actantial *schema* correspond to stable models whose structures and combinations have often been analysed over the past thirty years, their matter (all their "manifest" detail) is furnished by the leftovers of nominations, taxonomies, comic or heroic predicates, etc.: i.e. by fragments of scattered semantic sites. These heterogeneous – even opposite – elements fill out the homogeneous and given form of the narrative. Thus we have the actual relationship of the practices of space with the constructed order. On its surface, that is pierced and pitted by ellipses, asides and leakages of meaning, it is an order-sieve.

The verbal relics of which narrative is made up (fragments of forgotten

[41] Cf. F. Lugassy, *Contribution à une psychosociologie de l'espace urbain: L'habitat et la forêt* (Paris: Publ. de Recherche urbaine, 1970).
[42] Dard et al., *La ville*.
[43] Quoted in ibid., pp. 174, 206.
[44] C. Lévi-Strauss, *Tristes tropiques* (Paris: Plon, 1955) pp. 434–6.
[45] One could say as much of snapshots brought back from a trip, substituted for (and changed into) legends of the site from which one left.

stories and opaque gestures) are juxtaposed in a collage in which their relationships are not thought out and therefore form a symbolic whole.[46] They are articulated by lacunae. Thus, within the structured space of the text, they produce anti-texts, effects of dissimulation and fugue, opportunities for passage through to other landscapes, like cellars and copses: "Oh, massifs; oh, plurals!"[47] Through the processes of dissemination they open up, narratives contrast with *rumour*, which is always injunctive, the initiator and result of a levelling of space, the creator of mass motions that shore up an order by adding make-believe to make-do or -be. Narratives diversify; rumours totalize. Although there is always an oscillation from one to the other, it would appear that today there is more stratification: narratives are becoming more private and fading into out-of-the-way neighbourhoods, families or individuals, while rumour is rampant and, in the guise of the *City*, the key word of some private law takes the place of every proper name and obliterates or combats superstitions that are still guilty of resisting it.

The dispersal of narratives already means the dispersal of the *memorable*. In fact, memory is the anti-museum: it cannot be localized. Its remains can still be found in legend. Both objects and words are hollow. Some past lies sleeping there, as it does in the everyday gestures of walking, eating, sleeping – where ancient revolutions lie dormant. Memory is only a travelling Prince Charming who happens to awaken the Sleeping Beauty – stories without words. "*Here, there was* a bakery"; "*That* is where old Mrs Dupuis *lived*". We are struck by the fact that sites that have been lived in are filled with the presence of absences. What appears designates what is no more: "*Look*: here there *was* . . .", but can no longer be seen. Demonstratives utter the invisible identities of the visible: the very definition of the site is, in fact, to be this series of movements and effects between the shattered strata of which it is formed and to play upon those shifting levels.

"Memories are what keep us here. . . . It's personal – not interesting to anyone – but still, in the end that creates the spirit of the neighbourhood."[48] Every site is haunted by countless ghosts that lurk there in silence, to be "evoked" or not. One *inhabits* only haunted sites – the opposite of what is set forth in the *Panopticon*. However, like the royal Gothic statues of Notre-Dame that were walled up for 200 years in the basement of a building on the rue de la Chaussée-d'Antin,[49] such ghosts – broken, like the sculptures – neither speak nor see. A kind of knowing has fallen silent. Only whispers of what is *known* but is *silent* are exchanged "between us". Sites are fragmentary and convoluted histories, pasts stolen by others from readability, folded up ages that can be

[46] Terms whose relationships are not thought out but rather stated as necessary may be called *symbolic*. On this definition of symbolism as a cognitive mechanism characterized by a "deficit" of thought, see Dan Sperber, *Le Symbolisme en générale* (Paris: Hermann, 1974).

[47] F. Ponge, *La Promenade dans nos serres* (Paris: Gallimard, 1967).

[48] An inhabitant of Croix-Rousse, Lyon (interviewed by P. Mayol).

[49] Cf. *Le Monde*, 4 May 1977.

unfolded but that are there more as narratives in suspense, like a rebus: symbolizations encysted in the body's pain or pleasure. "I feel good here"[50] – an effect of space, set apart from language, where it suddenly bursts into light.

## The Infancies of Sites

What is memorable is what we can dream about a site. In any palimpsestic site, subjectivity is already articulated on the absence that structures it like existence, and the fact of "being there", *Dasein*. We have seen, however, that that being acts only in spatial practices, i.e. in *ways of passing to something else*. We must ultimately recognize here the repetition in various metamorphoses of some decisive and basic experience: the child's differentiation of himself from his mother's body. Here the possibility of space and of a localization (an "I am not alone") of the subject has its origin. Without going into Freud's famous analysis of this prenatal and natal experience while watching the games of his one-and-a-half-year-old grandson, who was tossing a spool and contentedly crying "O-o-o-o!" (meaning *fort*, i.e. *there, gone* or *can't*) and pulling it back to him by its thread with a joyful *Da* (i.e. *here, returned*),[51] suffice it to note this (perilous and satisfying) abrupt emergence from indifferentiation with the mother's body for which the spool is the substitute: this departure of the mother (that she both disappears and is made to disappear by him) represents localization and exteriority against a background of absence. The jubilant physical feat enables him to "make" the material object "leave" and to make *himself* disappear (for he is identical to that object) – to be *there* (because) *without* the other, but in a *necessary relationship* with what has disappeared – that creates an "original spatial structure".

Undoubtedly, we can follow differentiation further back to the nomination that already cuts off from its mother the foetus identified as male (but what about the daughter, who is henceforth placed in another spatial relationship?). What is important in this initiatory game – as in the "gleeful behaviour" of the child who, before a mirror, recognizes *one* (the totalizable *he*), whereas it is only the *other* (there, an image with which he identifies himself)[52] – is this process of "spatial cognition" that inscribes the passage to the other as the law of the being and the law of the site. To employ space, therefore, is to repeat the joyous and silent experience of childhood: it is, in the site, *to be other* and *to pass to the other* (figure 12).

Thus begins the progress Freud compares to strolling in the motherland.[53] This relationship of self to self controls the internal alterations of the site (inter-stratal play) or the promenade-like unfolding of the stories silted up on a

---

[50] See note 48 above.
[51] See the two analyses in *The Interpretation of Dreams* and *Beyond the Pleasure Principle*, as well as Sami-Ali, *L'Espace imaginaire* (Paris: Gallimard, 1974) pp. 42–64.
[52] J. Lacan, *Écrits* (Paris: Seuil, 1966) pp. 93–100.
[53] S. Freud, *Inhibition, symptôme et angoisse* (PUF, 1968).

Figure 12

site (movements and journeys). Childhood, which determines the practices of space, then augments its effects, proliferates and inundates private and public spaces and defaces their readable surfaces, and creates in the planned city a "metaphorical" city or a city in movement, like the one of Kandinsky's dreams: "A great city built in accordance with all the rules of architecture and suddenly shaken by an unpredictable and incalculable force."[54]

[54] N. Kandinsky, *Du Spirituel dans l'art* (Paris: Denoël, 1969) p. 57.

MICHEL DE CERTEAU

# The Jabbering of Social Life

> I love the word "believe". In general,
> when one say, "I know", one does not
> know: one believes.
>
> Marcel Duchamp, *Duchamp du signe*
> (Paris: Flammarion, 1975, p. 185)

Leon Poliakov once said that Jews are Frenchmen who, rather than no longer going to church, no longer go to the synagogue. In the humorous tradition of the *Haggadah*, that joke relegates to the past beliefs that no longer organize practices. Today political convictions seem to be following the same path. One becomes a socialist *to have been* one, without going to demonstrations, without attending meetings, without paying dues – in short, without cost. More ceremonial than identification, "membership" is shown by what is called a *voice*, that leftover of a word: one vote a year. By living on a kind of "trust", the party carefully collates the relics of ancient convictions and through that fiction of legitimacy it succeeds in managing its affairs. It only needs, by means of opinion polls and statistics, to proliferate its citation of those phantom witnesses, thereby re-citing its litany.

A fairly simple technique upholds the acting out of this credibility. The polls need only concern not what directly links the "adherents" to the party, but that which does not attract them elsewhere – not the energy of convictions, but their inertia: "If it is not true that you believe something else, it is therefore true that you are still with us." The results of this operation rely upon remnants of the membership. They reckon on the very attrition of any conviction, for those remnants indicate both the *reflux* of what the respondents had believed in and the lack of a stronger credibility that might lead them away: the "voices" are not withdrawing; they are staying put; they are still there where they were, they give rise to the same total. The account becomes an accounting. This fiction could well serve as an appendix to Borges' *Esse est Percipi*.[1] It is the apologue of a shift that figures do not show, one that affects beliefs.

By way of an initial approximation, I take "belief" to mean not what is

[1] See Jorge Luis Borges, *Chroniques de Bustos Domeq*, and the chapter "Esse est percipi" (to be is to be seen).

believed (a dogma, a programme, etc.), but the investiture of subjects in a proposition, the *act* of uttering it while holding it to be true[2] – in other words, a "modality" of the affirmation rather than its content.[3] Now, the capacity to believe seems to be receding everywhere in the political field. It underlay the functioning of "authority". Since Hobbes, political philosophy – especially in its English tradition – has deemed that connection to be fundamental.[4] Through that linkage, politics makes explicit its relationship of difference and continuity with religion. In both instances, however, the determination to inspire belief on which the institution lives is providing a respondent with a quest for love and/or identity.[5] It is therefore important to consider the forms taken by belief in our societies and the practices that form the origin of such displacements.

## The Devaluation of Beliefs

For a long time it was supposed that the reserves of belief were indefinite. On the sea of credulity one needed only create islets of rationality to set out and ensure the fragile conquests of a critical method. The rest, seen as inexhaustible, was presumed transferable to other objects and other aims, as waterfalls are harnessed and used for hydroelectric power. One tried to "capture" this force and to move it from one place to another: from those so-called pagan societies in which it was at home it was directed towards the Christianity it was supposed to support; from the churches it was then moved on towards a monarchical politics; next, from a traditionalist religiosity towards the institutions of the Republic, of National Education or the types of socialism. Such "conversions" consisted in capturing the energy of belief by transporting it. What was not transferable – or had not yet been transferred – to the new realms of progress was regarded as "superstition"; what was usable by the ruling order was deemed "conviction". The resources were so rich that in exploiting them one forgot the need to analyse them. Campaigns and crusades entailed "investing" the energy of belief in good sites and good objects (of belief).

Gradually belief became polluted, like the air or the water. This motive energy – still resistant albeit manageable – began to run out. It was noticed,

---

[2] Cf. the remarks in W. V. Quine and J. S. Ullian, *The Web of Belief* (New York: Random House, 1970) pp. 4–6.

[3] Cf. on this subject: Jaakko Hintikka, *Knowledge and Belief: An Introduction to the Logic of the Two Notions* (Ithaca, NY: Cornell University Press, 1969); Rodney Needham, *Belief, Language and Experience* (Oxford: Basil Blackwell, 1972); Ernest Gellner, *Legitimation of Belief* (Cambridge: Cambridge University Press, 1974); John M. Vickers, *Belief and Probability* (Dordrecht: Reidel, 1976); *Langages*, no. 43 on "modalities", September 1976.

[4] Cf., for example, R. S. Peters and Peter Winch, "Authority", in Anthony Quinton (ed.), *Political Philosophy* (Oxford: Oxford University Press, 1973) pp. 83–111.

[5] Pierre Legendre, *L'Amour du censeur* (Paris: Seuil, 1974) p. 28.

without knowing what it is. An odd paradox: all the polemics and reflections on ideological content and the institutional framework to be provided for it have not (except in English philosophy, from Hume to Wittgenstein, H. H. Price, Hintikka or Quine) been accompanied by any elucidation of the nature of the act of believing. Today it no longer suffices to manipulate, transfer and refine belief; its composition must be analysed, since we want to produce it artificially. Marketing (commercial or political) is still making only partial use of it.[6] Nowadays there are too many objects for belief and not enough credibility.

An inversion has taken place. The ancient powers managed their "authority" ably and thereby made up for their lack of technical or administrative machinery: this consisted of client systems, of allegiances, "legitimacies", and so forth. They tried none the less to make themselves more independent of the play of such fidelities through a rationalization, the control and organization of space. As an end result of that labour, the powers of our developed societies have fairly precise and compact procedures for the surveillance of every social network: such as the administrative and "panoptic" systems of police, school, health, security, etc.[7] However, they are slowly losing their credibility. They command more strength and have less authority.

Often the technicians do not concern themselves about this at all, busy as they are with extending and complicating the machinery for maintenance and surveillance. False confidence. The sophistication of discipline does not compensate for the disinvestment of subjects. In businesses the letting-go of workers is increasing more rapidly than the police control apparatus of which it is the target, the pretext and the effect. Waste of produce, misuse of time, "feather-bedding", job turnover and absenteeism among the staff, etc.: such things erode from within a system which, like the Toyota plants,[8] tends to become prison-like to prevent anything escaping. In administration, offices, and even in political or religious organizations, the cancer invading the machinery corresponds to the disappearance of convictions. It also causes it. Interest cannot replace belief.[9]

Belief is being exhausted. Or rather, it has sought refuge in the media and leisure activities. It has gone on vacation; yet it is none the less an object captured and dealt with by advertising, business and fashion. To regain those beliefs that are fading and becoming lost, business has set about manufacturing

[6] Cf., for example, Dale Carnegie, *Public Speaking and Influencing Men in Business* and, especially, Martin Fishbein and Icek Ajzen, *Belief, Attitude, Intention and Behavior* (Reading, Mass: Addison-Wesley, 1975).

[7] Cf. Michel Foucault, *Surveiller et punir* (Paris: Gallimard, 1975) etc.

[8] Kamata Satoshi, *Toyota: l'usine de désespoir* (Paris, Ouvrières edn, 1976): a system which is still "palaeotechnical", in which the goal is to *control* every activity; not make them cohere by means of values designed to create believers. See Miklos Haraszti, *Salaire aux pièces* (Paris: Seuil, 1976).

[9] Pierre Gremion further states that in local administration, and especially in the urban sub-system, the mechanisms of legitimation "no longer exist". See P. Gremion, *Le Pouvoir périphérique: Bureaucrates et notables dans le système politique français* (Paris: Seuil, 1976) pp. 416ff.

simulacra of credibility. Shell produces the Credo of "values" that "inspire" its management and that are to be adopted by its staff and its workers. The same holds true for a hundred other businesses, even if they are slow to take action and continue to rely on the fictitious capital of some outmoded "family" business or local "spirit".

The material with which to inject believability into the apparatus, where is it to be found? There are two traditional sources, one political, the other religious: in the first, the overdevelopment of administrative bodies and framework takes the place of mobility or reflux of convictions among militants. In the second, on the contrary, institutions in the process of decaying or of isolating themselves allow the beliefs that they had long fomented, maintained and controlled to become dissipated.

## An Archaeology: the Transits of Belief

The relationships between these two "bases" are strange and longstanding.

1. Religiosity seems easier to exploit. Marketing firms are turning back enthusiastically to fragments of beliefs that were only yesterday violently being combatted as superstitions. Advertising is becoming evangelical. Many administrators on the economic and social levels, who are disturbed by the slow sinking of the Churches in which repose the remains of the "values", are trying to re-enlist their services by christening them "up to date". Before these beliefs can go down with the ships that carry them they are precipitously being unloaded by businesses and administrations. The people who use these relics no longer believe in them. Nevertheless, they employ them and imbue them with kinds of "integrist" and ideological and financial associations in order to recaulk these old leaky tubs and turn the churches into museums of beliefs without believers, thus preserved for exploitation by liberal capitalism.

Such a salvage operation works on the basis of two tactical hypotheses – both probably false. The first postulates that belief remains attached to its objects and that by preserving the latter you retain the former. In fact (as demonstrated by both history and semiotics), the investment of belief passes from myth to myth, from ideology to ideology, or from utterance to utterance.[10] Thus, belief withdraws from a myth and leaves it more or less intact, but disarmed and changed into a document.[11] In the course of these transits, the conviction that is

---

[10] Cf. M. de Certeau, *La Culture au pluriel* (Paris: 10/18, 1974) pp. 11–34: "Les révolutions du croyable". From the standpoint of logic, it is precisely to these shifts of belief from utterance to utterance that Quine and Ullian devoted their first analyses (Quine and Ullian, *Web of Belief*, pp. 8–9).

[11] To the analysis of the journeys which lead the myth from tribe to tribe, and "wear it out" little by little into legendary tradition, fantastic elaboration or political ideology (see Lévi-Strauss, *Anthropologie structurale, deux* (Paris: Plon, 1973) pp. 301–15, "Comment meurent les mythes"), we must thus add that of these slow disinvestments through which belief moves away from a myth.

still attached to the terrain it is gradually abandoning cannot win out against the currents that are moving elsewhere. There is no equivalence between the objects that still cleave to it and those that mobilize it elsewhere.

The other tactic no longer assumes that belief remains tied to its prime objects, but rather that, on the contrary, it can be separated from them artificially; that its flight towards the narratives of the media, towards leisure "paradises", towards inner or communal retreats, etc., can be halted or diverted; that one might thus bring it back to the fold, to the disciplinary order it has left. However, conviction does not so easily resprout in the fields it has abandoned. It cannot be so easily brought back to administrations or businesses that have become "unbelievable". The liturgies that attempt to "enliven" and "revalue" the workplace do not transform its functioning; they do not therefore produce believers. The public is not that credulous. It is amused by such festivals and simulacra. It does not "go along".

2. *Political* organizations are slowly replacing Churches as the sites of the practices of belief, but because of this they appear to have been haunted by the return of a very ancient (pre-Christian) and very "pagan" alliance between power and the religious life. It is as though when the religions ceased to be an autonomous power ("spiritual power" as it was called), politics once again became religious. Christianity had cut through the interlacing of the visible objects of belief (political authorities) and its invisible objects (gods, spirits, etc.). But it retained that distinction only by establishing a clerical, dogmatic and sacramental power in the place left vacant by the temporary deterioration of the political at the end of the age of antiquity. In the eleventh and twelfth centuries, ecclesiastical power, under the banner of "The Peace of God", imposed its "order" on clashing civil powers.[12] Succeeding centuries were marked by the deterioration of that order to the benefit of princes. In the seventeenth century the Churches received their models and their rights from the monarchies, even if they still evidenced a "religiosity" that legitimized power and that it little by little turned to its credit. With the crumbling of this ecclesiastical power three centuries ago, beliefs flowed back towards the political, but without carrying with them the divine or celestial values the Churches had set aside, controlled and taken in hand.

This complicated round trip, which passed from politics to Christian religion, and from that religion to a new politics,[13] resulted in an individualization of beliefs (common frames of reference breaking down into social "opinions" or private "convictions") and of their fields of action in an increasingly diversified network of possible objects. The notion of democracy was consonant with the will to control this multiplication of convictions that had replaced the faith upon which an order had been based. It is striking that in

[12] See Georges Duby, *Guerriers et paysans* (Paris: Gallimard, 1976) pp. 184ff.
[13] See M. de Certeau, *L'Écriture de l'histoire*, 2. edn (Paris: Gallimard, 1978) pp. 152–212: "La formalité des pratiques. Du système religieux à l'éthique des lumières (XVIIe–XVIIIe siècle)."

breaking down the old system – i.e. the religious credibility of politics – Christianity finally compromised the feasibility of that religion it had detached from politics, it contributed to the devaluation of what it had appropriated in order to render it autonomous, and it thereby made possible the reflux of beliefs towards political authorities hitherto deprived of (or freed from) those spiritual authorities that had once been as much a principle of relativization as of legitimization. The return of a "pagan" repression had thus been affected by this fall from the "spiritual". The erosion of Christianity left an indelible mark on modern times: the "incarnation" or historicization that Rousseau, in the eighteenth century, was already calling a "civil religion".[14] In contrast to the pagan State, which "drew no distinction between its gods and its laws", Rousseau posited a citizen's "religion", "whose articles it was up to the sovereign to establish". "If anyone, after having publicly accepted those dogmas, behaves as if he does not believe in them, he is to be put to death." Different from this civil religion of the *citizen* was a spiritual religion of *man*: the individual, asocial and universal religion of *la Profession de foi du vicaire savoyard*. That prophetic view – far less incoherent than has been suggested – already articulates the development of a body of "civil" and political dogma on the radicalization of an individual conscience *freed* from all dogma and deprived of power. Sociological analysis has since proved that prediction to be correct.[15]

Hence belief is reinvested solely in the political system, to the extent that the "spiritual powers" – which had guaranteed civil powers in antiquity and which entered into competition with those of the Christian West – fall out of circulation and are disseminated or miniaturized.

## The Institution of the Real

The media change the profound silence of things into its opposite. Once constituted in secret, the real now jabbers away. We are surrounded by news, information, statistics and opinion polls. Never has history talked so much or shown so much. Never, indeed, have the gods' ministers *made them speak* so continuously, in such detail and so injunctively as the producers of revelations and rules do today *in the name* of topicality. Our orthodoxy is made up of narrations of "what's going on". Statistical debates are our theological wars. The combatants no longer bear ideas as offensive or defensive arms. They move forward camouflaged as facts, data and events. They set themselves up as messengers of a "reality". Their uniform is the colour of the economic and social earth. When they advance, the ground itself seems to advance. But in fact they manufacture it, they simulate it, they cover themselves with it, they believe in it – they thus create the stage of their law.

[14] J.-J. Rousseau, *Le Contrat social*, IV, ch. 8.
[15] Cf. Robert N. Bellah, *Beyond Belief: Essays on Religion in a Post-Traditional World* (New York, 1970) pp. 168–89, concerning "civil religion" in the United States.

Malville, Kalkai, Croissant, the POLISARIO Front, the nuclear question, Khomeini, Reagan, etc.: these fragments of history organize themselves into doctrinal articles. "Be silent!" says the speaker or the political officeholder. "There are the facts. Here are the data, the circumstances, etc. Therefore, you must. . . ." The real, as told to us, interminably dictates what must be believed and what must be done. And what can one reply to such facts? We can only bow down and obey what they – those oracles – "signify", as with the oracle at Delphi.[16] Thus the manufacture of simulacra provides the means of producing believers and, therefore, adherents. This institution of the real is the most visible form of our contemporary dogma. It is also, therefore, the most disputed among parties.

It no longer has its own site, its own headquarters or its own ultimate authority. Information, a private code, innervates and saturates the social body. From morning till evening, unceasingly, streets and buildings are haunted by narratives. They articulate our existences by teaching us what they should be. They "cover the event", i.e. they *make* our legends (*legenda* = that which must be read and said). Seized from the moment of awakening by the radio (the voice is the law), the listener walks all day through a forest of narrativities, journalistic, advertising and televised, which, at night, slip a few final messages under the door of sleep. More than the God recounted to us by the theologians of the past, these tales have a function of providence and predestination: they organize our work, our celebrations – even our dreams – in advance. Social life multiplies the gestures and modes of behaviour *imprinted* by the narrative models; it continually reproduces and stores up the "copies" of narratives. Our society has become a *narrated* society in a threefold sense: it is defined by *narratives* (the fables of our advertising and information), by *quotations* of them, and by their interminable *recitation*.

Such narratives have the strange and twofold power of changing sight into belief and of manufacturing reality out of simulacra: a dual inversion. On the one hand, modernity – once born of an observant will struggling against credulity and basing itself on a contract between the seen and the real – has now transformed that relationship and gives to be seen precisely what must be *believed*. The scope, the status and the objects of vision are defined by fiction. The media, advertising or political representation all function in this way.

Of course, fiction also existed in the past, but within circumscribed aesthetic and theatrical sites: fiction indicated itself as such (thanks to perspective, for example, the art of illusion); with its own ground-rules and production conditions, it provided its own metalanguage.[17] It spoke solely in the name of language. It narrativized symbolics, leaving the truth of things suspended and almost secret. Today, fiction claims to presentify the real, to speak in the name

[16] *To signify* in the sense of the Heraclitian fragment: "The oracle which is Delphi does not speak; it does not dissimulate: it *signifies*" (fragment 93, in Diels).

[17] See Erwin Panovsky, *La Perspective comme forme symbolique* (Paris: Minuit, 1975); E. H. Gombrich, *L'Art et l'illusion* (Paris: Gallimard, 1971) pp. 255–360; R. Klein, *La Forme et l'intelligible* (Paris: Gallimard, 1970).

of facts, and thus to cause the simulacrum it produces to be taken as a system of reference. Those to whom these legends are addressed (and who pay for them) are therefore no longer obliged to believe what they cannot see (the traditional position), but rather to believe what they do see (the contemporary position).

This inversion of the terrain on which beliefs develop is the result of a mutation in the paradigms of knowledge: the visibility of the real is substituted for the earlier postulate, its invisibility. The socio-cultural scene of modernity refers back to a "myth". It defines the social referent by its visibility (and thus by its scientific or political representivity); on the basis of this new postulate (the belief that the real is visible), it articulates the possibility of what we know, what we observe, our proofs and our practices. In this new arena – the infinitely extendable field of optical investigations and of a scopic drive – there still remains the strange collusion between *belief* and the question of the real. But now it is played out within the element of the *seen*, the *observed* or the *shown*. In short, the contemporary simulacrum[18] is the last localization of the belief in sight. It is the identification of the *seen* with what is to be *believed* – once we have abandoned the hypothesis that holds that the waters of an invisible ocean (the Real) haunt the shores of the visible and create the effects, the decipherable signs or the misleading reflections of its presence. The simulacrum is what the relationship of the visible to the real becomes when the postulate of an invisible immensity of the Being (or beings) hidden behind appearances crumbles.

## Society Recited

In the face of narratives of images – which nowadays are no more than "fictions", visible and readable productions – the spectator-observer *knows perfectly well* that they are but simulacra, the results of manipulations ("I know perfectly well it's a joke"), *but even so*, he assumes for those simulations the status of reality:[19] a belief survives the denial created by all that we know about their manufacture. As a television viewer has said, "Had it been untrue, you would have been able to tell." He postulated *other* social sites that could guarantee what he knew to be fictitious, and that is what allowed him to believe it "anyway": as though belief could no longer be couched in direct convictions, but only through the detour of what others are supposed to believe. Belief is no longer based on an invisible otherness concealed behind signs, but on what other groups, other fields or other disciplines are supposed to be. The "real" is what, in each place, the reference to another causes to be believed. And the same holds for the scientific disciplines. For example, the relationship between computing and history functions on the basis of an astonishing *quid pro quo*:

[18] On simulacra, see Jean Beaudrillard, *L'Échange symbolique et la mort* (Paris: Gallimard, 1976) pp. 75–128, "L'ordre des simulacres"; and, by the same author, "La précession des simulacres", in *Traverses*, no. 10 (1978) pp. 3–37.

[19] See O. Mannoni, *Clefs pour l'imaginaire ou l'Autre Scène* (Paris: Seuil, 1969) pp. 9–33: "Je sais bien mais quand même" (on belief).

from computers historians seek the accreditation of a "scientific" power that can lend a technical, real weight to their discourse; from history, the computer scientists seek validation through the "reality" created by "concrete" manifestations of knowledge. Each expects from the other a guarantee that gives weight to their simulacrum.[20]

The same holds true politically. Each party derives its credibility from what it believes and causes to be believed about its referent (the revolutionary "miracles" performed in the East?) or its adversary (the faults and woes of the wicked on the other side). Each political discourse creates effects of reality out of what it assumes and causes to be assumed about the economic analysis on which it is based (an analysis that is itself validated by this reference to the political). Within each party, the professional discourses of the "responsible" leadership *stand up* thanks to the credulity those leaders assume on the part of the rank and file militants or the voters and, on the other hand, the "I am well aware that it's a joke" of many voters is countered by what they postulate, out of conviction or out of knowledge, about the cadres of the political apparatus. Belief thus functions on the basis of the value of the real that is assumed "anyway" in the other, even when one knows perfectly well – all too well – the extent to which "it's all bullshit" on one's own side.

Quotation, then, is the ultimate weapon for making one believe. Because it plays upon what the other is assumed to believe, it is the means by which "reality" is instituted. To quote the other on one's own behalf is thus to make believable the simulacra produced in a particular place. Opinion "polls" have become the most elementary and the most passive procedure for doing this. Perpetual self-quotation – the proliferation of polls – is the fiction through which the country is brought to believe in what it *is*. Each citizen assumes for all the others what he takes to be their belief – without believing in it himself. By replacing doctrines that have become unbelievable, quotation allows the technocratic apparatuses to make themselves feasible for each person *in the name of the others*. To quote is to give reality to the simulacrum a power produces by causing a belief that others believe in it, but without furnishing any believable object. However, it is also to designate the "anarchists" or "deviants" (to quote them to the public), to hand over to the aggressivity of the public those who, affirming through their deeds that they do not believe in it, destroy the fictitious "reality" that no one can support "anyway" except as the conviction of the others.

To the extent that this "opinion-making" instrument can be manipulated by those who wield it, one is quite justified in wondering about the ability it offers to change "belief" into "distrust", into "suspicion" – even into denunciation, and about whether citizens can control politically that which provides the circular and pointless trustworthiness to political life itself.

---

[20] M. de Certeau, "Science et fiction: l'histoire, de l'informatique à l'anthropologie", in *Nouvelles littéraires*, January 1977.

# Part II

# Understanding the Meaning
of Signs

UMBERTO ECO

# How Culture Conditions the Colours We See

## I

Colour is not an easy matter. James Gibson, in *The Senses Considered as Perceptual Systems*, says that "the meaning of the term colour is one of the worst muddles in the history of science".[1] If one uses the term "colour" to mean the pigmentation of substances in the environment, one has not said anything about our chromatic perception. Johannes Itten, in his *Kunst der Farbe*, distinguishes between pigments as chromatic reality and our perceptual response as chromatic effect.[2] The chromatic effect, it seems, depends on many factors: the nature of surfaces, light, contrast between objects, previous knowledge, and so on.

I do not have any competence about pigments and I have very confused ideas about the laws governing chromatic effect; moreover I am neither a painter, nor an art critic. My personal relationship with the coloured world is a private affair as much as my sexual activity, and I am not supposed to entertain my readers with my personal reactivity towards the polychromous theatre of the world. Thus, as far as colours are concerned, I take the privilege of considering myself a blind man. I shall be writing about colours from a merely theoretical point of view, namely, from the point of view of a general semiotic approach.

Since I have assumed myself to be blind or at least a Daltonist, I shall mistrust my visual experience. I shall start from a verbal text, chapter 26, Book II, of Aulus Gellius' *Noctes Acticae*, a Latin encyclopaedia of the second century A.D.

To deal with colours by making recourse to a text of this period is rather

[1] James Gibson, *The Senses Considered as Perceptual Systems* (London: Allen & Unwin, 1968).
[2] Johannes Itten, *Kunst der Farbe* (Ravensburg: Otto Mair, 1961).

challenging. We are facing linguistic terms for colours, but we do not know what chromatic effects these words refer to. We know much about Roman sculpture and architecture, but very little about Roman painting. The colours we see today in Pompeii are not the colours the Pompeians saw; even if the pigments are the same, the chromatic responses are not. In the nineteenth century, Gladstone suggested that Greeks were unable to distinguish blue from yellow. Goetz and many others assumed that Latin speakers did not distinguish blue from green. I have found also somewhere that Egyptians used blue in their paintings but had no linguistic term to designate it, and that Assyrians, in order to name the colour blue, could do no better than transform the noun "uknu", naming lapis lazuli, into an adjective.

All of this is highly speculative, but we need not test every case. Let me concentrate on the following passage from Aulus Gellius. The reader is advised to hold his temper, since the passage is highly confusing.

Gellius is reporting a conversation he had with Fronto, a poet and grammarian, and Favorinus, a philosopher. Favorinus remarked that eyes are able to isolate more colours than words can name. Red (*rufus*) and green (*viridis*), he said, have only two names but many species. He was, without knowing it, introducing the contemporary scientific distinction between identification (understood as categorization) and discrimination, of which I shall speak later.

Favorinus continues: *rufus* is a name, but what a difference between the red of blood, the red of purple, the red of saffron, and the red of gold! They are all differences of red but, in order to define them, Latin can only make recourse to adjectives derived from the names of objects, thus calling *flammeus* the red of fire, *sanguineus* the red of blood, *croceus* the red of saffron, *aureus* the red of gold. Greek has more names, Favorinus says, but Fronto replies that Latin, too, has many colour terms and that, in order to designate *russus* and *ruber* (red), one can also use *fulvus, flavus, rubidus, poeniceus, rutilus, luteus, spadix*.

Now if one looks at the whole history of Latin literature, one notices that *fulvus* is associated by Virgil and other authors with the lion's mane, with sand, wolves, gold, eagles, but also with jasper. *Flavae*, in Virgil, are the hair of the blond Dido, as well as olive leaves; and the Tiber river, because of the yellow-grey mud polluting its waters, was commonly called *flavus*. The other terms all refer to various gradations of red, from pale rose to dark red: notice, for instance, that *luteus*, which Fronto defines as "diluted red", is referred by Pliny to the egg-yolk and by Catullus to poppies.

In order to add more precision, Fronto says that *fulvus* is a mixture of red and green, while *flavus* is a mixture of green, red and white. Fronto then quotes another example from Virgil (*Georgica*, III, 82) where a horse (commonly interpreted by philologists as a dapple-grey horse) is *glaucus*. Now *glaucus* in Latin tradition stands for greenish, light-green, blue-green and grey-blue; Virgil uses this adjective also for willow trees and for ulva or sea lettuce, as well as for waters. Fronto says that Virgil could also have used for his same purpose (his grey horse) *caerulus*. Now this term is usually associated with the sea, skies, the eyes of Minerva, watermelons and cucumbers (Propertius), while Juvenal employs it to describe some sort of rye bread.

And things get no better with *viridis* (from which comes the Italian *verde*, green), since in the whole of Latin tradition, one can find *viridis* associated with grass, skies, parrots, sea, trees.

I have suggested that Latin did not clearly distinguish blue from green, but Favorinus gives us the impression that Latin users did not even distinguish blue-green from red, since he quotes Ennius (*Annales*, XIV, 372–3) who describes the sea at the same time as *caeruleus* and *flavus* as marble. Favorinus agrees with this, since – he says – Fronto had previously described *flavus* as a mixture of green and white. But one should remember that, as a matter of fact, Fronto had said that *flavus* was green, white and red, and a few lines before that, had classified *flavus* among various gradations of red!

Let me exclude any explanation in terms of colour blindness. Too easy. Gellius and his friends were erudites; they were not describing their own perceptions, they were elaborating upon literary texts coming from different centuries. Can one say that they were considering cases of poetic invention – where, by a provocative use of language, fresh and uncommon impressions are vividly depicted? If that were the case, we would expect from them more excitation, more marvel, more appreciation for these stylistic *tours de force*. On the contrary, they propose all these cases as examples of the most correct and precise use of language.

Thus the puzzle we are faced with is neither a psychological nor an aesthetic one: it is a cultural one, and as such it is filtered through a linguistic system. We are dealing with verbal language in so far as it conveys notions about visual experiences, and we must, then, understand how verbal language makes the non-verbal experience recognizable, speakable and effable.

To solve Aulus Gellius' puzzle, we must pass through the semiotic structure of language. As a matter of fact, colour blindness itself represents a social puzzle, difficult both to solve and to detect, because of linguistic reasons. Let me quote this important passage from Arthur Linksz, which is later commented upon by Marshall Sahlins:

> To suppose color terms merely name differences suggested by the visible spectrum, their function being to articulate realities necessarily and already known as such is something like the idea that genealogical relations comprise a *de facto* grid of "kinship types," inevitably taken in this significance by all societies, which differ merely in the way they classify (cope with) such universal facts of "relationship." The point, however, in color as in kinship, is that the terms stand in meaningful relations with other terms, and it is by the relations between terms within the global system that the character of objective reference is sedimented. Moreover, the concrete attributes thus singled out by the semantic differentiation of terms then function also as *signifiers* of social relations, not simply as the *signifieds* of the terms. In the event, it is not even

necessary that those who participate in a given natural order have the same substantive experience of the object, so long as they are capable of making some kind of sensory distinction at the semiotically pertinent boundaries. Hence the cultural facility of color blinds, functioning on differences in brightness – in a world that everyone else sees as differentiated by hue. Red-and-green color-blind people talk of reds and greens and all shades of it [sic] using the same words most of us assign to objects of a certain color. They think and talk and act in terms of "object color" and "color constancy" as do the rest of us. They call leaves green, roses red. Variations in saturation and brilliance of their yellow gives [sic] them an amazing variety of impressions. While we learn to rely on differences of hue, their minds get trained in evaluating brilliance. . . . Most of the red-and-green blind do not know of their defect and think we see things in the same shades they do. They have no reason for sensing any conflict. If there is an argument, they find *us* fussy, not *themselves* defective. They heard us call the leaves green and whatever shade leaves have for them they call green. People of average intelligence never stop to analyze their sensations. They are much too busy looking for what these sensations mean.[3]

Commenting on this passage in his beautiful essay on "Colors and Cultures", Sahlins not only insists on the thesis that colour is a cultural matter, but remarks that every test of colour discrimination is rooted in a sort of referential fallacy.[4] Psychologists frequently assume that classifications of colours and utterance of colour names are linked to the representation of an actual experience; they assume that colour terms in the first instance denote the immanent properties of a sensation. Therefore, many tests are contaminated by this confusion between *meaning* and *reference*. When one utters a colour term one is not directly pointing to a state of the world (process of reference), but, on the contrary, one is connecting or correlating that term with a cultural unit or concept. The utterance of the term is determined, obviously, by a given sensation, but the transformation of the sensory stimuli into a percept is in some way determined by the semiotic relationship between the linguistic expression and the meaning or *content* culturally correlated to it.

Our problem, to quote Sahlins again, is "how then to reconcile these two undeniable yet opposed understandings: color distinctions are naturally based, albeit that natural distinctions are culturally constituted? The dilemma can only be solved by reading from the cultural meaning of color to the empirical tests of discrimination, rather than the other way around."

[3] Arthur Linksz, *Physiology of the Eye* (New York: Grune & Stratton, 1952) vol. 2.
[4] Marshall Sahlins, "Colors and Cultures", *Semiotica*, vol. 15, no. 1 (1975) pp. 1, 22.

## II

I shall begin with verbal language for practical reasons, for it represents the most powerful and therefore the most familiar instrument people use for defining the surrounding world and for communicating to each other about it. It is not, however, impossible to imagine another sign system in which colours and other elements of the world were indicated not by words but, say, by fingers (the thumb means red, the forefinger blue, etc.). Since we have more sounds than fingers at our disposal, we are verbal animals. But things might have gone differently: in the course of evolution we could have elaborated, instead of a very flexible phonatory apparatus, a particular skill in emitting, by chemical means, thousands of odours. Even if this were the case, our analysis of semiotic systems would not basically change.

If you look into a traditional handbook on communication, you see that such a process is represented as shown in figure 1.

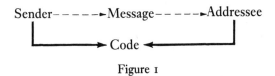

Figure 1

In order for a process of communication to be successful, a common code is the most elementary requirement. But the notion of code is still rather vague, abstract.

If dealing with the Morse code, the problem is rather simple: a code is a list of equivalences by virtue of which a given array of dots and dashes is made to correspond, element to element, to a given series of alphabetic letters. A natural language is a bit more complicated. We begin with a paradigm of phonemes which do not correspond to anything at all, then these phonemes are made to constitute a repertoire of meaningful units, lexemes. Lexemes are, in turn, made to correspond, roughly speaking, to certain cultural entities: let me call them, for the moment, meanings or concepts. Of course, the situation is not this simple – there are syntactical and co-textual rules, not to mention phenomena such as homonymy, polysemy and contextual meanings.

In order to make my discourse manageable for the present purpose, let me be outrageously simple and assume that in order to make communication possible, one needs a signification system. This principle holds for any sign system, from natural language to naval flag signals. A semiotic approach attempts to define the general conditions, for every system of signs, that allow processes of communication on the basis of a given system of signification. It is highly improbable to establish a communication process without an underlying signification system, whereas, theoretically speaking, it is not impossible to invent a signification system without using it in order to communicate – such a procedure, though, would seem a waste of time and energy.

A very schematic signification system can be represented as follows (figure 2):

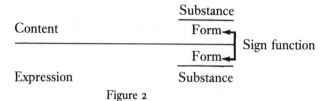

Figure 2

A system of general types of physical entities generates expressions: the general types are the form of the expression; their concrete and individual productions and manifestations are substances. Natural language, for instance, is based upon thirty or forty phonemes, organized by a phonological system establishing abstract types. We recognize these abstract types regardless of the various ways in which they are physically produced. Types, studied by phonology or phonemics, represent the *emic* aspect of language; concrete occurrences, studied by phonetics, represent the *etic* aspect. What is *emic* involves linguistic categories, whereas *etic* involves concrete sounds.

Phonemes are articulated to compose morphemes or – to be less technical – lexical entities or words. Type-phonemes and type-lexical expressions constitute a system of expression form, emically considered. The form of expression is used to convey contents, in the sense in which the sign is traditionally defined as *aliquid quid stat pro aliquo* or, as C. S. Peirce said, something which stands to somebody for something else in some respect or capacity. Units of the expression form are correlated to content units by a sign function.

What is content? Not the external world. Expressions do not *signify* things or states of the world. At most, they are *used* to communicate with somebody about states of the world. If I say that ravens are black and unicorns white, I am undoubtedly uttering a statement about a state of the world. (In the first instance, I am speaking of the world of our experience, in the second I am speaking about a possible world of which unicorns are inhabitants – the fact that they are white is part of the state of affairs of that world.) However, a term like "raven" or "unicorn" does not necessarily refer to a "thing": it refers instead to a cultural unit, to an aspect of our organization of the world.

The content of a signification system depends on our cultural organization of the world into categories. By "world", I do not necessarily mean physical world: Euclid's world is not a physical one, but a *possible universe* organized into points, lines, planes, angles, and so forth. It is a self-sufficient universe in which there are neither ravens nor unicorns, but only cultural units such as the concept of similitude and none such as the concept of love or justice. I can communicate about the Euclidean universe, making true or false assertions (I can, for example, assert truly that the sum of the internal angles of a triangle is equal to 180° and falsely assert that two parallel lines can meet in a given point of that universe), but the units "triangle" and "line" are, in themselves, neither true nor false. They are simply the pertinent or relevant elements of the Euclidean universe. Thus a signification system allows its possible users to isolate and name what is relevant to them from a given point of view.

Let us consider a classic example given by many semantic handbooks: Eskimos apparently have four words to designate four types of snow, while Europeans have only one word and consider relevant only one specific state of $H_2O$ in opposition to other states like ice and water. Of course a skier can recognize different qualities of snow, but he always sees, and speaks of, the same cultural unit, considered from different points of view according to certain practical needs. Eskimos, on the other hand, see, perceive and think of four different things in the same way in which I perceive, and speak of, two different things when, about to skate on a lake, I ascertain whether there is water or ice. This means that a given culture organizes the world according to given practices, or practical purposes, and consequently considers as pertinent different aspects of the world. Pertinence is a function of our practices.

According to a suggestion made by Luis Prieto,[5] if I have on a table before me a large crystal ashtray, a paper cup and a hammer, I can organize these pieces of furniture of my limited world into a twofold system of pertinences. If my practical purpose is to collect some liquid, I then isolate a positive class whose members are the paper cup and the ashtray, and a negative class whose only member is the hammer. If, on the contrary, my purpose is to throw a missile at an enemy, then the heavy ashtray and the hammer will belong to the same class, in opposition to the light and useless paper cup. Practices select pertinences. The practical purpose does not, however, depend on a free decision on my part: material constraints are in play, since I cannot decide that the hammer can act as a container and the paper cup as a missile. Thus practical purposes, decisions about pertinences and material constraints will interact in leading a culture to segment the continuum of its own experience into a given form of the content. To say that a signification system makes communication processes possible means that one can usually communicate only about those cultural units that a given signification system has made pertinent. It is, then, reasonable to suppose now that one can better perceive that which a signification system has isolated and outlined as pertinent.

Let us imagine an archaic community which has only two terms to designate every possible kind of human being: a term equivalent to "man" and a term like "barbarian" or "alien". The members of the community have two cultural units at their disposal: for them, the many-coloured universe of featherless two-legged mammals (among which we might distinguish black and Chinese, Dane and Dutch, European and American, East and West German) is a black and white universe split into "us" and "the others". Let us for the moment disregard the fact that further properties can be associated to these cultural units, namely that "men" are rational and friendly, while "barbarians" are stupid, irrational and dangerous. The problem of the organization of content is, of course, more complicated than this, and from the perspective of

---

[5] Luis Prieto, *Pertinence et pratique* (Paris: Minuit, 1975).

contemporary compositional analysis, what I called cultural units are more finely subdivided into a network of minor semantic properties. Yet even when we limit the domain of semiotic problems to be discussed, our fictional community retains a note of verisimilitude. The ancient Greek subdivision of humankind into Hellenes and "oi barbaroi" is more or less similar to my fictional model, as is the Nazi reorganization of humankind into Aryans and "inferior races".

Imagine a "sci-fi" situation in which our planet is invaded by monsters from two different galaxies. The aliens of Galaxy no. 1 are round, greenish and have three legs and four eyes; the aliens of Galaxy no. 2 are elongated, brown and have six legs and one eye. Certainly we would be able to distinguish and describe both species, but as far as our defence is concerned, the aliens are all "non-human". When the men of the terrestrial outpost first encounter the alien *avant-garde*, they will probably perceive and signal those they meet as simply aliens or monsters. Before we forge new terms to define their differences, we would need scientific interaction, and at some point we would enrich and reformulate our content form. But without such a collective reshaping of our content system, our very ability to recognize aliens will be strongly influenced by our cultural categories.

In the same way, for the members of our fictional ancient society, it will be difficult to ascertain the difference between a Viking and a Phoenician, as well as the difference between their languages: at first they will all be "barbaroi", speaking a non-language. Eventually, at a more advanced stage of inter-racial contact, someone will discover that Vikings are more aggressive and Phoenicians more eager to entertain commercial relationships, thus facilitating the reformulation of the content, the discovery of new pertinences, and the invention of new expressions to designate these pertinences. A sort of underlying discriminative ability will lead to a more refined system of identification and categorization. But in the early stages of contact, categorization will overcome discrimination.

At this point, I must introduce a new concept, the opposition between restricted and elaborated code. In a further stage of inter-racial contacts, our fictional society could split into two castes. Priests and merchants will be able to distinguish Vikings from Phoenicians, probably for different purposes (merchants because they are interested in dealing with the Phoenicians, and priests because they suppose that Vikings can be easily converted). These two castes will reorganize their content form, and coin new expressions to name these different cultural units. But the rest of the citizenry, in order to be employed as warriors, will still share a more restricted code; for them, "men" *versus* "barbarians" will remain the only pertinent opposition. Thus at the same moment in the same society there will be two different levels of social organization; therefore there will be two different ways of thinking, perceiving and speaking, based upon two different systems of signification or, better, upon two different stages of complexity of the same system. As the Italian playwright Dario Fo once said: the worker knows a hundred words, his master a thousand

– that is why he is the master. To know more words means to conceive of a more refined organization of the content. When our instinctive tendency to discriminate produces a more subtle categorization, we acquire a more powerful world view. In the course of this improvement, one changes one's codes.

Of course, such a passage from restricted to elaborated code happens not only infra-culturally but inter-culturally as well, and in space as well as time. Take the rodent universe. In Latin there is only one name to indicate two different kinds of animal that the English call, respectively, "mouse" and "rat" (figure 3).

| Latin | English |
|-------|---------|
| Mus | Mouse<br>· · · · · · · · · · · ·<br>Rat |

Figure 3

In Italian, we have two names, "topo" and "ratto", but many Italians today confuse the terms, using "topo" for both animals. This linguistic simplification deters them from paying attention to the morphological differences between a "little mouse" and a "big one" – an attitude that can produce a number of sanitary and social consequences.

Thus it is possible to say that the Latin term *mus* (and perhaps *topo* today) referred to a sort of homogeneous pertinent portion of the content, while the English names "mouse" and "rat" refer to two different pertinent units (figure 4):

*Latin*:

| E | C |
|---|---|
| mus | x |

*English*:

| E | C |
|---|---|
| mouse | $x_1$ |
| rat | $x_2$ |

Figure 4

The organization of content has to do with the empty cases I have filled up with variables. The important semiotic problem here is how to describe the content of these empty cases, as we are obliged to analyse them through other expressions – in their turn having to be analysed by other expressions, and so on *ad infinitum*. I return to the problem of colour and to the page of Aulus Gellius I mentioned earlier; the problem of the categorization of colours involves such empty cases.

## III

Perception occupies a puzzling position, somewhere midway between semiotic categorization and discrimination based upon mere sensory processes. Jean Petitot, who is working on the material roots of linguistic categorization based upon the mathematical theory of catastrophes, suggested to me that categorization and discrimination do not interact in the universe of sounds as they do in the universe of colours.[6]

We can, it seems, identify sounds with remarkable precision, but once we have perceived the emic difference between, say, *pa* and *ba*, we have difficulty in discriminating between the different etic ways in which *pa* and *ba* can be pronounced. Petitot suggests that this ability to categorize sounds is not culturally but innately grounded, and postulates a brain mechanism called "perceptual categorization" which would explain why verbal language is such a paramount semiotic system. Such an innate ability in sound identification, and such a difficulty in sound discrimination, are crucial for human language.

It is important that we can identify the thirty or forty phonemes which constitute the phonological paradigm of a given language, but it would be embarrassing (linguistically speaking) to be exaggeratedly sensitive to minimal individual differences between the etic ways of uttering the same phoneme. That is why, were I speaking, you could understand your native language even though many of you would be able to guess that I was not nurtured at Oxford. Your ability to discriminate accents has nothing to do with your etic competence – at most it has to do with paralinguistics or tonemics, which are entirely different. The more you were to focus your attention on my sounds, thinking of them as phonemes of your native tongue, the more you would be recognizing them emically, independently of the accent; you would forget the accent and directly catch phonological categories. Of course there are individuals specially trained in discriminating tonemes (that is, the subtle nuances in the etic production of sounds), such as actors or social workers interested in people's national or regional origins. But theirs is an etic training which has nothing to do with the emic training connected with the acquisition of a language as an abstract type.

Our discrimination ability for colours seems to be greater: we can detect the fact that hues gradually change in the continuum of a rainbow, though we have no means to categorize the borderlines between different colours. Nevertheless, when a given subject is exposed to a continuum of sounds ranging from the syllable *ba* to the syllable *pa*, uttered in many etic ways, "k" will be the

---

[6] Jean Petitot, work in progress (personal communication), with references to the work of A. Liberman, N. Studdart-Kennedy, K. Stevens (on perception of the speech code), Eimas, Massaro and Pisoni (on selective adaptation and features detectors), Eimas and Mehler (on innate bases of categorial perception).

"catastrophic point", where so-called feature detectors in the human brain isolate the threshold between two emic categories:

k
ba...............................pa

Figure 5

Our innate capacity for perceptual categorization enables a subject to perceive a clear opposition between the two emic entities, *ba* and *pa*, and disregard etic discrimination. But if the same subject is intensively exposed to the stimulus *ba*, the catastrophe point will slip to the left when he is once again intensively exposed to the full range of sounds represented in figure 5. This phenomenon is called "selective adaptation": the subject will acquire a quite severe notion of the emic type *ba* (and, probably, a snobbish sensitivity to accents).

The opposite happens with colours. Let us consider two colours, *a* and *b*, which are mutually adjacent in the spectrum. If the stimulus *a* is repeated, the catastrophe point will slip to the right rather than to the left. This means that the more a subject becomes acquainted with a stimulus, the more eager he will be to assign similar stimuli to the category to which he has assigned the original stimulus. Categorial training produces categorization ability for both sounds and colours; but sound categories become more restricted, while colour categories become more tolerant, and sensitivity in discrimination decreases.

Of course a painter can be trained more in etic discrimination than in emic categorization, but in the experiments above, the reaction of the subject is determined by the fact that he is not freely concerned with sense data, but is influenced by the aims of the laboratory experiment. He is encouraged to isolate categorial entities and reacts with categories already defined by language, even though he speaks only to himself.

These experiences have nothing to do with what I previously said about sign functions: to perceive phonemes or colours has to do with the emic analysis of expressions, not with the correlation between expressions and contents. But I smell in these experiences the presence of a more complicated semiotic question.

# IV

It has been said that colour discrimination, under laboratory conditions, is probably the same for all peoples no matter what language they speak, though psychologists also suggest that there is not only an ontogenetic but also a phylogenetic increase in discriminatory competence. The Optical Society of America classifies a range of between 7.5 and 10 million colours which can theoretically be discriminated.

A trained artist can discriminate and name a great many hues, which the pigment industry supplies and indicates with numbers, to indicate an immense variety of colours easily discriminated in the industry. But the Farnsworth-

Munsell test, which includes 100 hues, demonstrates that the average discrimination rate is highly unsatisfactory. Not only do the majority of subjects have no linguistic means with which to categorize these 100 hues, but approximately 68 per cent of the population (excluding colour defectives) make a total error score of between 20 and 100 on the first test, which involves rearranging these hues on a continuous gradation scale. Cases of superior discrimination (only 16 per cent) scored from zero to 16. The largest collection of English colour names runs to over 3000 entries (Maerz and Paul),[7] but only eight of these commonly occur (Thorndike and Lorge).[8]

Thus average chromatic competence is better represented by the seven colours of the rainbow, with their corresponding wavelengths in millimicrons (figure 6):

|  | Average chromatic competence |
|---|---|
| ⌈ 800–650 | Red |
| ⌊ 640–590 | Orange |
| ⌈ 580–550 | Yellow |
| ⌈ 540–490 | Green |
| ⌈ 480–460 | Blue |
| 450–440 | Indigo |
| ⌊ 430–390 | Violet |

Figure 6

Square brackets indicate the thresholds where, according to modern experiments, there are clear jumps in discrimination. This segmentation does seem to correspond to our common experience, though it was not the experience of Latin speakers, if indeed it is true that they did not clearly distinguish between green and blue. It seems that Russian speakers segment the range of wavelengths we call "blue" into different portions, *goluboj* and *sinij*. Hindus consider red and orange a unified pertinent unit. And against the 3000 hues that, according to David Katz,[9] the Maori of New Zealand recognize and name by 3000 different terms, there are, according to Conklin, the Hanunóo of the Philippines, with a peculiar opposition between a public restricted code and more or less individual, elaborated ones:

Color distinctions in Hanunóo are made at two levels of contrast. The first, higher, more general level consists of an all-inclusive coordinate,

[7] A. Maerz and R. Paul, *A Dictionary of Color* (New York: Crowell, 1953).
[8] E. L. Thorndike and I. Lorge, *The Teacher's Word Book of 30,000 Words* (New York: Columbia University Press, 1962).
[9] David and Rose Katz, *Handbuch der Psychologie* (Basel: Schwabe, 1960) vol. 2.

four-way classification which lies at the core of the color system. The four categories are mutually exclusive in contrastive contexts, but may overlap slightly in absolute (i.e., spectrally) or in other measureable terms. The second level, including several sublevels, consists of hundreds of specific color categories, many of which overlap and interdigitate. Terminologically, there is "unanimous agreement" (Lenneberg, 1953, p. 469) on the designations for the four Level I categories, but considerable lack of unanimity – with a few explainable exceptions – in the use of terms of Level II.[10]

Let us disregard Level II, which seems a case of many elaborated codes differing from males to females and even from individual to individual. Let us consider the various formats of Level II as idiolectal and quasi-professional codes.

The three-dimensional color solid is divided by this Level I categorization into four unequal parts; the largest is *mabi:ru*, the smallest *malatuy* [see figure 7]. While boundaries separating these categories cannot be set in absolute terms, the focal points (differing slightly in size, themselves) within the four sections, can be limited more or less to black, white, orange-red, and leaf-green respectively. In general terms, *mabi:ru* includes the range usually covered in English by black, violet, indigo, blue, dark green, gray, and deep shades of other colors and mixtures; *malagti*, white and very light tints of other colors and mixtures; *marara*, maroon, red, orange, yellow, and mixtures in which these qualities are seen to predominate; *malatuy*, light green and mixtures of green, yellow, and light brown. All color terms can be reduced to one of these four, but none of the four is reducible. This does not mean that other color terms are synonyms, but that they designate color categories of greater specification within four recognized color realms.[11]

Hanunóo segmentation follows our basic English paradigm only to a limited extent, since it involves black, white and grey in different ways. What is important for our present study is that the pertinentization of the spectrum depends on symbolic, i.e. cultural principles. Note that these cultural pertinentizations are produced because of practical purposes, according to the material needs of the Hanunóo community.

The basis of this Level I classification appears to have certain correlates beyond what is usually considered the range of chromatic differentiation, and which are associated with linguistic phenomena in the external environment.

First, there is the opposition between light and dark, obvious in the contrast of ranges of meaning of *lagti* and *biru*. Second, there is an

[10] Harold C. Conklin, "Hanunóo Color Categories", *Southwestern Journal of Anthropology*, vol. II (1955) pp. 339–44; see p. 341.
[11] Ibid., pp. 341–2.

opposition between dryness or desiccation and wetness or freshness (succulence) in visible components of the natural environment which are reflected in the terms *rara* and *latuy* respectively. This distinction is of particular significance in terms of plant life. Almost all living plant types possess some fresh, succulent and often "greenish" parts. To eat any kind of raw, uncooked food, particularly fresh fruit or vegetables, is known as *sag-laty-un* (*latuy*). A shiny, wet, brown-colored section of newly cut bamboo is *malatuy* not *marara*. Dried-out or matured plant material such as certain kinds of yellowed bamboo or hardened kernels of mature or parched corn are *marara*. To become desiccated, to lose all moisture, is known as *mamara* < *para* "desiccation." A third opposition, dividing the two already suggested, is that of deep, unfading, indelible, and hence often more desired material as against pale, weak, faded, bleached, or "colorless" substance, a distinction contrasting *mabi:ru* and *marara* with *malagti* and *malatuy*.[12]

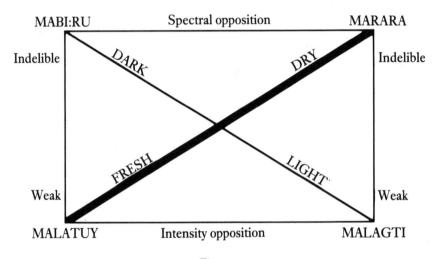

Figure 7

We have then a system of cultural units – lightness, darkness, wetness, dryness – which are expressed by four fundamental colours; these colours are, in turn, four cultural units expressed by four linguistic terms. This double organization of the content depends, as does any organization of this kind, on a system of disjunctions: it represents a structure. Just as a "mouse", within a semantic space concerning rodents, is everything which is not a "rat", and vice versa, so the pertinent content space of *malatuy* is determined by its northern borderline beyond which there is *marara*, and its southern borderline, below which there is *mabi:ru*.

Geopolitically speaking, Holland is a negative concept: it is the class of all

---

[12] Ibid., p. 342.

points adjacent to, but not, Germany, Belgium or the North Sea. The same principle holds for all other geopolitical expressions such as Germany or Italy or the Soviet Union. In any system, whether geopolitical or chromatic or lexical, units are defined not in themselves but in terms of opposition and position in relation to other units. There can be no units without a system. The different ways in which cultures make the continuum of colours pertinent, thereby categorizing and identifying hues or chromatic units, correspond to different content systems. This semiotic phenomenon is not independent of perception and discrimination ability; it interacts with these phenomena and frequently overwhelms them.

Consider again our diagram of colours (figure 8): it takes into account not only differences in the organization of content among different contemporary cultures, but also depicts different levels of complexity within a given culture as well as differences through the ages. It represents a reduced model of a tri-dimensional system of differences.

At this point we can probably tackle Aulus Gellius' puzzle. Rome, in the second century A.D., was a very crowded crossroads of many cultures. The Empire controlled Europe from Spain to the Rhine, from England to North Africa and the Middle East. All these cultures, with their own chromatic sensitivities, were present in the Roman crucible. Diachronically speaking, Aulus Gellius was trying to put together the codes of at least two centuries of Latin literature and, synchronically speaking, the codes of different non-Latin cultures. Gellius must have been considering diverse and possibly contrasting cultural segmentations of the chromatic field. This would explain the contradictions in his analysis and the chromatic uneasiness felt by the modern reader. His colour-show is not a coherent one: we seem to be watching a flickering TV screen, with something wrong in the electronic circuits, where tints mix up and the same face shifts, in the space of a few seconds, from yellow to orange or green. Determined by his cultural information, Gellius cannot trust to his personal perceptions, if any, and appears eager to see gold as red as fire, and saffron as yellow as the greenish shade of a blue horse.

We do not know and we shall never know how Gellius really perceived his *Umwelt*; unfortunately, our only evidence of what he saw and thought is what he said. I suspect that he was prisoner of his cultural mish-mash.

Yet it also seems to me (but obviously this hypothesis should be tested on more texts) that Latin poets were less sensitive to clear-cut spectral oppositions or gradations, and more sensitive to slight mixtures of spectrally distant hues. In other words, they were not interested in pigments but in perceptual effects due to the combined action of light, surfaces, the nature and purposes of objects. Thus a sword can be *fulva* as jasper because the poet sees the red of the blood it may spill. That is why such descriptions remind us more of certain paintings of Franz Marc or of the early Kandinsky than of a scientific chromatic polyhedron. As a decadent man of culture, Gellius tends to interpret poetic creativity and invention as a socially accepted code and is not interested in the relationships which colours had with other content oppositions in different cultural systems. It would be interesting to transform a given Latin chromatic system, that of

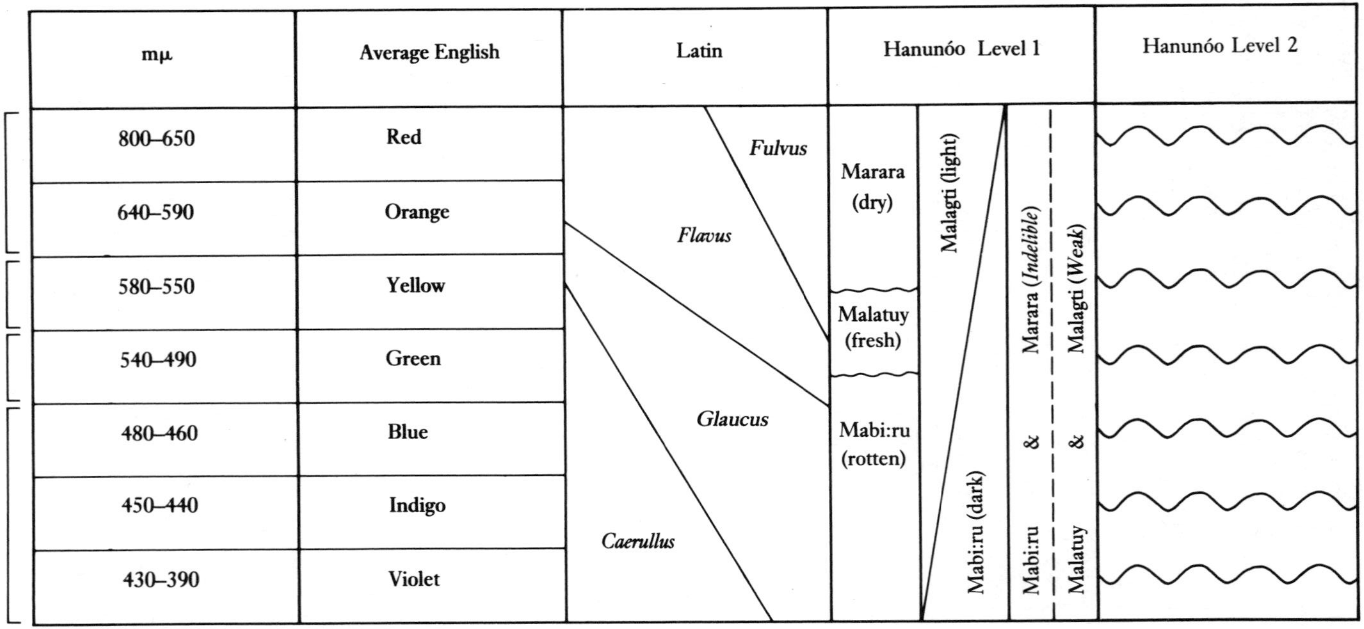

| mµ | Average English | Latin | Hanunóo Level 1 | Hanunóo Level 2 |
|---|---|---|---|---|
| 800–650 | Red | *Fulvus* | Marara (dry) | |
| 640–590 | Orange | *Flavus* | | |
| 580–550 | Yellow | | Malatuy (fresh) | |
| 540–490 | Green | *Glaucus* | Mabi:ru (rotten) | |
| 480–460 | Blue | | | |
| 450–440 | Indigo | *Caerullus* | | |
| 430–390 | Violet | | | |

Malagti (light) — Mabi:ru (dark)

Mabi:ru & Marara (*Indelible*)

Malatuy & Malagti (*Weak*)

Figure 8

Virgil for example, into a structure more or less like the one I proposed for the Hanunóo system, where the names of hues must be associated to opposition between dark and light (also in psychological and moral sense), euphoric and dysphoric, excitation and calm, and so on. The names of colours, taken in themselves, have no precise chromatic content: they must be viewed within the general context of many interacting semiotic systems.


## V


Are we, in any sense, freer than Gellius from the armour of our culture? We are animals who can discriminate colours, but we are, above all, cultural animals.

Human societies do not only speak of colours, but also with colours. We frequently use colours as semiotic devices: we communicate with flags, traffic lights, road signs, various kinds of emblems.

Now a socio-semiotic study of national flags[13] remarks that national flags make use of only seven colours: red, blue, green, yellow, orange, black and white. For physical reasons, the proportion of these colours is as follows:

| Colour combinations | Per cent |
| --- | --- |
| Red/white/blue | 16.8 |
| Red/white | 9.5 |
| Red/yellow/green | 7.3 |
| Red/white/green | 6.6 |
| Red/white/green/black | 6.6 |
| Blue/white | 6.0 |
| Red/yellow/blue | 5.8 |
| | 58.6 |

Orange, hardly distinguishable from red, is rarely used. What counts in the perception of a flag is categorization, not discrimination. If we were to look up the flags of the Scandinavian countries, we would realize that the blue of the Swedish and Finnish flags (which is light) is different from the blue of the Icelandic and Norwegian ones (which is dark). Now look at Sweden's yellow cross on a light blue field – there is not a flag in the world with a yellow cross on a *dark blue* background, and for good reason. Everyone would recognize such a flag as the symbol for Sweden. (And, thinking of Norway's dark blue cross on a red field, a flag with a light blue cross on red would similarly be recognized as Norway's symbol.) In national flags, categorization overwhelms discrimination.

[13] Sasha R. Weitman, "National Flags", *Semiotica*, vol. 8, no. 4 (1973) pp. 328–67.

This simplification exists not only for reasons of easier perception: such "easier perception" is supported by a previous cultural coding by virtue of which certain colours form a clear-cut system of oppositional units which are, in turn, clearly correlated with another system concerning values or abstract ideas.

In the study on national flags I have been referring to, it is interesting to check the symbolic values assigned by different countries to the same colour. Red, for example, symbolizes bravery, blood and courage in many countries (Afghanistan, Austria, Italy, Bulgaria, Burundi, Chile, Ecuador, etc.), but it also represents animals in Bolivia, faith in Ethiopia, soil in Dahomey. White, almost universally, stands for peace, hope and purity, but in Congo Kinshasha, hope is represented by blue which, for the majority of countries, stands for sky, sea and rivers. The colours of national flags are not colours: physical pigments; they are expressions correlated to cultural units, and as such are strongly categorized.

But the real problem is not – or not only – that our discrimination ability is limited to few colours. It is that the system of basic values to be expressed by colours is a limited one. The nature of these values (hope, peace, and so on) is irrelevant: what counts is the structural architecture of their basic oppositions, which must be clear.

One should remark that a greater variety of colours exists, or existed, in heraldry. But heraldry represents a case of an elaborated code for a cultivated minority able to discriminate more colours and associate more refined names to different hues, as well as memorize numerous aristocratic stocks.

The same strong categorization is at work in traffic lights and road signals. A traffic light can work and transmit its orders irrespective of the shade of green, red or yellow that, in terms of wavelengths, it emits. One would certainly stop at a traffic light with an orange light on, and continue moving even though the green light were a shade of blue. (Note that in the traffic light code, the signification of colours is reinforced by the position of the lights, which reduces the relevance of hues – and helps the colour-blind.) In any case, here too, in traffic regulation, people can only recognize a limited system of obligations. I do not think it is possible to found a system of communication on a subtle discrimination between colours too close to each other in the spectrum. This may seem strange since, as I have said, we potentially have a great capacity for discrimination, and with ten million colours it would be interesting to compose a language more rich and powerful than the verbal one, based as it is upon no more than forty phonemes. But the phonemes of verbal language are, in fact, a reasonable reduction of the great variety of possible sounds that our phonatory apparatus can produce. The seven colours of flags and signals are probably the most a human culture can recognize – by a general agreement as to categorizable expressive entities. This agreement has come about, probably, because verbal language has shaped our average sensitivity according to the macroscopic segmentation represented by the seven colours of the rainbow which is a Western conventional way of segmentation. The agreement has also come about because average verbal language, with its polysemy, works better for common people when many names stand synonymously for few basic concepts, rather than the opposite, when few names stand homonymously for thousands of concepts.

The fact that a painter (think of Paul Klee) can recognize and name more colours, the fact that verbal language itself is able not only to designate hundreds of nuances, but also describe unheard-of tints by examples, periphrases and poetic ingenuity – all this represents a series of cases of elaborated codes. It is common to every society to have members able to escape the determination of the rules, to propose new rules, to behave beyond the rules.

In everyday life, our reactivity to colour demonstrates a sort of inner and profound solidarity between semiotic systems. Just as language is determined by the way in which society sets up systems of values, things and ideas, so our chromatic perception is determined by language. You may look up your flags again: suppose there is a football match between Italy and Holland. One will distinguish the Dutch flag from the Italian one, even though the red of either of them, or of both, were looking orange. If, on the contrary, the match were between Italy and Ireland, the Italian flag would be characterized by a dark red, since white, green and orange are the Irish colours.

If one wants to oppose, for shorthand purposes, a Mondrian to a Kandinsky, Mondrian would be recognizable even though its reds were more or less orange, but in the course of an aesthetic discourse on Mondrian, and in judging the correctness of an art book's reproduction, one should spend much careful analysis in discriminating the better and more faithful colour among Mondrian reproductions.

Thus the artistic activity, be it the poetry of Virgil or the research on pigments by Mondrian, works against social codes and collective categorization, in order to produce a more refined social consciousness of our cultural way of defining contents.

If people are eager to fight for a red, white and blue flag, then people must be ready to die even though its red, due to the action of atmospheric factors, has become pinkish. Only artists are ready to spend their lives imagining (to quote James Joyce) "an opening flower breaking in full crimson and unfolding and fading to palest rose, leaf by leaf and wave of light by wave of light, flooding all the heavens with its soft flushes, every flush deeper than the other".

# UMBERTO ECO

# Producing Signs

At the opening of the First International Congress of Semiotics in 1974 in Milan, Roman Jakobson, speaking in French, outlined the thousand-year process by which semiotics, as a growing awareness of the centrality of the Sign in human affairs, elaborated its definition as a science. Semiotics, as Jakobson told us, is the science concerned with that basic *relation de renvoi* or relation of sending or referring back, where *aliquid stat pro aliquo* or, in C. S. Peirce's terms, something stands to somebody for something else in some respect or capacity.

But when semiotics had finally defined its own object, at that moment it launched an impressive series of critiques of the very notion of sign. This attempt to destroy its *raison d'être* has been interpreted as a suicidal syndrome on the part of a neurotic discipline too weak to trust itself and therefore condemned to die because of a lack both of self-identity and self-confidence. On the contrary, we have been witnessing a normal growth process. Even for a new-born discipline, maturity is everything, but the maturity test for a discipline is its capability of submitting to systematic doubt the definition of its field and of its methods.

Until most recently, semiotics was so sure of being concerned with the theoretic entity called "sign" that, since its prehistoric period, it has elaborated typologies of signs. From the first opposition between *nomos* and *physis* to the celebrated tricotomies of Peirce, from the subtle subdivision of Morris' *Foundations* to the most recent taxonomies of T. A. Sebeok, the entire history of the discipline is traversed by a classificatory compulsion to generate rhizomorphic trees (if the authors of the *Anti-Oedipus* will allow me to use this *contradictio in adjecto*).

This procedure has been of enormous importance because it permitted semiotics to outline a complex field of phenomena and to extend its province far beyond the realm of linguistics and the arbitrary paradigm modelled on the double articulation of verbal utterances. Semiotics has thus recognized as semiotic objects all cases in which, regardless of the continuum shaped, the channel used and the mode of articulation, certain physical objects are used to stand for something else.

But at the same time, we know that semioticians have widely discussed the tenability of the very notion of sign. On one side of the discussion, the awareness of the multiplicity of codes and sub-codes has made clear that so-called signs are transitory couplings of expressive and content units that can become differently coupled and correlated in different systems or, within the same system, in different contexts. On the other side, textual theorists have insisted on the fact that signification takes place through contextual and discursive strategies, through phenomena of topicalization, presupposition and other pragmatic paraphernalia. When semiotics approaches the problem of a pragmatic typology of discourse strategies, can it still pay attention to the traditional typologies of signs?

The whole of Peirce's theory seems to stress the enormous importance of discriminating among types of signs. It seems, or it seemed until recently, impossible to relinquish the triad of index, icon and symbol, and it would indeed be silly to neglect the differences existing between a picture and a word, a diagram and a pointing finger, a proper name and a cloud announcing a storm. But the most skilled of Peirce's interpreters know very well that never, in Peirce, does one meet a "real" icon, a "real" index or a "real" symbol, but rather the result of a complex intertwining of processes of iconism, symbolization and indexicalization.

The items of Peirce's celebrated trichotomy are not *types of signs* but rather *semiotic categories* by means of which one can describe more complex strategies of signification. If this were not so, it would be impossible to resolve the apparent contradictions which surface in various passages of Peirce's work, where Peirce seems to deny interpretants to icons and indices, and reserve only for the symbols the capacity to release an interpretative process. If this were true, then icons and indices would not be types of signs, since it is essential to a sign that it stimulate its own interpretations. Yet in other passages it seems that icons do have a sign-character since, for example, we can form a proposition by combining two icons (where an icon of a Chinese and one of a woman can be combined to form a proposition – "There is a Chinese woman" – and therefore an interpretable general term). Moreover in another passage Peirce clearly states that an icon "produces an interpretant idea".

These problems are clarified, however, when one understands that the term "icon" is often not used to indicate an abstract category, an instance of Firstness, but rather a *hypoicon*, that is an *iconic representamen*. In other words, Peirce means that a diagram may be called an icon in so far as an iconic mode is dominant, but in fact is a *hypoicon*. Only as a *hypoicon* is it semiotically understandable for it is constructed by employing symbolic and indexical modalities as well as iconic. Icons, symbols and indices are therefore not types of signs but types of semiotic functioning: signs, if any, are the result of just such global interaction of these modalities. Otherwise the sixty-six types of signs projected by Peirce (and the fifty thousand more he promised to Lady Welby) would be of no use. In fact, the promised typology dealt with signs, while the famous trichotomy dealt with abstract modalities of signification.

Why did Peirce not succeed in listing even the sixty-six types he promised, stopping instead after the first ten attempts? In his failure, we may see both the weakness of a project for an exhaustive typology of signs and the real purport of Peirce's suggestion.

The notion of *aliquid* which *stat pro aliquo*, or of something standing for something else, accurately defines the object of a semiotic enquiry – that is what Jakobson has called a *relation de renvoi*, or relation of sending back. But as far as the object of semiotics is concerned:

> *Aliquid stat pro aliquo*:
> That is all
> Ye know on earth, and all ye need to know.

Nobody has said that this correlation necessarily and exclusively constitutes what is commonly called a sign. Nobody has ever said that a sign is necessarily something homologous to a word. In fact, verbal language is perhaps the only semiotic system in which one gets the impression that to a single expression unit corresponds a single content unit. So it seems but, as with all other semiotic systems, an expression (a word) corresponds to a changing network of semantic components, content units. Any single expression unit refers back to a more complex portion of verbal discourse. A traffic signal with an arrow rarely means "here" or "there": it usually means "you are commanded to turn this way or that". It has often been observed that the image of a dog does not mean "dog", but rather "there is a black dog standing", and so forth. This kind of correlation between an expression and a content, called a sign function by many semioticians, can be either a unit-to-cluster or a cluster-to-cluster correlation, a coded or an uncoded correspondence. A verbal text is a sign function; a ready-made syntagm is a sign function; the Sistine Chapel is a sign function. Peirce suggested that even a book may be viewed as a sign – it all depends on the level at which we decide to make our analysis pertinent. The notion of sign is untenable only when confused with notions of elementary units and fixed correlations, for there are signs which result from the correlation of imprecise expressive textures and which convey vast unanalysable portions of content. There are expressive devices which convey different contents according to different contexts.

Peirce's final typology was an impossible dream. Once provided with a few modes of producing semiotic correlations, one can compose a great variety of signs. A complete typology is in principle impossible except for the purposes of *ad hoc* classification within the context of a precise descriptive project.

One may, for example, interpret a map of the London Underground as an iconic device referring back to the "real" layout of tracks in the city. But you can also look at it as the result of a symbolic convention which translates the uneven, fragmented route of the tracks into a series of straight unidimensional lines, and the complex interrelation of switch points, connections and stations into plain coloured circles. The straight lines represent not only the static intersection of the real tracks but also suggest, as vectors, the directions which trains must take. This map can be used for yet other signifying purposes; you could, for instance, interpret the lines and circles as an abstract, absolutely self-focusing construction – a map for map's sake. Or you could read the map as a reminder of personal experience: certain privileged routes would assume symbolic value, playing the role of both proper names and indices. The line connecting Piccadilly Circus to Victoria Station would then become the "sign" of my own personal stay or of a character in my own idiosyncratic novel. . . .

One could continue to play this sort of semiotic game, and the map would continue to change, assuming different roles as a sign function though always realizing its nature of something standing for something else by virtue of ever different modalities of sign production. Thus semiotics relinquishes the Utopia of an exhaustive list of *modi significandi* but must, in order to be a descriptive and predictive discipline, elaborate a typology of modes of production of sign functions. I have, in *A Theory of Semiotics*, attempted to outline such a typology. Here, I summarize its basic elements.

My classification of modes of sign production takes into account four parameters:

1 the physical labour needed to produce expressions, ranging from the mere *recognition* of existing phenomena through their *ostension* to the production of *replicas* and the effort to *invent* new expressions;
2 the relation between the abstract *type* of expression and its *tokens*;
3 the type of *continuum* or material substance to be shaped in order to produce physically an expression; and
4 the *mode and complexity of the articulation*, ranging from semiotic systems in which there are precise combinational units to those in which there are imprecise *texts* whose compositional units have not yet been fully analysed.

For simplicity's sake, let us consider only the first two parameters. As regards physical labour, we must consider:

(a) *Recognition*. Recognition occurs when a given object or event, produced either by nature or by human action, is correlated to a given content by a human interpreter who did not himself work to produce the object or event. Among types of recognition we find *imprints*, such as an animal's footprints, *symptoms*, such as traces of an internal illness left upon human skin, and *clues*, such as recognizable objects left at the scene of a murder.

(b) *Ostension*. Ostension occurs when a pre-existing object is selected and shown as the representative of the class to which it belongs. I can show an object as an *example* of a class (a cigarette in order to mean "cigarettes") or a part of an object or of a gesture as a *sample* of a more complex whole (an empty pack of cigarettes in order to mean "a [full] pack of cigarettes"). Ostension also includes *fictive samples*, as when one imitates the act of fencing without a foil (nevertheless accomplishing a part of the intended act) in order to say "I am (or one is) fencing", or more generally, "duel".

(c) *Replicas*. When a human being produces a token instance of a given abstract type, he is producing a replica. Words, for example, belong to a very restricted category of replicas, that of *combinational units*, which satisfy the requirements of the double articulation. The King of a deck of cards is a *stylization*, produced from a universal type which requires certain indispensable features but allows for a wide range of variants. In linguistics ready-made syntagms are stylizations, in architecture, an arch. *Pseudo-combinational units* are also replicas: like a Mondrian painting or the notes of a musical score, they are units combined according to certain rules, but we are uncertain whether their contents are correlated to a precise meaning. They may be inserted into a semiotic correlation, though they do not presuppose such a significant destination.

Expressions which the addressee does not perceive as semiotic constructs and reacts to with a merely physical response – though the sender uses them as semiotic devices whose effect he foresees, conventionally associating it to the stimulus – are called *programmed stimuli*. Finally, there are *vectors*. Vectors are features conveying a content which has the same temporal or spatial characteristics as the expression. For example, an arrow going from left to right which conveys the content "towards the right", or the temporal succession of the phrase "John beats Paul" may be called vectors. In the latter example, John is vectorially the performer and Paul the passive receiver of the action; by reversing the vectorial order, the content would also be reverse.

(d) *Invention. Congruences, projections* and *graphs* are examples of invention. In order to explain more clearly this last category of sign production, I must return to the type-token ratio.

When producing an expression, one usually physically produces a token according to a pre-established type. This relation of type to token is a *ratio facilis*. Verbal language is an example: German provides an abstract type of the word /Hund/, made of four phonemes to be syntagmatically linked in a precise way, and even an electronic oscillography, duly instructed, can produce a token utterance. The same thing happens, a phoneme less, with /und/. In these cases, the expression is correlated to its content by a cultural convention. This does not mean that *ratio facilis* governs only so-called arbitrary signs – symptoms, though motivated by a specific internal alteration of the body, are not iconically similar to the alteration they indicate. They can be artificially produced, and therefore falsified, according to an expression type registered in texts of medical symptomatology. They are both motivated and ruled by *ratio facilis*. A traffic signal, like an arrow pointing to the right, poses a different problem. It is arbitrarily correlated to the injunction "turn", but it is correlated by a motivation to the indication "to the right". This content may be applied to different referential or indexical situations. The arrow does not refer back to a given actual spatial position, but rather to an abstract portion of the semantic content. But this portion of the content, realized by the opposition between left and right, is nevertheless *space-sensitive*. Therefore the relationship between the arrow and its corresponding command is governed by *ratio difficilis*: the type of the expression is identical to the type of the content.

Note that my classification of modes of production is not a classification of types of signs. The arrow can be considered a sign, but as such it is the result of different modes of sign production. In so far as it pre-exists as a replicable model in the storehouse of traffic signals, it is a *combinational unit* governed by *ratio facilis*; since it can be reproduced in various ways as long as certain basic features are respected (size, colour, even form, are to a large extent irrelevant), it is a *stylization*; its efficacy depends upon its *vectorial* quality, governed by *ratio difficilis*.

The relation of correlation in *ratio difficilis* is *not* the relation described by naïve theories of iconism. It is, instead, a relation of the form of the expression to the spatial organization (or form) of a given content. Consider the case of a compass. The form of the expression does not imitate the structure of the terrestrial globe and its typical orientation. In order to represent our planet, our civilization has made pertinent only a few elements; its spheric structure has been reduced to a two-dimensional diagram in which only certain points are retained. The orientation of cardinal points is absolutely conventional: nothing obliges us to believe that North is up and South is down. In fact, in many medieval maps Africa is up and Europe is down, South is left and North is right. The image of the compass and its representation of the four winds is only one among the possible ways of organizing that portion of astronomical content. The *token* realization of a compass depends upon a previous model and is therefore ruled by *ratio facilis*. But the *type* of the compass is ruled by *ratio difficilis* because the expression possesses the same relations as the content to be expressed: if North is up, then South must be down and East right. There can be no arbitrary changes in the mutual orientation of the cardinal points. Thus the correlation between expression and content is partially ruled by projective conventions, or conventions in mapping (where "mapping" suggests motivation and "convention" arbitrariness). But "conventional" does not necessarily mean "arbitrary", and "motivated" does not exclude "cultural agreement". Thus convention relies upon a certain motivation, a motivation which requires the expression to embody the same form as the content *in some respect or capacity*.

Now let us return to the notion of invention, our last mode of sign production. Invention concerns those cases in which the expression can be neither elaborated according to an expression type (for it does not yet exist) nor according to a content type (as with the compass), because no type has yet been culturally defined. Let us consider an archaeological example: the invention of the sundial. The inventor projected (in the geometrical sense) data from concrete experience into an expressive diagram, thereby elaborating an expression and a content type at the same time. By *projection* I mean a set of culturized operations conceived in order to establish not only a vague relationship of resemblance but rather a precise relation of geometric similitude based on proportional rules. Only pertinent features are selected, as in the case, for instance, of the relation of similitude between triangles where the length of the angles and the proportion between sides are made pertinent, irrespective of the size of the triangles.

Invention ranges from a maximum of pertinent points in *congruence*, for example a death mask, through types of projection to the minimum of pertinent points as in *graphs*. Cases of invention are those in which the sign function is proposed and established, as is the code governing its correlation, for the first time. Imprints – think of a cat's paw – are not inventions because, even though ruled by *ratio difficilis*, the expression exists already, both in terms of recognition and of the possibility of producing a replica, and because it is culturally defined. (Everybody knows how to produce a cat's paw imprint, even though it has the same formal properties as the class of real paws.)

How, then, can this typology be applied to different semiotic phenomena? Let me consider two test cases: architectural objects and verbal phrases.

The semiotics of architecture has successfully established that architectural objects convey signification concerning both their function and their connotative value. But until now they have erroneously been considered signs, when in fact they are texts. A staircase, for example, is a stylization, an item of a very flexible architectural typology, as well as a combination of replicable units and a case of vectorialization, many of whose elements are pseudo-combinational units. A chair is a stylization made by an aggregation of pseudo-combinational units. In so far as it is reproduces the abstract posture of a seated body, it was originally a case of inventive projection which, through further catachresis, has become an imprint, an imprint of an abstract and very general content model. A number of pertinent features were selected so that it reproduces the posture of a seated body regardless of sex, age, size, colour and religion.

Verbal expressions can also be analysed in this way. Let us consider the following utterance in which a French speaker parodies an American accent: /Ah ah! Quand vous dites, 'Je vais au cabaréi', ça va sans dire que vous êtes américain!/ [Aha! When you say, 'I'm going to the *cabaréi*', it goes without saying that you are American!].

Each word is a combinational unit ruled by *ratio facilis*. But to get the general sense of the phrase, the sum of the units (along with their correlated contents) is not enough – many other modes of production are at work and you hear them:

*Ah ah*: this utterance is a *symptom*; the addressee detects that the speaker is happy or excited about telling what follows. It is also a *programmed stimulus*, aimed at attracting the addressee's attention. If the laugh is not spontaneous but emitted for linguistic reasons, that is with a phatic function, then it is also an example. If explicitly phatic, it is a fictive sample and a stylization. In any case, since it does not belong to the French lexicon, and is what in paralinguistics is called a "vocalization", it is a pseudo-combinational unit. The *ratio* is *facilis*.

*Quand vous dites . . . [alors] ça va sans dire que . . .*: logically speaking, this is an "if . . . then" clause expressing a causal dependence and a temporal succession. This double content relationship is grammatically expressed by a vectorialization. The two parts of the causal implication could be reversed in the surface representation, but they remain in the right order in the deep structure (where vectors are made metalinguistically clear by means of, for example, a tree structure). Even the verb phrase /vous dites/ works vectorially since if it were reversed (/dites vous/) the assertive modality would become an imperative one. These relations of vectoriality are governed by *ratio difficilis* because they mirror a consequentiality established by the content.

*"Je vais au cabaréi"*: this is a clear instance of ostension because it is a quote. In so far as it is the reproduction of someone else's utterance, it is a fictive sample. But it is produced and ostended as a symptom of ethnic origin. Tonemes are produced by vocal vectors, that is by raising and lowering the voice's pitch. As an attempt to reproduce a given national accent, the expression aims at being an imprint; but since a repertoire of standard caricatured accents already exists, the *ratio is facilis*. If, however, the accent attempted to reproduce a particular individual's way of speaking, then we would be dealing with a more or less successful case of invention. Such an invention would privilege only certain features of the caricatured accent (necessarily disregarding the timbre of voice) and thus would at most be a case of projection. In this case, the *ratio* is *difficilis*.

*Ça va sans dire*: as a ready-made syntagm, this is a blatant case of verbal stylization, that is, a rhetorical device.

The analysis could go on. I wanted only to show that in order to set up this complex sign function, it was necessary to use various modes of sign production related to different systems of operative convention, more or less formalized, weaker or stronger, displaying different types of correlation between expression and content. There is sometimes a unit-to-unit coupling; other times a cluster-to-cluster or a unit-to-cluster correlation. Within the contextural pressure created by different modes of production, the mocking phonetic monstrosity /cabaréi/ becomes a sign connoting "American-ness", only because a strategy of ostension has made it a significant feature. Otherwise it would have remained a mere ungrammaticality, a case of absolutely irrelevant mispronunciation.

Only through a typology of this sort can semiotics free itself from the blackmail of the linguistic model. The models listed in the above typology are neither linguistic nor purely extra-linguistic; they are pre-linguistic, pre-gestural, pre-visual. They are *autonomous* semiotic categories which can explain with equal force both linguistic and non-linguistic communicative procedures.

ROMAN JAKOBSON

# Dear Claude, Cher Maître

I like to recall the memory of our first meeting. The École Libre des Hautes Études was being set up in New York City. It was the first time I took part in one of the planning meetings for our Faculty of Letters. I knew almost none of my new colleagues, but I saw a young man – he was just half the age he is now – stand up and ask the dean a question that was, as I recall, on some minor matter, yet he framed it in such a cogent and unique way that I found myself a few moments later asking one of my neighbours, "What a sharp mind the man has – who is he?" Oddly enough, at the time a strangely similar experience I had had almost thirty years before at the Moscow Ethnological Society had slipped my mind; then, after having heard a young man raise a seemingly irrelevant question in the course of the discussion, I had also spontaneously sensed the presence of a real intellect and had felt impelled to ask his name. In both instances, the people I asked were less impressed than I, and I am now pleased to be able to report that, in both instances, their scepticism proved groundless. In 1914, the man had been Nikolaj Sergeevič Trubetzkoy, the great linguist of the interwar period, and in 1942 the man was Claude Lévi-Strauss, the great anthropologist of the years after the Second World War.

Now, what do the two episodes have in common? What is there about those seemingly unimportant details that make them stand out? It is the phenomenon (and it is quite a rare one) of having encountered a determined addresser, one who will not allow you to get by with half an answer, one who frames his question not only for the person he is addressing but for himself as well. What he is seeking, above all, is the answer – and anyone listening to him knows that he will find it. This supreme gift for posing questions is the exact impression we derive from every book and essay Lévi-Strauss has written and published.

An address given at a Tribute to Professor Claude Lévi-Strauss at the US Embassy in Paris on 8 November 1978.

I think I have the right to report a detail Lévi-Strauss once related to me during the École Libre days in New York. I do not know whether he still does this, but at the time he told me that he generally avoided directly addressing people he had to speak to; he did not use their names or titles, for the precise reason that he had a profound intuition of the distance so obviously required when a question is posed and when the answer must be independent of the allegiances of either addresser or addressee. What is being sought is an autonomous solution. What is peculiar in this instance is that we are not dealing with objects as objects, but rather with similarities, with distances, in short with relations which, as Lévi-Strauss has so clearly shown, are at once more simple and more intelligible than the very objects between which the mind perceives such relations.

Lévi-Strauss was able to bring out the continually dynamic, active, creative character of all such basic relations. When, for example, he speaks of the relationship between language and myth, he is able at the same time to make us aware of the distance, the ineluctable gap between those two domains. We are too used, when speaking of relations, to accepting a certain passivity, a stasis, between the objects being compared – and I am the first to admit that this was once one of my failings. At the time Lévi-Strauss posited for me, back in the École Libre days, the problem of the relations between *mytheme* and *phoneme*, I had trouble accepting it, whereas from the very beginning the author of *Mythologiques* had recognized both the similarity and the difference between linguistic and mythic utterances and between their basic elements.

Everyone has his favourite among the books of an admired author, and out of the marvellous panorama of Lévi-Strauss's writings it is his latest book, *La Voie des masques* (The Way of Masks), a classic contribution to the *Sentiers de la création* series, that particularly impresses me. The author succeeds in demonstrating that "a mask is not primarily what it represents" – and how often and in how many fields must we take this into account – "a mask is not primarily what it represents, but what it transforms", that is what it chooses either to represent or to omit. Like a myth, it excludes and denies as much as it states. This point is just as important for the student of masks as it is for the student of language. Diplomats have said that language exists not merely to reveal but, perhaps even more, to conceal. It is not enough simply to state this dual relationship; an explicit demonstration must be made of how a mask – and this of course applies not only to masks – is able to deny what it is affirming while simultaneously remaining affirmative.

*La Voie des masques* reveals masks in the full complexity of their oppositions. Care must be taken to avoid reducing their variety to some limited system. For masks – as for culture in general – there can be no spatial limitations. Lévi-Strauss rightly speaks of the vast international cultural current that filled the life of neolithic man with its constant ebb and flow, and he adds that the interchanging of masks among the various peoples of the Americas provides a pertinent analogy. It is not a matter of mechanical borrowings or of a preference for the masks of one's closest neighbours; it is rather an interchange of

*Box 1*                          *The Way of Masks*

Xwéxwé mask (Kwakiutl). Wood. 34.3 × 24.1 × 17.1 cm. Vancouver, Museum of
Anthropology, University of British Columbia.

### Reading what signs omit

Looking at the protruberant dance and dowry mask the Kwakiutls call Xwéxwé,
Lévi-Strauss exhibits the origin of the semiotic activity: unease in front of a
representation. For years justification of the Xwéxwé form escaped him. Why the
lolling tongue, the blazing, bulging eyes? "I was incapable of answering any of
these questions until I realized that masks, like myths, cannot be interpreted in
themselves and by themselves as separate objects. Seen from the semantic point
of view, a myth only acquires a meaning once it is returned to the set of its
transformations; so too, one type of mask, considered solely from the plastic point
of view, echoes other types whose lines and colors it transforms while assuming its
individuality."

Now, Xwéxwé, symbol of wealth and highest lineage, has a sordid character: in
dance, in myth, the mask signifies self-centered wealth, unshared copper
(currency of the Kwakiutl). Xwéxwé aims to account for a loss, an inequality of

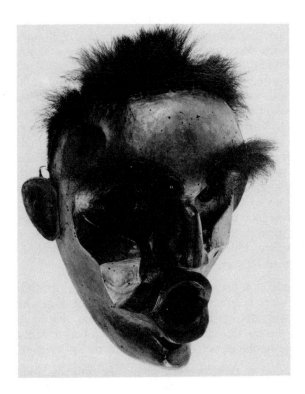

Dzonokwa mask (Kwakiutl). Wood, nails, roots, bear fur, graphite and cinnabar. 35.6 × 30.5 × 17.8 cm. Vancouver, Museum of Anthropology, University of British Columbia. (Photo, Johsel Namkung)

copper. How? By transforming and denying another mask, the Kwakiutl's coppery-colored Dzonokwa – hollow sockets for eyes, mouth pushed forward in a pout – Dzonokwa, the ogress-owner of the copper the lucky few wrest away from her. "Dzonokwa has eyes deeply buried in their orbits, or half-closed, because they are perpetually dazzled. [Xwéxwé], on the contrary, has protruberant eyes; this anatomical particularity thus signifies that *they cannot be dazzled* (my emphasis). The meaning of Xwéxwé is not what it first represents (I protrude), the meaning is what it denies: unlike the ogress, I am undazzleable by the copper I hypostasize. Because I have imperturbable vision, impervious to copper's gleam, the propriety of my ownership is undeniable.

Lévi-Straussian mind sees through the mask, through signs, to an activity of manipulation: ideology.

*Marshall Blonsky*

indigenous products with distant neighbours. We are dealing with intentional transfigurations, not with imitations; instead of a mere copy, we have the image transposed, inverted. This problem of masks in space and of the creative role of space in the history of masks or myths – the history of all human creation, in short – helps us to discern, *mutatis mutandis*, problems analogous to those that arise in relation to the temporal factor. Like spatial changes, temporal changes are phenomena that are as much of a mixed nature as of an intrinsic one. In both instances, they are part of an integrated system. Here, we must be aware of the risks any science runs: we either focus our attention on the utter uniqueness of a phenomenon or we attempt to discern the invariant among variables. For Claude Lévi-Strauss, "invariance" is a basic problem, but it also presupposes immense diversity. And that term "diversity" always had a distinctive emphasis in Lévi-Strauss: when he uses it, when he speaks of this question of diversity, we can hear, along with the scientist, the ordinary contemporary man who feels the need to preserve diversity in a world threatened by monotony and uniformity. How good and fitting it is that, whatever the variety of his citations, Lévi-Strauss should be so personal in his emphasis on individual and multifaceted variety, how fine that he should conclude his book on masks with this well-weighed statement:

> In claiming to be solitary the artist indulges in a perhaps fruitful illusion, but the privilege he grants to himself has no reality. When he thinks that he's expressing himself in a spontaneous fashion, that he does original work, he answers to other past or present, actual or virtual, creators. Whether aware of it or not, no one walks the path of creation alone.

It is in the finding of that dialectical path – the path combining diversity and unity – that we will manage to glimpse the science of the future, that science for which Claude Lévi-Strauss has been one of the first to clear the way.

ROLAND BARTHES

# Barthes to the Third Power

I suppose that if Barthes were asked for a critique of his own book *Roland Barthes by Roland Barthes*, he could only decline the request. He would doubtless have no difficulty in pointing out the shortcomings of his text, in drawing up his own balance sheet for his performance; but this would not take him out of the writer's operative field, which is more a matter of private conversation. Moreover, since criticism is traditionally never anything but a hermeneutics, how could he agree to give a meaning to a book which is altogether a refusal of meaning, which seems to have been written solely to refuse meaning?

Let us try to put him in his proper place, since he himself has bowed out (and since no one expects us to blame him for doing so). What is the meaning of a book? Not what it argues, but what it argues with. As an individual, bodily subject, Barthes is visibly at grips with two Figures (two Allegories in the medieval sense): *Value* (which grounds everything in taste and distaste) and *Stupidity*; as an historical subject he is at grips with two notions of the period: the *Imaginary* and the *Ideological*.

It is curious that an author, having to speak about himself, is so obsessed by Stupidity, as though it were the inner thing he most feared: threatening, ever ready to burst out, to assert its right to speak (why shouldn't I have the right to be stupid?); in short, *The Thing*. In attempting to exorcise it, Barthes plays the fool, he puts himself inside it; certain fragments of *Barthes on Barthes* are *short* ("It's a bit short, young man"); in a sense, this whole little book, in a devious and naïve way, plays with stupidity – not the stupidity of others (that would be too easy), but that of the subject *who is about to write*. What first comes to mind is stupid (all tangled up with the Other, who prompts me to my first discourse): spontaneity is imbecilic because it can only reproduce, imitate, and do so *with a completely clear conscience*. Though written in a somewhat distant and *matte* way (without *brio*), *Barthes on Barthes* gives a direct statement of ideas; a little more and this or that would perhaps have become an *avant-garde* idea; but this more is not given. One might say that Barthes experiments here with his own banality, that he descends into it. What does he find at the bottom of it? Ideology, of course. Ideology is not presented here as an external object of study or denunciation, but as a contaminating power, a worm which eats away at every utterance: ideology (bourgeois, petty-bourgeois) speaks within me and *Barthes on Barthes* can only make this speech understood *silently*, one might say stoically (nothing produces more guilt today than the ideological mark). The creation of which the book is the locus exists neither in the statements nor even in the writing, but essentially in the clandestine act whereby Barthes "imagines himself" an idea, puts himself in quotation marks and then removes them: a dislocation which obviously lends itself to every sort of misunderstanding, thereby beginning (intentionally or not?) to go unnoticed.

## The Imaginary

On the Ideological plane, Barthes the historical subject – or at least Barthes-in-the-process-of-expressing-himself – struggles with his class image, of which language is the inevitable mirror. Now Barthes takes up this struggle with the Image again elsewhere, through a psychoanalytic notion: the *Imaginary*. The Imaginary is not very highly regarded today, perhaps because it still has too many connections to classical moralism, which was a reflection of "*amour propre*", sincerity, and other ideal attributes of the Ego; at present any statement about Desire and Delight is preferable. By placing the Imaginary – his own Image-Repertoire – in the foreground of his book, Barthes dates himself somewhat; his book will appear to some as a retreat from *The Pleasure of the Text* (unless Fashion were soon to take a new turn and give a bit of prestige to this disinherited mode, shared only by little children and lovers). But could he have done otherwise? Having agreed to write about "him", he could utter only what belongs to him alone: not the Symbolic, Delight, but the Mirror – the varied, tiered, reflexive modes, always disappointing, in which *he imagines himself*, or even (it is the same thing), in which *he wants to be loved*. It is not for nothing, it seems, that the imagery of *Barthes on Barthes* (gathered symbolically before the text begins) is almost exclusively the imagery of childhood. It is not for nothing that the book is punctuated three times by the image of the Mother: first radiant, indicating the only *Nature* recognized by a subject who has not stopped denouncing the "natural" everywhere; then overflowing, enclosing the sad child in the dual relation, marking him with an eternal "demand for love"; lastly, sitting next to, in front of, and behind the mirror, thereby establishing the subject's imaginary identity. Creatively (for, after all, Barthes the "subject" interests only Barthes himself), the Imaginary, just like Ideology, leads to an utterance which endlessly undoes itself and, in the end, is anchored in no referent. Whence the framing of the utterances: discontinuous, circumscribed, "written", sometimes approximating the maxim, the *dictée*, the pastiche, the fragment, the grimace, taking on the "fixedness" of the image; one might say, vaguely, that they attempt to participate in that imaginary sideration which grips the animal confronting its trap.

## The Ideological

What is the Ideological? It is what goes into the making of an idea. And the Imaginary? What goes into the making of an Image. Once again we are dealing with a discussion about meaning, as it is "made up", as it "takes"; in short, we are dealing again with a semiology, but this time a tacit one, simultaneously undone, wild and icy, stripped of all scientific (or simply metalinguistic) purpose. This semiology is quite different from the old one, all its effort seems to be in assigning ideological and imaginary statements one and the same place: that of misapprehension – where I imagine myself, there I mistake myself. What? No truth? – Yes, for others, for the reader, for the Other. Prisoner of a collection ("X by X") which proposed to him that he "speak himself", Barthes could say only one thing: that he is the only one who is unable to speak *truly* of himself. Such is the "disappointing" meaning of his book. It would have been pointless for him to pile up declarations, interviews or articles, to surround himself with a cloud of commentaries; like the squid in his ink, nothing will come of it: as an imaginary and ideological subject, misapprehension (not error, but the infinite carryover of truth through language) is his lot, whatever he writes about himself and whatever name he signs it with – the most proven of pseudonyms: his own name, his Proper Name.

MICHEL DE CERTEAU

# What We Do When We Believe

In its Vedic (*'sraddhà*) and Latin (*credo*) origins, the term *to believe* presents a constellation of usages. Already it furnishes a field of hypotheses. "A true morphological fossil", sometimes it signifies having confidence in someone or something, sometimes believing in reality or in what one sees, sometimes trusting in what is said.[1] In these three forms, which concern either an actor (person or object) or a referential or a stating, belief posits a relationship to something *Other*. In this triple guise it always implies the support of the other, which stands for what we have to rely upon. In addition, in the examples cited by Georges Dumézil (Numa, etc.), this relationship has the form of some "commerce". It obeys the ethics of the *do ut des*. A loyalty is required of the partners, presumed to be "on the up and up". Thereby the shadow of the believer and its opposite, the *renegade* or traitor, is already evident.

Belief thus occurs between the recognition of an alterity and the establishment of a contract. It disappears if one of the two terms weakens. Belief no longer exists when difference is effaced by a process tending to equalize the partners and give them a mutual mastery of the contract; it no longer exists when difference becomes excessive through a breach of the pact. The oscillation between these poles, in the field of beliefs, makes for a first classification that could go, for example, from fidelity (which gives pride of place to alliance) to faith (which stresses difference).

Analysing the *Vocabulaire des institutions indo-européennes*, Émile Benveniste recognizes in the functioning of the word *kred* (*Credo*) – a function he ranks among "economic obligations" – a sequence linking a donation to a remuneration. To believe, he says, is to "give something away with the certainty of getting it back".[2] A coming and going of the "thing" marks, through a

---

[1] Georges Dumézil, *Idées romaines* (Paris: Gallimard, 1969) pp. 47–59 ("*Credo et fides*").
[2] Émile Benveniste, *Vocabulaire des institutions indo-européennes* (Paris: Minuit, 1969) vol. 1, ch. 15, pp. 171–9.

separation among moments, that which distinguishes its successive owners. The communication established by the goods put in circulation posits a distinction of sites (the detainers of the "thing") by that of *time*. It temporalizes the relation of the *one* to the *other*. The object of the exchange is itself altered by this distance between moments, since the due – or expected – is not the same as the given, but an *equivalent*: the analogy between the offered and the received would be the work of time on their identity. The sequence of the gift and restitution thus temporarily articulates an economy of exchange. It will develop on the side of *credence*, or "crediting", of the creditor or "believer" and, more explicitly, towards *credit*, where Marx sees "the judgment that political economy bears on the morality of man".[3]

Similar in its form to *seeing*, as analysed by Merleau-Ponty,[4] believing takes the form of an interlacing of operations, a combinative of gifts and debts, a network of "recognition". First, it is a "spider's web" organizing a social fabric.[5] The difference that distinguishes it from *seeing* or *knowing* is not at first notable for the truth value of which a proposition is susceptible – to which an entire epistemology has been devoted – but by this inscription of *time* in a subject-to-subject relationship. When this relationship can no longer be sustained and structured by temporalization, it will evolve into a relationship of (knowing) subject to (known) object. In social relationships, the question of belief is the question of time.

The "believer" abandons a present advantage, or some of its claims, to give credit to a receiver. He hollows out a void in himself relative to the time of the other, and, in the interests he calculates, he creates a deficit whereby a future is introduced into the present. Thus there takes form a problematic of society: independent wills are distinguished amongst themselves by the duration that retards appropriation. A *plurality* and a *historicity* are knotted into the act that posits, by the same gesture, a *different* partner and a *deferred* restitution. This temporal practice of difference endows *delay* with all its social pertinency. It is by this "deferred" that believing is separated from seeing.

However, it is also the acquisition of a right. It has the value of a "receipt". The thing given is exchanged for a right that places the other – and time itself – within a nexus of *obligations*. It enters into a field of socio-historical operations that allow for a collective management of the other and of time. The modes and duration of its circulation are placed under the guaranty and control of communication rules – a right, customs, etc. If the gift "sacrifices" to these rules (the act of "confiding something" also implies obligations), if thereby it actualizes them, it also derives a profit: it is sustained by them, and the donor, through his sacrifice, acquires the right to be sustained. The deferred thus equally marks the role and price of collective contracts. At the junction of a

---

[3] Quoted in Pierre Bourdieu, "Avenir de classe et causalité du probable", *Revue française de sociologie*, vol. XV, no. 1 (January–March 1974) p. 23, no. 29.
[4] See Maurice Merleau-Ponty, *Le Visible et l'Invisible* (Paris: Gallimard, 1964).
[5] See W. V. Quine and J. S. Ullian, *The Web of Belief* (New York: Random House, 1970).

practice of time and a social sym-bolics, belief, through its developments, retreats and displacements, is a strategic site of communication.

Most frequently it takes the form of a *speech* that fills the interval between a present loss (what is confided) and a remuneration to come (what will be recuperated). Bifaceted, speech derives from this present of a loss and from this discounted future. Its status (but is this not true of all speech?) is the simultaneous stating of the absence of the thing it represents and the promise of its return. It is a convention made with the thing that is no longer there but whose abandon has led to the birth of the word, and it is an acquired right to the future usage of its referential. In addition, speech enjoys a privileged relationship with belief: like the act of speaking, that of believing articulates onto the disappeared and expected thing the social possibility of a "commerce". In both cases, a loss authorizes a discount. Thus between the three terms that Dumézil distinguishes – an actor, a real, a stating – there is a disparity. In relation to believing, saying has in effect the dual function of indicating a particular type of object (one can believe in a speech, a narrative, etc.), and of furnishing a general model (saying and believing reproduce the same structure).

We can add to this homology between believing and saying that which brings belief closer to *sacrifice*, or at least the analysis that Durkheim makes of sacrifice. For Durkheim, sacrifice establishes and represents society: by what it takes from individual self-sufficiency, it marks on what is proper to each (on the body or on goods) the existence of the other, but the plurality thereby produced already has contractual value; the code of social exchange inscribed on individual nature, while mutilating it, transforms it into a blazon of sociality.[6] The place ceded to the other by the gift has a "conventional" value with the other. In the order of (re)cognition, believing would be the equivalent of what sacrifice is in the order of religious practices. It carves the mark of the other within an autonomy; it loses a present for a future; it "sacrifices", in other words "makes sense" (*sacer-facere*), by substituting a debit for a credit.

In a society, belief thus prevents the totalizing unification of the present. It creates in that society a return to the other and to a future. It also eschews dissemination. It creates a nexus of debts and rights amongst the group members. In sum, it guarantees a sociality based on a duration. It acts as the impetus to an insurance system in which social contracts are based on distinct periods of time. It is essential to the collectivities that temporally articulate human relationships. We can infer from it that the more a society evades the temporal law (for example by constituting scriptural sites where knowledge can be capitalized in a present), the less importance it accords to belief.

The same problematic can be encountered at the level of a group micro-sociology: everyday practices related to systems of *expectation* that refer to "a legitimate order of beliefs about life in society". Expectancies are supported by beliefs. A system of belief links present behaviour to a future that escapes them. Thus gestures of mutual aid, hospitality or courtesy function by the right

[6] Émile Durkheim, *Les Formes élémentaires de la vie religieuse* (Paris: PUF, 1968).

they give of trusting in a surety. Everyday practices are developed on a "background of expectations".[7] They presume all the social rites that play on deferred time. With greater or lesser virtuosity, they "execute" and they "interpret" (as we do a piece of music) the codes of expectancy proper to a group.

In this connection and anew, language here is a comprehensive model, organizing a formal network of mutual expectancies. For example, syntax foresees "linked probabilities", in other words what each position enables one to expect from the other and of the equivalent after it. More fundamentally, however, the entire language presumes that meaning must respond to what it articulates, and that it has acquired a symbolic right over the referential from which none the less it is separated. The act of speech is also founded on the expectation that there is a respondent, and that the utterance "given" to the other will, in the mode of an equivalence and not of an identity, be restored to the donor-speaker.

In many ways, a credibility network upholds the conventions that regulate social communication. Between partners, it also makes for all kinds of games, manipulations and surprise effects with these conventions (making believe that one believes, or that one does not, etc.). Essentially, however, believing makes a communication practice out of the alterity of time (or of non-immediacy). It functions where only a duration can reverse the donor's position to that of beneficiary; where a time of the other foreshadows some delay and thus the uncertainty of a difference onto the equivalency between the offered and the rendered. In contrast to this principle of historic sociality there is a principle of scientificity (or "truth") which, by eliminating the delay of a deferred time, by practising the immediate coincidence between the given and the received, has *seeing* as its index.

## Stating and Doing

The believer says: "I believe that you will (re)appear." He is sustained by the other, even if in many cases the other is tamed, sometimes controlled, even domesticated by the social rules that "insure" the creditor against the risk of time. He is situated in this interspace, in the suspense that separates what he has done from what the other will do. A stating occupies such a space: a promise, a convention, a confession of "faith", etc. However, that statement presumes and intends a doing. Believing is the link, distended, that connects by speech two distant gestures. It thereby ties a statement to a doing. Reciprocally, such an inscription of stating in doing, and doing in stating, turns belief into an expectational practice. From this point of view, the formula indicating his position to the believer could be: you believe it if you do it, and if you do not do

---

[7] Harold Garfinkel, "Studies in the Routine Grounds of Everyday Activities", in David Sudnow (ed.), *Studies in Social Interaction* (New York: The Free Press, 1970) pp. 1–30.

it you do not believe in it. This axiom holds true for a great many stable, traditional societies: for example, ancient Israel or Rome. There, beliefs had the form of practices. Thus, like Greek sacrifices,[8] they are interpreted by anthropology as a set of "ritualized activities"[9] that embody the promise or the trust in the objectivity of some gesture.

That they have been considered as *representations* capable or not of enjoying an individual or collective assent (of the type: "I believe in it" or "we do not believe in it") is, in part, an effect of historical interpretation, based on *utterances* that survive practices that have now disappeared. We thus endow such detached fragments with the value of assertions about beings (supernatural, divine, etc.) or truths that distance enables us to situate under the sign of credibility precisely because we no longer believe in them. In other words, belief becomes an utterance (an affirmation) when it ceases to mesh with some contractual practice. To posit the question: "Do I believe it?" is already to leave the field of belief and take it as an intellectual object independent of the act that affirms it as a relationship. Belief is no longer anything but a stating when it ceases to be a relational engaging, in other words when it ceases to be a belief.

The isolation of the stating also results from more recent history, which has, between beliefs and practices, made possible a break henceforth considered as a proof. Three centuries of polemic between "science" and "superstition" have divided practices themselves into two very unequal parts, each affected with a veritably different destiny: on the basis of such practices, one consists of mutual expectations, and it has become the superfluous remainder of a past, the illness that compromises the second position; the other, relative to an operativity of such practices, has become the object of a technical rationalization, an isolated portion, analysed, distributed into combinable elements in view of some improved efficacy. This sundering has given rise, on the one hand, to representations known as "beliefs" precisely because we do not believe them any longer, and they no longer function as social alliances, and, on the other hand, to objective behaviours (medical, commercial, educational, culinary, etc.) that it had brought to the status of techniques and thus treated as a series of gestures related to fabricational activities.[10]

Such a cleavage is accentuated in complex societies, in which heterogeneous, stratified and fragmented systems of credit coexist. The same practices obey codes that are divergent from what they allow one to expect. The same conventions of credit are practised in contradictory ways. Beliefs and conducts thus enter into increasingly unstable relationships. Combinations between what becomes of "convictions" and what becomes of "behaviours" increase. Contrary to what happened in many traditional societies, practice is no longer

[8] See Marcel Detienne and Jean-Pierre Vernant, *La Cuisine du sacrifice en pays grec* (Paris: Gallimard, 1979).

[9] Jean Pouillon, "Remarques sur le verbe *croire*", in Michel Izard and Pierre Smith (eds), *La Fonction symbolique* (Paris: Gallimard, 1979) pp. 43–51.

[10] See Michel de Certeau, *L'Écriture de l'histoire* (Paris: Gallimard, 1978) pp. 153–212 ("La formalité des pratiques").

the transparent objectivity of a belief. We must make a distinction between them, and that very distinction, verbal and operatory, has become our contemporary believing practice; it is among the gestures to which we presume a guarantee.

The autonomy of these two elements is neither so rapid nor so radical. Thus political action that takes the place of religious practices retains the trace of the salvational expectancies that it is trying to eradicate by means of some theory of revolution or well-being. Such outmoded "convictions", detached from the practices that articulated them, are objectified by the strategies that are supposed to replace them. Contrariwise, gestures that survive the collapse of the exchange system from which they derived their public legitimacy remain determinant, illegitimate as they may be, in the mental landscape that has become foreign to them. They are there, active but illicit, with the status of "superstitions": in other words, quite precisely "survivals".[11]

The important thing here is that even in such extreme cases, beliefs are still the index of practices that sustain them and that they intend. Writing about the evil eye, Benedetto Croce said: "It is false but I believe in it." That belief, exiled from scientific knowledge (it knows it is false), also cast out of the epistemological configuration to which it related (the remains of a cosmology), remains indissociable from things not to do (accepting praise means bad luck) or from precautions to be taken (wearing charms, saying or writing the number 5, etc.). Croce's belief is a gesture that transgresses cultural orthodoxy. The same holds true for many others, which are in fact practices that set up contracts with a future that has been more or less deprived of legitimacy by public discourse. Having been disinherited by the official credit system, they have received a new, more modest role. Within operations that, within a society, guarantee the "return" corresponding to an investment, "survival" no longer has a recognized *positive* function. However it retains – and often in this way receives – the *negative* role of restraining such public operations, of limiting them and even sometimes suspending them by "disastrous" procedures. The conventions agreed with partners outside of the social legality and identity cut, slash the field of legitimate expectations with silent gestures. Such ritual actions lay down invisible borders within the authorized culture.

At the end of the eighteenth century, Mme du Deffant stated: "I do not believe in ghosts, but I'm afraid of them." Through actions that prohibit her from being afraid, she nevertheless indicates what she still "believes". However, the term "belief" has become the object of wordplay, an equivocal site. In the "enlightened" discourse that is supposed to define the believable, in other words, in fact, the thinkable, the fragment of an illicit belief is still evidenced in behaviours, but in behaviours that, excluded from such discourse, limit belief

---

[11] See Émile Benveniste, *Vocabulaire*, vol. 2, pp. 273–9, *à propos of superstitio*, which designates that which "survives" or "subsists". Moreover, English anthropology has replaced "superstition" by "survival". See P. Saintyves, "Les origines de la méthode comparative et la naissance du folklore: Des superstitions aux survivances", in *Revue de l'histoire des religions*, vol. 105 (1932).

and stop it before phantoms. There is belief because there is still a practice, but discernible only through feeling (fear) that always burdens deficit with a logic of practices.

Recent studies on belief actually restore its relationship to a doing. Doubtless in a long, especially Mediterranean tradition, the *believed object* has been isolated from the collective and individual steps that it brought together in contracts. Cut off from the act that posited it, regarded as a "mental occurrence", belief received the comprehensively negative definition of corresponding to what one does not know or see, in other words, of being the *other* of knowledge or sight. It was labelled with such an identity by an epistemology that judged knowledge according to the truth value with which an utterance can be affected and which distributed this truth according to its two possible sources, memory or proof. In another, especially Anglo-Saxon tradition – one linked to the philosophical rigour of an "individualism" that distinguishes the act from its object – belief appears as the positive formality of an act of *uttering* related to a (willing) *to do* of the subject and to a *contract* entered into between social and/or symbolic partners. It thus refers to an acting.[12]

Alexander Bain has already stressed that the act of belief "has meaning only in reference to our actions".[13] R. B. Braithwaite regarded belief as a disposition to act "as if the proposition were true: belief", he said, is "being ready to act as if *p* were true".[14] Here the proposition is being judged according to the monotheistic rule of "true or false". Since Austin, we recognize a pullulation of utterances that escape this rule and that instead relate to the alternative "success or failure"; it works or it does not. Utterances of *belief* belong to this growing family. However, in Braithwaite's epistemology, still colonized by the question of truth, they have already been relegated to acting *vis-à-vis* the pertinent instance.

Belief, indeed, concerns "what makes it run".[15] It is perceived by the more or less strict links it maintains with what it makes happen and/or expects to see happen. Broadly, it relates to some salvation, to some efficacious reciprocity or to the success of some enterprise ("believing that the abyss is not so wide" makes it easier for me to cross over it).[16] On the other hand, it disappears when those links are broken. Even such propositions as "I believe that it will be nice tomorrow", or "I believe that the planet Mars is inhabited" do not at first refer to the validity of some knowledge; they are based on solidarities that the

---

[12] H. H. Price, *Belief* (London: Allen & Unwin, 1969), has worked extensively to extend and deepen the philosophical analysis of belief as a "disposition" to do.

[13] Alexander Bain, *The Emotions and the Will* (1859), quoted in Anthony Quinton, "Knowledge and Belief", in P. Edwards (ed.), *The Encyclopedia of Philosophy*, vol. 4, p. 351.

[14] R. B. Braithwaite, "The Nature of Believing", *Proceedings of the Aristotelian Society*, New Series, vol. 33 (1929–33) pp. 129–46.

[15] See Pierre Legendre, *L'amour du censeur* (Paris: Seuil, 1974).

[16] See Marcus G. Singer, "The Pragmatic Use of Language and the Will to Believe", *American Philosophical Quarterly*, vol. 8, no. 1 (1971) pp. 24–34.

respondants of projects or styles of action set up. The rejection of a planetary vacuum is none the less a sign of it. Also, contrary to what Anthony Quinton noted, it does not seem that there can be beliefs detachable from practical consequences.

All positions have doubtful elements. Nevertheless, one could adopt the thesis that a belief devoid of practical implications is not a belief. With the bluntness characteristic of the style of his later years, Pierre Janet rightly said: "For us, belief is nothing more than a promise of action: to believe is to act; to say that we believe in something is to say: we shall do something."[17]

## The Indefinite Surety

The "promise of action" also concerns a reality or an external partner. This leads us to what distinguishes belief from a contract and cannot be articulated into objects of exchange guaranteed by some law. In a society, this category of alliance consists of the region that is not yet or cannot be treated in the form of juridical links. The relationships it entails have the appearance of contexts, but they fall outside social instruments capable of objectifying their terms and thus of verifying or falsifying their rapports. Placed outside any legal control, beliefs compose a vast zone that is now open to the conquests of law (many trusts are transformed into contracts), now opposing it to a vast "balance" (resistant to juridical transformation).

Belief is differentiated by the role of the partners and their inequality. What it lacks in objectivation must be supplemented by the subjects. Lacking juridical assurances, the believer seeks, beyond the discounted "thing" (an advantage, a salvation, a truth), a surety upon which expectancy is based. He must not only "believe in", he must "have faith in". A trust doubles the belief and "comforts" it. (Trust comes from *fortis*: that which stands up.) We have to presume a guarantee from the other, in other words postulate an other (a person, a fact, etc.) endowed with power, will and knowledge that can mete out "retribution". In certain cases, *apropos* of God, spirits or humans, its very existence poses a problem, but in the end it is only a variant *vis-à-vis* the body of elements that constitute the competence of the surety and confront the hypothesis that, in one way or another, he is *absent*. The interrogation born from the possibility that he might default essentially bears on two points: that he recognizes himself as *obligated* and that he is *capable* of *paying up*. The first point is more relative to a stating; the second, to a doing. The guarantor is seen as the reflection of the characteristic features of the believer. He functions as his mirror.

However, the question is to know *if there is a surety*. When belief is directed to a person, it more clearly manifests a displacement that is ultimately to be found in all beliefs and that ends always to seek this surety *further on*. How can we be sure that the partner will *act* as *obligated*, that he will be "faithful" to what is

[17] Pierre Janet, *L'évolution de la mémoire et la notion du temps* (Paris: A. Chahine, 1928).

expected of him, or "straight" as Dumézil said? A first verification: in order to presume its object (the expected thing) believable, belief must also presume that the other, in a certain sense, also "believes" and that he considers himself obligated by the gift given to him. It is a *belief in the belief of the other* or in what he/one makes believe that he believes, etc. A belief *of* the other is the postulate of a belief *in* the other.

However, this guaranty is not a sure one, such that it will go behind the first obligator's back to seek, should one be lacking, an heir for him, a wider substitute (family, group, etc.) or higher up (a superior authority, a moral constraint, etc.), always more distant. A myriad of others must guarantee the other. By continually passing the hat and seeking guarantees above and beyond those it has already attained, belief seems to make itself independent of any particular interlocutor and to attempt to compensate the uncertainty of each debtor by an endless referral to others. If the entries in this eternal balance forward are not noted (but they are, by institutions),[18] the appeal to another converges towards a vanishing point of "fidelity" which under the name of God or society will be the very postulate of belief: there must be a guarantor for it. In an increasingly tautological and fundamental mode, belief goes back to the limit which is more than the condition proper to it: only the *a priori* of another who is "straight" makes it possible. In the last instance, it must presume that some Real will stand surety.

This general postulate (present even in scientific processes, as is all too evident) rises and falls on the scale of proximities, according to conjunctures and group types. In the village it takes the shape of the "straight" neighbour; in the party, that of the leader who has surety. On the other hand, in times of instability and/or under the questioning pressure of radical minds, this postulate becomes attenuated to the point that it is no more than the constraint of a hypothesis. Its sites of application and anchorage thus vary according to periods (times of crisis or tranquil periods), collectivities (even in a stable society there are outsider or marginal groups), and individuals (in a "closed village society", what attracts the belief of a dying man or a sceptical mind?). They also vary according to socio-economic configurations, medieval society, for example, was organized as a hierarchical combinative of "sureties" and "clienteles", whereas capitalism replaces that by the fiduciary system of a

---

[18] Social life tends to suspend this return of beliefs to their tautological principle. It even attempts to prevent it. Social life organizes itself in such a way that the indefinite carrying forward of the guarantor is stopped and that the secret of belief is hidden. Institutions are set up to respond to the breakdown of objective beliefs and to the needs of everyday practice. Such mediations serve both to buttress the interrogations that threaten the believable, as assurances against the vertigo of doubt, and as supports for the day-to-day relational activity. In a more or less transitory and respectable manner (they can change and/or lose value), such "authorities" are the pragmatic guarantors of social communication; they are the practical authorities of a system of credit.

common denominator, money. Differentiations still depend on the rise and fall of values: a decrease in practice leads to an increase in doubt, etc.

In principle, it should be possible to classify all the elements composing the successive geographies of such "authorities" having the value of guarantor and allowing for belief. However, their mobility is a dominant feature of such compositions of "sites" guaranteeing belief. It is as though the overall *a priori* according to which there had to be a guarantor somewhere, were, for pragmatic and contingent reasons, placed more or less near, dislodged, relodged elsewhere according to circumstances, and as if, under the pressure of crises and/or interrogations, it finally took refuge in that impregnable but inaccessible site, the impossibility of doing without it.

Each individual guarantor (who must exist on both sides) is thus the metonymy of an indefinite series of others who, behind him, also have the dual position of being missing – they are not (yet) faithful, or not (yet) there – and founders of belief: they "enable" believing, they authorize it, and the coincidence of absence and presence is one of the secrets of believing. However, it also defines the other himself: what I am lacking is what makes me work. And there is more here than a mere coincidence: belief, by means of a gift (or a sacrifice) creates the empty space that installs the other, but that other must fill the void. It produces this "other" presumed to insure against what it is losing. It is not surprising that belief should obey this dynamic circularity. Is this not the very structure of the lived present? This present is, in fact, what, by vanishing, constitutes the alterity of a future. Belief and time remain linked.

The "carrying forward" of the guarantor is also presented in a different form, which at first appears to concern the believer himself. Thus the peasants of Bocage refer not to what they believe, but to what others believe: "Some people believe . . . some people say . . ." Witchcraft, which they also speak about in this way, is "given as belief of the others".[19] On the part of those peasants, this is not only a tactic to keep "superstition" at a distance (a superstition with which the ethnologist identifies them); it is also a security taken against the scepticism that it introduces, and a balance forward that will in fact serve as guaranty of the existence and unknowable will of the other: "some people believe it". There is no certainty in belief. However, from the fact that many, or others, do believe, we can justifiably presume that there is a guarantor to what we fear or hope. The secret network of all these others answers for the witch.

The process of belief works starting not from the believer himself but from an indefinite plural (other/others), presumed to be the debtor and the guarantor of the believing relationship. It is because others (or many) believe it that an individual can take his debtor to be faithful and trust him. A plurality guarantees the guarantor. Can one believe alone in some thing or some one? No, whereas it *is* possible to see alone some thing or some one. Belief rests upon an anteriority of the other whose delegate and manifestation is the *fact* of a plurality of believers: "Some people believe . . . some people say. . . ." With

---

[19] Jeanne Favret-Saada, *Les Mots, la mort, les sorts* (Paris: Gallimard, 1977) pp. 28ff.

regard to witches and soothsayers, the Bocage peasants are more lucid in defining the belief of those who boast the naive formula, "I believe". They go to its true foundation: "Other people believe it."

This is the overall structure: as we know, "Children are in a way the basis for the belief of adults",[20] who only speak of their own beliefs on behalf of the other. Institutions of belief (religious or political) function in this way. Today, proliferating polls make use of the same structure: artificially, they produce for everyone a believable which is, in fact, what each person attributes to so many other people. Very familiar to religions, and now familiar to political powers, thousands of procedures produce believers by creating the belief that "there are many others who believe", or, an even surer technique, by noting those who turn to belief or no longer believe (who "converted"). Conviction is manipulated from a distance by an operation of what appears not to concern it, that of others. The effectiveness of this *quid pro quo* (one is dealt with instead of the other) is very like experiments in cross-breeding. For example, in many cases it is the "unbeliever" who believes that the "believers" believe, and this enables him to believe that he is not a believer[21] – or vice versa.

The fact, necessary to belief, that there may be others who do believe, continues, however, to be spread. The multiplication of pseudo-believers (proliferated by the interview) does not compensate for the decrease of their quality. The "I believe" of opinion oscillates between "it seems to me" and "I do not like". Their number is lessening and their attachment to particular practices is weakening, although they are all placed under the overall index of a societal transformation. All these "others", charged in principle with sustaining the "honesty" of the guarantor, are not "taken in" or they sustain nothing. Such inflation brings about a retreat to the overall postulate: there have to be those who believe. *Subjects supposed to believe* are, in fact, the condition of belief. In order for there to be belief, belief must be somewhere – not believable objects (that only constitute the object of exchange) but a positing of the subject (or quasi-subject) who is "straight" and does not deceive. Even scientific work presumes that "matter is not deceitful", so that although we deceive ourselves at least "it does not deceive us".[22]

What is ultimately questioned is the other even as a *subject*, a "guarantor" authorizing the relationship; the possibility for believing subjects is articulated on the existence of a subject. This question takes the form of what we *must suppose*. It plays on the relationship between a necessity and a supposition. Embodied in necessary fictions that are fictions of the other, this relationship is the vanishing point towards which belief tends in a society that has repressed the question of subject or which at least has isolated it from the practices cast in the form of objective techniques. By a series of referrals which multiply its initial *deferred*, belief continually carries forward towards the still other the unpossessable limit at which its status of possibility can be fixed.

[20] Octave Mannoni, *Clefs pour l'imaginaire, ou l'Autre Scène* (Paris: Seuil, 1969) p. 18.
[21] See Jean Pouillon, in *La Fonction symbolique*, p. 48.
[22] Jacques Lacan, *Séminaire sur les psychoses* (1955–6), lecture of 14 December 1955.

JACQUES LACAN

# Sign, Symbol, Imaginary

## Sign

We begin at the beginning. Saussure and the Prague Circle invented a linguistics that had nothing in common with previous work that had used the same name. They found its keys in the hands of the Stoics, but what did they do with them?

Saussure and the Prague Circle founded a new linguistics, and they founded it on a cut. This cut is the bar placed between the signifier and the signified. Its purpose is to bring into prominence the difference that constitutes the signifier absolutely. Thus the signifier was discovered to have an autonomous order that recalls the process of crystallization. This is especially evident in the systematization of phonemes which was the first success of the new linguistics.

There are some who have wanted to extend this success to the entire network of the symbolic order. They will admit a meaning only where the network guarantees it; they recognize effects but not contents.

This was the promise created by the cut that inaugurated the new linguistics.

The question was whether or not the signified could be studied scientifically. This was thought to depend on whether the field of the signifier was, by its very material, distinct from any physical field as defined by science.

This necessitated a metaphysical exclusion – this being understood as a *désêtre*, a de-being [resonates with *désastre*, disaster – Tr.]. No signification could henceforth be taken to be self-evident. It was no longer self-evident that light was present during the daytime, for example. Here, however, the Stoics were way ahead of us. And besides, as I have already asked, what was the purpose of this extension of the domain of science?

At the risk of being offensive I shall get right to the point. The term semiotics has undergone several redefinitions; notwithstanding, it refers to any discipline which begins with the sign taken as an object. My own definition of the sign (as representing something for someone) shows it to be an obstacle to the grasp of the signifier (defined as representing a subject for another signifier).

The sign presupposes the someone to whom one makes a sign of something. The shadow of this someone obscured the entry into linguistics.

Whatever you call this someone, there is no way around the silliness implicit in this notion. The sign of itself, taken as object, permits the someone to appropriate language as though it were a simple tool. The sign makes language the basis of abstraction and the means of discussion. This leads to the "progress" of thought in which the goal is criticism.

I would have to write, not *la chose*, the thing, but l'achose, the a-thing, to make you feel with what effect linguistics takes place. [Lacan's word-play puts us in mind of Hamlet's "a thing of nothing" – the things linguistics is about are nothings – Tr.].

This does not represent a progress; it is rather a regression. This is what we must fight against – the obscurantist unity which is already consolidated to prepare the a-thing.

No one seems to recognize what is at the centre of this unity. At a time when people gathered up the "signatures of things" for "someone", at least they did not refer to the elaborate idiocy we have which attaches language to the function of communication.

The recourse to the idea of communication protects the rear lines, if I may say so, from what linguistics bars and leaves to perish. Linguistics uses the notion of communication to cover over the ridiculousness that comes from reapplying its notion *a posteriori*, thus rendering language an occult phenomenon that is supposed to show something telepathic. Even Freud was taken in by this lost soul of thought – the idea that thought is communicated without words. Freud began to clean up this court of miracles but he did not unmask its secret king. So linguistics remains stuck to the thought that words communicate thoughts. This same miracle is invoked to convince you that you telepathize with the same material you use to make a pact. And the hypocrites draw you into their lair with the bait of "dialogue", and even with the social contracts they expect to come from it. The famous affect is still there hale and hearty to authenticate these effusions of feeling.

All men (who does not know what that is?) are mortal (let us gather round this equality communicable to everyone); and now let us speak of "all", let us speak together, passing quickly over whatever there is in the heads of the syllogists (not Aristotle, of course) who with one heart (since the time of Aristotle) want to put Socrates into the game in the minor premise. The result will be that death will be administered like everything else, both by and for men. But they will not be on the same side of the telepathic dialogue as it is communicated telegraphically. The syllogism creates a unifying concept of man for which the place of the subject will not cease to be an embarrassment.

Linguistics gets its force from the fact that the subject is marked from the beginning by division. This takes us beyond the pleasantries about communication.

Yes, linguistics has even had enough force to encompass the poet. It tells us that the poet is produced (permit me to translate my friend Jakobson who showed me this) by being eaten by verses. (In French *vers* also may mean worms.) The verses find their own arrangement without any concern for what the poet does or does not know about it. From this it follows that Plato ostracized the poets from his Republic, but also that he showed a lively curiosity in the *Cratylus* for these little animals that appear to him to be words with only care about their heads.

It is clear that formalism was vital in sustaining the first steps of linguistics. It is none the less true that linguistics was "anticipated" by the stumblings of language, or the stumblings of speech.

Freud proposed the following evidence to sustain the ordering he called the unconscious:

1 the subject is not one who knows what he is saying;
2 something is said by the word the subject cannot remember;
3 the subject behaves oddly and believes that his behaviour is his own.

It is not easy to find a place for this subject in the brain, especially when the brain shows itself to be most receptive to this subject when it is asleep – the current state of neurophysiological science does not contradict this.

Someone named Lacan who articulated the order of the unconscious will say that it is what Freud said it was and nothing else. Since Lacan, no one can fail to read Freud this way; and anyone who conducts a psychoanalysis according to Freud ought to regulate or to order his practice according to these agencies. Otherwise he will have chosen the path of ignorance.

Instead of saying that Freud anticipates linguistics, I introduce the following formula: the unconscious is the condition of linguistics.

Without the eruption of the unconscious, linguistics would never have left the dubious atmosphere of the university where, in the name of "human sciences", it finds itself eclipsed by science. Crowned by Baudouin de Courtenay at Kazan, it would have remained in the university.

But the university has not uttered its last word. It will make this whole story into a dissertation topic: the influence of Freud's genius on the genius of Ferdinand de Saussure. This will show how the one knew about the other before the advent of radio.

Do we pretend that the university did not always live without this radio which has deafened us so much?

And why would Saussure have recognized any better than Freud himself what Freud anticipated – that is, the Lacanian metaphor and metonymy: places where Saussure *genuit* Jakobson.

If Saussure did not publish the anagrams he deciphered in Saturnian poetry, it was because they would have wreaked havoc in the university. The dishonesty surrounding him did not make him stupid, this in distinction to what happens among analysts.

An analyst, on the contrary, who bathes in the procedures of the university and who is infatuated by it will be captured by its discourse and will make the blatantly erroneous statement that the unconscious is the condition of language. Those who say this make themselves into authors by disregarding what I told them, what I even incanted to them, which is, that language is the condition of the unconscious.

## Symbol and Imaginary

The notion of message in cybernetics has nothing to do with what we habitually call a message, which always makes sense. The cybernetic message is a succession of signs. And a succession of signs always leads back to a succession of o's or 1's. This is why what is called the unit of information, which is to say something against which the efficiency of the signs is measured, is always related to a primordial unit that is called the key and which is nothing other than the alternative.

The message, within this system of symbols, is part of a network. The network is that of combinations based on a unified scanning, on a 1 which is the principle of the scanning.

On the other hand, the notion of information is easy to understand in one of these little tables.

| O | O | : | O |
|---|---|---|---|
| O | I | : | O |
| I | O | : | O |
| I | I | : | I |

If we use this table, what it means is that in order to win, both elements must be positive. That means that at the beginning the probability of winning is 1:4. Let us suppose that I have already played once. If the element is negative, I have no chance of winning. If it is positive, I have one chance out of two, 1:2. This means that there are different levels of chances and that in moving from one to the other my chances have increased.

Phenomena that have to do with energy always tend to equalize the chances. When we are concerned with messages and with a calculus of chances, the greater the amount of information, the greater the differentiation of levels. I am not saying that it always increases, that my chances always increase, because there are cases where it does not increase; but when it decreases, it decreases toward differentiation.

What we call language can be organized around this base. In order for there to be language there must be little things like orthography and syntax. All of this is given at the beginning. These tables are precisely a syntax, and they show why machines can perform logical operations.

From this point of view syntax precedes semantics. Cybernetics is a science of syntax and it is made to make us see that the exact sciences do nothing more than link the real to a syntax.

But then what is semantics? It certainly has to do with the languages that people speak and that we as analysts work with; these languages have ambiguity, emotional content, and sense. Are we going to say that semantics is peopled or furnished with men's desires?

It is certain that we bring the sense to language: at least, for a large number of things it is certain. But can we say that everything that is circulating in the machine makes no sense? Certainly not in all the senses of the word *sense*, because, in order for the message to be a message, it is necessary not only that there be a succession of signs but that this succession of signs has a direction, an orientation. In order to function according to a syntax, it is necessary for a machine to move in one sense or another. And when I say *machine* you can see that I am not talking about some little thing which we usually call a machine. When I write on a piece of paper the transformations of the 1's and 0's, this production always has a direction.

Therefore it is not absolutely rigorous to say that human desire alone introduces sense into language. The proof is that nothing comes out of the machine except what we are expecting. This is to say, not so much what interests us, but what we have foreseen. The machine stops at a point that we have commanded it to stop at; that is where we shall read the results.

The base of the system is already present in the game we invented for the table above. How could we have established it if it did not rest on a notion of chance, on a certain kind of pure waiting; and this is already a sense.

Here, then, is the symbol in its purest form. This is certainly more useful for us than mistakes in syntax. Mistakes in syntax engender errors; they are accidents. But a mistake in programming will engender falsehood. At this level the true and the false are in play as such. But what does this mean for us analysts. What do we have to deal with when we encounter the human subject who comes to see us?

We can say that his discourse is *impure*. Is it impure because he makes syntactical errors? Of course not. Psychoanalysis is founded on the fact that finding something valuable in human discourse is not a problem of logic. Behind this discourse, which has its sense, we seek another sense, *the* sense. And we seek it in the symbolic function that is manifested through this sense. But this is another sense of the word symbol now.

Here there intervenes a precious fact manifested by cybernetics – something that is not eliminable from the symbolic function of human discourse, and this is the role the imaginary plays in it.

The first symbols, natural symbols as they are called, issued from a certain number of prevalent images – the image of the human body, the image of a certain number of evident objects, such as the sun, the moon, and others. This is what gives the weight, the vital force, the emotional vibration to human language. Is this imaginary homogeneous with the symbolic? No. And it would pervert the meaning of psychoanalysis to reduce it to the valorizing of these imaginary themes, to the coaptation of the subject to an elective, privileged, prevalent object; nowadays this is called the theory of object relations.

What cybernetics shows us is the difference between the symbolic order and the imaginary order. A cybernetician even admitted to me recently the extreme difficulty he has in finding a cybernetic translation for the functions of a Gestalt, which is to say the capture of good forms. Something that is a good form in living nature is a bad form in the symbolic.

As people have often said, man invented the wheel. The wheel is not in nature but it does have a good form, that of the circle. However there is nothing in the nature of the wheel that will describe the pattern of marks that any one of its points makes on each turn. There is no cycloid in the imaginary. The cycloid is a discovery of the symbolic (figure 1). And while a cycloid can easily be constructed in a cybernetic machine, people have the greatest difficulty, except in the most artificial way, in making one circle respond to another in the dialogue between two machines.

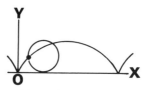

Figure 1    Cycloid

This brings to the fore the essential difference between the imaginary and the symbolic.

What the imaginary brings to a subject's discourse is an inertia. This inertia mixes up the discourse to the extent that when I want the best for someone, I really want the worst; when I love someone, it is really myself that I love; or when I think that I love myself, it is precisely at this moment that I love another. This imaginary confusion is precisely what the dialectical exercise of analysis should dissipate. To do so restores to discourse its sense as discourse.

The question is to know whether the symbolic exists as such or whether the symbolic is only the fantasy of imaginary capture taken to a second degree. This is where one has to choose between two different orientations for analysis.

Everyone, in the adventures of his history, has accumulated a certain amount of sense in the ballast of his semantics. Ought we to follow him in the sense that he has already given to his discourse, in so far as he knows that he is doing a psychoanalysis and that psychoanalysis has formulated certain norms? Ought we to encourage him to be very nice, to become a person who has attained instinctual maturity, having left behind the developmental stages in which one orifice or another is dominant? Do we try in analysis to capture these fundamental images, to rectify, to normalize these imaginary terms, or do we try to liberate the sense in the discourse, in this succession of discourse where the subject is engaged? The different schools diverge on these points.

Freud had to the highest degree this sense of sense, which explains why some of his works, for example "The Theme of the Three Caskets", read as though they were written by a master of the art of divination, as though he were guided by a sense which is like poetic inspiration. What is in question is knowing whether analysis will continue in the Freudian sense, not seeking the ineffable, but the sense.

But what is sense? The sense is that the human being is not the master of this primordial and primitive language. He has been thrown into it, engaged in it, caught in its gears.

We do not know its origin. We are told, for example, that cardinal numbers appeared in languages before ordinal numbers. This is not expected. One would have thought that man entered into the world of numbers through ordinals, through dance, through religious and civil ceremonies, through social hierarchies, through the organization of the village, which is nothing other than order and hierarchy. And yet linguists tell me that the cardinal number appeared first.

The paradox is none the less marvellous. Here man is not master of his own house. There is something into which he is integrated and which reigned already through its own combinations. The passage of man from nature to culture follows the same mathematical combinations which will serve later to classify and to explain. Claude Lévi-Strauss calls them the elementary structures of kinship. And yet, we do not suppose that primitive men were like Pascal. Man's entire being was taken into the procession of numbers, into a primitive symbolism which is distinguished from imaginary representations. It is in the middle of all that that something of man has to make itself recognized. But what has to be recognized, as Freud says, is not what is expressed, but what is repressed.

Something in a machine which does not get to the right place at the right time falls away and does not complain about it. With men things are not the same: the scanning is alive and what did not get there at the right time remains suspended. That is what is in question in repression.

Undoubtedly, something that is not expressed does not exist. But the repressed is always there – it insists, and it demands to come into being. The fundamental relation of man with this symbolic order is precisely the same one which founds this symbolic order itself – the relation of non-being to being.

That which insists on being satisfied can only be satisfied through recognition. The end of the symbolic process is that non-being comes to be, that he is because he has spoken.

JULIA KRISTEVA

# The Speaking Subject

I can summarize the contribution of Ferdinand de Saussure into two postulates which have inspired two corresponding currents of structuralism.

First, language is a system: it is this postulate, developed in the *Cours de linguistique générale*, which will become the foundation of the structuralist current which envisions all human practices, therefore all signifying practices as a system. I am here referring particularly to the work of Lévi-Strauss regarding systems of kinship and myths and to the whole current of structuralist semiotics. Secondly, language as a system is articulated through the signifier which exceeds the consciousness (and therefore the systematization) of the speaking subject. This is what is announced by Saussure's *Anagrammes* – a work on the underlying assonances in Latin and Vedic poetry, assonances which when assembled in an almost cabalistic manner, designate for Saussure a proper name of utmost libidinal and/or religious importance. It is precisely this tendency which will find its realization only after the intervention of psychoanalysis into the field of language, that is, when the Freudian notion of the unconscious will renew the classical or Cartesian concept of the speaking subject and permit the foundation in a materialist manner of a dialectical conception of signifying activity.

But before arriving at this eclipse of structuralism by the united efforts of Saussurian poetics and psychoanalysis, I shall say a few words about the conception of the speaking subject inspired by the first aspect of Saussurian intervention, that of language as a system.

## Theories of the Enunciated

In this type of theory, I include, first, structuralist theories, strictly speaking, which explore the articulations of the signified on the one hand, and of the signifier on the other, and the relationships (essentially displacing or isomorphic) between the two. Being only theories of manifestations, they are not interested in the *production* of the enunciated and consequently they foreclose the role of the speaking subject.

Secondly, I include generative theories. Apparently these theories postulate a two-tiered model (deep and surface structure) without there being a qualitative difference between the two: the same logical and syntactic categories articulate themselves at the surface and in the deep structure. This technical fact is a simple consequence of the epistemological postulate according to which a conscious subject, a Cartesian subject, preserves the deep as well as the surface structure.[1]

From this point of view (that is, from the point of view of the epistemological presuppositions concerning the speaking subject), the first aspect of Saussurian theory, like the generative theories, seems to me to share the same epistemological foundations.[2]

## Theories of Enunciation

In theories of enunciation, the notion of language as system is replaced by that of *discourse*: a system which can be produced under certain conditions (references, intersubjectivity, a modality emanating from the intention of the interlocutors). For enunciation theories, language is a practice as well as a system, a utilization of the system between speaking subjects. I represent the object of enunciation theories by the following adaptation of the Saussurian sign (figure 1).

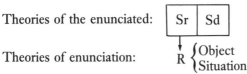

Theories of the enunciated: | Sr | Sd |

Theories of enunciation: R { Object / Situation

Figure 1

This tendency, represented in the United States by the sociological expansion of generative grammar and in France by theories of discourse, opens up the field of sense and signification beyond linguistics, towards sociology and psychology. This happens given the fact that the conditions surrounding the production of a system of meaning are none other than socio-historical and intersubjective. It is in this way that a first innovation appears in regard to the speaking subject in a *situation*.

If, however, we carefully examine this speaking subject, even in the context of

[1] Generative theories are a calculus assigning structural description to the sentences of the language; but this theory does not generate them in the sense of producing them from a heterogeneous level, as in Freudian theory.

[2] On this question, see "Épistémologie de la linguistique", in *Langage*, no. 24.

sociological and psychological adventure, it is nothing other than the phenomenological subject which Husserl defined as a transcendental ego. This subject is a logical and even metaphysical postulate which assures the permanence and fullness of meaning. The transcendental ego is the guarantor of a meaning always already there outside of which neither phenomenological reason nor the consequent theories of enunciation may venture.[3]

In other words, these theories remain pertinent for describing all signifying processes which are employed in the realm of the conscious and which presuppose the homogeneity, the unity of the speaking subject. But they are incapable of taking into account, first, sense as a practice; not a phenomenon but a process of production which presupposes a permanent dialectic (position and destruction) of the identity (which is as much the identity of the speaking subject as the identity of the signification produced for communication).

Also, these theories fail to take into account certain signifying practices which represent extreme states of subjectivity and of society; psychotic states and their corresponding discourse, as well as the sublimations which expand the limits of what I call the signifiable, to which I shall return almost immediately. For the moment I am referring generally to avant-garde art; to its poetry, music and plastic arts.[4]

---

[3] Within this limitation (reducing the speaking subject's activity to the systematicity of consciousness), there nevertheless is a real semiotic discovery which deeply marks the so-called "human sciences". What semiotics has discovered in studying "ideologies" (myths, rituals, moral codes, arts, etc.) as sign systems is that the *law* governing or, if one prefers, the *major constraint* affecting any social practice, lies in the fact that it signifies, i.e. that it is articulated *like* a language. Every social practice, as well as being the object of external (economic, political, etc.) determinations, is also determined by a set of signifying rules, by virtue of the fact that there is present an order of language; that this language has a double articulation (signifier/signified); that this duality stands in an arbitrary relation to the referent; and that all social functioning is marked by the split between referent and symbolic and by the shift from signified to signified coextensive with it.

One may say, then, that what semiotics has discovered is the fact that there is a general social law, that this law is the symbolic dimension which is given in language, and that every social practice offers a specific expression of that law.

But semiotics, by its attempt to set itself up as a theory of practices using language as its model, restricts the value of its discovery to the field of practices which do no more than subserve the principle of social cohesions, of the social contract.

It is not difficult to see why its strong point should be the study of the rules of kinship and myths as examples of community knowledge. Nor is it difficult to see that it cannot simply go on following the linguistic model alone, or even the principle of systematicity if it aims also at tackling signifying practices which, although they do subserve social communications, are at the same time the privileged areas where this is put to non-utilitarian use, the areas of transgression and pleasure: one thinks of the specificity of "art", of ritual, of certain aspects of myths, etc.

Its *raison d'être*, if it is to have one, must consist in its identifying the systematic constraint within each signifying practice (using for that purpose borrowed or original "models") but above all in going beyond that to specifying just what, within the practice, falls outside the system and characterizes the specificity of the practice as such.

Now in order to take account of the speaking subject as a process, that is, simultaneously a unity and the transition to zero[5] of this unity, I shall consider another parameter to be included in the preceding diagram. This is the signifiable (see figure 2).

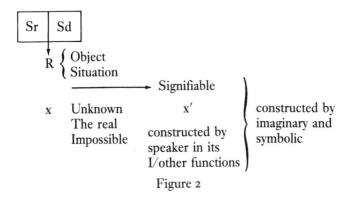

Figure 2

[4] I can summarize my criticism of these theories by saying that one phase of semiology is now over; that which runs from Saussure and Peirce to the Prague School and structuralism, and has made possible the systematic description of the social and/or symbolic constraint within each signifying practice. To criticize this phase for its "ideological bias" – whether phenomenological or more specifically phonological or linguistic – without recognizing the truth it has contributed by revealing and characterizing the immanent causality and in the presence of a social-systematic constraint in each social functioning, leads to a rejection of the symbolic and/or social *thesis* (in Husserl's sense of the word) indispensable to every practice. This rejection is shared both by idealist philosophy, with its neglect of the historical socializing role of the symbolic, and by the various sociological dogmatisms, which suppress the specificity of the symbolic and its logic in their anxiety to reduce them to an "external" determinant.

In my view, a critique of this "semiology of systems" and of its phenomenological foundations is possible only if it starts from a theory of meaning which must necessarily be a theory of the speaking subject. It is common knowledge that the linguistic revival which goes by the name of generative grammar – whatever its variants and mutations – is based on the rehabilitation of the Cartesian conception of language as an *act* carried out by a *subject*. On close inspection, as certain linguistics (from Jakobson to Kuroda) have shown in recent years, this "speaking subject" turns out in fact to be that *transcendental ego* which, in Husserl's view, underlies any and every predicative synthesis, if we "put in brackets" logical or linguistic externality.

Generative grammar, based firmly on this subject, not only expresses the truth of language which structuralism describes as a system – namely that it is the act of an *ego* which has momentarily broken off its connection with that externality, which may be social, natural or unconscious – but creates for itself the opportunity of describing, better than its predecessors, the logic of this thetic act, starting out from an infinity of predication which each national language subjects to strict systems of rules. Yet this transcendental subject is not the essential concern of the semiological revival, and if it bases itself on the conception of language proper to generative grammar, semiology will

The relationship between the referent (as object and situation) and what I have called the signifiable is never a relation of identity, but rather one of displacement: R $\diamondsuit$ signifiable where $\diamondsuit$ represents a contradiction. This relation is also one of emptiness, of the unnameable, of non-sense and of opaque experience which we could designate by the word increasingly haunting semiological theories: the body. One can ask: for linguistics, what is meant by "a body" and what is it one is calling "a body"? One can answer by asking: what appears when a signifier checks (as in chess) a signified?

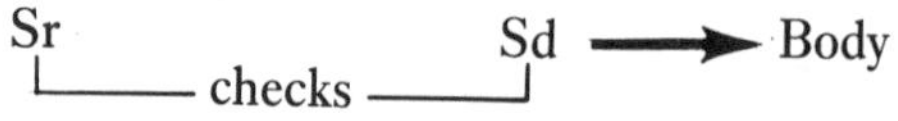

$$\text{Sr} \underline{\qquad \text{checks} \qquad} \text{Sd} \longrightarrow \text{Body}$$

Figure 3

A plurality of signifiers aims at and fails at being a signified. The signifiers check a signified in the sense of chess play, producing the sentiment of body. The diagram of contradiction is thus completed in the following way: R $\diamondsuit$ signifiable $\longrightarrow$ body. As for the signifiable, in a contradictory relation to the referent, it augments, in writing, in the attempt to signify everything, in order that there be no remainder, that the referent be caught exhaustively in the sign

---

not get beyond the reduction – still commonly characteristic of it – of signifying *practices* to their systematic aspect.

In respect of the subject and of signifying, it is the Freudian revolution which seems to me to have achieved the definitive displacement of the Western *épistémé* from its presumed centrality. But although the effects of that revolution have been superbly and authoritatively worked out in the writings of Jacques Lacan in France, or, in a rather different way, in the English anti-psychiatry of R. D. Laing and David Cooper, it has by no means reached far enough yet to affect the semiotic conception of language and of practices. The theory of meaning now stands at a cross-roads; either it will remain an attempt at formalizing meaning-systems by increasing sophistication of the logico-mathematical tools which enable it to formulate models on the basis of a conception (already rather dated) of meaning as the act of a *transcendental ego*, cut off from its body, its unconscious, and also its history; or else it will attune itself to the theory of the speaking subject as a divided subject (conscious/unconscious) and go on to attempt to specify the types of operation characteristic of the two sides of this split; thereby exposing them to those forces extraneous to the logic of the systematic; exposing them to, that is to say, on the one hand, bio-physiological processes (themselves already inescapably part of signifying processes; what Freud labelled "drives"), and, on the other hand, to social constraints (family structures, modes of production, etc.).

5 If we admit that the position of conscious mastery of meaning by the subject constitutes and guarantees the subject's unity, we are forced to state that the various *types* of signifying experiences suppose a relativity of this mastery whose limit would be its zero state, characterized by the afflux of unconsciousness logic alone even from drives or from affects. Knowledge and dream, mastery and psychosis, are the most striking images of these two shores of subjectivity which, nevertheless, far from excluding one another, can be considered reciprocal reverse sides (for example, the psychosis of knowledge, the dream of mastery).

(hence the infinity marker in figure 4). But something is left over, a remnant, experienced as the body. The original diagram can thus be modified again (see figure 4).

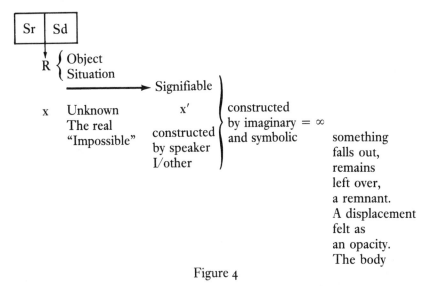

Figure 4

It is poetic language (in the Russian Formalist sense of the term, that is, poetry and prose) which best affects the never-ending process of the *rapprochement* between the signifiable and the referent. Poetic language accomplishes this function through two essential procedures: first, rhythmic and stylistic markings the logic is the motivation of the signifier, i.e. the repletion of the distinguishing or arbitrary void which separates the signifier from the signified. Secondly, poetic language accomplishes this function by operations which are more infrequent, found in marginal texts, operations which disturb the syntactic chain by means of ellipses or indefinite embeddings of grammatical categories.[6]

Given that the coherence of the sign and of the predicate synthesis are the guarantors of the unity of the speaking subject, any attack against the sign or syntax is the mark of a re-evaluation process *vis-à-vis* the speaking subject's unity. I say that the particularities of poetic language designate a subject, as we say in French, *en procès*, on trial and in process.

Any metalanguage (and any university discourse which is didactic and explicative is a metalanguage), however, preserves the coherence of both the sign and the syntax: the subject of a knowing discourse is not a subject on trial; its position equals essentially that of Husserl's transcendental ego.

Here we touch upon the limits of Western reason, which manifested themselves when knowledge confronted the so-called pathological functions

[6] See, for example, Mallarmé's *Un Coup de Dès*.

(insanity) or aesthetic functions (the avant-garde), which are not pure knowledge, and which are not limited to the redirection of sign and syntax matrices, but which break down these matrices in order to renew them.

I say limitations of Western reason because our knowing discourse and its transcendental subject are led to the point where they must take into account this specific practice ("art", "insanity" – but these are only the extremes of a true meaning on trial (*en procès*) which is intrinsic to every exercise of language). This practice does not limit itself to rationality, sign or syntax but operates with these only as its impetus as with any limitations.

Here we are faced with what I shall call the "penitentiary condition" of knowledge and of semiology in particular: imprisoned in meaning is to take into account the trial of meaning; walled into the transcendental ego is to outline the course of the subject on trial, in process: *en procès*.

I say straightaway that the wager which consists of postulating the possibility of knowing, of giving back the trial of sense and of the subject to semiology, is one that has the impertinence of the Pascalian wager. It is perhaps not insignificant that it is a woman who is announcing this while philosophy in France is abandoning, in large part, *any* metalanguage and replacing it with a discourse which calls itself fictional, and which is considered to be the only possible way to witness, if not to render, an accounting of the trial of sense and signification. The fact that this desire to push rationality to the limits of sense and of the ego is being expressed by a woman indicates, without doubt, the necessity of asserting oneself in a modality designated as paternal or phallic. But also and consequently, this indicates the fact that, in spite of appearances, women remain perhaps the ultimate guarantee of sociality after the crisis of reason and the crisis of paternal function, which the West is at present experiencing.

I should like to develop here an attempt to describe the trial of sense and the subject in the infinite–indefinite contest between the referent and the signifiable. I distinguish two modalities of signification: the semiotic and the symbolic.

By *semiotic*, I mean the primary organization (in Freudian terms) of drives by rhythms, intonations and primary processes (displacement, slippage, condensation). Genetically, the semiotic is found in the first echolalias of infants. Logically, it functions in all adult discourses as a supplementary register to that of sign and predicate synthesis. Plato speaks of this in the *Timeus*, in his invocation of a state of language anterior to the word, even to the syllable, and which, quite different from the paternal name, has a maternal connotation. Plato calls this the *chora*, the receptacle, the place before the space which is always already named, one, paternal, sign and predication.

By *symbolic*, I mean precisely the functioning of the sign and predications. The symbolic is constituted beginning with what psychoanalysis calls the mirror stage and the consequent capacities for absence, representation or abstraction. The symbolic is a matter, therefore, of language as a system of meaning (as structuralism and generative grammar study it) – a language with a foreclosed subject or with a transcendental subject-ego.

Sense as a trial and the speaking subject on trial articulate themselves precisely on the impetus of the interaction between these two modalities. The return, the emergence of the semiotic in the symbolic, is subservient to transformational conditions in the relation between subject and receiver: anguish, frustration, identification or projection all break down the unity of the transcendental ego and its system of homogeneous sense and give free rein to what is heterogeneous in sense, that is, to the drive. This heterogeneity (which is the materialistic postulate of the theory) manifests itself in the signifying chain only by the phenomena which I have just called semiotic.[7]

In these circumstances, the speaking subject undergoes a transition to a void, to zero: loss of identity, afflux of drive and a return of symbolic capacities, but this time in order to take control of *drive* itself. This is precisely what expands

---

[7] These will be the various deviations from the grammatical rules of the language: articulatory effects which shift the phonemative system back towards its articulatory, phonetic base and consequently towards the drive-governed bases of sound-production; the over-determination of a lexeme by multiple meanings which it does not carry in ordinary usage but which accrete to it as a result of its occurrence in other texts; syntactic irregularities such as ellipses, non-recoverable deletions, indefinite embeddings, etc.; the replacement of the relationship between the protagonists of any enunciation as they function in a locutory act (see, for example, the work of J. L. Austin and John Searle) by a system of relations based on fantasy; and so forth.

These variations may be partly described by way of what are called the *primary processes* (displacement, condensation – or metonymy, metaphor), transversal to the logico-symbolic processes that function in the predicative synthesis towards establishing the language system. They had already been discovered by the structuralists, following Freud, at the "lower", phonological, level of the linguistic synthesis. To them must be added the compulsion to repetition, but also "operations" characteristic of topologies and capable of establishing *functions* between the signifying code and the fragmented body of the speaking subject as well as the bodies of his familial and social partners. All functions which suppose a *frontier* (in this case the fissure created by the act of naming and the logico-linguistic synthesis which it sets off), and the transgression of that frontier (the sudden appearance of new signifying chains), are relevant to any account of signifying *practice*, where practice is taken as meaning the acceptance of a symbolic law together with the transgression of that law for the purpose of renovating it.

The moment of transgression is the key moment in practice: we can speak of practice wherever there is a transgression of systematicity, i.e. a transgression of the unity proper to the *transcendental ego*. The subject of the practice cannot be the transcendental subject, who lacks the shift, the split in logical unity brought about by language which separates out, within the signifying body, the symbolic order from the workings of the libido (this last revealing itself by the *semiotic disposition*). Identifying the semiotic disposition means, in fact, identifying the shift in the speaking subject, his capacity for renewing the order in which he is inescapably caught up; and that capacity is, for the subject, the capacity for enjoyment.

the limits of the signifiable: a new aspect of the displacement between the referent/signifiable, a new aspect of the body, has thus found its signification.

A mathematical theory could summarize the rules of this particular interaction between the semiotic and the symbolic: it is Thom's Catastrophe Theory. This theory, if one extrapolates it onto an epistemological plane, supposes that all structures are the result of the interaction between two communicating spaces; spaces, however, which do not obey the same laws. In this way, an external space, called the control, which is related to an internal space, can behave in such a way *vis-à-vis* the internal space, that a continual variation of the control, beginning at a certain degree, produces a bifurcation in the internal space of reference. This bifurcation, which is either discontinuity or conflict, is called, precisely, a catastrophe.

Within our semiotic and symbolic co-ordinates, the coherence of the symbolic, that is, the unity of the sign, of predication and of the speaking subject, depends on the "semiotic space of control" (let us say the sufficient repression of the semiotic). From certain socio-psychoanalytical conditions (this is where psychoanalytical thematic interpretation comes into play), the semiotic drive varies – the drive pressure is augmented continuously. Beyond a certain threshold, this quantitative pressure produces a catastrophe in the space of symbolic reference. For example, the unity of morphemes breaks down. Continually under the pressure of semiotic processes, there is produced by condensation (the primary semiotic process), in the place of a word selected from the normative lexicon, a portmanteau word. The most striking example of this process (which is only a simplification of the complex semiotic/symbolic relationship) can be found in Lewis Carroll:

> Take the two words "fuming" and "furious". Make up your mind that you will say both words, but leave it unsettled which you will say first. Now open your mouth and speak. If your thoughts incline ever so little towards "fuming", you will say "fuming–furious"; if they turn, by even a hair's breadth, toward "furious", you will say "furious–fuming"; but if you have that rarest of gifts, a perfectly balanced mind, you will say "frumious".

This description, like all descriptions and all metalanguage, remains essentially preoccupied with *sense*. But it considers sense as a heterogeneous dynamic: a two-tiered dynamic where one approaches sense without attaining it, in an unnameable manner. This conception of sense functions thanks to an interest directed beyond the linguistic phenomenon to the experiences of the speaking subject, and particularly to marginal experiences such as psychosis or art.

This seems to me to permit a new conception of praxis, a renewal of the Hegelian–Marxist dialectic at this level. This conception is opposed to the homogeneous direction of Hegel's Absolute Idea, because this idea, even while negating itself, never negates itself in and of itself, in its identity. It remains enclosed in the totality of logical knowledge. My conception is also opposed to a certain Marxist humanism which echoes the idealistic dialectical totality of

Hegel or concretizes it in the image of a providential proletariat, reducing the negation only to a merely economic externality.

The present renewal of semiology considers sense as a signifying process and a heterogeneous dynamic, and challenges the logical imprisonment of the subject in order to open the subject towards the body and society.[8] This seems to me to contribute to the elaboration of a more current conception of the subject in contemporary history: a subject precisely "on trial" as this is manifested in certain marginal experiences (modern art, psychoses, drugs). But also as this reveals itself in current political situations of the twentieth century, beginning with fascism, among other such manifestations. This is a subject in a crisis of rationality, struggling with its drives, the most impulsive of which Freud said was the death drive.

I can add that a textual study of Céline, undertaken in the methodical manner which I have just outlined, seems to me to show that the speaking subject, i.e. the author and the receiver, attempts a dynamic organization of the most profound crises of rationality. This dynamic organization is one which insures both social communication and the subject's pleasure or, as we say, *jouissance*, as characterized by the theories of catastrophe. This dynamic organization operates on two levels; first, on the level of fiction, i.e. as interrupted narrative structure, as thematic of death and of violence arising from the tradition of the apocalyptic genre, and also as thematic of laughter, the mask, nonsense and music, arising from the tradition of the carnival genre.

Secondly, and more importantly, this dynamic organization operates on a clearly definable linguistic level, effectuated by the usage of slang intended to introduce nonsense into the lexicon, and by frequent syntactical ellipses which

---

[8] We can remark that these two terms, today, can obtain a quasi-mystical value, outside of semiological and analytic rationality. We can even ask if modernity has not dethroned the monarch's body, if it has not already killed that body, in order to erect in its place the even more incontestable power of the social body, of the body and the social — full, opaque, unanalysable. It is not a matter either of sacralizing or avoiding these two domains (although perhaps it comes back to the same thing). However, in positing the *heterogeneity* (cf. this notion in my book *La Révolution du langage poétique*, Paris: Seuil, 1973) of the body with respect to sense, on the one hand we are led to consider many bodily manifestations as signifying in the sense of tributaries of sense and communication, and, on the other hand, we are led to pose *vis-à-vis* sense a zone of the *unknown*, which could be a guarantee against interpretative delirium, but also, in the consideration of human behaviour, maintain an infra-symbolic, ethological, biological or instinctual modality, which would function more according to the logic of the *automaton* than that of *adaptation*. Is not the semiotic body that I hear in pre-genital, narcissistic regressions of my patients – or even in such poetic elaborations – an exquisite encounter between this animal automaton body and the symbolic body which is only the body of the other? Finally, if it is true that we can call *perversion* this betwixt-and-between of the automaton body and the body of the other, we are compelled to state how much modern man – in his experiences of desire as well as politics deprived of a transcendental, even moral authority – finds himself deeper in perversion than ever.

cause the more primordial semiotic, rhythmic and intonational determination to appear beyond what I call the symbolic function.

These most profound crises of rationality, which are in this way dynamically organized, are accompanied by a rigid investiture of other archaic and repressive structures, when and if their attempts at becoming semiotic–symbolic fail. These archaic and repressive structures include order, the family, normalcy, normative classical psychological-tending discourse, all of which are just so many characteristics of fascist ideology. Consequently, we may conclude that texts on experiencing limits – this is modern art – constitute the most direct and risky approach to the fascist phenomenon. And parenthetically, we know how much the avant-garde artists have been tempted by fascism. At the same time, these texts constitute the fascist phenomenon's most radical opposition, that is, the defence which is most solidly anchored in the speaking being.

I conclude by indicating that, far from being simply a semiological preoccupation, the renewal of the conception of meaning and of the subject as practice and process concerns an entire socio-historical horizon.

VJAČESLAV VSEVOLODOVIČ IVANOV

# Eisenstein's Montage of Hieroglyphic Signs

Before he became a film director, Sergej Eisenstein had studied oriental languages, and this experience strongly influenced his later theoretical investigations of the sign nature of film language and his practical experiments in constructing cinematic "hieroglyphs".

John Dos Passos had an enthusiastic sketch of Moscow in the late twenties, and during his stay in Russia he underwent the strong influence of Russian art of the period: the device of the "Camera Eye" in his novels – indeed the very principles of compositional montage, testify to Vertov's and Eisenstein's influence, which he himself acknowledged.[1] In his diary, Eisenstein noted the sections of the film *October* that particularly appealed to Dos Passos, i.e. the shots of Napoleon, the montage sequence of the "Gods".[2] Many things in Moscow of that time struck Dos Passos by their unexpectedness, and among them the fact that Eisenstein, already a world-renowned film director, knew Japanese characters well.

In his memoirs Eisenstein relates that he entered the Department of Oriental Languages of the General Staff Academy in order to obtain permission to go to Moscow and have the possibility of studying art there. "For this," he writes, "I had to cope with thousands of Japanese words, mastering hundreds of whimsical hieroglyphic characters."[3] His notebooks bear ample witness to the

---

[1] See Dos Passos' interviews in *Cahiers du cinéma*, no. 1 (1967) and *Lettres françaises*, no. 1162 (22–28 December 1966) p. 9. On Eisenstein, Japanese culture and Moscow of the twenties see J. Dos Passos, *The Theme is Freedom* (New York, 1956) pp. 41, 67.

[2] Eisenstein's *Diaries* (Moscow: CGALI, Central State Archive) vol. 4c, p. 46, §6. Henceforth the *Diaries* are abbreviated as *ED*.

[3] Sergej Eisenstein, *Izbrannye proizvedenija v šesti tomax* (Selected writings in six volumes) (Moscow, 1964–71) vol. 1, p. 98; see the English translation, "How I Became a Film Director", in *Notes of a Film Director* (New York, 1970) p. 11. Hereafter, references to Eisenstein's *Izbrannye proizvedenija* are abbreviated as *IP*, and are followed by volume and page number. Hereafter, *Notes of a Film Director* is abbreviated as *NFD*.

seriousness of his study of Japanese.[4] As Eisenstein recalled, "memorizing words is not the most difficult thing about the Japanese language. The most difficult thing is to master the unfamiliar way of thinking determining the Eastern nuances of speech, sentence structure, word order, writing, etc." (*IP*, I, 98; *NFD*, 11). He concludes his description of the linguistic tortures he endured with the words: "How grateful I was later on to fate for having subjected me to the ordeal of learning an oriental language, opening before me that strange way of thinking and teaching me word pictography. It was precisely this 'unusual' way of thinking that later helped me to master the nature of montage" (*IP*, I, 99; *NFD*, 11).

Indeed, it suffices to read through Eisenstein's essays and diary of the period when the theory of the "intellectual cinema" was born (1928-9) to become convinced of the significance that the analogy with ideograms had for its formulation. Among the essays of those years "Beyond the Shot" (translated into English as "The Cinematographic Principle and the Ideogram"), which was written as an afterword to N. Kaufman's book *The Japanese Cinema*, is of particular interest.[5] It is devoted to an analysis of those features of Japanese culture which struck Eisenstein as cinematographic, even though at the time they seemed beyond the means of the cinema ("beyond the shot").

The essay begins with an analysis of ideograms. Eisenstein demonstrates how the ancient representation for "horse" is transformed into the ideogram 馬 "horse" (Chinese *ma*, Japanese *umma*): "In the fierily cavorting ideogram *ma* one can no longer recognize the features of the dear little horse sagging pathetically on its hindquarters, in the writing style of Ts'ang Chieh, so well known from ancient Chinese bronzes" (*IP*, II, 284; *FF*, 29). Here Eisenstein formulates a law characteristic of all typologically late ideographic systems of writing, such as Near Eastern cuneiform or Tangut hieroglyphics. In these systems the element of representationality, which is still preserved in the semi-pictographic (i.e. partly similar to drawing) signs of early Sumerian or ancient Chinese writing, is almost completely eliminated.

The transformation of the written sign's signifier, which becomes more and more conventional, is usually connected with the process that Eisenstein traces in detail in "Beyond the Shot" and other works of the same period. In semiotic terms it is a question of the transformation of iconic or indexical signs into symbolic ones.[6] Duality is characteristic of any sign, i.e. the presence of an

---

[4] CGALI (Moscow: Central State Archive) fund 1923, 1/892.

[5] "Za kadrom", *IP*, II, 283-96; see the English translation in *Film Form* (New York, 1949) pp. 28-44. Hereafter, *Film Form* is abbreviated as *FF*.

[6] For more details see V. V. Ivanov, "Lingvistika i gumanitarnye problemy semiotiki" (Linguistics and humanistic problems in semiotics), *Izvestija AN SSSR, Serija literatury i jazyka*, no. 3 (1963) pp. 236-45. On the semiotic terms "icon", "index" and "symbol", which go back to Charles Sanders Peirce, see J. K. Lekomcev, "O semiotičeskom aspekte izobrazitel'nogo iskusstva" (On the semiotic aspect of visual art), *Trudy po znakovym sistemam III* (Tartu, 1967) pp. 122-9; see the Italian translation in *I sistemi di segni e lo strutturalismo sovetico*, ed. U. Eco and R. Faccani (Milan, 1969) pp. 202-10.

external aspect (signifier), whether written or oral, which is correlated with a meaning, a concept (the signified) and an object or class of objects (the denotatum). The connection between the signifier, on the one hand, and the signified and the denotatum, on the other, may be various. In iconic signs, for example in a picture painted according to norms of representational art, the signifier reproduces the denotatum, even if only partially. An indexical sign, for example an arrow pointing in the direction one should go, is limited to a signal indicating an object. Finally, symbolic signs, for example the majority of words in a natural language, are characterized by the completely conventional nature of the connection between signifier, signified and denotatum.

The symbolic signs of ideographic writing that interested Eisenstein usually undergo an historical development from the most direct (representational) connection between the figuration and the meaning to the most roundabout, conventional type of connection. An ideogram whose very shape represents a concrete object, for example the two-leaved gates of a house (Chinese 门 *min*), later becomes a sign of grammatical meaning (in the case of *min*, it marks the plural number),[7] viz. 人门 *zhen min* "people", from *zhen* "man", which in antiquity was a pictographic representation of a man on two legs.

The transformation of an independent word into a sign conveying grammatical meaning is an instance of grammaticalization. In almost all the languages of the world, syncategorematic, purely syntactic words like postpositions and prepositions develop from nouns originally designating concrete parts of the body. Thus Latin *ante* ("before") and kindred prepositions in other Indo-European languages (Greek ἀντι, whence English *anti-*, etc.) develop from case forms of the noun "forehead" (cf. cuneiform Hittite *hant*, "forehead"), just as in north-western Caucasian languages words like Adygei *nate* ("forehead") gradually become postpositions with the meaning "before". Such an expression of abstract spatial relations through the use of words designating parts of the body is encountered as well in the earliest Sumerian texts, which are among the oldest written records of mankind. Such examples illustrate one of Eisenstein's favourite notions, namely that a human gesture lies hidden in the basic meaning of even the most abstract words: "historically, motion develops first, then the word and speech; finally, a pictographic written sign emerges" (*IP*, IV, 292).

The evolution of iconic signs into symbolic ones takes place not only in the transformation of drawn pictograms into stylized ideographic symbols and in grammaticalization, where an independent word becomes a grammatical sign, but also in the development of rituals and social institutions. As the outstanding English ethnologist Hocart has established,

> the comparative analysis of [social] institutions seems to have converged
> with the work of linguists on an important process in the evolution of
> thought and its expression. Man, it would seem, begins by putting

---

[7] On the historical connection between these two ideograms see E. D. Polivanov, *Stat'i po obščemu jazykoznaniju* (Essays in general linguistics) (Moscow, 1968).

together representations (a mode of thought we revert to in dreams). Gradually he disentangles relations and modes, and gives them separate expression. In order to express them he has to use existing material, which consists of representations. These are purged of all substance, so that they may serve only to bind the representations into a well-ordered whole.[8]

Hocart examined from this point of view the development of specific ritual symbols for the sky, the sun, thunder, or the bull, which later became syntactic signs for a particular social function, that of Kingship. (It is interesting to note that in Eisenstein's last film *Ivan the Terrible*, he reconstructed certain archaic rituals linked to the symbolism of kingship.) According to the extent of its development, the king's power is abstracted from its original symbolic function, as has indeed happened to the role of the king in all ancient societies that lacked a separate system of governing.

Similarly, the elimination of features of representationality also explains the development of games, where the division into two groups of figures (in the case of checkers or chessman, for example) or into two teams (as in soccer) reproduces the dualistic social organization at an earlier stage. Purely syntactic rules for the arrangement of the given game come only at a later developmental stage. The correlation of the two teams with the sun or night is still preserved in the games of ancient Mexico, whose archaic features so fascinated Eisenstein. The re-emergence of the ancient ritual function of the game – for example in soccer where each team is again correlated with a certain social group – is an example of a regression back to ancient forms which appears in contemporary life particularly under the influence of affect, a phenomenon Eisenstein studied attentively.

The same evolutionary pattern may also be observed in the case of ornament, where the original direct connection with a fixed denotatum can be established only historically, a task to which numerous studies on the history of ornament are devoted. Eisenstein was interested in ornament as a "prototype" of the fundamental features of all art and was an attentive student of its history in various cultures, as his library and numerous notes demonstrate. As he discovered, the most archaic form of ornament is that in which the object serves as a sign of itself: "in the earliest stage of ornament, representationality is entirely lacking. In place of a representation one finds simply the object as such: the claws of bears, or the teeth of ocean fish, perforated seashells, dried berries

---

[8] A. M. Hocart, *Kings and Councillors* (Chicago, 1970, 2nd edn) pp. 154ff. Hocart's remark about the possibility of comparing primal images to the dream processes is of importance in light of contemporary psychological theories of art. Since Freud, this juxtaposition has become a commonplace in the most diverse movements of psychological theory. In English sociological aesthetics one should mention the work of Christopher Caudwell, published almost simultaneously with the first edition of Hocart's book (1936): cf. his chapter "Poetry's Dream-work" in *Illusion and Reality* (New York, 1937).

or eggshells threaded on string."[9] Following Eisenstein's view, the display of the object as such in twentieth-century art – for example, in the collages of the Cubists – may also be considered as a sort of regression to a more elementary stage in the development of art.

In the case of ornament, its further evolution is marked by the gradual development of representational features, which slowly become more and more conventional. In Eisenstein's opinion, the paintings on Peruvian ceramics, which he analysed many times, are striking precisely because the degree of their graphic and chromatic stylization makes it "impossible to catch the sources of the external impressions which gave birth to them". In the case of Mayan ornaments, Eisenstein, with an aesthetic insight anticipating the conclusions reached by recent studies of ancient Central American art, made out "endless variations on the theme of the silhouettes of the upper jaw-bones of caymans and crocodiles".[10]

The loss of representationality, which thus appears to be the result of parallel developments in the most diverse sign systems, interested Eisenstein particularly in those cases where it was connected with the combination of two signs into one. In the essay mentioned above, "Beyond the Shot", he examines examples of the second category of ideograms (*huei-i*, "copulative", according to the Chinese terminology) and shows how the transition from representing an object to conveying a concept is accomplished by means of montage:

> The combination of two hieroglyphs of the simplest series is to be regarded not as their sum, but as their product, i.e., as a value of another dimension, another degree; each, separately, corresponds to an *object*, to a fact, but their combination corresponds to a *concept*. From simple hieroglyphs has been fused – the ideogram. The combination of two 'depictables' makes it possible to represent something graphically undepictable.
>
> For example: the picture for water and the picture of an eye signifies 'to weep'; the picture of an ear near the drawing of a door = 'to overhear';
>
> a dog + a mouth = 'to bark';
> a mouth + a child = 'to scream';
> a mouth + a bird = 'to sing';
> a knife + a heart = 'sorrow', and so on.
>
> But this is – montage!
>
> Yes. It is exactly what we do in the cinema, combining shots that are *depictive*, single in meaning, neutral in content – into *intellectual* contexts and series. . . .
>
> And we hail the method of the long lamented Ts'ang Chieh as a first step in this direction.[11]

---

[9] From a fragment characteristically entitled "I Can't Shoot: I Write Instead".
[10] "I Can't Shoot".
[11] *IP*, II, 284–5; *FF*, 29–30.

Eisenstein is often regarded as a theoretician who overrated the role of montage in film and extended this principle to all forms of art.[12] But he himself moved away from the extremes of his early theoretical works, with their emphasis on montage of short segments in the narrow (technical cinematographic) sense. In his later writings, as well as in the early essay "Beyond the Shot", Eisenstein is preoccupied less with montage in the generally accepted, conventional sense than with the "syntax of the language of artistic forms" (*IP*, III, 218), and in particular, "the audio-visual syntax of film" (III, 474). Even his terminology coincides with contemporary semiotics, which understands syntax as the rules for combining signs with each other in order to convey a meaning, whether that combination be one of sounds in a word, words in a sentence, brush strokes in a picture, hieroglyphs in an hieroglyphic inscription, or shots in a film. The first decades of our century were characterized by the exclusive attention paid to the syntax of various signs, both in art (Cubism, Dada, montage cinematography) and science (descriptive linguistics, logical syntax, etc.). In this sense Eisenstein's early films, with their emphasis on montage, as well as his accompanying theoretical declarations, answered the spirit of the times. Later on, however, even Eisenstein himself was to point to the "palpability of the contrapuntal construction" in *Potemkin* as a sign of immaturity (*IP*, III, 290).

For current semiotic studies of artistic works as sign phenomena, Eisenstein's aesthetic investigations are of less interest where, following the tastes of his time, he was occupied primarily with syntax as such, compared to where, as in the passage cited above from the essay "Beyond the Shot", he used syntax as a means of exploring semantics. As recent works on logical semantics demonstrate, "there is a sense in which semantics can be reduced to syntax".[13] This was essentially what Eisenstein was after when he examined how what is "graphically inexpressible" can be conveyed by the syntactic combination of two representations, for example of two pictographs or hieroglyphs. He regarded this principle to be fundamental for the "hieroglyph" of the "intellectual cinema", which was meant to go beyond mere photographic representationality.

Immediately after completing his work on the film *October*, Eisenstein sought to discover how in its successful parts he had managed to convey a single meaning by a sequence of representationally diverse shots. On 2 April 1928 he noted in his diary: "A brilliant way of imparting synonymity to a shot is simply to repeat it. The quite baroque complexity of the sequence of the Jordan stairs + Kerensky + the two adjutants + the statues, etc. – is quite unlike a 'monosemous' sign. But through repetition it acquires a single meaning – 'ascension'" (*ED*, IV, 20) (figures 1–12). Eisenstein marked this passage with three bold marginal strokes on either side and added in French: "Il se souligne

---

[12] Cf., for example, R. Micha, "Le cinéma, art du montage?", *Critique*, no. 51–2 (1951) pp. 723ff.; J. Carta, "L'humanisme commence au langage", *Esprit* (1960) pp. 1114ff.; C. Metz, "Le cinéma: langue ou langage?", *Communications*, no. 4 (1964) pp. 52ff., and *Essais sur la signification au cinéma* (Paris, 1968) pp. 40ff.

[13] A. Church, *Introduction to Mathematical Logic* (Princeton, NJ, 1956) vol. I, p. 65.

Figure 1    *The dictator*

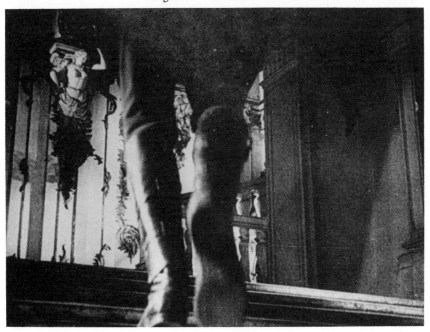

Figure 2    *The Commander-in-Chief*

Figure 3

Figure 4

Figure 5    *The Prime Minister*

Figure 6

Figure 7　*He – the Hope of the Country and The Revolution –*

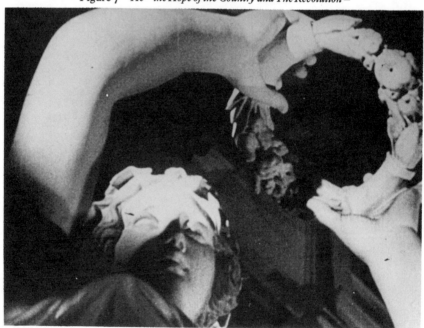

Figure 8

Figure 9   –A. F. Kerensky

Figure 10

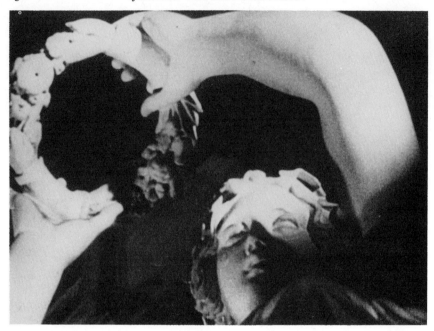

Figure 11

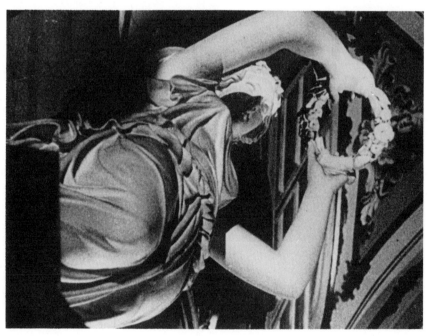

Figure 12

lui-même" ("It [the sign-shot] underlines itself"). His formulation reminds one of that given by the Dutch linguist van Ginneken for the sign nature of the ancient language of gestures and hieroglyphs: "le signe se signifie lui-même" ("the sign signifies itself").[14]

In Eisenstein's work on the theory of the meaning of the sign-shot in the "intellectual cinema", one is constantly struck by the analogy he makes between montage sequences and sequences of pictographic signs in oriental ideograms. In his own words, "I used as much as I could all the parallel readings and parallel significations" (*ED*, IV, 30); which reminds one of the structure of parallel phonetic readings of one and the same character in Japanese ideograms. In his copy of Granet's book on ancient Chinese thought,[15] Eisenstein underlined the description of the typical Chinese combination of meaningful (ideographic) signs (for example of the sign denoting "clothing") with phonetic signs (for example the sign *li*, which in its ideographic use signifies "village") to create complex hieroglyphs (for example *li* "lining"). He noted the similarity between the principles of construction of such combinations and the sort that he called "bimechanical".[16] For Eisenstein, what was essential was that in montage, i.e. the unification in a syntagmatic sequence of two iconic signs (hieroglyphs or film shots), each of which can be correlated with a concrete object or denotatum, there emerges a complex abstract symbol that correlates with a new concept rather than with the denotata of the iconic signs combined. The whole is more than the sum of its parts and different in nature: there is a movement from representation to abstraction, and from the concrete to the abstract.[17]

Eisenstein would have been happy to learn that the principle he formulated was rediscovered in the art of ancient Mexico, which he considered so close to his own work, thanks to the comparison with montage in film. In a book full of astute observations, the Americanist Ferdinand Anton notes "the juxtaposition of two distinct terms which tacitly express a third" as the most characteristic stylistic feature of Old Mexican poetry. Apparently, without knowing of Eisenstein's repeatedly expressed conviction that his own worldview and Mexican

[14] J. van Ginneken, *La Reconstruction typologique des langues archaïques de l'humanité* (Amsterdam, 1939) and "Ein neuer Versuch zur Typologie der alteren Sprachstructuren", *Travaux du Cercle linguistique de Prague*, no. 8 (1939).

[15] Granet, *La Pensée chinoise* (Paris, 1924).

[16] See Eisenstein's note "bimec!" in his copy of Granet's *La Pensée chinoise*, p. 77; see also p. 61, where a passage is underlined to the effect that the phonetic component parts of complex ideograms are preserved longer than their semantic components.

[17] M. Brystrzycka, "Eisenstein as a Precursor of Semantics in Film Art", *Proceedings of the First International Congress of Semiotics* (Warsaw, 1966), has noted that the principles formulated by Eisenstein for the combination of simple pictograms into complex signs are applicable not only to oriental languages, with which he was familiar, but to Egyptian hieroglyphs as well. A comparison of complex ideograms and film montage that coincides almost verbatim with Eisenstein's thoughts on the subject is to be found in J. Giono's essay "Écriture et cinéma", *L'Express*, no. 637 (1961), pp. 16–17.

234     VJAČESLAV VSEVOLODOVIČ IVANOV

culture were internally so very close, Anton writes that this method of old Mexican lyrical poetry "is not unlike the montage technique of the great Russian masters of the silent film, who were less concerned with narrative than with the evocation of specific associations by a juxtaposition of shots".[18] Anton has in mind such figures of speech in Aztec poetry as *choquitzli moteca ixayotl pixahui* ("sorrow increases, tears run") to express grief; the descriptive denotation "my body" by means of the double metonymy "my hand, my foot" (*pars pro toto*); and the designation of "precious, riches, beauty" by the juxtaposition "jade stones, quetzal feathers". Similar in construction are such pairs as "his word, his breath" meaning "his speech"; "water and hill" for "settlement"; "spear and lance" or "water and fire" for "war"; "mat and stool" for "authority" or "dignity"; "night and wind" for "unseen gods" (where the principle of conveying the unrepresentable and unseeable by combining two concrete representations is particularly clear); or "flower and song" for "poetry".

The device of constructing complex signs by combining simple iconic or indexical signs (in particular, signs indicating bodily parts) unites figurative systems like Aztec poetry and ideographic systems of writing with sign languages incorporating "lexical gestures" or gestures equivalent to words.[19] This may be seen as a confirmation of Eisenstein's idea of the interrelation between gesture, word and ideogram. In the sign language of Trappist monks, for instance, "wing" is denoted by an iconic gesture (the ends of the thumb touch the mouth while arms are extended and flap); "sweet" is signified by placing a finger between the lips and slowly vibrating them; "bee" by a combination of these two iconic gestures.[20] A similar complex gestural "hieroglyph" in the sign language of the American Indians is that for "wise", formed by combining simple iconic and indexical signs for "heart", "forehead" and "good".[21]

We have tried to show above that Eisenstein's cinematic concept of the "montage of hieroglyphic signs", like many of his basic concepts, goes beyond the realm of film language alone and has important consequences for semiotics in general. In this particular instance, the concept helps to explain certain synchronic facts of language and other sign systems, as well as certain aspects of their diachronic development. Eisenstein's research into the language of film always went hand and hand with insightful explorations in anthropology, linguistics and the history of artistic forms. Not only does the growing science of semiotics provide support for certain of Eisenstein's theoretical assumptions, but they in turn prove to be of tremendous significance for the

[18] F. Anton, *Alt-Mexico und seine Kunst* (Leipzig, 1965) p. 111.
[19] See M. Key, "Gestures and Responses: a Preliminary Study among Some Indian Tribes of Bolivia", *Studies in Linguistics*, no. 16 (1962) pp. 3–4.
[20] See E. Buyssens, "Le langage par gestes chez les moines", *Revue de l'Institut de sociologie*, no. 4 (1956) pp. 5–6.
[21] See Magnus Ljung, "Principles of a Stratificational Analysis of the Plains Indians' Sign Language", *International Journal of American Linguistics*, no. 31 (1965) p. 2.

development of semiotic methodology. Apart from his importance as a director and key theoretician of the new medium of film, Eisenstein emerges as a major precursor and theoretician of modern semiotics.

JACQUES DERRIDA

# To Speculate – on "Freud"

There is a mute daughter. And more than another daughter who will have used the paternal credit in an abundant discourse of inheritance – she will have said, perhaps, this is why it is up to your father to speak. Not only my father, but your father. This is Sophie. The daughter of Freud and mother of Ernst whose death soon will toll in the text. Very softly, in a strange note added afterward.

Freud sets the stage, and in his fashion defines the apparently principal character. He insists upon the normality of the child. This is the condition for justifiable experimentation. The child is a paradigm. He is therefore not at all precocious in his intellectual development. He is on good terms with everyone.

Particularly with his mother.

I leave it to you to juxtapose – to refold or to reapply – the content of the narrative with the scene of its writing, and to do so not only here, for example, but elsewhere too, and this is only an example, by exchanging the places of the narrator and of the principal character, or principal couple – Ernst–Sophie, the third character (the father – the spouse – the son-in-law) never being far off, and occasionally even too close. In a classical narrative, the narrator, who allegedly observes, is not the author, granted. If things were not different in this case, taking into account that it does not present itself as a literary fiction, then we would have to, will have to, re-elaborate the distinction between the narrator's *I* and the author's *I* by adapting the distinction to a new "metapsychological" toponymy.

Thus he is apparently on good terms with everyone, especially his mother, since (or despite the fact that) he did not cry in her absence. She occasionally left him for hours. Why didn't he cry? Freud simultaneously seems to congratulate himself for the child's not crying and to be surprised, that is sorry, about it. Is this child fundamentally as normal as Freud himself imagines him to be? For in the same sentence in which he attributes this excellent personality to the fact that his grandson did not cry for his daughter (the child's mother) during such long absences, he adds "although" or "and yet": the son was very attached to her, not only had she herself breastfed him, but she had cared for him with help from no one. But this small anomaly is quickly erased, and Freud leaves his "although" without consequences. Everything is fine, an excellent child, *but*. Here is the *but*: this excellent child had a disturbing habit. One does not immediately get over Freud's imperturbable conclusion at the end of his fabulous description of the disturbing habit: "I eventually realized that it was a game." Here is the description, and I shall occasionally interrupt my translation:

The child was not at all precocious in his intellectual development. At the age of one and a half he could say only a few comprehensible words; he could also make use of a number of sounds which expressed a meaning [*bedeutungsvolle Laute*, phonemes charged with meaning] intelligible to those around him. He was, however, on good terms with his parents and their one servant-girl, and tributes were paid to his being a "good [*anständig*, easy, reasonable] boy." He did not disturb his parents at night, he conscientiously obeyed orders not to touch certain things or go into certain rooms, and above all [*vor allem anderen*, before all else] he never cried when his mother left him for hours, although he was greatly attached to this mother, who had not only fed him herself but had also looked after him without any outside help.   (p. 14)[1]

I interrupt my reading for a moment. The picture painted is apparently without a shadow, without a "but". There is indeed an "although" and a "however", but these are counterweights, internal compensations used to describe the balance: he was not at all precocious, even a bit slow, *but* he was on good terms with his parents; he did not cry when his mother left him, *but* he was attached to her, and for good reason. Am I alone in already hearing a restrained accusation? The excuse itself has left an archive within grammar: "however", "although". Freud cannot prevent himself from excusing his daughter's son. What is he reproaching him for? But is he reproaching him for what he excuses him for or for what excuses him? – the secret fault for which he excuses him or precisely that which excuses him for his fault? And with whom would the prosecutor be identified in the mobile syntax of this trial?

---

[1] Citations from *Beyond the Pleasure Principle* refer to vol. XVIII of the Standard Edition (London: Hogarth Press, 1955), and are given by page number in the text. Derrida himself translated the passages cited from *Beyond*, and often more accurately than Strachey in the Standard Edition. Thus I have consistently modified the English translation. When the discrepancies between the Standard Edition (SE) and the German are major, I cite the German in these footnotes. All references are to the *Gesammelte Werke*, vol. 13 (London: Imago, 1940), and will be given as *GW* and a page number. Thus, here, *GW*, p. 13. As an example of the discrepancies between the *GW* and the SE: Strachey has divided into several sentences Freud's single sentence that begins "He did not disturb his parents at night . . ."; he has also translated Freud's "*wenn die Mutter es für Stunden verliess*" as "when his mother left him for a *few* hours". [Translator's note (hereafter TN).]

The big "but" will arise immediately afterward and this time as a shadow in the picture, although the word "but" itself is not there. It is translated as "however" (*nun*): "now, still it happens that", "none the less it remains that", "it must be said however", and "nevertheless, fancy that, 'This good little boy, however, had an occasional disturbing habit. . . .'"

What (despite everything) is satisfactory about this excellent child is his normality, his calm, his ability to bear the absence of the beloved daughter (mother) without fear or tears – all of which makes some cost foreseeable. Everything is very constructed, very propped up, dominated by a system of rules and compensations, an economy which, in an instant, will appear in the form of a disturbing habit. An economy which permits him to bear what his "good habits" might cost him. The child, too, is speculating. How does he pay (himself) for accepting the orders not to touch certain things? How does the PP[2] negotiate between good and bad habits? The grandfather, the father of the daughter and mother, actively selects the traits of the description. I see him rushing and worried, like a dramatist or director who has a part in the play. Staging it, *he hurries*: to have everything controlled, everything in order, before going off to change for his part. This is translated by peremptory authoritarianism, unexplained decisions, interrupted speeches, unanswered questions. The elements of the *mise-en-scène* have been put in place: an original normality in relation to the good breast, an economic principle requiring that the removal of the breast (so well dominated, so well removed from its removal) be overpaid by a supplementary pleasure, and also requiring that a bad habit reimburse, eventually with profit, good habits; for example the orders not to touch certain things. The *mise-en-scène* hastens on, the actor–dramatist–producer will have done everything himself, he also knocks three or four times,[3] the curtain is about to rise. But we do not know if it rises on the scene or in the scene. Before the entrance of any character, there is a curtained bed. All the comings and goings will have to pass before the curtain.

I myself will not open this curtain – I leave this to you – on to all the others, the words and things (curtains, canvases, veils, hymens, umbrellas, etc.) with which I have concerned myself for so long.[4] One could attempt to juxtapose all these things with each other, according to the same law. I have neither the time nor the taste for this task, which can be accomplished by itself or done without.

Rather, here is Freud's curtain along with the strings pulled by the grandfather:

[2] It is to be recalled throughout what follows that PP is not only the abbreviation of Pleasure Principle, but also the affectionate term for "grandfather" in French (*pépé*). It is always to be understood in both senses. [TN]

[3] Referring to the traditional knocks that precede the raising of the curtain in French theatre. [TN]

[4] Derrida is referring to many of his other works here, for example "The Double Session" in *Dissemination*, trans. B. Johnson (Chicago: University of Chicago Press, 1981) on the hymen, and *Spurs*, trans. B. Harlow (Chicago: University of Chicago Press, 1979) on the umbrella. [TN]

This good little boy, however, had an occasional disturbing habit of taking any small objects he could get hold of and throwing them away from him into a corner, under the bed, and so on, so that hunting for his toys [*Spielzeuge*, playthings] and picking them up [*Zusammensuchen*, to search in order to bring together, to reassemble] was often not easy work.  (p. 14)[5]

The work is for the parents, but also for the child who expects it from them. And the work consists of reassembling, of searching in order to bring together, in reuniting in order to *give back*. This is what the grandfather calls work, an often difficult work. In return, he will call play the dispersion which sends far away (the operation of distantiation), and will call playthings the collection of manipulated objects. The entire process is itself divided – there is a division between play and work: the child *plays* at throwing away his "toys", and the parents *work* at reassembling them, which is often not easy; as if in this phase of the operation the parents were not playing and the child were not working. He is completely excused from working. Who would dream of accusing him of this? But the work is not always easy, and one's breath grows heavy. Why does he disperse, why does he send far away everything he has at hand, and who and what?

The spool has not yet made its appearance. In a certain sense, it will be only an example of the process Freud has just described. But it will be an exemplary example, yielding a supplementary and decisive "observation" for the interpretation. In the exemplary example, the child throws away and brings back to himself, disperses and reassembles, gives and takes back by himself: he reassembles the reassembling and the dispersion, the multiplicity of agents, work and play, into a single agent, apparently, and into a single object. This is what the grandfather will understand as "a game", at the moment when all the strings are brought back together, held in one hand, dispensing with the parents, with their work or play which consisted in clearing the stage.

The spool has not yet made its appearance. Until now *Spielzeug* has designated only a collection, the set of toys, the unity of a multiplicity that can be scattered, that the parents work at reassembling, and that the grandfather here reassembles into a word. This collective unity is the apparatus of a game that can *dislocate* itself: can change its place and fragment or disperse itself. The word for things as a set, in this theory of the set, is *Zeug*, the instrument, the tool, the product – all these things, and, according to the same semantic transition in French or in English, the penis. I am not commenting on what Freud says, I am not saying that Freud is saying: by dispersing his objects or playthings into the distance the child not only separates himself from his mother (as will be said further on) and even from his father, but also, and primarily, from the supplementary complex constituted by the maternal breast and his own penis, allowing the parents, but not for long, to reassemble, to co-operate

[5] *GW*, p. 13. Freud's phrase is "*keine leichte Arbeit*", which Strachey has given as "quite a business". [TN]

in order to reassemble, to reassemble themselves, but not for long, in order to reassemble what he wants to dissociate, send away, separate, but not for long. If he separates himself from his *Spielzeug* as if from himself and with the aim of allowing himself to be reassembled, it is that he himself is also a collection whose reassemblage can yield an entire combinatorial of sets. All those who play or work at reassembling are participants. I am not saying that Freud says this. But he will say, in one of the two footnotes I have mentioned, that it is indeed himself or his image that the child "plays" at making appear–disappear. He is part of his *Spielzeug*.

The spool has not yet made its appearence. Here it is, again preceded by an interpretive anticipation:

> As he did this [throwing away his entire *Spielzeug*] he gave vent to a loud, long-drawn-out "O–O–O–O," accompanied by an expression of interest and satisfaction, which according to the common judgment of his mother and the writer of the present account [the daughter and the father, the mother and the grandfather are here conjoined in the same speculation] was not a mere interjection but represented the German word "*fort*" [gone, far away]. I eventually realized that it was a game and that the only use he made of any of his toys [*Spielsachen*] was to play "gone" [*fortsein*] with them. (pp. 14–15)[6]

Freud's intervention (I am not saying the grandfather's intervention, but the intervention of whoever recounts what the observer experienced, whoever finally realized that "it was a game": there are at least three instances of the same "subject", the narrator–speculator, the observer, the grandfather, the latter never being openly identified with the two others by the two others, etc.) – Freud's intervention deserves some analysis. He recounts that as an observer he has also interpreted. And has named. Now, what does he call a game, rather than work, the work itself consisting of reassembling? Well, paradoxically, he calls a game the operation which consists in not playing with one's toys: he did not employ them, he did not use (*benütze*) his toys, he says, he did not make them useful, *utensiles*, except by playing at their being gone. The "game" thus consists in not playing with one's toys, but in making them useful for another function, to wit, being-gone. Such would be the deviation or *teleological* finality of this game. But a teleology, a finality of distantiation with its sights set on what, on whom? For what and for whom is this utilization of that which is usually given as gratuitous or useless, that is, play? What does this non-gratuitousness yield? And for whom? Perhaps not a single profit, not even any profit at all, and perhaps not for a single speculative agency. There is the teleology of the interpreted operation and there is the teleology of the interpretation. And the interpreters are many: the grandfather, the so-called observer, the speculator, and the father of psychoanalysis, here the narrator,

[6] *GW*, p. 13. Freud's phrase is "*übereinstimmenden Urteil*" which Strachey has given as "were agreed in thinking". [TN]

and then, and then, conjoined to each of these instances, she whose judgement would have concurred, in coinciding fashion (*übereinstimmenden Urteil*), to the extent of being covered by it, with the father's interpretation.

This coincidence which conjoins the father and the daughter in the interpretation of the "O–O–O–O" as *fort* is odd for more than one reason. It is difficult to imagine the scene in detail, or even to accredit its existence and everything recounted within it. But it remains that Freud reports it: the mother and the observer are somehow reassembled in order to make the *same* judgement on the meaning of what their son and grandson articulated before, that is, for them. Try to figure out where the induction of such an identity, such an identification of point of view, comes from. But we can be sure that wherever it comes from, it has come round, and has linked the three characters in what must more than ever be called the "same" speculation. They have secretly named the "same" thing. In what language? Freud asks himself no questions about the language into which he translates the O/A. To grant it a semantic content bound to a determined language (a given opposition of German words) and from there a semantic content which surpasses language (the interpretation of the child's behaviour), is an operation impossible without multiple and complex theoretical protocols.

One might suspect that the O/A is not limited to a simple formal opposition of values whose content could vary without being problematical. If this variation is *limited* (which is what must be concluded from the fact – if, indeed, one is interested in it – that the father, the daughter and the mother find themselves reunited in the same semantic reading), then one can put forward the following hypothesis: there is some proper noun beneath all this, whether one takes the proper noun in the figurative sense (any signified whose signifier cannot vary or be translated into another signifier without a loss of signification induces a proper noun effect), or in the so-called literal, "proper" sense. I leave these hypotheses open, but what seems certain to me is the necessity of formulating hypotheses on the conjoining interpretations of "O–O–O–O", that is O/A, in whatever language (be it natural, universal or formal), conjoining the father and the daughter, the grandfather and the mother.

And the grandson and the son: for the two preceding generations have sought to be together; they have been, says one of the generations, conscious of being together in order to understand in their common verdict what their child intended to have them understand, and intended that they understand together. There is nothing hypothetical or audacious about saying this; it is an analytical reading of what Freud's text says explicitly. But we know now what a tautology can bring back by gushing over.

And what if this was what the son, I mean the grandson, was after, what if this superimposing coincidence in the judgement (*Urteil*) was what he believed without knowing it, without wanting it? The father is absent. He is far away. That is, since one must always specify, one of the two fathers : the father of a little boy who is so serious that his play consists not in playing with his toys but in distancing them, playing only at their distantiation. In order to make his play useful for himself. As for the father of Sophie and of psychoanalysis, he is still there. Who is speculating? The spool still has not yet made its appearance. Here it is. To send it off, the child was not lacking in *address*.[7]

It follows immediately:

> One day I made an observation which confirmed my view. The child had a wooden spool [*Holzspule*] with a piece of string [*Bindfaden*] tied around it. It never occurred to him to pull it along the floor behind him, for instance, and play at its being a carriage, but rather he held the spool by the string and with great address (*Geschick*) threw it over the edge of his little curtained bed [or veiled bed, *verhängten Bettchens*], so that it disappeared into it, at the same time uttering his expressive [*Bedeutungs-volle*, meaningful] "O–O–O–O." He then pulled the spool out of the bed again by the string and hailed its appearance with a joyful "*Da*" [*there*]. This, then, was the complete game – disappearance and return [*Verschwinden und Wiederkommen*]. As a rule one only witnessed its first act, which was repeated untiringly as a game in itself, though there is no doubt that the greater pleasure was attached to the second act.[8]

And with this word the call of a footnote, a footnote that I shall read presently.

"This then", says Freud, "was the complete game." Which immediately implies: this, then, is the complete observation, and the complete interpretation of this game. Nothing is missing, the game is saturable and saturated. If the completion were obvious and certain, would Freud insist upon it, remark upon it as if he quickly had to close, conclude, enframe? One suspects an incompletion (in the object, or in its description) all the more in that: (1) this is the scene of an interminably repeated supplementation, as if it never finished completing itself, etc.; and (2) there is something like an axiom of incompletion in the structure of the scene of writing.[9] This is due at the very least to the position of the speculator as a motivated observer. Even if completion were possible, it could neither appear for such an "observer", nor be declared as such by him.

But these are generalities. They designate only the formal conditions of a determined incompletion, the signifying absence of a particularly pertinent given trait: which may be on the side of the scene described, or on the side of the description, or in the unconscious which links the one to the other, their unconscious that is shared, inherited, telecommunicated according to the same teleology.

It speculates on the return, it is completed in coming back: the greater

---

[7] *GW*, p. 13. The pun on *address* exists in German as well (*Geschick*), and is crucial to Derrida's analysis of this passage. [TN]

[8] *GW*, p. 13. I have consistently modified Strachey's "reel" to read "spool" (*Spule*). [TN]

[9] The axiom of incompletion is related to the interminable supplementation, since the supplement is both the completing and the extra part. See *Of Grammatology*, trans. G. Spivak (Baltimore, Md: Johns Hopkins University Press, 1976). [TN]

pleasure, he says, is the *Wiederkommen* (the return), although the spectacle is less directly seen. And yet, that which again becomes a revenant must, for the game to be complete, be thrown away again, indefatigably. It speculates on the basis of the return, the point of departure of that which owes it to itself to return. On what has once more just returned from leaving or has just left again.

It is complete, he says.

And yet: he regrets that it does not roll along as it should roll along: as it should have rolled along if he himself had been holding the string.

Or all the strings. How would he himself have played with the kind of yo-yo that is thrown in front of or beneath oneself, and which returns as if by itself, on its own, by rolling itself up anew? Which comes back as if by itself, if it has been sent off correctly? One must know how to throw it in order *to make* it return by itself, in other words in order *to let* it return. How would the speculator himself have played? How would he have rolled the thing, made it roll, let it roll? How would he have manipulated this lasso? Of what would his address consist?

He seems surprised, adding to this surprise a confident regret, that the good little boy never seemed to have the idea of pulling the spool behind him and playing at its being a carriage: or rather at its being a wagon (*Wagen*), a train. It is as if one could wager (*wagen* again) that the speculator (whose contrary preference, that is railway phobia, is well enough known to put us on the track) would himself have played choo-choo train with one of these "small objects" (*kleine Gegenstände*). Here, then, is the first problem, the first perplexity of the father of the object or the grandfather of the subject, of the father of the daughter (mother: Ernst's object) or the grandfather of the little boy (Ernst as the "subject" of the *fort/da*): but why doesn't he play train or carriage? Wouldn't that be more normal? And why doesn't he play carriage by pulling the thing behind him? For the thing is a vehicle in convoy.[10] If he had been playing in his grandson's place (and therefore playing with his daughter since the spool replaces her, as he will say in the next paragraph, or at least, following its/his thread, is but a trait or train leading to her, in order to come just to depart from her again), the (grand-)father would have played carriage (I must be pardoned all these parentheses: the (grand-)father or the daughter (mother) are necessary in order to mark syntax in erasure of the genealogical scene, the occupation of all the places and ultimate mainspring of what I began by calling the athesis of *Beyond* . . .): and since the game is serious, this would have been more serious, says he, quite seriously. Too bad that the idea never occurred to him (for instance!) to pull the spool behind him on the floor and thus to play at carriages with it: *Es fiel ihm nie ein, sie zum Beispiel am Boden hinter sich herzuziehen, also Wagen mit ihr zu spielen, sondern es warf* . . . This would have been more serious, but the idea never occurred to Ernst. Instead of playing on the floor (*am Boden*), he insisted on putting the bed into the game, into play, on playing with the thing over the bed, and also in the bed. Not in the bed where the child himself would

[10] To indicate the impossibility of translating Derrida's sentence here, and the long commentary to which it could give rise, I shall simply cite it: "*Car la chose est une véhicule en translation.*" [TN]

be, for contrary to what the text and the translation have often led many to believe (and one would have to ask why), it appears that he is not in the bed at the moment when he throws the spool. He throws it from outside the bed over its edge, over the veils or curtains that surround its edge (*Rand*), from the other side, which quite simply might be into the sheets. And in any event, it is from "out of the bed" (*zog . . . aus dem Bett heraus*) that he pulls the vehicle in order to make it come back: *da*. The bed, then, is *fort*, which perhaps contravenes all desire; but perhaps not *fort* enough for the (grand-)father who might have wished that Ernst had played more seriously on the floor (*am Boden*) without bothering himself with the bed. But for both of them, the distancing of the bed is worked upon by the *da* which divides it: too much or not enough. For the one or for the other.

For the (grand-)father what is it to play trains? To speculate: it would be never to throw the thing (but does the child ever throw it without its being attached to a string?), that is to keep it at a distance continuously, but always at the same distance, the length of the string remaining invariable, making (letting) the thing displace itself at the same time, and in the same rhythm, as oneself. This trained train does not even have to come back, it has barely come to leave when it is going to come back.

It is going. This is what would go for the (grand-)father–speculator. Which enables him to be certain of the measure of the thing only by depriving himself of an extra pleasure, the very pleasure that he describes as the principal one for Ernst, to wit, the second act, the return. He deprives himself of this pleasure in order to spare himself the pain or the risk of the wager. And in order not to put the desired bed into play.

To play carriage also indeed would be "to pull" the invested object "behind him" (*hinter sich herzuziehen*), to keep the locomotive well in hand and to see the thing only by turning around. One does not have it before one. As do Eurydice or the analyst. For the speculator (the analyst) is obviously the first analysand. The analysand–locomotive for whom the law of listening is substituted for the law of looking.

It is not up to us to judge the normality of the child's choice, and we know about it only according to what the ascendant reports. But we might find the ascendant's inclination[11] strange. Everything occurs around a bed, and has never occurred except around a bed surrounded with veils or curtains: what is called a "skirted crib". If the child were indeed outside the bed but near it, which his grandfather seems to reproach him for, then these curtains, these veils, this cloth, this "skirt" that hides the bars, indeed form the inner chamber

[11] "*la pente de l'ascendant*": an elaborate play on words, since *pente* also has the sense of a cloth that goes over the canopy of a bed. *Ascendant*, of course, is the opposite of descendent, but has a resonance of *ascent*, again relating to the *pente* (literally and figuratively "inclination"). [TN]

of the *fort/da*, the double screen which divides it inside itself, dividing its internal and its external aspects, but dividing it only by reassembling it with itself, sticking it to itself doubly, *fort:da*. I am calling this, once more and necessarily, the *hymen*[12] of the *fort:da*. The veil of this "skirt" is the interest of the bed and the *fort:da* of all three generations. I shall not venture to say: it is Sophie. How could Ernst have seriously played carriage using a veiled bed, all the while pulling the vehicle behind him? One asks oneself. Perhaps quite simply it was his *duty* not to do anything with the object (obstacle, screen, mediation) named bed, or edge of the bed, or limen or hymen; it was perhaps his duty to stay off to one side completely and thereby to leave the place free, or to stay inside completely (as is often believed), which would have set loose less laborious identifications. But in order to have the *Spielzeug* or "small object" behind oneself, with or without bed, in order to have the toy represent the daughter (mother) or the father (the son-in-law, as will be envisaged further on, and the (grand-)father's syntax easily skips the parenthesis of a generation with a step to the side), one must have ideas. Follow the comings and goings of all these strings/sons (*fils*). The grandfather regrets that his grandson did not have them, these (wise or foolish) ideas of a game without a bed, unless it be the idea of a bed without a curtain, which does not mean without hymen. He regrets that his grandson has not had them, but he himself has not missed having them. He even considers them natural ideas, and this is what would better complete the description, if not the game. By the same token, one might say, he regrets that his grandson has indeed had the ideas that he has had for himself. For if he has had them for himself, it is indeed that his grandson has not been without having them also for him.

(This entire syntax is made possible by the graphics of the margin or the hymen, of the border and the step, such as it was remarked elsewhere.[13] I shall not exploit it here.)

For, in the end, was this bed with so necessary and so undecidable a border a couch? Not yet, despite all the Orphism of a speculation. And yet.

What the grand (-father-) speculator calls the complete game, thus, would be the game in its two phases, in the duality, the redoubled duality of its phases: disappearance/re-turn, absence/re-presentation. What links the game to itself is the *re-* of the return, the additional turn of repetition and re-appearance. He insists upon the fact that the greatest quantity of pleasure is in the second phase, in the *re-*turn which orients the whole, and without which nothing would come. Revenance, that is returning, orders the entire teleology; this permits one to anticipate that this operation, in its so-called complete unity, will be entirely

---

[12] *Hymen* is irreducibly both virginity and consummation (marriage), related here to the *conjoined* interpretations of father and daughter of what takes place around the bed. [TN]

[13] In addition to the works already indicated (*Grammatology, Spurs, Dissemination*), the undecidable syntax made possible by the graphics of the margin, hymen, border and step is also remarked (re-marked, re-inscribed) in *Tympan*, the "preface" to *Marges – de la philosophie*, and *Parergon*, in *La vérité en peinture*.

handed over to the authority of the PP. Far from being checked by repetition, the PP also seeks to recall itself in the repetition of appearing, of presence, of representation, and, as we shall see, via a repetition that is mastered, that verifies and confirms the mastery in which it consists (which is also that of the PP). The mastery of the PP would be none other than mastery in general: there is not a *Herrschaft* of the PP, there is *Herrschaft* which is distanced from itself only in order to reappropriate itself: a tauto-teleology which nevertheless makes or lets the other return in its domestic spectre. Which thus can be foreseen. What will return, in having already come, but not to contradict the PP, nor to oppose itself to the PP, but to mine the PP as its proper stranger, to hollow it into an abyss from the vantage of an origin more original than it and independent of it, will not be, under the name of the death drive or the repetition compulsion, an *other master* or a *counter-master*, but something other than mastery, something completely other. In order to be something completely other, it will have not to oppose itself, will have not to enter into a dialectical relation with the master (life, the PP *as* life, the living PP, the PP alive). It will have not to engage a dialectic of master and slave, for example. This non-mastery equally will have not to enter into a dialectical relation with death, for example, in order to become, as in speculative idealism, the "true master".[14]

I am indeed saying the PP as mastery in general. At the point where we are now, the allegedly "complete game" no longer concerns any given object in its determination, for example the spool or what it supplements. In question is the *re-* in general, the returned or the returning – to return in general. In question is the repetition of the couple disappearance/reappearance, not only reappearance as a moment of the couple, but the reappearance of the couple which must return. One must make return the repetition of that which returns, and must do so on the basis of its returning. Which, therefore, is no longer simply this or that, such and such an object which must depart/return, or which departs-in-order-to-return, but is departure–return itself, in other words the presentation of itself of re-presentation, the return-to-itself of returning. No longer an object which would re-present itself, but re-presentation, the return of itself of the return, the return to itself of the return. This is the source of the greatest pleasure, and the accomplishment of the "complete game", he says: that is, that the re-turning re-turns, that the re-turn is not only of an object but of itself, or that it be its own object, that what causes to return itself returns to itself. This is indeed what happens, and happens to the object itself re-become the subject of the *fort/da*, the disappearance–reappearance of itself, the object reappropriated from itself: the reappearance of one's own proper spool, with all the strings in hand. This is how we fall upon the first of the two footnotes. It is called up by the "second act" to which "the greater pleasure" is unquestionably attached. What does the note say? That the child plays the utility of the *fort/da* with

---

[14] On the non-dialectical relation with death, non-mastery, and the deconstruction of speculative idealism, see "From Restricted to General Economy", in *Writing and Difference*, trans. Alan Bass (Chicago: University of Chicago Press, 1978).

something that is no longer an object–object, a supplementary spool supplementing something else, but with a supplementary spool of the supplementary spool, with his own "spool", with himself as object–subject within the mirror/without the mirror. Thus:

A further observation subsequently confirmed this interpretation fully. One day the child's mother had been away for several hours and on her return [*Wiederkommen*] was met with the words, "Baby O–O–O–O," which was at first imcomprehensible. It soon turned out, however [*Es ergab sich aber bald*], that during this long period of solitude [*Alleinsein*], the child had found a method of making *himself* disappear [*verschwinden zu lassen*]. He had discovered his reflection in a full-length mirror which did not quite reach to the ground, so that by crouching down he could make his mirror-image "*fort*" [gone away].   (p. 15, n. 1)

This time, one no longer knows at what moment it came to pass, led one to think (*Es ergab sich* . . .), or for whom. For the grandfather–observer still present in the absence of his daughter (mother)? Upon the return of the latter, and conjointly again? Did the "observer" still need her to be there in order to reassure himself of this conjunction? Does he not make her return himself without needing her to be there in order to have her at his side? And what if the child knew this without needing to have his knowledge?

Therefore he is playing at giving himself the force of his disappearance, of his "*fort*" in the absence of his mother, in his own absence. A capitalized pleasure which does without what it needs, an ideal capitalization, capitalization itself; by idealization. One pays (with) one's head for what one needs by doing without it in order to have it. A capitalized pleasure: the child identifies himself with the mother since he disappears as she does, and makes her return with himself, by making himself return without making anything but himself, her in himself, return. All the while remaining, as close as possible, at the side of the PP which (who) never absents itself (himself), and thus provides (for himself) the greatest pleasure. And the enjoyment is coupled. He makes himself disappear, he masters himself symbolically, he plays with death as if with himself, and he makes himself reappear henceforth without a mirror, in his disappearance itself, maintaining himself like his mother on the line. He speaks *to himself* telephonically, he calls himself, recalls himself, "spontaneously" affects himself with his presence–absence in the presence–absence of his mother. He makes himself *re-*. Always according to the law of the PP: in the grand speculation of the PP which–who never seems to absent itself–himself from itself–himself. Or from anyone else. The telephonic or telescripted recall provides the "movement" by contracting itself, by signing a contract with itself.

Let us mark a pause after this first footnote.

For in having been played for ages, all of this has just begun.

## "La séance continue"

Return to Sender, the Telegram and
the Generation of the Sons-in-Law

The serious play of the *fort/da* couples absence and presence in the *re-* of
returning. It relates them, it institutes repetition as their relation, relating them
the one and the other, the one to the other, the one over or under the other.
Thereby it plays with itself *usefully*, as if with its own object. Thus is confirmed
the abyssal "juxtaposing" that I proposed above: between the object or the
content of *Beyond* . . ., between what Freud is supposedly writing, describing,
analysing, questioning, treating, etc., and, on the other hand, the system of his
writing gestures, the scene of writing that he is playing or that plays itself. With
him, without him, by him, or all at once. This is the same "complete game" of
the *fort/da*. Freud does with (without) his spool. And if the game is called
complete on one side and the other, we have to envisage an eminently symbolic
completion which itself would be formed by these two completions, and which
therefore would be incomplete in each of its pieces, and consequently would be
completely incomplete when the two incompletions, related and joined the one
to the other, start to multiply themselves, supplementing each other without
completing each other.

Let us admit that Freud is writing. He writes that he is writing, he describes
what he is describing, but this is also what he is doing, he does what he is
describing, to wit, what Ernst is doing: *fort/da* with his spool. And each time that
one says *to do*, one must specify: *to allow* to do (*lassen*). Freud does not do
*fort/da*, indefatigably, with the object that the PP is. He does it with himself, he
recalls himself. Following a detour of the *télé*,[15] this time an entire network. Just
as Ernst, in recalling the object (mother, thing, whatever) to himself,
immediately comes *himself* to recall *himself* in an immediately supplementary
operation, so the speculating grandfather, in describing or recalling this or that,
recalls *himself*. And thereby makes what is called his text enter into a contract
with himself in order to hold on to all the strings/sons (*fils*) of the descendance.
No less than of the ascendance. An *incontestable* ascendance. What is
incontestable is also that which needs no witness. And which, nevertheless,
cannot not be granted its rights: no counter-testimony appears to have any
weight before this teleological auto-institution. The net (*filet*) is in place, and
one pulls on a string (*fil*) only by getting one's hand, foot, or the rest, caught. It

---

[15] *Télé* is the French equivalent of the American expression TV – the English "telly" is
almost perfect here – as well as the prefix to "telecommunication", communication at
a distance, from the Greek *tele* (distant, *loin, fort*). Throughout the book from which
these chapters are extracted, *The Post Card – From Plato to Freud and Beyond*, Derrida
examines the relations between telecommunication and psychoanalysis. "Network" at
the end of this sentence translates *chaîne*, which has the sense of chain and of network
as a television or radio station, one of the tele-'s byways or detours. [TN]

is a lasso or a lace.[16] Freud has not positioned it. Let us say that he has known how to get caught in it. But nothing has been said yet, nothing is known about this knowledge, for he himself has been caught in advance by the catching. He could not have foreseen this knowledge entirely, such was the condition of the juxtaposition.

Initially this is imprinted in an absolutely formal and general way. In a kind of *a priori*. The scene of the *fort/da*, whatever its exemplary content, is always in the process of describing in advance, as a deferred joining, the scene of its own description. The writing of a *fort/da* is always a *fort/da*, and the PP and *its* death drive are to be sought in the exhausting of this abyss. It is an abyss of more than one generation, as is also said of computers. And is so, as I said, in an absolutely formal and general way, in a kind of *a priori*, but the *a priori* of an after-effect. In effect, once the objects can substitute for each other to the point of laying bare the substitutive structure itself, the formal structure yields itself to reading: what is going on no longer concerns a distancing rendering this or that absent, and then a *rapprochement* rendering this or that into presence; what is going on concerns rather the distancing of the distant; nor is the nearness near, nor the absence absent or the presence present. The *fortsein* of which Freud is speaking is not any more *fort* than the *Dasein* is *da*. Whence it follows (for this is not immediately the same thing), that by virtue of the *Entfernung* and the *pas* in question elsewhere, the *fort* is not any more distant than the *da* is here. An overlap without equivalence: *fort:da*.

Freud recalls himself. His memories and himself. Like Ernst in the glass and without the glass. But his speculative writing also recalls itself, something else and itself. And specularity above all is not, as is often believed, simply reappropriation. No more than the *da*.

The speculator himself recalls himself. He describes what he is doing. Without doing so *explicitly*, of course, and everything I am describing here can very well do without a thoroughly auto-analytic calculation, whence the interest and necessity of the thing. It speculates without the calculation itself analysing itself, and from one generation to another.

He recalls *himself*. Who and what? Who? Himself, of course. But we cannot know if this "himself" can say "myself"; and, even if it did say "myself", which me then would come to speak? The *fort:da* already would suffice to deprive us of any certainty on this subject. This is why, if a recourse, a massive recourse, to the autobiographical is necessary here, the recourse must be of a new kind. This text is autobiographical, but in a completely different way than has been believed up to now. First of all, the autobiographical does not overlap the auto-analytical without limit. Next, it demands a reconsideration of the entire *topos* of the *autos*. Finally, far from entrusting us to our familiar knowledge of what autobiography means, it institutes, with its own strange contract, a new theoretical and practical charter for any possible autobiography.

[16] Concerning the double stricture of the *lace* in relation to *fort:da*, I must refer to *Glas* (Paris: Galilée, 1974), and to "Restitutions – de la vérité en peinture", in *La vérité en peinture* (Paris: Flammarion, 1978).

*Beyond* . . ., therefore, is not an *example* of what is allegedly already known under the name of autobiography. It writes autobiography, and one cannot conclude from the fact that in it an "author" recounts a bit of his life that the document is without value as truth, science or philosophy. A "domain" is opened in which the inscription, as it is said, of a subject in his text (so many notions to be re-elaborated) is also the condition for the pertinence and performance of a text, of what the text "is worth" beyond what is called an empirical subjectivity, supposing that such a thing exists as soon as it speaks, writes and substitutes one object for another, substitutes and adds itself as an object to another; in a word, as soon as it *supplements*. The notion of truth is quite incapable of accounting for this performance.

Autobiography, then, is not a previously opened space within which the speculating grandfather tells a story, a given story about what has happened to him in his life. What he recounts is autobiography. The *fort:da* in question here, as a particular story, is an autobiography which instructs: every autobiography is the departure/return of a *fort/da*, for example this one. Which one? The *fort/da* of Ernst? Of his mother conjoined with his grandfather in the reading of his own *fort/da*? Of *her* father, in other words of *his* grandfather? Of the great speculator? Of the father of psychoanalysis? Of the author of *Beyond*. . . ? But what access is there to this latter without a spectral analysis of all the others?

Elliptically, lacking more time, I will say that the graphics, the autobio-graphics of *Beyond* . . ., of the word *beyond* (*jenseits* in general, the step beyond in general), imparts a command upon the *fort:da*, that of the overlapping by means of which proximity distances itself in *abyme* (*Ent-fernung*).[17] The death drive is *there*, in the PP, which is a question of a *fort:da*.

Freud, it will be said, recalls himself. Who? What? Trivially, first of all, he recalls himself, he remembers himself. He tells himself and tells us an incident which remains in his memory, in his conscious memory. The remembrance of a scene, which is really multiple, consisting as it does of repetitions, a scene that happened to another, to two others (one male, one female), but who are his daughter and his grandson. His eldest grandson, let us not forget, but who does not bear the name of the maternal grandfather. He says that he has been the regular, durable, trustworthy "observer" of this scene. He will have been a particularly motivated, present, intervening observer. Under a roof which although not necessarily his, nor simply a roof in common, nevertheless belongs to *his own*, almost, with an almost that perhaps prevents the economy of the operation from closing itself, and therefore conditions the operation. Under what headings can one say that in recalling what happens (on) to the subject (of) Ernst he is recalling himself, recalling that it happened to him? Under several interlaced, serial headings, in the "same" chain of writing.

First, he recalls to himself that Ernst recalls (to himself) his mother: he recalls Sophie. He recalls to himself that Ernst recalls his daughter to himself in

---

[17] "*Abyme*", the homonym of *abîme* (abyss), is the heraldic term for the shield within the shield, which Derrida often uses to connote infinite reflection. [TN]

recalling his mother to himself. The equivocal syntax of the possessive here is not only an artefact of grammar. Ernst and his grandfather are in a genealogical situation such that the more possessive of the two can always be relayed by the other. Whence the possibility immediately opened by this scene of a permutation both of places and what indeed must be understood as genitives: the mother of the one is not only the daughter of the other, she is also his mother; the daughter of the one is not only the mother of the other, she is also his daughter, etc. Already, even at the moment when the scene, if this can be said, took place, and even before Freud undertook to relate it, he was in a situation to identify himself, as is too readily said, with his grandson, and, playing on both sides, to recall his mother in recalling his daughter. This identification between the grandfather and the grandson is attested to as an ordinary privilege, but, and we will soon have more than one proof of this, it could be particularly spectacular for the forebear of psychoanalysis.

I have just said: "Already, even at the moment when the scene, if this can be said, took place." And I add *a fortiori* at the moment of desiring to write about it, or to send oneself a letter about it, so that the letter makes its return after having instituted its postal relay, which is the very thing that makes it possible for a letter *not* to arrive at its destination, and that makes this possibility-of-never-arriving divide the structure from the outset.[18] Because, for example, there would be neither postal relay nor analytic movement if the site of the letter were not divisible and if a letter always arrived at its destination. I am adding *a fortiori*, but let it be understood that the *a fortiori* was prescribed in the supplementary graphics of the joined reporting of what too hastily would be called the primary scene.

The *a fortiori* of the *a priori* makes itself (a bit more) legible in the second note of which I spoke above. It was written afterward, and recalls that Sophie is dead: the daughter (mother) recalled by the child dies soon after. It was in a completely different way recalled elsewhere. Before translating this sup-plementary note, it must be situated in the itinerary. It follows the first note only by a page, but in the interval a page has been turned. Freud has already concluded that no certain decision can be reached from the analysis of so singular a case. Such is his conclusion after a paragraph full of peripeteias, a paragraph which begins by confirming the rights of the PP: this is the moment when the interpretation (*Deutung*) of the game explains how the child compensates himself, indemnifies himself, reimburses himself for his pain (the disappearance of the mother) by playing at dis-reappearance. But Freud immediately distances, sends off his interpretation to the extent of its recourse to the PP. For if the mother's departure is necessarily disagreeable, how can it

---

[18] Derrida is referring to the ideas he elaborates in *Le Facteur de la vérité* ("The Factor/Mailman of Truth"), where he uses the structural possibility implicit in postal communication, that a letter can always potentially *not* arrive at its destination, to deconstruct Lacan's psychoanalytic interpretation of the signifier as the letter that always arrives at its destination. [TN]

be explained according to the PP that the child reproduces it, and *most often* in its disagreeable phase (distancing) than in its agreeable one (return)? It is here that Freud is obliged, curiously, to modify and to complete the previous description. He must, and in effect does, say that one phase of the game is more insistent and frequent than the other: the completion is unbalanced, and Freud had not mentioned it. Above all, he tells us now that the "first act", the distancing, the *Fortgehen*, was in fact independent: it "was staged as a game in itself" (*"für sich allein als Spiel inszeniert wurde"*). Distancing, departure, is therefore a complete game, a game quasi-complete unto itself in the great complete game. Thus, it is because distancing is itself an independent and more insistent game that the explanation by the PP must once more *fortgehen*, go away, distance itself in speculative rhetoric. And this is why no decision can be reached from the analysis of such a case.

But after this paragraph Freud does not simply renounce the PP. He tries it twice more, after the final resigned suspension of it in this chapter.

1. He tries to see in the child's actively assuming a passive situation (since he is unable to affect his mother's displacement), a satisfaction (and therefore a pleasure), but the satisfaction of a "drive for mastery" (*Bemächtigungstrieb*) which Freud curiously suggests would be "independent" of whether the memory was pleasurable or not. Thus would be announced a certain beyond of the PP. But why would such a drive (which appears in other texts by Freud, but which plays a strangely erased role here) be foreign to the PP? Why could it not be juxtaposed with a PP that is so often designated at least metaphorically, as mastery (*Herrschaft*)? What is the difference between a principle and a drive? Let us leave these questions for a while.

2. After this try, Freud again attempts "another interpretation", another recourse to the PP. It is a question of seeing it function *negatively*. There would be pleasure in making it disappear; the sending away that distances the object would be satisfying because there would be a (secondary) interest in its disappearance. What interest? Here, the grandfather gives two curiously associated or coupled examples: the sending away of his daughter (mother) by his grandson and/or the sending away of his son-in-law (father), who here – a significant fact and context – makes his first appearance in the analysis. The son-in-law–father appears only to be sent away, and only at the moment when the grandfather attempts a negative interpretation of the PP according to which the grandson sends his father off to war in order not to be "disturbed in his exclusive possession of his mother". This is the sentence that calls for the note on Sophie's death.

Before translating this paragraph on the two negative functionings of the PP, note included, I extract a notation from the preceding paragraph. I have extracted it only because it appeared dissociable to me, like a parasite from its immediate context. Perhaps it is best read as an epigraph for what is to follow. In the preceding paragraph it resonates like a sound from elsewhere, that nothing in the preceding sentence calls for, and that nothing in the following sentence develops: a kind of assertive murmur that peremptorily answers an inaudible question. Here it is then, to be read without premises or consequences: "It is of course naturally indifferent [*natürlich gleichgültig*] from the point of view of judging the affective nature of the game whether the child invented it himself or made it his own on some outside suggestion [*Anregung*]" (p. 15).[19] Oh? Why? Naturally indifferent? Really! Why? What is a suggestion in this case? What are its byways? From whence would it come? That the child made his own, appropriated (*zu eigen gemacht*) the desire of someone else, man or woman, or the desire of the two others conjoined, or that inversely he gave occasion to the appropriation of his own game (since the appropriation can take place in both senses neither hypothesis can be excluded) – all this is "naturally indifferent"? Really! And even if it were so for the "affective evaluation", which would therefore remain the same in both cases, would this be equivalent for the subject or subjects to whom the affect is related? What is incontestable is that all these questions have been deferred, distanced, dissociated.

I now translate the attempt at another interpretation, concerning the negative strength of the PP. In it, the successive sending away of the mother and father is pleasurable and calls for a note:

> But still another interpretation may be attempted. To wing away [*Wegwerfen*] the object so that it was "gone" [*fort*] might satisfy an impulse of the child's, which was suppressed in his actual life, to revenge himself on his mother for going away from him. In that case it would have a defiant meaning: "All right, then, go away! I don't need you. I'm sending you away myself." A year later, the same boy whom I had observed at his first game used to take a toy, if he was angry with it, and throw it on the floor, exclaiming: "Go to the war!" [*Geh in K(r)ieg!*, the *r* in parentheses taking into account the actual and reconstituted pronunciation of the child]. He had heard at that time that his absent father was "at the war," and was far from regretting his absence; on the contrary he gave the clearest indications that he had no desire to be disturbed in his exclusive possession of his mother. (p. 16)

Call for a note on Sophie's death. Before coming to it, I emphasize the certainty with which Freud differentiates between, if it can be put thus, the double sending away. In both cases, the daughter (mother) is desired. In the first case, the satisfaction of the sending away is secondary (vengeance, spite); in the second it is primary. "Stay where you are, as far away as possible" signifies (according to the PP) "I prefer that you come back" in the case of the mother, and "I prefer that you do not come back" in the case of the father. Or at least this is the reading of the grandfather, and of the indications which, he says, do not deceive, "the clearest indications" (*die deutlichsten Anzeichen*). If they do not actually deceive, one might still ask who they do not deceive, and

---

[19] *GW*, p. 13. Freud's phrase is *"für die affektive Einschatzung dieses Spieles"*, which Strachey mistakenly gives as "judging the *effective* nature of the game". (Perhaps this is an uncorrected typographical error?) [TN]

concerning whom. In any event, concerning a daughter (mother) who should stay where she is, daughter, mother. Wife perhaps, but not divided, or divided between *the two Freuds*, in their "exclusive possession", divided between her father and her offspring at the moment when the latter distances the parasite of his own name, the name of the father as the name of the son-in-law.

The name which is also borne by his other brother, the rival. Who was born in the interval, shortly before the death of the daughter (mother). Here, finally, is the second note, the supplementary note written afterward. The date of its inscription will be important for us:

> When this child was five and three-quarters, his mother died. Now that she was really *fort* ("O–O–O") [only three times on this single occasion], the little boy showed no signs of grief. It is true that in the interval a second child had been born and had roused him to violent jealousy. (p. 16)

This cadence might lead one to believe that a dead woman is more easily preserved: jealousy is appeased, and idealization interiorizes the object outside the rival's grasp. Sophie, then, daughter there, mother here, is dead, taken away from and returned to every "exclusive possession". Freud can have the desire to recall (her) (to himself) and to undertake all the necessary work for her mourning. In order to speak of this one could mobilize the entire analysis of *Mourning and Melancholia* (published several years before, three at most), and the entire descendance of this essay. I will not do so here.

In the most crushing psychobiographical style, there has been no failure to associate the problematic of the death drive with Sophie's death. One of the aims has been to reduce the psychoanalytic significance of this so ill-received "speculation" to a more or less reactive episode. Several years later, will not Freud himself say that he had "detached" himself a bit from *Beyond. . .*? But he had also foreseen the suspicion, and the haste with which he counteracts it is not designed to dispel it. Sophie dies in 1920, the very year in which her father publishes *Beyond*. On 18 July 1920 he writes to Eitingon: "The *Beyond* is finally finished. You will be able to certify that it was half finished when Sophie was alive and flourishing."[20] He actually knows, and says to Eitingon, that "many people will shake their heads over it [*Beyond. . .*]."[21] Jones recalls this request to bear witness, and wonders about Freud's insistence upon his "unruffled conscience over it [*Beyond . . .*]": is there not here some "inner denial"?[22] Schur, who is hardly suspect of wanting to save *Beyond . . .* from such an empirico-biographical reduction (he is among those who would wish to exclude *Beyond . . .* from the corpus), nevertheless affirms that the supposition of a link

[20] Cited in Max Schur, *Freud: Living and Dying* (New York: International Universities Press) p. 329. [TN]
[21] Cited in Ernest Jones, *The Life and Work of Sigmund Freud*, vol. 3 (New York: Basic Books, 1957) p. 40 [TN]
[22] Jones, *Life and Work of Freud*, vol. 3, p. 40 [TN]

between the event and the work is "unfounded". However, he specifies that the term "death drive" appears "shortly after the deaths of Anton von Freund and Sophie".[23]

For us, there is no question of giving credit to such an empirico-biographical connection between the "speculation" of *Beyond* . . . and the death of Sophie. No question of giving credit even to the hypothesis of this connection. The passage we are seeking is otherwise, and more labyrinthine, of another labyrinth and another crypt. However, one must begin by acknowledging this: for his part, Freud admits that the hypothesis of such a connection has a meaning in the extent to which he envisages and anticipates it, in order to defend himself against it. It is this anticipation and this defence which have meaning for us, and this is where we start to seek. On 18 December 1823, Freud wrote to Wittels, the author of *Sigmund Freud, His Personality, His Teaching, and His School*:

> I certainly would have stressed the connection between the death of the daughter and the Concepts of the *Jenseits* in any analytic study on someone else. Yet still it is wrong. The *Jenseits* was written in 1919, when my daughter was young and blooming, she died in 1920. In September 1919 I left the manuscript of the little book with some friends in Berlin for their perusal, it lacked then only the part on mortality or immortality of the protozoa. *Probability is not always the truth.*[24]

Freud therefore admits a *probability*. But what *truth* could be in question here? Where is the truth of a *fort:da* from which everything derives/drifts away (*dérive*), including the concept of truth?

I shall content myself with "juxtaposing" Freud's work after Sophie's definitive *Fortgehen* to the work of his grandson as *Beyond* . . . will have reported it.

1. The irreparable wound *as* a narcissistic injury. All the letters of this period speak of the feeling of an "irreparable narcissistic injury" (for example the letter to Ferenczi, 4 February 1920, less than two weeks after Sophie's death).[25]

2. But once she is *fort*, Sophie indeed can stay where she is. It is a "loss to be forgotten" (to Jones, 8 February 1920). She is dead "as if she had never been" (27 January, to Pfister, less than a week after Sophie's death). "As if she had never been" can be understood according to several intonations, but it must be taken into account that one intonation always traverses the other. And that the "daughter" is not mentioned in the phrase: "snatched away from glowing health, from her busy life as a capable mother and loving wife, in four or five days, as if she had never been".[26] Therefore the work goes on, everything

---

[23] Schur, *Freud: Living and Dying*, pp. 328–9. [TN]
[24] Cited in Jones, *Life and Work of Freud*, vol. 3, p. 41 (Freud's underlining). [TN]
[25] Cited in Schur, *Freud: Living and Dying*, p. 331 [TN]
[26] Cited in ibid., p. 330. [TN]

continues, *fort-geht* one might say. *La séance continue.*[27] This is literally, and in French in the text, what he writes to Ferenczi in order to inform him of his mourning: "My wife is quite overwhelmed. I think: *La séance continue.* But it was a little much for one week."[28] What week? Pay attention to numbers. We have pointed out the strange and artificial composition of *Beyond* ... in *seven* chapters. Here, Sophie, who was called "the Sunday child" by her parents, is snatched away in "four or five days", although "we had been worried about her for two days", from the arrival of the alarming news, on the very day of von Freund's burial. This is the same week, then, as the death of von Freund, which we know, at least via the story of the ring (requested by the widow of the man who was to have been a member of the "Committee" of 7, where he was replaced by Eitingon, to whom Freud gave the ring that he himself wore),[29] was another wound in what I will call Freud's alliance. The "Sunday child" is dead in a week after seven years of marriage. Seven years – is this not enough for a son-in-law? The "inconsolable husband", as we soon will see, will have to pay for this. For the moment the *séance* continues: "Please don't worry about me. Apart from feeling rather more tired I am the same. The death, painful as it is, does not affect my attitude toward life. For years I was prepared for the loss of our sons; now it is our daughter. . . . 'The unvaried, still returning hour of duty' [Schiller], and 'the dear lovely habit of living' [Goethe] will do their bit toward letting everything go on as before" (letter to Ferenczi, 4 February 1920, less than two weeks later).[30] On 27 May, to Eitingon: "I am now correcting and completing 'Beyond'. That is, of the pleasure principle, and am once again in a productive phase. . . . All merely [a matter of] mood, as long as it lasts."[31]

3. Third "juxtaposing" characteristic: ambivalence as concerns the father, the father of Ernst, that is, the son-in-law of the grandfather, and the husband of Sophie. The battle for the "exclusive possession" of the daughter (mother) rages on all sides, and two days after her decease (*Fortgehen*), Freud writes to Pfister: "Sophie leaves behind two boys, one aged six and the other thirteen months [the one Ernst would have been jealous of, as of his father], and an inconsolable husband [indeed] who will have to pay dearly for the happiness of these seven years. . . . I do as much work as I can, and am grateful for the distraction. The loss of a child seems to be a grave blow to one's narcissism; as for mourning, that will no doubt come later."[32] The work of mourning no doubt

[27] *La séance continue* means "the session proceeds, continues", in the sense of parliamentary procedure, but it also has the resonance of an analytic session. [TN]
[28] Cited in Jones, *Life and Work of Freud*, vol. 3, p. 19. [TN]
[29] Anton von Freund was a wealthy Hungarian supporter of psychoanalysis who donated several funds for analytic publications and instruction. The "Committee" was the unofficial, secret group that was formed around Freud after the break with Jung. Freud presented each member with a Greek intaglio ring. Communication was by circular letter. The original 1913 members were Jones, Ferenczi, Rank, Abraham, Sachs and Freud. [TN]
[30] Cited in Schur, *Freud: Living and Dying*, p. 331. [TN]
[31] Ibid., p. 331. [TN]
[32] Ibid., p. 330. [TN]

comes later, but the work on *Beyond* . . . was not disrupted for a single day. This letter is situated between Sophie's death and cremation. If the work is a "distraction", it is that he is not just working on just anything. This interval between the death and the cremation (a form of *Fortgehen* which can only have quite singular effects on a work of mourning) is marked by a *story about trains and even of children's trains*, an anecdote imprinted on all of Freud's letters of this week. No train to go to the deceased, she who is already gone (*fort*), before going up in ashes. A letter to Binswanger first alludes to von Freund's death:

> We buried him on January 22. The same night we received a disquieting telegram from our son-in-law Halberstadt in Hamburg. My daughter Sophie, aged 26, mother of two boys, was stricken with the grippe: on January 25, she died, after a four days' illness. At that time our railroads were shut down, and we could not even go there. Now my deeply distressed wife is preparing for the trip but the new unrest in Germany makes it doubtful that this intention can be carried out. Since then a heavy oppression has been weighing on all of us, which also affects my capacity for work. Neither of us has got over the monstrous fact of children dying before their parents. Next summer – this will answer your friendly invitation – we want to be together somewhere with the two orphans and the inconsolable husband whom we have loved like a son for seven years. If this is possible![33]

Is it possible? And in the letter to Pfister I have already cited in order to point out the allusion to the "seven years" and to the "distraction" of work, the problem of the train to the deceased is posed again, placed in a differentiated network:

> as if she had never been. We had been worried about her for two days, but were still hopeful [will she come back?]. From a distance it is so difficult to judge. The distance still remains. We could not, as we wished to, go to her at once when the first alarming news came, because there were no trains, not even a children's train. The undisguised brutality of our time weighs heavily on us. Our poor Sunday child is to be cremated tomorrow. Not till the day after tomorrow will our daughter Mathilde and her husband, thanks to an unexpected concatenation of circumstances, be able to set off for Hamburg in an Entente train. At least our son-in-law was not alone. Two of our sons who were in Berlin are already with him. . . .[34]

The "inconsolable husband who will have to pay dearly for the happiness of these seven years" will not have remained alone with the deceased. Freud is represented by his own, despite the suspension of the trains, by another

---

[33] Ibid., p. 329. [TN]

[34] Ibid., p. 329. Schur notes: "Children from starving Austria were sent abroad by an international children's aid association". [TN]

daughter and two sons, bearers of the name (recall his *preferred* game – the train kept at a constant distance).

The classical institution of a science should have been able to do without the Freuds' name. Or at least should have made of its forgetting the condition and proof of its transmission, its proper inheritance. This is what Freud believed or affected to believe, half believed, as in the classical model of science, the model which he fundamentally will never renounce *playing* at for psychoanalysis.

CHRISTIAN METZ

# Instant Self-Contradiction

There are still some typical forms of mental wit of which Freud does not speak – either because he forgot or overlooked them or because he implicitly linked them with one or another earlier technique. However, they are worth isolation and formal definition, even if this augmented list must also be incomplete.

We might call them *instant self-contradiction*. During a conversation with guests, a man explains that women have the fault of always "taking things personally", of taking as applying to themselves things said in a general way; his wife interrupts and cries, "Oh, I'm not at all like that!" By stating that she is "not like that", the wife unwittingly reveals that she "is like that": the two terms of the contradiction are almost intertwined; they are borne by the same words, and the listener hears them at the same time. It is this paradoxical compression that makes us laugh; it is also the innocence, the ease, the naturalness with which the contradiction is stated, for the protagonist does not notice it at all. Those two traits, as we shall see, can cover the whole of the category, heterogeneous as it may be in other respects.


As in the above example, the contradiction frequently arises between the utterance and its uttering. Or as in this story: a conversation on the usual superstitious tales about pregnancy. A woman gives birth to a child with a wolf's head because she had been frightened by a wolf in the forest, etc. One of those present breaks in with irritation: "Those are stories from the Dark Ages! Look – when I was expecting my second, I knocked over and broke a whole stack of records of which I was very fond. And yet I'm normal ... I'm normal ... I'm normal ... I'm normal ...", etc. Two friends at a concert: "Aren't they supposed to play the Ninth?" "But they just played it." "Well, they might have said something – it's my favourite piece!" (Variant: "What are they playing?" "It's the Ninth." "Then let's go, I know that one by heart!")

Road accident: nearby is a man who has had one too many and who claims to have seen it all. Policeman: "Is it true that you saw everything?" "As plainly as I see you, Father!"

Perhaps readers will recall an anti-German story that had its moment of popularity during the Liberation. A German learned English by memorizing all the words in the dictionary one by one, but awkwardly confuses two of them. He says: "I haf learnet all ze A's, end zen all ze B's, und zen all ze C's, and zo fort, and it iss all regordet bermanently here" – he taps his forehead – "in my ass!"

In an asylum, a patient who thought he was a chicken is cured and is authorized to leave the clinic. Fifteen minutes later, however, he comes running back in terror and goes up to the doctor: "Okay, *I* know I'm not a chicken. But do the foxes know it?"

In all of these stories, which are of a common type, the circumstances of the uttering instantly refute the affirmation of the utterance. It is not true that the woman with the records is normal, because she talks like a broken record; it is not true that the drunk could have seen the accident, because he confuses the policeman's uniform with a priest's cassock; it is not true that the pseudo-music-lover knows the Ninth well, because he does not recognize it, etc.: such is the structural "formula" of jokes of this kind (and each time, as I have said, the character is completely unaware). As to the circumstances of the uttering that re-establish the truth, they can be indicated to the listener by the context, as in the story of the woman who does not "take everything personally" or the man who loves the Ninth; or through the constraints of logical inference: the words of the madman who no longer thinks he is a chicken show that he still thinks he is a chicken; or, finally, by traces of the uttering in certain segments of the utterance (as is frequent in linguistics): the repetition of the words "I'm normal", indicating that the woman is not normal; the use of the word ass by the German, showing that there is at least one word that has not been properly "regordet"; and so forth.

In the darkness of a cinema, a dirty old man slips his hand on to the thigh of the woman sitting next to him. She exclaims, "You disgusting old man! Be so good as to remove your hand. I'll give you ten minutes, not a minute more!" Here again we see that the real contradiction is not between the two parts of the utterance, but between the explicit affirmation ("remove your hand") and the desire of the utterer ("do not remove your hand"). That wish does not figure in the utterance, but there is an anomaly (the "ten minutes") that enables us to discern it.

There is a similar mechanism in this story: "Your right stocking seam is crooked." "There: I've straightened it. How about the left leg?" "It's fine." "Are you sure?" "Sure! That one's a seamless stocking." It is the friend's "reassuring" phrase that informs us that the heroine is wearing obviously mismatched stockings.

A man goes to consult a clairvoyant. She lives on the third floor and the ground-floor door is locked. The client rings the bell and the clairvoyant opens her window and calls down. "Who's there?" The client is furious: "That's it! I get it. I'm leaving." The contradiction is between the clairvoyant's words and her professional gifts – something the listener would not necessarily have noticed; to "work", the joke requires a catalyst character, the customer; this is quite a rare case.

One of many "moocher" stories: "I'll bet you £100 you don't know why I've come to see you!" "I know perfectly well! You've come to put the touch on me!" "I have not! You're wrong! So you lose: hand over the £100!" Through the artifice of the pseudo-bet, the moocher manages to do his usual trick at the same time (and in the same sentence) as he is pretending not to.

A teacher before his class: "Only fools are positive; intelligent people are constantly in doubt." A mischievous student: "Are you sure of that?" "Absolutely!" Here the self-contradiction reminds one of certain classic paradoxes of the logicians, such as that of the Cretans who were deemed to be liars on the oath of a Cretan.

Dialogue between a man and woman in the dairy: "Do we need to order some fresh cheese?" "Of course not! We've had some in the storeroom for over three months!" Two words of the utterance – "three months" – reveal the true situation, one that contradicts the rest of the sentence, for the cheese is not fresh.

To the principle of contradiction between uttering and utterance we can add a sub-group of jokes that characteristically make direct use of language, correct and incorrect, its variations depending on social class, etc. Definition: the kind of language employed by a character simultaneously gives the lie to what he is employing to tell us. Two examples: a man considered by his acquaintance to be uncultivated and coarse finally gets angry: "I got nothing to say about education, but when it comes to manners – up yours!" A young woman introduces herself to the school principal: "It's me what is the English teacher who they told to right away come to see you."


The contradiction is often wholly contained within the explicit utterance; the utterance often employs both terms in their literal meanings. The fact of uttering and the placement of the word no longer intervene, or at least they are directly reflected in the utterance itself, which is now devoid of any oblique allusion. In the preceding examples, however, the sentence was not, strictly speaking, contradictory; it was contradicted by circumstances: the character speaking was contradictory. It is a matter of two clearly different forms of self-contradiction.

Even in the second, however, the joke can introduce a contradictory character, but only on condition that it "happens" completely in the character's words, without necessarily making any inference regarding the situation. A typical example is this phrase ascribed by H. Becque to a flirtatious woman: "I was mad about that boy, and now I can't bear the sight of him. How men change!"

Contradiction *per se* is no more amusing than non-sense, to which it is closely related. Such phrases as "He is big and small", "This hotel is expensive and cheap", and so forth, do not raise a smile. If certain contradictions are amusing, it is because they come very close to being reasonable statements, because they come within a hair's breadth of non-contradiction: for a fraction of a second the listener is taken in, and it is at this *logical surprise* that he will then laugh, at the contrast between the contradictory phrase and the semantically normal phrase that he had glimpsed or hallucinated an instant before – a phenomenon that was the basis for "nonsense" jokes. I repeat that it is neither on the primary nor the secondary process that the *witz* is based, but on their being simultaneous. In self-contradiction jokes it is also possible precisely to point out the words or expressions that "verisimilitudinized" the sentence or that made it resemble another, non-contradictory sentence – in short, those that momentarily tripped up the listener: the topsy-turvy tripping up of the illogical into the logical and not the reverse. Thus, the sentence "passes", until it is perceived, just afterwards, that it does not pass. Here we have something I have in my study of nonsense called "displacement of content": within a virtual class of sentences cut from the same pattern and nearly all of which are reasonable, the trick is to find the one that ends up in an internal contradiction while retaining the sensible echo of the others.

Georges Feydeau: if husbands allowed their wives to have a couple of lovers – for purposes of comparison – there would be far fewer wives (cf. sentences such as: "If husbands gave their wives more freedom . . ."). The director to the starlet, after an audition: "Very good. We will write to you. There's no need to leave your address" (cf. "There's no need to leave your photo for the moment"). An Edinburgh reader, writing to a London newspaper: "If you do not stop publishing stories on the so-called miserliness of Scots, I am going to stop borrowing your newspaper!" (resemblance to "reading your newspaper", or "buying your newspaper", which, furthermore, are what the listener expects: they become conjoined with "borrowing" to yield a comical sentence, half absurd and half normal; note that the rest of the utterance, as in all these stories, is completely reasonable). Another Scots story: "What do you think, Sir, about all those anecdotes about your national miserliness?" "I think they should be more sparing of them" (cf. "I think that they are false"). A poster: "You are in the free zone of Berlin. Photograph-taking forbidden!" (cf. "You are on a military base"). Another poster: "To fund a new animal home, the Animal Protection Society is holding a big bullfight tomorrow" (cf. "holding a big raffle"). "Not having children runs in that family" (cf. "bad eyesight"). Demonstration on the streets of San Francisco, banners reading: "Lesbian mothers demand their right to raise their children!" (cf. "unwed mothers"). Jules Renard: "Ah! To go on one's honeymoon all by oneself!" (cf. "to be all alone to work, to rest, etc."). Alphonse Allais: "If ever I get rich I shall buy a park, with hundred-year-old trees. If there aren't any, I'll plant them" (cf. "exotic trees, aquatic plants, etc."). Alphonse Karr: "There is an age at which one shares everything: when one has nothing" (= when one does not have much).

Among the jokes based on contradictions, there are also special cases whose structure does not seem to have given rise to a corresponding series of quips. They are "isolated", at least for the time being.

Post-office clerk to customer: "You will have to rewrite the address on your package; two words are illegible: the addressee, Martinet, and the town, Plougastel-Daoulas." Here the procedure that creates the contradiction – and at the same time confers on it a pseudo-normal air – is obviously the implicit telescoping between the clerk's knowledge ("I assert that it is not legible") and the customer's knowledge ("The package is for Mr Martinet of Plougastel-Daoulas"). In fact, if we heard the sentence at a post-office window, there would be a slight pause before we were surprised, since we would already know the two proper names. A grotesque illustration of a problem of everyday life: how to adjust the information level of our simplest phrases, for more often than not we do not know what our interlocutor knows or does not know.

Another rare variety: self-contradiction openly stated, as in this Israeli story: "Yesterday the owner of a café where I was having a drink looked at me as though I hadn't paid. Very irritating!" "So what did you do?" "Ah-ha! I looked back at him as though I *had*!" The internal contradiction of the discourse, which implies both that the character had paid and then that he had not paid, is combined here with another technique: unification, the echoing between two contrary, but very similar, propositions, "as though I hadn't paid" and "as though I had"; we must take care not to confuse contradiction and opposition; here both come into play.

Here is a quip from Alphonse Karr: "If you want to get along with your neighbours, don't have any!" Self-contradiction? Of course. But the way in which it is set up is unusual. In fact, the utterance is the result of "contamination" between two different sentences: "You can't be too careful if you want to live in peace with your neighbours", and, "Even then, that will not be enough: don't have any neighbours!" A typical manifestation of the primary process: the mental passage from one sentence to the other (displacement) has remained at the same level, so that the final utterance is a hybrid (condensation) that runs counter to the laws of logic. Metaphorically, we are faced with a device of generative linguistics: the "surface" sentence (the quip itself) has been spawned by two "underlying" phrases that do not appear directly.

A courtroom: the defendant has murdered his father and mother. As you can imagine, the prosecutor delivers a very harsh summation. However, he notes in conclusion: "Your only excuse is that you are an orphan!" Another very special type, because in one sense there is no contradiction – since his crime, the defendant has indeed been an orphan. What makes us laugh is that this came about because of the crime itself, and that before the crime he had not been an orphan (which thus cannot be his "excuse"). In short, for the *orphan/non-orphan* contradiction to arise, time and causality must come into play. On the other hand, one need only ignore those factors, as the prosecutor does, for the phrase to seem momentarily normal, while also remaining absurd (hence the slight disturbance it causes).

There are also (but quite rarely) delayed self-contradictions established only after the fact, retroactively, as in this anti-Soviet story: "Are you happy?" "Yes." "Do you have everything you need?" "Yes." "A refrigerator?" "Yes." "A radio?" "Yes: without a radio how would I know what I should answer?" Only the final sentence gives us the idea that this Soviet citizen was obviously not happy, that he did not have a refrigerator, etc.

The idea of contradiction plays a major role in Freudian metapsychology. It is related to the notion of ambivalence. The activity of the unconscious is constantly characterized by its indifference to the logician's principle of non-contradiction. The contradictory also evokes the absurd, of which Freud so often speaks in connection with witticisms. Finally, it will be remembered that he considers the antiphrasis, the figuration through contraries, to be one of the great principles of the spirit of thought. It is, therefore, surprising that he did not reserve a separate place for jokes based on internal contradiction. They are not to be confused with antiphrases, despite their common feature of playing on contraries: the antiphrasis tells us something *by means of* its contrary; a contradiction affirms a thing *and* its opposite; the first is essentially in the nature of a paradigm, the second of a syntagm.

Like all the "techniques" of witticism that I am attempting to catalogue and define one by one – let us remember that *technique* is Freud's own word – instant self-contradiction is at once a linguistic, psychoanalytic and social phenomenon. Those three dimensions are linked, at times confused.

As I have said, contradiction is often established between the uttering and the utterance, that is between the two great poles of language's very *machinery*, as described by, *inter alia*, Émile Benveniste and Roman Jakobson. You cannot say that you love the Ninth (= utterance) if you have not recognized it (= the circumstance of uttering, at the same instant): the hearers of a witticism, in effect, translate the uttering into an utterance such as "I do not know the Ninth". Even when the contradiction is within the utterance, it will still come up against linguistic (and not only logical) constraints and determinations, with the ensuing comic effect. In the story of the impresario and the starlet, the words "Very good. We will write to you" establish a great probability that the very next segment will be "leave us your address"; what we hear, however, is "there's no need to leave your address". Those are the laws of isotopy (in Greimas' sense) or of probability through partial redundancy (by linguistic psychologists) that are violated in the quip. In a more general way, it will be noted that the examples given in this article greatly resemble those employed by generative semanticists in their discussions and that such writers (Lakoff and McCawley, for example) often have recourse to jokes and witticisms.

Self-contradiction is also a psychoanalytic phenomenon, indeed a central one. I have just mentioned that for Freud the unconscious was indifferent to contradiction (as we note every day in our affective lives). Not only, as we have seen earlier, does contradiction facilitate the condensations and displacements that signal this category of witticism, but, more radically, it is very often the only way of giving conscious expression to feelings incompatible with practicality (= the reality principle), but peacefully coexisting in the great affective reserve of impulses (= the pleasure principle). Thus each of us desires both solitude and company ("Ah! To go on one's honeymoon all by oneself!"). Ordinarily we resolve this problem through alternation over time. However, if it is expressed in a *condensed* way, radically, far afield from our usual and precarious practical solutions, it becomes a witticism, as in that sentence about the honeymoon (which tells us many other things as well). The amusing effect also involves a factor of *surprise*: such "logic" is common in the unconscious, but after it has been censored it is rarely expressed consciously and explicitly: whether we know it or not, we laugh simply because we catch a glimpse of ourselves in a special light.

Self-contradiction is an excellent way of expressing or setting forth feelings regarding class, race, nationality, sex, etc. – in a word, social feelings. In the preceding examples, the reader will perhaps have noted the very high number of misogynistic stories. That is not fortuitous, for one of the dominant ideology's stereotypical reproaches of women is that they are illogical and contradictory. Suffice it to imagine a brief scenario in which a woman contradicts herself (but if we reread those examples we will see that they are perfectly applicable without modification to men; one simply does not do it). In the story about the Edinburgh man who borrows his paper from someone every day, we see a direct reflection of the French (racist) prejudice that Scots are miserly. That idea is not exterior to the structural mechanism of the witticism; it is not merely a prerequisite "theme". On the contrary, xenophobia penetrates into the internal configuration of the witticism: the term *borrow* (= avarice) is its point, through its implicit contrast with *buy* (= spend money), which is what was expected. As for contempt based on class, there is a good example in the story of the English teacher who makes mistakes in English when she introduces herself. Beyond the technical – and therefore professional – self-contradiction (this person does indeed seem to be a poor choice for teaching English to students), something else is easily seen to be surfacing: socially speaking, poor use of one's mother tongue is not the equivalent of having little talent for driving a car or for cross-country skiing, for it is a *déclassé* ignorance, in both senses of the word (belittling + assigning one to a lower social class).

Thus, the joke is one of many examples in which a *social practice* is mediatized by a (linguistic-psychoanalytical) *symbolic practice*. One can, of course, study the witticism using purely sociological methods: denomination of the themes (anti-Jewish jokes, jokes on the high cost of living, Communist jokes, etc.), polls and questionnaires about who laughs and who does not laugh, and so forth. The results might be interesting. However, a strictly linguistic study could also be carried out: jokes based on nouns, verbs, adjectives, and so forth. Or indeed, a purely psychoanalytic study: sadistic quips, exhibitionist quips, homosexual quips, etc. Yet it seems to me that the most interesting point of view is to be found where those three paths intersect.

LOUIS MARIN

# Writing History with the Sun King: The Traps of Narrative

## Introduction

For Benveniste, as we know, history, or purportedly objective narrative, is discourse *minus* the marks of uttering. In it, the features that utter it are obliterated or hidden. Narrative representation appears in the text as the presentation of the event itself. It recounts *itself*, presents *itself* in the representation, a presentation that is the presentation of truth itself seen as reconciling being and language. The truth is both particular and necessary, as Aristotle noted in *The Poetics* with regard to history: it refers to *one* event, to one action that *occurred at one time*. I can act only if it (that event, that action) has not occurred: the truth of the past.

Writing seems to be the operation proper of that reconciliation. "Because they can be recorded as though they had occurred," writes Benveniste, "such events must belong to the past." Benveniste, however, immediately corrects himself and inverts his statement: "It would certainly be better to say that from the moment they are recorded and uttered in a temporal historical expression, they are deemed to be past. The story-telling intent is one of the great functions of language; in it, it expresses its specific temporal nature." In other words, it is thus the absence of intervention by a narrator–utterer – characterized by writing – that specifies the narrative of an event as past. In contrast to the voice, which is always in the present, writing is always in the past, if only because the person speaking in and through the written signs is not *there* to say so. In the case of the narrative text, "Events seem to tell themselves as they loom up on the horizon of the story. No one is speaking here." To paraphrase Benveniste's observation, we would add that here *everything occurs* as though no one were speaking. "Story-telling" writing creates the simulation of an absence; it creates in saying what is said a semblance of silence.

We know the semantic and pragmatic elements of this simulation that define the modalities of utterance for the story-telling narrative. They consist of a series of exclusions: that of the relationship between persons – I–you – and of the adverbs linked with it – "here", "there", "now", "tomorrow", "yesterday"; and that of certain types of temporal relationships expressed in certain verb tenses: present, future or perfect. In short, as Benveniste says, "As a mode of utterance the story excludes every autobiographical linguistic form", i.e. all the formal machinery of discourse. Someone had to write the narrative, of course, but everything occurs as though it had been written by anyone: an effect of reading. Indeed, the reader forgets the subject of the written utterance in obedience to a command inherent in the very ordering of the text, through a power that is proper to story-telling. We are dealing with a semblance, because this power does not manifest itself as such in the narrative. The monument of story-telling, the narrative institution of memory, simulates oblivion of the narrator. In other words, everything occurs as though the fictional utterance, characterized by the absence of the marks of discursive uttering, had constructed itself by negating the whole nexus of the devices of utterance, from which it has, nevertheless, sprung.

This negation embodied in writing, this negation of writing, could also be analysed by a transference of the Freudian notion of de-negation. In this case, in fictional narrative it would entail de-negation that would reveal a simultaneous placing and suppression of the utterance itself. "When I dreamt of that woman," said Freud's patient, "I was not thinking of my mother." And Freud concluded, "The patient had therefore been dreaming of his mother." Thus, everything occurs as though, in fictional narrative, the subject, *by writing, had spoken*: and here we can note the contrast between the orality of speech and scripturality – "It is not I who say what I say [the instance of utterance]; it wrote itself [aoristic narrative], etc." Events seem to recount themselves: "It wrote itself, thus I am not speaking." That woman dreamt herself in my dream, who inscribed herself in my dream by appearing there; I say she is not my mother. Therefore, it is the mother who writes and represents herself therein.

The present and the subject are seen to be in a state of scission; in a state of syncope *qua syncope*, for this remarkably ambiguous term signifies both a temporary interruption of a body's consciousness, the suppression of a letter or syllable within a word, *and* the liaison of the last note of a measure of music with the first note of the next measure to make them appear to be one single note. Using another vocabulary, we could say that in its narrative the modality of the utterance of a story would consist in the expulsion from the narrating subject (the narrative) of its product, narrative; and in the return of the excluded as object to the real (history), but past. That would be the essential operation of writing: the present of writing is an eternally ensyncoped present, smoothly linked; that present of utterance would manifest itself therein as a representation of reality, as a past present in representation.

As de Certeau has clearly demonstrated, in recounting a tale (which is at once narration, narrative, story), "I" causes the dead to speak: by silencing "me" – this wrote itself, it was written – the silence of speech in the spoken.

However, in so doing, "I" silences the dead: "I" makes him die anew, and hence it is "I" who speaks, but what is writing itself is not what "I" am speaking. In recounting a story, "I" speaks well of someone to "you". But what "you" reads of him is different from that which "I" tells "you" of him: plotting, ruse, the trap of writing. Something, someone speaks of *itself/himself here and now*, but what "you" reads is the representation of a "he", of a "third party", absent in the past: the representation of the dead.

So what about the story narrative when it sets out to be contemporaneous with the action it narrates, to write a present, the single present of an action that is taking place? What of that narrative in which the historiographic pen-point is almost identical to the *stigma*, to the story's own created viewpoint. For such would be the narrative of the story of the King by his official historian.

The pure and simple internal requirement of totalitarian power, the pure and simple requirement of the absolute, entails – analytically speaking – its totalizing, absolute narrative, without a remainder and without exteriority. The King's story is, and cannot be other than, the text of its narrative. The King is truly the arch-actor of history and the metanarrator of his narrative. However, the gaze of the historiographer breaks the totalitarian adequation of history and its text; it introduces a dual polarity into the present presence of the royal action itself, that of doing and of seeing done, the first scission of the subject from the story; the first difference, which is immediately followed by another, between seeing and writing, the scission of time in the scission of the subject, the syncope of the present into the representation of a prior present.

To see the historic event from the King's angle, to be placed in that supreme – or nearly so – position is to see the birth of history itself, for the King is its sole agent. And because the gaze of the absolute master emits the light that enables us to see and produces what is to be seen, to be present at his side is to participate in his gaze and, in a way, to share in his power: to take his place and substitute oneself in the forthcoming narrative that this past presence not only authenticates, but that it enables and authorizes. The King's story, then, is actually the original history, in Hegel's sense; it is the narrative of the origin of history, history seized by the narrator at the origin of the historical event, worthy of being noted and retained at the very moment of its production by its agent.

However, to the extent that this power thinks itself and aims to be supreme, that it thinks itself and aims to be absolute, albeit an element of the site of that strength and that power, the historian does not participate in it: he has no share – by definition – in the act, in the word, in the thought of the absolute agent of history. Hence that odd value of the antique autopsy in modern royal history: it signifies, ascertains, the truth of the event and the veracity of the witness recounting it. Yet that witness is more than a witness. He *is sited at the point of view and the point of origin* that produced the event, but he has no share in them, lest he relativize that point of view and that origin, and yet the absolute agent of history is not its narrator. Arch-actor, he is its metanarrator through an intermediary person. It is not he who will write "*Veni, vidi, vici*", the minimal historical narrative of absolute political power. It is the historiographer who will take it down, "*Venit, vidit, vicit*". The passage from the first to the third person signals the theoretical gap between the narrator and the arch-actor or metanarrator.

In other words, the historian's position at the side of absolute political power, as close as can be to that power but not sharing in it, is very precisely *fiction as the subject of the theoretical representation of it it provides*, fiction, its double, its semblance: what political power needs *to be* represented, to represent to the future its own past, perhaps because the present of the absolute – because absolute – is forever opaque to it, perhaps because it is of the very essence of the absolute to be unable, without revitalizing itself, to reflect *itself* as such, to be aware of itself in an undistanced immediacy. Everything occurs as though, thanks to this fiction, absolute power were recounting its own story through the anonymous voice and writing of the narrator who sees only what it allows him to see. Thus the historian is the simulacrum of the King; his narrative, the simulation of the sovereign's history whose effect is perfect narrative representation, without excess or loss.

That is why only historical simulation and its representative effect have the power to write the present of absolute power, not at all as the present moment of its act, its word, its thought, but as the future–past.

By writing everything that it has been seen to do, say and think, history can write only what has already been seen, and thereby it writes what is *seen* so that those who will not have seen – and even those who, while seeing, do not know – will be made to see. In other words, by means of its writing, which will always follow the present moment of the act, absolute power, in the imaginary position it arrogates to itself by its simulacrum, is revealed and is written, is made known to the prior future: it will act, speak and think as though having acted, spoken and thought.

At the same time, however, and inversely, that temporal identity, that identification of the two broad categories of past and future in the present of the sovereign act, is but the effect of historical simulation, for that present is never spoken: it can only be so in writing, and that, in its very execution, will make it into a former present, a represented present. The miraculous instant of the absolute can never inscribe itself as such. We need only compare Racine's travel diary, the notes written as he accompanied the King from Paris to Gand in the winter of 1678, with the correspondong narrative of the royal historiographer in *L'Éloge historique du Roi*, to see the lived-through opacity of the miracle, at once perpetual and successive, manifest itself in the clarity and intelligibility of the narrative representation of the past turned into a monument for posterity: the power of simulation the absolute requires in order absolutely to constitute *itself*.

### The King is off to war . . .

Les Messieurs du Sublime, avec longue rapière
Et du mieux qu'ils pouvaient prenant mine guerrière,

Allaient, chacun monté sur un grand palefroi,
Aux bons bourgeois de Gand, inspirer de l'effroi.

[The Gentlemen of *le Sublime*, with long rapiers,
And adopting their best warlike expressions,
Went forth, each mounted on a great palfrey,
To inspire dread in the good burghers of Gand.]

(Pradon, quoted by R. Picard
in *La Carrière de Jean Racine*)

A little story:

His son Louis tells us that Racine had already written several large sections of *L'Histoire du règne de Louis XIV*, of which reign he was, after Pellisson and along with Boileau, the official historiographer. The manuscripts had been entrusted to Monsieur de Valincourt, Racine's friend; Louis tells us that "They perished in the fire in which everything Monsieur de Valincourt kept in his house at St-Cloud was consumed". La Beaumelle adds that Valincourt "gave twenty *louis* to a Savoyard to brave the flames to search [for the papers Racine had entrusted to him]. Instead of that invaluable manuscript, the Savoyard emerged with a bound volume of *Gazettes de France*."

So the King was out of luck. Of the Great Manufactory of Royal History there remain only a few fragments saved from a fire. The little story of the burning of Monsieur de Valincourt's house has outlived "The Great History in the Manner of Polybius, Livy and the Ancients". I cannot but read a sign into the anecdote: "The Master, the God, the All-Powerful Lord who serves as oracle neither speaks nor conceals: *he indicates*." Here the Master is another god more powerful than absolute power, thereby destroying his desire for history, his desire to find fulfilment in the narrative monument of his own story. Suddenly, that story is being told in a different way: a fire in a house at St-Cloud and a great heroic and imbecilic deed of a Savoyard, and the history written from the King's fiction, *his* historiographer, goes up in smoke: some ashes are all that remain of it. A fine end indeed for the effulgence of the Sun King, his lightning flashes and his light: to become fire and flame after the death of writing in the night. There is a god more powerful than the all-powerful Louis: the contingency of the event, the chance nature of the real, minor occurrence, here-and-now, in which the rationality of a great plan vanishes. The economy of politics is consumed in a fiery chance moment. The Great Politics of History, the grandeur of King immortalized in the Racinian monument, falls into the trap of anecdote, unforeseeable but terribly effective: one night at St-Cloud a house burns.

But that is not all. Chance, the fire-god, is having some fun. Instead of the manuscript/monument, the brave Savoyard emerges with a volume of *Gazettes de France*. What a substitute! Instead of marmoreal fiction, the ephemeral and trivial diary of the humdrum; the twenty-*louis* heroic act of an illiterate hero. A two-way exchange: everything must be paid for, even this unwitting substitution. The god laughs at this fortuitous parody of this Hegelian moment of heroic flattery in which the courtier trades his discourse – whose noblest form is history – to the King for abbeys, titles, pensions (in short, for money), to be remembered forever and yet, in the end, forgotten.

And yet the god laughs even harder, for Primi Visconti tells him another anecdote: "The Maréchal d'Estrades came up to me the other day and said to me with a smile, 'I told you that our historiographers would do better to go back to their versifying. Yesterday, at Madame de Montespan's, those gentlemen read out portions of their history; the King shook his head and, from time to time, he whispered to Madame de Montespan, "Gossip columns, gossip sheets!"'" The gossip sheets to which the writings of the royal historiographer were superior by dint of his patience and his labour, and even more because of the harsh discovery that the site of his discourse was that very one occupied by the absolute monarch whose great deeds he was to recount, behold, like his fiction, those gossip sheets would on the day of the "last" judgement rise up, substituted for the Great Narrative of the Royal Hero by some Savoyard – in his way a hero too, a hero of the "news item", of the "filler", his *alter ego*.

Or I can envision an allegory like those written by Racine and Boileau, detailing like commemorative medals the events of that reign they transformed into monumental signs of the deeds of Louis, an allegory as frontispiece to my discourse: the blind monster Chance lays waste the Temple of History while, amid the flames, idiot Ignorance tosses off gossip sheets to the winds.

So nothing but debris and ruins remains of the great Racinian monument. Yet we can see advantage in this distinction for our "critical" undertakings with regard to the texts, and particularly in the case of a text intended to indicate the pitfalls of the narrative of political power in general, and of absolute power in particular. The work of destruction is already done, the tripping mechanisms of the traps revealed. We have only to point them out in these fragmented texts; the ruin of the historical narrative monument provides the textual conditions for the reading and writing tactics we employ. Although the machinations of State power consist, together with the narrative of itself it creates, of the transformation of the event into marmoreal signs through which it can identify and authorize itself, eliminating from its own totality all exteriority, the fragmentation of those signs, by enabling us to spring the traps, marks the resistance of the event and the power of chance in the rigorous calculations of representation. Not the ruse of history, or even its irony, but its humour.

1. "The laws of history" are laws that power arrogates to itself in order to fulfil its desire for power: the contracts of the narrative representation of history.

2. If the god who guarantees these laws is named chance, the means that this guarantee is neither certain nor universal; that the laws and contracts are not absolutely binding; that the traps, so delicately set as to be perfectly effective, are always liable to jam, to seize up.

3. Better still, it can happen – not always, but sometimes – that an exact implementation of the planned manoeuvre can be, *simultaneously*, a failure, a breakdown.

Here is a case in point: one or two little tales I discovered among the notes for a travel diary by Racine the historian, including the journey to Gand, which was the first campaign on which he followed the King in 1678.

*Brie. Nangis. Provins. Sézanne.* Here one spent two days.[1]

*Fère Champenoise. Vitry.* The affection of the inhabitants; fires of joy, lanterns at all the windows. From the church where the King was to hear mass, they tore the tomb of one of their governors, who had been a member of the League, lest the King see in their church the name and epitaph of a rebel.

Now here are some reading notes of my own, my tactical landmarks in search of the broad strategy of the historical narrative that will be written based on this document.

Discerning a horizon of "reality" through place-names: the reality this text aims to put forward. For whom? For the man who writes it? The prime elements of his written memory, those names so easily forgotten. The (future) history of the King is first of all a journey. Whose? The hero's. I am going too fast, but I travel the text as swiftly as the hero travels in space. Here the scene that engenders the narrative, a simple network of named textual sites, is constructed. Those names – Brie, Nangis, Provins – have a dual function (the narrative machination begins): they *indicate*, beyond the text, the geographical "reality", but at the same time, they are uttered and read as if capable of entering a signifying network; they open a space in which sense, representation, can be produced. In other words, they stake out the boundaries of the textual system with its exterior, the index-names that also lay out a space of possibilities in which, with the fourth name, the meaning will emerge. We must perceive this, which is one way of unarming the trap of the impending narrative: these place names are written here solely to embody the narrator and his memory, or, the route of the hero of his narrative. I can skip over the text until the fourth name: for example, I can read the first three as an alphabetical list whose logic escapes me, the deployment of a pure code-space, both paradigm and syntagm, a print-loving child's reverie over a map, or a nursery rhyme.

Everything changes at Sézanne. "One's" two-day stay inscribes that name as a stop on the way, and, retroactively, the preceding three as places "one" has passed through. A time is inscribed in the text, that of a narrative backed up by geographical indices, a time that is the time of an actor, "one" who spent two days at Sézanne after passing through Brie, Nangis and Provins. "One" who? A neuter, indeterminate "someone", the hollow actor of this two-day visit, but, at the same time, the site, in the text, of the "I" who utters the narrative, but who is effaced. An "I" who recounts the narrative of the story anonymizes himself in the "one" of which he is a part and in which he nullifies himself: "I who am

---

[1] "On y séjourna deux jours" is better translated either in the first person plural or in the passive voice, but the author's exegesis requires the use of the less felicitous personal pronoun "one". [Translator's note]

telling you this history formed part of the group that spent two days at Sézanne. I was in the circle of the hero of the story I am recounting to you, but I am not recounting myself." The second springing of the narrative trap: "I" is both narrator and narrated, utterer and uttered; consequent value: it is *true*. Hence, the positioning of the reader (I, you, he): to take it or leave it. There is nothing to be said or to be read about "one's" journey to Brie, Nangis and Provins, nothing of interest for me who writes or, therefore, for you who read. You are bound by my law of discourse or you do not read. I lay down, without telling you so, a rule of selection regarding what I write. Perhaps you will try to guess it? Wait for the rest. Perhaps I myself do not know it. It could be that I am subject to another law of which my law is but the outward Sign. The law of the "one" of which I am a part? Only the two-day stop at Sézanne is worth noting, and not the passage through Brie, Nangis or Provins – or else the whole thing means that one was going so fast that one was forced to rest for two days at Sézanne.

Hence this remark: each named site is the repository of an action complete in itself; unity of action in unity of place. Topography is a topic – reservoir of notable actions – but not yet a topology, to the extent that this entire group of discourse sites is a succession of unoriented names/points. This document-fragment is a chronicle articulated to a topic. It is by delving into this topical reserve and finalizing it with a purpose, a strategy, that the monumental narrative of the royal history shall be constructed. It can be read in *L'Éloge historique du roi sur ses conquêtes*.

Here we are at Vitry: the narrative trap is perfected with a nominal phrase and an anecdotal narrative that is inserted into the great narrative syntagm of the King's campaign, a bit of gossip in which suddenly the trap is turned against the setter. The nominal phrase or trap: "*Vitry*. The affection of the inhabitants; fires of joy, lanterns at all the windows." Two brief notations of a *significant little* fact, underlying which we can recognize a causal, or rather, a significative, relationship: fires of joy, lanterns at all the windows indicate the affection of the inhabitants; that is the sign, the irrefutable sign that there is affection on the part of the inhabitants (for whom?). The notation is elliptical because of the near-insignificance of the fact – which is, however, significative. "I do not emphasize it, but, you see, it is notable." In my reading that notation enshrines a difference. Nothing of the sort happened at Sézanne, and yet "one" spent two days there: a point in Vitry's favour. (On the basis of that we can imagine whatever we like: for instance, a prefect's report on the occasion of the Prime Minister's visit on the eve of a general election.) And in addition, it is a still more significant anecdote of this affection for the King, for in the unimportant anecdote being recounted the King makes his first appearance. Until now the narrative stage had been bare. At Vitry it is populated. We must be very attentive as to the manner of this peopling, of the entrance of the actors on-stage, of the agent on to the "theatrical ground" which until now had been briefly sketched out with toponyms; although it was only a "private" travel diary, Racine made the trip only because he was the King's historiographer. He took notes in order to write *his* history (his: the King's). He was not sightseeing.

Thus the first note is a nominal phrase. Not "the inhabitants showed their affection by lighting fires of joy". No one must say, "It's very simple: he was in a hurry; he had no time to write". Read what follows: "From the church where the King was to hear mass, they tore . . . lest the King see. . .". Here a complex sentence unfolds its propositions, carefully articulated and organized into a hierarchy.

A nominal phrase, then; two even, linked by asyndeton, by the absence of a linkage. Here too, an ellipsis in articulation which on the surface *says* the ostensive meaning of which the notations are like two bearers.

And that is what is strange. This kind of writing is not strange because it is banal – banality: that is the art of the trap. That must likewise be the art of concealing art: to discover the strange in the banal – I mean to discover in the smooth surface of a discourse the minuscule indication of the hole into which I, the reader, without being aware of it, am about to fall; the trap being that I fall without knowing I am falling, that I tumble *into the hole* while continuing to walk *on the surface*, that I fall – prisoner – into the pit of a meaning while continuing to read, to produce meaning, continuously.

What is strange is precisely the following:

1. That "a minimum assertive utterance coincides with a syntactical element which, from the morphological point of view, belongs to the class of nouns", "that a form that is morphologically characterized as nominal assumes a function that is, syntactically, verbal".[2]

2. That this assertive utterance should in this case be a narrative utterance describing a way of being and a situation. Reread Benveniste's article on the nominal sentence. The strangeness in Racine's little notation, which I examine through it, is that the nominal phrase is employed here in the narration of an event and the description of a way of being of the subject. Its use discloses something of great importance: that the event, the subject's way of being are well narrated and described in their actuality, but as a complete essence, an absolute truth, a permanent value beyond time, beyond place, beyond all relation to the describing or narrative speaker; a definitive assertion, an authoritative argument. However, this strangeness must not conceal from us another strangeness that occurs in Benveniste's study, i.e. in my analytical and interpretive discourse on the utterance of the King's historiographer. In fact, the nominal assertion, whose characteristic is to place the utterance outside of any temporal or modal localization and outside the speaker's subjectivity, is always linked to the discourse; it presumes dialogue; it is introduced to act and to convince, not to inform. This means that, while being *outside discourse* (in Benveniste's sense) because of the traits of its *function*, it is *inside the discourse* because of the characteristics of its *use*. Demarcated from discourse in general, the nominal sentence is uttered by no one: the truth seems to speak of itself without the need of a spokesman, as it rests peacefully in the capital of a memory older than those of the speaking subjects; like the narrative of events,

---

[2] É. Benveniste, *Problèmes de linguistique générale* (Paris: Gallimard, 1966 and 1974).

the story (according to Benveniste), but from below, repose and not exertion, non-temporality and not chronological production, absolute expectation and not stunned surprise, identity and not difference. But now a speaker takes hold of it and utters it. Nevertheless everything occurs as though it had wrested away the presence of the speaking subject and taken possession of his voice. It is not I that speaks; it is truth that speaks in me, a truth that is neither mine nor yours: only *logos*, transcendent utterance without utterer, the absolutely pure force of assertion (whose favoured site is proverb, maxim, adage).

This then is the trap set by the historiographer in his travel notes: to transform by writing the narrative utterance of the event into a truthful sentence. That, however, is going too far, for if such were the case the trap would be sprung. We must add: while *causing* that sentence *to be read* as a narrative utterance; by a certain kind of writing to stimulate the reading of a narrative utterance and to present to be read, in that reading, the sentence of the truth itself, to produce a semblance of narrative with the effect of truth, to impose irresistibly a referential presupposition.

So the trap must be sprung, since it has been discovered. What is glaringly obvious is also what is self-evident, what prevents our seeing the surface clue to the trap beneath. And what is self-evident from the outset is the speed of motion shown by the fast-moving writing. "I have no time to make notes; I note only the noteworthy event, the essential feature." Now, this essential feature – which implies the omission of all the remainder I do not have the time to note down – is an essential trait: it is written as an essential trait. The immediate, remarkable impression, all at once, at Vitry, is immortalized in writing by a nominal sentence; the ephemeral notation, grasped in passing, written in passage, is suddenly the site of a transcendent utterance without utterer. Truth, and its assertive force, is being spoken here.

What operates this transformation, this springing of the trap? I in turn would note that it is at Vitry (in this site in the text) that the hero of the story on the verge of being told comes on-stage. It is established here that "one" is the King. Granted, he does not yet appear himself as a subject, but only through his "aura", his atmospheric presence. He is written of only in relation to the inhabitants of Vitry, in a presence that is hazy yet strong enough to be the sense of all their actions. The King is the finality of the narration, a simple modal function, and his subjects react to a possibility for action, to a presence not yet manifest on the narrative scene but nevertheless already there. That is what operates the transformation and the occultation of the transformation – in short, the springing of the trap: the King.

Or, to put it another way, the principle of selection of the esential is the essential presence of the King. It is he who, in this text, institutes the sentence of truth, who seizes the narrative proceedings with his presence and takes possession of its voice through the pure force of the assertion, by him *or* the narrator, *his* historiographer, in this *narrative sentence*: "The affection of the inhabitants: fires of joy, lanterns at all the windows." While being recounted as an event and as an aside, the nominal assertion, *in the narrative itself*, endows the fact with the character of an eternally necessary proposition, one that has always been inherent in the basic definition of the inhabitants of Vitry visited by their King. It is not the narrative that conveys the "real truth" of the story in its narrative utterances. Reality is the universal truth asserted by the nominal sentence which, because it too is a narrative utterance, states it in its existential singularity as an event, and the fact exists singularly as a true event. From this standpoint, the historical event – the King's most minuscule acts, those he performs as well as those he causes – is the universal singular of which narrative would be the ontological argument.

The denial of discursive utterance, a characteristic of the narrative, by nominalizing the event denies its historicity, and the utterance fades back into the story, but like the absolute power of the truth spoken in the utterance without anyone speaking it. Open your morning paper. Skim its headlines and its minor headings, the presages of your reading, your daily consumption of narrative utterances. The sentences of truth are spread out and expand: the narrative of twenty-four hours of *the history of the world*.

However, inside the trap, the counter trap – or rather the working of the trap – traps not only the reader, but even the writer who set it. In the nominalization of the event, a little story; at first sight a simple confirmation by stating facts: to what limit will the inhabitants of Vitry go to show their affection for the King? "From the church where the King was to hear mass, they tore out the tomb of one of their governors who had been a member of the League, lest the King see in their church the name and epitaph of a rebel."

A narrative which is a significant fact that gives significance to the fires of joy as signs of the affection of the people of Vitry for the King; a narrative which, at the same time, is already history. They tore: simple past tense. The present event, contemporary with the present utterance, is transformed into a past event when it is *written*. It is thus instituted in its *seme*, its sign, its memory: the historic past.

Now, the anecdote told to us is of the tearing out of a tomb on which are inscribed a name and an epitaph: a dead man's signs. In its narrative utterances the anecdote recounts (but in reverse) the very process by which the King's historian writes the narrative of his present story. It repeats the production of the historic past by its negative, and, in so doing, its narrator falls into the trap of the narrative he has himself set.

First there is the presence of the King whose history is the subject of Racine's forthcoming narrative, a presence that is a power of vision; not a gaze, but the power of a gaze, an eye: "lest the King see in their church". See what? A name and an epitaph that etch into the marble the claims to fame of he who bore them. What was he? A rebel governor, a representative of the King, the King himself present through delegation, in his province, who had been a member of the League half a century earlier.

In response to the absolute power of sight – to the eye of the master able to read the name of his own power turned against him – we have the act of obliteration of the tomb's signs, the gesture of de-nomination. Thus the motion of history returns to insignificance – an actor in the story who had made himself immortal makes a violent disappearance from the holy place where the King was to hear mass. What is occurring in this anecdote if not the tearing out of the story as a signifying mark by the power of the royal eye to make way for another mark, another movement, another tomb where power is re-established in its full immanence and where the Name and the Story of the power thus re-instituted are set up as historical narrative in the text of the historiographer, the artisan narrator of this reconstitution. By telling how the power of the royal eye can un-make history, Racine tells how that power can make history – he rewrites it with his pen. Power establishes the narration of its present as history only at the cost of tearing out another narrative, a name and an epigraph inscribed on a tomb, which had been the sign of its own scission. Then the new legend of Truth, Racine's narrative, the narrative of the King's historiographer, can be inscribed on the newly smooth marble of the church at Vitry. What keen eye could possibly make out what had been removed? What future reader read, in the narrative, the palimpsest of another past, power turned against itself? "*Vitry*. The affection of the inhabitants; fires of joy, lanterns at all the windows." Nobody. The trap is working.

However, it is working too well. It works to excess, quite simply because Racine, naïve as a cunning birdcatcher, has told how it works; and at the same time he has got caught in it: the utterance traps the uttering that was denying it. By narrating the anecdote of the ripping out of the rebel's tomb, Racine in his text brings back the tomb and the inscription and the past existence of the governor who had belonged to the League. By writing about the fact of eradication, the historiographer works the same transformation for the "eradicated" as he had created through the nomination of the brief passage about the King at Vitry: Truth pronounced its sentence therein through his pen and, at the same time, makes it eternal.

Such is the function of the denial represented here in narrative form: to reinstate what had been denied while continuing to deny it, and positing it only to the extent it was denied. The tomb that was in "reality" torn out recurs in the narrative as a "symbolic" tomb. And, to the extent that this action by the people of Vitry is an effect of the power of the King's history as a direct effect of royal power – without wishing to and without knowing it, it displays the power of its own narrative, in the King's service – and at the same time, by the very act of showing it, it turns that power against itself. The *real* negation that it recounts as a sign of the King's power somehow constitutes, *in the symbolic sphere*, the denied content, i.e. that of power divided against itself, of its narrative: a structure of conflict.

Denial of the utterance: an intellectual admission of the repressed, the essence of the repression none the less remaining. This means precisely – once the mechanism has been dismantled – that the subject of the utterance (while displaying within the narrative utterances he writes the power of his narrative, which is due to the fact that he does not appear therein) falls into his own trap every time he displays the power of the subject of his narrative (of which it is the fictive double, the semblance in the symbolic order), that is, he falls in continually without ever knowing it.

One more word: ripping a tomb out of the church at Vitry; narrative of that ripping out in Racine's notes: a stone set aside for the building of the King's own "tomb", his history. A house burns at St-Cloud and the tomb goes up in smoke. Nothing remains but the narrative of the fire by Louis Racine, his son. Nothing is left of the remains of the rebel governor in his tomb at Vitry but the narrative Racine made of them. Ruses follow upon ruses and imitate each other; through embedded repetitions counter-ruses create ruses by turning them around. The effaced returns in the narrative of its removal: the "narrated" make a brief appearance and then go away. Thus the "narrators"; power established, power denied and set up at the same time, but never at the point, at the site – or so rarely – never at the moment – or almost never – where it is expected.

Another little story: regarding a passive transformation:

*Toul.* One spent a day. The King toured the town, visited the fortifications and ordered two bastions by the river. . . .

*Metz.* One spent two days. Maréchal Créqui came and was ordered to leave the next day. . . . Great zeal of the inhabitants of Metz for the King.

Thus we have the following two narrative utterances:

1 The king ordered two bastions by the river.
2 Créqui was ordered to leave Metz the following day.

We can take (2) as the passive transformation of (1), but with two significant complementary side effects from one to the other. In (1) the omission of the object: the King ordered two bastions *from whom*? Going in reverse from (2) to (1), I note in (2) the manifestation of the "object" of the order – Créqui – and in (1) that of the subject ordering – the King. Everything takes place as though – in the text – the appearance of the object was correlative with the disappearance of the subject – as though both could not exist simultaneously on the same site of the text. Appearance and disappearance in and of the utterance of the subject and the object, revealing by their dual failure the site and time of the uttering.

I return to the analysis: names begin to separate from the anonymous "one", names that are named only through the nomination of the agent of the story: the King. In the narrative of *his* story, absolute power is first of all the power to elect the actors by distributing the effects of his power: he names. Thus Créqui, who comes to Metz, the site of "one's" stay: he is named only to receive an order. From whom? The King, of course. But the latter is not named at the source of the order as the word/name that issues it. All that is written down is the effect of the royal word in the form of propositions devoid of any strategic meaning. Why does Créqui come to Metz only to be ordered to depart the next day? We do not know. The King knows, but his historian, at the site of "one's" stay, knows nothing. He is content to note down the enigmatic royal signs emanating from the *numen* of power. From the King's innermost being arise uninterpretable signs, acts, movements. Racine was to recall them in *L'Éloge du Roi*: "In the history of the King, everything is alive, everything moves, everything is in action. One need only follow him if one can and study him carefully – him alone. There is a continuous series of miraculous deeds that he himself initiates, that he completes, deeds as clear, as intelligible when they are carried out as they are *impenetrable before they are carried out.*" With Racine, we are at that instant before the carrying out: the miracle of the impenetrable deed. A "notable", Créqui, arrives and leaves: a miracle; but what miracle? Créqui obeys a presence that is not manifested, that is, of itself, an issuer and enactor of orders.

The trace of this presence in the text is the omission of the "agent's complement". The absoluteness of the royal desire is shown through absence. That absence is the trace of the miraculous; in the text, the manner in which the narrator of this royal desire displays it; its effects, i.e. by summonses to exist, by naming of actors as objects/instruments whose military purposes and political ends are not specified. The infiniteness of the King's desiring substance can be represented only by its results.

In other words, the royal desire is manifested only through the syntax of the narrative utterance. The King is that syntax and he cannot be recaptured either as a semantic figure in that utterance or as its reference.

On the other hand, at the previous stop, "Toul", the King appears in the narrative as an actor: an acting, desiring, ordering subject. He appears on the narrative stage, but this time without an object. When the royal desire makes its entrance in the form of a deed, the object disappears, or rather – as the subject will later on – the object leaves a trace of its absence in the syntax of the utterance. Inversion of active into passive: the object appears as a narrative figure; it is, then, the subject that passes through the syntax when exiting the arena of the subject matter, leaving no trace in the discursive order but its omission. In other words, to sum up, we have a formula of this kind: (1) ← order → (you), where the two poles of the structure of the utterance, by their simultaneous complementary absence/presence, take form *on the basis of the verb in a neutral state* (the infinitive) and give *it* form as an uttered (conjugated) verb.

What is revealed in these notes, which in their fragmentary character make up a text, is absolute political power as fantasy, the fantasy of power and the power of fantasy in the writing of history; the structuring of the Power's desire for power, where its absolute attempts to define itself: a kind of primordial modalization that monumental history will narrate as a network of modalities whose circulation and transformation in the narrative replace – and we shall see this – narrative utterances.

To order: (1) to place in a certain arrangement; (2) to prescribe, enjoin. Near synonym: to command, to transmit a mandate.

Order: (1) arrangement of things according to a clear and constant relationship, either simple or complex; (2) law, a general rule depending on nature, authority, usage, etc.; (3) prescription, injunction.

The fantasy resides in this: if a relationship of order is non-reflexive, non-symmetrical and transitive, then *blocking* the flow of the transitive, the reference to the situation in the course of the process is tantamount to positing what, in the order, will have no more predecessors, but will have only successors: thus absolute order.

When the King takes form in the narrative as the subject of the utterance of order, there is absolutely no need to utter the object of the order, since "everything", all the elements of the whole furnished with the relation of order *can only be* the subject's "successors", and thus they are neutralized by the "ordering" of the subject/King. They become part of the syntax of the utterance, the order of this "ordering". They disappear as semantic figures or references.

When "Créqui" takes form in the narrative as the object of the utterance of order, there is no need to utter the subject of the order, since all the elements of the whole thus "ordered" can have only one single "predecessor". The "ordered being" can only be so if there is a subject King. He thus becomes part of the syntax of the utterance, the order of this "ordered being". He is the syntax of that order.

Here is Power's desire for power in the fantasy of the order: since the ordering process is blocked, since it is not process but structure, the order has always already been followed and thus the object of the order cannot single itself out as the "agent" of the order (to be given). It is immediately included in the "ordering" itself. That is why, as the subject of the "ordering" takes form on-stage, the object is caught up in the scene itself, in its syntax; and contrariwise, if the object takes form there, then it is the subject that is the "ordering" itself.

Therefore, if desire is the primordial modalization of utterance, the trace of the appearance of an uttering subject as the negation of an accomplished present and the assertion of an unaccomplished future, the "desire for power" of power within the fantasy structure of "ordering" neutralizes itself therein, since the future is never the assertion of the unaccomplished, the accomplished present is not denied there, all temporality is eliminated, and desire and power – secondary modalities of the primary modalization – are telescoped into an "always already done".

Racine will express this again with great clarity in a *Discours*: "Yet let us speak the truth, Sir: the path of negotiation is very short under a prince who, having power and reason always at his side, need only state his will to have it carried out. . . . [Our ambassadors] themselves confess that the king does everything and sees everything in the courts to which he sends them, and that all they have to take the trouble to do is to make known in a dignified manner what he had dictated to them with such wisdom." This text could pass for the political commentary on a verse of Pindar, or one of St Bernard's reflections as cited by Pascal: "When the gods have a desire, its fulfilment is swift and the paths to it are short" (*Pythiques*, IX, 67).

"With God, the word is not distinct from the intention, for He is true; neither the word from the effect, for He is powerful, nor the means from the effect, for He is wise" (*Ultimus sermo in Missus*).

Here is the conclusion of Racine's travel journal:

*Gand*, March 4th. The King, arriving at eleven o'clock, found Gand invested by Maréchal d'Humières. He dined and went to assign the quarters and tour the area . . . the lines of circumvallation had been begun and the King commanded that they be completed: they were seven leagues around. They began work to prepare the trench in the evening. . . . The following day, March 5th, the trench was opened on the left by the guards' regiment and was extended up to a front.

The King said, after the taking of Gand, that over three months ago the King of England had told Villa-Hermosa that he had to fear for Gand above all.

Miserable state of the Spanish troops: they surrendered because they had no bread. The governor, an old bearded man, spoke only these words to the King: "I come to surrender to Your Majesty; that is all I have to say to him."

Thus, the war, the campaign, the definition and taking of the strategic objective were carried out not in the absence of the King nor independently of him, but rather by a sort of *immediate action from afar*: there is but one example of this type of action, the light and, more precisely, the gaze; the power of the royal eye, the master's eye.

The same remarks hold for what follows: to tour the area is ritually to invest it with the royal presence. Majesty circumscribes the site, names it and takes possession of it. Likewise, the distribution of quarters superimposes on the geographical space and its natural articulations the strategic space of the royal will and substitutes one for the other, a strategic space marked out by the names of the delegated agents of the agent of the story, names that emerge from anonymity only to rename, at His Majesty's will, the sites of reality. Gand is already captured *ex opere operato* by the sacrament of the King's presence and movement even before actually being taken. Racine does not recount the event of the fall of Gand; for the historical event is only an immediate sequel to and, at most, a simple predicate of the substantive subject of the history. As proof, see this notation a few lines earlier: "A league from Valenciennes, he [the King] pointed out to me seven cities, all within view, which are now his; he said: You shall see Tournai, which is well worth my risking something to save." A gesture: pointing out; a totalizing gaze: representation is immediate appropriation of the things seen by the royal subject: and the seven towns are now his. They were not his, then, when he looked at them and pointed them out, but he took possession of them by the power of his eye: they were already his. The proof? They are his now.

"The King said, after the taking of Gand. . .": a commentary that reveals the underside of the strategic game. A knowledge; but this knowledge of the King's appears *after* the event of the taking of Gand, as if it had not appeared *before* as the goal of a movement, the objective of a strategic calculation, the aim of a policy, but as ever already essentially a part of the will of the subject of the history. The Racinian narrative is modalized by the King's knowledge, but retrospectively. The King has always known what has been afoot, from the beginning, even when "Court gossip was ... that one would be returning to Paris". And, at the same time, this knowledge, which here – at this point of the text – manifests itself, leads to closure and framework. The King's will, of which the narrator–reader has hitherto perceived only the signs, had been – as we learn at the *end* of the narrative – programmed *from the beginning* by his knowledge of the situation, of the intentions and calculations of his enemy.

And this retrospective knowledge, which inscribes the entire narrative between a viewpoint and a vanishing point, which establishes a perfect equivalent of it, because the "origin" is also the "end" of the narrative, which thereby makes of it *the* absolute viewpoint/vanishing point – this knowledge manifested in the utterance uttered by the King also says the enemy's name: "Villa-Hermosa". Against whom did the King go off to war? We learn it here, at the end, at the moment the narrative slips into its frame. And this word of the King *after* the event, by which he suddenly reveals his standing, *hidden*, knowledge of the historical situation, thus produces the event, since he names it: "The Siege and Taking of Gand".

### The King comes back from the wars . . .

> Seeing that I could not presently expect an illustrious occasion on which to distinguish myself, I attempted to illustrate my conquests by causing my name to be brought up everywhere I thought some honour could be gained.
>
> It ill behooved me however to speak any further of my glory in the presence of those who had witnessed it.
>
> That is why I shall leave it to my history to bring it out.
>
> ("Conversation de Louis XIV devant Lille", in Pellisson, *Oeuvres diverses*, vol. 2 (Paris: Didot, 1735) p. 336)

After the little tales comes the monument of the King's history: the rewriting of the journal of the trip to Gand, of the siege and taking of the town, in three great pages of the Great History written "in the manner of the Ancients, of Polybius and Livy".

First transformation of this rewriting: whereas in the *Notes de voyage* there were not enemies – except at the end, in an effect of retrospective framing – in *L'Éloge historique* they *occupy the foreground*, and are numerous, fierce and powerful, ranged against a lone man, the King: that is the setting of the prose epic.

Second transformation: whereas in the *Notes* Louis' statement – one sentence – after the taking of the town furnished the whole of the narrative through its retroactive effect upon it, with its closure, its framework, its unity of action, the *Éloge historique* reverses that importance: the strictly historical narrative will be no more than the projection on to the stage of its framework; in other words the narrative is, as it were, replaced by its programme; the narrative of action and of deeds by strategic calculation; the will of the King by his wisdom. The riddle that was created by the series of acts of power, by their impenetrability, is reversed: the narrative recounts to us nothing but the face turned toward the *enemy*, that of a rational, clearly and distinctly conceived calculation.

Thus – the third transformation – the narrative set forth in *L'Éloge historique* is, in fact, textually, in its historical rewriting, nothing but a huge syntagm of modal utterances that are no longer narrative. The primordial modalization of Power's desire for power has here become a concatenation of modalities. The writing of history is the transformation of the *libidinous* economy of power into narrative *political* economy: Power's desire for power is structured, in its written fantasy, as strategic rationality and programming politics, with neither residuum nor failure, as the *accomplished* historical action. Although you think you are reading a narrative, you are only reading the (strategic-political) calculation that produced the history that is taken on in the text by the narrative. You think that through the narrative utterances you are witnessing the rise of events on the horizon of history, as they appeared; you are only reading the all-powerful royal deliberation that *preceded* their emergence, as though the deliberation – that *political* discourse – had been the producer of the events, as though historical events had no end other than to manage to fill in the deliberative sequences. You think you are contemplating, in the distancing instituted by reading and by the past, an *accomplished* history; you are only reading its *plans for the future*, its model, or its operational matrix, but as *history in the making* (present tense).

That is why the event *as* historical event is neutralized, cancelled, in the narrative that utters it – a blend of surprise and expectation: in it the first affect is a symptom of the future, the uncertainty of what *is not yet*, and the second, of the past, is the expectation of what *has been* anticipated. There is indeed a narrative of events, but those events derive their "historicity" by emanating wholly and completely from a sovereign wisdom that has always known and understood them, from an absolute, timeless rationality that has always already performed them and that has thereby *achieved* them. There is indeed a narrative, a written narration of an accomplished past; but that past is, *in truth*, the timeless present of the royal essence, of its *verb*. The master of this transformation is the historiographer. He operates – through writing – this simulation; he is the depository, in the text he is writing, of reason as reason of

State = I, the "double", the simulation of the King, who is the depository of the reason of State = I as reason.

"The enemies evidently thought themselves to be. . .": such is the modal sphere reserved for the anti-subject at the narrative's point of departure: the enemy thinks he knows. He imagines and assumes he knows in order to will and to be able to achieve his plans: to the modalization of uncertainty (believe, claim, presume, doubt) from the dominant modality of knowledge the historiographer reserves for the enemy at the outset of his narrative, there is the hypermodalization of the dominant modality of the King, the subject: "The King could not bring himself to act." The King is powerless to refuse action. The King's will to act overflows the royal subject: to will is his fate.

Thus is the opening scene we see and the narrative production:

$$\begin{cases} \text{Enemy} \\ \text{Anti-subject} \end{cases} \quad \text{believe (to know)} \rightarrow \text{desire (to do)}$$

$$\begin{cases} \text{King} \\ \text{Subject} \end{cases} \quad \text{be unable (not to will [to do])} \rightarrow \text{to do}$$

Gand itself is under siege. This latest news is a thunderbolt for the enemy: for a long time he is loath to give credence to it. Thereupon the King, who was thought to be in Lorraine, appeared in the depths of winter to lay siege to the largest city of the Low Countries. . . .

The King, having calculated the time in which his orders could be carried out, leaves the Queen at Stenay, mounts his horse, traverses more than sixty leagues of countryside in three days, and joins his army before Gand. Upon his arrival he finds the circumvallation nearly completed and all the companies already in place according to the plan he himself had drawn up at Saint-Germain. . . . The city surrenders; and the citadel, although very strong, capitulates two days later.

Thus is the final scene that closes the narrative:

$$\begin{cases} \text{Enemy} \\ \text{Anti-subject} \end{cases} \quad \text{not to will (not to believe [to know])} \rightarrow \text{be unable (to do)}$$

$$\begin{cases} \text{King} \\ \text{Subject} \end{cases} \quad \text{to know (be able [to desire])} \rightarrow \text{to do}$$

Regarding the enemy (the anti-subject), I note, as concerns the first sequence:

1. a *permutation* of the category of "will", modalizing his action (to will to do), and that of "believe", modalizing his knowledge; and,

2. the *negation* of his dominant modality (to believe), the consequence of which is his powerlessness to act, the negation of his "to do".

On the other hand, the King's (the subject's) modal sphere becomes wholly positive: his action is the immediate result, as it were – or the projection – of the harmonious modal hierarchy of knowledge, power and will: whereas initially the King's conduct was the fated act of a will/destiny that overflowed and dominated the subject, by the narrative's end that will once again reintegrates the royal essence and becomes subordinated to the wisdom and omnipotence of the reason–State. Will and power are set in a hierarchy in and through the King's knowledge. The subject has taken over the modality of which it was – so it seemed – initially deprived: the knowledge which then – so it seemed – was characterizing the enemy.

How was such a transformation brought about? Through a remarkable operation, again bearing on the modalities which articulate the narrative of the conflict between the two adversaries, the enemy and the King; through a rational and strategic calculation that "stands for" the conflict by representing it within its operative matrix, with neither excess nor lack. As for the enemy, the narrative narrated by the historiographer restricts itself to developing its characteristic modality: to believe one knows. The anti-subject "recognizes his weakness in good faith"; consequently, he *wants* to make up for it by trying "to arouse compassion in the English"; he "wants to continue" the war; "he deludes himself that the King will at least leave Flanders in peace and that he will only have to cover the neighboring German provinces". The enemy's calculation is one that involves "thinking one knows", especially as regards the possibility of an English intervention on his behalf; the consequence of this is an "act" – but a defensive one that does not implement a willing, one that is not the implementation of some power or force, but one that contents itself with speculating on some partial and diminishing act on the King's part.

The site of the operation is with the King: the King *causes* the enemy to *believe* that he *wants to act* just as the enemy thinks he does. On the level of modalities what can this mean save that the royal subject is applying to the enemy's modality (belief) his own modality (will) and its consequence (act). The King acts, but in so doing he creates belief (on the part of the enemy, his adversary). The subject's "creating belief" is, so to speak, the conquest of the enemy modality through its will to power and action, but in two stages, at two strokes.

The first stage is that of modal syncretism: the modal category of will (to act) is encapsulated by the opposite category of belief (in knowledge) and, at the same "stroke", the royal subject acts, but what he does is finalized by the enemy's "belief": he creates belief. This is exact definition of "traitor", where the subject is split between being and appearance, truth and falsehood, the manifest and the latent. In other words, the syncretism of modalities entails the syncretism of the factors that act within a single subject. The King, the actor-agent of history, is also the subject, the hero: he wills and he acts, and the anti-subject betrays: he does not truly want what he apparently wants; he does not do what he appears to do; he does not truly say what he seems to say. He joins in the anti-subject's game; with his "act" he joins in the enemy's "belief". This logical-modal contradiction is a strategic "stroke" – a *ruse* – whose reversal is prepared in the next moment. Indeed, in the subsequent sequence the King no longer confines himself to doing what the enemy expects (thinks he knows) he will do. He acts – he takes the initiative of autonomous action: "However, the King takes to the road again and, arriving at Verdun, puts out the rumor that he is going to lay siege to Namur."

This is an action whose consequence is to arouse a new opinion on the part of the enemy. And that is the second stage, the second "stroke" of the strategic calculation: the King causes to believe what he wants because in the first stage he caused to be believed what he wanted to believe. Now it is the enemy who joins in the game; it is the enemy – and his characteristic modality "to believe one knows" – who joins in that of the King, "to will to act". The King creates belief in what he wants while waiting to do what he wants. Hence the logical-modal contradiction within the subject is resolved and the scission of the subject reversed with the dissolution of the enemy in the totalizing and totalitarian essence, the harmonious and altogether positive essence of the State = I, Louis. However, the subject's moment of "betrayal" is basic and necessary, for it provides the royal volitional substance with a logic, a wisdom that it had not initially had and that will in the end be stated by the historiographer's narrative as having always been present, active and "programming". Compare the utterance *in limine* – "The King, however, *could not bring himself to leave them at rest*" – with the utterance *in fine* – "*Upon his arrival* he *finds* the circumvallation nearly completed and all the companies already in place, *according to the plan he himself had drawn up at Saint-Germain.*" The moment of treachery is also necessary, for by rationalizing the sovereign will through wisdom, he rationalizes the secret and the riddle of State, of the reason of State, and of its (lightning) strokes. It makes it possible to endow the king-being with an infinite dimension, a maximal density, an opacity at once impenetrable and intelligible. In the end, after the event, all is explained: the agent of history (the King) is history itself in its agent, i.e. an all-powerful reason, which is a reason of State. The historical event is totally neutralized in its historicity, both because it is a miracle, a marvel and an irruption, in the time of deeds, of an omnipotent will to act, transcending its agent and its subject, and because it is the movement (the stroke) of a rational calculation, of a strategic matrix, a representative model produced by an all-seeing, omnipresent immovable logic, an ordering gaze that computes and stores up historical data. In the relationship I have sketched out here between the historical event and the all-powerful will and totalizing wisdom of the King, there also appears the structuring force of "ordering", in which Power's desire for power finds primordial expression because the following are unified by the historiographer's narrative power: (1) the whole, provided with a relationship of order; (2) the relationship of order itself; and, finally, (3) the injunction or instituting will of a structure of order.

A word in conclusion on this point: the King's *ruse* is essential, not only to assure his triumph at Gand, but also to gain for him a totalitarian and consistent substance, an absolute knowledge, an infinite will, a limitless power. He acquires his own substance only in the narrative written by his historiographer; to put it bluntly, the King's *ruse* is the *ruse* of his narrator, and the enemy who falls into the trap of the King's movements and counter-movements is also the reader who falls into the trap of this narrative, whose sole function is to operate the fantasy of Power's desire for power and there to subjugate it.

It can also be said that a history book encloses the narrative representation of an infinity of miracles concentrated in "very little space": the space of a book, homologous to the space of the body of the State. It is a container for keeping the representation, the narrative, always in view; a lasting presence wherein the special characteristics of the space and time are cancelled; a memory – permanence and immortality in a quasi-point – of what constitutes the favourite occupation of their thoughts. The spectator–readers raise their eyes to the infinite vanishing point on the horizon where universal power, the King's will, is condensed. In that process of containing and framing the narrative, it is not merely that the closure of the representation is itself represented at every stage of that process, but that it is – in its representation – nothing less than the setting out of the universal-singular will: the very purpose of representation. Perfect self-representation: the King's universal will – set out in all its exteriority – and singular will – condensed at the vanishing point – turns back upon its own desire: the very representation of absolute power.

Thus the eye (of the master) contemplates itself in its own gaze-light, universally present thanks to the receptive–reflective mechanism of the narrative of history, with which it endows itself.

UMBERTO ECO

# A Portrait of the Elder as a Young Pliny: How to Build Fame

In his Letter 6, XVI I, C. Pliny the Young (hereafter the Young) writes to Tacitus about the death of his uncle, Pliny the Elder (hereafter the Elder), who perished during the eruption of Vesuvius at Pompeii, A.D. 79.

The letter is written to provide Tacitus with material for his *Historiæ*. As can be understood from the letter, the Young had first-hand evidence of the start of the events and first-hand reports about the circumstances of the death of his uncle. This fact is very important for the purpose of the following analysis: at the beginning of the letter there is an implicit Ego (the Young) writing presumably around A.D. 104 to his addressee, and the only true proposition one could identify in this text is "I, Pliny, am writing in this moment to you Tacitus saying p." The whole set of propositions labelled as "p" should be referentially opaque. But the letter implies a sort of performative mode, as if it said: "I swear that p is true." There is a sort of authentication agreement[1] between the Young and Tacitus, by force of which Tacitus – and any other possible addressee of the letter – must take "p" as pure matter of fact. Besides, Tacitus asked the Young for reliable information just because he thought and assumed that his correspondent would have told a true story. As far as we know, the story is true, indeed: in any case it mirrors the only historical truth we recognize as such, since it has contributed (together with some other texts) to what our cultural encyclopaedia records as truth.

But we have improperly defined what the Young says as a set of propositions labelled as "p". As a matter of fact, the Young narrates something, but his narration, like every other narration, is made up of two components, the

---

[1] Algirdas J. Greimas and J. Courtés, *Sémiotique: Dictionnaire raisonné de la théorie du langage* (Paris: Hachette, 1979): on this point they would have said "*contract of veridiction*".

underlying *fabula* (or story) and the vehicular *discourse* (or plot, or discursive arrangement of events).

The aim of the present analysis is to show that the story (once it has been isolated by a reader in the form of a series of macropropositions chronologically ordered) says one thing. However, the discourse says, if not something else, at least something more, in such a way that it is difficult to isolate clearly the two levels.

This *double jeu* is clearly evident in the opening lines of the letter: Tacitus asked for a description of facts but the Young understands very well that what is at stake is an account for posterity – that is, a cultural monument.

Petis ut tibi avunculi mei exitum scribam, quo verius tradere posteris possis. Gratias ago; nam video morti eius si celebretur a te immortalem gloriam esse propositam. Quamvis enim pulcherrimarum clade terrarum, ut populi ut urbes memorabili casu, quasi semper victurus occiderit, quamvis ipse plurima opera et mansura condiderit, multum tamen perpetuitati eius scriptorum tuorum aeternitas addet. Equidem beatos puto, quibus deorum munere datum est aut facere scribenda aut scribere legenda, beatissimos vero quibus utrumque. Horum in numero avunculus meus et suis libris et tuis erit. Quo libentius suscipio, deposeo etiam quod iniungis.

Thank you for asking me to send you a description of my uncle's death so that you can leave an accurate account of it for posterity; I know that immortal fame awaits him if his death is recorded by you. It is true that he perished in a catastrophe which destroyed the loveliest regions of the earth, a fate shared by whole cities and their people, and one so memorable that it is likely to make his name live for ever: and he himself wrote a number of books of lasting value: but you write for all time and can still do much to perpetuate his memory. The fortunate man, in my opinion, is he to whom the gods have granted the power either to do something which is worth recording or to write what is worth reading, and most fortunate of all is the man who can do both. Such a man was my uncle, as his own books and yours will prove. So you set me a task I would choose for myself, and I am more than willing to start on it.

Pliny the Young is explicit: Tacitus can provide immortal glory to the Elder by representing him as a scientific hero. Such an introduction can be taken in two ways. It looks as if the Young were saying "I provide you with the facts, and they will speak by themselves – all the rest is up to you"; on the other hand, the Young is providing facts and comments, or fact wrapped with comments. Only he is not so naïve as to put forth comments as comments. He follows a different persuasive strategy. Let us follow the second part of the letter:

Erat Miseni classemque imperio praesens regebat. Nonum kal. Septembres hora fere septima mater mea indicat ei adparere nubem inusitata et magnitudine et specie. Usus ille sole, mox frigida, gustaverat iacens studebatque; poscit soleas, ascendit locum ex quo maxime miraculum illud conspici poterat. Nubes – incertum procul intuentibus ex quo monte (*Vesuvium fuisse postea cognitum est*) – oriebatur, cuius similitudinem et formam non alia magis arbor quam pinus expresserit. Nam longissimo velut trunco elata in altum quibusdam ramis diffundebatur, credo quia recenti spiritu evecta, dein senescente eo destituta aut etiam pendere suo victa in latitudinem vanescebat, candida interdum, interdum sordida et maculosa *prout terram cineremve sustulerat*. Magnum propiusque noscendum ut eruditissimo viro visum. Iubet liburnicam aptari; *mihi* si venire una vellem facit copiam; respondi studere me malle, et forte ipse quod scriberem dederat.

Egrediebatur domo; accipit codicillos Rectinae Tasci *imminenti periculo exterritae* (nam villa eius subiacebat, nec ulla nisi navibus fuga): ut se tanto discrimini eriperet orabat. Vertit ille consilium et *quod studioso animo incohaverat obit maximo*. Deducit quadriremes, ascendit ipse non Rectinae modo sed multis (erat enim fre-

My uncle was stationed at Misenum, in active command of the fleet. On 24 August, in the early afternoon, my mother drew his attention to a cloud of unusual size and appearance. He had been out in the sun, has taken a cold bath, and lunched while lying down, and was then working at his books. He called for his shoes and climbed up to a place which would give him the best view of the phenomenon. It was not clear at that distance from which mountain the cloud was rising (*it was afterwards known to be Vesuvius*); its general appearance can best be expressed as being like a pine rather than any other tree, for it rose to a great height on a sort of trunk and then split off into branches, I imagine because it was thrust upwards by the first blast and then left unsupported as the pressure subsided, or else it was borne down by its own weight so that it spread out and gradually dispersed. Sometimes it looked white, sometimes blotched and dirty, *according to the amount of soil it carried with it*. My uncle's scholarly acumen saw at once that it was important enough for a closer inspection, and he ordered a boat to be made ready, telling *me* I could come with him if I wished. I replied that I preferred to go on with my studies, and as it happened he had himself given me some writing to do.

As he was leaving the house he was handed a message from Rectina, wife of Tascus, whose house was at the foot of the mountain, so that escape was impossible except by boat. *She was terrified* by the danger threatening her and implored him to rescue her from her fate. He changed his plans, and *what he had begun in a spirit of*

quens amoenitas orae) laturus auxil-
ium. Properat illuc unde alii fugiunt,
*rectumque cursum recta gubernacula in
periculum tenet adeo solutus metu*, ut
omnes illius mali motus omnes figuras
ut deprenderat oculis dictaret
enotaretque. Iam navibus cinis incide-
bat, quo propius accederent, calidior
et densior; iam pumices etiam nigri-
que et ambusti et fracti igne lapides;
iam vadum subitum ruinaque montis
litora obstantia. Cunctatus paulum an
retro flecteret, mox gubernatori ut ita
faceret monenti *"Fortes"* inquit *"fortuna iuvat*: Pomponianum pete." Sta-
biis erat diremptus sinu medio (nam
sensim circumactis curvatisque litor-
ibus mare infunditur): ibi *quamquam
nondum periculo adpropinquante*, con-
spicuo tamen et cum cresceret proximo, sarcinas contulerat in naves,
certus fugae si contrarius ventus
resedisset. Quo tunc avunculus meus
secundissimo invectus, complecitur
trepidantem consolatur hortatur,
utque timorem eius sua securitate
leniret, deferri in balineum iubet;
lotus accubat cenat, aut hilaris aut
(quod aeque magnum) similis hilari.

*inquiry he completed as a hero*. He gave
orders for the warships to be launched
and went on board himself with the
intention of bringing help to many
more people besides Rectina, for this
lovely stretch of coast was thickly
populated. He hurried to the place
which everyone else was hastily leaving, *steering his course straight for the
danger zone. He was entirely fearless*,
describing each new movement and
phase of the portent to be noted down
exactly as he observed them. Ashes
were already falling, hotter and
thicker as the ships drew near, followed by bits of pumice and black-
ened stones, charred and cracked by
the flames: then, suddenly they were
in shallow water, and the shore was
blocked by the debris from the mountain. For a moment my uncle won-
dered whether to turn back, but when
the helmsman advised this he refused,
telling him that *Fortune stood by the
courageous* and they must make for
Pomponianus at Stabiae. He was cut
off there by the breadth of the bay (for
the shore gradually curves round a
basin filled by the sea) so that *he was
not as yet in danger*, though it was clear
that this would come nearer as it
spread. Pomponianus had therefore
already put his belongings on board
ship, intending to escape if the contrary wind fell. This wind was of
course full in my uncle's favour, and
he was able to bring his ship in. He
embraced his terrified friend, cheered
and encouraged him, and thinking he
could calm his fears by showing his
own composure, gave orders that he
was to be carried to the bathroom.
After his bath he lay down and dined;
he was quite cheerful, or at any rate
he pretended he was, which was no
less courageous.

Interim e Vesuvio monte pluribus locis latissimae flammae altaque incendia relucebant, quorum fulgor et claritas tenebris noctis excitabatur. Ille agrestium trepidatione ignes relictos desertasque villas per solitudinem ardere in remedium formidinis dictitabat. Tum se quieti dedit et quievit verissimo quidem somno; nam meatus animae, qui illi propter amplitudinem corporis gravior et sonantior erat, ab iis qui limini obversabantur audiebatur. Sed area ex qua diaeta adibatur ita iam cinere mixtisque pumicibus oppleta surrexerat, ut si longior in cubiculo mora, exitus negaretur. Excitatus procedit, seque Pomponiano ceterisque qui pervigilaverant reddit. In commune consultant, intra tecta subsistant an in aperto vagentur. Nam crebris vastisque tremoribus tecta nutabant, et quasi emota sedibus suis nunc huc nunc illuc abire aut referri videbantur. Sub dio rursus quamquam levium exesorumque pumicum casus metuebatur, quod tamen periculorum collatio elegit; et apud illum quidem ratio rationem, apud alios timorem timor vicit. Cervicalia capitibus imposita linteis constringunt; id munimentum adversus incidentia fuit.

Meanwhile on Mount Vesuvius broad sheets of fire and leaping flames blazed at several points, their bright glare emphasized by the darkness of night. My uncle tried to allay the fears of his companions by repeatedly declaring that these were nothing but bonfires left by the peasants in their terror, or else empty houses on fire in the districts they had abandoned. Then he went to rest and certainly slept; as he was a stout man his breathing was rather loud and heavy and could be heard by people coming and going outside his door. By this time the courtyard giving access to his room was full of ashes mixed with pumice-stones, so that its level had risen, and if he had stayed in the room any longer he would never have got out. He was wakened, came out and joined Pomponianus and the rest of the household who had sat up all night. They debated whether to stay indoors or take their chance in the open, for the buildings were now shaking with violent shocks, and seemed to be swaying to and fro as if they were torn from their foundations. Outside on the other hand, there was the danger of falling pumice-stones, even though these were light and porous; however, after comparing the risks they chose the latter. In my uncle's case one reason outweighed the other, but for the others it was a choice of fears. As a protection against falling objects they put pillows on their heads tied down with cloths.

Iam dies alibi, illic nox omnibus noctibus nigrior densiorque; quam tamen faces multae variaque lumina solvebant. Placuit egredi in litus, et ex proximo adspicere, ecquid iam mare admitteret; quod adhuc vastum et adversum permanebat. Ibi super

Elsewhere there was daylight by this time, but they were still in darkness, blacker and denser than any night that ever was, which they relieved by lighting torches and various kinds of lamp. My uncle decided to go down to the shore and investi-

abiectum linteum recubans semel atque iterum frigidam aquam poposcit hausitque. Deinde flammae flammarumque praenuntius odor sulpuris alios in fugam vertunt, excitant illum. Innitens servolis duobus adsurrexit et statim concidit, ut ego colligo, crassiore caligine spiritu obstructo, clausoque stomacho qui illi natura invalidus et angustus et frequenter aestuans erat. Ubi dies redditus (is ab eo quem novissime viderat tertius), corpus inventum integrum inlaesum opertumque ut fuerat indutus: habitus corporis quiescenti quam defuncto similior.

gate on the spot the possibility of any escape by sea, but he found the waves still wild and dangerous. A sheet was spread on the ground for him to lie down, and he repeatedly asked for cold water to drink. Then the flames and smell of sulphur which gave warning of the approaching fire drove the others to take flight and roused him to stand up. He stood leaning on two slaves and then suddenly collapsed, I imagine because the dense fumes choked his breathing by blocking his windpipe which was constitutionally weak and narrow and often inflamed. When daylight returned on the 26th – two days after the last day he had seen – his body was found intact and uninjured, still fully clothed and looking more like sleep than death.

Interim Miseni ego et mater – sed nihil ad historiam, nec tu aliud quam de exitu eius scire voluisti. *Finem ergo faciam.* Unum adiciam, omnia me quibus interfueram quaeque statim, cum maxime vera memorantur, audieram, persecutum. Tu potissima excerpes; *aliud est enim epistulam aliud historiam, aliud amico aliud omnibus scribere.* Vale.

Meanwhile my mother and I were at Misenum, but this is not of any historic interest, and you only wanted to hear about my uncle's death. *I will say no more*, except to add that I have described in detail every incident which I either witnessed myself or heard about immediately after the event, when reports were most likely to be accurate. It is for you to select what best suits your purpose, *for there is a great difference between a letter to a friend and history written for all to read.*[2]

The first impression one receives in reading this letter is that the Elder was indeed a hero of science who lost his life sailing courageously to the source of the eruption because of his sense of duty and his erudite curiosity. The acknowledgement of such an effect is not only a matter of intuition. Unfortunately, we do not know how Tacitus, as an empirical reader, reacted to the letter, since his *Historiæ* stop at A.D. 70 and their second part is lost. But we

---

[2] Pliny the Younger, *Letters and Panegyrics*, trans. Betty Radice (Cambridge, Mass: Harvard University Press, 1969; London: Heinemann, 1969), author's emphasis.

know how other readers reacted, since our encyclopaedia records the fate of the Elder as a paramount example of scientific holocaust.

Nevertheless, if one puts the underlying *fabula* into a sequence of propositions, the crude facts are the following: the Elder moves towards the eruption before knowing that it is an eruption (moreover, at that time nobody considered Vesuvius as an active volcano and the same Pliny the Elder in his *Naturalis Historia* (III, 62) describes Vesuvius as a pleasant and harmless component of the Neapolitan landscape.[3] Even when he arrives at Pomponianus' home in Stabiae, he is still unaware of the proportions of the disaster, understanding neither its format nor its definitive effects. He says with nonchalance that the flames raging on the mountain are only bonfires left by the peasants. It is true that, according to Younger's interpretation, he says so in order to allay the fears of his companions; but afterwards he *really* goes to sleep without realizing that he was risking burial by ashes if somebody had not awakened him. When he finally understands that there is no escape and that the situation is really dramatic, it is too late. He dies as quickly as possible, because he was also asthmatic, as some commentators suggest.

When one carefully reconsiders the bare *fabula*, one gets the impression of reading the story of a very narcissistic and narrow-minded Roman admiral, completely unable to cope with the situation (in short, this efficient rescuer not only did not help anybody but also succeeded in depriving the fleet of its commander-in-chief, just when some efficiency was needed from the local military authority). Pliny the Young does not conceal anything: if Tacitus had wished he could have extrapolated the real story (perhaps he did it) precisely as we are now doing.

The Tacitus we are interested in, however, is not the 'real' Tacitus: it is the planned addressee of Pliny's letter, that is, what I have elsewhere called the Model Reader of a text.[4]

Pliny's letter is a text which, as any other text, is not empirically addressed to an empirical addressee: it builds up, by a discursive strategy, the type of reader who is supposed to co-operate in order to actualize the text such as the Model Author (that is, the objective textual strategy) wants it to be. We can refuse to play the role of the Model Reader, as we are presently doing; but we must recognize the kind of reader that the text not only presupposes but also produces through the use of given linguistic strategies.

To read the discursive manoeuvres of the Young at a metatextual level means to acknowledge the way in which the text gives its Model Reader the appropriate instructions as to how to realize a certain persuasive effect. This letter not only aims at saying something "true" (in an assertive mode); it also wants to make Tacitus (or every other possible reader) believe that the Elder was a hero, as well as wanting Tacitus to write that the Elder was one. Greimas

[3] A. N. Shewin-White, *The Letters of Pliny* (Oxford: Clarendon Press, 1966) p. 375, n. 5.
[4] Umberto Eco, *The Role of the Reader* (Bloomington, Ind.: Indiana University Press, 1979).

would speak of modalities; *faire croire* and *faire faire*: or, how to do things with words.

In order to produce the "right" co-operation of his Model Reader, Pliny the Young plays upon a complicated gamut of discursive operations, mainly temporal shiftings in and out (*embrayages* and *débrayages*, according to Greimas' terminology) and a planned confusion between the subject of the speech act and the subject of the narrative utterance (the *instance de l'énonciation* suddenly intruding on the course of l'*énoncé*). Moreover, as we shall see, the *fabula* does not only concern the world of events but also the epistemic worlds (or the propositional attitudes) of the characters, and these epistemic worlds continually overlap with the supposed epistemic world of the Model Reader (different propositional attitudes are thus *focalized* at the same moment). The final result is that the reader does not understand (provided he does not perform a metatextual analysis) *who* is speaking at a given moment.[5]

## A Portrait of the Young Pliny as an Old Reporter

At the beginning of the letter (1–3) there is an implicit *Ego* (the subject of *scribam*) which clearly refers to an individual, Pliny the Young, author of that letter, presumably in A.D. 104. Let us define *this* Pliny as $P_1$, writing at a time-moment $t_0$, in a world $W_0$ conventionally taken as the real world. This is an oversimplification due to the fact that we assume that the letter is not a piece of fiction but of natural narrativity (like a newspaper article). If it were a piece of fiction (like the letters of *Clarissa* or of *Les Liaisons dangereuses*) we would assume that there is another subject (a $P_0$), the empirical producer of the speech act, while the *Ego* of the discourse is a fictive subject, not to be identified with the author. In other cases (fiction written in third person) the subject of the speech act can interfere with the discourse as a semi-fictive subject, an *Ego* who comments on the facts, and who can or cannot be identified with the empirical author (see, for instance, the comments provided in the first person by Fielding or by Manzoni throughout *Tom Jones* or *The Betrothed*).

In our case we can assume that the historical Pliny and the Ego speaking from 1 to 3 can be taken as the same entity, the Sender of the letter whose Addressee is Tacitus.

However, from 4 onwards, $P_1$ tells Tacitus a story concerning $P_2$, that is, what happened to himself twenty-five years before, at Misenum, in A.D. 79, 24 August. Thus we have a letter written in $t_0$ which tells about another time, or a given series of temporal states that we shall register as follows:

$t_{-3}$ = 24 August, afternoon, when the cloud appears and the Elder decides to sail;

$t_{-2}$ = The lapse of time or the series of temporal states occurring from the

[5] For such a dialectic of *voices*, see also Gérard Genette, *Figures III* (Paris: Seuil, 1972).

departure of the Elder to his death (the evening of the 24th and the following day, the 25th);

$t_{-1}$ = 26 August, when the Young receives fresh news about what happened.

The moment in which $P_1$ shifts out to the time of the *fabula* ($t_{-3}$) is marked by the passage from present to the imperfect tense ("*erat Miseni . . . regebat*"). The narrative mood is also stressed by the insertion of chrononyms ("*Nonum kal Septembres*") and by the introduction of individuals belonging to a former temporal state (the uncle, the mother – the former as the implicit subject of *erat* and by the attribution of some functional properties, as *regebat classem*). All these grammatical devices mark clearly the passage between the introductory part, where the Young speaks as $P_1$, and the second one, where the explicit or implicit Ego is $P_2$ (see figure 1).

$P_0$ The historical
    Pliny the Young
    Subject of the
    speech act
    (*sujet de l'énonciation*)

$P_1$ Narrator
    Pliny the Young
    as the subject
    of the uttered
    discourse, in $t_0$
    *Énonciation*
    *énoncé* or spoken
    speech act

$P_2$ as one of the
    characters of the
    narration along
    with:
$E$ the Elder
$M$ the mother . . .
all in $t_{-3} . . . t_{-1}$

Figure 1

One should notice that the second box of the above diagram, embedded in the first one, does not necessarily represent the level of the *fabula* as opposed to the level of discourse. As a matter of fact the *fabula* of $P_2$ is still told in a discursive form and must be extrapolated from the discourse by the co-operative reader.

What the reader extrapolates are different states of the same narrative sequence, that is, different states of the same narrative world. According to the definitions proposed in Eco,[6] passing from one state to another, the individuals of such a world change some of their *accidental* properties, without changing their *essential* properties. Thus, in the narrative state corresponding to the time $t_{-3}$, the Elder is a living Roman admiral, in $t_{-2}$ he is the same Roman admiral undertaking certain unpleasant experiences, and in $t_{-1}$ he is a Roman admiral who is accidentally dead.

Nevertheless what interests us is not a comparison between these different states of the same narrative world (which incidentally coincide, as far as we know, with the "real" world, as it has been recorded by our encyclopaedical

[6] Eco, *Role of the Reader*, 8.6.

competence). What interests us is that $P_1$, as the subject of the uttered discourse in $t_0$, shares with Tacitus (as his Model Reader) some knowledge *apropos* of the death of the Elder. At the same time, $P_1$, telling Tacitus what happened in $t_{-3}$ attributes to the Elder and to himself a different sort of knowledge.

We are thus concerned with two epistemic worlds, the world $W_0$ of the beliefs shared by $P_1$, by Tacitus and by ourselves as contemporary readers, and the $W_{Nc}t_{-3}$ of the knowledge attributed by $P_1$, as narrator, to the characters of the narrated events: $P_1$ is telling the story of himself and of his uncle who, twenty-five years before, saw a strange cloud and believed $p$ ($p$ being the content of the epistemic world $W_{Nc}t_{-3}$).

In plainer words, the Young in A.D. 104 knew what he himself and his uncle could not know on 24 August A.D. 79, namely that the cloud of unusual size came from the eruption of Vesuvius and that it was made up of poisonous ashes and other harmful materials. To $P_2$ the cloud was an amazing phenomenon (and so it was to $E$) while for $P_1$ (and for Tacitus) it was, in short, Death.

This means that the *fabula* should tell about certain individuals of a given narrative World $W_N t_{-3}$, the individuals being $P_2$, $E$, $M$ along with $C$ (the cloud) and $V$ (Vesuvius), this world hosting at least one narrative subworld $W_{Nc}$ representing the beliefs of the characters of the story (since it happens that at that moment the Young, the Elder and the Mother share the same epistemic world). In such a subworld $W_{Nc}t_{-3}$ the cloud is not yet linked with the volcano, is still amazing but not necessarily harmful and, what is more important, is not supposed to represent the element that will kill the Elder.

On the contrary, the epistemic world of $P_1$ and of his Model Reader contains at $t_0$ the same individuals, but endowed with rather different properties: $E$ is a dead scientist, the cloud has a volcanic origin, Vesuvius was the cause of the disaster, the disaster (or Vesusius itself) was the agent which provoked the death of the Elder.

It is important to maintain the difference between these worlds, since in $t_{-3}$ the Elder believes that the cloud is harmless, does not suspect that Vesuvius had something to do with the phenomenon he is watching, and does not know that he will die: all elements that make his decision to go a little less courageous than if he had known what was to be the later course of events.

Let us assume that we are dealing with two narrative worlds: $W_{Nc}t_{-3}$ is the world of the narrated beliefs of the characters of the story told by $P_1$ – for the sake of economy we shall consider only the beliefs of the Elder – that coincide with those of both the Young and his mother, at that time. On the contrary $W_0t_0$ is the world of the story such as it is known by $P_1$ and Tacitus.

From this point of view we can consider these two worlds as structured according to $S$-necessary properties,[7] that is, those that link the individuals of the *fabula* by strict textual interdependence, so that one individual cannot be defined except in terms of another.

---

[7] Ibid., 8.7.3.

Thus we can outline two world-matrices in terms of the following individuals and of their $S$-necessary properties, where:

$E$ = Elder,
$C$ = Cloud,
$V$ = Vesuvius,
$cRe$ = the relation defining a cloud as the one actually perceived by the Elder in $t_{-3}$,
$cRv$ = the relation defining a cloud as being produced by the eruption of Vesuvius, and
$vRe$ = the relation defining Vesuvius as the fatal agent of Elder's death.

The resulting matrices will then be as shown in figure 2.

| $W_{Nc}t_{-3}$ | $cRe$ | $cRv$ | $vRe$ | $W_0t_0$ | $cRe$ | $cRv$ | $vRe$ |
|---|---|---|---|---|---|---|---|
| $C_1$ | + | − | − | $C_2$ | + | + | |
| $E_1$ | + | | − | $E_2$ | + | | + |
| $V_1$ | | − | − | $V_2$ | | + | + |

Figure 2

One then realizes that none of the individuals of the first world shares the same $S$-necessary properties of the homonymous individuals of the second one. Thus the individuals are designated by the same names but they are not the same: the cloud of the second world is the one perceived by the Elder and at the same time the one produced by Vesuvius, while in the first world, had there been by chance a cloud with the property of being erupted by Vesuvius, it would not have been the same as $C_1$. And so on.

Two possible narrative worlds furnished with individuals sharing different $S$-necessary properties are not narratively accessible. In the same way, a heretic Gospel telling the story of a man called Jesus who is not the Son of the Father does not speak about the same theological character as the Canonic Gospels.

Such is the difference between the epistemic world of $P_1$ (and of Tacitus) and the epistemic world of $P_2$ (and of the Elder).

## A Portrait of the Old Pliny: the Young as a Young Informant

Now we can come back to the discursive surface of the story of $P_2$ told by $P_1$. Notice that $P_1$ should make it clear that $P_2$ and the Elder shared the epistemic world $W_{Nc}t_{-3}$. A good narrator interested in the psychology of his characters and in the dialectics between reality and illusion, should insist on this gap (think of the energy with which Sophocles shows Oedipus blinded by a set of propositional attitudes that do not correspond to the real course of past events).[8]

Which is on the contrary the discursive strategy of $P_1$?

From 1 to 3 the *Ego* who speaks in $t_0$ reminds Tacitus of what he is supposed to know very well, namely that the Elder perished in that catastrophe, that the catastrophe was memorable and that because of this his name will live for ever. Why such an insistence on this piece of encyclopaedical information? The Young is clearly preparing his Model Reader to think of the Elder in terms of $W_0 t_0$.

From 4 on, the Young operates a temporal shifting-out: the change of tense produces – so to speak – a flash-back and puts the Model Reader in a previous state of the same world. But in this previous state of the same world the characters nourished propositional attitudes which cannot cope with those of the Model Reader. The Young is prima facie very honest. He says that neither he (twenty-five years before) nor his uncle knew where the cloud was coming from. But immediately afterwards he opens a parenthesis and reminds Tacitus that it was coming from Vesuvius: the parenthesis marks a new temporal and epistemic shifting-in (an *embrayage*, a return to $t_0$), expressed by the use of different tenses: *cognitum est postea . . .Vesuvium fuisse*. But, though the move is grammatically correct, both from the semantic and syntactic point of view, its pragmatic effect is quite different: it reintroduces in the core of the epistemic world of $P_2$ and of $E$, the epistemic world of $P_1$ and of Tacitus. The cloud is without any shadow of doubt the one that the Model Reader is supposed to know as *cRv* (knowing also that *vRe*).

The following move is more interesting: $P_2$ and $E$ are watching a cloud which is *candida interdum, interdum sordida* (sometimes white, sometimes dirty) and these are indeed the accidental properties of *cRe*, the cloud such as the Elder witnessed it in $t_{-3}$. But the Young (who in this case seems to be the *Ego* $P_2$, but who in fact, by a sudden shifting in $t_0$, is $P_1$) says that the cloud looked so *prout terram cineremve sustulerat* (according to the amount of soil and ashes it carried with it): a property that could not be scored as belonging to $C_1$ since it was typical of $C_2$, the cloud of the later epistemic world of $P_1$, the cloud coming from Vesuvius, the dangerous one, the one that *now* (in $W_0 t_0$) everyone knows as the mythical co-agent of the subsequent disgrace.

This time, the Young has not signalled his shifting-in by a parenthesis: on the contrary, he has further confused the temporal situation, using a pluperfect (*sustulerat*) against the imperfect of the surrounding discourse (*diffundebatur*, *vanescebat*). He thus stresses the obvious fact that (from the point of view of the logic of events) the presence of soil and ashes was prior to the spreading out of the cloud. That is correct from the point of view of the *fabula*, but not from the point of view of the epistemic world of $P_2$, who knew all this only *afterwards*. $P_1$ is telling *his* truth; which also happens to be the truth of the Reader, but which was not the truth of $P_2$ and of his unfortunate uncle. The Reader could become

[8] Ibid., pp. 243–5.

conscious of this subtle operation, if he wanted: but how can he want it since he is so cordially invited to disregard this sudden *embrayage–débrayage*?

At this point it becomes difficult for a generously co-operating reader to avoid the conviction that the Elder in $t_{-3}$ is courageously facing his *evident* destiny. The *double jeu* of shifting has, so to speak, projected onto a mirror, or a screen, the future that the encyclopaedia has definitely recorded: the Model Reader is the only one able to watch that mirror, but he nourishes the impression that the Elder is watching with him.

Thus it is very easy for $P_1$ (always acting as $P_2$) to say that, since Rectina is "terrified", the Elder, "*vertit . . . consilium et quod studioso animo incohaverat obit maximo*" (the translator, caught in the trap displayed by the text, emphasizes, and writes "as a hero"). One can suspect that, from the moment the Elder receives Rectina's message, he already knows that *cRv*. In any case, he does not know that *vRe*. But the text is shameless: the Elder "*rectumque cursum recta gubernacula in periculum tenet adeo solutus metu*", hurries to the danger (his own danger!), steering his course straight, entirely fearless (fearless of *his* incumbent death!): the same Elder who, according to $P_1$, after his arrival, goes peacefully to bed! The Model Reader, confused by a double flickering mirror where two epistemic worlds collide and vanish one into another, may now admire the sublime decision of the hero: *Fortes . . . fortuna iuvat*, let us proceed, I don't care about *my* death!

In a hiccup of honesty, $P_1$ cannot avoid telling the truth: "*quamquam nondum periculo adpropinquante*", the Elder does not feel himself in any immediate danger, Pomponianus' spot where the Elder lands is still relatively safe. But the Reader *knows* that this spot is exactly the one where the Elder will lose his life. The Elder has sailed from $W_{Nc}t_{-3}$ towards $W_0t_0$ as if he knew everything about the furniture of that world, as if he were Ulysses crossing the Pillars of Hercules.

This story of temporal shiftings-in and out is also a story of rapid switchings in focalization. It happens as if a moving spotlight were throwing its rays, alternatively, on two different epistemic worlds so that, by a sort of optical effect, one never realizes which world is being focused on; or, as happens in so-called "three card monte", where the trickster manoeuvres his cards at such a speed that his victim cannot any longer understand which card is where: a paramount example of discursive manipulation determining the extrapolation of the *fabula*'s level. Really Pliny the Young (or his text) are *doing* things with words.

The last instruction of Tacitus (after having again shifted-in at $t_0$, from line 22 to the end) is a masterpiece of hypocrisy. "*Finem ergo faciam*", "I stop representing $P_2$ and the Elder in $t_{-3}$ as I did until now (what a supreme lie!), let me come back to the present, notice, my dear Tacitus, that until now we were in another world, let us return to our own which has never interfered with that one" (such is indeed the rhetorical function of *finem ergo faciam*). "What I, $P_1$, have said until now (from 4 to 21) is only what I have witnessed at *that* time, what I knew at *that* time, what I believed together with my uncle at *that* time, what I have heard from my first-hand informants" (who obviously, let me add, knew a little more than the Elder at $t_{-3}$). "Now, Tacitus, it is you who must transform my honest report into a cultural monument, for there is a great difference between a letter to a friend and history written for all to read."

In fact, as we well know, the letter was already written for posterity, but to become effective (as it did) it had to conceal its purpose from its Model Readers.

Fortunately every text is always, more or less consciously, conceived for two kinds of Model Reader. The first is supposed to co-operate in actualizing the content of the text; the second is supposed to be able to describe (and enjoy) the way in which the first Model Reader has been textually produced.

One wonders whether Pliny the Young would have preferred a Reader accepting his glorious product (monument to the Elder) or a Reader realizing his glorifying production (monument to the Young).

ROMAN JAKOBSON

# Supraconscious Turgenev

In the memoirs of Count V. A. Sollogub (1813–82)[1] one finds a curious biographical episode recounted, apparently, directly by his guest Ivan Sergeevič Turgenev: "I like to amuse myself occasionally with a typically Russian word. I'll never forget a little incident that happened to me in London in this regard." N. M. Žemčužnikov, the brother of the famous poet, who had settled in England, once invited Turgenev to dine "at one of the grandest clubs", where the writer was promptly "overcome by the frigidity of the overwhelming ceremoniousness". Around the two newcomers three butlers took up the solemn, ritualistic performance of their duties.

Here, in Sollogub's rendering, is the kernel of Turgenev's memorable "sketch" of the club: "I felt that I was beginning to get the creeps. The luxurious hall, gloomy despite being fully illuminated; the people, looking quite like shadows made of wood, scurrying about all round us; the whole ambience of the place began to exasperate me to the extreme." The apogee neared. "I was suddenly seized by some sort of frenzy. With all my might I banged my fist on the table and started screaming like a madman: *Réd'ka! Týkva! Kobýla! Répa! Bába! Káša! Káša!* 'Radish! Pumpkin! Mare! Turnip! Peasant Woman! Kasha! Kasha!'"

Turgenev's "outburst", as the journal version of Sollogub's memoirs christened it, is formed of seven exclamatory holophrases, consisting of seven

The title adjective, *zaumnyj* ("supraconscious"), alludes to the particular form of poetry practised by the twentieth-century Russian Futurists, *zaum'*, which in its most outrageous instances verges on total verbal delirium. The literal meaning of the term is "going out of one's mind", "trans-sense". The title could be translated into colloquial English as "Turgenev Leaves His Senses", or "senseless Turgenev". [Translator's note]

[1] V. A. Sollogub, *Vospominanija*, ed. S. P. Šesterikov (Moscow and Leningrad, 1931) pp. 445–8 (a critical edition of the memoirs prepared before the author's death and first published in the journal *Istoričeskij Vestnik* in 1886, and as a book in 1887).

nouns of feminine gender in the nominative singular, with the ending "*a*" and with stress on the penultimate syllable. Five inanimates – two initial, one central, and two final – are opposed directly on both sides of the central word by two animate nouns. The latter are distinguished by the voiced prevocalic /b/ of their stressed syllable, and both semantically convey sexual information: *Kobýla!* ("mare"), *Bába!* ("peasant woman").

None of the seven words contains a rounded vowel. The central noun *Répa* ("turnip") shares with the initial *Réd'ka* ("radish") the same combination /ré/, whereas the intervening words repeat a stressed "*y*", thus forming a kind of embracing rhyme /é–í–í–é/.

The entire verbal effusion numbers five velar consonants, to be more precise, five unvoiced plosive /k/s, concentrated in the three initial and two final nouns. This same verbal chain is endowed with five labials, encompassing all the words from the second word, *Týkva!* ("pumpkin") to the fifth, *Bába!* ("peasant woman"). Thus labial consonants gravitate toward the centre of the cry, whereas velars are distributed along its borders. Five of the seven words begin with plosive consonants, as do five out of the seven stressed syllables.

It is appropriate in this context to recall the persistent testimony of the great Russian Futurist poet Velimir Xlebnikov: "I studied models of selfsome speech (*samovitaja reč'*) and found that the number five is extremely significant for it, just as it is for the number of our fingers and toes."[2] It turns out, for example, that in the first four-line proposition of the poet's *Kuznečik* ("The Grasshopper") – "apart from the desire of the one who wrote this nonsense, the sounds *u*, *k*, *l*, *r*, each repeat five times". Xlebnikov finds a parallel to this "law of freely flowing selfsome speech" in the "five-rayed make-up" of honeycombs and starfish.[3]

The structure of the peripheral three-word groups – the initial and the terminal – sharply differs. In distinction to the terminal word group, the initial is characterized by a variation in the number of syllables and in the stressed vowel, which is, moreover, consistently different from the unstressed vowel. On top of this, the initial three-word group displays a skilfully co-ordinated variety of consonants.

The three initial words contain three consonants, and the rest two each. The repertoire of consonantal classes, revealed in the first three words, i.e. in the words consisting of three consonants each, includes liquids (/r'/ and /l/), labials (/v/ and /b/), dentals (/t'/ and /t/), and velars (/k/).

The make-up and sequence in which the consonants of the various classes appear in the initial word (liquid–dental–velar) corresponds to the make-up and sequence of the same classes in the beginning of all three initial words

[2] V. Xlebnikov, *Sobranie proizvedenija*, vol. 5 (Leningrad, 1933) pp. 185, 187, 191. [*Samovitaja reč'*, a neologism coined by Xlebnikov, has been variously translated as "self-centred", "self-moving", "self-sufficient" or "autotelic" speech. We render it by an analogous English neologism, "selfsome". – Translator's note]
[3] Cf. my analysis of Xlebnikov's poem "The Grasshopper" in "Subliminal Verbal Patterning in Poetry", *Selected Writings*, vol. 3 (Paris and The Hague, 1981) pp. 137ff.

(liquid–dental–velar). The make-up and sequence of the last word of the initial group (velar–labial–liquid) correspond to that of the same classes before the final vowel in all three initial words. The make-up and sequence of the consonants of the second word in the group (dental–velar–labial) correspond to that of the identical consonantal classes in the middle of all three initial words.

In short, between the position of all three consonants in the word and the position of the word in the structure of the initial three-word group the strictest symmetry reigns. The initial and final consonant of the first word (liquid–velar) form a mirror symmetry with the initial and final consonant of the third word (velar–liquid). The velar occupies in the three initial words a position of mirror symmetry (3–2–1) in relation to the order of the words (1–2–3). In the limits of the word the velar may be preceded only by a dental and followed only by a labial. Thus the distribution of consonants in the three words of the initial group follows an unwavering scheme:

liquid–dental–velar
dental–velar–labial
velar–labial–liquid

The vocalism of unstressed vowels in all the words consistently amounts to the phoneme /a/: such, for example, are both unstressed vowels in the word *Kobýla!* In the three words of the terminal group the phoneme /a/ appears not only in the unstressed, but also in the stressed syllables, whereas, as we noted above, in the rest of the words the unstressed /a/ is opposed to a stressed /é/ or /í/. The terminal three-word series differs in general in its tendency toward homogeneity, or, more precisely, in its repetition of words (*Káša! Káša!*), in its direct repetition of syllables (*Bába!*), and in the identity of the stressed and unstressed vowels throughout the sequence (/á–a–á–a–á–a/). The compactness of the stressed vowels in the whole terminal three-word unit and the compactness of both consonants (the velar and palatoalveolar) in the last, doubly-repeated word create an apex of consonantal and vocalic compactness: *Bába! Káša! Káša!*

"I can't stand it any longer" (*moči moej net*) runs Turgenev's commentary to his incantatory improvisation as rendered by Sollogub: "I'm suffocating here, suffocating. . . . I have to calm myself down with a few Russian words!" Thus the unexacting peasant woman with her kasha turns out to be victoriously opposed to the three majestic butlers and the pair of gentlemen of "an ever more lifeless appearance" eating in the hall. The feminine gender and sex in Turgenev's attack are contrasted to the masculine, stuck-up ambience of the club.

Turgenev's reply to the "religious rites" (*svjaščennodejstvija* – "no other word", he says, "could possibly be used for it") performed by the trinity of butlers, who seemed "more like members of the House of Lords than servants", was simple. He answered with a string of names for country vegetables that developed into a craving for the peasant woman managing the estate and for kasha, the highest attainment of Russian folk cuisine. "The most imposing of the butlers", as if to emphasize the consummate ceremoniousness with which he was observing the ritual of the relentless diet poor Žemčužnikov's doctor had prescribed, served one identical dish after another in succession, majestically announcing: "First Cutlet! Second Cutlet! Third Cutlet!" As Ivan Sergeevič puts it, "there are no words in any human language" to express the irritation he experienced. Watching the ritualistic appearance of the invariable viands served on a silver plate covered by a silver bell-glass, he experienced something, as it were, beyond words: the five velar consonants of his feverish tirade – concluding in the hypnotic catchword "Kasha! Kasha!" – alliteratively echo the overwhelmingly crushing, thrice-repeated announcement: "Cutlet!"

It is quite likely that later embellishments by Turgenev crept into the narrative, as Sollogub hints, noting Ivan Sergeevič's "impeccable upbringing". One might well ask whether he actually spoke or merely thought up his seven-word table formula. It is possible, finally, that the memoirist himself is guilty of certain "exaggerations". Nevertheless, it is incredibly difficult to believe that this masterful experiment in creatively soldering together "disjointed Russian words" was not created by the courageous and mighty artist of the "free Russian tongue".

Frustration of anticipated *consummatum*, a characteristic motif of Turgenev's life and work – "Oh, why did I not answer her", and so on – makes itself felt in the writer's late peripheral activities: not only in the escapade at the London club, but also in the grotesque little "fairytales" (*des choses bien invraisemblables*) which, on the threshold of the seventies and eighties, Claudie (1852–1914), the daughter of Pauline Viardot, received in the form of letters from Turgenev, "ton vieux qui t'adore" or "ton éperdument ahuri Iv. Tour".[4] In connection with the supraconscious symbolism of these tales, their Parisian editor quite correctly predicts their future inclusion in "anthologies of Surrealism".

The substitution, common to both Turgenev's tales and fables, of unrestrained scatology in place of elevated eroticism must have affected the young recipient of his epistolary *épanchements* with a force matching the fright of his London table companion (Turgenev relates: "He thought that I'd lost my mind."). Such, for example, is the narrative letter of 3 September 1882, in which "a pale youth *au teint maladif*" utters an entreaty to his beloved German virgin. He contemplates suicide, hoping only that his beloved will allow him to share not her inaccessible bed but her private lavatory or, at the very least, her latrine "in the bosom of nature". This viscous motif is developed into a florid dialogue. One is tempted to compare it to the Indian taboo against a woman performing her natural needs in a place where a man has urinated.

In Turgenev's extravagant behaviour at the London club as well as in the delirious phantasmagoria of his French epistles, the extreme shift toward the primitive is decked out in whimsical verbal figures that endow the text with a

---

[4] I. Turgenev, *Nouvelle correspondance inedité*, vol. 1, ed. A. Zbiguilsky (Paris: 1971) XLIII–LII, pp. 278–80, 310–12.

mad, unexpected, incontestable persuasiveness akin to the supraconscious "wisdom in a snare" (*mudrost' v silke*) that inspired Turgenev, half a century before Xlebnikov, in his "tale of the nightingales". In it, Turgenev renders the "summit" (*desjatoe koleno*) of the nightingale's art: "With a good throaty nightingale here's how it goes. First there's a 'tee-eé-wheet!', then there's a 'took!' They call that the 'knock'. Then again: 'tee-eé-wheet ... took! took!' A double 'knock', with a half stroke on the second – it's too much! Then, the third time around: 'tee-eé-wheet!' Damn, it scatters so fast in a tap or a peal, the son of a bitch, you can hardly stand on your feet, it burns so!"[5]

[5] I. Turgenev, *Sočinenija*, vol. 14 (Moscow and Leningrad, 1967) p. 174; V. Xlebnikov, "Mudrost' v silke", *Pervyj Zurnal russkix futuristov* (1914).

ROBERT SCHOLES

# Is There a Fish in this Text?

1 Let the pupil write the description of a tree.

2 Of a tree without mentioning the name of the tree (larch, pine, etc.) so that the reader will not mistake it for the description of some other kind of tree.

(Ezra Pound, *ABC of Reading*, Norfolk, Conn., p. 66)

If I am a woodcutter and I am led to name the tree I am felling, whatever the form of my sentence, I "speak the tree," I do not speak about it. This means that my language is operational, transitively linked to its object. . . . But if I am not a woodcutter, I can no longer "speak the tree," I can only speak *about* it, *on* it. . . . I no longer have anything but an intransitive relationship with the tree; this tree is no longer the meaning of reality as a human action, it is an *image-at-one's-disposal*.

(Roland Barthes, *Mythologies*, New York, 1972, pp. 145–6)

To write the tree, or to write *about* it – that is the question posed by these two texts from Pound and Barthes. For Pound, we have only to avoid the name, and the real tree in all its treeness may be captured in words by the alert pupil. For Barthes, only a person who is productively linked to the tree can speak of it authentically. The very same words, whether they name the tree or describe it, will embody either a transitive or intransitive relationship between the writer and the object of writing.

There are some problems in both of these formulations. Barthes' notion that a productive relationship with the tree guarantees the transitivity of the woodcutter's discourse partakes of Marxist and existentialist formulas that mythologize the world in ways not unlike the myths of capitalism. Still, as a critique of Pound's apparently neutral and natural position, Barthes' view can be helpful. Pound *does* want an *image-at-one's-disposal*. He is an imagist, after all, and what imagism offers is a kind of licensed fetishism, a world neatly packaged for possession and consumption. This packaging is accomplished by the gaze, by looking at the object until it has been really seen. This principle emerges very clearly in Pound's exemplum of Agassiz and the fish:

> No man is equipped for modern thinking until he has understood the anecdote of Agassiz and the fish:
> A post-graduate student equipped with honours and diplomas went to Agassiz to receive the final and finishing touches. The great man offered him a small fish and told him to describe it.
> Post-graduate student: 'That's only a sunfish.'
> Agassiz: 'I know that. Write a description of it.'
> After a few minutes the student returned with the description of the Icthus Heliodiplodokus, or whatever term is used to conceal the common sunfish from vulgar knowledge, family of Heliichthinkerus, etc., as found in textbooks of the subject.
> Agassiz again told the student to describe the fish.
> The student produced a four-page essay. Agassiz then told him to look at the fish. At the end of three weeks the fish was in an advanced state of decomposition, but the student knew something about it.[1]

In the anecdote, it is strongly suggested that we learn by looking at things. Above all, the student is held to have learned about the fish by repeatedly gazing at it. The student looks and writes, looks and writes, until he sees the fish well and truly – as Pound's disciple Hemingway might have said – and can describe it as it really is. But, using Barthes' perspective, we may ask if he knows the fish as a fisherman might know the fish. He knows something *about* a dead and decomposing creature – but he does not know the fish and cannot speak it. He *can*, however, now speak and write Agassizese, for this is what he has really learned: to produce the sort of writing his teacher wants.

It is a parable of all schoolrooms, is it not, and perhaps a parody of them as well. The student seems to be learning about the subject, but what he is truly learning is to give the teacher what he wants. He seems to be reporting about a real and solid world in a perfectly transparent language, but actually he is learning how to produce a specific kind of discourse, controlled by a particular scientific paradigm, which requires him to be constituted as the subject of that discourse in a particular way and to speak through that discourse of a world made visible by the same controlling paradigm. The teacher's power over the

---

[1] Ezra Pound, *ABC of Reading* (Norfolk, Conn., 1934) pp. 17–18.

student is plain in Pound's example, and the student's ritual suffering as he endures the smell of the decomposing fish and the embarrassment of the teacher's rebuffs is part of an initiation process he must undergo to enter a scientific community. As Michel Foucault puts it: "First question: who is speaking?":

> Who, among the totality of speaking individuals, is accorded the right to use this sort of language? Who is qualified to do so? Who derives from it his own special quality, his prestige, and from whom, in return, does he receive if not the assurance, at least the presumption that what he says is true? What is the status of the individuals who – alone – have the right, sanctioned by law or tradition, juridically defined or spontaneously accepted, to proffer such a discourse?[2]

To have the right to speak as a biologist or naturalist, Agassiz's student must be indoctrinated in a set of discursive procedures. To "speak the fish" as a biologist or a fisherman or a poet is to speak in a particular discourse. But we English teachers have been slow to acknowledge this.

The entire edifice of American instruction in written composition rests on a set of assumptions much like Ezra Pound's. We have all been brought up as imagists. We assume that a complete self confronts a solid world, perceiving it directly and accurately, always capable of capturing it perfectly in a transparent language: bring 'em back alive; just give us the facts, ma'am; the way it was; tell it like it is; and that's the way it is. Perhaps some of our difficulty in teaching composition results from our operating uncritically on this set of assumptions – all of which have been questioned so thoroughly, now, that the whole naïve epistemology upon which they rest is lying in ruins around us. In response to this situation, we can assume that our practice has nothing to do with theory, or we can make the opposite assumption, and try to use the new developments in structuralist and post-structuralist theory as the basis for a new practice in the teaching of composition. Many will choose the former of these two assumptions, and perhaps they will be right to do so, for it will not be easy to found an American practice upon these largely European theories. Nevertheless, that is what I would urge upon my fellow-teachers of reading and writing.

To make the case for such a project, and in so doing to take a few steps in the direction of a more fully developed semiotics of composition, will be my object in the remainder of this discussion. My method will be to apply a semiotic procedure of analysis to Pound's parable of instruction, returning, like the student of Agassiz, to this specimen again and again until it stinks in all our nostrils. Like the student in the parable, we shall have to learn to "see" our object. Pound's anecdote comes to us in the form of a text. To see it with some degree of thoroughness, then, we must see it "transtextually" (in Gérard Genette's terminology), as a text related to other texts. First, we shall work

[2] Michel Foucault, *Archeology of Knowledge* (New York, 1972) p. 50.

backwards from Pound towards the texts that he had adapted in creating his own, and then outward to some other texts by and around Agassiz, concluding with some texts related mainly by their own concern to speak, in some way, the fish.

The anecdote of Agassiz, the student and the fish might have come to Pound in any number of ways, written and oral, but there are two versions available to us in print, which were also available to Pound before he wrote the *ABC of Reading* in 1934. They are Nathaniel Southgate Shaler's recollection of his initiation into Agassiz's world in 1859, as recorded in *The Autobiography of Nathaniel Southgate Shaler* (Boston, Mass, 1907); and Samuel H. Scudder's recollection of his very similar experience at about the same time, but first published in the magazine *Every Saturday* on 4 April 1874. Both of these versions of two very similar experiences were extracted from their original texts by an English Professor at Cornell University, Lane Cooper, and published in 1917 in a little volume called *Louis Agassiz as a Teacher: Illustrative Extracts on His Method of Instruction*. There is a strong presumption that Pound, in fact, knew Cooper's little volume and drew his anecdote from it. I say that the presumption is strong, because it is Cooper who draws the parallel between biology and the study of poetry, between the natural scientist and the English teacher. As he puts it in his preface, the reason why an English teacher should be moved to issue a book on Agassiz is that "I have been taught, and I try to teach others, after a method in essence identical with that employed by the great naturalist" (p. v).

In his "Introductory Note" Cooper develops this theme further:

> Within recent years we have witnessed an extraordinary development in certain studies, which, though superficially different from those pursued by Agassiz, have an underlying bond of unity with them, but which are generally carried on without reference to principles governing the investigation of every organism and all organic life. I have in mind, particularly, the spread of literary and linguistic study in America during the last few decades, and the lack of a common standard of judgment among those who engage in such study. Most persons do not, in fact, discern the close, though not obvious, relation between investigation in biology or zoology and the observation and comparison of those organic forms which we call forms of literature and works of art. Yet the notion that a poem or a speech should possess the organic structure, as it were, of a living creature is basic in the thought of the great literary critics of all time. . . . We study a poem, the work of man's art, in the same way that Agassiz made Shaler study a fish, the work of God's art; the object in either case, is to discover the relation between form or structure and function or essential effect.[3]

---

[3] Lane Cooper, *Louis Agassiz as a Teacher: Illustrative Extracts on His Method of Instruction* (Ithaca, NY, 1917) pp. 2–4.

Forty years later, when Northrop Frye suggested that the study of literature be made more like the study of biology, this came as a great shock, even at Cornell University, where I happened to be studying at the time, and where Lane Cooper's memory was still green. The shock, I submit, was not so much in the suggestion that literary study learn from science, as in the different notion of biology put forward by Frye:

> As long as biology thought of animal and vegetable forms of life as constituting its subject, the different branches of biology were largely efforts of cataloguing. As soon as it was the existence of forms of life themselves that had to be explained, the theory of evolution and the concepts of protoplasm and the cell poured into biology and completely revitalized it.
>
> It occurs to me that literary criticism is now in such a state of naive induction as we find in a primitive science.[4]

Frye drew a careful parallel between biology and literary study, arguing that biology became a fully fledged science when it went beyond close observation of the individual object to study the systems by which individual objects were, in fact, ordered and perceived. Frye was attempting in his own way (as Geoffrey Hartman noticed long ago) to move toward a structuralism in literary study. It was this that made his work so startling and refreshing at the time, and it was this that prepared those Anglo-American critics influenced by Frye to receive structuralism hospitably when it began to be exported from the continent of Europe.

The shift in literary studies indicated through the different uses of the biological analogy by Lane Cooper in 1917 and Northrop Frye in 1957 is only part of the history we are considering. The scientific metaphor itself conceals something in the agendas of both Cooper and Frye that must also be considered, and in the case of Cooper this is especially important. Stripped of its scientific cloak, what precisely was the method of literary study that Cooper was advocating back in 1917?

Cooper offered a method that was essentially hermeneutic: "We study a poem, the work of man's art, in the same way that Agassiz made Shaler study a fish, the work of God's art." The appearance of God in this equation is no accident but part of its design. Substitute a tree for the fish and Joyce Kilmer's infamous poem can be generated by a simple, almost mathematical operation: "Poems are made by fools like me,/But only God can make a tree." And who makes the fools, one wishes to ask? This excessive anthropomorphizing of the creative principle in the universe is a major problem in Western theology, but it is a kind of red herring in the present discourse and we must abandon it. For our purposes, what is important in Cooper's formulation is its focus on the single object, fish or text, the meaning of which is guaranteed not by its place in

---

[4] Northrop Frye, *Anatomy of Criticism* (Princeton, NJ, 1957) p. 15.

an order or system, but by the creator whose creature it is and whose presence in the object is signified by the object's structure. Before fish or poem, we are in the presence of presence, of metaphysical presence, that is, which guarantees the object's meaning. As Cooper himself observes, "Agassiz, considered in his philosophical relations, was a Platonist, since he clearly believed that the forms of nature expressed the essential ideas of a divine intelligence".[5]

There is more to Pound's fish than meets the eye. He has suppressed the Platonism of his model, of course, but his procedure should make us wonder how much latent Platonism there may be in all attempts to see the object as in itself it really is, whether the object be a tree, a fish or a text. For here is the point at which the older criticism and pedagogy is confronted most directly by semiotic theory and practice. Is the object's meaning guaranteed by reference to its creator's intention in making it, or is its meaning a function of its position in a system of objects linked to it by paradigmatic and syntagmatic processes? Taking Pound's anecdote of the fish as our object, I wish to argue that we can interpret it best only by taking our eyes off it, denying it status as a thing in itself, and reading it as intertextually as we can within the limits of the present discourse.

We can begin by looking at the actual pre-texts that lie behind Pound's text. In considering them, we shall see what Pound retained, what he suppressed, what he added, and what he transformed for his own purposes. Before receiving his fish, Nathaniel Shaler was given a preliminary oral examination, which revealed that he knew some Latin and Greek, some French and a good deal of German. It was also determined that he had read Agassiz's *Essay on Classification*, and "had noted in it the influence of Schelling's views".[6] The exam ended with a fencing match (quite a literal one, with masks, foils and swords in play). Only after all this came the famous fish:

> When I sat me down before my tin pan, Agassiz brought me a small fish, placing it before me with the rather stern requirement that I should study it, but should on no account talk to anyone concerning it, nor read anything related to fishes, until I had his permission so to do.[7]

For a week Agassiz refused to hear a report on the fish. As Shaler tells us, "At first this neglect was distressing; but I saw that it was a game, for he was, as I discerned rather than saw, covertly watching me".[8] Shaler looks, Agassiz watches him looking, and Shaler discerns rather than sees Agassiz watching him looking. Gazes run rampant here. At the end of the week Shaler made a one-hour oral report, to which he received the response, "That is not right". Recognizing that "he was playing a game with me to see if I were capable of doing hard, continuous work without the support of a teacher", Shaler went to

[5] Cooper, *Agassiz as a Teacher*, p. 3.
[6] Ibid., p. 19.
[7] Ibid., p. 22.
[8] Ibid.

work for another week and at last satisfied Agassiz. "The incident of the fish", he writes, "made an end of my novitiate".[9]

At this point I wish to draw a few of the conclusions that the juxtaposition of Shaler's and Pound's versions of the fish incident makes available to us. First, it was obvious to Shaler that he was involved in a power game, a ritual, a novitiate. Secondly, the rules of the game – no reading up on the subject, strict concentration on the single object – are remarkably like the techniques developed by I. A. Richards and the New Critics for the teaching of poetry. Thirdly, the candidate, having read his teacher's essay on classification before being given his object for analysis, is remarkably *un*like the untutored undergraduate confronting a poem or the freshman composition student told to describe a tree. Fourthly, in this version of the fish story, the fish itself is not named, nor is there any *writing* about the fish beyond the taking of notes. The reports to Agassiz are made orally, not in the form of written compositions as they are in Pound's anecdote. Now let us look at Scudder's report on his very similar experience.

Scudder, who wanted to study nice clean insects, was nevertheless given a fish, a *haemulon*, to study. Scudder makes much of the fish's disagreeable smell, its "ghastly" and "hideous" appearance, and the limitations under which he worked: "I might not use a magnifying-glass; instruments of all kinds were interdicted".[10] At last, he got the idea of drawing the fish, and began to see features in it he had not noticed before. For this he was rewarded by Agassiz, who told him, "That is right, a pencil is one of the best of eyes".[11] But, when questioned, he did not satisfy the master. He was told he had not seen "one of the most conspicuous features of the animal, which is as plainly before your eyes as the fish itself; look again, look again!" and, as Scudder tells us, he was then left to his "misery". When he had not found the missing "conspicuous feature" by the end of the afternoon of his second day with the fish he was told to go home and report in the morning for an examination *without looking at the fish*. He says that he walked home, spent a wakeful night, and returned in the morning to face "a man who seemed to be quite as anxious as I that I should see for myself what he saw. 'Do you perhaps mean,' I asked, 'that the fish has symmetrical sides with paired organs?'" To which the "thoroughly pleased Professor Agassiz" replied, "of course! of course!".[12]

From this version, too, some conclusions may be drawn. This has less the air of an initiation than Shaler's experience, and more that of a puzzle or riddle: guess what the professor has in mind! Here, too, the examination is oral, not written. It is Pound who has brought writing into his exemplary fable. Seeing is emphasized here, too, but the final problem is not exactly a problem in vision. Scudder is, in fact, told to solve the problem without looking at the fish. And solve it he does. But bilateral symmetry is a feature of a classification system

[9] Ibid., p. 25.
[10] Ibid., p. 43.
[11] Ibid.
[12] Ibid., p. 45.

rather than a simple fact of nature. It cannot be "seen" apart from the concept that gives it status, and it certainly cannot be drawn easily in the case of fish, since its flat shape leads us normally to draw either one side of a fish or the other. Scudder's anecdote would seem, then, to illustrate superbly the principle that vision is always mediated, that the concept enables the perception. "Seeing" itself is not a simple function but a complex one, and scientific seeing is always dependent upon instruments. If not the microscope, then the pencil; if not the pencil, then the conceptual system, which is itself, of course, an instrument, an apparatus that enables a certain sort of vision. Shaler had read Agassiz's *Essay on Classification* before he was given *his* fish. It is, by the way, an essay on the classification of fish, not simply on classification in general. And what of Scudder? What did he do during his sleepless night? Did he just lie there thinking of fish? Or did he talk to anyone about them? Might he have consulted Agassiz's own essay on the classification of fishes? Whence came his miraculous vision of a fish with "symmetrical sides and paired organs"? What organs did he "see" and how did he see them? He does not tell us. Pound, of course, tells us more. Let us return to him like a good student to his ghastly fish and examine him yet another time, for as he says himself, "The proper METHOD for studying poetry and good letters is the method of contemporary biologists, that is careful first-hand examination of the matter, and continual COMPARISON of one 'slide' or specimen with another."[13]

Pound presents the anecdote to us *as* an anecdote, which allows him a raconteur's licence to improve his material, and improve it he does, for he is a superb raconteur and a well-schooled rhetorician. First, he gives us an arresting generalization: "No man . . .". Then he introduces an alazon in the form of a *discipulus gloriosus* with "honours and diplomas" seeking "final and finishing touches". Agassiz, a "great" man, is our *eiron*, offering a small fish to the proud student, who remarks in his pridefulness, "That's *only* a sunfish." Only! He will rue that only, will he not? The student returns in a matter of minutes with a textbook description of a fish with a Latin name. Here Pound, who often had no quarrel with either learning or Latin, makes fun of the name as obfuscatory. He associates the student, not the teacher, with this name by an intricate metonymy that includes a partial homonymity between the student's *diplo*mas and the name Helio*diplo*dokus. We may speculate that Pound vaguely remembered Scudder's *haemulon* in inventing the Heliodiplodokus, but he is merely having fun. One could have had fun with Scudder's original fish, too, for the *haemulon* is better known as the "grunt", because of the noise it makes when taken out of the water. But how could a student of Agassiz ever learn about the reason for the common name by simply examining a dead fish? It does not grunt when removed from the alcohol bottle. We are back to the question of what it means to know the fish, but Pound is our fish for the moment and we must continue to play him.

Pound's student next produces a four-page essay, perhaps because of

---

[13] Pound, *ABC*, p. 17.

Pound's interest in writing, perhaps simply as a way of making his efforts concrete. Pound's fish decomposes badly, while Shaler's and Scudder's do not, because they keep them wet and replace them in their alcohol bottles every night like good little students, but it certainly makes a fine story this way, a far better story than those of Scudder and Shaler themselves. Pound's student suffers these indignities for three weeks, Shaler for two, and Scudder for only three days. Pound's exaggeration improves the tale, of course, and is of the essence of the anecdotal mode. One suspects, however, that Shaler has "improved" his material in this respect, too; that for him Scudder is a pre-text. The story grows in each retelling, like many fish stories. But what should we, looking at Pound, looking at Agassiz, looking at Shaler, looking at Scudder, looking at their fish, learn from all this?

We may ask ourselves what is the reality, the truth behind the incident, but we will find no ready answer. Pound's distortions are clear enough, but what is he distorting? Shaler, boxer and fencer, gives us an initiation ritual. Scudder, the fastidious entomologist, gives us a puzzle. Both students pass their tests and go on to become professors themselves. What we see is a stage in their learning a discourse (as Foucault puts it, or, in Thomas S. Kuhn's terminology, acquiring a paradigm). Pound, the imagist, gives us a recipe for imagism: look at the object and write about the way it looks without naming it and you will capture its truth. Each one sees what his own discourse lets him see. And what do we see? Why, the truth, of course.

"What is Truth; said jesting Pilate; And would not stay for an Answer" – so grumbles the father of British empiricism, Francis Bacon, in the opening sentence of his Essayes, but those who stay with Bacon himself to learn what truth is may not be satisfied. Observing in passing that poets lie for pleasure's sake, Bacon goes on to tell us that "This same Truth, is a Naked, and Open day light, that doth not shew, the Masques and Mummeries, and Triumphs of the world, halfe so stately, and daintily, as Candle-lights." In short, he offers us metaphors, or poetry, for both lies and truth, as indeed must all who speak of either.

To tell the truth, to capture reality in writing, is a noble aim, and to teach such skill is to make instruction in composition a high calling indeed. But such work is not easy. I propose to consider some of the difficulties by taking an example or two from Agassiz, since he has been put before us by Pound and Cooper as an exemplar of both instruction and accurate perception. Confronted with a new phenomenon in his own experience, how did he perceive it, in what terms did he write about such a thing himself?

In 1846, Agassiz visited Philadelphia, where we are told he encountered black Americans for the first time. His biographer, Edward Lurie, has given us a brief extract from a letter Agassiz wrote to his mother upon that occasion:

> I hardly dare to tell you the painful impression I received, so much are the feelings they gave me contrary to all our ideas of the brotherhood of man and unique origin of our species. But truth before all. The more pity I felt

at the sight of this degraded and degenerate race the more . . . impossible it becomes for me to repress the feeling that they are not of the same blood we are.[14]

In public essays, he repeated the same themes, arguing that blacks were by nature submissive, obsequious and imitative, and that "white relations with colored people would be conducted more intelligently if the fundamental differences between human types were realized and understood".[15]

"Many an eye / He trained to Truth's exact severity", said the poet Lowell in his encomiastic verses upon the great man. And "Truth before all", said Agassiz to his mother, but what is truth? What did Agassiz *see* when he looked at black Americans? What he saw was surely not an unmediated vision. It was, in fact, what many other "cultivated" individuals of his time saw, but he was not an ordinary individual. He was a scientist, a zoologist, and his views carried weight. He developed a theory of humanity, asserting that there were eight distinct types – Caucasian, Arctic, Mongol, American Indian, Negro, Hottentot, Malayan and Australian – insisting that these types were distinct in origin, with "their differences", as Lurie puts it, "stamped on them from the beginning". In the decade leading up to the Civil War, these views were of more than passing interest. His biographer, in fact, comes to the following melancholy conclusion: "within ten years Agassiz had provided racial supremacists with primary arguments. . . . That Agassiz permitted his reputation to support doctrines of social and racial inequality was indeed tragic."[16]

Truth before all, said Agassiz, but what is truth? For Agassiz, truth had, as Lane Cooper pointed out, a very Platonic cast. This emerges clearly in his response to Darwin's work, where his refusal to accept the theory of evolution gradually undermined his standing as a scientist. He became a forerunner of our contemporary "creation scientists", in fact, and did everything he could to reconcile scientific findings with received religious truths. In the *Essay on Classification* itself, he had argued that reality was regularly found to agree with *a priori* conceptions of it, which, he maintained, demonstrated that the human and the Divine intellects were linked by "an identity of operations".[17] This view led him to assert that all species were absolute, fixed from their creation, and hence to reject all fossil evidence for evolution. There were no variants from species, he claimed, asserting at a meeting of the Boston Society for Natural History that, "in 6,000 fishes, he had not seen a variety".[18]

We are back to looking at fish again, but on a grander scale, and we must ask a question: why could Agassiz not *see* the evidence in fish and fossils that many other scientists of his time saw in them. The answer, as Thomas Kuhn elaborates it for us in so many passages of *The Structure of Scientific Revolutions*,

[14] Edward Lurie, *Louis Agassiz: A Life in Science* (Chicago, Ill., 1960) p. 257.
[15] Ibid., pp. 260, 262.
[16] Ibid., p. 265.
[17] Ibid., p. 283.
[18] Ibid., p. 297.

is because vision depends upon expectations to a considerable degree. Because Agassiz refused to accept the paradigm shift in his discipline, he could not "see" the evidence that might have persuaded him to accept the shift. We "see" and "are" in discourse.

The lesson to be drawn from this example of Agassiz and the fish is that what the student needs from the teacher is help in seeing discourse structures themselves in all their fullness and their power. The way to see the fish and to write the fish is first to see how one's discourse writes the fish. And the way to see one discourse is to see more than one. To write the fish in many modes is finally to see that one will never catch *the* fish in any one discourse. As teachers of writing we have a special responsibility to help our students gain awareness of discourse structures and the ways in which they both enable and constrain our vision. And the only way to do this is to read and write in a range of discursive modes.

Having made this point, I wish to add a necessary qualification. The existence of specific discursive codes seems to me beyond argument, and their constraining effect on the actual practice of writing a necessary corollary of their existence – but it would be unwarranted to assume from this that such constraints are absolute and fixed. Codes change. Discursive practice modifies discursive systems, which are never completely closed. In short, there is always room for creativity in any discursive order, but it is attained by mastering the practice of the discourse to a degree that enables new utterances to be formed, which in turn become a part of the body of discursive models and finally effect changes in the code itself.

I should like to conclude by offering an example of creativity at work in what has been widely recognized as one of the most rigid discursive systems ever to operate in English literature: Augustan poetry, with its heroic couplets and poetic diction, so severely criticized by Wordsworth and others as unnatural, artificial and totally incapable of seeing or writing "the fish", offering us instead such locutions as "finny tribe" and "scaly breed". The indictment is certainly correct, up to a point, but in acknowledging it we should also recognize that there is nothing especially fishy about such scientific statements as Scudder's "symmetrical sides with paired organs". Every discourse is a net that captures some aspects of its objects at the necessary cost of allowing others to slip through. Even "finny tribe" captures something of the reality of fish. But let us look at the actual practice of an Augustan poet. Here is a teenage versifier of some talent working in the pastoral mode. He has, in fact, just committed a "scaly breed" two lines before, but he goes on:

> Our plenteous streams a various race supply
> The bright-eyed perch with fins of Tyrian dye,
> The silver eel in shining volumes rolled,
> The yellow carp in scales bedropped with gold,
> Swift trouts, diversified with crimson stains,
> And pikes, the tyrants of the watery plains.
> (Pope, "Windsor Forest", ll. 141–6)

This is a decorative art, meant to recall the known rather than reveal the unknown, and not simply to recall it but to clothe it in elegant connotations of art, riches, power and learning. But, for all that, one would not wish to say that the young Alexander Pope had failed, here, to capture something of the colour, movement, and even the behaviour of his quarry. His pike, for instance, are well cast as tyrants of the underwater world. He is using an obvious formula – adjective, fish name, prepositional descriptive phrase – and he is taking his colours from a rich and royal palette: gold, silver, crimson, Tyrian (purple) and yellow. But there are some creative strokes, none the less, and his "silver eel in shining volumes rolled" manages, as he might have said himself, "to snatch a grace beyond the reach of art".

In short, even as a youthful apprentice, wandering in fancy's maze, he had begun to achieve a mastery of his discourse that enabled him to rewrite its possibilities. He became, of course, a master of English literary history as well as of his own form of discourse. He edited Shakespeare; he knew well the work of Chaucer, Spenser and Milton; and he had a superb critical eye for the best in his own era. As even Ezra Pound says of Pope, "He is constantly fishing out the better writers. Sic Dunciad II, 124: Congreve, Addison, and Prior. 127: Gay, sieved out from seven authors now completely forgotten."[19] Pope not only mastered his own poetic discourse; he also cast a wide net and drew upon many other texts to enrich his own.

Among the forty or fifty lines from Pope's work that Pound selects to illustrate his strengths as a poet in the *ABC of Reading* is one couplet that will serve to conclude this attempt to illustrate how what we call "creativity" works to transcend the limits of discursive practice. These lines are taken from Book I of *The Dunciad*. They are part of a speech in which the goddess of Dullness is described as showing to her chosen disciples the proper ways to achieve dullness themselves. One thing she shows them is

> How Index-learning turns no student pale,
> Yet holds the eel of science by the tail:

George Sherburn, whose edition of Pope I used as an undergraduate, found "the eel of science" a "sparklingly trenchant" bit of "verbal marksmanship". I, too, think well of the image, though it seems to me more a matter of constructing something that was not there before than of hitting a pre-existing target. Surely, the eel of science is not a matter of seeing at all. What Pope wanted was an image that would convey something that ought to be a difficult task – the acquisition of learning – the sort of task that might well turn a student pale. He personified the abstraction, index-learning, as a kind of cheap substitute for real learning, an easy way to fake an actual acquaintance with texts. Holding an eel by the tail came to him as the image of difficulty – but from where did this image swim up into his consciousness? I think it came from the River Thames of "Windsor Forest", his youthful exercise in pastoral verse.

[19] Pound, *ABC*, p. 170.

The image in "Windsor Forest" of "the silver eel in shining volumes rolled" contains in that word "volumes" the connecting link between the two poems. The word "volume" comes from a Latin work meaning "coil", "roll" and hence, "scroll". When parchment scrolls gave way to bound books the word volume was extended to rectangular books as well as rolled scrolls. Pope's "shining volumes rolled" is a clever archaism, restoring to the word "volume" its sense of "scroll". In "Windsor Forest" some learning attaches to the eel, even as political power attaches to the pike. In *The Dunciad*, the learning which is rejected by those index-learners who do not read their volumes is signified by the absence of the volumes in this new image of the eel of science. The eel of science is an eel and not some other kind of fish because only the eel comes in the form of a volume. The eel, of course, is also slippery and hard to hold, but index-learning, tutored by Dullness, can reduce both the lustre and the slipperiness of those shining volumes, and hold the eel of science by the tail.

I am suggesting that what we are normally content to accept as hidden within the black box called creativity can here be glimpsed as an intertextual process, the suppression of which generates the power of the final image. The startling or surprising aspects of the image of the eel of science in *The Dunciad* – which is to say the unexpectedness that gives it a high level of information and hence much of its poetical quality – is achieved by Pope's erasure of some parts of his train of thought, crudely measurable here by the disappearance or non-appearance of the word "volumes". This train of thought itself is an aspect of Pope's mastery of his discipline, his knowledge of languages, his recollection of pre-texts, in this case one of his own, and his habit of searching for images to give substance to a developing flow of thought.

> Some beauties yet no Precepts can declare,
> For there's a happiness as well as care.
> Music resembles Poetry, in each
> Are nameless graces which no methods teach,
> And which a master-hand alone can reach.
>       (Pope, "An Essay on Criticism", ll. 141–5)

GEOFFREY H. HARTMAN

# The Unremarkable Wordsworth

> wreaths of smoke
> Sent up, in silence, from among the
> trees!
> With some uncertain notice. . . .
> (Wordsworth, "Tintern Abbey")

## I

It is a general proposition in semiological analysis that signs are not signs unless they become perceptible, and that their perceptibility as signs depends on a contrast set up within the signifying system. Some parts of the system are "marked" and some "unmarked"; this contrast shapes perceptibility, and there is a conventional rather than inherent relation between linguistic features and their marked/unmarked status. Now this matter of perceptibility (or noticeability) affects the reader as well as the writer: in remarking what has been written the reader may see a different set of contrasts than the writer. Doubtless there are limits to this process of remarking; yet we all know that what is merely a primrose to one person may be a wonderful and complex world to another.

It is interesting that for a long time Wordsworth's poetry seemed so natural to readers that many considered it not poetry so much as a form of prose. Even when the distinction between prose and poetry had been modified to the point of breaking down, Cleanth Brooks, who used "paradox" and "irony" to define what was specifically poetic in all language, said that Wordsworth's paradoxes were peculiarly unemphatic compared to those of an earlier Poetry of Wit. Yet one could still uncover them by close analysis. Michael Riffaterre, similarly, points out in a recent essay that "smokeless", describing London in the sonnet "Composed Upon Westminster Bridge, September 3 1802",

> All bright and glittering in the smokeless air,
> (l. 8)

calls up, without stress, its opposite: it cancels yet preserves the commonplace image of the city as a dirty, crowded place. Through "smokeless" the "latent intertext surfaces into the text": the word is a "hostage from the sociolect" which "forces" readers to apprehend a stereotypical contrast between Edenic countryside and corrupt, rapidly industrializing city.

Like Brooks, Riffaterre is seeking to smoke out the technique of a subtle poet. One cannot deny that there are contrasts in this poem: it is a question of how and where they operate, and why we have trouble in spotting them or making them significant. (Wordsworth was thoroughly abused by Jeffrey and other critics of his time for imposing unremarkable sights or sentiments on his audience.) "Smokeless", like the contrast of "wear" and "bare", or "theatres" and "temples", in

> This City now doth, like a garment, wear
> The beauty of the morning; silent, bare
> Ships, towers, domes, theatres and temples lie
> Open unto the fields, and to the sky,
>
> (ll. 4–7)

or like the adjacency of majesty and intimacy, might and stillness, in

> Dear God! the very houses seem asleep
> And all that mighty heart is lying still!
>
> (ll. 13–14)

can be made perceptible by careful readers, whether or not they back what they do with a theory of literary, as distinguished from non-literary, language. This gain in perceptibility, however, does not resolve but focuses the quiet action or special negativity of Wordsworth's style.

## II

Rather than insisting on paradox or the cancelled presence of the opposite term, it would be better to acknowledge that contrast in Wordsworth points beyond the activity of pointing. "Smokeless" signals, as it were, the absence of a signal, and comes close to subtly thematizing Wordsworth's wish not to violate – by "poetic diction" or some other artifice – nature's own mode of expression. Nothing here is forced on our awareness: what halted the poet–spectator then, and what allows him to halt us now (via this sonnet-tribute) is precisely not characterized by the usual trappings of picturesqueness or sublimity. It was a moment – who could pass it by? – of the "poetry of earth" and does not need the heightening of rhetoric.

> Earth has not anything to show more fair:
> Dull would he be of soul who could pass by
> A sight so touching in its majesty. . .
>
> (ll. 1–3)

Yet the poet *is* passing by; and one of the contrasts, barely perceived, is between the curious specificity of the title with its temporal marker ("September 3, 1802"), and the poem's first culminating image of repose of will, also temporal in its association, however modified: "The river glideth at his own sweet will". Riffaterre might say that the structure here is the same as in "smokeless": a commonplace ("the river of time") is both cancelled and preserved. Yet Riffaterre passed this one by; and we are left, in any case, with an unstable rather than stable contrast, for we do not know how to interpret, even should we notice it, the relation of "passing by" to these temporal markers, whether stressed or unstressed.

To talk of reserve or indeterminacy would be to praise Wordsworth's style without understanding it. How can a poem put on so much pressure without the reader feeling pressured, without, for example, overconscious dictions, paraphrases, and cryptic veilings? Goethe said of Nature that its secrets were in the open. In Wordsworth, too, there is no masque that obliges us to question what Parsifal failed to question. We can let things pass by: even the theme of "passing by". A Wordsworth poem often has no point. As readers we respond to the mystery of his response. That the poem exists at all, that it emerges into "answerable style" has to be understood together with that style.

At a very basic level, then, the present sonnet is simply an extended lo! or behold!, though these markers remain subvisionary. Nature works rarely by signs and wonders, and what matters in any case is "soul" as Wordsworth calls it in line 2: the poet's, not only nature's, capacity for "timely utterance". This phrase, from the *Intimations Ode*, reinstates the Parsifal moment: there must be – as a moral obligation, even if self-assumed – a capacity for response in the poet. This responsibility is involved with voice, or poetry as the temporality of rhetoric, as the pulse-point in the "incumbent mystery of sense and soul". Telling the time (which may go wrong), is always a prophetic venture yet absolutely ordinary. The initiative, moreover, cannot be nature's alone; the poet anticipates what may be coming his way and has to reform (re-mark) an inarticulate or mute code. Whether or not there is a language of nature there is a language of the heart that goes out to nature; and this going out, or being called out, brings Wordsworth to the subject of nature-personification when he writes programmatically about poetics, as in the famous Preface to *Lyrical Ballads*.

The theme of time, then, does not settle into such conventional frames as transience, regret, seizing the moment. Instead, as at the beginning of *The Prelude* (Wordsworth's autobiographical epic), a "correspondent breeze" within him joins the "congenial" power of a "half-conscious" external breeze that brings a blessing or invitation from nature. So also the Westminster Bridge sonnet's many eulogistic terms (fair, touching, beauty, bright, beautifully, sweet) suggest a *temporal greeting* rather than something purely descriptive. It is as if nature herself were saying "Good morning" to the wayfarer.

The "telling", of course, is all on the poet's side; only the "show" is nature's. Yet Wordsworth is uneasy with the deictic (epideictic) mode: something more direct, approaching apostrophe or prayer, a naïve or commonplace and absolutely basic vocative swells up, like the supreme cliché "Dear God!" which climaxes the sonnet and is in the place of a point, had he written in the pointed style.

Comments like this take up from what Schleiermacher defined as the "grammatical" to the "divinatory" level of interpretation. This is where a certain risk comes in: where the interpreter has to anticipate the poem, in the direction it is going. We know from other celebrated episodes that splendid evenings or mornings are "trials of strength" for the poet. In the most famous dawn-scene of them all (*Prelude*, Book IV) he becomes, without knowing it, a "dedicated spirit": that is, devoted to poetry. "I made no vows, but vows / Were then made for me." What kind of vow or utterance can we associate with the simple, descriptive verses of the Westminster Bridge sonnet?

The poet, I suggest, is met on the way by a natural sign, a "good morning". Yet his passing by gives it the virtual status of a good-bye or farewell. We do not know the locus of that "Good-bye", whether it is from nature or from the responsive soul; we know only that promise and parting coincide as in the blessing: "God be with you." Some sort of timely utterance, *parole* or password, is offered from within the tacit, natural spectacle. ("Day unto day uttereth knowledge.") Yet there is no word except these verses. And whatever is heard (or seen rather than heard) culminates in a vision of repose:

> Never did sun more beautifully steep
> In his first splendour, valley, rock, or hill;
> Ne'er saw I, never felt, a calm so deep!
> (ll. 9–11)

### III

Wordsworth, looking at a city, sees "something like the purity of one of nature's own grand spectacles", as his sister wrote in her journal. That is clear. Yet how far back in time does the "first splendour" reach? Wordsworth suggests not only an extraordinary coincidence of urban and natural perspectives but the vision of a pristine urban landscape. At the very point that factories and urbanization are threatening the rural character of English towns, Wordsworth glimpses a radiant city established, as it were, from the beginning of time. By a quiet cliché ("in his first splendour") the poet travels back to the dawn of creation, now recaptured or renewed. It is this elision of time – this repetition in and despite time – which is part of the calm he feels.

The curious vigour of Wordsworth's clichés (or unremarkable phrases) remains to be explored. They function faintly like the classical "constant epithet" in that they are tautological as well as autological. Yet this constancy, in Wordsworth's case, is temporal rather than antitemporal. It remains closely linked to the immediate if repeated experience of the poet who recalls them.

There is something like Proust's involuntary memory, as an experience repeats itself, or gives the impression of repetition, even if in fact two or more incidents are conflated. The poet is faced by an illusion of time dissolving, of being able to travel back to the origin (to an *illo tempore* or "first splendour"), or travelling even now among "Powers and Presences". So it is possible to draw a wayside omen and silent blessing from the Westminster Bridge sonnet, or to re-mark the position of the poet–traveller as, prophetically, "telling time". A further temporal aspect is disclosed by the rhetorical movement of the sonnet's second part.

This "glides" from a glimpsed origin to a calm that suspends the flow of time and could intimate a final repose. There is nothing sinister in this convergence of origin and end. The effect is more like an unexpected bridging or a time-dissolve. In this and other poems, moreover, the traveller does not cross, like Coleridge's Mariner, the border of naturalistic perception into some other world. Yet "travelling" does reveal an indefinite figural extension. Though it remains secular it authorizes us to view even the self as a figure: acting within a larger drama or frame, acting out a fantasy-role that remains, however, completely in touch with the familiar world.

The withholding of fantasizing, even in the legitimate or formal mode of myth, is, of course, Wordsworth's distinction among the English Romantics. His yearning for those nourishing pagan myths is not in question; and he can write about it as in a famous passage of *The Excursion* and in his well-known sonnet conjuring up Proteus and Triton. But his strength, and perhaps limitation, lie in his refusal of romantic classicism's liberal attitude towards myth. Keats, who placed myth-making on the side of a generous and impersonal imagination, suspected that Wordsworth's great refusal was really in the service of the ego, and so denounced his style as the "egotistical sublime". The puzzling strength of it does indeed lie in this area: the poetry is occasional, the depicted experience usually quite ordinary, and the narrator, though quirky, no more than a passing observer or very sensitive tourist. Yet the fantasy within stirs like a coiled snake. The challenge is to define Wordsworth's interiority (or is it exteriority?) which has frustrated so many interpreters who have turned to vague concepts of the unconscious or subconscious.

The fantasy-content of the present sonnet is clear enough despite its character as a poetry of earth. The toll or touch of time – the mortal nature of earthly things[1] – is made unimaginable by a style of weightless clichés and

---

[1] I do not know whether it has been noticed, but something in the enumeration "Ships, towers, domes, theatres and temples" may call to mind Prospero's famous lines (*The Tempest*, IV.iv.) on the vanished rural masque. He foretells a similar vanishing to the more substantial "pageant" of earth: "And, like the baseless fabric of this vision, / The cloud-capt towers, the gorgeous palaces, / The solemn temples, the great globe itself, / Yea, all which it inherit, shall dissolve". It would be too tenuous an exercise to compare Shakespeare's "baseless" and Wordsworth's "smokeless"; but the fair show seen from Westminster Bridge is viewed by the poet as Earth's own "majestic vision" (*The Tempest*, IV.iii) that promises to stand more firmly than Prospero's enactment of his "present fancies".

timeless (unpointed) contrasts. The deep calm, therefore, "seen" by the poet, could frighten us: such a heart, alive yet lying still, what response is it capable of? Does the poet desire a peace close to death after all?

A later sonnet, in a rare moment of surmise, depicts earth or the nether sphere "Opening to view the abyss in which she feeds / Her own calm fires". A *calm fire* is the carefully framed visionary oxymoron to which the present sonnet also tends. But if its imagery is wishful beyond the restlessness of wishing, there is another fantasy that removes from the poet the weight of "timely utterance", together with the risk of untimely – unnatural – prophecy. I have suggested that the sonnet is a reflection on an utterance of nature's: an omen that cannot be called an omen, an oracle that is not an oracle but simply a temporal greeting. The fantasy in this is not the experience itself but that the poet may feel he has the blessing, or that his journey, at least, is blessed. For what journey is it? Is he privileging by the inscribed date the act of composition rather than his first experience of the prospect, or is there a conflation of his journey to Calais and back?[2] Or is he travelling another route altogether, that of his vocation as poet, which was assured in a previous dawn (1805 *Prelude*, Book IV, 330 ff.) but which must always be confirmed by such intimations? If that is so, we are suddenly in a biblical as well as vernacular world, "touching in its majesty" indeed. As with the resonance of "first splendour", the poet becomes a figure travelling mentally along switching or conflating tracks of time. How does he compose all this into a semblance of unity, and may the title-phrase "Composed . . ." connect with the calm he so strongly images?

## IV

"Composed . . ." is utterly conventional, and occurs in many sonnets written during that journey of 1802. "Composed by the Sea-Side near Calais, August, 1802"; "Composed near Calais, on the Road Leading to Ardres, August 7, 1802"; "Composed in the Valley near Dover, on the Day of Landing". Traditionally, "composed in" or "upon" refers to drawing a picture (impression) on the spot, under the very influence of the scene. It is not really different from "Lines written in" or "near" a certain place. The tradition of those poems, their inscription of time and place, is not innocent: the tradition evokes or re-animates a buried consciousness; it puts the genius of the writer into relation with genius or spirit of place – and again raises the question what sort of signing is going on, by nature, or by the undulled soul strong enough to meet or complete nature's message. Tradition can be used to sensitize as well as

---

[2] Time-switching is felt even on the simplest biographical level. There is evidence that the poem was composed (or started) on the way to France at the end of July; by 3 September Wordsworth was back in London and must have recrossed the bridge, so that there may be a conflation (or mental retravelling) as so often in his poetry. For another conflation, also involving bridges and morning, see my "Blessing the Torrent", *PMLA* (1978) pp. 196–204.

desensitize a formula, so that "Composed . . ." is not ruled out as a significant phrase.

It is, in fact, one of those clichés that pass by us in common usage, but draws a response from us in poetic language. Riffaterre, whose distinction I summarize here, insists on two kinds of perceptibility. Without the commonplace, or phrases from the sociolect, there could be no perceptibility; yet it is the literary intervention which moves the commonplace from indeterminate to determinate and meaningful status.[3] "Smokeless" needs the context of the elided sociolect with its simple contrast of Edenic countryside and corrupt city to gain the point and pathos it has.

"Composed . . ." is even more unassuming, and only the title foregrounds it. Titles belong, however, more than other parts of the literary work, to the sociolect. When a title is particularly long – longer than the poem itself in some epigrams – then of course we discern a playful or literary dimension. This is the case even in "Tintern Abbey", whose full title, "Lines Composed a Few Miles above Tintern Abbey, on Revisiting the Banks of the Wye during a Tour, July 13, 1798", seems over-elaborated. But the title of the Westminster Bridge sonnet does not draw attention to itself, except for the specified date, also present in some other poems.

The reader, then, can only value the word "Composed" by a general hermeneutic principle, namely, that in literature (as in Scripture) every word counts, whether or not that is apparent in the immediate context. According to this view it is not the individual poem that determines the meaning of indeterminate phrases but the poem as part of an intertextual corpus which the skilled interpreter supplies. Alternatively, the poet could be using everyday speech so effectively that it becomes scriptural, even without a hermeneutic principle ("poetry is like Scripture"). The poet undoes the separation of literary (hieratic) and common speech.

The first principle, transferred from sacred hermeneutics to secular occasions, may have a heuristic value, but it is clearly the second principle which points beyond theory to a fact Wordsworth was able to create. I do not mean that he programmatically views vernacular or colloquial expressions as having scriptural dignity. I am talking about poems, not programmes or intentions. The natural sight, like the casual salutation ("*Good-morrow, Citizen*", in the sonnet "Composed on the Road Leading to Ardres"), is amplified by means that reinstitute the temporality of rhetoric. "Composed", without separating itself from its ordinary language or traditional status, raises a question about the poem as a response in time: to this place, this moment, this journey. Is his destiny as poet linked in any way to his destination: travelling to Calais during the Peace of Amiens, meeting his natural daughter for the first time, and returning around 3 September?

[3] See especially the section "The Poem as Response" in Michael Riffaterre's still valuable essay called "Describing Poetic Structures: Two Approaches to Baudelaire's *Les chats*", in *Structuralism*, ed. Jacques Ehrmann (New York: Anchor Books, 1970).

Wordsworth undertook the trip during an armistice and in view of a momentous step: his plan to marry an Englishwoman that autumn. The sonnet may be about crossings and thresholds, yet no liminal anxiety is allowed to come through, and only the title indicates something via its mention of a bridge. It is the reader who has to take responsibility for heightening the common word, which is neither transformed nor reified.

Yet "Composed", however ordinary, contrasts in the body of the poem with an emotion which is not only recollected *in* tranquillity but is an emotion *of* tranquillity. The one self-reference, "Ne'er saw I, never felt, a calm so deep", depicts that tranquillity as it affects the person of the poet. The composed – composured – mind then produces, by a stunning natural transfer, a sublime personification, first of the river, then of the houses and the city as a whole:

> Ne'er saw I, never felt, a calm so deep.
> The river glideth at his own sweet will:
> Dear God! the very houses seem asleep;
> And all that mighty heart is lying still!
>
> (ll. 11–14)

This transfer from person to personification is the point at which the poem becomes "touching". A curious, even contradictory personification (the City wearing bare beauty like a garment) falls away, and an altogether different kind of visionary metaphor appears. That new personification absorbs the poet, who is now only one locus of being, so that the line between person and personification is erased, or personification becomes what it should be. It is a moment Coleridge would have identified with the workings of Imagination rather than Fancy, and concerning which, as at the end of chapter 12 of *Biographia Literaria*, he might have quoted Jeremy Taylor: "He to whom all things are one, who draweth all things to one, and seeth all things in one, may enjoy true peace and rest of spirit."

It cannot be said that this sabbath vision reposes the will entirely but it does distinguish between the world as will and as representation. The "Dear God!" at the poem's climax not only recapitulates casually the paradox of intimacy and might, but reproduces as a verbal flow, as a spontaneous utterance, the "sweet will" attributed to the river. The cornerstone of Wordsworth's poetics, of his subtle style, is not to reject but to justify the personification of nature by grounding it once more in this excursive and animating language of the heart.

## V

"Open unto the fields, and to the sky" so extends the horizon of visibility that it evokes a state "which knows not any line where being ends". The technique again is subtle: things "lie/Open", and the qualifying "unto" intimates not only a horizontal direction (open as far as the sight can reach, even to the sky) but also a metadescriptive or mythical direction (open *to* the fields, and so undoing the boundary between city and country, yet also *up to* the sky in a vertical, ascensional manner). In "Tintern Abbey" a secluded rural scene connects with "the quiet of the sky"; here the city itself exceptionally points upwards, as if it belonged to that region, more earthy or substantial than that sky, more firm than the firmament. Wordsworth will write in a sonnet of 1806:

> Nor will I praise a cloud, however bright,
> Disparaging Man's gifts, and proper food.
> Grove, isle, with every shape of sky-built dome,
> Though clad in colours beautiful and pure,
> Find in the heart of man no natural home:
> The immortal Mind craves objects that endure. . . .

The emphasis, in the Westminster Bridge sonnet, should be on its initial word: "Earth". The thematic contrast, at least the emergent one, is between earth and sky rather than between Edenic countryside and smoky city. The image of the city, when industry begins to alienate it as a natural home or enduring object, is represented as a site of organic human power ("all that mighty heart") and saved from the temptation of visionary fantasies, skiey adventures. Wordsworth writes against his own foreboding, against nature's diminishing hold on the imagination during a revolutionary era of industry and war. This poem, consequently, as much an epitaph as a descriptive sonnet, is a faithful sign of the times. As a poetic marker, as an inscription, the sonnet can neither insist on itself by artificially heightening an effect of nature, nor not insist on itself as a memorial trace – for such impressions may be all of nature a future generation will know. The poet's reticence is considerable. He does not allow us to upset the wavering balance of his design by interpreting the tranquillity of this naturalized city as a dying rather than as a vital sign. A "good-bye" may ultimately have to be said to earth itself, to that world "which is the world of all of us", but here it is in the form of a blessing, not a viaticum, and a silent intuition, not an oracle. Yet the line, the border, between these states is as indeterminate and extensible as the prospect of the city itself, lying open in the way it lies open.

The act of description, in Wordsworth, tends to "compose" a precarious relation between signs and sensibility, between what befalls – accidents, incidents – and imaginative character – the active or prophetic mind, and perhaps the poetical character as such. Rarely has the very process of composition been regarded so intensely as a divination ("Another omen there!" Yeats writes, but far more comfortably). Wordsworth weighs every thought, every feeling; and the balance in which they are weighed is the poem, his composition of signs that, like absences ("smokeless") or uncertain presences ("wreaths of smoke"), may not be passed by.

Keats objected to the "palpable design" of some of Wordsworth's lyrics, accusing the poet of not remaining long enough in a state of "negative capability". It would be fairer to say that Wordsworth was literally worn out by "dim sadness and blind thoughts" that encompassed his perception of nature and made him cling to every auspicious hint that might counter them, even "one soft impulse saved from vacancy". This movement into vacancy, this dying of nature to the mind, is the condition he confronts; he would like to read it as a dying into the mind, a providential process related to the growth of a poet's mind ("internalization" we might now say), but he cannot neglect other, untoward readings. One is that nature is dying indeed, in the sense that the industrial revolution, or the era of which it is a symptom – an era racked by other turmoil also – is despoiling nature and destroying natural rhythms, so that by prophetic extension the human sensitivity to nature as a benevolent and calming force (a sensitivity which had barely developed in the century before Wordsworth) will soon be but a memory. Wordsworth, the poet of nature, is he already an Ancient of Days? The other fearful thought is simply that of mortality: a growing anxiety that his penchant toward repose and tranquillity is a leaning, however premature, toward the grave.

> How strange, that all
> The terrors, pains, and early miseries,
> Regrets, vexations, lassitudes interfused
> Within my mind, should e'er have borne a part,
> And that a needful part, in making up
> The calm existence that is mine when I
> Am worthy of myself! Praise to the end!
>                          (1805 *Prelude*, Book 1)

Even this "Praise to the end!" is not a simple benediction. It may be saying: I laud the end (calm of spirit, an assured identity) which those strange and adverse means have produced. It may also be saying: may I have the strength to praise what has happened to me, as I am doing now, to the very end – the end of my days. But if this second meaning is admitted, the word "end" in "Praise to the end!" anticipates death, and so praise of nature's role in the poet's psychic development becomes a praise of the death-principle, lending further precision to Freud's startling epigram: "The aim of life is death".

The careful reader cannot fail to catch the complex tenor of Wordsworth's utterances, especially when his theme is praise or complacency. It is often in these moments, foreign to a more modern sensibility, that Wordsworth is most elusive and most original. "Praise to the end!" seems to impose an optimistic turn on experiences that are dark or perplexing. I would agree that the optimism is sometimes stuck on; but I would also argue that it arises from an extraordinary resilience having to do with the *reading of signs*: with events that impinge like omens, sometimes even bad omens, yet are converted, explicitly or implicitly, into blessings.

## VI

In the Westminster Bridge sonnet I have dealt with a tenuous and fortunate incident. It is time to adduce more dramatic examples. One is close to a literal curse and focuses on the shock words can give. When the young poet travelled to London at the age of 18 or 19, he heard, as he tells us in the *Prelude*,

> and for the first time in my life,
> The voice of woman utter blasphemy –
> Saw woman as she is, to open shame
> Abandoned, and the pride of public vice;
> I shuddered, for a barrier seemed at once
> Thrown in, that from humanity divorced
> Humanity, splitting the race of man
> In twain, yet leaving the same outward form.
> (1805 *Prelude*, Book VII, ll. 332–9)

This "first time" – it comes surprisingly late – produces a double image: a separation from simplicity, a "splitting" like a psychic wound. ("This is, and is not *Cressid*", Shakespeare's Troilus cries when he has ocular proof of Cressida's infidelity. And Wordsworth in effect: this is, and is not, woman.) Yet there is no wound except in the consciousness of the poet, since "the same outward form" remains. His "shudder" is therefore like a mimicry of what should be rather than what is: the *poet* intuits a visible wound; he wants the outward form changed to harmonize with inner reality. What is terrible is not simply the conjunction of "voice of woman" and "blasphemy" but that *the internal cause of this conjunction is not clearly marked*, not overt. The darkness is not made manifest except by a seeing through the ear.

Yet that there is no visible mark ultimately shelters the eye. Wordsworth may be afflicted with the thought that appearances betray, that the evidence of sight is deficient, and even when not deficient, unable to overcome (as was the case with Alypius in Augustine's *Confessions*) the power that images of shame ("open shame . . . pride of public vice") exert. Primarily, however, Wordsworth's anxiety focuses on the absence of correspondence between what is seen and what is heard. The fact that the human form is relatively immune to internal shock or change does more than disable sight: it saves it from the breach opened by words.

Let me follow more closely this movement toward immunity in Wordsworth. In the seventh book of *The Prelude* he describes another shock on a later visit to London, when he spotted a blind beggar in the midst of a crowd. It comes while he is distracted, even oppressed by the thought that his mind, in this overcrowding, cannot grasp what it sees: "The face of every one / That passes by me is a mystery". Again, he does not wish simply to pass by or be passed by, dull of soul.

                                                     lost
        Amid the moving pageant, I was smitten
        Abruptly, with the view (a sight not rare)
        Of a blind Beggar, who, with upright face,
        Stood, propped against a wall, upon his chest
        Wearing a written paper, to explain
        His story, when he came, and who he was.
        Caught by the spectacle my mind turned round
        As with the might of waters; an apt type
        This label seemed of the utmost we can know,
        Both of ourselves and of the universe;
        And, on the shape of that unmoving man,
        His steadfast face and sightless eyes, I gazed,
        As if admonished from another world.
                        (1805 *Prelude*, Book VII, ll. 636–49)

This, too, is a picture of "open shame". But the values of the "spectacle" are very different. Eye and voice are both sheltered here, so that the shock comes not from a radical disparity of sight and sound, of voice and human form, but from the character of the signpost or marker, which intimates a state of quasi-divine impassibility – nothing is left to be wounded. Life is reduced to a marker, a living stele with its inscription. This is, indeed, a sight that lies "beyond / The reach of common indication" (1805 *Prelude*, Book VII, ll. 635–6).

The absence of wounds is relative, of course. The poet's eyes are still vulnerable (he is "smitten") even if blindness makes the form of the beggar seem steadfast: the "written paper" is still like a voice in effect, even if as mute as the beggar is blind. The desire for immunity is stronger than the achieved immunity. Perhaps the subtlest distancing of shock comes in the very description of the effect of the beggar on Wordsworth. "My mind turned round" describes a reversal, a recognition strong enough to be traumatic, but it is naturalized by being deprived of specific direction and being subtly associated with the earth's own motion, the wheeling or rolling of the seasons prominent in Wordsworth's consciousness. What does the mind turn to, or turn back to? There are no signs here as a road, however crooked, might supply. "Indication" merges with the "dark, inscrutable workmanship" of natural process (1805 *Prelude*, Book I, ll. 341ff.).

This movement beyond markings or the desire for them, even beyond anything "exposed", I have discussed elsewhere, and linked to the wishful possession of a psyche "From all internal injury exempt".[4] The desire for an invulnerable or immortal state of being, as Freud realized in *Beyond the Pleasure Principle*, is hard to tell from the desire for inertia and even death. Seeking

---

[4] Geoffrey H. Hartman, "A Touching Compulsion", *Georgia Review*, vol. 31 (1977) pp. 345–61.

immunity, the psyche transfigures the wounded part. We approach here such a transfiguration. Wordsworth's stated moral concerns the simplicity or limit of what we can know of the "mystery" behind the human face, but that moral is conveyed through eyes that are baffled, smitten, occluded. To turn the catatonic image of a blind beggar, propped up like a stick, into a symbol of impassive, quasi-divine, invulnerable being, reveals, on the poet's side, a euphemism so extraordinary that we can risk the contagion of the episode, and call it blind as well as tacit. Wordsworth in his way stages as remarkable an act of blessing, saved from the jaws of its opposite, as when Job's wife is made to say to her suffering husband, "Bless God, and die" rather than "Curse God, and die".

LOUIS MARIN

# The "Aesop" Fable-Animal

What, in the discourse of fable, is the significance of the *talking animal?* An allegory of man? All right. What does it indicate? The fiction of the "clinamen", the tangential point at which "speaking" and "eating" meet, where the verbal and the oral, the instinct of self-preservation and the linguistic urge, come together. "Thesis": the talking animal of fable, the embodiment of that kind of fiction of the infinitesimalness of the clinamen, of that "original" fault. A devouring and a devoured body, the fable-animal also speaks. Within the fable, the animal is the simulation of a symbolic regression to the instinctual: the fiction of an origin of discourse in Eros and in destruction, one whose function is to rob the masters of their power of discourse.

At the very beginning of *La vie d'Esope*, as told by La Fontaine (1668), I found a little narrative in the guise of an introduction to the *Premier Recueil de Fables Choisies*: a fable that (by chance?) tells the origin of fable by telling the origin of the fabulist himself. Thus, in this odd narrative, the production of narrative is narratively exposed, the fable recounts itself recounting a fable, an endless referring of the narrative to the narration that produces it, and of the narration to the narrative that narrates it.

In this little story, however, that referring stops short simply because this narrative is a sequence of gestures, a silent narrative, one mute before language. Its narrator is not a voice at all, but a body, a fable-animal. The animal of fable is a devouring–devoured body, but one that, in addition, *speaks*. Here the fabulist man is an animal, a (devouring–devoured) body that cannot yet speak; a body that has, through the moral of the tale, been given speech, gestures, to which a story has been given, in conclusion, in addition. And throughout, there is the question of master and slave, of strength and justice, of accusation and rebuttal; throughout there is a question of power and discourse.

. . . Aesop was a Phrygian from a town called *Amorium*. He was born around the fifty-seventh Olympiad, some 200 years after the founding of Rome. It is difficult to say whether he had reason to thank Nature or to make complaint to her; for while endowing him with a very fine mind, she caused him to be born misshapen and ugly of visage, barely having the form of a man; indeed, she almost withheld from him totally the power of speech. With these defects, while he was not at all suited to be a slave, he could not have failed to become one. Yet his soul remained ever free and independent of fortune.

At the beginning of the tale one notes the irremediable ambiguity of the Phrygian; a fine mind shut up in a deformed body, human intelligence in the body of a wild beast. To go a bit further: Aesop does not have – or barely has – a human form because he does not speak: an animal or quasi-animal. He grunts; he gibbers. According to Rousseau, the first man was "nothing ... he is an animal".

His first master sent him out into the fields to till the soil, either because he adjudged him incapable of anything else or to remove so disagreeable an object from his sight. Now, it came to pass that his master, having gone out to inspect his country house, was offered some figs by a peasant: he thought them very fine and had them very carefully put aside, ordering his butler, Agathopus by name, to bring them to him after his bath. It so happened that Aesop had business in the house. As soon as the master had gone in, Agathopus seized the opportunity and, with a few of his companions, ate the figs; he then blamed this mischief on Aesop, never thinking he could ever clear himself, for he was such a stammerer and seemed such an idiot! The punishments to which the ancients subjected their slaves were very cruel, and this offence was highly punishable. Poor Aesop fell down at the feet of his master; and making himself understood as best he could, made him understand that he was requesting, for pity's sake, that his punishment be delayed for a few moments.

Now the story proper begins, and with it the first fable: a silent narrative, a gestural narrative. The first gesture of this narrative is one of supplication, its effect is to introduce a difference that is at once temporal and spatial: to stave off for a moment his punishment. Here, perhaps, is one of the cruxes of the story of origin: the delay, or as St Augustine would say, the distancing; the setting aside, the apostasy of the now, as Aristotle would have it. The prolonging of the moment is the basis on which narrative is possible. In our story, the "originating" gesture is not – as it is in the first chapter of *The Phenomenology of Mind* – the *stigmè*, the pointing, the indicating finger ... the *deixis* of the gestural instant; it is, rather, the gesture of a hand fending off an imminent blow, slowing down the "all of a sudden"; it is a "suddenly" that opens up, temporally, spatially, the site or the stage for a play. Or, to put it another way, the gesture of delay, or averting or of spacing out, of opening a gap or of divergence, is "something like" the creation of a clinamen, of a tangent at one point on the arc; it is a tiny angle, a small gap in an urgent chain. Or, to put it trivially, Aesop goes off on a tangent: a kind of duplicity.

After gesture, the body: the constitution of the narrative and the narrating bodies, a complex process. I recall the beginning of the story: the master wanted to eat some figs when he emerged from his bath. The butler, Agathopus – the good-looking one, the *kaloskagathos* – and his companions had eaten the figs instead of the master. They ate them out of gluttony, greediness. The figs were gone: the tasty morsel has been introjected, incorporated, assimilated, its exteriority, its thingness, has been destroyed; consumed. Agathopus and his companions blame Aesop. They speak. They tell lies, all the more secure in their (verbal) falsehood because they think – correctly – that the manipulating of words, the discourse of the strong, functions, on the one hand, as something representational and, on the other, as something monologous. First represen-tation: the discourse articulates the being, the situation, the state of affairs. It articulates them falsely, but *it does articulate them*. And by describing a past situation the discourse also takes the form of narrative discourse: Agathopus tells what has happened, what is past. In this sense his narrative is the outline of a situation, an action. "Aesop went into the house; the figs have disappeared; Aesop ate the figs." The narrative discourse constitutes (falsely) the record of the past situation; it outlines it and is its only trace. Thus, the tale told by Agathopus is not only the narrative representation of the past, but also – and this goes without saying – this narrative representation discursively creates an explication: the historical narrative, because it is re-presentation, explicates the absence, the disappearance, of the figs.

Next, narrative representation is monologous: there is, there will be, there can be no reply on Aesop's part – because he cannot speak. The animal can provide no counter-narrative, no counter-explanation. However, let us imagine that possibility – let us give Aesop speech for a moment. What could Aesop have *said?* "I did not eat the figs. Yes, I did go into the house, but by *chance*. Besides, I don't like figs. . . ." And so on. "Prove it", the master would have said. It is impossible for him to produce proof: the *corpus delicti* has disappeared. A good fictive example of dual discourse as understood by ancient sophistry: between the *pro* and the *con*, an undecidable truth, but one whose undecidability resides in the disappearance of the object. The thing has been consumed. It is rediscovered, of course, but as representation in the narrative. "It is Aesop who ate the figs", says Agathopus. "It was Agathopus", Aesop would have said, had he been able to speak. It is thus the adversary who shapes the narrative body "Aesop", the fig-eater, the assimilating stomach: a body of speech, a body of words. The animal is a voracious one – that is well known. In Agathopus' narrative, the accusation is given an embodiment. Its ineluctable conclusion is punishment. The master–judge passes sentence. Aesop is condemned to death: that is the urgent, immediate implication of the narrative, of Agathopus' monologous narrative representation.

Aesop, however, does reply to the accusation: his first gesture of reply is – as we have seen – a gesture of delay, which, at the moment of urgency, creates a field of play: the stage for a counter-discourse, but a discourse that will not be *uttered*. Here I would stress the contrast between the accusing narrative of Agathopus, which is representational and monologous, and the "discourse" of Aesop, who does not tell a tale, who does not revive the past in story form. His reply is on the spot, instantaneous, of the moment, the setting aside of the moment. He replies to the verbal narrative body, the representational archive of the past, by means of another body, a counter-body – neither anti-*logos* nor anti-*mythos*, but anti-body, one whose temporal characteristic is the present, the now; a "now" contained in the apostasis, in by-passing the now of the stage that has been created by the supplication–distancing gesture.

Of what does this fable-making anti-body consist? Aesop drinks some warm water, puts his fingers down his throat and vomits the water he has ingested. Thus two bodily functions are enacted: a rhythm of the body, filling–ingestion, excretion–rejection. I say "enacted" because Aesop drinks without thirst and vomits intentionally. The anti-body is a "produced body", which is quite different from "the natural body". To drink warm water rather than cold water is obviously to drink without thirst; to put one's fingers down one's throat is the accepted gesture for provoking vomiting, vomiting which is not at all the natural result of indigestion. Perhaps I have not been totally exact in saying that Aesop does not tell a tale. By *pro*-ducing in his body the rhythm of repletion–excretion (and we should recall, in this connection, the famous passage from Plato's *Symposium*), by acting with his body, he narrativizes it. And it is of this narrativization that La Fontaine tells: "He went to get some warm water, he drank it in the presence of his master, he placed his fingers in his mouth, and he vomited only the water." Aesop's anti-*mythos*, which is a body-game, the body put into play, consists precisely of this fact – it is his response to Agathopus' narrative – that repletion and excretion, ingestion and rejection, assimilation and expulsion are linked. To introduce is to reject; to incorporate is to exclude; to eat is to expel. The body is rhythm, yes and no, Eros and destruction.

At the same time, the lying accusing body, the monologous, narrative, historical body of Agathopus, the body of language, is replaced by the pro-duced body of the accused, the rhythmic body of interior-ization–exteriorization, shown by the acting to be a kind of "YES!": the water disappears–reappears, is lost – is found again. In addition, the clinamen, the divergence to which I referred, is here accentuated. In a sense, Aesop reproduces the past scene of the crime recounted by Agathopus (he reconstitutes the crime), but now he also reinscribes it on the spot with his own body, in the different gap of the clinamen, in divergence; he repeats the difference in an acting body. If there is an Aesopian narrative, that narrative is not a body of narrative but a narrating body. Words are not substituted for things by representing them as having disappeared – that is Agathopus' task – but things are substituted for words in this "point of origin".

> After having thus cleansed himself, he made a sign that the others should do the same. Everyone was surprised; they would not have believed that

Aesop could be so inventive. Agathopus and his companions tried not to show their surprise. They drank some water as the Phrygian had done, and placed their fingers in their mouths; but they tried with all their might not to put them too far back. The water, however, had its effect, and the figs were brought to light, all raw and ruddy. Thus, Aesop saved himself; and his accusers were doubly punished both for their gluttony and for their malice.

The anti-body of the fable-maker is a body of dialogue. Aesop gestures to each of the others to repeat in turn his own bodily scene, his pro-duced body, to put the rhythmic functions into play. *After* the "originating" gesture of setting aside, we have the gesture of indication, the finger pointed at Agathopus and his companions; not at all, however, in accusation, but as a signal of the time for reversal, for reply: the time for *metabolè*; it is not a question of saying the opposite (anti-*logos*), but of doing the same (*homopoièsis*) and, by doing the same, of producing the opposite. However, the reply required from Agathopus, precisely because it is demanded by the gesture of pointing, is situated, if one can put it thus, in the pro-duced body used for Aesop's enacting. He is directing the play. His body, in acting, becomes in turn the stage for acting by the bodies of the others. It absorbs them. The slave has become the master's master. With water he brings back the thing assimilated, the clueless occurrence. "To eat the figs" reappears on stage, but inverted: the figs will be vomited up, "all raw and ruddy". An impossible occurrence, unless Agathopus was so gluttonous as to have gulped down the figs without chewing them. Agathopus is the animal, yet Aesop is not quite a man. The lost object has been *found just as it was*: the same – we have homoeostasis, but in the meantime the fable has been born.

What can we say excepting that the narrative of Agathopus, the pleasant-looking man, a narrative indexed on the referent, the occurrence over and done with, on the death and disappearance of the object, a narrative endowed with a value of truth, a language narrative, a narrative representation of the voracious beast – what is there to say save that that narrative is replaced, within two gestures, one of setting aside, one of indicating, by a narrative body of fiction neither true nor false, by a performative dialogic body, by a narration-body that achieves and produces here and now another, a different, event, and one that re-produces, but in reverse, the past and lost event? That body even undertakes, in fact, an analysis of the story the narrative has recounted in language, not as a meta-discourse on the narrative of the past event, but as the production of a body-narrative that inverts its effects.

Let us listen again to Agathopus' narrative: "While the master was bathing, Aesop went into the house and ate the figs." Let us look at the body-narration of the fabulist: "I drink water, I put my fingers down my throat, I vomit up the water. Agathopus drinks water, he puts his fingers in his mouth, he vomits the figs." Such are the narrative body of the adversary and the "narration-body" of the fabulist: a fiction of consumption – *hic et nunc* – whose effect is the rejection of the thing that is good to eat and at the same time the deconstruction of the verbal narrative, of the narrative with the value of truth; it is the actual moment of doing, of a bodily acting, of an action-fiction that brings the truth into being as an effect of the interlocutor's discourse.

Thus we can imagine, as a pragmatic consequence of Aesop's gesticulation, the master's discourse: "While I was asleep after my bath, Agathopus went into the house and ate the figs." Which is, we are told, the truth. Thence Agathopus' punishment both for his gluttony and his maliciousness, for having *eaten* the figs and *told* a story. Thence the position of Aesop who, by drinking the water and vomiting it up, by making others drink and vomit, between a gesture of distancing and a gesture of indication, attains something that is not yet verbality, but not yet quite orality either; something I have called the "narration-body-fiction". In other words, the simulation of the body in the body, the constitution of a simulacrum with the dual gesture of distancing and indicating that forms the basis for possibility.

In urgency, in imminence, the temporal distancing of a now opens up a stage *for the present*. Spatial indication entails a repetition not of the "same" past, but of an *immediate* or present *difference*, with the effect of truth in the master's discourse. Hence the notion of simulacrum and that of fiction or corporal simulation as a defensive retaliatory tactic. In silence, with his gestures and his body, Aesop repeats the narrative of his accusers, but shifting and inverting in his own body the syntagmatics of his accusers' statements. The rhetorical denial of the accused – "No, it is not true; I did not eat the figs" – is thus transformed into a bodily reaction of rejection, of vomiting. To recall here Freud's famous text on de-negation, we might say that symbolic negation regresses to the archaic reaction of vomiting. However, because it is intentional, desired, *acted*, it retains its symbolic dimension, but conserves it in the present, in the immediate, in the now. In other words, "neither yes nor no", but *fiction*, or simulation, whose perlocutionary force in the master's discourse will be: "Agathopus ate the figs, not Aesop."

I have already noted that Aesop does not accuse. He points to his accusers not to accuse them, not in order to say "no" with his hand, but to call upon them silently to repeat his fiction and the simulacrum he has just acted out with and in his body and his gestures. In so doing, Aesop's accusers repeat his gesticulation, but in that very repetition they produce a supplement, a supplement whose effect of truth will be affirmed by the master's discourse: "Yes, they ate the figs." Thus the accusing, offensive force is inscribed and turned back in the acting body, articulated in and by the signs of the narrative, in the language of the strongest. It might well be that the "fable" in general, the narrative of the weak and of the marginal is – in the element of the discourse itself – a device for the displacing and turning back, by the weakest, of the force of the discourse of the strongest.

The next day, after their master had gone and the Phrygian had returned to his usual labours, some travellers who had lost their way (some say they were priests of Diana) asked him, in the name of Jupiter the Hospitable, to point out the road to the city for them. First of all, Aesop made them rest in the shade; then, having offered them a light meal, he insisted on acting as their guide and did not leave them until he had set them on their road. The good men lifted up their hands to heaven and prayed Jupiter not to leave this charitable act unrewarded. Hardly had Aesop left them when the heat and his weariness led him to lie down to sleep. During his slumber he imagined that Fortune stood before him; she untied his tongue and at the same time made him a gift of that art of which he can be said to be the author. Rejoicing at this adventure, he awoke with a start and, as he awoke, he said, "What is this? My voice has been freed; I can say quite clearly, 'Rake', 'Plow' – anything I want."

The moral of this tale can be found in the next episode: accession to verbality. I shall not analyse it, but it would be easy to find there, on another level, all the elements I have tried to discern in Aesop's silent gesticulation before his accusers. The priests of Diana wish to know the way, the road to the city. They no longer accuse; they ask for information, they, the learned, ask to be shown the way. The slave has become the master of an item of knowledge – of a road, of a route, of a direction. Here again he first makes the gesture of distancing, of spacing out the urgency: here it will be a rest in the shade of a tree to take a light meal, to eat, to restore strength and recover from fatigue. Once again, Aesop now makes a gesture of indicating but here he makes it with his whole body: he accompanies the travellers on the right road. He causes them to *do* what he *knows*; he transmits to them his knowledge, not through the mediation of the signs of discourse, but by simulating a journey with them; he causes them to do what he does and/or knows. The priests of Diana pray to Jupiter on Aesop's behalf. When they have gone, Aesop sleeps: a repetition of the spacing out, but this time as the opening up of the space for *oneiric* enactment; Aesop dreams. But in his dreams it is not Jupiter, the all-powerful Master, the Master of masters, who unties his tongue, but Fortune; it is through the power of chance, the event of the fortuitous, that language comes, and with it fable: language, the supplement of gesture and the body, narrative supplementing the fiction of the pro-duced body, the simulacrum of simulation. Aesop awakens: "What is *this*? This is a rake, a plow; I can say anything I want." Aesop is now a logothete. "This" – a deictic word that reflects in language the gesture of indication and silently opens up the field of nominal definitions, the field of signs, the domain of the symbolic, at the will, at the desire of the slave, the founder of language. The animal is speaking. The fables are recounted.

A. J. GREIMAS

# The Love-Life of the Hippopotamus: A Seminar with A. J. Greimas

I should like to begin at the beginning by asking the question: when we have a text like this one (see box 1) before you, what do we do with it? How do we proceed to analyse it? The first problem we find ourselves confronted with is the problem of segmentation. Well, to solve it, we can very easily divide the text along temporal criteria. You see at the beginning "one African afternoon", then "later that evening", and, finally, "after midnight". Thus, we have the text following temporal deictics and separated into three parts – the temporal parts,

"afternoon" *vs* "evening" *vs* "after midnight"

let us call them, which correspond to the three segments of the text on the spatial plane, since our text is spatially distributed. Thus, we can say that we have three segments we can consider to be autonomous (see box 2).

There we have the overall scheme of the text, the result of segmentation. Notice that I have placed the 6 in the middle. Why? Because this segment is where story number one, about the parrots, ends, and also where story two, about the hippopotamuses, ends. It is the point of convergence of the two general parts of the narrative. You can thus see that the way in which the text is composed reminds us more of a poem than it does of a piece of prose, so severe and rigorous is its organization. What I have done so far is follow a formal procedure that yields a rather rigorous and convincing schema. We have no need to rely on intuition. The text itself provides criteria of mark and dimension.

We have undertaken so far to articulate, to segment the text, which is completely normal because we are engaged in analysis, and analysis is the

*Box 1*

## James Thurber
### The Lover and his Lass

An arrogant gray parrot and his arrogant mate listened, one African afternoon, in disdain and derision, to the lovemaking of a lover and his lass, who happened to be hippopotamuses.

"He calls her snooky-ookums," said Mrs Gray. "Can you believe that?"

"No," said Gray. "I don't see how any male in his right mind could entertain affection for a female that has no more charm than a capsized bathtub."

"Capsized bathtub, indeed!" exclaimed Mrs Gray. "Both of them have the appeal of a coastwise fruit steamer with a cargo of waterlogged basketballs."

But it was spring, and the lover and his lass were young, and they were oblivious of the scornful comments of their sharp-tongued neighbors, and they continued to bump each other around in the water, happily pushing and pulling, backing and filling, and snorting and snaffling. The tender things they said to each other during the monolithic give-and-take of their courtship sounded as lyric to them as flowers in bud or green things opening. To the Grays, however, the bumbling romp of the lover and his lass was hard to comprehend and even harder to tolerate, and for a time, they thought of calling the ABI, or African Bureau of Investigation, on the ground that monolithic lovemaking by enormous creatures who should have become decent fossils long ago was probably a threat to the security of the jungle. But they decided instead to phone their friends and neighbors and gossip about the shameless pair, and describe them in mocking and monstrous metaphors involving skidding buses on icy streets and overturned moving-vans.

Later that evening, the hippopotamus and the hippopotama were surprised and shocked to hear the Grays exchanging terms of endearment.

"Listen to those squawks," ruffled the male hippopotamus.

"What in the world can they see in each other?" gurbled the female hippopotamus.

"I would as soon live with a pair of unoiled garden shears," said her inamoratus.

They called up their friends and neighbors and discussed the incredible fact that a male gray parrot and a female gray parrot could possibly have any sex appeal. It was long after midnight before the hippopotamuses stopped criticizing the Grays and fell asleep, and the Grays stopped maligning the hippopotamuses and retired to their beds.

MORAL: *Laugh and the world laughs with you, love and you love alone.*

From *Further Fables for Our Time*
London: Hamish Hamilton, 1956

*Box 2*                          **At the Blackboard**

"For these temporal spaces," Greimas says rising, "there is for the first one, afternoon, the character parrots." He draws the following table on the blackboard:

(a) "afternoon" – the parrots
(b) "evening" – the hippopotamuses
(c) "after midnight" – the parrots and hippopotamuses

Standing before his drawing, Greimas asks the students to notice that the story's last sentence, from which came entry (c), is made of two co-ordinate clauses – the first with its subject the hippopotamuses, the second with its subject the parrots; and both having the same predication. The overall structure of the text appears and is binary – and if binary, he notes, the class is going to find parallelism between the parrot and hippopotamus parts.

What interests him is to segment the parts, seeking each segment's parallel. He finds the opening – Mr and Mrs Parrot listening – paralleled by the hippopotamus lovers being "surprised and shocked to hear". Comparable predicates, comparable objective complements (lovemaking parrots/lovetalking hippos). This state of affairs enables Greimas to announce a principle of entire comparability, and he draws the following:

| | |
|---|---|
| Sg 1 An arrogant gray parrot and his arrogant mate listened, one | Sg 1′ Late that evening, the hippopotamus and the hippopotama were surprised . . . to hear |
| Sg 2 "He calls her snooky- "I don't see how any "Capsized bathtub | Sg 2′ "Listen to those squawks "What in the world "I would as soon live |
| Sg 3 But it was spring, and the lover and his lass . . . green things opening. | Sg 4′ To the Grays, however, the bumbling romp . . . threat to the security of the jungle. |
| Sg 5 But they decided instead to phone up their friends and neighbors and gossip | Sg 5′ They called up their friends and neighbors and discussed the incredible fact that |

Sg 6 It was long after midnight

It is simple for Greimas to find the comparable segments 2 and 2′: the graphic presence of the quotation marks signalled him, he says. To find his next comparability, he notices a terminal bit of text immediately after the hippos' dialogue: "They called up their friends and neighbors . . ." Part two is ending here, the co-ordinated part three ("It was long after midnight . . .") is about to begin. To this terminal bit corresponds the termination of the first part: "But they decided instead to phone their friends and neighbors . . ." "Friends and neighbors" in each piece: the uttering subject is purposely repeating the formulaic object to call attention to the parallel temporality. Greimas has found segments 5 and 5′.

Now he looks at the long section following the parrot dialogue, starting with "But it was spring" – it ends with the disjunction "but": "But they decided . . . " Between the two "buts" is another disjunctor, "however" – "To the Grays, however . . ." – cutting this part. Without knowing anything of the content, he knows that he has found two segments, 3 and 4, disjoined by the pivot "however". And segment 6 is simply the third temporal part, "It was long after midnight."

The comparabilities he has noticed are similarities which will enable him to discern differences, and thus specify each part *vis-à-vis* the other.

*Marshall Blonsky*

articulation into parts. The object is dissected and separated into parts; then it has to be put back together. The first phase is the phase of destruction. If you prefer, I can use a fashionable term and say "decomposition", even "segmentation", but it is all the same thing. Now, the next phase is to see whether there is a way of giving a syntactic and semantic representation of this text, in other words, of passing from the level of the manifested text to that of its representation. Let us begin gradually, by taking little steps.

## The Subjects

If a subject is repeated in several sentences, we call it the discursive subject, while next, if we manage to give it a syntactico-logical status, we call it the narrative subject. Progressing by steps, we can say that the discursive subjects are of two types: on the one hand, the parrots, and on the other, the hippopotamuses. Let us call the parrots $P$ and the hippopotamuses $H$:

| $P$ | $vs$ | $H$ |
|---|---|---|
| (1) The Grays | | hippopotamuses |
| (2) they | | they |
| (3) Gray vs Mrs Gray | | the hippopotamus and the hippopotama |
| (4) A male parrot and a female parrot | | the male hippopotamus $vs$ the female hippopotamus |
| (5) a gray parrot and his mate | | the lover and his lass (+ her inamoratus) |

Thus, on the one side, you have the use of the plurals, the "Grays", to which correspond, on the other side, the hippopotamuses. Here the plurals have dual value, neither plural being a true one, because the real opposition here is between bourgeois values and Rousseauist happiness, the vulgar, simple, somatic joy of existing. The next plural is the dual "they" of "they decided to phone", corresponding to which we have another "they": "they called up", etc. The third is "Gray and Mrs Gray" on the one hand, and the "hippopotamus and hippopotama" on the other. Fourth is a male parrot and a female parrot, the same being true for the hippopotamuses; in other words, there is no seme of individuation other than one of sexual opposition. Finally, fifth, you have a gray parrot and his mate, and the lover and his lass – with an unexpected denomination, "her inamoratus". That is all – there you have the exhaustive list of the denomination of the subjects: the whole thing enabling us to say that sometimes we have an individual subject and sometimes a dual one; in other words, that the couple is only a single subject, sometimes manifesting itself in the form of two actors, sometimes not.

Of course, things get a bit more complicated when the text says that there is a lover and his lass, already announced in the title and revealing the unpardonable androcentrism of our cultural tradition with its male predominance. And here we are led into error for the following reason. For a long time, full of liberalism, we thought that love could be defined as amorous communication, bipolar; but no, that analysis ran into difficulties, so we then thought that there was amorous communication and that it had to be contrasted with social communication. As you can see, the text *could* be articulated in that way. However, amorous communication is not a reciprocal communication here, it is solely an amorous *doing*, in other words, a programme of behaviour aimed at or directed at an object of value, which therefore supposes quest, conquest, amorous bliss, etc. These characters, husband and wife, are interchangeable, but love is considered from only one viewpoint: there is a love subject, a love object, there is the quest, conquest and so on. It is thus as amorous doing – if you will permit my speaking this way – that we have to see the description of the lovemaking of hippopotamuses and parrots.

## Doings

In a general way, we can distinguish two levels of narration, two distinct types of doing met with in the narrative discourse. On the one hand, there is the pragmatic or what I call occurrential doing. I am loath to use the term "pragmatic" in the United States because the way we French use it is exactly the opposite of what we understand "pragmatic" to be in the language of American logicians. For us, their "pragmatic" is almost metaphysical, whereas by "pragmatic" we simply mean the chain of events or occurrences. Thus we can use the term occurrential – equivalent to the word I use in French, *événémentiel*. So there is an occurrential doing, of a somatic type, let us say; and, on the other hand, there is a cognitive doing, whose object is to acquire knowledge. So I can call $D1$ the occurrential or pragmatic doing and $D2$ the cognitive doing.

Cognitive doing is true doing, it has a subject and that subject aims at an object. In that way we can write that as an entire narrative programme. However, if you take cognitive doing, the subject intends an object but that object is, as we said, knowing; it involves knowing what? Another object, and, especially, what I call the doing of someone with someone else. A simple example is the parrots that listen to the amorous doing of the hippopotamuses – they learn, they acquire knowledge about the hippopotamuses' doing.

Now, the cognitive doing can obviously be broken down. It can be simply situated at the level of reception and you can see the difference between "listen" and "hear". "To listen" is an active doing, "to hear", a passive one. It has to do with "editing", with communication of knowledge. On these cognitive levels, we can thus glimpse different cognitive operations: the reception of knowledge, its interpretation and its transmission, the communicating of knowledge. You will see that things are organized something like that. In our text, the reception of knowledge is "to listen . . . to hear", and the interpretation of already-received knowledge is "with disdain and derision". Thus from the second line on, knowledge about "lovemaking" is received and interpreted with disdain and derision. Obviously, the author is going to vary the grammatical construction somewhat, and we can view that as a stylistic labour, because here we have the substantives *disdain* and *derision* whereas in the second part we shall have *surprised* and *shocked*, past participles used in place of nouns. And, finally, the third cognitive doing is the communication of already-interpreted knowledge found in the verbs *to gossip* and *describe, to discuss*, etc.

So we have a mechanism for the predicates we have set up, with this complication: when dealing with interpretive doing, we can distinguish verbalized doing from non-verbalized doing – dialogues represent verbalized doing while the non-dialogical parts represent only interpretive doing.

Now, for the subjects. If there are two subjects, we shall have to baptize them. We can take $S$ and say that that is the parrot subject, and non-$S$ – $\bar{S}$ the hippopotamuses. Now each of them, the $S$ and $\bar{S}$, are able to be both subject of the occurrential doing and of the cognitive doing. Consequently, they can be broken down, and we have $S_1$, $\bar{S}_1$ – subjects of occurrential doing – and $S_2$, $\bar{S}_2$ – subjects of cognitive doing. The parrot, in other words, exercising a cognitive activity, will be called $S_2$, while the hippopotamus, as lovemaker, will be called $\bar{S}_1$ – the non-subject the parrots perceive. Do not take this formalization too seriously. Take it only to the extent that it sheds some light and does not create obscurity.

Now, let us proceed. When we have broken the subjects down we have four of them; the question now is what does the presence of two subjects in a single parrot mean? What guarantees the permanence of a single being, of a single individual, a being exercising itself now as subject of the occurrential verb, now as subject of its cognitive doing? And a second question: what establishes the difference between the parrots and the hippopotamuses? – for some are indulging in an amorous doing and the others are mocking them, then the roles are inverted; everything happens as if there were no difference between parrots and hippopotamuses, particularly since the author himself, the subject of the uttering, says upon introducing the hippopotamuses: "who happened to be hippopotamuses". It is a matter of chance, no? They could have been other parrots, could have been doves.

## Actantial and thematic roles

In an early phase of research into narrativity, I tried to interpret Propp by saying that in each narrative there was a subject, an object, a sender and a recipient, and I called them *actants*. After a few years, examining things a bit more closely, I realized that it was a much more complicated matter and that, although one could by and large assign those roles, the subject does not remain a subject all the time, or rather, it changes. In other words, when we have a character at the beginning of a novel, the character is not the same as at the end. Things are as stupid and as simple as that. Only, I had to think of it. Literary critics have contributed to the confusion of our minds because they speak of the

Stendhalian hero or the Balzacian hero as if a character of Balzac or Stendhal were a hero all of the time, which is not the case. The hero becomes a hero only at a given moment in the narrative route; earlier he was not a hero, and perhaps at a given moment he will cease to be a hero. In other words, the subject is defined not only as a subject, but is further determined by the position he occupies in the narrative journey – a journey often characterized by the acquisition of competences.

Thus we can call "hero" a competent subject who has the will to do and power to do. That is a hero. If there were no will-to-do, there would be no hero, but what if one can *will* but not be able to *do*? The examples are obvious. According to the position on the narrative route, according to the modalization that characterizes an actant, such an actant is a dynamic being, he can alter modal content, and from that point of view I call these different and changing modal contents *actantial roles*. The hero is an actantial hero, he is the subject that can become, can take the actantial role at a given time, etc. The traitor is an actantial role, and so on.

Now, we also have thematic roles. These are roles that embody an entire programme and that are, at the same time, capable and competent to make this programme a reality. You can see that a thematic role sums up a whole body of activities already semantically specified, and are not purely grammatical. This enables us to make a linkage: if you take an actantial role and add a thematic one to it, if at a moment you take grammar and add to it semantics, you have a total character, a character I call an *actor*. The actor is a site where both an actantial role and a thematic role – at a minimum, one – are invested. Now, from this point of view, if we look at occurrential doing, we can see that it is defined simply as pragmatic – we define it on the grammatical level, let us say – but given the semantic investiture we can say that we have business with amorous doing – lovemaking. You see, there is semantics there; otherwise it would be the occurrential doing that produced and ordered the events, whereas we know that it is on the level of "love" that the occurrences are situated. Now, following this line, if you take the cognitive activity, cognitive doing, whether it concerns parrots or hippopotamuses, it is a denigratory doing. It is a matter of denigrating, of making fun of someone else, and so we have two thematic roles pertaining to two types of doing – a thematic occurrential role, that of the lover, and the cognitive role, the denigrative one.

Perhaps we have taken a small step forward. However, we have not resolved the problem of the difference between the parrots and the hippos (let us call them because it is too much trouble to keep saying "hippopotamuses"); we have not resolved the problem of difference because according to the position of the hippo in the narrative, he sometimes occupies the lover's role and sometimes the denigratory role, and the same thing is true for the parrots. Thus we can see that as soon as one reaches a certain level of abstraction, we can no longer distinguish – in spite of the two very different figures that hippos and little parrots cut – between the two.

Let us say that when we already have an apparatus of this sort, we can attempt to operate a semiotic transcription of the text. I am not going to indulge in redoing the transcription on the blackboard. Let us say that such tasks are logicians' games. There is a segment 1 and a segment 1'; segments 2 and 2'; segments 3, 4, 5, 5', 6 – I have only given you positions of segment, and now we have to fill these positions, by inscribing narrative utterances – in other words, by specifying in each case what is the subject and what it does. Whichever doing is being put into play, we have $S$, $S_1$, $S_2$ and the non-$S$, the $\bar{S}$. We have four subjects, and we have occurrential and cognitive doings, with this little *combinatoire*, and we can make various utterances. Thus we can say that the parrot, as a cognitive subject – let us call it $S_2$ – listens, it exercises a cognitive doing, and that cognitive doing enables it to gain a knowledge object, and that object-knowing has to do with what the hippos are doing, and the hippos, since they are making love, are not $S_2$, they are $S_1$ with the negative sign $\bar{S}$: there you see the type of the narrative utterance. In other words, we are dealing with a very simple symbolic notation with elements that have been provided by four subjects and two types of doing. And then, with a very little bit of sophistication we can say that cognitive doing can be receptive, and then one could put the letter $R$ next to it; it could be communicative, and one would put the letter $C$; or interpretive, putting $I$ there, plus a $V$ for verbal, if the interpretation is in words; if it is not, if it is non-verbal, as it can be, you write the interpretive $I$ with a barred or denied $V$.

However, such transcriptions are boring, and I shall make do with as little as possible because I am lazy. I would have to get up and clean the blackboard and then write it out . . . so I shall rely on your intelligence and your logical know-how – logic is really very simple, do you not agree, and rather childish. We only have to have a few ounces of wit, then, to understand how to construct any logic.

## Commentary

Now, I would rather give you a commentary on what is going on. You see, at the moment of segmentation, we divided the text into two parts. Now, when we transcribe those parts – let us say into narrative utterances – such parts become narrative programmes. Thus we have two narrative programmes corresponding to the two parts. Then, in order to be taken seriously, we can call the first programme $NP_1$ and $NP_2$ – obviously – and we must not forget the remainder of the text that you have already gone through – and then we go on.

Now, so long as we stay on the level of filling actantial and thematic roles, we can see that in narrative programme 1 we have the subject $S_2$ – in other words the cognitive parrot – and $\bar{S}_1$, the amorous hippo, while in narrative programme 2 we have $\bar{S}_2$, in other words, the cognitive hippo, and $S_1$, the amorous parrot. In other words, the two programmes are identical save for an inversion of heroes. And such takes place, this interchangeability of roles that we find in segments 1, 2 and 5, and gives the impression that at a certain level the narrative suspends the oppositions between the subjects *hippos* and *parrots*, and that in the end both these programmes are recurrent and can be reproduced *ad infinitum*.

There are popular narratives that have been studied by Hannah Jason, narratives in which there is a swindler and his dupe. In the first part, the swindler deceives. Then in the second part, the person who was earlier tricked turns into a swindler himself and tricks some other creature. And then in the third part, these roles are once again reversed, and reversed again and reversed again – the stories are endless. Now almost every folklore in the world has this kind of story, and on the surface the kind of fable we are studying at present has this kind of popular archetype.

Now, obviously, if this kind of story can be reproduced *ad infinitum* it is because it produces a particular effect of meaning. Which?

There are lovers who are stupid and lovers who make fun of them who are stupid in turn. All this does not seem very serious, but only because it produces the surface level. What is happening is that the textual narrative is organizing itself in a paradigmatic way. As Jakobson said, we finally have the projection of the paradigmatic on to the syntagmatic, and this makes things repeat themselves, do you see? And at the same time the action stops and the question becomes: is this projection merely the principle of poeticity or is there something, a transformation, a change, that is going on in spite of this level of appearances of immutability? You probably know the quarrel of Jakobson's cats. Now, that cat problem is something like ours. There are the cats, our parrots and hippos, interpreted in the spirit of Jakobson as the projection of the paradigmatic. For us, however, the problem is to know if, in spite of such recurrence of categories, there is a narrative that is subjacent to this story of cats. I can see that the publication of that text by Jakobson and Lévi-Strauss gave rise to immense progress in semiotics, but since that time we have become aware that this paradigmaticized surface is only a level of appearance that hides deeper transformations and my task is to reveal that our text does not just mark time. There is a narrative progress to it.

When we have to deal with a closed text, we must regard it as an entire, completed semiotic object and proceed to its analysis by cutting it up, by segmenting that object into small pieces in order to proceed to reunite the disparate pieces into a whole reconstituting the object's globality. It is easy to see that the first part, the analytical part, would be nugatory if we could not reconstitute later the object. There would be a loss of signification that would not justify our effort – and that, unfortunately, is very often the case with narrative analysis. If we merely project what we know on to the narrative organization without seeking to globalize it, that projection would be at once a scholarly and scholastic exercise.

Now, faced with a textual fact, there has for a while – not for very long – been a fashion of giving titles, or entitling, these texts in order to separate title from text. There is a whole propaedeutics of the relationships between the title and the subjacent narrative text. When, for example, we take a simple thing such as a newspaper item about a run-over dog, we can easily see that the title is nominal in character, it is fairly paradigmatic, whereas the narrative is set forth as a syntagmatic expansion of the title. This by way of example, with the relationships much more complex in our case. We are dealing with morality, something that distinguishes the written from the oral fable – which does not deal in morality. In passing from the oral to the written genre, we have to disjoin the text – why? Because the moral is supposed to represent the deep signification of the fable, but nine times out of ten we see that that deep moral, that deep signification, does not correspond to the signification offered to us, as we obtain it from analysing the text. There is also, on the one hand, an ignorance of the author, and of what he is doing, and, on the other hand, there are often stylistic effects that are designed to displace the moral by a stylistic relationship – let us call it metonymic – *vis-à-vis* the whole. Thus, the beauty of the genre is the creation of such gaps in signification, which is why, in possession of the bare text, we proceeded to a segmentation that was very simple.

That segmentation, whose criterion we picked to be temporal, was laid out in three segments, to which spaces corresponded: spatial units populated by events and characters. Now, starting from there we can distinguish between the graphic space and the imaginary space, which is constructed out of the signifieds. As for this imaginary space, you have already noticed that the parrots are above and the hippos below. If they were not fictional hippos we would say that it was natural that they should be beneath the parrots, since the author tells us that these amorous creatures "happened to be hippopotamuses", that is, it is happenstance, and we could put anything in the place of the hippos; their low position *vis-à-vis* the high position of the parrots therefore signifies something.

This position could be an interesting study from the point of view of the euphoric co-location in our Western culture whereby everything elevated is deemed euphoric and everything cast down, in an abyss, is deemed to be dysphoric. Here, then, from this point of view, we can frame certain texts that are obedient to the cultural sociolect, or even others that are disobedient and reverse the euphoric category. True, this is a small matter – it may not even be worth mentioning. I do so only in passing because I am sure that some of my students have tried to play with this spatial connotation. You can even see that it has given me a pretext for distinguishing the graphic space from space constructed in an imaginary way.

So once this segmentation has been accomplished, we can see that the two parts can be used, each part seemingly symmetrical with respect to the other, and that we thus have a structure we call binary, that is, a two-part binary contrast. Now, space is worthless, it signifies nothing if it is not linked to amorous living characters, to direct actors – which allows me to broaden the characters to include other than humans. Space becomes a signifier only to the extent that it is connected to the appropriate actors, and we can thus see that we have parrot spaces and hippo spaces. That already gives us a binary, poetic structure of narrativity. There is thus a subject and an anti-subject. No need to moralize, agreed? The tactic of moralization, the naming of one of the subjects as a hero and the other as a traitor, comes later, accidentally.

For example, take Hop o' My Thumb – he acts like a traitor, he behaves in exactly the same way as the traitor in Propp's stories, only he is made sympathetic to us. This is, let us say, a surface phenomenon of the second order; the essential thing in a narration or narrative discourse is that there be two subjects, that there be a polemical structure. I believe that this is one of the functioning modes of the human image system – we have to create obstacles in order to surmount them. That is how man imagines his life. I would not dare pronounce on the universality of this category, but it is, I believe, very widespread.

Thus, we are faced with a subject, an anti-subject – we can call them merely $S$ and $\bar{S}$. Now, we can see that on the other hand there are two types of doings, that is, two dimensions along which the narrativity develops. The first dimension, I have called the pragmatic one. I have called pragmatic or occurrential events those that describe behaviours, human actions, at the bodily level of their performance. The pragmatic, however, is not wholly the somatic, since now that I have named this activity the bodily, I could also get a gestural language alongside the occurrential, where this gestural decidedly does not belong. After all, I can make myself understood, by my interlocutor, let us say; I can not only make myself understood, but I can deceive myself or, inversely, conceal certain things with gestures. Well, all that is no longer pragmatics, it is no longer the occurrential, it is already the cognitive.

It is because of this that the terms somatic and bodily do not work to distinguish this genre. We can call this activity occurrential because in the end what is an occurrence, an event? I would naïvely say that an event is the action accomplished by a subject but seen by an observer. Thus, we cannot know events other than by examining the actions, the doings, of subjects. Well, then, if we recognize two kinds of acquired knowledge and two autonomous levels of discourse – the occurrential and cognitive dimensions – we must then distinguish subjects. There are cognitive subjects and subjects of occurrential doing, acting subjects. Now, and at the same time, you have an actor, a person – I do not say *personne*, character – who can simultaneously be the subject of a pragmatic activity and the subject of a cognitive activity. It is in this sense that in this text we are dealing with four subjects. The subjects are not characters – and we must understand this – but syntactical constructs. That is why we can speak of narrative grammar and thus no longer of the doings of characters; and it is in this sense that semiotics begins. It is in the domain of literary criticism that we speak of heroes, of characters; with semiotics there is an organization of positions, no longer of characters. In semiotics we can make distinctions within a single actor by considering that actor as an empty continuum that is progressively filled. You can put two subjects into it. That is why a hippopotamus can be simultaneously the subject of the occurrential doing and the subject of the cognitive doing.

To be sure, often as not he does not exercise both of those doings at the same time, which means that, first, he is busy lovemaking and, next, he watches the parrots doing the same thing. It is all by chance but not really, because the author has wanted it thus. However, we can easily imagine both activities occurring at the same time. I would only point out that in the fifth paragraph of the text, the second sentence – "The tender things they said to each other during the monolithic give-and-take of their courtship sounded as lyric to them as flowers", etc. – shows that at the same time they are busy lovemaking and that their love seems to them like this or that, in other words, they are the cognitive subject of their own doing.

This is a very elementary kind of grammar. There are subjects, there are verbs, predicates. In a sense it is when you have a predicate and a subject that you can make a sentence. In order to distinguish these sentences from the sentences in so-called natural language, we shall call them utterances. Thus we have narrative utterances, and with such narrrative utterances we can write a text, by putting one after the other, and we have the sum of all the utterances appearing as a narrative utterance.

Now we proceed to a homogeneous writing of the text. We can make a representation of the text, and that representation is more abstract; it does not retain overall the manifest text, it is rather a translation of the uttered text, a representation of a certain level of coherence, a certain isotope wherein all the elements are contained and inscribed and that we have selected. Having done this, we should not be accused – semiotics should not be accused – of having expelled lived experience, of not being interested in it. The lived and the felt are not denied or expelled. They are set aside provisionally and then, later, we integrate things in order to reconstruct as well as possible the total thing. That is our procedure – I dare not call it scientific, but rather of scientific intent. Let us understand, finally, semiotics; let us say that semiotics has two components: one, grammar and syntax, and two, a semantics. Now, when we speak of the subject and its doing, we inscribe the whole thing in a kind of narrative syntax. However, we still have to deal with semantics; and that semantics tells us that one of the ways of integrating it consists in saying that the actor is, on the one hand, an actant, i.e. that he plays an actantial role (we know what that means – it is the way in which he is syntactically defined). On the other hand, there is a thematic role, and it is the reunion of the thematic with the actantial role that creates the actor.

That is the experience that can shed light on this concept, and I believe that at first glance it may seen all too obvious or too complicated, but it is perhaps a way of accounting for this text. Thus, we have seen that with regard to the pragmatic, occurrential doing, the two subjects, as pragmatic subjects, exercised what we called amorous doing, lovemaking. So you see that to speak of pragmatic doing, in other words performing actions, means behaving. And if I inject amorous doing, lovemaking, I am adding semantics. Now if you take cognitive doing, you notice also that the two – parrots and hippos – are engaged in a certain cognitive doing, in other words, they are interpreting behaviours in a certain way, and that interpretation is an essentially negative one. We have said that the cognitive doing is denigratory. It consists of speaking ill of someone else. Well, all these are semantic elements that we add to the syntax, and thus, from this viewpoint, you can see the text emerging as a kind of mechanism that has been created in a simple and clear manner. There is only this interchangeability of roles: when the hippos are concerned with lovemaking, the parrots make fun of them; when the parrots are making love, the hippos find it ridiculous. Thus, we are dealing with a recurrent structure. Since the author has warned that these two characters who have tender feelings towards each other happened to be hippos, we can imagine or invent new paragraphs concerning other animals, human beings, and then the story, in principle, would never stop because we are dealing with a recurrent fact that has a kind of actantial distribution, the siting of actants, and I would call this structure an ideology.

I say this to make a distinction from axiology. Let us say you have a semiotic square with life and death (see figure 1). If you add value to the life and non-value to death, or a negative value to death, you then have a small axiologic, and not ideologic system, whereas ideology is already the siting of a device with an actantial distribution. There are subjects, there are designed objects, there are senders, etc. Now you can see that what I have been saying has been from the grammatical point of view. You can see that we can very easily inject semantics and obtain ideological variations. Following the semantic injections that you put into one single model, you will obtain different ideologies, and thus you will have a possible typology of ideologies.

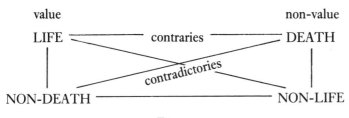

Figure 1

Our own example is clear. The hippos invest tender lovemaking and that is a model of romantic ideology. If you take the parrots, they act like the upper-class bourgeois. This is bourgeois ideology. Mr and Mrs Gray are a married couple, whereas the hippos practise free love. Saying this, we already have a semantic problem, but here I insist on demonstrating what the relations are between syntax and semantics. We can now take a small step forward.

I am going to attempt to prove that if we adhere solely to the interpretation suggested to use by the textual layout – i.e. the repetitions, first the hippos, then the parrots – and so long as we adhere to this recurrence and interchangeability, the textual signification is very clear. These people are stupid. When they are making love they find it completely natural, but when they see others doing so, they find it unnatural and disgusting. Yes, from that we can, let us say, add a pinch of literary spice and see what comes out.

In addition to noticing what occurs in the text, you have obviously noticed that I have spoken also of the cognitive dimension. Armed with the concept of dual dimension, if you reread the text you will notice that, in fact, it almost *never* speaks of occurrential, pragmatic doing. From the first line, you encounter "an arrogant gray parrot and his arrogant mate *listened*". To what are they listening? They are listening to lovemaking, that is, lovemaking is already an utterance subordinated to listening, and finally, what reunites the fact and what creates the continuity of the text is the cognitive, not the occurrential, level, because sometimes the occurrential level disappears, and all that is left is cognitive doing. In the end, if we pose the question in this way, we can see that the text is, finally, speaking about something other than love. It is asking the question: What do we know? How do we know? Under what conditions can we know? What do we know about ourselves? About others? You see, this is what I call the cognitive dimension. Finally you see that we could easily conceive that in place of love, the author could have put another human activity and have obtained the same results. There is a hierarchy of dimensions and of textual readings – the pragmatic ruled by the cognitive.

I have told you already that this narrative is dramatizing cognition. First there is reception, a receptive doing, and I told you that it could at once be classified as active or passive, that with "listen" *vis-à-vis* "hear", "listen" is active and "hear" is passive, so we have possible modalities of this receptive doing. Then, on the other hand, we have emissive, communicative doing, since the parrots and the hippos call in their friends and neighbours and let them in on this astonishing news. Between these two poles of common communication, right in the middle of the text, we see the interpretive part.

There is receipt of a message, which is given here as positive, resounding – but not in the end quite so resounding, since the author describes forms of receiving. You see, therefore, that the reception here is a general cognitive proceeding in which unique news reaches us by all the sensorial channels and not necessarily by sounds alone. The closest thing to logic is to have proof, redundancy of reception. I believe that this is what usually predominates in description, and therefore while the author says "listened", mere listening is not normal. We can therefore say that to "listen" here is only in a metonymic relationship to the receptive doing as a whole.

Now, between the poles, we have the interpretive doing. In other words, after having received the world's message, the interlocutors interpret it, and the threefold dialogue is devoted to that interpretation, and is even the central section of the narrative. We can think what we like about their interpretive doing, but we must not become vexed by it. It is an extremely important activity in human life. Consider, finally: what does a professor of literature do if he does not throughout his life perform such interpretive doing? He interprets texts, as we all know – and here I am speaking only of professors, but in general our life consists in interpreting the words and gestures of others, because we have to know what we are dealing with in our relationships with others in our lives. What they say can be either true or false; the way in which they behave is never presented as raw data, it always calls for a cognitive activity to codify it, to believe it or not believe it. Thus in the text the interpretive period is appropriately longer than the reception or emission.

And so we have the organization of the superficial text, the surface organization. To recap: it is first presented as a binary symmetry, as a projection of the paradigmatic. Each part, since it is composed of two parts, gives an aspectual programme, that is, begins with the receiving of a message from on high, continues with its interpretation and then ends by the emission of a new message, the diffusion of the message. This holds true for each of the parts. And that is the surface. Now, according to certain semioticians, there is where we should stop since we have the organizational principle. Indeed, so long as we remain on the surface, that *is* how things appear and they are fairly satisfying.

## Modalization

I do not reject any of this, but I would draw your attention to the semiotic placement, which must integrate all the levels of explanation and not reject them – only be aware of the textual complexity. Now, then, knowing may be subdivided into instances where the cognitive doing is exercised. You have already remarked that, with regard to the examples I have given, knowing entails an objective complement, knowing is knowing something. Very simply, in this case, we can say that knowing can bear either on others or on oneself. We are going to call that knowledge directed towards others a transitive knowing, while the knowledge about oneself is reflective knowing (see figure 2).

$$S1 \cap 0 \text{ or } \begin{matrix} S_2 \\ S_1 \end{matrix}$$

Figure 2

We have a subject that exercised a knowing and which thus conjoins itself with a knowledge. That is, its object is knowledge, but the object of the knowing can also be $S_2$, that is, another subject, or even $S_1$, oneself. In the latter case, knowing bears on the subject itself, on its being and not on what it does. There is a *conte* of Voltaire in which we are told that the king, having learned so many things, now learns – what? He learns the doing of the hero, and thus, "he shall have my daughter and half my kingdom". His knowing thus bears upon the hero's doing. Now, we almost have the distinction we want. We can apply all this to knowing – not about the others but about oneself. This is typically the definition of reflexive knowing, but reflexive knowing bearing upon doing – and on those who do not know what they are, which is perhaps very grave – a reflective knowing about being. You see, I am making you a typology, giving the elements of a new grammar. I am setting forth a morphology and from that morphology we can construct a syntax.

I believe that these distinctions are practical ones because they replace the concept "conscious". We know how to deal with consciousness, whereas in the text we have a sub-articulation of consciousness. It also might be helpful to think of the narrative of the artist. It is on his doing that all knowing bears, but one cannot speak, so to say, of the direct life of the artist. That life, if it were described, would be described as weak. What is described is the artist's consciousness of weak events, so to say, or unconsciousness of the weak. In such a text, one has a certain typology and already one has a dispensation from taking into consideration either consciousness or unconsciousness. The concept of "unconscious" exists, of course, but it is very difficult to speak simply about, especially from the linguistic point of view. What can we say of a grammar, your English grammar? I believe that grammar is a bit like an iceberg. The mass of this grammar is unconscious but perhaps there are certain parts that you exercise consciously. There are small-natured types, like me for example, who, as soon as they consciously take account of grammatical rules, do not know how to speak any more.

So, pursuing knowing and dispensing with consciousness, and the unconscious, we can also speak of meta-knowing: this is when my knowing bears not on someone's behaviour or his being, but on the knowledge he has, his own knowing. In such a case, we are dealing with a meta-knowing and not a simple knowing. Now this knowing or this meta-knowing can also be transitive or reflexive. When it is a question of a knowledge a subject can have about the knowledge of another subject $S_2$ bearing on itself, it will therefore concern a transitive knowledge. But if it concerns the knowing of a subject $S_1$ bearing on the knowing of subject $S_2$ vis-à-vis and occurrential doing of $S_1$, then in that case it is a question of a reflexive meta-knowing.

Thus, take for example paragraph five, the second line, "and they were oblivious of the scornful comments of their sharp-tongued neighbors". Now, replace "oblivious" with "conscious". So they were conscious and thus they possessed a knowing about the comments, i.e. about the cognitive doing of the anti-subjects bearing upon *their* own doing – not on the doing of the parrots but on that of the hippos.

You see, knowing is in three stages. What I am giving you is a kind of technique that can enable you to resolve the kind of problem that is like a riddle: if I take a piece of chalk and you try to guess which hand it is in, you either guess or you do not. I then change hands. Then in order to guess, you will say to yourself, "Ah, it must be in the other hand now". However, since you think that I think that you think I am putting it in the other hand, I will keep it where it was. And so on. And this can be carried forward indefinitely. This is the psychology of bluff. All of it goes to bring us to the last category, the knowledge-making, *making know*.

If we have an emission, a communication, this is a making know. In this case, making is an optative modality, a making that is active, that consists of rendering possible the transmission of the knowledge-object. We can see that it, too, can bear on such objects as knowing, or on persons. Take persons: you can have a suit made – what does it mean, make a suit be made? It means that we are making the other move, alter, so making know means making the other change knowledge, to yours. From there we can conceive a new domain, a reflection on the manipulation of beings and things.

If we analyse sentences or parts of sentences, it is a question of occurrential doing, of amorous doing, and we see that the hippos are exercising that doing quite naturally. So we have a more or less detailed description. It is, then, a question of what? A question of performance. As I have said, every performance presupposes competence, and in consequence it is not a matter of exercising an amorous doing, but rather, of being competent to exercise it. Indeed, I remember that during one of Jakobson's visits to Paris, the question was strongly debated between Jakobson, Lévi-Strauss and Lacan whether, if two young people had been raised following the precepts of Jean-Jacques Rousseau, "naturally", without knowing the laws of love, could they or could they not exercise amorous doing? This is an eminently metaphysical problem, and the votes were divided, obviously. I recall that Lévi-Strauss was categorical in saying, "No, they cannot make love", whereas Jakobson sided with nature.

So in that connection, let me get back to the hippos. You need a certain competence for any kind of labour, such as shoe-repairing. We can say that the doing of a shoe-repairer is a performance, but that means that the shoe-repairer knows how to and can make shoes. Thus, what I am saying here is that in our text the narrator is speaking not only of amorous doing, but of competence. This competence is implicit and logically presupposed. The same thing would hold true if we were dealing with a fisherman fishing with rod and reel. Even if the writer does not mention his competence, it is presupposed that he knows how, either well or badly; it is not very important which, only that his competence exists. What I mean is that there is a canonical schematics of narrativity in which each performance presupposes competence, but such schematics is not co-extensive with the text. The text can only manifest a small part of the narrative programme, and thus we must not try, as certain people do, to take Propp's model and stick solely to the text we are studying. That is not semiotics. Semiotics is the pure construction of an object the manifestation of which can be partial, or extensive, or hypertrophied.

We have here divided the text into a number of lines. They are disproportionate, but that does not mean that the two parts are not proportional; we have a problem of expansion, of restriction. Thus, what I am saying is that, with regard to occurrential doing, the competence of the subjects is presupposed. Why do I say that? Not just because I want to say it, but because I need this affirmation. If, for the occurrential level, performance presupposes competence, then if we go on to the cognitive level, the same holds true: to exercise a cognitive doing one has to have a cognitive competence. That cognitive competence is, quite simply, Chomsky's competence, pure and simple. You can decompose it: to be competent to speak a natural language is to want to be able and to know how to speak it. Thus, what we are doing is decomposing competence into different modalities and applying it to all human acts, not only the acts of language. The acts of language are only one aspect of human competence. That is in total correspondence with that seventeenth- and eighteenth-century philosophy or psychology of the faculties in which Chomsky sought his competence. He sees himself as a Cartesian – those are his philosophical presuppositions and he does not hide them. Linguists are honest and have no need to hide their references. If someone before you has already thought something, it makes things easier, you no longer have to invent things for yourself.

Now, let us say something about competence. If we are talking about knowing on a cognitive level, it is as though competence consisted of wanting and of being able to know. Take the sentence in paragraph 5, because paragraph 5 is still there to be explained, "But it was spring, and the lover and his lass were young, and they were oblivious of the scornful comments of their sharp-tongued neighbors and they continued to bump each other", etc. What do we have business with? What we have to do with in the first sentence is knowledge of the hippos that bears on the knowing of the parrots. And the knowing of the parrots bears on the lovemaking of the hippos. After this lengthy excursus, I now believe that our sentence is very clear. If you read "and they continued to bump each other", etc., you can see that this second part, which is not co-ordinate, is the description of the hippo's lovemaking. Finally, the next sentence, "The tender things they said to each other during the monolithic . . . sounded to them as flowers", is about what? Reflective knowing by the hippos bearing on the hippos' amorous doing, on their lovemaking.

So there are three sentences, and each has a modal status. In the centre there is the amorous performance that thus presupposes, as I have said, competence. However, this is preceded by a construction on three levels. There is amorous doing, lovemaking; there are the commentaries, that is, the knowledge or knowing of the parrots; and there is the knowing of the hippos *vis-à-vis* the doing of the parrots. But the knowing of the hippos *vis-à-vis* the knowing of the parrots is said how – how is it manifested? "They were oblivious" – as we say in French, they were *"ignorants"* – or they, reflexively, were "self-ignorant". Now let us approach the modalities. They did not want to know; they wanted to act as if the commentary did not exist. I am not betraying the text. We believe that their knowledge exists, but that knowledge is over-modalized by will. Thus, we can describe this situation as not-wanting-to-know about the knowing of others. Whereas in the sentence – "sounded to them as flowers" – there is knowing *vis-à-vis* the very doing of the subjects themselves: now we can speak of the will or non-will of the subject. These modalities presuppose the power of the subject to want to know or not to want to know. However, here it is an active knowing that is being exercised and that is simply denied. And this tells us one of the reasons why we must exclude the problem of consciousness from semiotic research: it is because when we are exercising a structural approach, we not only have knowing, but also non-knowing, which is another term of knowing. In this case we no longer know how to articulate this with consciousness or non-consciousness.

If, thus, the first structure is characterized as being able-to-not-want-to-know, the second is to be able-to-want-to-know, without the object's changing. And if you interpret,

and they were oblivious of the scornful comments . . .

the tender things they said . . . sounded as lyric to them as flowers . . .

if I can put that into a formula, what I mean is that there are two moral propositions that we can translate almost in the following way: if we are capable of not-wanting-to-know, of ignoring what others think of us, we are capable of being conscious of our own doing, our own being, and that is our sentence, i.e. the amorous doing, the lovemaking of the hippos seeming to them like budding flowers, etc. In other words, we can know ourselves so long as we ignore what others think of us.

Once again we have arrived at a great truth that is very simple. What I mean is that simple truths rest on a relatively complex and multi-levelled modal structure. Perhaps I should not leave this first part without saying something about spring. You will have noticed that there is an actor, "spring", who appears here – "but it was spring and the lover and his lass were young", etc. The fact that "spring" precedes "oblivious" clearly indicates that here spring is playing the part of sender. It is the sender who allows them to ignore the comments of the parrots. And when you have spring, you can then understand the last part of this section. There is a whole naturist and romantic imagery represented here that lends a kind of grotesque semantic coloration. What enables me to say that? It is because I am looking at the second part of the text, which deals with the parrots. I can see that the parrots wanted to call the ABI (the African Bureau of Investigation), which would have been their receiver. Here we have an essentially cultural instance, in contrast with spring, a natural instance. So we have once again rediscovered a basic semantic structure, i.e. nature and culture, homologous with life and death. We can also see that the language is not the same. Not only do the parrots not want to understand, not only are they unable to understand, but they cannot tolerate. This is a power language. The sender of the hippos is the sender through will, through desire, whereas here we are dealing with a sender through power, according to the modality of domination. The text is very clearly articulated in this sense.

Now, from the modal point of view, what does our second part mean? "To the Grays, however, the bumbling romp of the lover and his lass was hard to comprehend" – *comprehend:* here we have the form by which knowledge is evidently manifested. Now, "hard" corresponds to the modality of power. Thus I am translating a semantic language by saying that it consists of not-being-able-to-know. Whereas in the first part of the text we were dealing with the negation of wanting, here we have the negation of power. And if we are dealing with the negation of power, things seem very strange. For on the one hand, we can now say that it was difficult for them, impossible for them to comprehend, whereas on the other hand the entire text states that the parrots are sure they can understand. Thus the famous question is put: who is speaking in the text? On the one hand, the parrots are presented as endowed with the competence of being able to want to know. On the other hand, there is the narrator's intrusion into the text, who, in parentheses, states that they do not understand. In other words, here we have the fact that when the parrots think they are able, that they have power, a question comes: is that power true or is it false? Or is it a lie? Now we see that what the narrator, the subject of the utterance, is introducing is an over-modalization with regard to the true and the false, in other words, with regard to secret and lie. The parrots' power appears true to them, but it is not true. Here I have to draw it all inside a small square (see figure 3). I put being as *B* and appearing as *A;* I link appearing to non-appearing and being to non-being. Now, there are things that are and that appear; these are true. Things that do not appear and that are not are false; false and inexistent. Things that are but that do not appear are secret things, and things that appear but that are not are lies. We call this the square of veridiction. This square works at what level? At the level we call uttering. This is the relationship between the subject of uttering and the readers. At the level of the utterance, the text, produced by the same utterer, states that the parrots are sure of their knowledge. Whereas the contract that the subject of the uttering offers to the reader is of quite another sort: "the competence of the parrots is a falsehood, while the competence of the hippos is true", says that contract. It is as if the good Lord had decided to insert marks of the uttering in the text, enabling us to accept the contract offered to us by the introduction of that text.

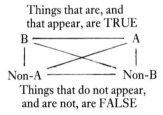

Figure 3

**The uttering**

I earlier said that there is an intervention by the subject of uttering in the sentence "who happened to be hippopotamuses". Let us understand that then, as now, this is no longer the utterance, it is the utterer who intervenes directly to tell us, here the parrots' competence is lie, there the lovers just happened to be hippopotamuses but could have been anything, but were not. I should like to say, briefly, what I think of the subject of the uttering or the utterer, a few words having to do with the would-be scientific semiotic attitude we can adopt. Either we are content with the indications of the text and we say: "Outside the text, no salvation!", or we bring in psychology and psychoanalysis and history and sociology and we no longer have semiotics: there is a great deal of intelligence, genius, but no longer any coherent analysis.

So in addressing this problem, semiotics says that the text is the product, the result of the production of what we call a verbal activity, of someone who is the subject of the uttering. The text is an uttered thing, and every such utterance presupposes an uttering. But the uttered and the uttering do not occur on the same level. The uttering is always implicit. When I formulate the utterance, "The earth is round", the round earth is the thing uttered; my speech act, however, the act of language, is not verbalized. I can say, "I said that the earth is round", but in that case I am presupposing another "I say", saying that the earth is round, and so on. In speaking about true uttering, we can only speak about it as a logical construction, logically presupposed by the existence of the text. I am not saying that the subject of the uttering does not exist; but it is not Thurber, it is everything the text, as utterance, implies, presupposes. Thus the subject of the uttering is the master of ceremonies, but at the same time is outside the text, a set of logical presuppositions.

Now, notice that it is different when it comes to the uttering that is set up within the discourse, because together with "the earth is round" I can say "I said that the earth is round". That *I* is sometimes considered by some semioticians – incorrectly – as the subject of the uttering. That notion is wrong because the *I* of Marcel Proust and Marcel Proust himself are two different things. As a result, a distinction has to be made between the subject of the uttering *per se* and the subject of the uttering already uttered or reported or set up in the discourse. It makes little difference what terminology we use; but it must be remembered that we are dealing with two different things. It is from that point of view that I introduced the subject of the uttering and talked about it, and I have wanted to make clear my theoretical position because this topic gives a lot of trouble to untrained minds. For on the pretext of speaking of the subject of the uttering, people reintroduce all the old psychology, psychoanalysis, etc., and there is no semiotics left. It has taken us twenty years to get rid of the author and biography and all of that – and now all of a sudden we have the subject of the uttering, and we can do just what we used to twenty years ago! Everyone – or nearly everyone – becomes happy, and the professor can say, "Now we don't have to wear ourselves out"!

That is not my way. I say let us modernize the sauce a bit. And I have given you a concrete example so that now we know how the lie, how falsehood functions as the utterer, or uttering, in the text. Finally, it is this level of true and false, of lie and secret, that is the most profound, if you like, hierarchical level, dominating the text. This is a *deus ex machina*, virtually. The decision must be made that the symmetry, as posited at the outset and on the surface of the text as two equal parts, is a false symmetry – false because the hippos are right and the parrots, wrong. Thus, what I call the second reading of the text takes on a very different cast.

Now, based on that, we can perhaps wonder whether there might not be a third reading. It would be introduced by a word I do not like very much because I do not know its definition: irony. The irony that kills the text, that, in this sense, is the higher form of negation. And since the author is speaking about hippos, on the one hand we have this whole metaphorization of capsized bathtubs and overturned moving-vans, but, on the other hand, there is the amorous isotope of flowers in bud and so on, a whole bursting spring-time. In spite of the reading we previously undertook, which is inscribed in the text, there are still new words like "capsized bathtub" . . . the text capsizes, and the result of the final signification of the text is derision. In other words, both couples are derisory and the whole thing is meaningless. Irony negates the signification that is posited.

And there I shall stop.

# Part III

# Signs of Life

# Nel Mezzo del Cammin di Nostra Vita

"In the middle of the path of our life." This is the beginning of Dante's *Divine Comedy*. Of course, this middle of our life, this middle of the path of our life, it's clearly not an arithmetic point, is it? It's not a geometric middle. How would I know the total quantity of my life so as to divide it in two? Consequently, the middle of the path of my life is a point that I would call *semantic*. It is the moment when there is produced in my life, the moment, whenever it happens, perhaps extremely late, perhaps a few days or a few months or a few years before my death, little matter, but this moment when there is produced in my life the call for a new meaning, the active desire for a mutation, to change the life, to inaugurate, to undertake an initiation, such precisely as Dante plunging into the *selva oscura* under the direction of a great initiator, Virgil.

(Roland Barthes, "Proust and Me")

# MICHEL FOUCAULT

# Sexuality and Solitude

In a work consecrated to the moral treatment of madness and published in 1840, a French psychiatrist, Louren, tells of the manner in which he treated one of his patients – treated and, of course, as you may imagine, cured. One morning he placed Mr A., his patient, in a shower room. He makes him recount in detail his delirium.

"But all that", says the doctor, "is nothing but madness. Promise me not to believe in it any more."

The patient hesitates, then promises.

"That's not enough," replies the doctor. "You've already made me similar promises and you have not kept them."

And he turns on the cold shower above the patient's head.

"Yes, yes! I am mad!" the patient cries.

The shower is turned off. The interrogation is resumed.

"Yes, I recognize that I am mad", the patient repeats. But he adds: "I recognize it because you are forcing me to do so."

Of course another shower.

"I assure you," says the patient, "that I have heard voices and seen enemies around me."

Another shower.

"Well then," says Mr A., "I admit it. I am mad and all that was nothing but madness."

And of course he is cured.

To make somebody suffering from mental illness recognize that he is mad is a very ancient procedure in traditional therapy. In the works of the seventeenth and eighteenth centuries, one finds many examples of what one might call truth therapies. But the technique used by Louren is altogether different. Louren is not trying to persuade his patient that his ideas are false or unreasonable. What happens in the head of Mr A. is a matter of perfect indifference for Louren.

The doctor wishes to obtain a precise act, the explicit affirmation: "I am mad." Since I first read this passage of Louren, about twenty years ago, I kept in mind the project of analysing the form and the history of such a bizarre practice. Louren is satisfied when and only when his patient says: "I am mad", or "That was madness." Louren's assumption is that madness as a reality disappears when the patient asserts the truth and says that he is mad.

We have, then, the reverse of the performative speech act. The affirmation destroys in the speaking subject the reality which made the same affirmation true. What conception of truth of discourse and of subjectivity is taken for granted in this strange and yet widespread practice? In order to justify the attention I am giving to what is seemingly so specialised a subject, let me take a step back for a moment. In the years that preceded the Second World War, and even more so after the war, philosophy in continental Europe and in France was dominated by the philosophy of subject. I mean that philosophy took as its task *par excellence* the foundation of all knowledge and the principle of all signification as stemming from the meaningful subject. The transcendence of the ego reigned. The importance given to this question was, of course, due to the impact of Husserl, but the centrality of the subject was also tied to an institutional context, for the French university, since philosophy began with Descartes, could only advance in a Cartesian manner. But we must also take into account the political conjuncture. Given the absurdity of wars, slaughters and despotism, it seemed to be up to the individual subject to give meaning to his existential choices. With the leisure and distance that came after the war, this emphasis on the philosophy of subject no longer seemed so self-evident. Hitherto hidden theoretical paradoxes could no longer be avoided. This philosophy of consciousness had paradoxically failed to found a philosophy of knowledge, and especially of scientific knowledge. Also, this philosophy of meaning had failed to take into account the formative mechanisms of signification and the structure of systems of meaning.

With the all too easy clarity of hindsight, let me say that there were two possible paths that led beyond this philosophy of subject. The first of these was the theory of objective knowledge as an analysis of systems of meaning, of semiology. This was the path of logical positivism. The second was that of a certain school of linguistics, psychoanalysis and anthropology – all grouped under the rubric of structuralism. These were not the directions I took. I have tried to explore another direction. I have tried to get out from the philosophy of the subject, through a genealogy of the modern subject as a historical and cultural reality. That means as something which can eventually change, which is, of course, politically important. One can proceed with this general project in two ways. In dealing with modern theoretical constructions, we are concerned with the subject in general. In this way, I have tried to analyse the theories of subject as a speaking, living, working being in the seventeenth and eighteenth centuries. One can also deal with the more practical understanding found in those institutions where certain subjects became objects of knowledge and at the same time objects of domination: asylums, prisons and so on.

I wished to study those forms of understanding which the subject creates about himself. But since I started with this last type of problem, I have been obliged to change my mind on several points. Let me introduce a kind of autocritique. It seems, according to some suggestions of Habermas, that one can distinguish three major types of techniques: the techniques which permit one to produce, to transform, to manipulate things; the techniques which permit one to use sign systems; and finally, the techniques which permit one to determine the conduct of individuals, to impose certain ends or objectives. That is to say, techniques of production, techniques of signification or communication, and techniques of domination. But I became more and more aware that in all societies there is another type of technique: techniques which permit individuals to affect, by their own means, a certain number of operations on their own bodies, their own souls, their own thoughts, their own conduct, and this in a manner so as to transform themselves, modify themselves, and to attain a certain state of perfection, happiness, purity, supernatural power. Let us call these kinds of techniques technologies of the self.

If one wants to analyse the genealogy of subject in Western civilization, one has to take into account not only techniques of domination, but also techniques of the self. One has to show the interaction between these two types of self. When I was studying asylums, prisons and so on, I perhaps insisted too much on the techniques of domination. What we call discipline is something really important in this kind of institution. But it is only one aspect of the art of governing people in our societies. Having studied the field of power relations taking domination techniques as a point of departure, I should like, in the years to come, to study power relations, especially in the field of sexuality, starting from the techniques of the self. In every culture, I think, this self-technology implies a set of truth obligations: learning what is truth, discovering the truth, being enlightened by truth, telling the truth. All these are considered important either for the constitution or for the transformation of the self.

Now, what about truth as a duty in our Christian societies? As everybody knows, Christianity is a confession. This means that Christianity belongs to a very special type of religion – those which impose obligations of truth on those who practise them. Such obligations in Christianity are numerous. For instance, there is the obligation to hold as truth a set of propositions which constitute dogma, the obligation to hold certain books as a permanent source of truth, obligations to accept the decisions of certain authorities in matters of truth. But Christianity requires another form of truth obligation. Everyone in Christianity has the duty to explore who he is, what is happening within himself, the faults he may have committed, the temptations to which he is exposed. Moreover, everyone is obliged to tell these things to other people, and hence to bear witness against himself.

These two ensembles of obligation – those regarding the faith, the book, the dogma, and those regarding the self, the soul and the heart – are linked together. A Christian needs the light of faith when he wants to explore himself, and conversely, his access to the truth cannot be conceived of without the purification of the soul. Maybe you will object that you can find the same two obligations in Buddhism. The Buddhist also has to go to the light and discover the truth about himself. But the relation between these two obligations is quite different in Buddhism and in Christianity. In Buddhism, it is the same type of enlightenment which leads you to discover what you are and what is the truth. In this simultaneous enlightenment of yourself and the truth, you discover in Buddhism that your self was only an illusion. In Christianity, these two types of truth obligation, the one concerned with access to light and the one concerned with discovering truth inside oneself, have always kept a relative autonomy – even after Luther and Protestantism.

I should also like to underline that the Christian discovery of the self does not reveal the self as an illusion. It gives place to a task which cannot be anything else but undefined. This task has two objectives. First, there is the task of clearing up all the illusions, temptations and seductions which can occur in the mind, and discovering the reality of what is going on within ourselves. Secondly, one has to get free from any attachment to this self, not because the self is an illusion, but because the self is much too real. The more we discover the truth about ourselves, the more we have to renounce ourselves; and the more we want to renounce ourselves the more we need to bring to light the reality of ourselves. That is what we could call the spiral of truth formulation and reality renouncement which is at the heart of the Christian techniques of the self.

Recently, Professor Peter Brown stated to me that what we have to understand is why it is that sexuality became, in Christian cultures, the seismograph of our subjectivity. It is a fact, a mysterious fact, that in this indefinite spiral of truth and reality in the self sexuality has been of major importance since the first centuries of our era. It has become more and more important. Why is there such a fundamental connection between sexuality, subjectivity and truth obligation?

Our point of departure is a passage of St Francois de Sales. Here is the text in a translation made in the beginning of the seventeenth century:

I will tell you a point of the elephant's honesty. An elephant never changes his mate. He loves her tenderly. With her he couples not, but from three years to three years. And that only for five days, and so secretly that he is never seen in the act. But the sixth day, he shows himself abroad again, and the first thing he does is to go directly to some river and wash his body, not willing to return to his troupe of companions till he be purified. Be not these goodly and honest qualities in a beast by which he teaches married folk not to be given too much to sensual and carnal pleasures?

Everybody may recognize here the pattern of decent sexual behaviour: monogamy, faithfulness and procreation as the main, or maybe the single, justification of sexual acts – sexual acts which remain, even in such conditions, intrinsically impure. Most of us are inclined, I think, to attribute this pattern either to Christianity or to modern Christian society as it developed under the influence of capitalist or so-called bourgeois morality. But what struck me when I started studying this pattern is the fact that one can find it also in Latin and even Hellenistic literature. One finds the same ideas, the same words, and eventually the same reference to the elephant. It is a fact that the pagan philosophers in the first centuries before and after the death of Christ proposed a sexual ethics which was partly new but which was very similar to the alleged Christian ethics. It has been very convincingly stressed that this philosophical pattern of sexual behaviour, this elephant pattern, was at that time the only one to exist.

During this period we may witness an evolution towards the nuclear family, real monogamy, faithfulness between married people and distress about sexual acts. The philosophical campaign in favour of the elephant pattern was both an affect and an adjunct of this transformation. If these assumptions are correct, we have to concede that Christianity did not invent this code of sexual behaviour. Christianity accepted it, reinforced it, and gave to it a much larger and more widespread strength than it had before. But the so-called Christian morality is nothing more than a piece of pagan ethics inserted into Christianity. Shall we say then that Christianity did not change the state of things? The thesis I propose is that early Christians introduced important changes, if not in the sexual code itself, at least in the relationships everyone has to his own sexual activity. Christianity proposed a new type of experience of oneself as a sexual being.

To make things clearer, I shall compare two texts. One was written by Artemidorus, a pagan philosopher of the third century, and the other is the well-known fourteenth book of the *City of God* by Augustine. Artemidorus wrote a book about the interpretation of dreams in the third century after the death of Christ, but he was a pagan. Three chapters of this book are devoted to sexual dreams. What is the meaning, or, more precisely, what is the prognostic value, of a sexual dream? It is significant that Artemidorus interpreted dreams in a way contrary to Freud, and gives an interpretation of sexual dreams in terms of economics, social relations, success and reverses in political activity and everyday life. For instance, if you dream that you have sex with your mother, that means that you will succeed as a magistrate, since your mother is obviously the symbol of your city or country.

It is also significant that the social value of the dream does not depend on the nature of the sexual act, but mainly on the social status of the partners. For instance, for Artemidorus it is not important in your dream whether you had sex with a girl or with a boy. The problem is to know if the partner was rich or poor, young or old, slave or free, married or not. Of course, Artemidorus takes into account the question of the sexual act, but he sees it only from the point of view of the male. The only act he knows or recognizes as sexual is penetration. Penetration is for him not only a sexual act, but is part of the social role of a man in a city. I would say that for Artemidorus sexuality is relational, and that sexual relations cannot be dissociated from social relations.

Let us now turn to Augustine's text, whose meaning is the point at which we strive to arrive in our analysis. In *The City of God,* and later on in the *Contra Julian,* Augustine gives a rather horrifying description of the sexual act. He sees the sexual act as a kind of spasm. All the body, says Augustine, is shaken by terrible jerks. One entirely loses control of oneself. This sexual act takes such a complete and passionate possession of the whole man, both physically and emotionally, that what results is the keenest of all pleasures on the level of sensations, and at the crisis of excitement it practically paralyses all power of deliberate thought. It is worthwhile to note that this description is not an invention of Augustine: you can find the same in the medical and pagan literature of the previous century. Moreover Augustine's text is almost the exact transcription of a passage written by a well-known pagan philosopher, Cicero in Otensius.

The surprising point is not that Augustine would give such a classical description of the sexual act, but the fact that, having made such a horrible description, he then admits that sexual relations could have taken place in Paradise before the Fall. This is all the more remarkable since Augustine is one of the first Christian Fathers to admit this possibility. Of course, sex in Paradise could not have the epileptic form which we unfortunately know now. Before the Fall, Adam's body, every part of it, was perfectly obedient to the soul and the will. If Adam wanted to procreate in Paradise, he could do it in the same way and with the same control as he could, for instance, sow seeds in the earth. He was not involuntarily excited. Every part of his body was like the fingers, which one can control in all their gestures. Sex was a kind of hand gently sowing the seed. But what happened with the Fall? Adam rose up against God with the first sin. Adam tried to escape God's will and to acquire a will of his own, ignoring the fact that the existence of his own will depended entirely on the will of God. As a punishment of this revolt and as a consequence of this will to will independently from God, Adam lost control of himself. He wanted to acquire an autonomous will, and lost the ontological support for that will. That then became mixed in an indissociable way with involuntary movements, and this weakening of Adam's will had a disastrous effect. His body, and parts of his body, stopped obeying his commands, revolted against him, and the sexual parts of his body were the first to rise up in this disobedience. The famous gesture of Adam covering his genitals with a fig leaf is, according to Augustine, not due to the simple fact that Adam was ashamed of their presence, but to the fact that his sexual organs were moving by themselves without his consent. Sex in erection is the image of man revolted against God. The arrogance of sex is the punishment and consequence of the arrogance of man. His uncontrolled sex is exactly the same as what he himself has been towards God – a rebel.

Why have I insisted so much on what may be nothing more than one of those exegetic fantasies of which Christian literature has been so prodigal? I think this text bears witness to the new type of relationship which Christianity established between sex and subjectivity. Augustine's conception is still dominated by the theme and form of male sexuality. But the main question is not, as it was in Artemidorus, the problem of penetration: it is the problem of erection. As a result, it is not the problem of a relationship to other people, but the problem of the relationship of oneself to oneself, or, more precisely, the relationship between one's will and involuntary assertions.

The principle of autonomous movements of sexual organs is called libido by Augustine. The problem of libido, of its strength, origin and effect, thus becomes the main issue of one's will. It is not an external obstacle to the will. It is a part, an internal component, of the will. And it is not the manifestation of petty desires. Libido is the result of one's will when it goes beyond the limits God originally set for it. As a consequence, the means of the spiritual struggle against libido do not consist, as with Plato, in turning our eyes upwards and memorizing the reality we have previously known and forgotten. The spiritual struggle consists, on the contrary, in turning our eyes continuously downwards or inwards in order to decipher, among the movements of the soul, which ones come from the libido. The task is at first indefinite, since libido and will can never be substantially dissociated from one another. And this task is not only an issue of mastership but also a question of diagnosis of truth and illusion. It requires a permanent hermeneutics of oneself.

In such a perspective, sexual ethics imply very strict truth obligations. These do not only consist in learning the rules of a moral sexual behaviour, but also in constantly scrutinizing ourselves as libidinal beings. Shall we say that after Augustine we experience our sex in the head? Let us say at least that in Augustine's analysis we witness a real libidinization of sex. Augustine's moral theology is, to a certain extent, a systematization of a lot of previous speculation, but it is also an ensemble of spiritual techniques. The techniques were mainly developed in the ascetic milieu and monastic institutions, and those relayed by the Augustinian theory of libido had, I think, a huge influence on Western technologies of the self. I shall be very brief about those spiritual techniques.

When one reads the ascetic and monastic literature of the fourth and fifth centuries, one cannot but be struck by the fact that these techniques are not directly concerned with the effective control of sexual behaviour. There is very little mention of homosexual relations, in spite of the fact that most ascetics lived in permanent and numerous communities. The techniques were mainly concerned with the stream of thoughts flowing into consciousness, disturbing, by their multiplicity, the necessary unity of contemplation, and secretly conveying images or suggestions from Satan. The monk's task was not the philosopher's task: to acquire mastership over oneself by the definite victory of the will. It was perpetually to control one's thoughts, examining them to see if they were pure, whether something dangerous was not hiding in or behind them, if they were not conveying something other than what primarily appeared, if they were not a form of illusion and seduction. Such data have always to be considered with suspicion; they need to be scrutinized and tested.

According to Cassian, for instance, one has to be towards oneself as a money-changer who has to try the coins he receives. Real purity is not acquired when one can lie down with a young and beautiful boy without even touching him, as Socrates did with Alcibiades. A monk was really chaste when no impure image occurred in his mind, even during the night, even during dreams. The criterion of purity does not consist in keeping control of oneself even in the presence of the most desirable people: it consists in discovering the truth in oneself and defeating the illusions in oneself, in cutting out the images and thoughts one's mind produces continuously. Hence the axis of the spiritual struggle against impurity.

The main question of sexual ethics has moved from relations to people, and from the penetration model, to the relation to oneself and to the erection problem: I mean the set of internal movements which develop from the first and nearly imperceptible thought to the final but still solitary pollution, through those ascetic techniques, as through the Augustinian theology. However different and eventually contradictory they were, a common effect was elicited. Sexuality, subjectivity and truth were strongly linked together. This, I think, is the religious framework in which the masturbation problem – which was nearly ignored or at least neglected by the Greeks, who considered that masturbation was a thing for slaves and for satyrs, but not for free citizens – in our society is one of the main issues of sexual life.

FREDRIC JAMESON

# The Realist Floor-Plan

The hypothesis to be tested in the following essay is a conception of the moment of novelistic "realism" as the literary equivalent (both on the level of discourse and on that of "realistic" narrative) of what Deleuze and Guattari (in the *Anti-Oedipus*) call "decoding": the secularization of the older sacred codes, the systematic dissolution of the remaining traces of the hierarchical structures which very unequally and over many centuries characterized the organization of life and practices under the *ancien régime* and even more distantly under feudalism itself. The process is evidently at one with the whole philosophical programme of secularization and modernization projected by the Enlightenment *philosophes*, who thematize it essentially in terms of the defence of nascent science and the elimination of superstition or error, as well as the subversion of the older forms of theological power in the church and the monarchy.

I call this enormous process of decoding on all levels the *bourgeois cultural revolution*: a formulation which suggests that we cannot be content with a merely negative account of the whole Enlightenment demolition programme, but must also attempt to convey what "positively" was set in place in the moment of desacralization. Even on a first approach, one would assume the emergence of a new space and a new temporality, a whole new realm of measurability and Cartesian extension, as well as of measurable clock time, a realm of the infinite geometrical grid, of homogeneity and equivalence.

All this can be said in a somewhat different way if we pause to interrogate the function of the writers and the artists of this transitional period, and the culture they produce, in that immense "great transformation", in which the production of legitimizing ideologies by the philosophers, journalists and scientists is only one component. The artists also are to be seen as *ideologues* but not in the narrow and debunking sense of the producers of false consciousness: their service to ideology in the vastest sense of daily practices is a virtually demiurgic one, the production of a whole new world – on the level of the symbolic and imaginary – which will henceforth constitute the objective lived appearance of that equally objective production of the infrastructure of the emergent market system of industrial capitalism. What is at stake in their cultural production is therefore the retraining, the collective re-education, of a whole population whose mentalities and habits were formed in the previous mode of production, feudalism or the *ancien régime*. This is of course, no punctual event, and in the case of this particular "transition" extends from the sixteenth century (Weber's Protestant ethic is one of the early key mechanisms in such a cultural revolution) all the way to the late nineteenth century in France, in which a landed aristocracy and an old agriculture still largely survive. (Indeed, under the direction of what is euphemistically called "modernization", this particular cultural revolution is still going on in the Third World today, although sometimes combined, in the sense of Trotsky's permanent revolution and "uneven development", with a more properly socialist cultural revolution.)

In general, only the negative or destructive features of the bourgeois cultural revolution have been insisted on: most particularly the vast demolition efforts of the Enlightenment *philosophes*, as they seek to clear a space for what will become contemporary science. But the positive features of such a revolution are no less significant, and essentially include the whole new life world to which people are to be retrained: a new form of space, whose homogeneity abolishes the old heterogeneities of various forms of sacred space – transforming a whole world of qualities and libidinal intensities into the merely psychological experience of what Descartes called "secondary sensations", and setting in their place the grey world of quantity and extension, of the purely measurable – together with the substitution of the older forms of ritual, sacred or cyclical time by the new physical and measurable temporality of the clock and the routine, of the working day. In this sense, we may go even further in our account of the ideological mission of the nineteenth century realistic novelists, and assert that their function is not merely to produce new mental and existential habits, but in a virtual or symbolic way to produce this whole new spatial and temporal configuration itself: what will come to be called "daily life", the *Alltag*, or, in a different terminology, the "referent" – so many diverse characterizations of the new configuration of public and private spheres or space in classical or market capitalism. When we think of the genealogy of the Renaissance city itself, which derived from the painters' invention of perspective, itself derived from late medieval theatrical space, this productive function of the novelists may seem less paradoxical: at least it usefully underscores the active role of Flaubert's linguistic revolution, and offers a characterization of "realism" less passive than the conventional notions of "reflexion", "representation" and the like.

But something else follows from our initial hypothesis, namely, that we must not be content to model this process as two distinct and discontinuous moments, related to each other only by the rubble of some incomprehensible restructuration. Rather, recoding, realism, desacralization (what I shall call in a moment the production of the referent and of daily life) is all to be seen as a production process in which the older forms and structures now serve as the *raw materials* to be worked over and transformed into the new system. The two moments of the *ancien régime* and the bourgeois market system are therefore here to be described as a synchronic coexistence, as a dialectical surcharge, in which old and new find themselves locked at every instant in a grisly cannibalization: the new drawing its vitality from the old and draining it off, as has often been pointed out by those who have perceived the degree to which the culture of capital – the most sterile of all human cultures – is constantly obliged to renew itself by drawing on more vital precapitalist forms.

I have found it useful to describe this process as the virtual production of the referent or of daily life in order to underscore the radical difference between the secular life of modern times and the industrial city, in this immense new world which has become one gigantic factory, and the older kinds of communal experience which organized the life of the village or the peasant or aristocratic *Gemeinschaft* (and still minimally do so, as John Berger's account of peasant life in *Pig Earth* vividly conveys). As for the referent itself, the sense of raw data existing objectively out there, the object so radically sundered from the subject that our language and symbolic systems can do no more than designate it from afar, it is for modern linguistics and post-structuralism a myth, a mirage, or an ideology. Indeed, the text we are about to examine, from Flaubert's tale *Un Coeur simple*, is particularly strategic at this point, since it was the occasion for Roland Barthes' most powerful attack on precisely the concept of reference and realism, in his article *"L'effet de réel"* (in *Communications*, vol. II, 1968). From my own point of view, however, which is that of a radical historicism, we can bracket the truth-claims of both positions, of the nineteenth-century "belief" in science and the referent, as well as of late-twentieth-century scepticism in this respect. What is significant for us, even if reference is taken to be a mirage, lies in the "reality of the appearance" and the way in which belief in reference governs the practices of nineteenth-century daily life and of the nineteenth-century "realistic" aesthetic. But historicism will also want to bracket or to estrange the "beliefs" of the late-twentieth-century linguistics and post-structuralism as well: and indeed, in our subsequent exhibits, one of the key stories we shall have to tell will be very precisely the curious and complex, dialectical ways in which the referent has slowly been effaced again.

This is, however, the moment to turn to the text itself, which is a description of the provincial house in which the maid Félicité will pass the rest of her earthly existence:

Cette maison, revêtue d'ardoises, se trouvait entre un passage et une ruelle aboutissant à la rivière. Elle avait intérieurement des différences de niveau qui faisaient trébucher. Un vestibule étroit séparait la cuisine de la *salle* où Madame Aubain se tenait tout le long du jour, assise près de la croisée dans un fauteuil de paille. Contre le lambris, peint en blanc, s'alignaient huit chaises d'acajou. Un vieux piano supportait, sous un baromètre, un tas pyramidal de boîtes et de cartons. Deux bergères de tapisserie flanquaient la cheminée en marbre jaune et de style Louis XV.

La pendule, au milieu, représentait un temple de Vesta, – et tout
l'appartement sentait un peu le moisi, car le plancher était plus bas que le
jardin.

[This house had a slate roof and stood between an alley-way and a lane
leading down to the river. Inside there were differences in level which
were the cause of many a stumble. A narrow entrance-hall separated the
kitchen from the parlour, where Madame Aubain sat all day long in a
wicker easy-chair by the window. Eight mahogany chairs were lined up
against the white-painted wainscoting, and under the barometer stood
an old piano loaded with a pyramid of boxes and cartons. On either side
of the chimney piece, which was carved out of yellow marble in the Louis
Quinze style, there was a tapestry-covered armchair, and in the middle
was a clock designed to look like a temple of Vesta. The whole room smelt
a little musty, as the floor was on a lower level than the garden.]

We must look at a description of this kind in a new way, as a form of
programming. The house itself is a pretext, and in that sense Barthes was not
wrong to isolate a detail from this paragraph as his central illustration for what
he calls "*l'effet de réel*", a purely connotative function in which a wealth of
*contingent* details – without any symbolic meaning – emit the signal, "this is
reality", or better still, "this is realism". Balzac's houses are indeed so many
signs: materiality in Balzac, the quantities of objects and descriptions which
freight the lengthy preparatory work of a Balzacian narrative, are in this sense
quite unmaterial, and when examined closely have all the transparency of the
sign or symbol – designating meanings, serving as shorthand for the social
condition of the inhabitants or for their moral qualities. This is not noticeably
the case with the Flaubert description in question here: on the other hand, it is
difficult to accept Barthes' conception of an empty sign – a passage which
would function as pure connotation without any denotative content (inasmuch
as for him this content is contingent, or meaningless, anything would do, any
house would do).

Our characterization of the work of Flaubert's *écriture* as a form of
programmation – as unlovely as this terminology may be – will allow us to
isolate some of these mechanisms in a way which is usefully distinct either from
stylistic analysis (which presupposes the modernist aesthetic of a unique
personal style) or from current forms of structural analysis which essentially
foreground the systemic content of such texts.

The active remoulding of the reader's "mentality" begins at once, with a
sentence in which the central object – the house – is immediately decentred by
its twin boundaries, the alley-way and the lane. The only thing we are told
about the ostensible object of description in this initial sentence concerns its
roofing; and roofs obviously also at once empty down into the adjacent spaces,
spilling the reader with them. This "dominant" is clearly an abstract form: it
does not yield qualities or adjectives of any kind, but rather sensitizes us to the
empty fact of a dual system of proximate levels, levels which are neither liminal

nor forms of closure, which have no particular content in their own right but function simply as the parallel lines of a grid. What is imposed on the reading mind here is a training in uneven surfaces, in the abstract, empty feeling for the inequality of adjacent co-ordinates.

This characterization may well seem an excessive deduction from the relatively impoverished data of the initial sentence: it is, however, largely confirmed by the second, which rematerializes the abstract form of this experience in terms of "*différences de niveau*" – virtually the first information we are given about the interior of the house, and surely a peculiar feature by which to introduce it. Yet the "stumbling" over this uneven surface subliminally inscribes this empty form on the reading body itself: the sentence is no longer inert or denotative, but has gestural content and energy: this tripping over the levels within the house is thus what Bakhtin calls a chronotope – a spatio-temporal unity – albeit a deliberately anonymous one, belonging to no particular individual or character of the tale, an experience of the Heideggerian "man" or nobody, which is thus fully as abstract as the empty form which it undertakes to dramatize for us.

A dual system of parallel lines, an abstract experience of sheer unevenness extending in all directions: let us relate all this to Cosimo Tura's painting *Flight into Egypt* and grasp these two parallel lines as analogous to the stripes of Joseph's switch on the donkey's flanks, an alteration meant to drive the donkey forward in a straight line, just as it here programmes the reader to drive forward head-on into the infinite space of Cartesian extension. All this now combines in the third sentence to model the interior of the house as a dual and uneven world: the kitchen on the one side (uncharacterized, yet already marked by our knowledge of the central character of the tale to come, whose privileged space this is) and the parlour on the other, in which the mistress passes her days looking out of the window, much like Proust's Tante Léonie. This comparison reinforces a significant distinction that must be stressed between the empty form or spatial grid in question here and the conventional "structural" conception of a binary opposition. The latter is a form of closure, in which the twin terms are fatally asymmetrical to each other, and enforce a generally repressive system of essential and inessential terms, of self and other, or centre and margin: the binary opposition thereby becomes the generator or marginality and marginalization in general. But we have already noted that the "boundaries" of the house are not closed limits of this kind: the space of extension stretches far beyond "alley-way" and "lane" to include the village and ultimately France and Europe itself. "Alley-way" and "lane" are thus not marked terms of the binary type, and what is generated by their juxtaposition is a system of dual inequality, a most unstable dualism in which "two" is not a meaningful unit in itself, but rather a deconstructive weapon against "one", against the conception of the house as a central substance in its own right.

This is why it would be a mistake to assume that the third sentence of our paragraph, in which the inhabitants of the house finally seem to make their appearance, has as its primary function the expression of some hierarchical relationship of domination between mistress and servant. Domination and hierarchy are certainly present, but of a peculiarly decentred kind, as I now want to show. Félicité is, of course, so far present only as the "implied subject" of the kitchen space; but this shadowy absence is emblematic enough of her marginalization throughout the tale, which insistently stages her life by proxy through the children and destinies of the family she serves, and later on, through the metonymic–metaphoric displacement of her libido onto the wellnigh Benjaminian allegorical relics of that family history.

I think that it is important for interpretive purposes, however, to understand the peculiar class position of servants as such in this world, who are neither working-class people (with at least a potentiality for a genuine, centred class culture of their own) nor peasants – a class position explicitly abandoned by Félicité in the opening pages of our story. An adequate social and historical interpretation of Félicité's peculiar vacancy is possible only if we keep in mind the uniquely parasitical situation of the *servidumbre* of these periods, who can attain no class consciousness of their own, but must necessarily in one way or another reflect the class consciousness of their masters.

On the other hand – and this is equally crucial – it would be a great mistake to read Madame Aubain as a simple representation of the place of the master, whether the latter is understood as a decaying feudal aristocracy or an emergent business or bourgeois caste. The master, in that sense, is dead; his place is vacant: it is not Madame Aubain's class affiliation but her status as a woman which assigns her a position not less marginalized than that of her own servant. She also lives by proxy, her affairs managed by a male surrogate, whose very defection is itself another demonstration of her marginality. Indeed, a more ambitious study of the social investments of Flaubert's libido – the privileged relationship between woman's experience, as in *Madame Bovary* itself, and the construction of narrative – would probably explain this affinity less in terms of sexuality than in terms of social marginalization. At any rate, the twin and parallel spaces of kitchen and parlour – however binary and hierarchical with respect to one another – are in their symbiosis both uniquely marginalized and decentred by this new space of infinite divisibility, a space which knows no sacred centres any longer, and which might, following Sartre, be described as the space of seriality, of serial flight, in which the centre is always *elsewhere*.

But then this makes for an unusual compositional problem: Flaubert will have to describe the contents of this ec-centric room, and convey the latter's structural displacement in what must remain essentially positive terms, terms of existing things, terms of a present of visible contents. It is the solution to this dilemma which we observe in the next four sentences, beginning with the chairs, which, counted up and indifferently substitutable for one another, become detached from their blank support, as though the room were nothing but a wall on which they were hung when not in use: an additive space is here clearly replacing an organic or qualitative one.

Yet this cultural revolution – this infinite process of quantification, before which the older primary perceptual qualities dry up and evaporate, this universal process of what Max Weber called *"Entzauberung"*, the disenchant-ment or the desacralization of the older pre-capitalist life world – such a cultural revolution does not make its way without certain resistances, which are slyly registered in Flaubert's text. Thus, in our next three sentences, it is *culture* which stages a holding operation, a desperate pitched battle of resistance. This resistance can essentially be described as the attempt to recentre space, to stem the serial flight of infinite divisibility, to pull back the contents of the room into a genuine centred hierarchy. So in the second of these two moments, the mantelpiece draws the two armchairs around itself in an elaborated version of that "pyramidal structure" already emerging in the first sentence, that "crowns" the piano. But such an operation demands the power of a specified agency; it is scarcely an automatic momentum that can resist the momentum of quantifi-cation under its own steam – it needs the rallying point of some ideological slogan, in short, it needs content.

The agency of our first sentence here is, of course, the barometer, well known from Roland Barthes' remarks on the subject in his essay "L'effet de réel". I find that my own reading is perturbed by a very peculiar slippage from barometer to metronome; and it would be interesting to see whether other people find the sentence rewriting itself in those terms against its and their own will. None the less, the barometer itself proves to be a most ambiguous symbol of resistance indeed, marking if anything the triumph of science and measurement over the older cyclical and qualitative time of the seasons. In the next two sentences, therefore, a more symbolic and ideological slogan or pretext will be devised: a most classical bourgeois solution indeed, which always finds it convenient to identify the opposite of science as *culture*, in the most limited and pejorative senses of that term. Now the realignment of space, the two armchairs flanking the mantelpiece, will be staged under the sign of bourgeois taste – the temple of Vesta – kitsch culture, the cultural bric-à-brac and decorative allusion to which, in the new middle-class world, the great collective styles of the past are reduced. It is not inappropriate here, I feel, to juxtapose this dramatic moment of Flaubert's paragraph with Heidegger's account, in *The Origins of the Work of Art*, of the sacred temple as the recentring of the world and deconcealment of being itself. To that august collective and social function of the temple in the ancient *polis*, Flaubert's art-object makes a trivializing and desolately ironic allusion.

But the problem with the little temple of Vesta can be underscored in another way, by remaining within the text itself – for this decorative emblem houses that very different thing, the clock: which, like the barometer or metronome, is as E. P. Thompson and others have shown, one of the prime agencies for the rationalization of time and the organization of the modern labour process. The counter-offensive, the attempt to recentre, organized around the vacuous ideology of culture, is thus contradictory in its own terms, and, as the final Flaubertian cadence confirms, it is doomed in advance to failure: *"car le plancher était plus bas que le jardin"* ("as the floor was on a lower level than the garden"). Here, in the so characteristic afterthought, the process of infinite fission and metonymization returns with a vengeance – once again the two levels, in their inequality, floor and ground level outside: and the return of the process, sealed by the great Flaubertian mannerism, the seemingly aimless rationalizing and logical connective "*car*" ("as" or "since") which offers the very symptom of a cause-and-effect logic running wild and consuming the universe.

One final textual event must, however, be noted, and it is a significant one, significant in its very triviality: "The whole room smelt a little musty." A further contingent or meaningless detail, documenting the Barthesian reality-effect and giving further, quite unnecessary evidence as to the "concreteness" and solidity of this textbook piece of realistic representation? I think not; and our reading of Cosimo will have alerted us to something very different at work here. For this is the only perceptual sentence in the entire description – the only one which flexes what survives of the older bodily sensorium, the only concrete practice of perception still feebly surviving in a new odourless and qualityless universe. This musty hold of a forgotten past – this faint trace of some olfactory historicism, last survival of what Adorno called the most archaic of all the senses – this event (for it is just that, the only genuine *event* in this lengthy paragraph) marks an indispensable stage of the process, but one which has seemingly been omitted until now. However abstract and impersonal the world which has here slowly been set in place, it will necessarily be accompanied by forms of subjectivity specific to it, of which we can expect that – in the historically original situation of a radical split between subject and object – they will necessarily be historically original as well. The musty smell, in my opinion, is to be seen as the place of the emergence of the new bourgeois subject, a process which has most strikingly been described by Deleuze and Guattari in the following terms:

> Something on the order of a subject can be discerned on the recording surface: a strange subject, with no fixed identity, wandering about over the body without organs, yet always remaining peripheral to the desiring-machines, being defined by the share of the product it takes for itself, garnering here, there and everywhere a reward, in the form of a becoming or an avatar, being born of the states that it consumes and being reborn with each new state: "*C'est donc moi, c'est donc à moi!*" .... The subject is produced as a mere residue alongside the desiring-machines: a conjunctive synthesis of consumption in the form of a wonderstruck: "*C'était donc ça!!*" ["Wow"] (Gilles Deleuze and Félix Guattari, "The Desiring-Machine", *Anti-Oedipus*, New York, 1977, p. 3)

On my reading, therefore, this sudden and unexpected burst of "affect" announces the fitful emergence of the subject in Flaubert's text: the "musty smell" inscribing, with a triumphant, desolate flourish, the place of subjectivity in a henceforth reified universe.

I want to conclude this reading with two very suggestive objections that have been made to it, or rather with two interesting alternative readings which my critics have proposed, and which will allow us to return to our initial model of "cultural revolution" and to dramatize it in an unexpected way. These are, briefly, "symbolic" readings of Flaubert's passage, interpretations which to my mind return us to the earlier critical moment of high modernism and propose the kinds of image-unification practised by such canonical but now rather archaic myth-critical studies as those of Wilson Knight on Shakespeare's imagery, for instance.

My own reading of the text as a kind of programmation is admittedly a purely formal one, if by that you understand the description of an abstract process whose contents are relatively indifferent. What my critics pointed out was that there existed a functional content in this passage which retained an essentially symbolic value: thus, the temple of Vesta is to be grasped, not only as the mere abstract place of culture, not as a mere empty gratuitous decoration, but as staging a very immediate symbolic reference to the destinies of the two women protagonists – themselves virtual vestal virgins in the isolation of the bourgeois household. Meanwhile, the "musty smell" at the conclusion of the fragment is not "innocent" either – not some mere abstract marker which signifies "perception" and "subjectivity" – but stages a far more meaningful reference to the increasingly dominant role of odour in this tale, and can already stand as a symbolic prefiguration of the ultimate destiny of Félicité, and her olfactory ecstasy in death as she inhales the incense of the religious procession outside her open window.

Now these are very interesting proposals indeed and I am very far from thinking that the interpretations they propose are in any conceivable sense *wrong*; I shall also only too readily agree that such interpretations or readings are radically incompatible with the one I proposed above. Our business, however, is less to choose between them and to make some ultimate *decision* about the meaning of the text one way or the other (after all, was it not the very author of our textual exhibit who once told us: "*La bêtise consiste à vouloir conclure*"?). The existence of two distinct type of reading now transforms our text into the place of what Ricoeur called the "conflict of interpretations", and on the methodological level presents a historical overlap between two moments of theory and critical practice, two moments which you will not be surprised to find me identifying as those of high modernism and postmodernism respectively.

In order to situate this conflict more sharply, it may not be inappropriate to return one last time to the essay of Roland Barthes we have had several occasions to mention here; and to quote briefly from his own suggestive account of the emergence of contemporary sensibility:

> The pure and simple "representation" of the "real," the naked account of "what is" (or what has been), thus proves to resist the meaning; such resistance confirms the great mythic opposition between the *vécu* [the experiential, or "lived experience"] (or the living) and the intelligible; we have only to recall how, in the ideology of our time, the obsessional evocation of the "concrete" (in what we rhetorically demand of the human

sciences, of literature, of social practices) is always staged as an aggressive arm against meaning, as though, by some *de jure* exclusion, what lives is structurally incapable of carrying a meaning – and vice versa. (Barthes, "L'effet de réel")

I believe that the symbolic and iconographic readings which have been proposed of the temple and the "musty smell" correspond to a nostalgia for meaning in the sense of Barthes' diagnosis; a high modernist longing for symbolic unification which seeks to convert the work of art into an immense organic totality, most frequently under the sign of "myth". I happen to believe that at the present time we feel a certain historical resistance to such symbolic interpretations as well as to the practice of symbolism in the literary texts themselves (wherever such a relatively archaic practice persists in contemporary writing). Yet this overlap between two moments of theory and criticism cannot be said to be a false one: it is an objective feature of the discontinuous world in which we still live, and such ideologies of the symbolic are no doubt among the traces, survivals and anachronisms which our own cultural revolution – that of late or multinational capitalism – has as its mission to transform and to eradicate.

Yet we will not fully understand the consequences of all this unless we return to Flaubert's text itself, where I am equally willing to believe that such interpretative *temptations* – the persistence of the iconographic meaning and of the symbol – also retain an objective existence, albeit of a ghostly and fantastical type. But the opposition, the coexistence, the overlap, in Flaubert is of a different kind historically: not, as for us, on the level of theory, between the moment of high modernism and that of postmodernism, but rather between the older still feebly sacred iconology of the *ancien régime* and the new abstract decoding apparatus of a middle-class realism. But at this point we return to the model of cultural revolution as the synchronic work of the new forms on the persistent and inherited raw material of the older content. The symbolism of the temple and of incense is really present in Flaubert, but on the point of extinction: it hovers above the textual apparatus as a ghostly remanence, as the faint after-image of what the text was called upon to transform and to suppress, of what is, in the very process of this paragraph, in the course of dissolution. Far from constituting a damaging alternative to the interpretive model I have proposed here, therefore, the symbolic readings I have alluded to end up as a dramatic reconfirmation of an ideological and formal production process which works the raw materials of the older mode of production over in the very moment in which the forms, practices and daily life of the new mode of production are being for the first time produced, and as the bourgeois floor-plan of the new society is being set in place.

I had already completed the preceding essay when, returning after an absence of some thirty years to Pound's *Cantos*, I happened with some astonishment on the following, once cryptic allusion:

> Un peu moisi, plancher plus bas que le jardin.
> "Contre le lambris, fauteuil de paille,
> "Un vieux piano, et sous le baromètre . . ."
> (Ezra Pound, *The Cantos* (New York:
> New Directions, 1970) p. 24)

I was now in a better position to admire a translation process whereby a classic Flaubertian sentence is transformed into an all-too-characteristic Poundian idiolect, into the fragmentary notation of the *Cantos'* archaic potsherds. But the unidentified reference projects, I think, a more substantive comment on the passage that interests us here, a comment developed by Pound's juxtaposition of the French stylist with his English-language opposite, Henry James. Both are, more generally in Pound, the objects of a professional admiration limited and qualified by their own restriction to the medium prose, but also by their historical situation, as this Canto makes clear.

For Canto VII is the place of the great transitional moment, in which for the first time the epic swings away from that archaic immediacy in which the gods existed in the early *Cantos* toward the junk-filled contemporary space of a *belle époque* on its way to the First World War. The James alluded to here ("the great domed head . . . weaving an endless sentence") is one whose work is evaluated by means of the spatial co-ordinates which govern all the early *Cantos*, a James who is defined principally, not by the late novels, with their intricate psychology, but rather by the ghost stories, most notably "The Jolly Corner":

> We also made ghostly visits, and the stair
> That knew us, found us again on the turn of it . . .

Both Flaubert and Henry James, in other words, are in Canto VII presented to us as committed, self-punishing artists whose fundamental historical raw material is the empty room, the room in which life once was lived (Flaubert) or in which it might have been lived (James), but in which it is present no longer, a vacant interior space overlaid with unnecessary ornament and decoration and inhabited by the husks and shells of former human beings. Unlike Mallarmé's empty rooms, however, virtual mausoleums through whose casements a distant constellation shines, the Poundian drawing room is haunted by the surcharged energy of older dwellings ("house expulsed by this house") in a way that makes historical commemoration possible, and epic, dialectical, retrieval of the past. The spatial implications of Pound's montage, in Canto VII, can at the least be taken as confirmation of the privileged, historically exemplary nature of the descriptive text of Flaubert with which we have been concerned.

EDMUNDO DESNOES

# Cuba Made Me So

I

Almost twenty years ago, I was rash enough to write something on how they see us in the North and how we see ourselves in the South. This dialogue came out with a descriptive, if clumsily worded, title: "The Photographic Image of Underdevelopment". I have just reread it, and it creaks with the sound and fury of the sixties. How much of it has survived and how much is dead?

Photography is no longer the Cinderella of the fairy-tale of criticism. Within the visual arts, it now has its body of ideas, its beauty parlour, and even an incipient grammar. A respectable discourse that allows it to look and be looked at in galleries and museums.

Excuse the irony. It is the irritating question of where and how one breathes the atmosphere of culture. We Latin Americans complain when doors are closed to us and nobody wants to listen to us, and if some doors are then opened and we are observed attentively, we suspect that we are being manipulated and turned into court buffoons. The world is impure – and we should be glad not to be angels – but if life is being used, knowing *how* to use is creation. Photography is in fashion – and we are glad.

"Photography", I wrote then, "has fooled the world. There's no more convincing fraud. Its images are nothing but the expression of the invisible man working behind the camera. They are not reality, they form part of the language of culture."

Today it would be going too far to insist that "reality and photography *are not* the same thing". Roland Barthes and Susan Sontag have done for photography what those of us on the outskirts of Western culture could only have dreamed of offering you: they have defined and minutely examined its cultural operations and ambiguous spiritual impact.

Photography is not reality, but it does have a special relationship with reality.

It is another of art's plausible lies, as Picasso thought. But it would not be a bad idea to give this lie a special place.

I am interested in the space (a word I would not have used ten or fifteen years ago) of photography and the way it functions. If in those days a sad ignorance prevailed, today too much critical competence can succeed by its subtleties in breaking down the obvious image and causing it to evaporate. Physical reality is the specific raw material of photography. The environment, the people, the objects are physically present – found, surprised, placed or arranged – they are outside, before the camera, not in memory.

Let us take a look.

"As she stared she found herself wondering why it was that a diseased face, which basically means nothing, should be so much more horrible to look at than a face whose tissues are healthy but whose expression reveals an interior corruption. Port would say that in a non-materialistic age, it would not be thus. And probably he would be right." The heroine of Paul Bowles' novel *The Sheltering Sky* is contemplating the face of a North African beggar.

That diseased face, or that face of healthy tissues, is photography's point of departure.

The novelist could have recorded or invented the scene, but the photographer could only have been there, stolen the reality, and snatched a face from the beggar.

The existence of the photographic camera allows man's intervention to be reduced to a minimum, but at the same time it forces him to impose his presence at the moment of creation, to establish a living relationship with the subject, and to initiate a hand-to-hand struggle. He disappears behind the keyhole but he cannot separate himself from the door. His absence is his presence.

The inexhaustible material world and the camera – the black artefact of the profession – create a new space for photography, a space of its own, a breach that henceforth will always belong to the photographer.

There is no more down-to-earth art than photography – beside it, the cinema is dreamland, a composite of time and space, a daydream in the darkness. Next to this red fringe come dance, theatre, painting, literature, and music. Photography is always the same temperature as the planet.

And everything comes out in the interpreter of photographs: in the reaction of the spectators of photographic violence; in the perceptual penetration of the image and its effect in the field of consciousness. Let us go back to our specific theme and continue with what I wrote in 1966: "Photography is just as closely tied to economic and political interests as to dreams and art. The photographic image of underdevelopment, for example, impinges constantly on our experience and is a decisive ingredient in our vision of the Third World. We live in that world and we are not sure to what extent we are conditioned by the gaze of the other one. Our thoughts are often based on press, propaganda, fashion, and art photographs that claim to express our surroundings. Photography is a much more influential and penetrating cultural ingredient than the great majority of people are capable of realizing. The visual code – and here one can only agree with Barthes – depends on language. And language in its turn on social action, without separating us from certain fundamental Marxist formulations."

Photography is an index of values. Both in production and consumption. Photographs are matter in cultural movement. In order to live, they include their time and space. The analysis or contemplation of photographs as objects in themselves, independent of their context, outside the system of social circulation, is an illusion, a methodological trap. There is no great difference, and we should not, or rather we cannot, separate looking from seeing, perception from the perceived. What our eyes propose and what we see. Photographs are detonators. They explode in us. We are the gaze as well as the gazed-at. The observer and the observed.

## II

What we observe today in the Third World has changed little since the middle of the sixties – that is, if we go by the tourist business. Travel folders still insist on a photographic utopia of endless, deserted, unpolluted beaches. We may travel accompanied by our partner, or meet her/him at the hotel – the photograph is not clear on this point – but the sea, rippled by the breeze, and the soft white sand are both obvious and real, as is the protective shade of the palm trees that have sprung up at the proper distance so that we can stretch our hammock and relax. It remains only to buy the airline ticket and make our hotel reservations. Hardly any changes are to be seen in these photographs over the last ten years. They form part of a conservative and effective advertising method. Our Caribbean goes on being a tropical paradise.

If some inhabitant of paradise appears, he/she is being photographed to show that the natives are obliging and of an innocent and exotic beauty. If we are unable to travel, a photograph then helps us to travel as consumers. The products of our world are pure, free of chemical contamination; sweaty black hands separate the two halves of a wholesome green coconut and from its heart emerges the white bottle of CocoRibe liqueur. Naturally, the sharp machete cannot fail to be seen in the foreground (figure 1).

In recent years, alongside the well-behaved savage and the traditional planter, alongside the profitable local product, a worldly native middle class has emerged. The last advertising campaign for Puerto Rican rums offers us a gallery of elegant professionals from the national bourgeoisie, with drinks in their hands and on the table, made with island rum. Architects or horse trainers. This new and accordingly young bourgeoisie is the one appointed to know and relish the major products of its native land. It is a campaign that also indicates the growing importance and strength of the national white elite of dark-skinned America.

Certain advertising appeals have disappeared. The sixties were marked by

Figure 1

radical political tremors and wars of national liberation in Asia, Africa and Latin America. Advertising then helped to neutralize political anxiety. At first it made use of the social prestige, the impact of revolutionary ideas; the revolution was a fabric, and men wore Tergal shirts and pants, with Mexican hats and decorative guns (figure 2); only the most resistant gear survived lawful violence; the women's revolution was Popoff, the underwear that set off the sensual lines of the body. Photographs demonstrate the commercial effectiveness of advertising pseudo-reality.

"Advertising based on situations of political confrontation", Umberto Eco pointed out as early as 1971, "is declining. A recent statistic shows a shrinking of the political theme, an obvious sign that the public at large is entering a phase of proletarian tranquillity and middle-of-the-road indifference." The observation can be extended to the whole capitalist world; by the mid-seventies it develops into a sharp turn to the right. However much it uses its voice, advertising is still an echo – and there is every reason to suspect that since 1968, fear has elicited pacifying advertising campaigns.

Figure 2

For the moment, it is preferable to bathe with Vita-bath of the forest, amid delicate ferns and beneath refreshing waterfalls as seen in an Italian advertisement: to return to the condition of the noble savage, guided by the nostalgic text reinforced by the photograph, in order for men to "feel like Tarzan" and women to come back into their own.

The social revolution might have gone on being a necessity, but it was no longer in fashion; fear clothed itself with loathing. In the twilight of the seventies, fashion was playing with Arab oil. The West was contemplating the world of the petrodollar with fear and fascination. Models posed like odalisques on soft cushions, and even a towel could be converted, at least in the pages of *Vogue*, into a chaste and perilous veil. And from there to the social tranquillity, preserver of poverty, of India and its worn-out mystery. They went back to posing in front of an elephant (though Richard Avedon had already placed Dovima between two elephants in 1955) or a camel for variation.

Today, revolution in the United States is no longer related to sex, as during the sixties, but to food. Food is the sex obsession of the eighties. *New York* magazine, in its 1 August 1983 cover, refers to the new conservative orgasm:

food – "You've had sushi, falafel, dim sum, bacon cheeseburgers and tandoori chicken. Now it's time for the Mexican Revolution." At the table, eating next to the gringo, sits a taciturn survivor of the troops of Pancho Villa (figure 3). The food is as hot as the revolution: and as they eat under the burning title, the revolution in Central America is just a distant echo, one of the possible connotations of the image. Taming the barbarian, the heathen, has been a lucrative game. Some southern countries will be swallowed up by the attractive skin of the consumer society; others will find their own way. But the most deplorable, perhaps inevitable, aspect is the interiorization in underdeveloped countries of the metropolitan vision, and the squandering of photographic opportunities to affirm our identity and create or reflect adequate values. Creating values, and disputing them if they are empty – these are the two sides of cultural activity.

Fashion photographs are an even more critical field, since clothes do indeed make the man. Our manner of dressing – the fashion photographs in our publications – indeed transmit popular values and cultural identity. On our continent, the photographs of clothed (and even unclothed) models imitate like

Figure 3

parrots when they exaggerate colours, or like monkeys when they copy the styles of Paris or the dynamic capitalism of New York. Latin American magazines, from the Rio Grande to Patagonia, operating in the fertile soil of a middle-class subservience to the industrial centres of capitalism, are a warning to the countries of Africa and Asia that are still capable of learning from the mistakes of others. These two continents still have a strong identity in their wearing apparel, adapted to the cultural and climatic realities of each region.

Photography, by its special relation to reality, plays a decisive role in this implacable dream. A dream fabricated and conditioned by base interests, but with a credible face thanks to this blessed or cursed photography. The advertising world, fashion as we know it today, would collapse without it. Painting and the written word lack the realistic charms of a photograph.

As a young man in Cuba I saw the world, history, in photographic imagery. History took place where photographs were taken, shot. I remember how stupidly thrilled I was, at the age of twenty-four, when I saw the island in *Harper's Bazaar*. "Flying Down to Cuba"; who is up and who is down in a round earth? I felt the pulpless fashion model was validating the island by coming down to sight-see and be seen in a magazine that infused meaning into every sight she appeared before (figure 4).

Even the discourse of travel was convincing, sequential: the Angel announced our existence as she landed at the Havana airport; the proof was there: the airstrip, the fuselage of the plane, her expensive suitcase. A "Cadillac from Havana's Amber Motors" arrived to pick her up. The Hotel Nacional, the Plaza de la Catedral, the sugarcane fields, the cock fights. It was true, because I recognized the background; she was beautiful because she was powerful (her name never appeared in the captions, only the price of the garments). I was being culturally colonized by the Annunciation.

If the image had the strength of physical existence – regardless of how impossible the model was as a prop for the camera statement – the text of the photograph essay reveals the weaving of arbitrary relations. The Cuban background for the fashions is justified because, for example, they are "in colours that happen to be native to the Cuban scene". "Daiquirí white fleece. The whipped, golden white that foams on the rim of your Bacardí daiquiri", and "under it, rich pungent brown – Tobacco brown". Words reveal the gimmickry of a meaning the photographs hide in their contrived physicality.

"Native to the Scene", a double-spread tryptich of photographs, enhances the packaged model as she deigns to chat with smiling, ragged toothless *campesinos*. The model, like the ladies of the Spanish court, uses wasted creatures to heighten her beauty.

The model wears white gloves to avoid the dangerous parasites that lodge under your fingernails in the tropics as she talks to a child, as she looks down to a child while a creased old man admires her androgynous presence. Or she stands before an ox-cart as she shows off her calm, cool clothes and blesses poverty; she spreads her arms, palms out, as a saint or a magician.

Cuba – then an economic colony of the United States – made me see the

## Native to the Scene

• Calm, cool clothes indigenous to travels in the tropics: photographed here
against a lush stand of sugar cane at the Finca Santa María,
in the Cuban savannah country near Matanzas. And: from the cane come molasses
and *bagasse*—that make the Bacardi that makes the daiquiri that foams
in to a delectable cooled-off white—the white of the season.
FROSTED GRAY LINEN (above left). Smooth, straight fitted dress,
cooled off around the edges with white, and accompanied by a bolero. By Paul
Parnes, in Moygashel Irish linen. About $111. Milgrim; Marshall Field.
SILK LINEN (above right), a new silken climate to move in, in the
newest white—daiquiri white. A curve-collared jacket over a strapless dress.
By Hannah Troy, in Bianchini silk. About $155. Bonwit Teller; Saks.
SILK LINEN (opposite) paled to the fresh-white on top of a daiquiri; curved to
show the collarbone and given a light suggestion of sleeves. By B. H. Wragge,
in Couture silk. About $50. Bonwit Teller; Bullock's-Wilshire; Hudson's.

Figure 4

ideal, the rag flower doll; Cuba – as a country involved in building a socialist society – made me appreciate the fruit, the wound hidden behind the froth of a daiquirí. I decode within a cultural context. I can't help it, Cuba made me so.

## III

Only a few attempt, in press photographs and reports, to reveal the true face of the world, the scar hidden under the froth. Various traps are customarily laid.

The true scar of Africa, one of the deepest wounds of the world, is the work of white men in the name of European civilization; there is nevertheless an insistence on black barbarism, on the dark-skinned savage as an irresponsible murderer. The skill displayed in the photographs of the innocent whites of Kolwezi, that froth of the world, those inert, blond, white-skinned bodies rotting amid the demolished equipment of the mining camp, is proof of the effectiveness of the press, of its power of empathy, in the insolent capitalist world (figure 5). Next to the full-colour photograph of the livid corpses, there had to be, of course, a black-and-white reproduction of the true wounded of the continent, forced to prostrate themselves on the ground before soldiers of the French Inquisition. These two pages of *Newsweek*, published on 5 June 1978, are an admirable treatise on the photographic wisdom of the historical murderers.

And to make you shriek with laughter there is the grotesque coronation of Bokassa, in full imperial colour, with his uniform, arrogantly bracing himself on his Napoleonic throne. The naïve savage repeats history as a farce. The reporting takes advantage of the context to reinforce prejudices and profound myths of Western Culture.

In October 1978, *Life* came out with an article on the Shah of Iran and his royal family. On the last page, a general, having just arrived from Teheran, receives instructions from the monarch. Everything is in order, to the point of reverence. Then an explosion: but the American press reports that the armed forces are keeping the situation, a popular uprising, under control. The army always manages to disperse the demonstrators. Baktiar stands fast, and lets himself be photographed next to a picture of Mossadegh. The carrot and the stick. Tanks patrol the calm streets. The Ayatollah Khomeini is neither seen nor spoken of. He does not exist.

This is the way they write history. Readers are always informed by what the press wants to see and to say with photographs. And even as it misinforms, it does not lose credibility. Yesterday's news stories and photographs are forgotten. It is an absence. It is the final trap. The lies of yesterday are always the truth of today.

Faced with photographic pseudo-reality, one can only rely on one's memory and an inconsolable intelligence.

Rebellion in the Third World has passed to urban centres without abandoning the rural areas; from Beirut and Teheran to Soweto and San

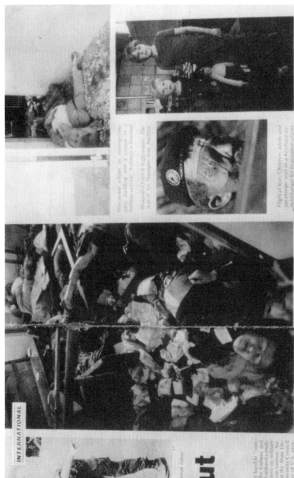

# The Fallout In Zaire

## HORROR AND HOSTAGES

Figure 5

Salvador the masses are taking to the streets, burning the symbols of consumerist colonization, and defying the military repression. It is a new revolutionary reality, a new photographic countenance.

Nicaragua, because of the feudal cruelty of Somoza, counted for a moment on the sympathy of the world. The pictures of the young people of Masaya, León, Jinotega and Matagalpa filled us with astonishment. The bandit's kerchief has become the uniform of urban revolution in Central America. The pistol is added to the rifle, and carnival masks protect the identity of the new urban guerrilla. Susan Meiselas' photographs, taken inside the liberated towns and not from behind or in the footsteps of the National Guard, seize us with their sensual texture and pierce us by their political sympathy. The tension is overwhelming. The position of the photographer and the angle of press photographs are what is most difficult to neutralize: though not impossible.

These photographs followed two paths: they fell on the cushion of established publications, and they circulated in a series of projections designed to collect funds to continue the struggle against Somoza. A lone photographer, no matter what his or her photographs may say, is powerless unless he functions within a definite context, unless the pressure of other bodies exists behind his images. If five years ago the photographs of revolution in Nicaragua were used to support the Sandinistas, today the photographs of revolution in El Salvador are used against the rebels. Yet it is the same Central American revolution.

The least deceitful publications acknowledge a political party, a stated bias; they can be mistaken and often are, but we know beforehand what their viewpoint is.

When we read the newspaper *Granma*, we hold in our hands the official organ of the Cuban Communist Party; we understand why a picture of a brigade of sugarcane cutters that have downed a million juicy stalks takes up more space than one of Carter, Giscard, Callaghan and Schmidt holding a summit meeting on the island of Guadalupe in 1979. It is a value judgement, and these everyday images correspond to a well-defined, consciously motivated social plan.

The decade of the seventies opened with an irreproachable figure in the Moneda Palace. Salvador Allende holds the office of President of Chile under all the provisions of the law. His noble portrait appears repeatedly on the pages of the world press, while the millions of faces and bodies that make up Chile leap in the streets, without weapons, to show that they are not starving. The tragedy is summed up in two indelible moments: the burning of the Moneda Palace and the dignified President in his white helmet, gripping a rifle given to him by Fidel (figure 6), and with this image he defends his words: "I am not made of the stuff of martyrs, I am a simple social fighter, but I want it clearly understood that I am fulfilling the mandate of the people, and to get me out of the Moneda Palace they'll have to take me out dead."

So much for press photographs.

Figure 6

## IV

There is a kind of photography that has a refined presence in the history of images stolen from reality. It is the art photograph as a lie. It transcends fluid reality and creates a closed unity. When it achieves an aesthetic synthesis, it immediately attains static unity. Cartier-Bresson's photographs taken in Indonesia, for example, have this paralysing effect. One is compelled to believe in the perfection of the original reality; the image is a harmonious entity in itself. "Do not change a single thing!", one feels inclined to exclaim, like a stupid tourist in any "exotic and primitive" country. The closed architecture of the image is beauty that tends, as the Greeks thought, to be its own justification. Art frequently creates a comfortable world that detaches itself and becomes independent from action. The photographs of Edward Weston, for example, are closer to the world of painting than to the active realism that characterizes impure photography. Weston's sensual texture or Cartier-Bresson's implacable composition are apt to close over themselves, attaining the perfection of a certain sensual and harmonious bliss. We see textures, volumes, equilibrium – and reality, open and ragged, is lost and transcended. Images as self-sufficient, perceptually and culturally, as Velásquez's *Las Meninas*, irreproachable in their own space.

There is another manner of escaping: the effects obtained through excessive interference when the photograph is taken and especially when it is processed in the darkroom. Effects that break the obvious, recognized connection with physical reality.

On emerging from the embrace of reality, photographs do not remain floating in a no-man's land: they cross the frontier and surrender to the world of painting. They are perceived and analysed within a sensibility refined by painting: texture, composition, equilibrium and spatial tension, eternal harmony. If painting is already this archetypal world of absolute and eternal truth, photography governs the field of the contingent, the temporal, the broken, and the scattered, the interrupted.

This, roughly speaking, is the way to read the kind of photography that has matured in our time. An unsettled composition, an uprooted space, an intercepted light. The other way of producing images, of seeking closed and organized images, belongs to painting. From a Weston nude to a crumbling wall by Enrique Bostelmann. It is photography but we read it as painting.

This is not an absurd excommunication, it is a distinction. Let us for the moment assign to the established canons of painting the photograph that longs for fluid reality. A photographic genre in no way to be despised, it would merit a separate analysis of its own – both for the pleasure and the astonishment it sometimes affords us. Modern man's avidity is constant because insatiable: no one, especially today, voluntarily resigns himself to limiting his intake. Not to speak of the Latin American, who, with his broad context and cultural pressures, has a universal curiosity well expressed by Pablo Neruda: "I am omnivorous of feelings, beings, books, events, and battles. I would eat the whole earth. I would drink the whole sea."

This vast and recognizable link with reality has special importance for the critical photography of the emerging South. Our America (Latin, not Anglo-America), particularly now that its economic, political and cultural development allows it to speak out vigorously on an equal footing, requires the weight of the planet. Now that we can travel all over the world like exotic Indians and obliging blacks, we must develop photography as a critical attitude revealing and directing a world that can offer a possible alternative, another reality, to the Euro- and USA-centric vision and cultural conceptions. Not only do we live other economic and social problems, but we live them differently.

We are recognized for artistic imagination, elemental strength and creative exuberance. I have given a certain weight to theoretical and ideological discourse in this essay because it is less important to affirm our presence than to define our outlook. Our criticism and thought have consumed our creative energies from Simón Bolívar to Fidel Castro, in the struggle for political independence. "There is no literature that expresses anything" – I extend José Martí's words to culture as a whole – "so long as there is no essence in it to be expressed. There will be no Hispanic American literature so long as there is no Hispanic America."

If we judge the photography of our continent – the most advanced and aware in the southern world – by some of its more striking recent examples, we can recognize that, on the one hand, it largely satisfies the requirements of a critical and orienting vision and, on the other, gives evidence of a sensibility open to all currents.

These photographs have freed themselves from certain deep and recurrent myths that have been imposed on us and which we sometimes internalize: archetypes that have accompanied us since the Conquest. In press and advertising photographs, for example, the view of the noble savage or the atrocious cannibal is obvious. Either we are innocent and docile, living in surprising harmony with our surroundings, or this natural beauty turns into the ferocious grimace of the irrational savage, who manifests his discontent by overturning cars and setting fire to shops and proconsular offices, incapable of understanding the civilizing influence of Europe and the United States. Either we are noble examples of utopia, or we are soulless inferior beings, incapable of joining the modern world: docile parrots or dangerous jaguars.

Three friendly female natives offer themselves smiling to the colonizer in a girlie magazine, *Hustler*. The metaphor could not be more eloquent. The women open themselves, surrender willingly to the new God (figure 7). A double oppression, as natives and as women. Could this posed photograph fail to explain why many women's organizations in the United States support revolution in Latin America?

In the field of artistic photography, the myths live on by the eternal return: the immensity of nature, the vastness of rivers, plains and mountains; the delicate beauty of the hummingbird or the endless voracity of the boa constrictor; the utopian beauty of civilizations destroyed by the Conquest; ruins with ruined people, who are nevertheless deserving in their beautiful handmade rags.

When some of these subjects appear, their idealist and exotic burden may be neutralized by their position in a specific historical and social context. Or they may be converted into symbols, like the photograph of the destroyed, roofless colonial church by the Mexican Renato von Hanffstengel; the typical hut is also destroyed by fire in the pathetic desolation of the touristic development of Brazil, depicted by Adriana de Queirós.

The urbanized Indian affirms his stubbornness before a wall that shrieks Coca-Cola; as a mother with her baby on her back, sitting on the sidewalk with her miserable subsistence merchandise, this Indian suffers under the circumspect and classical gaze of the white stone sculpture adorning so many parks and residences of the New World; and he even appears with class-conscious satisfaction when he sits in the colonizer's chair in front of the photographer Pedro Meyer. Blacks and mestizos are men and women in the

Figure 7

photographs of the Panamanian Sandra Eleta; to be men and women is not an easy thing for the Latin Americans who sustain the continent. Photographing men and women, as men and women, is here a positive and vital feat.

It is not an easy vision. It involves a knowledge that is erotic and at the same time rational. The eros of knowledge must join with the logos of our America. Without knowledge, intuitive or conscious, of the structure of the world around us, we are lost.

Alejo Carpentier, in touching on the present problems of Latin American fiction, opened his eyes to the continent: "Someone has written a novel about the jungle after peering at it for a couple of days. As for myself, I believe that certain American realities, for not having been exploited in literature, not having been named, require a prolonged, vast, patient process of observation. And that perhaps our cities, for not having yet entered into literature, are more difficult to handle than the jungles or mountains."

Carpentier is speaking of the novel, but he conjures up our photography as well. Naming things can be confusing and tiring for the reader of novels. Photography, with its immense visual ambiguity, its ability to cover so much in the little time it takes to absorb it, is different.

Our cities *have no style*. And yet we are now beginning to discover that they have what we might call a *third style*: the style of things that have no style ... What happens is that the *third style*, just as it defies everything that was hitherto been taken for *good style* and *bad style* – synonyms for *good taste* and *bad taste* – is usually ignored by those who contemplate it every day, until a clever writer or photographer proceeds to reveal it . . . . It is difficult to *reveal* something that offers no preliminary information in books, an archive of emotions, contacts, epistolary exclamations, personal images and approaches; it is difficult to see, define, weigh something like what Havana was, scorned for centuries by its own inhabitants, the object of allegations expressing tedium, the wish to escape, the inability to understand.

This necessity, although it can manifest itself as pure scenography, answers to a real need to name our things and situate them in a real context.

> The coexistence of people of the same nationality belonging to different races, Indians, blacks, and whites, of different cultural levels, often living simultaneously in *different periods*, if you consider their degree of cultural development. . . . The political and military context of Latin America has inexhaustible implications. Though it should be taken into account, one must be careful not to fall into a facile and declamatory literature of *denunciation*. . . . Valid connections should be established between the man of America and chthonic contexts, without resorting to the exploitation – in any case, discredited – of the bright colors of the shawl, the charm of the sarape, the embroidered blouse, or the flower worn over the ear. *Distance* is another important context, as is the *scale of proportions*. The dimensions of what surrounds the American man. . . . The disproportion is cruel insofar as it conflicts with the module, Pythagorean eurhythmy, the beauty of number, the golden section.

All this has to do with photography.

The Latin American photographer has the possibility, and the means, for naming the things of our world, for demonstrating that there is another kind of beauty, that faces of the First World are not the only ones. These Indian, black, plundered white and mestizo faces are the first element defining the demographic content of our photography. Cultural, economic and social conflicts are also obvious in many photographs. An eagerness to name our reality is present in the dark splendour of most of these images, as well as the need to reject the exploitation of exotic colours so as not to fall into a facile and declamatory photography of denunciation.

The military and religious contexts also appear in our photography, without resorting to the visual pamphlet. As heirs of Spanish colonization, we are still countries of soldiers and priests. But although the priests are privileged, many Latin Americans are genuine believers, poor devotees of syncretisms of Afro-Spanish origin. "Religious suffering is, on the one hand, the expression of real suffering, and on the other a protest against it": Marx's acute observation now applies more to us than to the North. The two faces of religion, oppression and escape, are nevertheless a powerful refuge in this uncertain and fluid decade.

The same cannot be said when we find the military in certain photographs: it is always the naked form of power, deciding national destinies and repressing genuine aspirations, those aspirations that have continued to propel us since the emancipation struggles of the last century. This active, revolutionary face seldom appears. The rebellion of the continent appears in a photograph of Allende in the hands of the Chilean people and in the frustrated scrawl of the word "revolution" on a rough wall.

The revolution in power is the presence of Cuba. Yet historic images appear in many Cuban photographs: militiamen of Playa Girón, armed peasants, popular demonstrations, grimy machete wielders more staunch than smiling. Cuban photographs have the force of nostalgia, they are historical pictures, imbued with the spirit of the sixties. The image of the sixties is the most powerful and recognized one of Cuba. It is a real vision, but already stereotyped. The decade of the seventies is visually almost unknown. Enough of scratching the surface, naming the absent appearances: the jeans of the high-school student in the Campo, the white helmets of the members of the micro-brigades, the epaulettes and uniform caps of the military. Adventure has given way to order. Images have to be analysed for a programmed response. Critical photography of everyday life is inseparable from cultural dialogue.

The style of Cuban photographs can be recognized by a certain frontal candour. The photographer seems to be arrested frontally before a powerful reality where the struggle is as obvious as an open smile, where social homogeneity produces a photography of pure denotation, with no remote connotations. These are testimonies that open like fruits in the smile of Nicolás Guillén or the worker with the machete standing with his trophies in his hands on a vast field of cut sugarcane. Mayito and Marucha artfully transcend this ingenuous frontality.

I would say it is no accident that the least regional photographs, those most obviously related to international photography – both in theme and in the way of treating the theme – are made in Mexico and Brazil, the countries with the highest level of economic development, and where modern neocapitalist society is already the lifestyle of a substantial minority. They are authentic photographs of a real colonization.

Theft, as Picasso used to say, is only justified when it is followed by a murder. In many photographs we easily discover the chicken thief. Chickens from another roost: desolate urban landscapes, ostracized transvestites, fragments of figures, surrealistic montages, hygienic textures, and so on.

Perhaps the only excusable case might be that of Francisco X. Camplis, with his photograph of a Chicano nude (figure 8). Faced with the erotic buffetings of Anglo-American beauties, he gives us the female beauty of his own race. It is an ambiguous photograph, as ambiguous as the difficult position of the Chicano artist in the United States. The photographer himself acknowledges it: "I am keenly aware of the influence, subliminally or otherwise, upon my work by the plethora of American designed imagery . . . . We continue to hold a fascination for things European, for *gente güera*, for *la gabacha* or *gringa* and so forth. In effect, we help to perpetuate the myth that beauty solely resides in creatures

Figure 8

blonde and blue-eyed." Latin American photographers in the United States suffer – with greater violence – the same contradictions when they speak or look at themselves in the mirror. The face and features are Chicano, but the whole body responds to the aesthetic standards of the North. Their graphic style could have been used to specify another physical type: strong face, short legs, broad hips. The photograph is a sweet trap. On a macho continent, marked by rigid and watertight sexual definitions.

Centred around the positive social pole are the photographs of Paolo Gasparini, a critical artist committed to one of the most difficult tasks of Latin American photography: to clean away the golden, filthy cobwebs that hinder moral clarity. His work has dwelt for the past twenty years on the revealing contexts of our southern world: the vast American geography marked by the exploitation of its natural resources and by immense garbage dumps of consumerism. The geography that Gasparini has shown us includes not only the tenacity of its men but also its cemeteries of crosses and oil rigs. The money that reposes on the neoclassical columns of the banks and the garbage that the many mestizos of the continent transport in order to live.

His pictures today preach about diamonds and children. One series is devoted to the exploitation of diamonds in Venezuela. They are images of the hellish circle of plunder. Earth and men plundered by livid, invisible hands that create a vicious circle, which in San Salvador de Paúl wastes away "a small mirror in which the history of lost humankind is concentrated." These are his own words: "Children looking without much astonishment at wealth consuming itself, wealth that generates poverty right there in the very place where the offense, the crime against nature, was committed. The diamond becomes poverty despite the mirth of the prostitute, in the greed and futility of the middleman."

Children, for Gasparini, have taken on the role of witnesses; Latin American children, who will inherit what we, the adults, are already revealing and imprinting on their minds.

When he gets to this point, Gasparini breaks out in curses. His voice is the most despairing of all. "Each image can be read in many ways", he remarks in connection with his Venezuelan diamonds. "In a Finnish museum, these photographs might simulate exotic appetites, in a European or American magazine they would form part of one more 'coverage,' in socialist Cuba they might illustrate an article in *Prensa Latina* on the inconsistencies of democracy, in the house of a friend they would appear as 'the body of Maria Luisa inviting you to go to bed,' to the squinting eyes of some museum curator the out-of-focus hand of the same Maria Luisa would be disturbing, and for me it will go on being a vivid experience, an apprenticeship in memory that draws me back to the garden of childhood."

Gasparini's perplexity emerges from the monstrous distance between creation and distribution: between creation and the form of consumption. This distance, which erodes or destroys the work and the original intention, is more pronounced and exaggerated with photography.

Its images are scattered, they do not have the inner cohesion of the cinema film nor the precise location of a projection room. The ambiguity of the image, including the documentary reportage, requires definition, demands a context. Inexorably we fall into the trap: be it the magazine with its columns of print or the museum wall with its antiseptic time and space. In a magazine, the photograph usually argues as it informs, and in the museum it casts off its historical and social moorings.

Museums and galleries are a new element; they increase the distance but satisfy a repressed vanity of the creator of photographs: to be recognized as wholly an artist in society. Yet photography triumphs when "the press photograph merges with world news, the family portrait with everyday life, and the photo in a magazine or book with countless cups of coffee". This is the greatest and most ambiguous triumph of photography.

But the photographer who has very precise intentions feels himself at a loss. "Is photography capable of giving a good version of reality? At least an adequate version of our intentions? I don't think so, nor am I even sure of what photographs really say", the despairing Gasparini concludes.

# V

There throbs in all of us a certain overevaluation of photography, art and the mass media. Despair, the need to entrust everything to the effectiveness of creative beauty, the hope of concentrating everything in the content of a message, is an illness, a form of alienation. It is not art, photography included, that will liberate us but a revolution in our way of working and living. Photographs and art are indexes of value. They are elements for cultural dialogue. They refer to our existence but they are not our existence.

Let us not reject the aesthetic, humanizing function. The young Marx based his work on the prospect of placing man in the centre of his world: "The eye has been transformed into a human eye, just as man has become a social, human aim, an aim flowing from man for man."

It is not, however, an isolated element.

The richness of our contemporary visual world must be seen as a danger. It is an overwhelming and oppressive world. A world that manifests itself fundamentally through the image is only a few steps from totalitarian manipulation. Images, the visual power of present-day capitalism, like the ritual constructions of ancient Egypt, are refined ways of inhibiting and crushing man. I have lived more than twenty years with these anxieties. I am convinced of the effectiveness of shared, collective work, and of the decisive importance of dialogue among people. I have learned much more by conversing, in animated exchanges and collective discussions, than in eyeing and reading the barrage of information that imposes on us a docile passivity. That is the lure of pseudo-reality.

The photographs in magazines and books, or blown-up on posters and billboards, have the limited power of a watchword, of visual phraseology. We do not commit ourselves by giving our word, we do not assume a real and considered position within the group. The image only incites us, it does not commit us. It customarily manipulates us. For better or for worse. The visual image has a limited value within a social and cultural system.

The Greek habit of dialogue continues to be a liberating principle; and when this dialogue becomes universal among men and bases itself on work, on coherent action – only then will the image be able to play a humanizing role.

The prestige of the visual image is out of all proportion. Photographs are ideas, memories, feelings, thought – and thought devotes itself only to death, to what is mechanical in life, to regularities or distortions. Life is first action, then words, and a photograph in death. It is an instantaneous truth that has already ceased to exist.

Photography has taught us not to twist ourselves around a discourse that should always be an open dialogue. It is what we have been, and not necessarily what we will be. We are ignorant of the future.

There are one, two, three paths . . .

MICHEL DE CERTEAU

# The Indian Long March

"Saturday afternoon, 14 July, 1973. The roads leading to Guambia began to be filled with Indians (*compañeros*). The first came from the neighbouring '*resguardos*',[1] – Jambalo, Pitayo, Quisgo, Totoro, Paniquita and other nearby hamlets. Next came the Inganos and Kamsa,[2] who had travelled from Putumayo, and the representatives of the '*parcialidades*' of Narino,[3] along with the Aruacos of the Sierra Nevada of Santa Marta,[4] who had been travelling four days by foot, train and bus in order not to miss the Meeting.

"And later came those from the West, and after midnight the comrades from the East, from Tierradentro, who had come by way of the '*paramo*'.[5] There were already around two thousand of us. Since it was very cold and as our comrades from the hot climes[6] hadn't even a *ruana* to put on, we made eleven fires to warm ourselves, then began warming ourselves, some chatting, others playing music and singing.

"From time to time we would drink a little coffee to stave off hunger. Sunday, 15 July, broke full of sunlight, and we were full of contentment. . . ."[7]

---

[1] *Resguardos*; land reserved for the Indians by the Spanish Crown, then by the Colombian Republic: the *Cabildo* (Indian government) distributes the land among families so that they can cultivate it, but the ownership of the land is held by the community. The following names of the *resguardos* are those of the Cauca.

[2] *Kamsa*: groups, tribes.

[3] *Narino*: state in the South, on the border of Ecuador.

[4] *Santa Marta*: in the north of Colombia, between the coast and Venezuela.

[5] The *Paramo*: a very cold zone, situated above 3000 metres.

[6] As there are no seasons in Colombia, although the climate varies with the altitude, one currently speaks of hot climes, cold ones and the *paramo*, the three stages of Colombia.

[7] Indian meeting of the Cauca, in Colombia, according to the account given by the regional Council of Cauca "as a contribution to our common struggle". The text has been published in *La Lettre*, no. 188 (April 1974) pp. 14–15.

"Some people walked all night to join the Indian *compañeros*", adds the editor of *La Lettre*. They are heading towards another morning. No longer devoured by poverty, as they were when I knew them in Misiones in Argentina; no longer stricken by those "simultaneously mystic, social and political crises" that Alfred Métraux once noted in their treks towards the Land Without Evil, or in the solitary suicides of the Indians of the Grand Chaco[8] – but determined to forge their own history. "Recent actions have changed our perspective: today more than reacting against imminent extinction, growth and development are our objectives."[9] The Meetings of Tribes and Assemblies of Chiefs are aimed at a reconquest. For both peasant and Indian a revolution is taking form in fact and in consciousness; it is already stirring up hitherto silent depths in the Latin American countries.

### Memory or the Tortured Body

The time of oppression is still not over. On the contrary, by asserting their rights to the earth and organizing autonomous associations, the Indians are being met with a renewed wave of repressive measures. Recent events tend to prove this: the destruction of the El Cedro hamlet in the Indian region of Veraguas by the Panama National Guard (15 March 1976); the military interventions in the communes of Palenque Ocosingo and Chinon in Mexico, that led to the pillage and burning of hundreds of houses, the expulsion of 2400 inhabitants, to mistreatment and rape (12–13 June 1976); the murders and imprisonment of Indians in Merure (Mato Grosso, Brazil) designed to prevent the creation of a reservation for the Bororo and to sustain the great landowner holdovers from the colonial tradition (15 July 1976); etc. A list of further misdeeds that echoed in the national or international press would be lengthy. Yet these bloody marks on the surface of news transmissions are far from signalling the ordinariness of the violence. And the imprisonments, the arsons, even the murders are probably less destructive than the economic alienation, cultural domination and social degradation – less dangerous than the entire process of an on-going, day-by-day ethnocide.

"You know," said Russell Means, "the Indian has a long memory. He doesn't forget his murdered heroes or his land occupied by the foreigner." In their villages, the Indians retain a keen awareness of their four and a half centuries of colonization.[10] Dominated but not subjugated, they also remember what

---

[8] Alfred Métraux, *Réligions et magies indiennes d'Amérique du Sud* (Paris: Gallimard, 1967) esp. chs 1 and 6. Cf. M. de Certeau, "Terres lointaines", *Études*, April 1968 pp. 582–90, and his *L'Absent de l'histoire* (Tours: Mame, 1973) pp. 135–50, "Réligion et société: les messianismes".

[9] Declaration of ANUC, and the indigenous regional Council of Cauca, Bogota, 31 August 1974.

[10] Jean-Loup Herbert, *Indianite et lutte des classes* pp. 227–8.

Westerners have "forgotten" – a continuous succession of uprisings and
awakenings that have left almost no traces in the written historiographies of the
occupiers.[11] As much as and more than in the handed-down narratives, this
history of resistance punctuated by cruel repression is marked upon the Indian
body. This writing of an identity recognized through pain constitutes the
equivalent of the indelible markings engraved on the bodies of the young in
initiation tortures.[12] In this form too "the body is a memory". It bears, it writes
the law of the equality and non-submission that regulate not only the relation of
the group with itself, but also its relations with the occupiers. Among the ethnic
Indian groups (some 200) that inhabit "Latin" America, this tortured body and
this other body, which is the altered earth, form the beginning from where once
more the will to construct a political association is reborn. A unity fashioned by
unhappiness and the resistance to unhappiness is the historic site, the collective
memory of the social body, from whence originates a will that neither ratifies
nor denies this writing of history and that deciphers the scars of the body itself –
or the fallen "heroes" and "martyrs" who reflect them in narrative – as the
index of a history to be made. "Today, in the hour of awakening, it is we who
must be our own historians."[13]

The relationship of the "Race of the Sun" with the "scattered blood" that
"obliges" and with which the lost earth awaits its "masters" seems to articulate
fully the Indian political speech on the effectiveness of associative and rural
strategies. In any event, ideology is most often absent from demands. In effect a
common language would merely provide the groups with a substitutional body.
It would finally replace ethnic groups by a unitary, comprehensive discourse.
Here, on the contrary, the instituting alliance of each community with a body
and with land upholds the real difference between specific situations. Action is
thus aimed less at the construction of a common ideology than at the
"organization" (this leitmotif word) of tactics and operations. In this
connection, the political pertinence of a geographic distinction between distinct
sites repeats – at the level of the association among ethnic groups – the
distribution of sites of power and the rejection of centralization that is
characteristic of the internal functioning of each of them.[14] The Indian
awakening thus takes on a democratic, autonomous form that can be recognized
in the specific features of its political organization and in the objectives it
concludes with its analyses.

[11] Ibid., pp. 216–17, the series of resistances and rebellions which, in Guatemala, were
kept silent.
[12] Cf. Pierre Clastres, La Société contre l'état (Paris: Minuit, 1974), the chapter on
initiation: "De la torture dans les sociétés primitives", pp. 152–60.
[13] Speech of Justino Quispe Balboa (Aymara, Bolivia) to the first Indian Parliament of
South America, 13 October 1974, before the Paraguayan authorities and observers.
J. Quispe Balboa was then twenty-one years old. Dial Document no. 196.
[14] Cf., among many others, Clastres, La Société contre l'état, chs 2 and 7, pp. 25–42 and
132–6.

## A Political Awakening

What strikes us in the Indian manifestos is the distinction between, and yet the connection with, two essential givens: on the one hand a proper political form (which entails, for example, the refusal to participate in political parties – "foreign to our American reality",[15] declared the Indian parliament that met in Paraguay in 1973); on the other hand, an economic situation common to an entire rural Latin American proletariat (agricultural or underdeveloped journeyman workers, without contracts or guarantees, indebted victims of loans at exorbitant rates of interest; overtaxed small producers swallowed up by intermediaries who purchase their goods). The narrow articulation of the political and the economic avoids two quite frequent reductions: either the assimilation of the "proper" to a cultural "identity" frozen by the anthropologist (when he does not substantialize it!), isolated from society as a whole, withdrawn from history and destined to be repeated quasi-mechanically; or the effacement of an ethnic and political specificity by the generality of production relationships and class conflicts. To the alibi of a cultural identity (fairly prestigious and nostalgic) constructed by the science of anthropology or to the loss of self under the (effectively imperialist) control of socio-economic laws and conflicts imposed by the international market,[16] the Indians prefer a third political path: that of changing by means of appropriate strategies a reality that gives them solidarity with other, non-Indian, peasant movements.

Thus, specificity no longer leads to a given, to a past, to a system of representations, to an object of knowledge (and/or exploitation), but is affirmed in a set of procedures – a way of doing – in the field structured by a global economic system that also sets up among those oppressed the bases of revolutionary alliances. "Cultural" specificity takes the form of a style of action that can be articulated on situations established by capitalist imperialism.

This political determination of cultural specificity is obviously the effect of a long historic experience, of a difference maintained through the anchoring of such ethnic groups on a homeland and their particular resistance to ideological seduction. Three aspects must be stressed.

First, the Spanish institution of the *encomienda* in the earliest colonial era, the privatization and capitalization of the land by its occupiers, the subsequent demographic foundering of the Indians, the artificial regrouping of the rest of the indigenous population into *reducciones* (those factory cities of the seventeenth century) or the institution of forced labour for groups brought

---

[15] The word "American" here means the time preceding colonization.

[16] These two "reductions" go together, anyway: the ideological and fixing construction that ethnology produces as its object, the "indigenous" culture, reinforces and camouflages the loss of *socio-economic* autonomy produced by capitalist domination. Knowledge and power are conjugated in order to impose simultaneously representations and Western laws on societies that often end up by interiorizing both.

together on large estates or in the mines[17] – all these forms of colonization, and others as well, dissociate the labour force and the means of subsistence; they superimpose upon the destruction of former systems (which sometimes, as in Inca society, prefigured "feudal" organization)[18] the framework of a palaeotechnical capitalism whose first proletarians were the Indians. The manipulations – already commercial and industrial – that made possible the distancing of a colonial power and the ethnic separation of dominators and dominated were widely tested before being replicated and perfected in colonizing nations, as divisions of labour and class struggles. In this connection we can say that the critique of capitalism in recent Indian Declarations goes back to their earliest witnesses, to those whose experience extends over more than four centuries and who, today safe from the catastrophes it has brought down upon them, cannot dissociate the struggle for their political existence from a lucid analysis of that economic system.[19]

Secondly, if the resistance of those spared has a political aspect, it is because despite the arrogation of the best land by the colonizers, despite the reduction and spatial distortion caused by the geographic expansion of those colonizers, as well as the pressure exerted on the Indian lands by smaller-scale colonial adventurers (failures in the dominant system and determined to get ahead), and, finally, despite the movement (also centrifugal, but in the opposite direction) that forced the Indians to abandon land too poor to nourish them and to find work elsewhere as agricultural or factory labourers, the surviving communities have never stopped making a periodic return to the village, to assert their rights to the land, and thus, through this collective alliance to a land, to maintain an anchorage in the particularity of a site. More than representations of beliefs (often hidden and fragmented by the occupier's systems[20]), this referential land has bolstered and defended a "proper" claim against every superimposition. It was and remains a kind of palimpsest: the scription of the foreign *gringos*[21] does not eradicate the first text, which remains traced there, illegible to the passers-by who have manipulated these regions for four

[17] Cf. the analysis of Nathan Wachtel, *La Vision des vaincus: Les Indiens du Pérou devant la Conquête espagnole* (Paris: Gallimard, 1971) pp. 134–211: "destructuration". On the historic effects of this destruction, see Sakari Sariola, *Power and Resistance: The Colonial Heritage in Latin America* (New York: Cornell University Press, 1972) pp. 266–92: and especially Stanley and Barbara Stein, *L'Héritage colonial de l'Amérique latine* (Maspero, 1974) pp. 34–58 and 167–75.
[18] Wachtel, *La Vision des vaincus*, pp. 105–33.
[19] See, for example, the remarkable dossier of André Gunder Frank, *Capitalism and Underdevelopment in Latin America: Historical Studies of Chile and Brazil* (Harmondsworth, Middx: Pelican Latin American Library, Penguin Books, 1969).
[20] See J. E. Monast, *On les croyait chrétiens: les Aymaras* (Paris: Cerf, 1969) and M. de Certeau, "Le danger de l'insignifiance ou l'évangélisation superficielle", *Spiritus*, no. 44, pp. 86–90.
[21] *Gringo*: the white man, the European or North American foreigner.

centuries, sacredly silent with "maternal forces", a tomb of fathers, and an indelible seal of a contract between members of the community.[22]

The earth "retains" an undecipherable Indian secret in spite of the alterations this Testament, this Table of the collective Law – the land – has suffered. It has not ceased and it continues to render possible the marking of a proper and own place. It helps resistance to prevent its being disseminated in the network of occupying forces, and not to allow itself to be captured by their dominant or interpretive discourses (or by the single inversion of these discourses, which does not escape their logic). It "retains" a difference that is rooted in an opaque and inaccessible belonging to violent appropriation or to the recuperation of wisdom. This is the mute foundation of affirmations that have political sense in that they depend on the consciousness of being from a "different" (and not merely contrary) place from that occupied by the omnipresent conquerors.

Lastly, the style of Indian resistance is attached to the Indians' typical internal social organization. What has often been stressed (sometimes to the point of turning it into one of the anthropologists' "myths") is the lack of coercive power – in wartime – in their communities. "It is the fault of social stratification and authority of power that must be retained as a pertinent feature of the political organization of the majority of Indian societies."[23] The hive provides a metaphor for such egalitarian societies.[24] Instead of referring to an overt rejection of centralizing institutions, such a structure refers to a society that has no one particular representative (the chief) of the power that organizes it. In it, the law acts as a tacit co-ordination of received practices. It is the very functioning of the group – a non-isolated authority invested in practised norms. As linkage to a land minimizes the role of a system of representations and is articulated in gestural relationships between the body and the mother earth, the concert of social practices and functions composes an order that no single figure of power detach itself from the group or become visible in order to impose duties of submission or offer, to all, the opportunities for control or revision. "Societies of the multiple",[25] Indian ethnic groups no longer endow their present demands with a recapitulating representation or integrating organism, such as a strategic discourse, for example, supposedly able to manage the particular actions, or a central power whose role it is to cover local groups. A plurality of communities and practices is still its structural form. At the level of the Association between communities it reproduces the type of organization proper to each of them. An ethnic difference is thereby affirmed in a different political model instead of being aligned upon ours to defend it.

[22] T. C. McLuhan and Edward S. Curtis (eds), *Pieds nus sur la terre sacrée* (Paris: Denoel, 1974) pp. 14, 35ff.
[23] Clastres, *La Société centre l'état*, p. 26.
[24] Pierre Clastres, *Chronique des indiens Guayaki* (Paris: Plon, 1972) p. 219.
[25] The definition given by Pierre Clastres of "primitive societies". See "Entretien avec Pierre Clastres", in *L'Anti-mythes*, no. 9, p. 5.

## A Revolution: Autonomous Federated Communities

In assembling the features that emerge from the Indian Manifestos, we have the following model: an associative tissue of socio-political micro-units, each characterized by an autonomous communality of goods (basically land) – in other words, by a distribution of complementary rights and duties over the same wealth and attributed to different parties over which no one possesses, with private title (as a physical or moral person), what we have called the right of property. Its mode of explicitation in the present case – or, let us say, the work of making conscious that makes for the political utterance of this model – follows procedures that conform to the structure that designs it: by a series of local, regional, national and federal Councils, incessant returns to a "permanent consultation of the communities" are effected; furthermore, group orientations are constantly controlled, confronted and enriched in the course of the visits, reunions, consultations, seminars and direct oral discussions (preferred to radio) that guide the construction of the federation to its plural reality.

Thus as was stated in the Constitutive Act of the *Confederación de Indigenas de Venezuela* in 1973, the Indian communities "posit other models of society for developmental alternatives".

At a time when the notion and effectiveness of Western democracy are everywhere being undermined by the spread of economic and cultural technocracy and are slowly foundering with their inherent possibilities (a difference of local units and an autonomy of their socio-political representations[26]), at a time when the micro-experiences and research inherent in self-management tend to compensate for this centralizing evolution by recreating a diversity of local democracies, we have the Indian communities, oppressed and occulted by the Western "democracies", declaring themselves capable of offering self-management models supported by hundreds of years of history. The whole process is occurring as though the chances for a socio-political renewal were emerging on the outskirts of Western societies, precisely where they had always been most powerful. From the area those societies have most despised and that they fought and endeavoured to subjugate, there have emerged political alternatives and social models that may in themselves represent a corrective to the massive acceleration and reproduction of the totalitarian and levelling factors created by Western structures of power and technology.

As early as 1971, Georges Balandier, based on his analyses of African countries, noted the fundamental practical and theoretical changes that were

---

[26] This *autonomous* "research" remains in great part *utopian*, simultaneously mobilizing and mythic, indicative of experiments and studies to be undertaken, similar in this respect to the *democratic* utopias that in the eighteenth century led the way to the great revolutions of that century or of the nineteenth century.

emerging in the so-called "underdeveloped" societies.[27] The search for different models should, he said, be oriented towards the very regions upon which the "benefits" of colonization had purportedly been bestowed. Since then, studies of this type, in economic science, for example, have been concerned with the work of Ignacy Sachs on the politics of development,[28] or, in the field of ethnology, with the new "political anthropology" championed by Pierre Clastres.[29] To these examples we must add research into the origins of political power[30] or on the further implications that the examination of the structures of thought and political power in "primitive" societies have had for Marxist analyses of production relationships.[31]

This is precisely what Francisco Servin, *Pai-Tavytera*, stated at the Indian Parliament held in Paraguay in October 1974: "We were masters of the land but we have become veritable pariahs since the gringos came. . . . We have a hope that a day will come when they will realize that we are their roots and that together we must become a great tree, with all its branches and flowers."[32] Indeed, the dawn of this day has broken. The image of this tree, which once signified revolutions of liberty and popular solidarities, seems to be rising once again with the Indian awakening and with its correspondences in Western experiments and investigations. Perhaps an "age of autonomy"[33] has been inaugurated by these odd coincidences between phenomena produced in rising and declining societies and by the different forms political change can take.

A maintenance and deepening of these differences will only add to the autonomous project that is taking shape. The political feature of Indian practices does not therefore set an example. It would serve only as a mystification, it would be merely an object produced by our discourse, were we to transform it into some utopian model, into a dream solution to all our difficulties or into some ideological substitute for the technical problems the autonomous project encounters in our societies. The Indian Declarations, however, are explicitly opposed to such ideological exploitation. They preach a labour of differentiation and egalitarian co-operation that can work both in favour of the relationship between communities and of their relationship with foreign societies. It is in that way that possible paths are defined and questions posed. A rapid summary of them serves to indicate the bases for demonstrating solidarity with the movement embodied in these Declarations.

[27] Georges Balandier, *Sens et puissance: Les dynamiques sociales* (Paris: PUF, 1971). See also, from the same author, *Anthropo-logiques* (Paris: PUF, 1974).

[28] Ignacy Sachs directed an important study: *Le Changement technologique comme variable des politiques de développement et l'avenir des rapports entre le tiers monde et les pays industrialisés* (IRED, 1974). See also from the same author, *La Découverte du tiers monde* (Paris: Flammarion, 1970).

[29] See Clastres, *La Société contre l'état* and his *Chronique des Indiens Guayaki*.

[30] See J. W. Lapierre, *Essai sur le fondement du pouvoir politique* (publication of the Faculté d'Aix-en-Provence, 1968).

[31] Maurice Godelier, *Horizon, trajets marxistes en anthropologie* (Maspero, 1975).

[32] See Dial Document no. 196.

[33] Pierre Rosanvallon, *L'Âge de l'autogestion* (Paris: Seuil, 1976).

First, the passage from a micro-politics (autonomous communities) to a macro-politics (federation), whereas in our societies such a passage corresponds to a hitherto uncrossed frontier created by the integrating structures of the State.

Secondly, the collective contracts with the land in their dual aspect – economic (rural co-operatives) and ecological (a harmony with nature) – whereas Western development, through the two-fold privilege it accords to industrialization and social conflicts, has acquired a "history" in which "nature" figures merely as the object of labour and the arena of socio-economic struggles that have no value other than the negative one of a peasant "resistance" to be overcome, of a biological limitation that must constantly be surmounted or of some traditionalist ballast to be cast overboard. In this connection, Indian statements concerning some duty to the earth, water, forests (as well as instruction in traditional medicine and medicinal plants) are as important as plans for rural co-operatives: a different relationship with nature comes into play in various other areas as well.

Lastly, and equally essential to any autonomous plan, there is a cultural pluralism that assigns to schooling, which is brought under the control of the community and of "sages" (*amautas*), the task of teaching the social processes of a rural "co-operatism", the necessary agricultural know-how, the history of relations with the West, the mastery of the mother tongue as well as of the national language – in other words, the tools which enable one to use and to symbolize various practices, whereas the dominant culture and the "rural schools" established so far (a catastrophe) have hierarchized such practices and have debased or crushed the differences and thereby deprived democratic enterprise of all cultural content and technological wherewithal.

A space of exchange and of sharing[34] is thereby set up: without fanfare. It is accompanied – and this ought not to astound us – by references to the Great Spirit, references that are modest because the "everyday knowledge of the Invisible and the Eternal is "mute": "The sun of the morning, the sweet new earth and the great silence, each soul must encounter them alone."[35] Around such silences, the "cornerstones" of the community, the gestures, groups and federations of Indians form networks. On the frontiers of these Indian lands another sort of silence seems to reply to the inhabitants: the militant, unspectacular activities of the various religious or civil associations which, in Latin America,[36] in the United States,[37] in Germany,[38] Sweden,[39]

---

[34] Robert Jaulin, *Gens du soi, gens de l'autre* (Paris: 10/18, 1973) pp. 377–427.
[35] McLuhan and Curtis (eds), *Pieds nus sur la terre sacrée*, p. 42.
[36] See, for example, in Mexico, *Eco: primer periódico Bicultural Bilingue de Información general en la Zona Mazahua* (Temascalcingo Edo. de Mexico); in Brazil, the CIMI (Conselho Indigenista Missioñario) of Brasilia, and its *Boletim*; in Paraguay, the *Coordinación pastoral de la Selva* (Asunción) and its publications in *Catequesis Latinoamericana* (see especially the number of July–September 1974).

Denmark[40] and in many other distant countries, are devoting themselves to sharing information and to active solidarity. Since Barthélémy de las Casas, the rumblings of such solidarities have shaken the colonizing West. In this task, born of concern for others and destined to increase in concert with the Indian awakening, we readers are, in our turn, invited to join.

[37] See, for example, in Berkeley (California), *Indigena* and *American Friends of Brazil*, which published *Supysáva: A Documentary Report on the Conditions of Indian Peoples in Brazil* (1974); the *Akwesasne Notes*, the official publication of Mohawk Nation at Akwesasne, New York.

[38] For example, in Hamburg, the *Gesellschaft für Bedrohte Völker*, which publishes *Pogrom*.

[39] For example, the *Syd Amerikansk Chaski*, whose first issue appeared in Stockholm in June 1976.

[40] Thus, in Copenhagen, the *International Work Group for Indigenous World* (IWGIA), which publishes a remarkable series of documents.

JEAN FRANCO

# Killing Priests, Nuns, Women, Children

The murder of three American nuns in El Salvador in December 1980, the murder of priests in Brazil and Argentina, the torture of pregnant women in Uruguay, the farming out of "terrorists'" children to military families in the southern cone, the admonitory raping of women in front of their families in several Latin American countries, the Mexican army's attack on unarmed male and female students in Tlatelolco in 1968, the recent kidnapping in broad daylight of a well-known writer, university teacher and feminist, Alaíde Foppa in Guatemala, the dislodging of Indian communities from traditional lands, plus countless other incidents, all appear more and more to be the well-thought-out atrocities of a concerted offensive. It is part of a war that has pitted unequal forces against one another – on the one hand, the overarmed military who have become instruments of the latest stage of capitalist development and, on the other, not only the left but also certain traditional institutions, the Indian community, the family, and the Church (which still provide sanctuary and refuge for resistance). These institutions owe their effectiveness as refuges to historically based moral rights and traditions, rather like the immunities which (before the recent attack on the Spanish embassy in Guatemala) had accrued to diplomatic space. Homes were, of course, never immune from entry and search but until recently, it was generally males who were rounded up and taken away, often leaving women to carry on and even transmit resistance from one generation to another. Families thus inherited opposition as others inherited positions in the government and bureaucracy.

But what is now at stake is the assault on such formerly immune territories. The attack on the Cathedral in El Salvador in 1980 and the assassination of Archbishop Romero, for instance, showed how little the Church could now claim to be a sanctuary. The resettlement of Indians in Guatemala, of working-class families from militant sectors of Buenos Aires, the destruction of the immunity formerly accorded to wives, mothers, children, nuns and priests have all taken away every immune space. This assault is not as incompatible as it might at first seem with the military government's organization of its discourse around the sanctity of Church and family. Indeed these convenient abstractions, which once referred to well-defined physical spaces, have subtly shifted their range of meaning. Thus, for instance, the "saucepan" demonstrations of Chilean women during the last months of the Allende regime plainly indicated the emergence of the family as consumer in a society which, under Pinochet, was to acquire its symbolic monument – the spiral-shaped tower of the new labyrinthine shopping centre. The Church, once clearly identified as the Catholic Church, and the parish as its territory, has now been replaced by a rather more flexible notion of religion. The conversion of massive sectors of the population all over Latin America to one form or another of Protestantism, the endorsement by Rios Montt, when President of Guatemala, of born-again Christianity, and the active encouragement, in other countries, of fundamentalist sects, all indicate a profound transformation which, until recently, had gone almost unnoticed. Radio and television now promote a serialized and privatized religious experience which no longer needs to be anchored in the physical reality of the parish and in the continuity of family life.

This process can be described as "deterritorialization", although I use this term in a sense rather different from that used by Deleuze and Guattari. In their view (see Gilles Deleuze and Félix Guattari, *Anti-Oedipus: Capitalism and Schizophrenia*, New York, 1977), primitive society (the social machine) does not distinguish between the family and the rest of the social and political field, all of which are inscribed on the socius (that is, the social machine that distinguishes people according to status and affiliations). In the primitive tribe, the socius is the mother earth. What Deleuze and Guattari describe is a process of abstraction which takes place with the emergence of the despotic state that now inscribes people according to their residence, and in doing so "divides the earth as an object and subjects men to a new imperial inscription, in other words to the abstract unity of the State". This they call "pseudo-territoriality", and see it as the substitution of abstract signs (e.g. money) for the signs of the earth and a privatization of the earth itself (as state or private property). Advanced capitalism carries this abstraction much further, recoding persons and making repression into self-repression, exercised not only in the workplace and the streets but within the family, the one place under capitalism where desire can be coded and territorialized (as with Oedipus).

What seems unsatisfactory in Deleuze and Guattari's description of the family is that even though, reading these authors, we may recognize the family's restrictive and repressive qualities, we do not recognize the family's power as a space of refuge and shelter. What seduces us about the home (and what seduces some people about the convent) is that it is a refuge, a place for turning one's back on the world. Max Horkheimer saw (albeit in an idealized fashion) that the family could nourish subjectivities that were alien to capitalism. (Thomas Mann's *Buddenbrooks* is a good example of the subversive effects of the mother inculcating into her son all that will make him incapable of reproducing the work ethic.) In Latin America, this sense of refuge and the sacredness that attaches to certain figures like the mother, the virgin, the nun and the priest acquire even greater significance, both because the Church and the home retained a traditional topography and traditional practices over a very long period, and also because during periods when the state was relatively weak these institutions were the only functioning social organizations. They were states within the state, or even counter-states, since there are certain parishes and certain families which have nourished traditions of resistance to the state and hold on to concepts of "moral right" (E.P. Thompson's term), which account for their opposition to "modernization" (i.e. integration into capitalism). This is not to say that the patriarchal and hierarchical family, whose priority was the reproduction of the social order, has not rooted itself in Latin American soil. But the family has been a powerful rival to the state, somehow more real, often the source of a maternal power which is by no means to be despised, particularly when, as in contemporary Latin America, the disappearance of political spaces has turned the family (and the mother, in particular) into a major institution of resistance.

It is only by recognizing the traditional power of the family and the Church and the association of this power with a particular space (the home, the Church building) that we can begin to understand the significance of recent events in Latin America. Beginning in the fifties and early sixties, "development" brought new sectors of the population, including women, into the labour force. The expansion of transnational companies into Latin America depended on the pool of cheap labour formed from the uprooted peasantry and the ever-growing sector of urban under-classes. The smooth functioning of this new industrial revolution was imperilled by the guerrilla movements and movements of national liberation which, in turn, confronted the counter-insurgency campaigns of the sixties that "modernized" the armies of Latin America, making them pioneers in the newest of torture methods and inventive masters of the art of "disappearance". It is this counter-insurgency movement which has destroyed both the notion of sacred space and the immunity which, in theory if not in practice, belonged to nuns, priests, women and children.

Though women have never enjoyed complete immunity from state terror – indeed rape has been the casually employed resource of forces of law and order since the Conquest – the rapidity with which the new governments have been able to take immunity away from the traditional institutions of Church and family calls for explanation. Such an explanation would involve understanding not only the particular incidents mentioned at the beginning of this essay, but the profound consequences of destroying what Bachelard, in *The Poetics of Space*, called the "images of felicitous spaces", or topophilia. Bachelard's investigations "seek to determine the human value of the sorts of space that may be grasped, that may be defended against adverse forces, the space we love. For diverse reasons, and with the differences entailed by poetic shadings, this is eulogized space. Attached to its protective value, which can be a positive one, are also imagined values, which soon become dominant" (Introduction,

p. xxxiii). In this essay, I want to give these felicitous spaces a more concrete and historical existence than Bachelard's phenomenology allows, for only in this way can we understand the really extraordinary sacrilege that we are now witnessing.

Although it is impossible to separate the literary from the social, literature is a good place to begin to understand this Latin American imaginary with its clearly demarcated spaces. In common with Mediterranean countries, public space in Latin America was strictly separated from the private space of the house (brothel), home and convent, that is spaces which were clearly marked as "feminine". These spaces gave women a certain territorial but restricted power base and at the same time offered the "felicitous" spaces for the repose of the warrior. Nothing illustrates this better than the description of the return of José Arcadio Buendía's blood to its place of origin in his mother's kitchen in García Márquez's *One Hundred Years of Solitude*. The thread of blood "passed along the street of the Turks, turned a corner to the right and another to the left, made a right angle at the Buendia house, went in under the closed door, crossed through the parlor, hugging the walls so as not to stain the rugs, went on to the other living room, made a wide curve to avoid the dining-room table, went along the porch with the begonias, and passed without being seen under Amaranta's chair as she gave an arithmetic lesson to Aureliano José, and went through the pantry and came out in the kitchen, where Ursula was getting ready to crack thirty-six eggs to make bread."

The blood of one of the most *macho* of the Buendias thus follows the order of "feminine" domesticity, traces its path through the women's peaceful and comforting everyday activities which stand in stark opposition to the male world of physical and intellectual prowess and war (the virile or in its most recent and reduced game-cock version – the *macho*).

To view the home thus as a sanctuary obviously makes it into a male-idealized otherness (the Utopia) whilst locking women into this pacific domesticity. House, home and convent are undoubtedly constructions produced by a sex-gender system in which feminine categories are organized in relation to the presence/absence of the phallus, understood in this case as the source of symbolic power. The "logic" of this organization can be illustrated by a semiotic quadrangle (see figure 1).

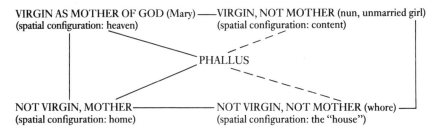

VIRGIN AS MOTHER OF GOD (Mary) ——VIRGIN, NOT MOTHER (nun, unmarried girl)
(spatial configuration: heaven)          (spatial configuration: content)

PHALLUS

NOT VIRGIN, MOTHER——————— NOT VIRGIN, NOT MOTHER (whore) ——
(spatial configuration: home)          (spatial configuration: the "house")

Figure 1

Because there can only be one mother of God (Mary), all other women fall into one of the three remaining categories of which only one (the mother) can receive the legitimate seed that will allow the system to be reproduced. The extent to which the mother is not only sanctified by this function but is converted into the temple of the species, whose bodily configuration is identical to that of the home, is illustrated in a poem by César Vallejo. Imagining his return to the family home, his mother's body is re-entered as if it were a building:

> Your archways of astonishment expects me,
> The tonsured columns of your cares
> That have eroded life. The patio expects me
> The hallway down below with its indentures and
> its feast-day decorations. My grandfather chair expects me
> that good jowly piece of dynastic leather,
> that stands grumbling at the strapped and strapping
> behind of great great great grandchildren.

The father alone has the right to enter this temple and when he does so, it is on his knees in acknowledgement of an irreversible event.

> Between the colonnade of your bones
> That cannot be brought down even with lamentations
> And into whose side not even Destiny can
> place a single finger!

The reference in the last line is to the doubting finger of Thomas who wished to test the resurrection of Christ by touching the wound. In Vallejo's human mother/temple, no such doubt is possible, for the matrix offers the only unequivocal faith in a chaotic world.

The very structure of the Hispanic house emphasized that it was a private world, shut off from public activity. It was traditionally constructed around two or more patios, the windows onto the street being shuttered or barred. Inside, the patios with their plants and singing birds represented an oasis, a domestic replica of the perfumed garden. Respectable women only emerged from the house when accompanied and when necessary. Their lives were almost as enclosed as those of their counterparts, the brothel whore and the nun. In the fifties, I lived in such a house where windows onto the outside were felt to mark the beginning of danger as indeed, after curfew, they did. A prison yes, but one that could easily be idealized as a sanctuary given the violence of political life.

The convent was also a sanctuary of sorts, one that gathered into itself the old, the homeless and the dedicated to God. In José Donoso's novel *The Obscene Bird of Night*, the convent has become an extended building housing the archaic, the mythic and the hallucinating desires which are outlawed from the rest of society. It is this aspect of the Hispanic imaginary which Buñuel's films also capture. Archaic in topography, its huge, empty, decrepit rooms not only sealed it off entirely from the outside world but made it into a taboo territory, the violation of which tempted and terrorized the male imagination.

Finally there was the brothel, the house whose topography mimed that of the convent, with its small cell-like rooms and which, as described by Mario Vargas Llosa in his novel *The Green House*, was another version of the oasis. As the convent gathered to itself the women who were no longer sexual objects, the green house offered them as the common receptacles of a male seed absolved from the strict social rules that governed reproduction.

> Blacks, mulattoes, mixtures of all kinds, drunks, somnolent or frightened half-breeds, skinny Chinese, old men, small groups of young Spaniards and Italians walking through the patios out of curiosity. They walked to and fro passing the open doors of the bedrooms, stopping to look in from time to time. The prostitutes, dressed in cotton dresses were seated at the back of the rooms on low boxes. Most of them sat with their legs apart showing their sex, the "fox" which was sometimes shaved and sometimes not.   (José María Arguedas, *The Fox Above and the Fox Below*)

In describing these spaces, I am not describing categories of women but an imaginary topography in which the "feminine" was rigidly compartmentalized and assigned particular territories. Individual women constantly transgressed these boundaries but the territories themselves were loaded with significance and so inextricably bound to the sacred that they were often taken for spaces of immunity. With the increase in state terrorism in the sixties, mothers used this traditional immunity to protest, abandoning the shelter of homes for the public square, taking charge of the dead and the disappeared and the prisoners whose existence no one else wished to acknowledge. With the seizure of power by the military, the dismantling of political parties and trade unions, this activity acquired a special importance. Homes became hiding places, bomb factories, escape hatches, people's prisons. From the signifier of passivity and peace, "mother" became a signifier of resistance. Nothing illustrates this in more dramatic fashion than an article by Rodolfo Walsh (an Argentine writer who would himself "disappear" shortly after writing this piece). His daughter, who was the mother of a small child and whose lover had already disappeared, was one of a group of *montoneros* killed in the army attack on a house, an attack which deployed 150 men, tanks and helicopters. A soldier who had participated in this battle described the girl's final moments.

> The battle lasted more than an hour and a half. A man and woman were shooting from upstairs. The girl caught our attention because every time she fired and we dodged out of the way, she laughed. All at once there was silence. The girl let go of the machine gun, stood up on the parapet and opened her arms. We stopped firing without being ordered to and we could see her quite well. She was skinny, with short hair and she was wearing a nightdress. She began to talk to us calmly but clearly. I don't remember everything she said, but I remember the last sentence. In fact, I

could not sleep for thinking of it. "You are not killing us," she said, "we choose to die." Then she and the man put pistols to their foreheads and killed themselves in front of us.

When the army took over the house, they found a little girl sitting unharmed on the bed and five dead bodies.

The significance of such an event goes far beyond the rights and wrongs of local politics. Like the murder of the nuns in El Salvador and the kidnapping and killing of Alaíde Foppa in Guatemala, it is a cataclysmic event which makes it impossible to think of the Utopian in terms of space or of the feminine in the traditional sense. Most disconcerting of all, the destruction of these Utopian spaces has been conducted not by the left but by the right-wing military who have nothing left to offer but the unattainable commodity (unattainable, that is, for all but the army and the technocrats). It is true that the military of some southern-cone countries are now in (temporary?) eclipse, but the smell of the cadaver will not be dispelled by the commodity culture, a debt-ridden economy and the forms of restored political democracy.

It is some time since Herbert Marcuse drew attention to the terrors of a desublimated world, one in which such spaces and sanctuaries had been wiped out. His analysis and that of Horkheimer can be seen as overburdened with nostalgia for that *gemütlich* interior of European bourgeois family life in which all the children played instruments in a string quartet. But even if we can no longer accept the now challenged Freudian language of his analysis, he undoubtedly deserves credit for monitoring the first signals from an empty space once occupied by archaic but powerful figures. Feminist criticism based on the critique of patriarchy and the traffic in women has rightly shed no tears for this liquidation of mother figures whose power was also servitude. Yet such criticism has perhaps underestimated the oppositional potentialities of these female territories whose importance as the *only* sanctuaries became obvious at the moment of their disappearance.

This is, however, an essay without a conclusion. I wrote it, thinking of an old friend of mine, Alaíde Foppa, who in 1954 provided sanctuary for those of us left behind in Guatemala and trying to get out after the Castillo Armas coup. I have a vivid memory of her reciting a poem about her five children "like the five fingers of her hand". Today there are only three children left. During the 1960s and 1970s, Alaíde became the driving force behind the feminist movement in Mexico. She was used to going back home once a year to Guatemala to visit her mother. In 1980 she did not come back. A Guatemalan newspaper reported that her whereabouts and that of her chauffeur were "unknown". To this day, Alaíde "continues disappeared" in the words of the newspaper, like many other men, women, priests, nuns and children in Latin America who no longer occupy space but who have a place.

WLAD GODZICH

# The Semiotics of Semiotics

On 28 September 1982 there appeared in *The New York Times* an article on the subject of semiotics. This was a significant event for it brought to the attention of the larger literate public a form of enquiry that is still far from having gained general acceptance in the academic world in which it is mostly practised. But, to semioticians, *The New York Times'* choice of location for the printing of the article was even more significant than the publication itself: it appeared within the pages of the Science supplement, appropriately called "Science Times". From its authoritative position, *The New York Times* appeared to have decided one of the longer lasting controversies within the field: is semiotics a science? a discipline? or a mode of dealing with signification that cuts across disciplines? Since it is unlikely that the editor of "Science Times" was familiar with the intricacies of this debate, it may prove enlightening to enquire into the reasons that led him to include semiotics within the scope of science. For, suddenly what is at stake here is no longer the status of claims made by semioticians about their own field, but rather the way in which that field is perceived and in which it makes sense to someone outside of it. In other words, what *The New York Times* report precipitated is the need for an enquiry into the semiotic status of semiotics.

## The Crisis of Meaning and the Commodity

### *1. Boot Fetish at "The New York Times"*

*The New York Times* is a thorough newspaper: it knows what it wants and knows how to get it. The author of the article on semiotics, Maya Pines, spoke to many people calling themselves semioticians or so called by others. In every instance she asked them to define their field and to provide examples of what they did.

She also asked them if they had anything "semiotic" to say about the fact that a number of erstwhile and affluent New Yorkers were wearing cowboy boots as part of their daily attire. In fact, the question is reproduced as the lead sentence of the article: "What does it mean when a man wears cowboy boots, even though he lives in a city?" (see figure 1).[1]

It soon became apparent that this was far from an idle question. Pines and her editor had little patience with those explanations that related the wearing of cowboy boots in urban settings to machismo, American myths about the cowboy, or the desire for wide-open spaces. Such interpretations struck them as neither novel nor especially semiotic; they could have thought them up themselves, they argued, with a little help from scholars in American Studies or, more generally, from students of American culture. The semioticians interviewed were uneasy with the concentration on the boots, fearing that the example was too trivial, and offered instead to discuss matters more representative of semiotic enquiry, such as stop signs and their manufacture, table manners, or the conventions of landscape painting. But *The New York Times* was not to be deterred, and the matter was pursued until an explanation satisfactory to Pines and the editor was provided. Such doggedness in the pursuit of cowboy boots deserves some attention.

## 2. On Cowboy Boots

Before we enquire into the *The New York Times'* preoccupation and fascination with cowboy boots, we need to restate, in a fuller version than was ultimately published, the explanation that satisfied "Science Times".

Cowboy boots, with their special cowhide, leather-tooling and design, have been part traditionally of the attire of the cowboy. Designed to be worn during lengthy sojourns on horseback, they had a specific use value to the cowboy. Rapidly, together with other elements of the cowboy's dress (the hat, the belt, and the waistcoat, in particular), they became emblematic of a certain mode of life and began to be adopted as the distinctive wear of certain regions of the United States: the West and the Southwest. In this guise, their value resided primarily in their signalling one's belonging to a larger community of individuals sharing a relation to the land and, presumably, some values; they were community-integrative.

In the seventies, there opened up two additional avenues for the wearing of cowboy boots. The first was the relatively short-lived yet highly significant emergence of the long-distance trucker as a sort of cowboy of the highways. Depicted as a genuine working-man, though in actual fact frequently self-employed or the equivalent, in the service sector, of a sharecropper, the trucker, as hero of country music and as the vehicle for the promotion of CB radios, was treated as a populist enemy of the system symbolized by the "bears"

---

[1] *The New York Times*, 28 September 1982, p. 36.

of the highway patrol, and of the regulatory power of government most evident in the imposition of a lowered speed limit.

As a wearer of cowboy boots he was, in the language of the article, "virile, self-reliant, free to roam over the wide-open spaces" of America, like his mythical cowboy predecessor of Western romance and film. The myth of the trucker occulted the genuine crisis that was then shaking that sector of the economy: strikes, take-overs and moves toward monopolization. Much of this resulted in violence in the mid-seventies, especially on the Pennsylvania Turnpike. But, of course, the largest crisis was due to the petrol and diesel fuel shortages caused by the oil embargo and the ensuing imposition of controls over the supply of energy by the oil cartels. The cowboy boots were an ironic sign since alongside their obvious reference to the overt features of the cowboy myth, they also seemed to allude to the less reassuring aspects of that myth by foretelling the obsolescence and eventual demise of the trucker who may have had the desire to run (through) America but literally did not have the energy.

The second track was precisely the energy track. The boots, as part of the old Western gear, were inherited, and adopted, by the new oil and gas money-makers of the energy-producing states, to such an extent that not only the latter but those who, for professional reasons, came in contact with them, began to wear cowboy boots, frequently of very expensive quality. Here another aspect of the boots – or to speak the language of semiotics, another semic feature – was being reactivated: vitality, which, in the seventies and eighties, translates itself into the possession or the supplying of virtually limitless energy.

At this moment in time (1980–1) then, cowboy boots constitute a rather complex and internally contradictory semiotic entity. They partake of all the following: the old American myth of the cowboy, the trucker's seemingly populist and semi-anarchic dream of unregulated wandering and enterprising, the *gemeinschaftlich* uniform of the West rising against Washington in the so-called "sagebrush rebellion", and the new oil money effectively capturing the apparatus of the state with the election of a new President who, quite appropriately, ties these various strands together: he has played cowboys, comes from the West, owns a ranch, ran against the regulatory power of so-called "big government", was bankrolled by oil-interests, and is frequently photographed wearing cowboy boots both functionally, in horseback riding, or socially, at Santa Barbara receptions.

It becomes clear that, with the final nudge into aesthetic conversion provided by John Travolta in *Urban Cowboy*, and with the sartorial extravagance authorized if not demanded by New York discotheques, a number of affluent New Yorkers who normally care and know as much about cowboys as about cowpats, should begin to adopt cowboy boots. As the article states quite accurately, "New Yorkers don't want real cowboy boots – just the *idea* of cowboy boots. So they buy boots made of lizard or snake that serve as symbols or signs of cowboy boots, in which they can roam the city with a feeling of power, but wouldn't be much good for rounding up cattle." These boots, frequently costing over a thousand dollars a pair, serve then a phantasmatic

# What's the Real Message of 'Casablanca'? Or of a Rose?

By MAYA PINES

**W**HAT does it mean when a man wears cowboy boots, even though he lives in a city? Why do advertisements often show laughing young women being carried piggy-back by young men? And what accounts for the extraordinarily enduring appeal of the movie "Casablanca"?

The world is filled with such questions, say members of a rapidly growing and fashionable academic discipline called "semiotics," which has influenced the study of English, comparative literature, philosophy, religion, sociology, political science, anthropology and other fields.

Everything we do sends messages about us in a variety of codes, semioticians contend. We are also on the receiving end of innumerable messages encoded in music, gestures, foods, rituals, books, movies or advertisements. Yet we seldom realize that we have received or sent such messages, and would have trouble explaining the rules under which they operate.

Semiotics is an attempt to decipher these rules and bring them to our consciousness. Though its name comes from a Greek root meaning "sign," and semiotics is often defined as the study of signs, in fact it has become the study of the codes through which people communicate, verbally or nonverbally. Understanding these codes should give us a clearer view of our own actions and those of others, semioticians say, as well as a new way of think-

Unhappy Love

"Myths of sacrifice' such as Unhappy Love are seen pervading 'Casablanca.'"

Culver Pictures, Inc.

ing about books, movies, art and foreign cultures.

Nothing seems too trivial or too complicated for semioticians to analyze. Take the matter of cowboy boots, for instance. A New Yorker who buys such boots is actually responding to well-established myths about the cowboy in our culture, and also to the new power of the oil millionaires and ranchers who support the Reagan Administration, says Dr. Marshall Blonsky, a semiotician in the department of comparative literature at the State University of New York at Stony Brook.

"In both myths, the wearer of cowboy boots handles the world masterfully," says Dr. Blonsky. "He is virile, self-reliant, free to roam over the wide-open spaces that New Yorkers lack, and has or supplies virtually limitless energy." Nobody cares that real cowboys often lead humdrum lives, he points out. New Yorkers don't want real cowboy boots — just the idea of cowboy boots. So they buy boots made of lizard or snake that serve as symbols or signs of cowboy boots, in which they can roam the city with a feeling of power, but wouldn't be much good for rounding up cattle.

"Semiotics is the discipline of studying everything that can be used in order to lie," declares Dr. Umberto Eco, holder of the world's first professorship in semiotics (at the University of Bologna, Italy). Therefore semiotics can be used to see through lies or efforts at manipulation, from individual attempts at conveying a macho image to worldwide efforts at promoting certain ideologies.

*Continued on Page C6*

Figure 1

Continued From Page C1

The method of semiotics is, first, to separate an act, called "the signifier," from its meaning, called "the signified." When a man offers a woman a red rose, for instance, the signifier is the act of giving the rose, but the signified is romance. The rose itself has little importance.

To understand the signified, the semiotician looks for connotations — meanings that have been attached to a signifier by its history of use, or by other aspects of our culture. According to Dr. Blonsky, the key question is: "Where have I seen this before?"

Why, for instance, do men playfully attack women with pillows or sprays of water, or else carry women on their backs, in some advertisements? The sociologist Erving Goffman, who analyzed male and female roles in his book, "Gender Advertisements," noted that he had seen exactly the same kind of "mock assaults" when men play with children and treat them like prey under attack by a predator.

The hidden message of the ads, therefore, is that women should be placed in the subordinate and indulged position of children, Dr. Goffman says. He adds that "underneath this show a man may be engaged in a deeper one, the suggestion of what be could do if he got serious about it."

Signs don't mirror reality, but bring echoes of some of the received ideas that we carry around in our heads — old narratives, myths, events, or values, says Dr. Blonsky. To be effective, political images or art must trigger some received ideas, The nearly universal fascination with the movie "Casablanca" in Western nations can be attributed to the film's lavish use of archetypes which have shaped stories through the ages, according to Dr. Eco.

The movie "opens in a place already magical in itself: Morocco, the exotic," he writes. "The city is the setting for a Passage, the Passage to the Promised Land. . . . But to make the Passage one must submit to a test, the Wait." The Passage also requires a Magic Key — in this case a visa allowing the anti-Nazi activist (Ingrid Bergman's husband) to leave Casablanca and carry on the good fight. The movie's passions revolve around the winning of this visa.

The myth of sacrifice runs through the film, Dr. Eco continues. There is Unhappy Love, Civilization against Barbarism, Redemption, and the Triumph of Purity. "Casablanca brings with it, like a trail of perfume, other situations which the viewer brings to bear quite readily," says Dr. Eco. Ironically, some of these echoes come from films or situations that occurred years after the movie was actually made. It wasn't until "To Have and Have Not," for instance, that Humphrey Bogart actually played the part of a Hemingway hero. But now that these images are part of our culture, however, we tend to see Bogart as a Hemingway hero even in Casablanca, which was made years earlier.

There have been several practical applications of semiotic analysis in recent years. One of the most dramatic involves predictions made by Polish semioticians for the use of the Polish labor union Solidarity.

Last year, Solidarity's leaders were very concerned that the Polish propensity for uprisings and acts of heroism might lead to a bloody Soviet response, says Dr. Wlad Godvich, a professor of comparative literature at the University of Minnesota. To help them forestall such a response, a group of Polish semioticians began to analyze Soviet writings and speeches about the Soviet Union's satellite nations, looking for incongruencies that would

# Semiotics find little too trivial or complex to analyze

reveal some of the codes under which the Soviets operated.

This allowed the group to build a model explaining how the Soviet Union viewed its dependence on the satellites. The group, which worked anonymously, then predicted that if Solidarity opened its ranks to peasants (who, under some Marxist interpretations, are considered remnants of a feudal society and enemies of the working class) the Soviet Union would believe that Solidarity was no longer a labor union but had become a political movement aimed at overthrowing Poland's Socialist order.

Forewarned by the semioticians' prediction, Solidarity's leaders emphasized that they were, indeed, a real labor union and pre-empted the issue, Dr. Godvich says; they were not challenging the Soviet Union, they said, but were simply advancing a different kind of Marxist analysis which did not assume a class antagonism between workers and peasants.

According to Dr. Godvich, these efforts helped blunt the force of the Soviet response, and although the Soviet Communist Party did attack Solidarity, its attacks were not so virulent as they might have been. Nor was there an invasion.

Analyses of this sort will be increasingly important in the future, Dr. Godvich believes; they "are applicable in negotiations of all kinds, as well as in establishing communication with people from other cultures."

Semiotics was founded by a Swiss linguist, Ferdinand de Saussure, and an American philosopher, Charles S. Peirce, in the early part of the 20th century. Its growth was also strongly influenced by the French structural anthropologist Claude Levi-Strauss. However, it did not begin to spread around the world until the publication of "Mythologies" — a book which has been called a sarcastic Marxist critique of everyday life — by the French philosopher Roland Barthes in 1957. In the past 15 years, semiotics has taken such a firm hold in the humanities departments of major American universities that few professors now dare to talk about the meaning of a literary or artistic work; instead, they teach their students to look for the work's underlying codes, and to analyze how certain images are used to manipulate the reader or viewer.

As the semiotic approach has spread from architecture to zoology, however, it has encountered increasing resistance. Some academics accuse semioticians of "a limitless imperialistic desire," to take over all other disciplines. And even the most committed semioticians agree that semiotic techniques lack precision, remaining somewhat speculative and unjelled. Nevertheless, semioticians maintain that they are placing a conscious framework around reality which allows us to see many kinds of deception and self-deception that might otherwise escape us.

Meanwhile the word "semiotics" itself has acquired so much value that some intellectuals now bandy it about as a sign of their worth — much in the same spirit as New Yorkers who buy cowboy boots.

integrative function that unites their wearers into some sort of brotherhood of mastery: those who handle the world masterfully. The New York wearer of boots is a latecomer to this amalgamation since his role was generally limited to *not* voting for Carter, thus permitting the election of Reagan in 1980. The purchase of the boots is his first affirmative act in this respect.[2]

### 3. Crisis of Meaning

This answer was acceptable to Pines and to the "Science Times" editor, both in its own terms (it does explain the puzzling occurrence of expensive cowboy boots on some New Yorkers' feet), and as an example of semiotic analysis (scholars in American Studies could talk of the myth of the cowboy, psychologists, of the New Yorker's feeling of powerlessness, but the ability to weave complex historical and contemporary data with behavioural patterns, psychological motivations, political effects and ideological resonances, had to be the hallmark of a new science).

   Semiotics had provided an answer to the question of what it means when a New Yorker wears cowboy boots in the city. But the question itself deserves scrutiny. Clearly, this sartorial development must have been very puzzling to "Science Times" since it was willing to grant its imprimatur to the explanatory and analytic system that accounted for it. I am going to suggest that it is because it was far more perceptive than many literary scholars, and indeed many semioticians, of something that has been going on around us without our being able or willing to recognize it, whereas "Science Times" not only did so but found its strategic location.

[2] This, indeed, *is* fuller, more analytic than what *The New York Times* published. Since the short entry it *did* publish was attributed to the editor of this volume, he is perhaps justified in printing here what he more fully told the *Times*: "Look at the coalition perceived as being uniquely powerful in the United States today – the so-called 'sagebrush rebellion', oil millionaires, ranchers and others who grouped together to produce the current administration. New Yorkers are far removed from these social classes, both in terms of mileage and psychology, and there's precious little we can share with them to leach out some of their perceived power. The superficial signifier of fashion is perhaps as good a steal as we can ever get. The New Yorker adopts the oilman's unfamiliar outfit as a sign of power in the midst of his own powerlessness, as an imitation of activity and capacity for activity elsewhere. So when you wear the $700 lizard or ostrich boots or the $250 rooster feather hat, it's an unconscious acknowledgement on your part that the people who control much of our destiny today are those who wear their cowboy boots seriously. It will be interesting to see if the boots and hats aren't relegated to the closet at about the time our present administration is." The quotation told too much of the origins and contrivance of Reaganism – a contrivance *The New York Times* has faithfully been *acting* to dismantle in favour of another contrivance (and another administration) more liberal. Sartre once said that the United States is a monster with many heads. One head may, as now, be quarrelling with another, but under no circumstances must the monster's entrails be exposed. *The New York Times* cut semiotics short because it had and has other things to do than print theory. It has Reagan to dismantle. [Editor's note]

What has been going on is what the Germans have lately taken to calling a *Sinnkrise*, a crisis of meaning.[3] Its manifestations are multiform: the great explanatory systems of the West are felt to be inadequate, if not obsolete, whether they be of a social-democratic, Marxist or educated-liberal variety. The master narratives are dying for lack of credibility, as Jean-François Lyotard has argued in *The Postmodern Condition*,[4] and nothing is taking their place. Politics appear to take on more anarchic forms, or to adopt previously inconceivable dimensions. Here it will suffice to invoke the example of the emergence and rise of the Solidarity movement in Poland, a phenomenon that has proved to be beyond the explanatory powers or the conceptual scope of either the traditional Left or Right, and equally troublesome to both.

But a diagnosis formulated in such broad terms as the "crisis of meaning" does not lend itself to any sort of resolution, but, at best, a description of its aetiology. What "Science Times" experienced was more specific, and therein lies its value: it felt the crisis as a crisis of a specific artefact, the cowboy boots, and we, in turn, can see this crisis as a more general, yet specific, crisis of the commodity. *The New York Times* could have seen it as a broad existential crisis, or as a mere fad, localized at that, or as a psychological condition affecting a restricted population, but it did not seek philosophical, sociological, group- or individual-psychological explanations. The mystery was *in* the boots, and the old reliable explanations of the behaviour of commodities were inadequate to the mystery they posed. These boots were not part of that system of commodity behaviour, and therefore a new explanatory regress had to arise to explain them. I belabour this point for its significance can scarcely be exaggerated: such means as are available to "Science Times" for the uncovering, description and analysis of the meaning of a certain commodity were unequal to the task. Given the role played by commodities – their production, distribution and consumption in our social life – such an inability was potentially catastrophic.

Since these means (historico-cultural, economic, psychological, etc.) had been developed in response to, and as an accompaniment to, the production of commodities, then their inadequacy in the instance of the cowboy boots logically suggested that these boots had got on New Yorkers' feet by means of a different mode of production, one that was unknown to "Science Times" as of yet, but which, the writer and editor correctly averred on the basis of their knowledge of the laws pertaining to modes of production, had to have also given rise to an explanatory system that could, among other things, explain the phenomenon they found so puzzling. And clearly, the descriptive and analytic regress of a mode of production deserves the name of *science*. *The New York Times* knows what it is doing.

We are led then at this juncture to the following set of considerations: if the

---

[3] See the discussion of this term in Manfred Frank, *Der kommende Gott* (Frankfurt: Suhrkamp, 1982).

[4] Jean-François Lyotard, *The Postmodern Condition*, trans. by Geoffrey Bennington and Brian Massumi (Minneapolis, Minn.: University of Minnesota Press, 1983).

intuition of the "Science Times" is correct, then we are at present dealing with a new mode of production; if we fail to describe it, then we shall certainly fail to understand what semiotics is all about. Thus the first task we face is an enquiry into, and a description of, this mode of production. It should be followed by an examination of the question whether semiotics is adequate to this mode of production, in the sense that it is its product as well.[5]

## The Mode of Production of Semiotics

My discussion of the mode of production, though conducted in economic terms, will be aimed principally at the status of meaning in the mode of production. Such an approach is, in any case, further justified by the fact that it was in the form of a "crisis of meaning" that this mode of production disclosed itself to us in the first place.

### 1. Productive and Unproductive Labour

A discussion of the meaning of commodities must, in classical terms, invoke the value of commodities. The apparently self-evident notion that too high a price in relation to the use value of a commodity inhibits its purchase is clearly challenged in the case of the cowboy boots New Yorkers formerly wore to discotheques, theatres and restaurants, before fashion turned its page on the boots.[6]

The discussion of value is best framed in terms of productivity. For classical economics, a product brings wealth if it increases the real salary of its recipient by making him or her more efficient. Strictly speaking, the degree of productivity is independent of the socio-economic status of the producer, who may be an artisan, a salaried worker or a mass-production financier. For Marxist political economy, which starts from the point of departure of classical

---

[5] For strategic reasons, this commissioned article was written in the formal mode of a learned discourse. Given its serious implications, the editor will from time to time intervene to cast the language in a more popular style. As now. Godzich is asking *sotto voce* whether university-taught semiotics, whether the semiotics bought at bookshops and accepted by the press, has in fact been co-opted within the system. Explicating film, poetry and the like, might semiotics be fulfilling a need our culture has for indicating that meaning is not altogether vanishing? That there is still use value to be found in our commodities and lives? [Editor's note]

[6] I was wrong in my remark to *The New York Times*: "It will be interesting to see if the boots and hats aren't relegated to the closet at about the time our present administration is." The boots went into fashion's closet *much earlier*. Why? Because they were a part of a strategy for *gaining* power, but inappropriate for the exercise of power. Gaining power required only a semblance of consensus whereas the exercise of power requires domination of one group, one class, one section of the country over another. Boots would be too overt for this – they had to retreat behind more benign symbols. [Editor's note]

economics, money is produced only in the making of a material object by *salaried* individuals.

Such a formulation leads to a certain amount of conceptual difficulty when one attempts to think of the status of writers, composers, playwrights and generally other producers of artistic artefacts, as producers of market wealth. The difficulty lies in the applicability of the question of surplus-value to their productions: what kind of labour produces surplus-value? This question in turn leads to the distinction between productive and unproductive labour, where the former is defined as labour that creates value and permits the accumulation of capital while the latter does not. In other words, productive labour leads to the growth of capital and the creation of surplus-value, while unproductive labour is of interest to the purchaser of labour only through the use-value of the product. For Marx, under capitalism only salaried individuals can be productive since, by selling their labour power, they create capital. As a result, and against the tenets of classical economics, unsalaried workers – those who receive royalties, for example – or even salaried workers who create capital only implicitly (through the consumption implied in their activity), are not productive. They do create wealth within the capitalist mode of production but it is a type of wealth that, properly speaking, is external to this mode. It is important to bear in mind that an activity that may promote consumption or production is not in itself productive of wealth in this analysis.[7]

## 2. Productive "Unproductive Labour"

A *locus classicus* of philosophy and political economy is the artisan who produces an artefact and proceeds to sell it. When I purchase a basket from a basket-weaver, I deal with him or her as a seller of merchandise and not as a seller of labour even though it is his or her labour that produced the basket. In this sense, an artisan is unproductive, although it would probably be better to say that the distinction between productive and unproductive labour is alien to this category of producers.

But what happens in the case of those producers we have identified as troublesome? Let us follow Jacques Attali's analysis of the musical composer who has written a song. Since he is paid by royalties, he is, technically, unproductive, yet his product is not fixed the way a basket is: it may be printed by salaried workers, sold to musicians, create surplus-value and then a salaried musician may perform it, giving a formal representation of it. It is, in fact, in this performance that we feel that the song, as the composer's product, has truly come into its own. Yet, from our present perspective, the composer's status, and especially the status of his labour, leaves all of this quite perplexing with respect to the issue of productivity. Clearly the composer is at the origin of the process

[7] My entire discussion of the mode of production of repetition is indebted to Jacques Attali's reflections on the subject, in connection with his theorizing on music. See his *Bruits: Essai sur l'économie politique de la musique* (Paris: Presses Universitaires de France, 1977).

that leads to the performance; yet, just as clearly, since he sells his song against a part of the surplus-value obtained through the use-value of the song (the royalty on the performance), he is at once unproductive in the sense we have defined, yet a part of each performance. His remuneration is paid in the form of a royalty. In a sense, he manages to keep ownership of his labour power. How is that possible? The explanation lies in his distinction from the basket-weaver. Unlike the latter, the composer does not really sell an artefact that is a finished commodity. Rather, he produces a programme in an almost cybernetic sense, for further investment of labour power. In fact, this programme is taken over by capitalist production which purchases labour power from salaried individuals to realize it. The composer is then not an artisan but what Attali calls a "designer" and he enjoys a status more akin to that of a *rentier* than that of an artisan with whom he is frequently confused. Writers and composers are not the only ones in our society to enjoy such a status; anyone who designs programmes for further production is a designer. Our economy is replete with such designers, many of them self-employed. Those who are salaried cannot, of course, be considered as enjoying *rentier*-like status.

The Marxian distinction between salaried and unsalaried is all-important here: the self-employed designer – the composer in our example – is not paid for his labour since what he is paid is independent of the quantity of labour that he will have furnished, whereas his salaried counterpart, whether paid by the hour or the year, is paid on that labour. The self-employed designer's income depends upon the quantity of demand that the product of his labour generates. It is in this sense that the designer creates a programme that gives rise to, and sustains, an entire industry.

Though it permits us to comprehend the specific differential status of the designer, Marxian economics has paid scant attention to the role played by this individual, focusing rather upon those who sell their labour: the proletariat. Classical economics has been more concerned with investors and the accumulators or creators of capital, and has paid equally little attention to the designer. Though equally necessary in both frameworks for an analysis of capitalism, the designer seems to have escaped the attention s/he deserves. We shall see that the crisis of meaning and the crisis of the commodity have a great deal to do with this function.

### 3. The Production of Demand

If we return to the basket-weaver, we can observe that, as an artisan, he manufactures unique artefacts and sells them. No two of his baskets are quite alike. In fact, he is likely to vary the design somewhat with each object, even though he may be conforming to a general pattern of his own invention or to one prevalent in his community. The same situation obtains in early capitalism, though for somewhat different reasons. A design is used but once, primarily because the technical means for its reuse are not available. Under such circumstances, every object is, if not custom-made, at least of sufficient difference from other objects of the same class to permit easy identification and differentiation, and thus the establishment of a specific relationship with its owner. Attali calls this mode of production the "mode of representation", for here the product *represents* the labour that has gone into its production. If, however, the design is used over and over again, then we are dealing with the "mode of repetition". In this mode, the product no longer stands in relation to the labour that has produced it.

In the market system, then, representation refers to that which results from a singular act, whereas repetition holds sway as soon as serial organization prevails. Books, records, designer clothes and cans of tomato purée are all instances of repetition, while custom-built cabinets, a dress by a grand couturier, a painting or a lecture are instances of representation.

Representation emerges with capitalism, but it does little to sustain the latter's appetite for profit. By contrast, repetition permits one to capitalize upon the designer's work by creating use-value out of his product over and over again. But the kind of use-value created here differs from the one created by the basket-weaver, for example. When I purchase a basket from the individual who wove it, I may be attracted by its shape or colours, or I may be in need of a basket in order to carry some groceries I have just purchased, or, perhaps, I intend to make a gift of it to someone. In any case I envisage some use of it as I acquire it, and, generally, I arrive at this notion by myself. The weaver has not taken any part of the surplus-value he has created and used it to stimulate my interest in the basket.

A somewhat different situation arises in the case of serially produced artefacts. The integrity of the old use-value has to be broken up here since some of the surplus-value produced has to be used to pay a royalty to the designer on the one hand, and an additional portion of the surplus-value – and it is an ever-increasing one – has to be devoted to giving meaning to the artefact, on the other. In a market situation, to give meaning to an artefact is to convince a potential buyer that the artefact has a use-value. For, indeed, the serially produced object does not evidence its use-value as readily as our basket.

Indeed, to deflect a part of the surplus-value in order to establish the existence of use-value, as is commonly done with advertising, is to acknowledge that the meaning of the commodity (that is, its use-value) is not necessarily obvious. Of course, this procedure is used in order to promote sales, that is to increase, or, properly speaking, to *produce demand*. But the logic of this mechanism is ultimately self-defeating: repetition requires that a substantial portion of the surplus-value obtained in the production of the supply be spent to produce demand; the production of demand requires that use-value be established; the establishment of use-value requires a further deflection of surplus-value, making less of it available for the production of the object and its actual use-value as opposed to the establishment of the latter. In other words, repetition is a mechanism for the progressive diversion of surplus-value away from investment in the production of additional use-value, and its rechannelling into the *establishment* of use-value or the production of demand.

Under the regime of repetition, then, use-value must be established for commodities, otherwise there is likely to occur loss of meaning. Labour is used to produce demand, and production proper becomes increasingly reproduction and payment of royalties. The production of demand, as establishment of use-value, thus becomes a wholesale production of meaning, carried out principally by the economic sphere itself, with the assistance of the public sphere when the state intervenes to promote further meaningfulness, that is demand. For very rapidly here, one goes from producing demand to producing consumers.

But, as Attali is quick to point out, the necessity of investing surplus-value in order to establish use-value takes on increasingly the appearance of disorder: the disorder that is inevitable in replication from a mould, where flaws occur with ever greater force and frequency with each copy. The logic of repetition is such that the increasing difficulty of producing begins to put strains on the system's ability to produce supply. The state of the US car industry is an eloquent testimony to this fact. The mode of repetition is then faced with its breakdown. It produces artefacts whose use-value cannot be easily (read: cheaply) established, and which therefore remain unsold; it then uses up surplus-value in the attempt to sell them, that is in the attempt to make them meaningful to buyers, and thus it begins to use up capital that otherwise would have been invested in the production of commodities. In the mode of production of repetition, the system feeds upon itself: it is forced to use profit in unproductive ways. Paying royalties to designers and paying for the establishment of the meaning of its productions, it fails to accumulate the capital necessary for further production. One recourse is to establish an internal designing unit and thus remove the designers from the unproductive, in our sense, system of royalty payments to the productive one of salaried labour. This is done more and more often. None the less, the dangers are sufficiently great that the very codes of production are endangered.

This, in fact, is what seems to be happening; to such an extent that whole modes of analysis, based upon the existence of these codes and the existence of these processes of production (the classical as well as the Marxist), are being rendered obsolescent since they are suddenly left without any object upon which to train their analytic power.

### 4. The Production of Semiotics

It is in this context that semiotics is produced. The effect of the mode of production of repetition is an increase in disorder and an endangering, and a diminution, of use-value, that is thematized as an endangering and a loss of meaning. Under such circumstances, the uncovering, localization and preservation of meaning acquire urgency. Yet, these are tasks to which analytical instruments, concepts and explanatory regresses, derived from the mode of production of representation, are, by definition as well as a matter of empirical fact, unequal. They cannot be altogether jettisoned, of course, for we do have many artefacts dating from representation around, but they do need to be reterritorialized so that they can be recycled under repetition. The relationship of "American (cultural) Studies" to semiotics in the case of the cowboy boots is a good instance of such a remapping, one that, it should now be obvious, does not derive from some will to power or imperial imperative of semiotics, but is a systemic necessity under repetition.

The question that now arises is whether semiotics, or more specifically, semioticians, are aware of the historical role they are called upon to play (see box 1). What is at stake here is not the frequently made distinction between a materialist and an idealist semiotics. Such a distinction is, in any case, dependent upon, and concerned with, two concepts that are concepts of the mode of representation and thus of antiquarian interest within the mode of repetition that has given rise to semiotics. Rather, what is at stake is whether semiotics, as a product of the mode of repetition, is to serve that mode by providing it with its alibi – an alibi to be construed quite literally since it would consist in claiming that meaning, though not immediately apprehensible, is none the less localizable and therefore recoverable – or whether semiotics will be the science through which we shall know that mode and be able to overcome it: that is whether semiotics can be a critical practice.

The prospect of the latter option does not appear too promising, at first. For repetition does not let itself be known as such, that is as repetition, but rather, because it offers itself through its artefacts and not its process, and because of its insistence upon the production of demand as the establishment of meaning, it gives itself in the guise of representation. A semiotics that would serve repetition would be then a semiotics of representation, blind to its inscription within repetition. Such, unfortunately, appears to be the case with the bulk of semiotics being practised today. It is a semiotics of representation *for* repetition.

The possibility of a critical practice of semiotics hinges on the ability of semiotics to remap semiotically the historical, and it is to this that we now need to turn.

## Semiotics and History

It is generally held, by its promoters and detractors alike, that semiotics is not a form of historical thought, although it is acknowledged that, through the distinction between diachrony and synchrony, it provides conceptual and operational room for history. Such a tenet requires examination for at least two reasons:

1. If semiotics is indeed a theory of signification, then history must be signified in it not only under such guises as it had previously but in some specifically semiotic ways.

2. For the sake of its self-constitution, semiotics must examine its own system of inclusions and exclusions.

In both cases, the apparent neglect of history should constitute one of the

*Box 1*
## Semiotics in the Marketplace:
## a Test Case

To test the Godzich theory in experience – and using a prestige he and I enjoyed after *The New York Times* article – I did not throw away an opportunity that I was given. Which? To lend myself toward illustrating that semiotics may be *en route* toward uncovering, stabilizing and refining meanings for marketers of repetitive products.

Shortly after the article appeared, I received a telephone call from the research director of a large advertising agency. His firm represents one of the seven American women's service magazines. He wanted to know its "significancies" (his word) – *vis-à-vis* the meaning of the magazine's closest competitor. The magazine's editors felt they knew too little of the magazine's meaning or its audience. They felt they were editing without a law, or with such a weak rule as to make that rule almost inoperable. I was asked to uncover the meaning, to read issue after issue, article upon article, of the magazine and *abduce*, as we say, a law for the future. "'Adso,' William said, 'solving a mystery is not the same as deducing from first principles. Nor does it amount simply to collecting a number of particular data from which to infer a general law. It means, rather, facing one or two or three particular data apparently with nothing in common, and trying to imagine whether they could represent so many instances of a general law you don't yet know, and which perhaps has never been pronounced'" (Umberto Eco, *The Name of the Rose*).

Now, one can scrutinize a magazine for its model, implicit reader, or go right to the empirical one. I did both. I sifted the magazine for the truth of its reader, and I stared at her – at a group of women through a one-way mirror – hearing, really hearing, the discourse of this reader.

The audience perceives itself as mediocre – given the values of a class/sexist society. One of the women speaking of her life said: "It's family life, everyday hum-drum stuff" – interrupted by laughter, then, her voice raised: "Well, that's what we're *in*." Guilt-ridden, their guilt seems to extend down to the most trivial of their object relations. "I feel guilty if I sit with Michener's novels, they're so long" (*Poland* had just appeared). Another: "I feel guilty about buying magazines – $2, my God! I could buy a gallon of milk for that. That's why I buy *Woman's Day* – it's 75¢, like a candy bar." They are subordinated: to the family, to children, to their husbands. A speaker: "To me, a family is parents and children, not a man and a woman and a child that someone got from somewhere." Taking the child's part, she hints of a pregnancy produced by infidelity. And of a strange indefiniteness. A being without identity gets a child from an unknown place (the child also without identity). This is regression to the point of the child asking "where do I come from?" "I will lose all identity, become child again, if I enter the couple man–woman", she is saying. It's the loss of distinction, of culture, that terrifies these women if they are women.

And they cannot read for catharsis, for the adventure of the strange that might cleanse or ameliorate them. Criticizing *Redbook* (recreated by editor Sey Chassler to be aligned with the liberal branch of the women's movement), a woman whom I am watching says: "I'm not real happy with it now: so much emphasis on sexual permissiveness, not interesting anymore. Its articles aren't realistic. College kids – surveys – who can drink the most beer – the professor feels this way – this is how you should do for your children." "My job is homemaker and mother", another says. "I want to know what pertains to your life right now." Mired in the now, they are self-referential. The trouble with *People*? "It's not going to change your life if you know who did what to whom how many times."

In exchange for what do they read? Their repression maintained, solidified, made finer. A fiftyish-year-old woman, addressing the group (of twenty- and thirty-year olds): "I used to look for hamburger recipes. Now I'm looking more for the entertainment." Once, like you, I was drowning in hamburger recipes; now, in the second stage of my life, my *vita nuova*, as yours will be, I am serenely transcendental: "[Where you are] you're looking for the hamburger recipes, it's a different stage of one's life. It's not oriented towards the career couple who have a swell apartment." In a first moment, they know about the other life, then: they will *not* to know it. On *Cosmopolitan*: "You don't want it to be constant [read it constantly] because you might learn how to have dinner with a man and pay the check." Hear the woman, willing her repression. And recall the bait: here, as with all subjection systems, while the prince takes his pleasure (those on my side of the mirror live well), the people get bliss – deferred, of course.

*Q*: When do you read?

*A*: After the kids go to bed – in bed under covers [giggles]. I get comfortable with a magazine.

Not with my husand – this, amongst other things, is what the little text says in not saying, in covering up. In exchange for what do they read in the bath, in the bed? To glorify the family. Not to see their submission. For a treat. For the mirror to see . . . the now. The here. For a bath of magazine. They read not to spend money. They read to chase away desire to protest at being buried in hamburger. They read to feel lucky they are wives, mothers, custodians of the family.

The magazine whose agency called me was giving all this – giving it in greater doses than its rival, giving it more intensely, without distraction. Pasta-pronto . . . boost your energy . . . blah to beautiful . . . trim your tummy . . . hair colour magic . . . cakes, cookies, breads, preserves, more! Marie Antoinette had it right.

And that is why it was beating its rival. The search for an explicative law in these natural facts led me to this line of reasoning: that a woman's day cannot accept a break in the family circle, that a family circle cannot accept that a woman has a day except in the sense that every dog should have its day.

This is the truth of the signs I saw, which I told to the agency that had asked my opinion. High over the city, someone has just said (the US having just invaded Grenada): "It's not fair-play – us being so big and them like that" – pointing to the bit of city below us. One of the executives is responding to me: "It's a myth that women all want to be liberated. Myth that those in the home are oppressed. The readers we saw *call* themselves mediocre because of guilt fostered by a minority. The women's movement."

To help the readers meet this myth, he recommended to the editorial staff, to whom he told the rule, "Don't open the iron circle."

*Marshall Blonsky*

privileged modes of access to semiotics, since it would also permit us to determine whether semiotics can be a critical practice. It should be borne in mind that Saussure himself, far from being ignorant of, or oblivious to, history, was, before inventing modern linguistics and semiotics, a brilliant student of Indo-European comparative linguistics; indeed it is upon the work he had done in that most historical of fields that the reputation he enjoyed in his lifetime rested. Yet, most contemporary semioticians ignore Saussure's early work, and, in fact, act as if the opposition diachrony *vs* synchrony were not just a systemic one but the operator of a periodization in Saussure's own career, neatly separating his diachronic comparative linguistics from his synchronic theoretical work in structural linguistics. It will be my contention that this *parti pris* unnecessarily impoverishes our understanding of semiotics and prevents the latter from achieving the status that Saussure envisaged for it: that of a form of *social psychology*.

## *1. Substance and Substance-Effect*

Comparative linguistics, one of the nineteenth century's great historical sciences, came into being to reconstruct Indo-European, the lost parent language of most European languages. In common with the procedures of most other historical endeavours, it relied heavily upon substantive evidence, in this case the occurrence of, and patterns of repetition in, some sounds in the same words in the descendent languages. By way of illustration, let us consider the following example:[8]

| | |
|---|---|
| Sanskrit | mātā |
| Doric | mātēr |
| Latin | māter |
| English | mother |

Trying to reconstruct the word for "mother" we find that every descendent language that retains that word has an *m* in the initial position. We can proceed then to reconstruct the *m* as the initial sound in the parent language in the word for "mother". Such reasoning is based entirely upon the evidence we observe, and, more specifically, upon the fact that we observe the recurrence of the same substance (the sound *m*) in the same position. The comparative method, which consists in the reconstruction of the elements of the parent language on the basis of a comparison of the features of the descendent languages, does not rely upon arguments from substance alone, for, if it did, it would rapidly run into unresolvable situations caused by anything from an unwanted proliferation of

[8] I follow here the excellent discussion of Saussure's achievement in the *Mémoire* by William Diver in his "Substance and Value in Linguistic Analysis", *Semiotexte* vol. 1, no. 2 (Autumn 1974) pp. 11–30.

forms in the descendent languages to a paucity of evidence. But as in all the other historical disciplines, the evidence provided by substance was considered the most telling one because irrefutable.

Yet, inevitably, as in other fields of historical enquiry, some of the evidentiary substance would be missing or prove contradictory, thus impeding the reconstruction of the parent language. The co-occurrence in similar environments of two distinct phonemes,[9] the middle consonants *d* and *t* in the words *Bruder* and *frater*, for example, would either necessitate the positing of both in the same location in the parent language – a step that would destroy the functionality of the language since it would then have to contain all the sounds to be found in all of the descendent languages – or it would require the formulation of a rule that would account for such a co-occurrence. It is, of course, the latter procedure that was followed, and, indeed, all the great achievements of historical linguistics lie in this domain.

The formulation of such explanatory rules, or laws as they became known in the field (Grimm's Law, Werner's Law, etc.), represented an accommodation to discontinuity in the chain of substantive evidence, whether the latter was due to divergent evolution or to the outright loss of some forms. In other words, the reconstruction of substance in the parent language could not proceed on the basis of substance alone, but had to rely upon the introduction of the complementary notion of "significant difference" or "value". Prior to Saussure's contribution to this field, all work in Indo-European reconstruction involved a greater or lesser mix of substance and difference in the reconstruction of the original language. Yet, there occurred problems that seemed beyond solution, no matter how ingenious a mix of substance and difference was concocted. It is to one of these problems that Saussure devoted his *Mémoire sur le système primitif des voyelles dans les langues indo-européennes* of 1879. In order to appreciate Saussure's boldness of thought – a *Denkgestus* that, I shall argue, led him to invent semiotics – it is useful to follow William Diver's description of Saussure's solution to the problem of semi-consonants.

Apparently, in the course of the evolution of the parent language, some consonants were lost during the pre-historic period of every descendent language. What makes the problem of their reconstruction arduous is the fact that they left very clear traces but that these traces took on the "appearance of an almost entirely regular correspondence of long vowels" which suggested the possibility of formulating a law that would explain their occurrence.

In Greek, for example, there are a number of morphological irregularities such as the following:

| | | | |
|---|---|---|---|
| leipō | lipemen | loipos | "leave" |
| thēka | themen | thōmos | "put" |
| dōka | domen | dōron | "give" |

---

[9] The term "phoneme" is, of course, a later coinage; I use it for ease of discussion, given its widespread usage today.

In each instance we have a singular verbal form, a plural verbal form, and a verbal noun. The irregularity we shall consider is the variation in appearance of the vowel of the first syllable, where we observe diphthongs such as *ei, oi*; short vowels and long vowels. Saussure took this data and looked at it somewhat differently:

|          |         |         |
|----------|---------|---------|
| leip-ō   | thē-ka  | dō-ka   |
| loip-os  | thō-mos | dō-ron  |
| lip-emen | the-men | do-men  |

Saussure then argued as follows: in the first column, we observe the alternation *e, o* and ø. Perhaps the variations in the second and third columns are disguised versions of what occurs in the first, namely that the *e* and the *o* of the bottom words of these columns (*themen* and *domen*) are not the usual *e* and *o*, but that they are part of the root remaining after the real vowel had dropped out, leaving in actual fact nothing, which we mark, as in the first column, by ø. These *e* and *o*, if we are to compare them to the sounds of the first column, are not equivalent to the *e* and *o* of the two top forms (*leipo* and *loipos*), but to the *i* of the bottom form *lipemen*. The *e* and *o* would thus be the vestiges of a consonant that was lost pre-historically in all known languages. We should rewrite our data then as follows:

|          |          |          |
|----------|----------|----------|
| leip-o   | theE-ka  | deO-ka   |
| loip-os  | thoE-mos | doO-ron  |
| l ip-emen| th E-men | d O-men  |

where the capital letter is used to indicate a lost element. Now all three columns present the same form as far as the vowels are concerned: an *e* in the top form, an *o* in the middle one, and ø in the bottom one. In the bottom forms, what is left has to take over the function of the vowel.

In the first column, then, the *i* is part of the root in all three forms, while the *e* and the *o* are part of the morphology. The *E* and the *O* in the other two columns are part of the root as well, but they have been lost in the evolution of the languages. They subsist in the form of a lengthening of that verbal element which had to take over their vowel function as they disappeared, or become the vowel itself in the bottom forms. What was confusing about this problem is that the kind of correspondences which then appeared on the surface resembled vowel variations that had been studied in the nineteenth century. These correspondences had been called *Ablaut* and they had been collected wherever they occurred.

What Saussure did was to cut the Gordian knot of this problem by positing the existence of a single relation, a "common value" as Diver accurately dubs it, among all the various types of *Ablaut*. This was tantamount to asserting that all the variation of substance could be explained by a single relationship of value. Saussure did start from the contradictory nature of the substantive evidence, but, unlike his predecessors or his contemporaries, instead of arriving at a significant difference that would apportion the substance into two or more meaningful ensembles, he derived sets of differences that, he claimed, were possible only if some substance, the lost semi-consonant whose properties he described, had been present initially and then had been lost. In other words, Saussure did not reconstruct substance by looking at substance or by mixing substance and difference, but by turning his back to substance altogether. He brought to bear upon each other columns or chains of differences, and he set them up so that they would lead to further chains of differences, finally claiming that at the intersection of the latter, there had to have been substance.

Linguists of Saussure's day, though impressed with the elegance of his solution, and not a little swayed by the power of his reasoning, none the less rejected it because they could not accept its radical departure from substance. Quite correctly, they perceived the incompatibility of the procedure followed by Saussure with the very project of historical linguistics, which was so dependent upon substance. The story does have a happy ending in that Saussure was ultimately vindicated: in 1903, there were discovered some inscriptions, which, when deciphered by the Polish linguist Kuryłowicz some twenty-seven years later – long after Saussure's death – proved to be in the then undescribed Indo-European language Hittite, and contain substantive evidence that the semi-consonant postulated by Saussure did exist. It was then duly reconstructed into the Indo-European parent language.

I have discussed this early work of Saussure at length because it provides not only evidence of his preoccupation with historical data but also because the solution he proposed to the problem was to prove determinant not only to his rethinking of linguistics and to his invention of semiotics, but also to the specifically semiotic way of envisaging the historical. We ourselves lack the evidentiary chain from the *Mémoire* to the lectures that would ultimately become the *Cours de linguistique générale*, and the explanation proposed here will have none of Saussure's elegance nor its probative value. It is not meant to be conclusive in respect of the historical question of Saussure's own evolution, but rather to draw attention to the link between the two periods in his career, and through them, to the relationship of historical linguistics to semiotics.

## 2. The Substance-Effect and its Locus

There is no doubt that what comparative linguists could not accept was but the point of departure for further thought on Saussure's part. If he could reason his way to the reconstruction of a specific substance on the basis of differential chains of difference alone, what was the necessity of substance in the first place? He had been able to assert the absence of the lost substance because he had been able to *read* the effect of the latter in the differential organization of the chains of differences. But to reason thus was still to reason historically, that is from substance. If substance were not to be invoked at all, Saussure would be truer to his actual procedure, which consisted in reasoning from sets of differences. To restate then the reasoning, but by taking difference and not substance as one's point of view, one would assert that, *at the intersection of two or more differential chains of structured differences, there would be produced an effect equal to that produced by the occurrence of substance at that point* (see box 2).[10] The historical perspective of the *Mémoire* required the assertion of an attestable (i.e. reconstructable) substance, whereas a differentialist one would be content with the notation of the substance-effect.

It is far from clear that the significance of this paradigmatic shift, in Kuhn's terms, has been fully appreciated until quite recently, when Umberto Eco, in his *A Theory of Semiotics*, proceeding purely deductively, reformulated the description of the sign as the intersection of two codes, which he previously described as chains of structured differences.[11]

What I have called the substance-effect takes place then in the very locus that will be occupied by the sign. It would be tempting to conflate sign and substance-effect on the basis of this positional commonality, but to do so would be to blind ourselves to the specifically semiotic mode of historical inscription.

Substance-effect is a differentialist concept that marks the location where an inscription can take place.[12] To be sure, it imposes restrictions on the sort of

[10] Why "equal to that"? Godzich is using a mathematical notion: when chains of difference intersect, an effect is produced *having the same value* as that produced by the occurrence of substance – of a sign. The system capable of producing meaning, the *semiosis*, produces a point where substance may be called for – but it may not. One possibility is that there be no substance, no visibility. Another is that one combines the various features the substance can have in this or that way. It is here that ideology, decisions, manipulations take place. Godzich is concerned with the point at which the system able to manufacture meaning opens and is available for an inscription, for signs.

Alexander Zinoviev, the Soviet dissident, has written that the logic of planning in the USSR sometimes requires an absence of sign, when a sign might be at odds with Soviet ideology. Under such a circumstance, the planners have either the choice of falsifying their plans or writing a plan in such a way that the logic is left – the plan, however, pretending ignorance of what is to take place. Soviet planners are producing a substance-effect. They are writing the plan in such a way as to indicate a formal place, but claiming ignorance of what that place entails, of the material sign to be inscribed there; for example, financial incentives, a means of economic stimulus contrary to doctrines.

[11] Umberto Eco, *A Theory of Semiotics* (Bloomington and London: Indiana University Press, 1976) pp., 36–70.

[12] We can say more about what is intended by the term substance-effect. It is the idea of not being blinded by the signs we see, the idea of seeing not the sign but the place or function it fills. Reasoning this way, we can understand that other signs could be in this place. For instance, looking at the Miller image in figure 2, we can imagine the black with his head held high, not posing as *The Thinker*, and ask what decisions led to the exclusion of such a pose? Thinking of the substance-effect, of the substance-site, we reason toward the range of possible signs that could go into this locus. By conflating the concept of sign with that of the locus of substance-effect, the semiotics that only looks at representation, only at manifestations – that only asks what does this film, fashion, etc., mean? – such a semiotics endows the sign and the place where it

*Box 2*

## When Chains of Difference Intersect:
### A Lesson

I have found it helpful in teaching this at first difficult idea to resort to an advertisement for Miller beer. It presents the still image of a black man, about thirty years old, sitting on the end of a pier, his chin on his right fist, bent forward over his upraised arm (see figure 2). He is seen in profile, eye, cheek, mouth deeply shadowed. His left hand, resting on his thigh, holds the Miller bottle – it juts up at a 45-degree angle between his opened legs. He stares over the water into infinity and in the distance the sun sets behind some buildings on the spectator's horizon. "Miller time", says the headline. "If you've got the time, we've got the beer." As Roland Barthes used a racist example to illustrate connotation (a *Paris Match* cover showing a black soldier giving the French salute), so I have used this racial advertisement to teach what Godzich calls chains of differences.

Figure 2

The lesson starts with the concept of code – the force that correlates an expression with a content. Expressions are physicalities: a number on a door, the words "I love you", a dozen roses. Contents are ways in which a culture has made its world pertinent. A world, for instance, once carved into Greeks and barbarians (see Eco, pp 163–4), now into the US and the Evil Empire.

Neither an expression nor a content is (according to semiotics) recognized in itself, but only in opposition to other units. "[T]he important thing about a word is not the sound in itself, but those phonic differences which allow this word to be distinguished from all other words ... phonemes ... have a solely differential value, thus a purely negative value" (Roman Jakobson, *Six Lectures on Sound and Meaning*, 1978). As the word, so the content: a mouse, for semiotics, is everything within the semantic space of rodents that is not a rat; Holland is the class of all points next to but not Germany, Belgium and the North Sea. Because of a code, which is an order, a prescription, I correlate chains of differences to one another. A chain of phonemes to a chain of contents. Thereby I make sense.

"A French speaker may not be familiar with either the slang word *mek* (*mec*, 'bloke') nor with the specialized word *mok (moque*, a nautical term for a particular kind of wooden pulley), but hearing these words he will assume that they signify two different things because they differ in one of their phonemes" (Jakobson). I correlate the chain *m-ɛ-k* to the chain of contents: "undifferentiated person", "without civil title", etc.

With this in mind and looking at the Miller image, I can speak of the elements of one system, call it "The Modelling System" – the medium-skinned model puts his chin on his hand, light and dark alternate to make facial planes and hollows, light shines through the yellow bottle, sun blazes behind irradiated top of distant building. Also, I can speak of another system, call it "A White Look at Black Life" – "when your ass is in the mud, you stare at the fruit in the treetop" (Afro-Cuban saying), time-out from work and dreaming of making it ... how much? All of it, that's what the gaze at the horizon means, and of course his penis erected. As I stare at the image, I realize that two sets of differences have come together. Here is how.

I start with the White Look/Black Life system. It is a signification system (see Eco, pp. 162–5), a mental set. What does a white person "off the street" think a black knows of art? *The Pietà, Mona Lisa, The Thinker*, very little else. (And of course the advertisement forcibly connotes Rodin's *The Thinker*.) Of what is the black man's sexual system composed? It is a set of two elements, erection, deflation, with the first always privileged. And the dedication of his work life? A job that bores him, seen as an undifferentiated oppressive whole – the black man can't wait to be off work to do nothing. His leisure also an undifferentiated whole of drink and dream. Analysis of popular racist literature, direct analysis of everyday conversation of whites: by numerous ways we arrive at these gross categorizations, this poverty of contents by which to imagine the black. *Pietà, Thinker*, penis erect, down, erect; at work, at dream; these are positions occupied in the sub-systems of a dominant mental set. This is the way American society has focused on blacks and made them pertinent.

I can speak in a similar way of "The Modelling System". "I don't want this one or that one or that one", says a casting director looking at photos of possible models, on the way to selecting the man whose image we see. "Raise the bottle more, turn it left, turn your face right" – says the photographer, making just the shadow he wants, and the irradiation of the bottle. "Spread your legs a bit. . . "

We the spectators are encountering two sets of differences. *First*: bottle not on a surface (readiness to drink: first step in the pleasure sequence), not on its side (agrammaticality – a bartender, a supermarket assistant, will always pick it up, right it); model not deep black, nor dark brown; head not seen in light, etc. And *second*: not *Pietà*, not *Mona Lisa*, not the 3-D Christ that stares at you as you pass; not flaccid; not burdened by work; not a well-lit, frontal face of two eyes that grip you. The *first* system, The Model's, was made to be the expression conveying us – how? by iconic, iconographic, rhetorical and other conventions – to the *second* system, the Racist, whose parts are kitsch, sexual impulse, laziness/fantasy. As we gaze at the image we are living with this correlation of the two sets of differential chains, as Godzich puts it. We live with a correlation that has produced an effect of substantiality, of presencing. Nothing appears to have been held back, everything has been given. A black man on a pier *is all there is* . . . is the gripping message emanating from the image.

The gift of presence conceals that there are undetectable segmentations that produce the presence. The casting agent rejected the too-black models – the model before us takes on significance in relation to the rejects: he is not black ("If you're black, get back", goes the racist ditty), nor brown (". . . if you're brown, stick around"). "Not . . . nor . . . nor" is what subliminally we say as we instantaneously process the chain of colour, the chain of sex, of work. However, the manifestation seems separate from such segmentations, from the rules that produced this concrete instance. What is called the sign, therefore, is a euphoric life with the category of the present, of the instance – and no thought given to another category, that of the absent, of the form; of the rules making possible this instance.

Signs banish our grasp of the segmentations of experience, the numerous ways in which culture has made its experience pertinent. This is why Godzich is saying that the sign, properly understood, is not substance, it is the relation between ordered sets of differences. The proper study of semiotics becomes, not the sign as such, but the rules whereby items of one set of differences have been coupled to items of another set – producing the sign, the presence-effect. What we call signification occurs when chains of differences are conjoined; then we transcode, pass from the one to the other. The one has played the role of expression for us; the other, that of content. Nothing, however, is sacred about the roles, they are reversible. With training, a consumer could look at our image and go: "Why that's a male model not letting the bottle dangle. . ."

*Marshall Blonsky*

---

appears with a givenness, a naturalness. A critical practice of semiotics, however, would open the sign up, see through it to a space of decision where power has exercised itself. Such a semiotics enquires into motivation and decisions. Thus why in the autumn of 1984 did fashion so emphasize the "brights"? The reds, for instance? The return of primary colours – after the subdued colours of the previous few years – created a general feeling of euphoria, one of the functions of red, as we know. We could analyse the subdued colours that led to the autumn of 1984, understand them as meant to produce quiescence, to calm the alarms of people. Whereas *vis-à-vis* 1984, we can reason our way to an attempt to rechannel this quiescence into a state of euphoria. For a function of that euphoria, its intentionality as well, see pp. xxxii–iv and following. [Editor's note]

inscription that it can be; none the less, it retains the important possibility that no inscription will occur. The sign, on the other hand, is always some materiality, some substance. It is in so far that it is a substance that, in the act that summons it forth into the locus of the substance-effect, it can become inscription, an inscription that both fulfils the positional substance-effect requirements of the differential chains of structured differences, and exceeds them. It exceeds them because the very substantiality of the sign is, strictly speaking, not required by the purely structural determination of the substance-effect. Yet, the substance of the sign, its materiality, is necessary to mark the inscription, but it does so by operating a swerve: the materiality of the sign not only serves to mark the inscription of the substance-effect, it also marks the sign's appurtenance to an order other than that of pure signification.[13] The materiality of the sign is already charged with the previous history of that sign, the history of its previous placements, and that history is sufficiently strong to obscure the play of pure semiosis that the substance-effect was to mark.[14] Instead of having the exact and determinate structural position of signification,

[13] Signs are not merely elements in a communication system, in a mind set, in an intentionality. They connect to the world, they refer to history, to class struggles, to justices, injustices. [Editor's note]

[14] Godzich is saying that from a sign we can read to the set of the previous environments in which that sign has occurred, in which it may have had different meanings, different connotations. Looking at the Miller image, we understand that the statue of *The Thinker* has been transplanted to a water site, removed from the environment of the aesthetic, the art-book, the museum, to the space of the quotidian and the quotidian black. "Here is instant culture," says the ad – "no need to read, to travel to the university, to the museum." We have begun to reason to forces at work diminishing the drive for literacy, knowledge, in America's working class. *These forces issue no signs.*

We also know that this image is a citiation – of Rodin's 1880 *The Thinker*. Look at the original in the Rodin Museum, Paris: six foot and seven inches, head deeply bowed, what can be taken for leg veins popping. What doubtless the art director for Miller did not know was this: *The Thinker* was a preliminary execution for the central figure that would later be carved into the top of the *Gates of Hell* (1880–1917, now at the Philadelphia Museum). A head bowed because *The Thinker* is descending to hell. A deep subject of conscience, of contemplation, the humanist subject is seen here through the eyes of Miller – lightened, less muscular, a head that raised itself. This is the place only to touch on the mode of enquiry Godzich proposes: Rodin humanism – so useful in the mind-set of power – this humanism is here adulterated almost to nil in this image, this gift of the imaginary, for the black viewer. Miller quoted Rodin but Rodin quoted Michelangelo – the unfinished Slaves, or Captives, who appear to be writhing to free themselves of their encumbering stone. Rodin was fascinated by the immediacy, spontaneity, torsion of these captives – they seemed to express depth, an interiority, a nature and subjectivity that he would imitate in the chiselling of *The Thinker's* foot, leaving jagged edges, making planes. Given that our Miller Thinker is black, we are returned to the Michelangelo original – and perhaps to a deep and unsymbolized portion of the Miller Brewing Company's collective mind. We return to the Michelangelo original, while seated before us is America's slave, not writhing nor muscular; quiescent, assimilating the horizon, that is everything, in his gaze. Or he would be, if he gave off the sense of being alive. But he does not. Although the planes

we get the latter overlaid with a materiality that brings with it the history of its past instantiations. And, of course, such a process is not limited to one locus in the production of the utterance, but pervades it through and through, indeed becomes its law.

In other words, the distinction between substance-effect and sign – a distinction that semiotics has so far failed to make, for, quite rightly, it may have feared that it would wreak havoc with one of the features of semiotics that has proven very appealing to many, namely its susceptibility to formalization – and the distinction between position and substance, permit us to think both the syntactico-logical requirements of semiosis and the historical excedent of semiosis that the materiality of the sign brings into the process. The substantiality of the sign marks the fact that a substance-effect is all that semiosis requires, but that the inscription of the position of this substance-effect, because it can be only inscribed by a substance, displays a substance in that locus in a swerve that necessarily draws in areas of semiosis other than those involved in the production of meaning at that point, thereby producing the paradoxical effect of a simultaneous incompleteness of meaning (positionally) and a proliferation of meaning (substantially). The excedence of the sign brings into play other considerations than those of the pure semiosis;[15] its externality to the semiotic process underway marks the introduction of other interests and of a temporality that recasts the semiosis by inscribing it within history, but a history that must be first understood as operating in the gap between the determination of the substance-effect and the inscription of a substance into that locus.

By introducing a distinction between the locus of the substance-effect, defined as the space of the inscription of the sign to come, and that inscription, semiotics opens up a new way of considering such problems as the historical process, freedom, determination, etc. This is not the place to enquire into them, even though they constitute the semiotic reinscription of the historical, but I should like to underscore the link between this conception of semiosis and Saussure's description of semiology as a branch of social psychology,[16] a statement often remarked upon, yet still considered obscure.

---

of his face are angular, he seems made of a substance lighter than Rodin's bronze. Might we not say that images of bronze, that a muscular Image-repertoire, would be too galvanizing for our captive class? The most vital element in this image is not the human, it is the sun, intense behind the building in which others, not blacks I daresay, plan and decide. [Editor's note]

Godzich has in mind reading signs for a portion of the history, let us say, of an imperceptible, systematic exclusion of blacks from humanism and its swelling of the subject. [Editor's note]

[15] Inevitably my discussion introduces a temporal gap into a process where none exists. The mechanism can be described logically only at the cost of such deferral being built into the description.

[16] *Course in General Linguistics*, trans. by Wade Baskin (New York: McGraw-Hill, 1966) p. 16.

One of the most unfortunate consequences of the occultation of semiotics' handling of history, has been the development of a purely static concept of the semiotic, with until recently, little attention paid to the actual production of signs. Yet, if the social realm is to be treated as a social text, that is as the locus of semiotization, it is the very process at work in the gap between the substance-effect and the inscription of substance into its locus that is most deserving of enquiry.

Let us connect this analysis with the previous analysis of the mode of production of repetition developed in the first section. We then obtain the following: at the systemic level, the mode of production of repetition so taxes the surplus-value of the commodity, in order, it will be recalled, to produce demand by establishing meaningfulness, that it grinds up its own productive codes and resources, and produces greater disorder and less meaning. Systematically then, a convergence of codes, in Eco's conception of sign-formation, is produced in such a way as to achieve the locus of a substance-effect that, ideally within the logic of repetition, should be occupied by a meaning localizing, preserving and indexing entity. Now, following our own analysis of Saussure's distinction between the locus of the substance-effect and the sign that comes to occupy that locus, we see that the locus of this substance-effect is at present occupied by the entity called semiotics.[17] The Saussurean analysis requires that we recognize, and indeed enquire into, the provenance of this materiality which, though it occupies the locus of the substance-effect, is not fully coincident with it and may either exceed it or come short of its requirements,[18] but, in any case, by its own inscription into that locus, it establishes links to other realms and thus lays the ground for the eventual skewing of the system into which it has just been inscribed (in such a way as to produce its demise, or more precisely, its passing into another

[17] Let me make this explicit: the establishment needs what Godzich calls the semiotics of representation – the semiotics that only analyses signs, never forms, only analyses them for their meaning and connotation. The establishment requires such *simple* semiotics because we live today with a universal loss of meaning. The practitioners of this semiotics think of themselves as being in command, as master analysts, whereas they are servants of the system, providing only the reassurance that meaning in everyday experience is available to those who look for it very hard. Of course the meaning they provide is only the meaning the system authorizes. [Editor's note]

[18] Again, I shall make this explicit: at the same time that the system authorizes an official, university-taught semiotics, it requires a semiotics much cleverer than the disipline the semioticians have. Such a semiotics produces no signs. It exists only to provide artefacts in the world that produce effects. Artefacts such as John Loring's Tiffany windows (see Endword). The function of the Endword is to start to corroborate what Godzich is claiming at the theoretic level. There is a semiotic know-how, as opposed to a semiotic theory, that is operative in the marketplace amongst the best designers, marketers, advertisers. Semioticians are running behind, not even suspecting how sophisticated *is* this semiotics. It is not that the semioticians who read papers and teach students are the tip of an iceberg. Rather they are like a little floe that has broken off; the iceberg has drifted in another direction, and they cannot locate it. [Editor's note]

system).[19] In other words, I am only making explicit now what I have been doing all along in this article, which is treating semiotics as a sign in a manner consonant with my interpretation of the problematics of the sign and substance-effect in Saussure. I am claiming then to have been doing semiotics and not merely to have been writing about it.

---

[19] The claim being made is that if we can bring to the surface this hidden iceberg, the system will have to play by different rules. The sign as a deceit may be fully assumed by both sides, sender and receiver, with more attention paid to playfulness and pleasure, rather than to blind manipulation. [Editor's note]

THOMAS A. SEBEOK

# Pandora's Box: How and Why to Communicate 10,000 Years into the Future

# Preamble

Shortly after the inauguration of Ronald Reagan as the fortieth President of the United States, my services were engaged by the Bechtel Group, Inc., as a consultant to the Human Interference Task Force, assigned responsibility for "reducing the likelihood of future human activities that could affect geologic high-level waste repositories". The specific assignment of this Task Force was to prepare a report on this topic for submission to the US Nuclear Regulatory Commission, via the US Department of Energy.[1] It was prepared under the

---

[1] Some of the concern motivating the Task Force project may be read in the Task Force report to the Department of Energy ("Reducing the Likelihood of Future Human Activities that could Affect Geologic High-Level Waste Repositories" (September 1981): "The scenarios of most concern are those in which the interference either direct or indirect takes place without knowledge of the repository's existence or with insufficient knowledge of its significance, because of the potential for exposing unsuspecting populations to releases of radioactive materials for extended periods" (Section 1.2). On the one hand, the Task Force is concerned about, and against, an avaricious, almost a bumbling and certainly unreflecting population. On the other hand, it is concerned about, and *in favour of*, a quite different population: "The security of protective systems engineered today cannot be guaranteed against the potentially advanced technologies of future societies. Moreover, future societies may need to use the materials at present considered to be wastes. For that reason draft EPA [Environmental Protection Agency] criteria would preclude tamperproof nonretrievable systems" (Section 1.6). The Task Force is imagining a technically superior yet energy-inferior US of the future: "This society's obligation should be discharged by providing a secure isolation system that would continue to function if left undisturbed. The prime objective therefore should be to transmit knowledge of the repository to

auspices of the National Waste Terminal Storage Program, which directs both the development and the implementation of the technology required for designing, constructing, licensing and operating repositories. In September 1981, the report of our Task Force was duly submitted, but the opinions expressed and positions stated by the members have, as of the summer 1982, not yet been endorsed by the Department of Energy. The article that follows constitutes an updated version of my own report to the Bechtel Group; although I have, of course, learned a great deal from my collaborators, and have profited from the draft document mentioned, it contains solely my personal views on the specific problem on which I was asked to work: designing a reasonably fail-safe means of communicating information about the repository and its contents, such that the system's effectiveness would be maintained for up to 10,000 years.

The 10,000-year limitation forecast – roughly equivalent to 300 generations, according to current actuarial tables – is clearly an arbitrary limit. While the projection is consistent with the Department of Energy's Statement of Position on the Nuclear Regulatory Commission Waste Confidence Rulemaking (DOE/NE–0007, 15 April 1980), and with certain preliminary criteria of the Environmental Protection Agency (40 CFR 191, Working Draft no. 19, 1981), one must nevertheless be mindful that the radioactive half-life of, for example, the metal thorium 232 is 10 billion years, more or less, by contrast with, say, that of plutonium 214, which is a mere fraction of one second.

Since I submitted my formal report, Fred C. Shapiro's exhaustive study of radioactive wastes, *Radwaste* (1981), appeared.[2] This is an invaluable source of reliable information on the entire range of depressing issues involved in the disposal of radwaste, awesome mountains of which continue to accrete inexorably while our Federal Government and the States of the Union argue over a "permanent solution" for getting rid of these toxic materials.

As I wrote this preamble, to accompany the published version of my report, *The New York Times* informed its readership:

---

future generations, allowing them to plan their activities accordingly. The principal concern in communicating such knowledge is to avoid a situation where interference activities take place with no, or insufficient, knowledge of the existence and significance of the repository and therefore the consequences proceed unchecked" (Section 1.12). Motivated by civic virtue, by the loyalty of forebears to a responsible future, the Task Force seeks semiotic aid in transmitting knowledge that will be effective for 10,000 years. The importance of the author's proposal in response can be perceived by reading the present account of it together with Umberto Eco's "Towards A New Middle Ages" (p. 488). Thereupon, the proposal makes sense as a trace of élite thinking *vis-à-vis* the present (and not only a future) situation of the US and the West. For the elaboration of this conjoined reading, see the editor's "Wes Geistes Kind ist die Atomsemiotik?" ("Whose Inspiration is Atomic Semiotics?"), in *Zeitschrift für Semiotik*, vol. 6, no. 3 (1984): (*Und in alle Ewigkeit . . . Kommunikation über 10000 Jahre*) pp. 311–24. [Editor's note]

[2] Fred C. Shapiro, *Radwaste* (New York: Random House, 1981).

"In a sealed carbon-steel tank" in West Valley, a community near Buffalo, "encased in concrete walls eight feet below the earth, is 560,000 gallons of poisonous waste, produced by the only commercial nuclear-fuel reprocessing plant ever to operate in the United States. The liquid will be dangerously radioactive for thousands of years; the tank has a life expectancy of 40." (11 July 1982, pp. 1 and 17). The Department of Energy proposes to mix the radioactive waste with glass, and then emplace the 300 or so vitrified logs formed in a metal mould overpacked by some combination of cement, clay and/or metal that will protect the logs, each about ten feet long and two feet in diameter, from corrosive elements for 1300 years. Four years ago, it was estimated that the cost of this solidification would be $130 million; the current estimate for doing the job, which is still in the "design" stage, is that it will cost "under $500 million". There are serious questions about whether the glass, now favoured as a permanent storage medium, would nevertheless allow some radioactivity to escape into the environment. It is problematic whether the use of horosilicate glass would be secure. According to present plans, the wastes will be stored in salt formations – precisely where has not yet been decided – which are supposed to persist for the tens of thousands of years that the waste will be so radioactive that its isolation is desired. On 27 April of this year, the Senate endorsed the Nuclear Waste Policy Act (S. 1662), which called for the development of a plan for determining suitable sites to store, bury and isolate radioactive waste, some containing materials predicted to be lethal for 240,000 years. The House has yet to act on a comparable measure (H.R. 3809). The Department of Energy estimates that the earliest date a final repository could be available will be in the year 2000; some scientists criticize this target as impossible to make. As Eliot Marshall has noted: "Even if enacted this year, a bill like this would have to be considered only a hesitant first try at solving the nuclear waste problem. It deals with none of the technical disputes and leaves the highly difficult task of site selection to the bureaucracy."[3]

Finally, it should be mentioned that ocean-dumping of radwastes is again under active consideration, in an atmosphere of both concern and controversy.[4] However, my job was to focus on geological repositories deep beneath the earth's surface, and to ignore, for purposes of this report, marine disposal of waste materials, as well as other options which have variously been put forward.

This paper is concerned with neither engineering nor economic problems – and not at all with their international dimensions – but solely with the design of a method to prevent human interference with repositories during the first 10,000 years after their closure.

## Introduction

Any viable strategy for radioactive (hazardous) waste disposal, in which the repository would be situated in a crystalline rock mass beneath a blanket of

[3] Eliot Marshall, "The Senate's Plan for Nuclear Waste", *Science*, vol. 216 (1982) pp. 709–10.

sedimentary rocks whose physical characteristics are well understood, entails the possibility of human intrusion, which must and can be minimized. The present paper deals with semiotic techniques designed to restrict, if not altogether prevent, access to the material.

Semiotics is the name of the discipline which brackets the conjoint scientific study of both verbal and averbal systems of communication. It is thus focally relevant to the problems of human interference and message exchanges involving long periods of time, over which spoken and written languages are sure to decay to the point of incomprehensibility, making it necessary to utilize a perspective that goes well beyond linguistics (the formal study of verbal messages), which, traditionally (mainly in the nineteenth century), has dealt with the relatively brief diachronic past, or (mainly in the twentieth century) the synchronic present. Workers in semiotics, or in its narrower branch called linguistics, have very seldom been called upon to make projections into the short-range future, let alone the long-range future, which, in the case at hand, must take into account up to 10,000 years.

It is generally believed that the "social function of communication is the ensuring of continuity in society through access to the experiences and ideas of the past, expressed in (loosely speaking) symbols for transmission across space and through time. This is the 'time-binding' function of social communication".[5] Man's time-binding ability arises from his usage of "language, number, gesture, picture and other symbolic forms",[6] enabling him to transcend the limitations of inherited characteristics and the seemingly insurmountable barrier of "time". It should be noted, in passing, that an era will come when messages vitally important to the race, affecting its survival, will be transmissible by microsurgical intervention with man's molecular blueprint, but the technology required for this form of temporal communication is far from available as yet. Therefore, in what follows, this theoretical possibility will not be considered further.

## Some Basic Principles of Semiotics[7]

*Semiotics,[8] the pivotal branch of the integrated science of communication,[9] is concerned with the formulation and encoding of messages by *sources, the transmission of these messages through *channels, the *decoding and *interpretation of these messages by *destinations, and their *signification. The

---

[4] Colin Norman, "U.S. Considers Ocean-Dumping of Radwastes", *Science*, vol. 215 (1982) pp. 1217–19.

[5] A. Neelameghan, "Expressions of Time in Information Science and their Implications", in F. Greenaway (ed.), *Time and the Science* (Paris: UNESCO, 1979) pp. 103–18, see p. 103.

[6] Ibid.

[7] Sebeok's original report to Bechtel's Human Interference Task Force included a discussion of basic semiotic principles as a sort of primer for the scientists, engineers,

entire transaction, or *semiosis, takes place within a *context to which the system is highly sensitive and which the system, in turn, affects. Any living entity, or its products, can be either message sources or destinations. Humans are unique in being able to process both verbal and averbal messages. Semiosic acts are monitored by *feed mechanisms,[10] which can variously function to fine-tune performances. Differences between input and output are due to "noise", which can, however, be counteracted by *"redundancy". The process of message interchanges, or *semiosis*, is held by many to be an indispensable characteristic of all terrestrial life forms. It is this capacity for containing, replicating and expressing messages, of extracting their significance, that, in fact, distinguishes them more consistently from the non-living – except for human agents, such as robots, that can be programmed to engage in quasi-semiosis – rather than other traits often cited, such as the ability to reproduce (e.g. mules or neutered cats do act as message sources and destinations, but none can reproduce).

All human messages fall into two distinct categories: *verbal messages and *averbal messages. *Language – as the array of verbal messages is collectively referred to – has, so far, been found only in our own species; biologists would thus say that language constitutes a "species-specific" trait. The study of this unique yet "species-universal" attribute of man, his language, is the subject matter of *linguistics, which is one of the most sophisticated, partially formalized branches of semiotics. Man's rich repertoire of averbal messages – by sharp contrast with his language – has not comprised a unified field of study, and therefore lacks a positive integrative label. Averbal messages are, by definition, *not* linguistic. This negative delineation has led to terminological chaos, which is manifoldly compounded when the multifarious message systems employed by the millions of speechless creatures are additionally taken into account.

Averbal messages can be distinguished from one another according to several criteria of semiotic relevance. Let me briefly illustrate this point by going back to a classical discussion found in the Hippocratic writings on medical semiotics, where *sémeion* – from the same root as both *"semiotics" and *"semiology" – is used to refer to the observable "symptoms" by which a physician identifies a disease ("makes a diagnosis") and forecasts its outcome ("makes a

---

executives and others in the thirteen-person Task Force and its consultants. Enough of this primer is reproduced here to suggest the development of its argument. [Editor's note]

[8] Expressions preceded by an asterisk are defined in the "Glossary of Technical Terms", to be found at the end of this article.

[9] See Roman Jakobson, *Main Trends in the Science of Language* (New York: Harper and Row, 1970) p. 33.

[10] Dodd H. Bogart, "Feedback, Feedforward and Feedwithin: Strategic Information in Systems", *Behavioral Science*, vol. 25 (1980) pp. 237–49.

prognosis").[11] This standpoint of Hippocrates (*c.* 460–*c.* 377 B.C.) – whom historians have sometimes reverentially regarded as "the father and master of all semiotics" – hinges on an ancient but still widely prevalent distinction drawn between two kinds of messages: "conventional" *vs* "natural". *Conventional messages are those whose power to signify is thought to depend on some prior agreement, presumed to have been reached at some temporal juncture and thereafter accepted as a matter of custom – such as, most importantly, messages cast in spoken or written utterances, but also frequently messages that are embodied in the shape of a parochial gesture, a tradition exercised and understood by one group of persons but not necessarily by their neighbours. The meaning of a conventional message – whether verbal or not – is invariably circumscribed to a time and place. So-called *natural messages, on the other hand, have the power to signify the same things at all times and in all places, precisely because their interpretation does not presuppose a familiarity with the conventions of a particular group. For this reason, "natural messages", as defined here, are particularly pertinent to the present responsibility of the Human Interference Task Force.

After describing certain averbal symptoms (*sémeia*), Hippocrates does go on to say, in his treatise on *Prognostic*, that these "prove to have the same significance in Libya, in Delos, and in Scythia". Given the quasi-universality of the class of averbal messages physicians call symptoms, he does not deem it "strange that one should be right in the vast majority of instances, if one learns them well and knows how to estimate and appreciate them properly".[12]

By contrast, there is also something designated as a *"multimessage", i.e. a conventional gesture that has a number of totally distinct meanings, the choice of interpretation depending on the time and the place. Thus all Americans are familiar with the raised hand gesture, such that the thumb and forefinger form a circle. This essentially signifies that something is OK. In other countries, however, the same configuration may mean something totally different: for example, in Japan, "money", in the South of France, "zero" or "worthless"; in many places it may convey an obscene comment or an insult, as it did in Greece more than two thousand years ago; again, in some other areas it may betoken nothing at all.[13]

A message can now be provisionally defined as a selection out of a *code* by a *source*.[14] A very important component is the message *context*, or setting, in

---

[11] Eugene S. Miller, "Hume's Reduction of Cause to Sign", *The New Scholasticism*, vol. 43 (1979) pp. 42–75, see p. 44.

[12] Ibid., p. 45, after Hippocrates' *Prognostic*, xxv.

[13] Desmond Morris, *Manwatching: A Field Guide to Human Behavior* (New York: Harry M. Abrams, 1977) pp. 39–40.

[14] In his original report to the Bechtel Task Force, the author presented the well-known communication diagram representing one box, a source, connected to another, a destination; the line connecting them signifying the message; the source formulating and encoding the message, the destination decoding and interpreting it. Enveloping these linked boxes, like an atmosphere, is the context. The lesson in its entirety may

which the entire transaction takes place. The context in which any message is emitted, transmitted and admitted decisively influences its interpretation, and vice versa: the context of transactions is continually modified by the messages being interpreted; messages, in brief, are always more or less context-sensitive. This much is well known, but just *how* an organism takes its environment into account remains unclear. The notion of "context" has been employed differently by various investigators, but, broadly speaking, the term refers to the organism's cognizance of conditions and manner of appropriate and effective use of messages. Context includes the whole range of the animal's cognitive systems (i.e. "mind"), messages flowing parallel, as well as the memory of prior messages that have been processed, and no doubt the anticipation of future messages expected to be processed. Some semioticians have consigned the study of contexts to a nebulous subdivision of the field called "pragmatics" (complementing "syntactics" and "semantics").[15]

Context is often the crucial factor in resolving the significance of a message. Thus messages encoded in the chemicals isolaveric acid and methyl mercaptan are components, respectively, of human body malodour and halitosis. This notwithstanding, the same chemicals and, consequently, the same odours, are responsible for some of the bouquet and flavour of cheese – contexts account for the difference in interpretation.

The verbal context may subtly yet decisively affect memory, as was shown in a remarkable experiment by Loftus and Palmer.[16] These two psychologists showed a film of a car accident, and questioned two different groups of "witnesses" about it in two slightly different ways. One group was asked, "How fast were the cars going when they smashed into each other?" The other group was asked, "How fast were the cars going when they hit each other?" A week passed. Then all "witnesses" were asked, "Did you see any broken glass in the accident?" Although there was no broken glass, those who were cued with the verb "smash" were more than twice as likely to erroneously report the presence of broken glass than those originally cued with the verb "hit".

The context often determines whether the addressee believes the message. A little boy exclaims, "Mummy, there is a tiger in the backyard." Mummy's reply: "Johnny, stop making up stories!" Suppose the family lives in Venice, Florida, next door to the circus's winter quarters: very different reply.

All semiotic systems are not only dynamic but adaptive, that is, self-regulated to adapt both to the external context (conditions of environment) and the internal context (circumstances inherent within the system itself). At successive

---

be found in *General Semantics Bulletin: Yearbook of the Institute of General Semantics*, vol. 49 (1982) pp. 27–30 [Editor's note].

[15] See Charles Morris, *Writings on the General Theory of Signs* (The Hague: Mouton, 1971) pp. 359–68 (Glossary), and Colin E. Cherry, *On Human Communication: A Review, a Survey and a Criticism* (Cambridge, Mass.: MIT Press, 1978), Appendix, pp. 339–43.

[16] Elizabeth F. Loftus, *Eye-witness Testimony* (Cambridge, Mass.: Harvard University Press, 1980).

points, intelligence mechanisms come into play about system conditions which can, accordingly, activate and shape coping responses; their flow is commonly described as *"feed process".[17] Feed processes typically move, in mutually complementary fashion, forward as well as backward, forming loops. Thus the source normally checks whether the launched message stream reaches the destination according to expectation (*"feedforward"), whereas the destination tends to continually confirm or disconfirm this (*"feedback") to the source. *Feedforward* is like a trend forecast that biases perception and enables the source to adjust its performance in anticipation of changeful happenings; in the favourable case, it may facilitate the avoidance of mistakes. *Feedback* brings into the frame information about the working efficiency of the system itself – information which is then "fed back" into the system, thus enabling adjustments on the basis of results accomplished.

An example of feedforward, taken from familiar organizational surroundings, is budgetary planning: the Vice-President for Research and Engineering (the source) tells a department manager (the destination) by a memo (the message) how much money the department, say, of the Apex Corporation, may spend during the coming year, and he then designs, or redesigns, the department's activities on the basis of this "foreknowledge". A different example: many predators (the source) – including various birds of prey, bats, wolves, lions, polar bears – capture their prey (the destination) by a manoeuvre called "interception" (of the message). This means that the predator aims not at where the quarry *is*, but where it is most likely to be at the moment of impact, that is, a precise point *ahead* of the quarry in its calculated trajectory.

Feedback is so well known as not to need exemplification.

The message received (and finally interpreted) by the destination is, in practice, seldom identical with the message sent (after being formulated) by the source; in other words, the output of the channel generally does not agree with its input. The discrepancy $M\hat{s} \neq M\hat{d}$ may be due to random and persistent disturbances that variously intrude into the system and obscure the clarity or quality of the message or, in extreme cases, obliterate its comprehension entirely. A channel might also, say, for secrecy, contain a cryptographic scrambling device. Such disarrangements, which make the output unpredictable even when the input is known, are called *noise*. To circumvent noise and thereby to decrease the probability of transmission errors, the source habitually introjects *redundancy*. There are many kinds of noise and many techniques for overcoming it, but always at a price – as, for instance, slowing the source (and thus the entire transaction) down, or in other ways.

## Types of Messages

We have already seen that human beings are capable of dual means of communication: verbal and averbal. These are, in daily practice, intimately

[17] Bogart, "Feedback, Feedforward and Feedwithin".

intertwined, and either mutually redundant, reinforcing, or, as the case may be, contradictory.

Another classification cross-cuts the above. Message types – ideally conceived – are either *iconic*, or *indexical*, or *symbolic*. In actuality, most messages are a combination of two or all three aspects, stacked in a contextually appropriate hierarchy, which shifts over time as the context alters. Every natural language consists of a complex interplay of subtly shifting iconic, indexical and symbolic signs.[18]

An iconic message is one which resembles – according to some conventionally accepted criterion – some agent of the real world to which it refers. When Julius Caesar said: *Veni, vidi, vici* ("I came, I saw, I conquered"), the order of the three verbs he used iconically represented the order of his three successive actions in Gaul. This is an example of verbally expressed syntactic iconicity. Images, such as drawings or photographs, are commonly utilized icons in our culture: there is an assumed isomorphism between the pictorial representation and the thing represented. An example is the Star-Spangled Banner: what is iconic about the flag of the United States is the fact that each of the fifty white stars in a single blue canton "stands for" one of the fifty states in the present Union, whereas each of the thirteen stripes "stands for" one of the colonies that originally formed the Union.[19] The important point here is that their iconic relations can be grasped only by those already informed of the code, or convention (viz. American history) being used. There are other aspects of the flag which are indexical and symbolic; the aspect that predominates is always a function of the context.

An indexical message is one which "points to" an object or is a sample of it. Verbal indexes are, for one set of examples, all pronouns: "I" means "me" when I utter it; but when Ronald Reagan utters the same combination of phonemes, they add up to "Ronald Reagan". "Today" means "Monday" as I am writing this sentence; had I written it yesterday, "today" would have meant "Sunday". If I place onto a marker a tiny box containing radioactive waste from a nuclear powerplant, this could (in that context) be an index of a larger quantity of waste resulting from reprocessed spent fuel in the vicinity – say, encapsulated in a canister sunk far beneath the surface sample.

A symbolic message is one whose relationship to the "state of affairs" that it purports to represent is arbitrary, that is, understandable because of a pre-existing social convention which specifies that the message will, to all who concur, stand for thus-and-so. For instance, the spoken word "dig" will be understood by all who are privy to the code known as "modern spoken English" as, roughly, equivalent to "excavate" (and associated notions), given the right context (in other contexts, the same morpheme might mean "thrust", "reside",

---

[18] Roman Jakobson, "Quest for the Essence of Language", *Diogenes*, vol. 51 (1965) pp. 21–37, see in particular p. 26.

[19] Thomas A. Sebeok, *Contributions to the Doctrine of Signs* (Lisse: de Ridder Press, 1976) p. 121.

"poke", "apprehend", "enjoy" and so forth – derivative extensions commonly called "metamorphic meanings"). Symbols, of course, can be encoded in various other modalities. The American flag is also a symbol triggering deep emotional responses – say, in the context of a burial at Arlington National Cemetery.

The technical word used for highly formalized symbols in the visual mode is *emblem*. Examples of emblems are the abstract wheelchair design (figure 1), widely recognized as a way of making it known that there is a facility nearby giving access to a handicapped person; and the so-called trefoil (figure 2), generally accepted as a biohazard warning. Situated within a downward directing arrow in a canary-yellow triangle (figure 3), the trefoil is meant to be

Figure 1    *"Access for the handicapped"*

Figure 2    *Trefoil for biohazard warning*

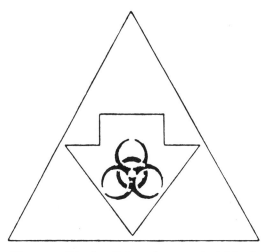

Figure 3    *"Caution: biohazardous waste buried here"*

interpreted as "Caution, biohazardous waste buried here", i.e. below where the arrow points.

Each mode of communication – iconic, indexical, symbolic (or emblematic) – has a set of advantages and a corresponding set of disadvantages, which are both context-bound.[20] Since the context is far from predictable at any stage over the next 10,000 years, and, with the passage of time, is bound to become increasingly equivocal, it will be recommended that all signs be constructed of a mixture of the three modes. While this intermingling will still not be fail-safe, it is certain that the more redundancy is built into the system, the more this will tend to ensure accurate decoding by any destination. The implications of this statement are further developed below.

## Some Problems of Imaging

At this point, some comments are in order about certain predictable problems involving iconic, specifically, image-based coding. It should be stressed that there is substantial disagreement on the extent to which pictorial perception depends on specific cultural experience, certainly a major source for human individual differences. Obviously, pictures give some humans some information on some occasions; but the "how" and "when" are complicated questions, and the answers are neither obvious nor should they be taken for granted in circumstances as delicate as our project demands. There are stick-figures, cartoons, sketches, paintings, photographs and a host of other possibilities for pictorial representation, with varying degrees of accuracy; the perception of all depictions, moreover, varies across species, cultures and times. For example, in the crowd scene in figure 4,[21] are the people fighting, dancing or engaged in some other activity? What is intimated here is by no means that images should

Figure 4

[20] *Ibid.*, ch. 8.
[21] This figure is based on figure 10 in John M. Kennedy's *A Psychology of Picture Perception* (San Francisco, Calif.: Jossey-Bass, 1974) p. 70.

not be used, but rather that they be selected with extreme forethought, and that they should always be incorporated into a framework that judiciously intermingles icons with symbols, supplementing the pair with indexes whenever that, too, is feasible.

## Channels

Every form of physical energy propagation can be used as a channel for conveying messages. To mention only the most common links used in one corner or another of the animal kingdom, these are: chemical, optical, acoustic, tactile, electric, temperature-based, different combinations of the afore-mentioned, and others. It is important, furthermore, to appreciate that human senses register only a small portion of ambient stimuli. Acoustically and optically, for example, as already pointed out, we are dependent upon a narrow range of hearing and seeing, i.e. we can register only restricted frequencies. It is very difficult to foretell what sensory prostheses will be at man's disposal in future decades and centuries, and one must further allow for the possibility – indeed, in the opinion of many, likelihood – that "human interference" will be carried out only indirectly by man, through the mediation of programmed robots equipped perceptually by unpredictable bionic devices. The problem of what constellation of channels are to be used to store the information to be transmitted into the future thus assumes considerable importance; here, once again, redundancy offers the best hope; all channels that seem technically feasible should be utilized. For instance, if the site can be rendered repulsively malodorous for a lengthy period, that would be, at least provisionally, a deterrent against casual exploration; no one, however, would advocate exclusive reliance upon the olfactory channel as a "final solution".[22]

## Recommendations (and Related Considerations)

(A) The opening sentence of Jane Harrison's classic survey of Pandora's Box,[23] on the changing aspects of this celebrated mythical symbol, begins: "There is a strange fascination about a mythological character that has retained its vitality up to our own day." This familiar myth – which occurs in countless verbal and pictorial variants since Hesiod's famous account of the Pandora story in his *Works and Days*[24] – deals with the woman, fashioned, upon orders from Zeus, by Hephaestus into a body out of clay and water, endowed by vital force

[22] The original Bechtel Report contains a bibliography on ancient writing systems and their decipherment. See *General Semantics Bulletin* pp. 35–6 [Editor's note].

[23] Jane E. Harrison, "Pandora's Box", *The Journal of Hellenic Studies*, vol. 20 (1900) pp. 99–114, see in particular p. 99.

[24] Dora Panofsky and Erwin Panofsky, *Pandora's Box: The Changing Aspects of a Mythical Symbol*, Bollingen Series LII (New York: Pantheon, 1962).

and a human voice and sent by the ruler of Olympus as a gift to Epimetheus, the brother of Prometheus, who was enchanted by Pandora. The beautiful mischief brought in her arms a great vase, raised its forbidden lid, thus enabling every evil the flesh is heir to to escape and spread about the earth (Hope alone remained). Pandora and her proverbial box (or jar,[25] or cask, or vase) often appear as an emblem of misery and destruction (see, for example, figures 5 and 6).

These persistent and widely diffused mythological and iconographic resonances of the assignment to which the Task Force is seeking a resolution lead to the first recommendation, to wit: that information be launched and artificially passed on into the short-term and long-term future with the supplementary aid of folkloristic devices, in particular a combination of an artificially created and nurtured ritual-and-legend. The most positive aspect of such a procedure is that it need not be geographically localized, or tied to any one language-and-culture (although, clearly, when linguistic and ethnic boundaries are crossed, both the verbal component and the associated set of rites are likely to undergo changes and an attenuation of the original rationale).

The legend-and-ritual, as now envisaged, would be tantamount to laying a "false trail", meaning that the uninitiated will be steered away from the hazardous site for reasons other than the scientific knowledge of the possibility of radiation and its implications; essentially, the reason would be accumulated superstition to shun a certain area permanently.

A ritual annually renewed can be foreseen, with the legend retold year by year (with, presumably, slight variations). The actual "truth" would be entrusted exclusively to an – as it were – "atomic priesthood", that is, a commission of knowledgeable physicists, experts in radiation sickness, anthropologists, linguists, psychologists, semioticians, and whatever additional administrative expertise may be called for now and in the future. Membership in this elite "priesthood" would be self-selective over time. The notion of a "priesthood" created to watch over "waste" has also been suggested by Arsen Darnay;[26] it is, of course, merely a colourful term for a self-perpetuating, government-independent committee. In another, wider, context, the more menacing expression, the Nuclear Barons, is used for "an international élite of scientists, engineers, politicians, administrators and military officers who brought atomic energy under control".[27]

The best mechanism for embarking upon a novel tradition, along the lines

---

[25] The original Greek word *píthos*, commonly mistranslated as "box", referred to a huge earthenware storage jar, "often large enough to serve as a receptacle for the dead", i.e. that either stands *on* or is partly buried *in* the earth (see Harrison, "Pandora's Box", p. 100, and Panofsky and Panofsky, *Pandora's Box*, p. 7.

[26] Arsen Darnay, "Aspic's Mystery", in Isaac Asimov, Martin Harry Greenberg and Charles G. Waugh (eds.), *Space Mail*, vol. 2 (New York: Fawcett Crest, 1976; 2nd edn 1981) pp. 42–65.

[27] Peter Pringle and James Spigelman, *The Nuclear Barons* (New York: Holt, Rinehart and Winston, 1981) p. ix.

Figure 5    *"Man's Opening the Fateful Vessel" (an engraving by Giulio Bonasone, 1531–74)*

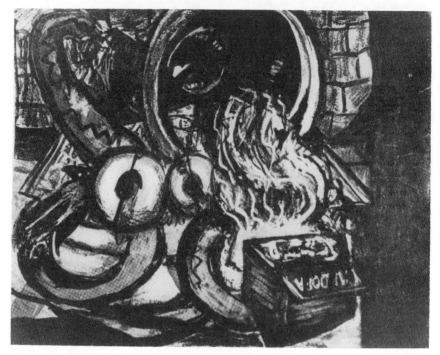

Figure 6    *"Pandora's Box" (gouache by Max Beckman, begun in 1936*
*but thoroughly repainted in 1947)*

suggested, is at present, unclear. Folklore specialists consulted have advised that they know of no precedent, nor could they think of a parallel situation, except the well-known, but ineffectual, curses associated with burial sites (viz. pyramids) of some Egyptian Pharaohs, e.g. of the eighteenth dynasty, which did not deter greedy, and, presumably, illiterate graverobbers from digging for "hidden treasure".

(B) Although the problems of waste storage are being studied in other countries – among them, Canada, France (which began research on vitrification and other forms of waste solidification in the late 1950s), Sweden and West Germany (which alone has chosen a site for the final resting place of some of its garbage) – and demonstration projects underway abroad are, in some places and some respects, technically further along than those in the USA, the human intrusion factor is scarcely studied abroad.[28] This means that planning should begin immediately to internationalize the kinds of communication measures discussed in this paper, and other Task Force reports. The ultimate design adopted should enjoy the benefit of worldwide thinking about the problems we face and their worldwide implications.

[28] See, however, Thomas B. Johansson and Peter Steen, *Radioactive Waste from Nuclear plants* (Berkeley, Calif.: University of California Press, 1981).

It should be noted that the first issue of *Nuclear and Chemical Waste Management: An International Journal of Hazardous Waste Technology* was begun in 1980, its announced purpose being to serve "as a forum to facilitate the communication in this area on a global basis".

(C) Consideration should be given to communication in artificial languages, which are mainly of two kinds: general purpose languages and languages restricted to the communication of some specified subject matter. The use of mathematical formulae is an old and conspicuous special purpose language, and may safely be assumed to embody the physical laws of the universe, understandable throughout the cosmos. Usually, mathematical communication consists of formulae surrounded by bits of vernacular. While the exclusive use of mathematical communication is not recommended, especially not for rite-bound messages, it is reasonable to anticipate a limited use in (a) metamessages and (b) technical messages to be "permanently" stored in archives, libraries, computers and other long-term repositories.[29]

(D) One of the pivotal concepts undergirding this whole paper is the notion of *redundancy*. In information theory, this term refers to a property of an information source whose *entropy,[30] $H$, is less than the maximum entropy, $H_{max}$, that could be obtained with the same string of messages. Redundancy (or one minus the relative entropy of the source, i.e. the ratio of the actual entropy to $H_{max}$) is an extremely important matter because it reflects the extent to which the efficiency of a communication system can be brought up to the desired standard by improvements in the encoding source (i.e. in our present time).

When the channel is noisy – as it is often bound to be – so that some messages are received erroneously, containing certain distortions, certain extraneous material, the introduction of redundancy will make it much more probable that some or all of the errors may be corrected. Therefore, the purpose of error-correcting codes is to intromit redundancy in a known manner such that corrections can be made at the receiving point – that is by the destination (i.e. in a future era) – without any further reference to the message source (which, by the nature of the case we are considering, would be impossible).

(E) Finally, a carefully considered overall recommendation is urged about the entirety of the communication system under deliberation. This is based on the conviction that all human thinking must be in continuity with the past, but also on an ineluctable corollary of this proposition, namely, that information tends to decay over time (i.e. the entropy continues to increase, eventually resulting in total incomprehensibility). This is not merely an empirical observation – witness the evolution of Modern English from Anglo-Saxon, through Middle English – but a consequence, more generally, of the Second

[29] On this subject, see further Hans Freudenthal, "Cosmic Language", in Thomas A. Sebeok (ed.), *Current Trends in Linguistics*, vol. 12 (The Hague: Mouton, 1974) pp. 1019–42, and the same author's earlier thesis, *Lincos: Design of a Language for Cosmic Intercourse* (Amsterdam: North Holland, 1960).
[30] See Jeremy Rifkin, *Entropy: A New World View* (New York: Viking Press, 1980).

Law of Thermodynamics. These related concepts are authoritatively discussed, in layman's language, by Norbert Wiener;[31] the fact, he says,[32] that information may be dissipated but not gained is one form of the Second Law of Thermodynamics, which also states that (in an isolated system) the probability that the entropy shall decrease is zero.[33]

What to do to counter the passage from negentropy to ultimate entropy?

What is being proposed here is a so-called "relay system" of information transmission, which rests on a very simple scheme: to divide the 10,000-year epoch envisaged into manageable segments of shorter and, presumably, reasonably foreseeable periods. Assuming that 10,000 years is equivalent to 300 generations of humankind, it is recommended that the messages at the burial site be designed for only three generations ahead, to wit, our children, grandchildren and great-grandchildren. A clear advantage of any such system would be that the verbal portion could be Modern English, while the averbal portion could easily be extrapolated from existing and universally understood pictorial emblematic strings (e.g. cartoons, stick-figures, or the like).

This message, however, would have to be supplemented by a metamessage – coded in the same combination of familiar verbal/averbal signs – incorporating a plea and a warning that the object-message at the site be renewed by whatever coding devices seem to be maximally efficient, roughly, 250 years hence. That future object-message should, in turn, incorporate a similar metamessage for the generation 500 years from now to act comparably, and so on, and on, up to 10,000 years ahead.

As for the more permanently stored, elaborated and scientifically accurate information in archives of the future, a similar set of instructions should make it clear that, as the information begins to decay, it should be updated, and also expanded in the light of improved science, engineering and technology.

The disadvantage of the relay system is, of course, that there is no assurance that future generations would obey the injunctions of the past. The "atomic priesthood" would be charged with the added responsibility of seeing to it that our behest, as embodied in the cumulative sequence of metamessages, is to be heeded – if not for legal reasons, then for moral reasons, with perhaps the veiled threat that to ignore the mandate would be tantamount to inviting some sort of supernatural retribution.

### Glossary of Technical Terms

AVERBAL: not linguistic.
CHANNEL: a medium wherein a message travels from source to destination.

---

[31] Norbert Wiener, *The Human Use of Human Beings: Cybernetics and Society* (Boston, Mass.: Houghton Mifflin, 1950).
[32] Ibid., p. 88.
[33] Ibid., p. 22.

CODE: an agreed transformation, or set of unambiguous rules, whereby messages are converted from one representation to another.

CONTEXT: broadly, the environment of a message; narrowly, all preceding and/or following messages that bear on their significance.

DECODING: a transformation, whereby, by operation of code rules, a destination alters an incoming message from one representation to another.

DESTINATION: where a message ends, i.e. is successively decoded and interpreted.

EMBLEM: a highly formalized symbol, usually in the visual modality.

ENCODING: transformation, whereby, by operation of code rules, a source alters a message from one representation to another.

ENTROPY: a term strictly used in statistical thermodynamics; and loosely used in semiotics to refer to the information rate of a message source.

FEEDBACK: a kind of feed mechanism that functions to detect an error in a communication system after the error has already occurred.

FEED MECHANISM: a cover term for three types of self-regulated control systems: FEEDBACK, FEEDFORWARD, FEEDWITHIN.

FORMULATION: an electro-chemical precoding process assumed to occur in a vertebrate's central nervous system prior to the recoding of a message in an externally communicable representation; generation.

ICON: a sign is said to be iconic when there is a topological similarity between the signifier and its denotata.

INDEX: a sign is said to be indexic in so far as a signifier is contiguous with its signified, or is a sample of it.

INTERPRETATION: an electro-chemical postcoding process assumed to occur in a vertebrate's central nervous system after the recoding of the message as received.

LANGUAGE: a uniquely human modelling system, such that signifiers (commonly: sounds or their graphic representation) and signifieds (meanings) are coupled over an infinite domain; verbal communication.

LINGUISTICS: the academic discipline devoted to formal studies of language and of natural languages.

MESSAGE: in communication, a sign or string of signs.

MESSAGE, CONVENTIONAL: a sign or a string of signs whose power to signify is thought to depend on prior agreement.

MESSAGE, NATURAL: a sign or string of signs signifying the same things at all times and in all places.

MULTIMESSAGE: a signifier that has a number of distinct meanings, the choice of interpretation depending on the time and/or the place.

NOISE: disturbances which do not represent any part of the messages from a specified source; unwanted signs.

PRAGMATICS: that branch of semiotics which studies the uses and the effects of messages; a term parallel to "syntactics" or "semantics".

REDUNDANCY: a property assigned to a source by virtue of an excess of rules whereby it becomes increasingly likely that mistakes in reception will be minimized.

SEMIOLOGY: one common synonym for "semiotics".

SEMIOSIS: the action of a sign, involving three subjects – a sign, its object and its interpretant.

SEMIOTICS: the doctrine, science or theory of signs; the subject matter of semiotics is the exchange of any messages whatever and of the system of signs which underlie them.

SIGNIFICATION: the meaning, or sense, of a message.

SOURCE: where a message begins, i.e. is successively formulated and encoded.

SYMBOL: a sign without either similarity or contiguity, but only with a conventional link between its signifier and its denotata, and with an intensional class for its designator.

TRANSDUCTION: transformation from one form of energy into another.

VERBAL: linguistic.

# MILTON GLASER

# I Listen to the Market

It is a very odd process by which, in our time, art exerts its power. You have to have an extraordinary system of introduction into the culture to *go through* the commercial channels, the art galleries, publishers and so on. Yet for social reasons you may take the extreme position of challenging the culture and find yourself being co-opted by commercial channels. "Going through" means that people begin to make money from the art. They encourage it and modify it. It is a fascinating process by which significant art finally penetrates cultural resistance – such art being, in its original state, difficult or incomprehensible and saying of the culture's values: "There's another way to look at this." If the art does offer an alternative vision, most people do not want it.

And yet, deeply we understand (or else it would never happen) the need for these transformations. Culture understands the need for these eccentric, difficult, incomprehensible elements to keep us alive.

That is the most curious thing when you think about the arts, that artists, on the one hand, are held up as the most important figures in the culture, but on the other hand, they are humiliated constantly, they cannot survive economically, they are unsupported, they are laughed at, they are portrayed as wastrels and weirdos. We have these two attributes held simultaneously in the mind, really an odd configuration when you stop to think that the artist exists on both poles at once. Celebrated for being what is best in the culture; despised for not being "productive". And these attributes are constantly and simultaneously held, by *all* cultures, I suspect. By all contemporary cultures.

It is astonishing to me how artists make the breakthrough. How they impose their vision on the world. I mean, Picasso is a fabulous case of someone who really out of willed talent and monstrous appetite transformed the world. He transformed the vision of our time. Picasso, Matisse, de Kooning, Duchamp, all the great figures of the twentieth century who insidiously transformed our culture.

That you could stylistically move from one position to another, that you do not have to be true or faithful, or believe in any of the work as being an answer to anything – that was for me the most important idea that I got from Picasso. That idea of your own sort of mobility in life. That you can abandon your own history and move on and give up and say, "I was wrong then", or, "I don't believe that now". That belief as such, in terms of the Platonic ideas of form, truth and beauty, was nonsensical.

My whole work from a career point of view has been to try to abandon what I knew how to do. I started out doing humorous illustrations, then doing more serious illustrations, then I became more interested in design, then I became a magazine designer, then I suddenly found myself doing interiors; now I am designing supermarkets and play parks for children and new petrol stations and so on. And I always realized that if you are lucky, you can abandon your own mastery. Learn how something is done and do it well, and then move on to something else.

I think that more than anybody else Picasso was really responsible for that basic insight: that you could just move along and leave all the baggage behind. You do not necessarily have to stay with it forever.

I stopped doing whole kinds of work; yet I also tried to use what I had learned in a given area. For example, I tried to use what I learned in the magazine business in designing supermarkets. I find that when you are in the business of communicating ideas and information, you are always dealing with the same questions of understanding novelty, familiarity, duration.

The first thing I did for the Grand Union supermarket was to introduce a table of contents. It has become a sign that tells you where everything is that you want to find (see figure 1). It seemed to me it was silly not to have one in a supermarket. "Magazine", after all, means a storehouse of random objects. That is what a supermarket is – a storehouse of random objects. When you design a magazine, what you try to do is move people in time through the magazine, keeping them informed and interested as they make their passage. You have to keep them turning the pages, being surprised, being led, being informed. A supermarket is the same. You have to take somebody in space, move them around, keep them informed – but that is not usually the way supermarkets are conceived. They are just conceived as a series of aisles which people get through as quickly and efficiently as possible.

However, in the supermarkets we have been designing, we are trying to change the experience to deal with compression, expansion, information, novelty and so on. And those are the same issues you deal with in a magazine. It is basically a problem of keeping people interested in what they are doing. How do you make them pay attention? At the same time, our supermarkets use many of the traditional concepts, because you cannot disrupt familiarity. You cannot have somebody come into a place and say, "What the hell is this?" or "I don't know where to go". So we make a real combination of old and new forms, trying to get people to understand the form of the aisle and the sequence of events, but

Figure 1

also trying to inform them more clearly and less capriciously as they go along. We also try, as they turn a corner, to surprise them.

However, we rely very heavily on the conventions of the marketplace. You have to always work within what is known. What does this person frequenting the supermarket know? What does he or she understand? And then, how much can you introduce the idea of novelty without disrupting, without making people feel that they are in a strange place or reading strange information?

It is very delicate, this interface between what is truly new and what is already familiar. Painters do not have this problem because the issue of the public and the media *understanding* is not one of their concerns. They are concerned with the bigger issue of transformation. But as a designer you are always concerned with the medium understanding, getting the message across, making a deviation or not, when such an event will take place, how much something will cost, what the benefit and value is if you, the customer, buy such and such. We are always involved with the reality of the need and desire between, usually, a client and its customer. We are the mechanism for transformation – taking an idea, bringing it to the customer and making it effective in terms of being able to produce the effect the client wants.

Packaging is very interesting from this point of view. You have to understand the exact audience you are speaking to in every case. The cases change, so the form of address has to change.

For instance, we are doing a lot of generic packaging for one line called "Basics". Now, there are two problems. One was to make the packaging look slightly better than the existing generic packaging, which is all black and white.

But basically, generic packaging is supposed to look terrible. Its intention is to produce the impression that no time was spent doing it and no cost. The truth of the matter is that generic packaging costs exactly the same to produce, from a physical point of view, as conventional packaging. It is run on the same press, and the fact that you do not use all the colours does not mean a thing. In the end the cost is the same.

But it is very important to signal that no costs are involved. In the same way, when we built a marketplace called "Basics", it was important for it to look as though no money had been spent on it. We used cardboard on top of pressed plywood to give the appearance of three layers of corrugated cardboard.

A very funny story is that we were doing this market and the client decided that it was essential to have a concrete floor. Why? Because one of the signals that it is not a fancy place is that you have a concrete floor. They took over an old failed market. It had a perfectly good tile floor. And at a cost of $50,000 they tore up that perfectly good tile floor so that they could reveal the rather crummy-looking concrete underneath! Semiotics!

There used to be a whole category of products called Packers' Labels, which were for A, B and C vegetables: perfectly good products, but they had broken stems and pieces and so on. They have now all been repackaged under the generic brands. They do not exist now as Packers' Labels. They used to be available to people who wanted a less expensive product. But it has suddenly become fashionable, not only fashionable but essential, for some people to buy less expensive products. So actually it was already in the market and available to everyone, but what has happened is that under this buzzword name "generics", it has now become a sort of official way to save money with a clear signal for people. So that is what they are buying, fashionably, in the light of day now. They are buying a level of product that was always available, but never so coherently presented.

We are so used to colours that when we see black and white it is like a kick in the stomach, yet it is a clear signal. And the satisfaction comes out of the reassurance that it is a plain operation. You are really getting good value because "look how skimpy and lousy the package looks. They really went out of their way to cut corners." We are really in a very odd position in the packaging that we did. It is slightly better than generic packaging. It looks as though somebody actually designed it, but it still is a clear signal.

There was one other thing that was required. And that came from the fact that people really hated the idea that there was nobody behind the product, that if you got some bum tunafish there was nobody to complain to. So we actually put a brand name on the generic. We called it "Basics", so that people could have a sense that there was some responsibility for the stuff.

There is, of course, a difference, one of quality, to generically packaged food. It is nutritious but certainly of lesser quality than brand-name food. Now the funny thing is that they had this category in the market for years not moving, and now it has become the hottest part of the supermarket. Why?

People are much more serious. The truth is that probably people realize, with or without the packaging, that they can use broken mushrooms to make their stew and it will taste the same, and it will be nutritionally the same, and they do not have to get a national brand for the purpose. The stringency of just trying to make ends meet and the increased consciousness of being ripped off – the combination of these two elements moves people towards generic products. Generic marketing is a response to a kind of calculating consumer able to read through the myth of ads and know that he or she does not require the fancier food.

Basically I am responding to what is a clear culture-societal desire – and taking advantage of it. Our designs are always trying to take advantage of what is occurring. Both shaping it and responding to it. Somebody once gave the best definition of design I have ever heard, and I give a rough paraphrase of it here: "Design is the intervention in the flow of events to produce a desired effect." A general definition: where something is happening, and you say, "Well, if we move here and do this, this will happen." Basically that is what you are always involved with in design practice. It is very hard to subvert events, although sometimes you want to. Recently we tried to participate in a project to encourage coffee drinking, because coffee drinking has been declining. The client was General Foods' Maxwell House. I worked with George Lang, a very well-known restaurateur, and with another team, to create a coffee house as a new kind of space form.

The idea was to open a new kind of restaurant. And Lang did a fabulous job. It was an informal place to really revive coffee conversation as a premise. And the problem, as I saw it originally, was that coffee had just been replaced as a drug of choice. It had been replaced because now people are not that interested in conversation, which is basically what coffee used to stimulate in the old days. We used to sit down, have a cup of coffee, basically as a conversation mode. I mean, it stopped the action. You sat and talked. Now people use drugs and they do so in a very different way. They do it because they want to be isolated. They do not want to talk; they do not want to have that former kind of interaction.

As a designer you may very well be acting against the direction of a culture by trying to replace where the culture is going with an alternative, and trying to convince people that it is a viable alternative or an interesting alternative. In other words, you may find yourself in a position of trying to make the culture turn, as well as just swimming along with it. We have both responsibilities, always in the context of overlapping our design on to the marketing objective. We try to isolate what the marketing objectives are and see how design reinforces those objectives. We have been doing much more of it in the last three years than I ever did before in my life.

We have done a tremendous amount of the propositions for Grand Union, for instance, in terms of changing their attitude towards food, the way they prepare their food, the criteria by which they package their food, doing their advertising, creating a store that is basically non-directional. The old stores were militaristic in the way they were designed. Now we create a store with a piazza in the middle, which is our newest model, so that you see an open space to come into the store (figure 2). And then you move through the store at your discretion, without having the old sense that you had to pass down all the aisles in order to pick up stuff along the way. The most important thing I saw in researching for Grand Union was the fact that very few people thought of it as their favourite store. When people thought of a store as their favourite, they tended to shop there frequently, and they bought more. The issue with Grand Union was therefore the transformation of people into believing that it was their favourite store. What do you do for these people?

The first thing is to really get on their side and try to think about what it is to shop. For you. So that instead of this idea of lockstep, going through efficiently and getting it over with – which is the way most people thought about Grand Union or other kinds of shopping – since shopping is the second largest leisure activity in the United States, shopping instead should be conceived of as a pleasurable activity. And what do you have to do to make shopping an awaited, important part of the day? You restore the marketplace to its real information resource status to people – with promotional books, with guides, with information and ultimately with product systems somewhere down the line. People now love to shop at Grand Union. You revitalize and bring back the marketplace to its real role.

One of the great losses to civilization is the movement to shop outside the city. I mean, the out-of-town shopping area is the most hideous thing that ever happened to America. You take the marketplace, which is really a place where

Figure 2

people come together and exchange ideas and things, and move it out into isolation where there is no function except selling and buying as an activity, and you tear the heart out of city life. The heart of the market is that it be accessible for the exchange of information. We must think of the market as a place that you can learn from. Or share information at.

There is more than one kind of exchange. One of them is "your cash for my product". And the others are every other kind of experience that you can have: personal interaction with others. In terms of learning about food or any other product, or learning other things as well. I do not mean learning in the sense of somebody in a class; I mean experiential learning.

When you go to a market in Europe, or an old market in South America, you really see how essential learning is to the life of the community, how it is the centre of the community's life. And then every once in a while you go to a market here in a small town which has that attribute, where the market is the heart of the town and where life revolves around it in terms of information, of posting information on the boards and other similar activities. In Woodstock, New York, where I live and where there is a Grand Union, they have just put in a fish counter for the first time. It is the first fresh fish that you have been able to get in that area for years. And it is a civic event. It is not just fish. They have a lobster tank and fresh lobsters swimming around. It is a big deal in a small town.

My vision of the world was transformed by Duchamp who taught me that you did not necessarily have to make objects for bourgeois consumption. When you look at the earthworks, and works of artists that were essentially polemic, or works that were essentially ideas, works that could not be displayed in galleries, that could not be sold – all of that comes from Duchamp: a resistance to playing the art game, increasing the prices, protecting deals, all that fraud that is supposed to be art. I also try to turn the culture but within the flux of the marketplace and in design for clients like Grand Union. The design-users, those who are susceptible, can develop an appetite for the original, and can go back. I do not think that always happens, but when it does not, it is a matter of personal limitation. If the potential for appreciation is there, the vulgar form can eventually lead you to the original.

In fact, this state of affairs is almost so by definition, by the definition of art; it could not be any other way. If high art is by definition incomprehensible, which it is, and difficult, which it is, and challenging, which it is, then it is going to be rejected, misunderstood and feared in its original manifestation, which it is. There has to be some mitigating circumstance, or a series of events that make it accessible to more than just this very refined group of super-intellectuals who can understand the emerging form.

And part of the whole vulgarization – I use vulgarization in its best sense – is a process which comes through exploitation, through social manipulation, through replication, through counterfeit, through copying, and the breakdown of values that occurs as problematical works are attacked. And eventually, the best thing that can happen is that the original work (and its integrity) emerges unscathed by reasserting its value in some way, after you have seen all the counterfeits and vulgarizations.

I think, if you examine it, that this is probably what happens. Otherwise there would not be any way for new forms to enter a culture. I mean, how else could they enter if not through the vulgar link?

RONALD WEINTRAUB

# Lifting the Veil

To be successful, a company must develop a strategy which enables it to earn profits consistently in competition with other companies, some of which have greater resources. In a consumer-products company new products are the key to earning profits consistently over an extended length of time. To facilitate the creation of new products, Flexnit Company, a manufacturer of intimate apparel, has always followed the prime rule of product development: find a need and fill it. Discovering unfilled needs requires skill, imagination and luck; finding them consistently requires a methodical approach. We use a process of consumer-focus-group research which uncovers explicit information and also facilitates intuition and creative interpretation.

A focus group is a panel of ten to twelve people selected on the basis of certain demographic criteria. We usually choose women between the ages of eighteen and forty-five, whose family income is between $15,000 and $25,000 per year and who shop in department stores in major cities or suburbs. The discussion is led by a moderator skilled in psychology and group dynamics. All sessions are tape-recorded and our product development staff sit in an adjoining room to view the proceedings through a one-way mirror. The panelists know they are being observed and recorded but this seems not to inhibit their spontaneity. The research is not statistically projectable but does provide us with clues and insights which are helpful in developing new products and creating advertising campaigns.

Two groups are conducted on the same subject on three consecutive days in order to counterbalance a possible aberration in one group, and to verify clues and conclusions. There are three sets of these groups. The first is for concept, and a wide assortment of product prototypes is shown. In the second, the number of products is narrowed down and specific styles are selected. In the third group, an attempt is made to select a name, an advertising theme and a photograph.

Over the past fifteen years we have developed many products through this technique but the most successful have come since 1978 when we added the insights of semiotics to the systematic procedures of focus-group research.

In the autumn of 1978 we were conducting a focus group on a novel brassière design. The idea being explored was rejected but as often happens, another idea was uncovered. A semiotic consultant attended this focus group at my invitation after expressing curiosity about this technique. Afterwards, in the "debriefing" session where we discuss what the panellists said and felt, he pointed out, by employing insights from semiotics, that three of the women made hostile comments and sat for much of the time with arms folded across their chests. He hypothesized this as a sign of defensiveness, of "covering up", and we were sufficiently intrigued to investigate further.

In seeking some connection among these three women, we finally discovered that all had A-cup breast size. Normally we select a random assortment of women based on our demographic criteria, and try to have a balanced representation of all sizes ranging from A- to D-cups. These three women were sending a message about their feelings of being size A. To probe further, we conducted two more focus groups with only A-cup women and showed prototypes of bras made in their size.

The response was enthusiastic. They were grateful that a brassière manufacturer recognized their need for attractive products in their particular size. It was difficult, they said, to find attractive styles in size A because many manufacturers make only B- and C-cups, the bestselling sizes. Others make some styles in A but often fail to offer all the popular fashion colours.

Before proceeding further we had to determine if the market was large enough to justify a line just for A-cup women. No explicit numbers were available but we were able to find some statistics as the Department of Health and Human Services that implied that between 15 and 20 per cent of the adult female population might be this size. Also, we used our computer to analyse past sales of our basic styles, and we satisfied ourselves that the market potential justified developing a line of bras for this market segment.

When we began to design new styles we discovered that there were physiological differences in the chest development of size-A women. We accommodated these in the design and fit of our products. Also, all manufacturers, including Flexnit, had made A-cup patterns simply by mathematically downgrading patterns from size 34B, which is the standard on which all designers fit. Our products were developed on A-cup models, which resulted in a more precise fit. Not only did we have a unique marketing concept but also a superior product by virtue of the improved fit.

After a series of focus groups, which gave us guidance on styling, we conducted additional groups to select a name and advertising copy. Ultimately, the "A-OK" was chosen, and the copy headline "Beautiful bras designed especially for A-cup women" was adopted. This has recently been revised to "You're an A-cup woman and you're A-OK".

Since its introduction in August 1979, A-OK has been highly successful. In 1981 the line of seven bras, some with matching panties, had retail sales of over

$5,000,000. Thus, using focus groups as a means of exploration, and adding the insights of semiotics, we discovered and met an unfilled customer need.

After A-OK we looked for another unfilled need and decided to investigate cotton. Cotton bras were very successful in Europe and we believed the American market was ready because of the emphasis on natural fibres and the natural look in clothing. In early 1980 we conducted focus groups at which we showed prototypes of cotton bras of our design as well as some from European collections.

Our growing interest in semiotics attuned us to listen closely to the words consumers used and to observe the intensity of their feelings. Some women viewed cotton as old-fashioned, "the kind of bras my mother used to wear", but we discounted this because the old bras were made of woven cotton broadcloth, which is different from the knitted cotton and Spandex blended fabric we were planning to use.

There were many positive comments about cotton. It was described as comfortable, absorbent, easy to wash, soft and pure. It was viewed with favour despite a "conventional" image; it was considered rational and practical, not sensual.

This faint praise should have caused us to drop the project but sales reports from Europe were very positive and, more importantly, we learned that two of our competitors were also working on cotton bras. An irrational desire to beat the competition overcame us; we were not going to let someone else capture a new market when we had a head start.

We ignored the negative indicators and concentrated on the positive features of cotton. The product was named "Stay Natural" and the advertising headline was "The new cotton blend seamless bra that feels as natural as you".

The product failed after less than twelve months in the market despite wide distribution in most major department stores. The products offered by our competitors also failed quickly, one because it was made in a bold striped fabric, the other because it was plain and conventional like ours. They compounded the error by naming theirs "Le T", which to many consumers had the connotation of a man's T-shirt, even though the manufacturer meant that it was to be worn under T-shirts which were in style at the time. It was evident that consumers decode products in terms of their own prejudices and emotions despite efforts by the manufacturers to influence them. Even the most imaginative theme backed by large ad budgets would not have succeeded. Cotton is fine for sheets, bandages, panties and men's underwear but does not meet the American consumer's criteria for brassières. Also, while some women ask for a "natural" look, even very attractive women believe their figures to be in some way flawed. Thus, they want bras that will enhance their figures, not just conform to their natural shape. Unfortunately, we learned this at focus groups held later to help us analyse why our cotton products failed.

Fortunately, the good that emerged from this experience far outweighed the cost of the failure, for it was during the cotton focus groups that our next and most important new concept was discovered.

During the cotton focus groups some of the women who were critical of cotton asked for products that were more sensual. We followed this clue and conducted some focus groups at which we showed prototypes of very sexy bras and panties. The initial response was encouraging, so at the next series of groups we showed not only sensual products but also photographs of fantasy scenes as we were looking for a unique advertising approach. The photographs showed men and women in exotic costumes, women in gauze fabrics swinging on boughs of flowers, a woman under an umbrella made of daisies and other fantasy scenes in exotic colours.

These photographs proved to be a kind of Rorschach test in that they stimulated the women to express themselves openly about their sexual fantasies. We were surprised to hear so many frank comments about sex because in the prior fifteen years of research on intimate apparel, sex was seldom mentioned. It was also unexpected because the moderator was male, and the women knew there were people behind the one-way mirror and that the session was being tape-recorded.

In spite of these inhibitors they wanted to talk freely about sex. One woman related in detail how she would dress up, including sexy underwear, on Saturday nights, go out with her husband to a nice dinner with a few drinks, in order to come home released from conventional restraints. Her husband recognized the clues and became sexually aroused, unlike on other nights. She said she used her intimate apparel as one of the tools to seduce her husband. She was not embarrassed to tell this to the group but was ashamed of having to arouse her husband in such a deliberate and calculating manner. Sex in our society is supposed to be spontaneous and she was violating the rule.

Another woman said that before going on vacation with her husband she bought new underwear to look sexy. She shopped for "low-cut things" because they made her "feel good, new and sexy". Another said, "When I go out with my husband I want to look good for afterwards." Still another stated, "When I was single I would buy sexy bras and colour-co-ordinated sets. I wanted to feel sexy, be sexy and wanted to look sexy if anything should happen."

Some told rather sad stories of their dull sex lives. Married many years, they said the romance had gone out of their relationship with their husbands. Others were more tightly bound by convention and had rarely experienced sexual excitement. One said, "Sexiness is only for single girls." Another commented, "I have girl friends who live for lingerie. It makes them feel good. Pretty lingerie is an indulgence." Yet another said, "I want to be noticed; I don't want to be a neuter" and "I don't want sex, I want a very pretty silk dress."

We heard many other revealing statements, such as "I want to wrap myself in prettiness", and "I make a sentence out of my body by the clothes I wear". Most wanted co-ordinated colours in their underwear because, as one put it, "Colour makes me feel better and sexier". Another said, "There is a difference between getting dressed in the morning and getting dressed to go out in the evening." One said she was "glad that underwear is getting sexier", and one summed it all up by saying "If I look good with my clothes on, why shouldn't I look good with my clothes off?"

Our industry had missed the sexual revolution! Of course there were companies making attractive and sensual brassières but this usually meant that lace was added to the bra to signify femininity. Others had used sensual themes in their advertising but often the product did not live up to the claim or the image. We had discovered a market segment that could be defined in terms of psychographics rather than demographics or body type, a consumer whose lifestyle included a need, as yet unfulfilled, for exciting, sensual intimate apparel. We decided to be the first to develop a line of truly sensual products with an advertising campaign that was consistent with and enhanced the imagery of the products.

In the next series of focus groups, women told us they wanted intimate apparel that was sexy yet in good taste. They referred to merchandise in the Frederick's of Hollywood catalogue but asked for products that were less risque and gaudy, and wanted to buy them in department stores. They were telling us that sex is a fact of life, and rather than treat it as something tawdry they wanted to make it more beautiful, more full of excitement and delight. The human body is more inviting and mysterious when covered. The veil of lingerie enhances the attractiveness of the body and heightens the degree of pleasure when lifted. Intimate apparel can be a powerful aphrodisiac. Even the most practical women said that while colourful, sensuous lingerie was no substitute for real romance, it did embellish their fantasies and was viewed as perfume or cosmetics, a symbol of hope and a means of covering their bodies in an attractive manner.

After more focus groups to select styles we sought an appropriate name. Panellists selected "Ce Soir", which they told us sounded sexy because it was French and because of the alliteration of the soft "s" sounds. The dynamic blue script of the "Ce Soir" logotype – rising from the lower left across the model's legs – evoked a sinuous being coiling and uncoiling rapidly upwards: desire itself in its movement. The model, the environment, the pose they selected all reflected their consensus version of sensuality: outspoken but not blatant, frank but in good taste.

"Ce Soir" is today two collections of eleven styles including four bras, three bikinis, two teddies and two suspender belts, with retail sales in 1985 expected to reach $10,000,000.

From this experience we learned that the way in which the product is communicated is as important as the actual product, but the product has its own image which must be consistent with and enhance the advertising theme. Many advertising professionals believe that a product should have an image or personality. To establish a personality some campaigns employ a celebrity spokesperson who becomes the identity of the product. In our industry, Playtex uses Jane Russell in their television commercial for one of its lines of heavy support bras and control girdles. Other industries' products are given a personality using animation, like the Pillsbury Dough Boy or the Jolly Green Giant of vegetable fame.

Semiotics has taken us beyond personality to "resonance". We know our products fill distinct consumer needs because the ideas come directly from consumers. Some may quarrel with the particular execution of our ads and no doubt improvement is always possible. The model in the "Ce Soir" ad is an evidently sexy woman in a mauve bedroom, deep reddish throw pillows on the bed behind her. Her hair is Botticelli-like and her gaze is into *your* eyes: you are looking at *will*. We might have selected another model and projected an entirely different image and hence resonated with another type of consumer. The potential market for "Ce Soir" products is large and comprises many different types of women so it is obviously impossible for one photograph to resonate with all of them. We do not have the budget to create and run a wide range of ads so we attempt to resonate with some and for all others to project a prototypical sign of sensuality that all can understand. This is highly subjective, and some women may ignore or reject the sign just as others will read it and understand and act on the message.

To understand how to make and sell lingerie you must listen "between the lines" to women. Not an easy task, but it is possible to improve insight by employing focus groups to explore systematically the underlying attitudes and by using semiotic analysis to lift the veil.

MATTHEW KLEIN

# And Above All, Please Do Not Disturb

I have my imitators as well, you know. When I constructed an Arcimboldesque head out of a fish, a shrimp, a lemon and so on and photographed it for the cover of *New York* magazine, a restaurant asked to buy the rights to it, but did not want to pay me a reasonable amount. I rejected the proposition, whereupon the restaurant's art director said: "Well, to hell with it, *I'll* make a head, too", and proceeded to make a weak semblance of my vegetable face. He used a radish for an eye, another radish for a mouth – because a radish is red and has a little tail and looks, supposedly, like lips, although a radish looks no more like lips than many another thing. He used an abstraction instead of telling a visual lie.

You could make a tree out of pineapples, a fish out of trees, who would care? What is interesting, phantasmatic about Arcimboldo is that it is a *face*, a human face, and more: it is a person. Arcimboldo has embodied a personality: there is as much rich expression in his heads as in a good portrait.

It is a contingent person, yet this person also refers you to a type. In Arcimboldo you will find a happy person surprised, a dumbbell expressing joy. It is the person-type undergoing a momentary affect. Never in the imitators of Arcimboldo do you get such a disturbance of the person. You easily read the imitation, understand, identify it as a face of eggplants or of pickles: never do you like or dislike it. No movement (of your body) of attraction or repulsion.

Stealing from Arcimboldo, I have obviously read his commentators – and one of the best of them has this to say on the springs of Arcimboldesque affect:

Arcimboldo's heads are monstrous because they all go back, whatever the charm of the allegorical subject (Summer, Spring, Flora, Water), to a malaise of matter: the *swarm*. The jumble of living things (vegetables, animals, children), arranged in compact disorder (before taking their place in the intelligibility of the final figure), evokes a whole larval world, a

Figure 1

tangle of vegetative creatures, worms, fetuses, viscerae, lying at the edge of
life, as yet unborn and nevertheless already subject to putrescence. Now,
the "marvel" – or the "monster" – is essentially what transgresses the
separation of realms, mixes the animal with the vegetable, the animal with
the human; it is *excess*, insofar as it changes the quality of the things
to which God has assigned a name: it is *metamorphosis*, which overturns
one order into another; in short, to use another word, it is *transmigra-
tion* (Roland Barthes, "Rhetor and Magician", in *Arcimboldo*, trans. by
John Shepley, Parma: Franco Maria Ricci, 1978).

Barthes was able to see an immense *gravity* of these heads: the face, the final
intelligibility, always being pulled apart by the primal parts and swarm – a
wonderful thought, but interestingly enough, no one sees it this way except
Barthes. Barthes' is a personal, an elaborated eye. There is a dominant,
contemporary – a psychologizing – viewpoint quite contrary to that of Barthes. If
you were to ask ten thousand "common" people, the proverbial 9999 would say

"Those are vegetables in the shape of a face", not a face in the shape of vegetables – whether you show them Arcimboldo or Matthew Klein.

I recall another remark of Barthes:

> For Arcimboldo's century, the monster is a marvel. The Hapsburgs, patrons of the painter, had cabinets of art and curiosities (*Kunst- und Wunderkammern*), in which strange objects were collected: freaks of nature, effigies of dwarfs and giants, or hirsute men and women: everything that "astonished and caused one to reflect"; these cabinets, it has been said, had some of the characteristics of the laboratories of Faust and Caligari.

The determinants of my life are different from Arcimboldo's. Mine emphasize the building process – vegetables becoming man – more than do his: which is to say, my works deconstruct less forcibly than his – granting Barthes' idea – perhaps even very little or not at all. His images are, for a number of reasons, more sophisticated than mine. First, because they give off more semes, and interestingly, since the seme is the connoter of the person, an arch-seme in Arcimboldo would be – for the elaborated, the refined eye, I insist – the decomposing person, the person becoming unperson.

My goal is to amplify the person, to share my model and its time with the spectator. This is the purpose of communication – to create the illusion that the spectator and the photographic model, receiver and sender, share time and concepts.

Unlike Arcimboldo, who made use of allegorical iconography ("Summer", "Winter", "Calvin", "Water", "Fire"), I make new icons. For *New York* magazine, I made an image of a fat face out of food that people eat when they are dieting – fish, shrimp, grapefruit, lettuce, nuts. The image did not involve a grand issue, as Arcimboldo's Jurist does – a much more potent image (see figure 2). (Perhaps today diets *are* more potent images than jurists.) In any case, the image is not archetypal, it is local. People are always going to be interested in, and have always been interested in, myth. People have only been interested in diets for the last fifteen years in America. You can find a Biafran to talk to you about myth; you will not find one to talk to you about his diet, particularly his slimming diet.

I am a photographer who had an assignment from *New York* magazine, which is for people whose preoccupations are Upper East Side elegance. These people think less archetypally than locally – although the image they want to have of themselves is that they think universally, which is just part of their local myth: that New York and this Upper East Side district in New York is where the world is – the best stuff, the right stuff is there. All the rest of the stuff of the world is the wrong stuff. We are trying to seduce these people to fork over a couple of bucks to buy the magazine.

A friend of mine who was working as an art director wanted to become a photographer. He talked to his boss, a friend of Irving Penn, who had worked with Penn. The boss said, "Well, Irving is looking for a new assistant. Why don't you go speak to him? I'll set up an appointment." Penn is a commercial and artistic god in the business. He is a very profound photographer and has cunning commercial instincts. My friend showed Penn his pictures, reflections in puddles, young lovers, people walking around gloomy – deep, sombre kinds of moods. Penn looked at all the pictures, looked at each photograph for a minute. He did not say a word. He went through the whole stack, then went through it again backwards. My friend was thinking, "He loves it, it's terrific, I'm going to be his assistant and then I'm going to have a big studio." Penn got through the group a second time, put them all together, handed them to this man and said, "Young man, I can't hire you." My friend asked why. "Because the most important thing in commercial photography is that the world should be imbued with a sense of well-being. Really, nothing else matters. It's irrespective of your formidable talent."

I am working in the commercial marketplace and my work, if it is grotesque, still must be imbued with a sense of well-being. The fat person on a diet cannot be grotesquely fat. The fruits shown cannot be about to explode from their own juice pressure. The face has to be benevolent, has to smile and say "I'm doing fine and everybody involved in my construction was doing fine and you'll be doing fine if you come and shop here, or buy my product, or associate with me, or eat at my restaurant." That is a basic metonymy of commercial behaviour.

*Vis-à-vis* the *New York* magazine cover, here is a person smiling, obviously on a diet; and even though his or her diet is not working (the face, by the way, is deliberately androgynous), there is a certain good humour about it. We all know your diet did not work, neither did mine. This person is not going to jump out the window and is not demented. No one is going to kill Dr Tarnower because her diet did not work. It is a happy, healthy look we are after – always. In anything commercial, you never can show anything negative.

Look at my face again on that cover. Here is a face that is pleasant and happy, without anomaly. If you want, the anomaly is the fatness which the title and article refer to and describe, and not in an unpleasant way. You could eat this face – with pleasure. Arcimboldo has one such face, the Gardener. He really looks like he is saying: "Not so bad for a bowl of vegetables, huh?" The rest, you could not eat. They are putrescent. Look at Summer. It is food, yet something is in the expression – a bulge of the eyes about to burst – that makes it shocking. Herod – a sense of babies, pink things crawling over each other, like a catch of crustaceans, shelled yet still moving. Babies? We look again: larvae, primal creatures that disfigure the civilized self.

In commercial art, the personality portrayed, whether it be portrayed by a model or an actor or a gang of vegetables, has to be pleased with itself and especially pleased with its association with the product. Pleased with itself means that the personality has a limit, a property, and stays within that limit and its property.

Let us look at Arcimboldo's people in Barthes' way for an instant, as if they were people becoming vegetables rather than vegetables becoming people. It is as though they were escaping into vegetableness, fishness and so on. They *prefer* to be going the wrong way, so to say – to be leaving their skin. "I don't want to be a person any more, I want to be a bunch of fish." There is tremendous anxiety in Arcimboldo's heads. An anxiety at being proper and property, at being this and not that. Never an "I respect that I'm this and not that, I respect my difference from other things." Arcimboldo's heads always seem eager to become something other than what they are, eager to become components, fruits and vegetables, fish and animals – whereas in my heads, if there is an eagerness, it is an eagerness *not* to be lowly fruits and vegetables, but to be a person, to be an identity and a commercially wholesome identity: a local not archetypal person, an Upper East Side person, slightly androgynous, the definition of modern man.

Contrary to Barthes' opinion, the heads of Arcimboldo cause little suffering, little anxiety inside our culture. The swarming and putrefaction only slightly deconstruct our pretence of unity and identity. Why? Because to us they are archaic, not from our time; much in the same way that we are not threatened by, say, a photograph of a madman from the 1820s.

Figure 2

*I* can think my way into some of the affective power of Arcimboldo's heads –
the Jurist who passes judgement on other people thinks he is better than you –
and that idea will rot his soul. That is what the bulbous chicken-nose says, that
is what the rigid fish-tail beard says. It is a moral portrait (see figure 2).

But the commercial audience does not think in this way, it does not think
morally, archetypally; it is local in thought. When we "target" Americans in the
commercial marketplace, we are conceptualizing a population with a common
culture or, putting it technically, signification system – a restricted, highly
restricted culture. Think of the "sit-coms" on television; they barely differ. The
various writers and products have found an essentially single way of
approaching Americans. This approach tends, by synecdoche, to define the
culture at large.

I could make a grotesque head. I could use as a model a moral, unlocal,
un-upper bourgeois appearing head. I would photograph not paint it.
Photography, with its reality claim, is today's dominant code. That head might
be under your bed when you close your eyes and try to sleep at night. It might

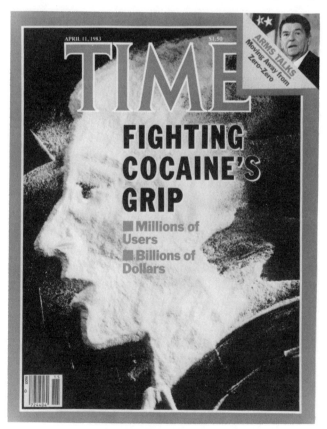

Figure 3

come out and grab you. And turn *you* into a bunch of vegetables. Now those are *real* fears.

I only did that once, to frighten the population a bit, to ride the cocaine fright-consciousness (see figure 3). *Time* magazine excepted, the faces I make are benevolent because they are commercial faces. I would never think, commercially speaking, of deconstructing the pretence of being an identity, that happy-go-lucky and well-adjusted person you are. I would do it myself, for my own personal cynical reasons, but I would not do it in the marketplace because that would not pay.

I know how hard it was at the beginning to get the ego *I* have now got. I worked at it. And Arcimboldo – seeing him through Barthesian eyes – is the one who tries to deconstruct all this illusion and pretence of being a unity. He tears it to pieces and leaves the pieces, propped up against one another. There it is, the body before the mirror-stage.

What Arcimboldo shows – barely noticeable in our ego-reigning, happiness culture – is the fragility of the face, the person, the construct. Rule: never let that happen in the marketplace. All images have to be absolutely solid. So my vegetables become a whole and will stay that way by virtue of their cement. What is the cement? Goodness. The personality I have made is a "good" person – fun-loving, adjusted, ignoring his locality, etcetera, etcetera.

UMBERTO ECO

# Towards a New Middle Ages

Recently, and from several quarters, we have begun to hear our period spoken of as a new Middle Ages. The question is whether we are dealing with a prophecy or a statement of fact. In other words, have we already entered the New Middle Ages or, as Roberto Vacca puts it in a disturbing book (*Il Medio Evo prossimo venturo*), "will there be a Middle Ages in the near future"? Vacca's thesis involves the decay of the great systems characteristic of the era of technology; too vast and complex to be co-ordinated by a central authority or even to be controlled individually by an efficient managerial organization, they are doomed to collapse, and through a series of chain reactions to bring about a retreat of all industrial civilization. Let us take a brief look at the most apocalyptic hypothesis conceived by Vacca, as a sort of "scenario", seemingly quite persuasive, for the future.

## Design for Apocalypse

One day in the United States a traffic jam and a tie-up of train transportation will combine to prevent the night-shift personnel from reporting to work at a major airport. Overcome by fatigue, the overworked air-controllers cause a collision between two jumbo jets, which plunge on to a high-tension power line, whose load, redistributed on other already overloaded lines, results in a blackout similar to the one experienced by New York some years ago. However, this time its effects are more serious and last for days. Since it is snowing and the roads remain clogged, cars create monstrous traffic jams; fires are lit for

These pages were written in 1972. Many things of course have changed, many of the examples have changed as well. So the pages have to be read as pages written in 1972 – in which, from today's vantage point, we see social forces in a quite early form.

warmth in offices, leading to blazing conflagrations that firemen are unable to reach and put out. The telephone system is jammed under the impact of fifty million isolated persons trying to call one another. People begin forced marches in the snow, with the dead left by the wayside.

Lacking provisions of any kind, the wayfarers try to commandeer food and shelter, and the tens of millions of firearms sold in America are put to use. All power is taken over by the armed forces, although they too are victims of the general paralysis. Supermarkets are looted, the supply of candles in homes runs out, and the number of deaths from cold, hunger and starvation in the hospitals rises. When, after a few weeks, things have with difficulty returned to normal, millions of corpses scattered throughout the city and countryside begin to spread epidemics, bringing back scourges on a scale equal to that of the Black Death, which in the fourteenth century destroyed two-thirds of the European population. "Contamination psychoses" emerge and the search for scapegoats leads to increasingly savage witch-hunts. Political life, engulfed in crisis, becomes split up into a series of subsystems separate and independent from the central authority, with mercenary militias and autonomous courts of justice. As the crisis spreads, those best equipped to survive it will be the inhabitants of underdeveloped areas, already prepared to live under elementary conditions of life and competition. Mass migrations will take place, accompanied by racial intermingling and the importation and diffusion of new ideologies.

With the decline of the rule of law and the destruction of land registers, ownership will rest on the sole right of possession; on the other hand, rapid decay will have reduced the cities to a series of ruins alternating with inhabitable houses in the hands of squatters, while minor local authorities will be able to maintain a degree of power by building enclosures and small fortifications. At this point, a complete feudal structure will have taken over. Alliances among local powers will rest on compromise and not on law; individual relations will be based on aggression, friendship or common interest; and the elementary custom of giving hospitality to travellers will re-emerge. In the face of this prospect, Vacca tells us, all we can do is to think of preparing the equivalent of the monastic communities that, in the midst of such decay, would henceforth train themselves to keep alive and transmit the technical and scientific knowledge needed for the advent of a new revival.

One must decide whether the above thesis is an apocalyptic scenario or the exaggeration of something that already exists. And then one ought to free one's conception of the Middle Ages from the bad name with which it was saddled by a certain cultural approach fostered by the Renaissance. Let us try to understand what the term "Middle Ages" means.

## Alternate Design for a Medieval Age

For one thing, we notice that the term designates two quite distinct historical moments: one extending from the fall of the Roman Empire in the West to the year 1000, a period of crisis, decay, violent shifts of populations and the clash of cultures; the other from the year 1000 to the rise of what in our schools is called Humanism. It is not by chance that many non-Italian historians consider this second period as already in full flower by this time; indeed, they speak of three revivals, the Carolingian one, another in the eleventh and twelfth centuries, and the third which is known as the actual Renaissance.

Assuming it is possible to synthesize the Middle Ages into some sort of abstract model, to which of the two will our own era correspond? Any one-to-one correspondence would be naïve, if only because we live in a period of enormously accelerated processes, whereby what takes place in five of our years can sometimes correspond to what then took five centuries. In the second place, the centre of the world has expanded to cover the entire planet; civilizations and cultures and different stages of development all co-exist nowadays, and common sense leads us to speak of the "medieval condition" of the populations of Bengal, while we look on New York as a flourishing Babylon, or Peking as the model for a new Renaissance civilization. Thus the parallel, if there is one, must be traced between certain moments and situations of our planetary civilization and different moments of a historical process running from the fifth to the thirteenth century A.D. To be sure, comparing a particular historical moment (today) with a period of almost a thousand years has all the look of a pointless joke, and pointless it would be if that were what we were trying to do. But here we hope to develop a "hypothesis of the medieval" (almost as though we were proposing to construct a Middle Ages and were trying to decide what ingredients were needed to produce an effective and plausible one).

This hypothesis, or model, will have the characteristics of all laboratory creations: it will be the result of a choice, a filtering, and the choice will be governed by a precise purpose. In our case, the purpose is to come up with a historical image against which to measure tendencies and situations of our time. It will be a laboratory game, but no one has ever seriously maintained that games are useless. It is by playing that a child learns to get along in the world, precisely because he is pretending to do what he will later be forced to do.

What is needed for a good Middle Ages? First of all, a great Peace that is breaking down, a great international state power that had unified the world in language, customs, ideologies, religion, art and technology, and which at a certain point, by its actual ungovernable complexity, collapses. It collapses because its borders are being pressed by "barbarians", who are not necessarily uncivilized but who bring new customs and new visions of the world. These barbarians may penetrate by violence because they want to take for themselves a wealth that has been denied them; or they may insinuate themselves into the social and cultural body of the ruling Pax, thereby causing the circulation of new faiths and outlooks. The Roman Empire, at the beginning of its fall, was not undermined by the Christian ethic; it had already undermined itself by syncretistically accepting Alexandrian culture and the Eastern cults of Mithras and Astarte, and toying with magic, new modes of sexual behaviour, and various hopes and images of salvation. It absorbed new racial groups, eliminated out of necessity many rigid class distinctions, reduced the differences between citizens and non-citizens, patricians and plebeians, and kept the divisions based on wealth but diluted the differences between social roles. Nor could it have done otherwise. It witnessed examples of rapid acculturation, raised to positions of power men belonging to races that two hundred years earlier would have been judged inferior, and reduced the dogmatic content of many theologies. In the same period, the government could worship the classical gods, the soldiers Mithras, and the slaves Jesus Christ. It instinctively persecuted the faith that by and large seemed most lethal to the system, but in general a great repressive tolerance allowed for the acceptance of everything.

The collapse of the Great Pax (military, civil, social and cultural at the same time) starts a period of economic crisis and weak authority, but it is only a justifiable anti-clerical reaction that has prompted us to see the Dark Ages as all that "dark". Actually, even the Early Medieval period (and perhaps more than the Middle Ages after the year 1000) was one of incredible intellectual vitality, of impassioned dialogues between barbarian civilizations and the Roman heritage, seasoned with Eastern and Christian elements; of journeys and encounters, with the Irish monks who criss-crossed Europe spreading ideas, encouraging the reading of books, and inventing all kinds of madness.

In short, this is where modern Western man ripened, and it is in this sense that a model of the Middle Ages can help us to understand what is happening in our times: the collapse of a Great Pax gives way to crisis and insecurity, different civilizations clash, and the image of a new man slowly takes shape. Only later will that image appear clearly, but the basic elements are already there, simmering away in a dramatic cauldron. Boethius, as he expounds Pythagoras and rereads Aristotle, is not reciting by heart a lesson from the past but is inventing a new way of creating culture, and while pretending to be the last of the Romans, actually constitutes the first Research and Development office of the barbarian courts.

## Crisis of the Pax Americana

That today we are experiencing the crisis of the Pax Americana has become a commonplace of contemporary historical writing, but it would be silly to attempt to isolate the "new barbarians" in a precise image, if only because of the negative and misleading ring that the word "barbarian" always has for our ears. It is hard to say whether they are Chinese or the peoples of the Third World, or the sub-cultures or the Central American rebels "manipulated" by Fidel Castro, or the southern Italian migrants who, in Turin, have created a new Piedmont that never existed before; or whether, like the Mexican aliens, they press in at the borders (where such exist) or, like the Colombian cocaine dealers, are already at work inside the social body (see figure 1). On the other hand, who were the barbarians of the centuries of imperial decline – the Huns

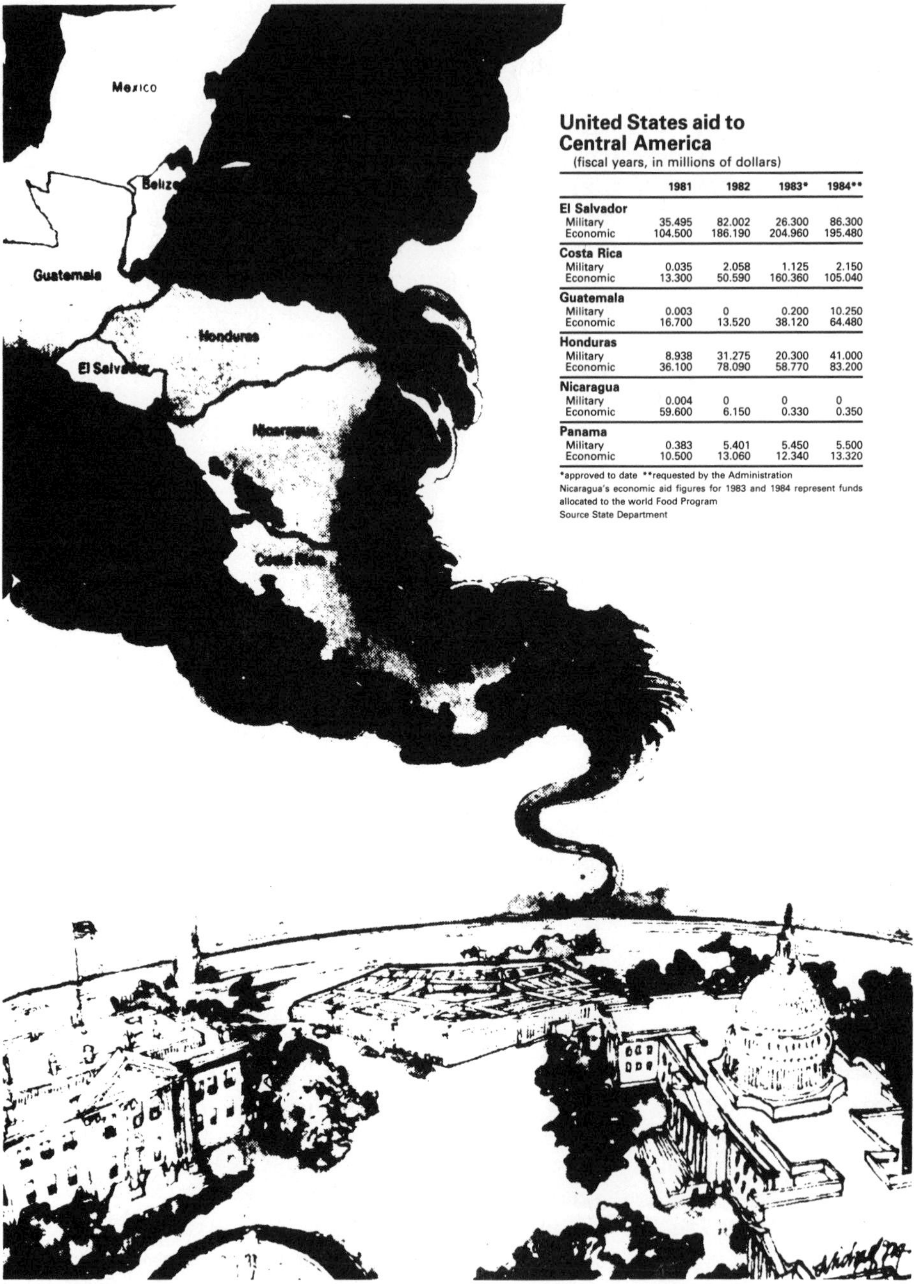


**United States aid to Central America**
(fiscal years, in millions of dollars)

| | 1981 | 1982 | 1983* | 1984** |
|---|---|---|---|---|
| **El Salvador** | | | | |
| Military | 35.495 | 82.002 | 26.300 | 86.300 |
| Economic | 104.500 | 186.190 | 204.960 | 195.480 |
| **Costa Rica** | | | | |
| Military | 0.035 | 2.058 | 1.125 | 2.150 |
| Economic | 13.300 | 50.590 | 160.360 | 105.040 |
| **Guatemala** | | | | |
| Military | 0.003 | 0 | 0.200 | 10.250 |
| Economic | 16.700 | 13.520 | 38.120 | 64.480 |
| **Honduras** | | | | |
| Military | 8.938 | 31.275 | 20.300 | 41.000 |
| Economic | 36.100 | 78.090 | 58.770 | 83.200 |
| **Nicaragua** | | | | |
| Military | 0.004 | 0 | 0 | 0 |
| Economic | 59.600 | 6.150 | 0.330 | 0.350 |
| **Panama** | | | | |
| Military | 0.383 | 5.401 | 5.450 | 5.500 |
| Economic | 10.500 | 13.060 | 12.340 | 13.320 |

*approved to date **requested by the Administration
Nicaragua's economic aid figures for 1983 and 1984 represent funds allocated to the world Food Program
Source State Department

Figure 1 *The liberal American press (The New York Times, 6 March 1983) managing the culture's contents: here, the Barbarian from the South, burning our borders.*

and Goths, or the Asian and African peoples who involved the centre of the empire in their religions and trade? The only thing that was definitely disappearing was the Roman, just as today it is Liberal Man that is endangered, that English-speaking entrepreneur who had found his primitive epic in *Robinson Crusoe* and his Virgil in Max Weber.

The American middle-level executive in his suburban home is still impersonating the Roman of ancient virtues, while his son is letting his hair grow, wearing a Mexican poncho, playing the Indian sitar, reading Buddhist texts or Leninist pamphlets, and often successfully harmonizing (as happened in the Late Empire) Hermann Hesse, astrology, alchemy, Mao's thought, drugs and the techniques of urban guerrilla warfare. On the other hand, even this Roman throwback would play at wife-swapping in moments of boredom, thereby threatening the fabric of the Puritan family.

Ensconced in a large corporation (a great system on the downgrade), our latter-day Roman is already experiencing the total decentralization and crisis of the central power (or powers) reduced to a fiction (as the Empire by now was) and to a system of increasingly abstract principles. One does not have to be a sociologist to recognize the extent to which government decisions in our society are already mere formalities with respect to the seemingly peripheral decisions made in large economic centres, which not by chance are setting up their own private CIAs, even employing the forces of the public one, and their own universities, tailored to turn out particularly efficient graduates, with a view to the collapse of the Central Training Office. How absolutely independent the policy of the Pentagon or FBI can be from that of the White House is confirmed daily by our newspapers.

## The Vietnamization of Territory

In this play of private interests that manage themselves and succeed in maintaining compromises and mutual checks and balances, served by private and hired police forces, and with their own multi-towered storage and defence centres, we are witnessing what Furio Colombo[1] calls a progressive Vietnamization of territories, patrolled by new bands of mercenaries. When you land in New York on a TWA flight, you enter an absolutely private world, a self-contained cathedral that has nothing to do with the International Arrivals terminal. Everything depends on the flying feudal lord to whom you give your allegiance, and the *missi dominici* (who are also invested with the power of ideological condemnation and absolution) will lift excommunications for some and apply them all the more dogmatically for others.

One does not have to go to America to notice how the outer aspect of a bank lobby in Milan or Turin has changed, and to measure, in trying to enter the State Radio and Television building, the system of checkpoints, run by internal

[1] Furio Colombo et al., *Documenti su il nuovo medioevo* (Milan: Bompiani, 1973).

police, that one must pass through before being allowed to set foot in a castle more fortified than others. In Italy, the example of the fortification and pre-militarization of factories is one of daily experience. At this point, the cop on the beat is both useful and not; he confirms the symbolic presence of power, which some-times can become the actual secular arm, but often the internal mercenary forces are enough. When, however, the heretical fortification (think of the State University in Milan, its campus a free territory endowed with *de facto* privileges) becomes embarrassing, the central power intervenes to re-establish the authority of the Image of the State; but when the Milan School of Architecture turned itself into a citadel, the central power moved in only after feudal lords of various extraction – industries, newspapers, municipal Christian Democrats – had decided that the enemy citadel should be wiped out. Only then did the central power realize, or pre-tend to believe, that the situation had been illegal for years, and indicted the faculty council. So long as the pressure of larger feudal lords had not become unbear-able, this little fief of aberrant Templars, or that monastery of dissolute monks, was left to govern itself by its own rules and fasts, or by its own licentiousness.[2]

An Italian geographer, Giuseppe Sacco, developed in 1971 the theme of the medievalization of the city. A number of minorities who refuse to be integrated set themselves up as clans, and each clan picks a neighbourhood that becomes its – often inaccessible – stronghold (this is the medieval "contrada", as Sacco,

---

[2] Students protest because classrooms are overcrowded and the instruction too authoritarian. The teachers would like to organise the work in seminars with their pupils, but the police intervene; five students are killed in a clash (1200 A.D.). A reform is launched granting autonomy to teachers and students; the chancellor will not be allowed to deny a teaching certificate to a candidate supported by six teachers (1215 A.D.). The chancellor of Notre Dame bans the works of Aristotle. Students, protesting exorbitant prices, invade and demolish an inn. The provost of police intervenes with a company of archers and wounds some passers-by. Groups of students arrive from the adjoining streets and attack the forces of law and order, ripping up the pavement and hurling the stones. The provost of police orders his men to charge; three students are killed. General strike at the university, the building is barricaded, and a delegation is sent to the government. Students and teachers disperse towards outlying universities. After lengthy negotiations, the King establishes a law regulating low-cost student lodgings and sets up university residences and mess halls (March 1229). The mendicant orders occupy three out of twelve faculty chairs. Revolt of the lay teachers, who accuse them of constituting a baronial mafia (1252). The following year violence explodes between students and police, lay teachers abstain from classes out of solidarity, while the lecturers from the regular orders continue to hold their classes (1253). The university comes into conflict with the pope, who upholds the teachers of the regular orders, until finally Alexander IV is obliged to grant the right to strike if the decision is taken by a two-thirds majority of the faculty assembly. Some teachers reject the concessions and are fired: Guillaume de Saint-Amour, Eudes de Douai, Chrétien de Beauvais and Nicolas de Bar-sur-Aube are put on trial. The dismissed teachers publish a white paper entitled *The Peril of Recent Times*, but the book is condemned as "iniquitous, criminal, and execrable" by a bull of 1256 (see Gilette Ziegler, *Le Défi de la Sorbonne*, Paris: Julliard, 1969).

who teaches in Siena where the word is still used, calls it). The well-to-do classes also revert to the clan spirit by pursuing the myth of nature and withdrawing to the suburbs, a garden quarter with autonomous shopping precincts, thereby giving rise to other kinds of microsocieties.

Sacco, too, takes up the theme of the Vietnamization of territories, theatres of permanent tension due to the breakdown of consensus: one of the responses of the authorities is the trend toward the decentralization of large universities (a sort of student defoliation) to avoid dangerous mass concentrations. Within this framework of permanent civil war, governed by the clash of opposed minorities and without a centre, cities will increasingly come to resemble what we already find in certain Latin American localities accustomed to guerrilla warfare, "where the fragmentation of the social body is aptly symbolized by the fact that the concierges of apartment houses are customarily armed with machine guns. In these same cities, public buildings in some cases look like fortresses, such as presidential palaces, which are surrounded by a sort of earthwork to protect them from bazooka attacks."

Of course, our medieval parallel must be sufficiently flexible as to be able to withstand diametrically opposed images. For while the other Middle Ages show a strict connection between a decline in population, the abandonment of the cities and famine in the countryside, difficulties in communication, deterioration of roads and Roman posting stations, and the breakdown of the central authority, today the opposite phenomenon (in relation to and despite the crisis of the central authorities) seems to be taking place: an excess of population interacts with an excess of communication and transport to make cities unliveable, not through destruction and abandonment, but through a paroxysm of activity. It is not ivy which corrodes crumbling buildings and walls, but atmospheric pollution and garbage dumped in front of every apartment building, which disfigure them and make city air minimally breathable. The city fills up with new immigrants, but is being emptied of its former inhabitants, who use it only as a place to work and then scurry home to the suburbs (increasingly fortified after the Bel Air massacre). Manhattan is on its way to being inhabited, not counting the international businessman and other stars, only by blacks and other Third World peoples, Turin by Southern Italians, while on the surrounding plains and hills rise new lordly castles, linked by rules of good neighbourliness, mutual distrust and great ceremonial get-togethers.

## Ecological Deterioration

On the other hand, the large city, which today is not invaded by warlike barbarians and devastated by fires, suffers from water shortages, power failures and traffic jams. Vacca mentions the existence of underground groups who seek to impair technological society at its roots by urging people to blow out all the power lines by simultaneously using as many electrical household appliances as possible, and by leaving the refrigerator open to cool the house. As a scientist,

Vacca notes that leaving the refrigerator open raises the temperature rather than lowering it, but pagan philosophers had much more serious objections to make against the sexual or economic theories of the early Christians. Nevertheless the problem was not of seeing whether such theories were effective, but rather of suppressing, beyond a certain limit, abstention and the refusal to co-operate. The dismissal of university teachers for refusing to take the roll call of their classes is equivalent to punishment for not sacrificing to the gods. Power fears the slackening of ceremonies and the absence of formal obeisance to institutions, in which it sees a desire to sabotage the traditional order and introduce new customs.

The Early Middle Ages are also marked by a sharp technological decline and the impoverishment of the countryside. There is a shortage of iron, and the peasant who drops his one and only sickle in the well must (as the legends testify) await the miraculous intervention of a saint to get it back; otherwise he starves to death. The fearful decline in population is reversed only after the year 1000, with the introduction of bean and lentil cultivation, highly nutritious food items without which Europe would have died of constitutional weakness (there is a positive connection between beans and cultural revival). The parallel today is the other way around: an immense technological development causes malfunctions and bottlenecks, and the expansion of the food industry turns into the production of poisonous and carcinogenic foods.

On the other hand, the consumer society at its height does not produce perfect objects, but gadgets that easily deteriorate (if you want a good knife, buy it in Africa; in the United States it breaks after being used once), and technological civilization is well on its way to becoming a society of used and useless objects. In the countryside we witness deforestation, the abandonment of cultivation, water, air and plant pollution, the disappearance of animal species, and so on. Whether beans or not, the introduction of at least some authentic elements is becoming increasingly urgent.

### Neonomadism

When we come to the fact that man today simultaneously travels to the moon, broadcasts sports events by satellite, and invents new compounds, we might note that it very well matches the other and largely unknown side of the Middle Ages straddling the two millennia, a period that has been seen as that of an early and highly important industrial revolution: in the span of three centuries stirrups, the horse collar which increases the animal's efficiency, the jointed stern rudder which allows ships to navigate by tacking against the wind, and the windmill were all invented. Strange as it may seem, one had much less chance of seeing Pavia in one's lifetime than of ending up in Santiago de Compostela or Jerusalem. Medieval Europe was criss-crossed with pilgrim routes (listed in their excellent tourist guides, which mentioned abbey churches the way motels and Hilton hotels are mentioned today), just as our skies are criss-crossed by airline routes that make it easier to go from Rome to New York than from Spoleto to Rome.

Someone might object that the semi-nomadic society of the Middle Ages was one in which travel was uncertain; to leave on a journey meant making one's will (think of the departure of the old man Anne Vercos in *L'Annonce faite à Marie* by Claudel), and to travel meant to run into bandits, gangs of vagabonds and wild beasts. But the notion of the modern journey as a masterpiece of comfort and safety came to grief some time ago, and to board a jet by passing through the various electronic devices and body searches whose purpose is to prevent hijacking restores that old feeling of adventurous insecurity, one that is presumably destined to increase.

## Insecuritas

"Insecurity" is a key word. It is necessary to include this feeling within the framework of millenarian or "chiliastic" anxieties: the world is about to end, a final catastrophe will write finis to the millennium. The famous terrors of the year 1000 have now been shown to be a legend, but it has also been shown that fear of the end circulated for the whole tenth century (except that towards the close of the millennium the psychosis had already abated). As for our own times, the recurrent themes of nuclear holocaust and ecological disaster (apart from the present survey) are enough to indicate strong apocalyptic currents. As a Utopian corrective, there was then the idea of the *renovatio imperii;* today there is the sufficiently flexible one of "revolution", both with real and solid goals that have not always worked out according to plan (the Empire was not to be renewed, but there would be a rebirth of cities and towns and the national monarchies would exercise some control over insecurity). But insecurity is not only historical, it is also psychological, and is part of the relationship between man and landscape, man and society. Man used to wander in the woods at night, seeing them populated by evil spirits; he did not easily venture outside settled areas, and usually went armed. This is a condition being approached today by the inhabitant of New York, who worries about setting foot in Central Park after dusk or is afraid to take a subway that might let him off by mistake in Harlem; nor does he ride the subway alone after midnight, or even earlier in the case of a woman. Meanwhile, if everywhere the forces of law and order are beginning to suppress crime by indiscriminate massacres of the innocent and guilty, the practice of revolutionary bank robbery and the kidnapping of ambassadors is being established, just as a cardinal and his entourage might be captured by some Robin Hood and exchanged for a couple of his Merry Men sentenced to the gallows or the torture rack. As a final touch to this picture of collective insecurity, there is the fact that now as then – and as a departure from the practice established by modern liberal states – war is no longer declared (except perhaps when the conflict is over, as in the case of India and Pakistan), and one never knows if one's country is in a state of belligerency or not. For the rest, one has only to go to Leghorn, Verona or Malta to realize that troops of the Empire are stationed in various national territories as a permanent garrison, and there are multilingual armies whose commanders are constantly tempted to use this force to wage war (or dictate policy) on their own.


## Vagantes

Through these broad areas in the grip of insecurity wander adventurers, mystics and bands of the dispossessed. Apart from the fact that with the general crisis of the universities, students, when equipped with individual scholarships, have reconstituted themselves as *vagantes* in order to seek out transient teachers, while rejecting their own "natural instructors", we have seen on the one hand bands of hippies – actual mendicant orders – living on public charity in their search for mystical happiness (whether drugs or divine grace makes little difference, since various non-Christian religions peep from the folds of chemical bliss). Local populations have not accepted them and have persecuted them, and once he has been kicked out of all the youth hostels the flower child writes that he has found perfect happiness. As in the Middle Ages, the borderline between the mystic and the cut-throat is often minimal, and Charles Manson is nothing but a monk who, like his predecessors, had gone too far in Satanic rites. (On the other hand, even when men of power give offence to the legitimate government, it involves them, as it did Philip the Fair for the Knights Templars, in homosexual scandal.) Mystical excitation and diabolical rites are very close, and Gilles de Rais, burned alive for having devoured too many children, was the comrade-in-arms of Joan of Arc, a warrior as charismatic as Che. Other types, similar to those in the mendicant orders, gravitate in another key to political groups, and the moralism of the Union of Marxist–Leninists has monastic roots, with its summons to poverty, austerity of behaviour and the "service of the people".

If the parallels seem haphazard, think of the enormous difference, under the apparent covering of religion, between contemplative and lazy monks, who within the walls of the monastery pulled out all the stops – active and populist Franciscans, doctrinaire and intransigent Dominicans, but all of them in their different ways deliberately withdrawing from the current social context, which they despised as decadent, diabolical, the source of neurosis and "alienation". These societies of renovators, divided between furious practical activity in the service of the dispossessed and violent theological debate, are torn to pieces by mutual imputations of heresy and a constant volley of excommunications. Every group creates its own dissidents and its own heresiarchs, and the attacks that Dominicans and Franciscans directed at each other are not unlike those indulged in by Trotskyites and Stalinists. Nor is this the indication, facetiously underscored, of an aimless disorder; on the contrary, it is the indication of a society in which new forces are seeking new images of collective life and discovering that they cannot impose them except through a struggle against established "systems", by exercising conscious and rigorous intolerance on both the theoretical and practical levels.

## Auctoritas

There is one aspect of medieval civilization that our secular, enlightened and liberal outlook has led us, because of an excess of necessary controversy, to distort and misjudge, and this is the practice of having recourse to *auctoritas*. The medieval scholar is always pretending to have invented nothing and constantly quotes some previous authority. It may be the Fathers of the Eastern Church, it may be Saint Augustine, it may be Aristotle or the Holy Scriptures or scholars from barely a century before, but one must never put forward something new without making it seem to have been already said by someone in the past. If we stop to think about it, this is exactly the opposite of what will take place from Descartes to our own century, in which the philosopher or scientist who is worth anything at all is precisely the one who contributes something new (and the same, ever since Romanticism and perhaps as early as Mannerism, goes for the artist). Not medieval man, who does just the opposite. Thus medieval cultural discourse seems to an outsider to be an endless, undifferentiated monologue, since all are committed to the use of the same language, the same quotations, the same arguments, the same vocabulary, and it appears to the outside listener that the same thing is always being said, exactly as happens if one attends a student gathering or reads the newspapers of radical splinter groups or the writings of the cultural revolution.

Actually the student of medieval matters is able to recognize fundamental differences, just as the politician of today navigates with aplomb by singling out differences and deviations from one speaker to the next, while knowing how to classify each according to his alignment. The fact is that medieval man knew very well that one can do as one likes by the use of *auctoritas*: "Authority has a wax nose that can be twisted any way you like", says Alain de Lille in the twelfth century. But even before him Bernard de Chartres had said: "We are like dwarfs on the shoulders of giants." The giants are the undeniable authorities, so much more lucid and far-seeing than ourselves; but we, small as we are, can see even farther when we stand on them. There was thus an awareness of originality and progress, but the originality was required to rest on a cultural *corpus* that ensured unquestionable convictions on one side and a common language on the other. This was not simply – even if it often became – dogmatism, but constituted the way by which medieval man reacted to the disorder and cultural extravagance of the Late Empire, and to the crucible of ideas, religions, promises and languages from the Hellenistic world, in which each found himself alone with his store of knowledge. The first thing to do was to reconstruct a set of themes, a rhetoric, and a common vocabulary by which to recognize one another, otherwise there could no longer be any possibility of communication or (more important) of throwing open a bridge between intellectuals and the people – something that, unlike the Greek and Roman intellectual, medieval man did, paternalistically and in his own way.

Now the attitude of political youth groups today is exactly of the same kind, and represents a reaction against the extravagance of Romantic and idealist originality, and the pluralism of liberal outlooks, which are seen as ideological disguises intended to conceal, under the patina of varying opinions and methods, the massive reality of economic domination. The search for sacred texts (be they Marx or Mao, Guevara or Rosa Luxemburg) has first of all this function: to re-establish a basis for common discourse, a body of recognizable authorities on which to initiate a play of differences and proposals for conflict. All this with an entirely medieval humility, just the opposite of the Renaissance, bourgeois, and modern spirit; the personality of the speaker no longer matters, and the proposal does not have to pass as an individual discovery, but as the fruit of a collective decision, always and strictly anonymous. Thus an assembled meeting unfolds like a *quaestio disputata*, which gave the outsider the impression of a monotonous and Byzantine game, while in it not only the great problems of man's fate were being debated, but also questions concerning property, the distribution of wealth, relations with the ruler, and the nature of terrestrial bodies in motion or of motionless celestial bodies.

## Forms of Thought

Now for a shift in scene (in terms of today), but without budging an inch as far as the medieval parallel is concerned: if we were to make a circuit of university lecture halls in the 1970s, we would find Chomsky grammatically splitting our utterances into atomic elements that then branch into two, or Jakobson reducing phonological emissions to binary principles, or Lévi-Strauss structuring kinship and the fabric of myth in sets of antinomies, or Roland Barthes reading Balzac, Sade and Ignatius of Loyola the way medieval man read Virgil, pursuing opposite and symmetrical illusions. Nothing is closer to the medieval intellectual game than structuralist logic, just as nothing is closer to it, after all, than the formalism of logic, physics and contemporary mathematics. That in the same old territory one can find parallels with the dialectical debate of politicians or the mathematical descriptions of science should come as no surprise, if only because we are comparing a current reality with a condensed model, but what we have in both cases are two ways of confronting reality that do not have satisfactory parallels in modern bourgeois culture, while both derive from a plan for reconstitution in the presence of a world whose official image has been lost or rejected.

The politician reasons subtly, basing himself on authority, in order to establish a developing praxis on theoretical foundations; the scientist tries to restore form, through classifications and distinctions, to a cultural universe exploded (like the Graeco-Roman one) by too much originality and the conflict-ridden convergence of too many diverse factors: East and West, magic, religion and law, poetry, medicine or physics. It is a matter of showing the existence of abscissas of thought that make it possible to regroup moderns and primitives under the sign of the same logic. The formalist excesses and anti-historical tendency of structuralism are the same as in the debates of medieval scholastics, just as the pragmatic eagerness for change of revolutionaries, who were then called reformers or heretics *tout court*, has to (and had to) be based on furious theoretical diatribes, and every theoretical nuance involves a different praxis. Even the debate between St Bernard, advocate of a terse and severe art without images, and the Abbé Suger, champion of a sumptuous cathedral swarming with figurative messages, finds its counterpart, at various levels and in various ways, in the conflict between Soviet Constructivism and Socialist Realism, between abstract and neo-baroque painters, and between strict theorists of conceptual communication and MacLuhanite partisans of the global village of visual communication.

## Art as Bricolage

When we go on, however, to cultural and artistic parallels, the panorama becomes much more complex. On the one hand, we have a fairly close correspondence between two periods that in different ways, with equal educational Utopias and with their paternalistic plans for directing people's minds likewise ideologically disguised, try to fill the gap between high and low culture by means of visual communication. Both are periods in which a chosen elite argues over written texts with an alphabetical mentality, and then translates into images the essential data of knowledge and the structures conveying the ruling ideology. The Middle Ages constitute a civilization of vision, in which the cathedral is the great stone book, as well as the advertising poster, the television screen and the mystical comic strip that must tell and explain everything: the peoples of the earth, arts and crafts, the days of the year, the seasons of sowing and harvest, the mysteries of faith, anecdotes of sacred and profane history, and the lives of the saints (great role models, like today's singers and film stars, an elite without political power perhaps, but with enormous charismatic power).

Alongside this massive enterprise of popular culture runs the operation of composition and collage that high culture carries out on the debris of the past. Take a magic box by Cornell or Arman, a collage by Ernst, a useless machine by Munari or Tinguely, and you are back in a landscape that has nothing to do with Raphael or Canova but has much in common with medieval aesthetic taste. In poetry there are centos and riddles, Irish kennings, acrostics, and verbal textures of multiple quotations that remind one of Pound and Sanguineti; there are the mad etymological games of Virgil of Bigorre, and Isidore of Seville, which go so far as to suggest Joyce (as Joyce himself knew), the temporal exercises in composition from treatises on poetics, which seem like a programme for Godard, and above all the taste for collections and inventories.

This took concrete form at the time in the treasures of rulers and cathedrals, whose indiscriminate collections might include a thorn from the crown of Jesus, an egg found inside another egg, a unicorn's horn, St Joseph's engagement ring, and the skull of St John at the age of twelve [sic].[3]

A total lack of distinction between aesthetic and mechanical objects held sway (an automaton in the shape of a rooster, artistically embossed, was presented to Charlemagne by Harun al-Rashid, a kinetic jewel if ever there was one), and there was no difference between a "created" object and a curio, and no distinction between craftsmanship and artistry, between a "multiple" and an individual example, and especially between a lucky find (the Art Nouveau lamp, the whale's tooth) and a work of art. All this governed by a shrill sense of colour and of light as a physical element of pleasure, and it makes no difference if then it was necessary to have gold vessels inlaid with topazes placed to reflect the sun's rays as refracted by a stained-glass window, and now it is the multi-media orgy of some Electric Circus, with strobe lighting and shimmering, watery Polaroid projections.

Huizinga has said that in order to understand medieval aesthetic taste one should think of the type of reaction experienced by an astonished bourgeois in looking at a curious and precious object. Huizinga was thinking in terms of post-Romantic aesthetic sensibility; today we would find that this type of reaction is the same as that felt by a youth towards a poster representing a dinosaur or a motorcyle, or towards a transistorized magic box in which bands of light rotate, something halfway between the small technological model and the promise of science-fiction, with elements of barbaric goldsmith's work.

Like the medieval, ours is a non-systematic but additive and composite art. Today, as then, the refined elitist experiment coexists with the great enterprise of popularization (the relationship between illuminated manuscript and cathedral is the same as that between the Museum of Modern Art and Hollywood), with reciprocal and uninterrupted exchanges and borrowings. And the apparent Byzantinism, the mad taste for collecting, listing, assembling and amassing different things is due to the need to take to pieces and reconsider what is left of a previous, perhaps harmonious, but now obsolete world, to be experienced, as Sanguineti would say, as a stinking swamp that has somehow

---

[3] *Objects contained in the treasure of Charles IV of Bohemia:* the skull of St Adalbert, the sword of St Stephen, a thorn from the crown of Jesus, pieces of the Cross, tablecloth from the Last Supper, one of St Margaret's teeth, a piece of bone from St Vitalis, one of St Sophia's ribs, the chin of St Eobanus, a whale rib, an elephant tusk, Moses' rod, clothing of the Virgin. *Objects from the treasure of the Duc de Berry:* a stuffed elephant, a basilisk, manna found in the desert, a unicorn horn, a coconut, St Joseph's engagement ring. *Description of an exhibition of Pop Art and Nouveau Réalisme:* disembowelled doll from which protrude the heads of other dolls, a pair of glasses with eyes painted on them, cross inset with Coca-Cola bottles and a lamp at the centre, multiple portrait of Marilyn Monroe, blow-up of Dick Tracy comic strip, electric chair, ping-pong table with plaster-of-Paris balls, compressed car parts, motorcyclist's helmet decorated with oil paint, electric battery in bronze on pedestal, box containing bottle caps, vertical table with plate, knife, packages of Gitanes and shower hanging over an oil landscape.

been crossed and forgotten. While Fellini and Antonioni attempt their Infernos and Pasolini his Decamerons (and Ronconi's *Orlando* is not at all a Renaissance spectacle but a medieval mystery play performed in the street for the common people), others, thinking themselves invested with an intellectual mandate, try desperately to save the old culture, and they accumulate the encyclopaedias, digests and electronic stores of information on which Vacca has been counting to transmit to posterity a treasure of knowledge that threatens to be dissolved in nuclear catastrophe.

## The Monasteries

Nothing more resembles a monastery (lost in the countryside, walled, surrounded by alien and barbarian hordes, and inhabited by monks who have no contact with the outside world and pursue their own private researches) than an American university campus. Sometimes the ruler summons one of these monks and makes him his adviser, sending him on a mission to Cathay, and he moves from the cloister to secular life imperturbably, becoming a man of power and seeking to govern the world with the same ascetic perfection with which he collected Greek manuscripts. He may be called Gerbert of Aurillac or Kissinger, Bernard of Clairvaux or Brzezinski; he may be a man of peace or a man of war (like Eisenhower, who wins battles and then retires to a monastery, becoming president of a university, only to return to serve the Empire when the crowd calls him forth as a charismatic hero).

But it is doubtful that it will be up to these monastic centres to record, preserve and transmit the heritage of past culture, even by means of complicated electronic devices (as Vacca suggests) that can restore it a little at a time, encouraging its reconstruction without ever revealing all its innermost secrets. The other Middle Ages produced in the end a Renaissance that amused itself by indulging in archaeology, but actually the Middle Ages did not carry out a systematic plan of preservation but an operation of casual destruction and disorderly preservation: essential manuscripts were lost and utterly ludicrous ones saved; wonderful poems were obliterated so that riddles or prayers could be written over them; sacred texts were falsified by interpolating passages, and in so doing the Middle Ages wrote their "own" books. It was a period that invented municipal society while knowing very little about the Greek *polis;* it arrived in China expecting to find people with only one foot or with their mouths on their stomachs; and it may have reached America before Columbus by using the astronomy of Ptolemy and the geography of Eratosthenes.

## The Permanent Transition

It has been said that this new Middle Ages of ours will be a period of "permanent transition", for which new methods of adaptation will have to be adopted. It will be less a problem of scientifically preserving the past than of exploring possibilities for turning disorder to account by entering into the logic of conflict. A culture of continual readaptation, nourished by Utopia, will be born – is already being born. This is how medieval man invented the university, with the same impartiality with which today's wandering scholars are destroying or, if you like, transforming it. In their own way, the Middle Ages preserved the heritage of the past, not by hibernation but by constant retranslation and reuse. It was an immense operation of bricolage, balanced above nostalgia, hope and despair.

Under an appearance of immobility and dogmatism, it was, paradoxically, a time of "cultural revolution". The whole process was, of course, marked by plagues and massacres, intolerance and death. No one says that the new Middle Ages offer an exactly cheerful prospect. As the Chinese used to say when they wished to curse someone: "May you live in an interesting age."

MARSHALL BLONSKY

# Endword
## Americans on the Move: a Dossier

### *In Salute to Laurie Anderson*

In the New York boardroom of BBDO International, a $2.4 billion advertising agency, I sat in March 1979 with Lewis Pringle, now Executive vice-president and I uttered some theory about his firm's practice. BBDO had and has for years guided the corporate and product images of General Electric. Pringle asked, "What can semiotics say about–" . . . and we watched BBDO's latest commercial for GE, a domesticated duel between Mr Universe, all opulent muscles, and "Ellen Walsh" – around forty and thereby, in today's mythology, without body. The voice-over: "Ellen Walsh has more muscle in one finger than Mr Universe has in his whole body." And all that followed occurred on a split screen – the primitive work on the left, the same work technologized, elevated on the right; the system of household work, chopping, crushing, washing, drying, warming, cooling; Mr Universe using the hand and arm, Ellen Walsh using only the finger (see figure 1). To press, to turn.

There he is peeling potatoes while she reads a book in bed (see figure 2). The covers are over her stomach. Underneath she wears a nightgown. Very well protected, her body. She is, as we say, "comfy", whereas he, as she reads, has drawn "KP", that lowest of culinary acts – to peel potatoes. She goes to bed alone – and look at her smile: what a pleasure! – *while he is humiliated.* Why? Because of his maleness. And why does she sleep alone? To be maleless. His skin had glistened all along, his breasts neatly separated ("cut", as body builders call it) – pectorals, abdominals, biceps neat and pure, sensuously there. The Male Image-repertoire.

I, talking: "He provokes by skin and muscle – then *revokes* by his excess." It was a life-encrypting commercial. Female life kept safe, sealed in a box – the tiniest house or apartment. Merely kitchen and bedroom. The Image-repertoire of the safe house, I explained.

What had BBDO wrought? A powerful image of pleasure, for it united three ideas: mastery over property, the stability of the home and the comfort of

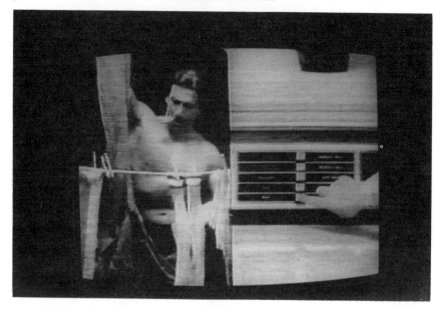

Figure 1

Figure 2

technology. It is almost sleep time, the house is safe, the lamp is lit. Here is extraordinary ego reinforcement, the unconscious and its drive muffled. This is an Imaginary, a model for solitary living in the Pleasureland of America *fin de siècle*.

Pringle was attracted, fascinated, worried whether semiotics was a science – my assertions could not be empirically tested, he said. He brought me to Allen Rosenshine, now Chief Executive Officer of BBDO. A similar analysis.

Pringle was attracted: an applied semiotics had described a communication act as ruled by a system of signification, had given more order to a parcel of empirical data. He was also concerned: what degree of scientificity had these rules? Unlike *evidently* grammatical systems commercial discourse seemed to him to be a "twilight zone", its phenomena relatively unstable. Working in this field, a specific semiotics would be deprived of the power to construct reliable theoretic objects. It could never claim the status of a natural science: in the last analysis, it could make only some predictions about the behaviour of this or that planned communicational act.

A fragment of the commercial world had grasped that semiotics was at most a human science; such a notion still is controversial. And so, governed by the natural sciences model, institutional attention waned. Freud described the modalizing power of not being recognized: it made him doubt his speculations. The encounter with commercial life made me doubt that the advertising institution had understood, or that I had understood its signs in the first place.

In February 1984, in the BBDO house organ, Rosenshine published an article, "The Image of . . ." I had nothing to do with it. Here is an extract:

> Too often we hear – and ask – "Are we talking about the product, or are we doing imagery?" It's the wrong question. Everything is imagery. . . . We don't really remember the facts, the figures, the classic copy-points of the strategy. What we do get is a net impression, a sense of what the brand is about. This is what we call imagery. . . . Every brand creates through its advertising a brand imagery which in a very real sense is the consumer's only perception of the brand. The brand image, above all else, is the brand reality. . . .
>
> Let me suggest an example taken from a very famous and often-talked-about advertising campaign, the Mercedes-Benz "long-copy" approach. It was called "long-copy" because the agency literally packed the page, and often a two-page spread, with copy, copy and more copy. This is not to say that the ads weren't attractive. They were beautifully laid out with draftsman's diagrams, exploded views, all surrounded with words punctuated by automotive jargon. When you glanced at a Mercedes-Benz ad, you saw an engineering treatise. So where's the imagery? That *is* the imagery. It didn't matter whether you read a single word of the copy. You got a net impression just from seeing the ad, for even a few seconds, that Mercedes-Benz was state-of-the-art, a marvel of automotive design, a car so replete with quality that it took all those words and drawings to get it said. . . .

[We are] devoting a great deal of time, effort and money to developing research methodology that identifies, quantifies and communicates the parameters of performance and user imagery in advertising.

Belief is being exhausted. To reattract it, conventional business has been telling its consumers/employees its "philosophy", "values", "credos". Rosenshine is signalling the end of such ideology – and a substitution of the image and of a nascent semiotics of the Imaginary. We can better understand his idea through a comment by the designer Massimo Vignelli:

The image in our time – its expressive plane as well as its content – has to deploy pleasure to the point of euphoria. An example is our recent project of creating an identity program for the IBM personal computer. Notwithstanding the personal in its name, the PC is an entity felt by many to be hostile. How, therefore, to valorize the personal? We arrived at the soft pastels, colors not taken into consideration in the seventies. We settled on a light blue, a foam green, a rose – lingerie coloration – for the surfaces of the PC software "library". Being a library, its different entities were to have the appearance of books – precious ones. Each was given a binding of cloth and made to fit into a cloth slipcase. We sought to create a soft love affair with these surfaces and finally with the centerpiece of our technology, that bland box whose outer shell seems to be keeping in reserve some unknowable machination and meaning. In the decay of the Book Age, at the end of the era of the Logos, aware of the irony of it, we fashioned the content of this image from the Book.

The message is: "We are not going to argue with you – henceforth we are going to captivate you." Advertisements, even print, and everything commodified, will be produced to be splendidly seen, not read.

Here, another entry in this dossier, is Charles King, for many years a creative director at Grey Advertising, telling me of the Cola-Coffee Wars:

In the 1950's the great cultural beverage in America was coffee. The secret slogan of the culture was "Father Knows Best."

Coffee sales peaked in 1962. At that point the colas began to challenge coffee for the young adults market with another slogan: "Think young." Over the past twenty years, they have spent hundreds of millions of dollars playing the Eden Tape. Quick cuts of Adam and Eve running into the surf. Instead of eating apples they're drinking colas.

"It's the Pepsi Generation, comin' at you, goin' strong. Put yourself behind a Pepsi. If you're livin', you belong."

The commercial they never did:

OPEN ON A YOUNG ADULT COUPLE AT RESTAURANT TABLE.

BOY: I'll have coffee.

GIRL: I'll have coffee, too . . . wait, change that to a cola.

BOY: Cola? Instead of coffee?

GIRL: Sure. Colas are cool, refreshing. They go great with food.

BOY: You're right. From now on, it's cola for me.

No, you never saw a commercial like that. Because it would have started an argument in your mind. Which *is* better? Cola? Or coffee?

Instead, they used unarguable, low-definition signs.

The signs he is talking of correspond, in fact, to the category, the image, the Imaginary. And the image, a "net impression", *is* reality to its spectator. BBDO's Rosenshine is saying that people's knowledge of reality, or the real as we like to say, will henceforth be an illusory condition of their comprehension of/captivation by images. He has internalized the lesson we learned in the Introduction of this volume: signs do not give access to things but we forget this. This is why the designer/advertising celebrity George Lois wrote:

> As a professional designer and creator of advertising I have a nagging respect for semiotics – not because of its dissection of "lies," but because of its emphasis on sign, symbol and myth, the hard stuff of mass communication – and, indeed, of high art. That's why I've always been entranced by Picasso's startling observation that "Art is the lie that tells the truth" – especially relevant to advertising.
>
> Getting down to cases, in our market-wise culture almost all products happen to be comparable in quality (or, in the jargon of marketing, America is a land of "parity products"). Except for the first years of Xerox, when advertising for a duplicating process spawned what I like to describe as "The Xerox Culture," I have never worked on a product that was significantly better than its competitors – except, possibly, a politician.
>
> Therefore, when advertising is *great* advertising, it fastens on the myths, signs and symbols of our common experience and becomes, quite literally, a benefit of the product. Picasso's cherished "lie" thus becomes the truth. As a result of great advertising, food tastes better, clothes feel snugger, cars ride smoother. The stuff of semiotics becomes the magic of advertising. ("An Ad Is the Lie that Tells the Truth", *The Market Stops To Think* (ed. M. Blonsky), forthcoming)

We learn from Lois and the other sample entries here that the Establishment has been asystematically teaching itself codes which have no responsibility *vis-à-vis* history or the test of the real. On the other hand, the consumer is knowingly buying the illusion of signs – "prestige" with Eco's bestseller, "power" with a business suit, "knowledge" with a magazine or newspaper. The Establishment controls the entire code, the citizen lives with and as fragmented signs and images, like Humpty Dumpty, unable to ever put himself together again.

Here, at perhaps the extreme of Establishment power to theorize, is John Loring, Design Director of Tiffany & Company. I present a final text of commercial semiotics – Loring telling how he brings the New Yorker through the looking glass of Tiffany:

Today's pedestrian is given over to hurrying. He wants to get from one place to another as quickly as possible. It's as if he were propelled by some unknown whose message were: "You must get from here to there as quickly as you can. Don't waste time. Don't waste time." You may have nothing to do but don't waste time.

With this increase of tempo since the twenties and thirties, this neurotic compulsion to move quickly, the crowd has geared itself up to such a point that you can't draw people into a store with the twenties and thirties technique of making the window go out to the sidewalk. People have no time to be impeded in their "walk." They can only cast their eyes sideways, glimpse what you're showing, as they hurry by.

At Tiffany we're limited to two tiny windows for each of the two streets – Fifth Avenue and 57th Street – that we abut. Our windows therefore *must* be more violent in their effects, more arresting than windows of former time. At all costs must the window stop the propulsion, take you out of yourself, make you disappear – you and your daily problems, everything – in your involvement with it.

Look at a particular window designed for us by Gene Moore – who is the foremost window designer of our day. Gene placed a doll in the window that was four stories high in comparison to the people working on it (figure 3). He presents an abrupt shift of scale, exhilarating to the

Figure 3

passer-by who has had to walk in front of Tiffany daunted by a gigantic piece of stone towering above him.

However, the shift isn't stable. Gene is imagining a child's relation to its doll: as the child to its doll, so the doll to something even smaller: Gene has begun a regress. A child, frequently probably, thinks it would be wonderful to switch the relationship, the doll becoming enormous. Look at the dolls of F.A.O. Schwarz, up the street. Schwarz has made dolls so big now that the child frequently is not larger than the doll. Some dolls are absurdly large, eight feet, nine: that doll could lose you! They put in play, and we did too, the fantasy of shrinking – there's something thrilling about it. Disappearing.

The most troubling of our recent windows was that doll being served. She's not a simple country girl; rather, slightly menacing, a rather violent figure. Some pins stick in her, sharp edges, spikes; and the stance and the gesture are abrupt, brittle, commanding.

The marketplace once was bazaar, arcade. Gene Moore and others have changed the entire look and effect of windows all over the world. Once, the arguing, the jostling of which Benjamin wrote. Now, in New York, on the street, the private experience produced by our windows, and others'. You scarcely want someone next to you to share it. Personally, I love nothing more than the bazaars of North Africa, to spend days arguing over pieces of merchandise. Unhappily, that is not the logic of New York, or contemporary capitalism. ("Through the Looking Glass of Tiffany", in *The Market Stops To Think*)

You have been reading an uncodified semiotics, nevertheless a theory of the Imaginary. You have been reading Loring tell of the fading self, all too susceptible to images of itself as missing – having lost – something. One then makes an image of deconstitution – sticks pins in the doll, makes her attendants seem to be shrinking to the point of disappearance. As if by a blow, the passer-by is stopped, drawn to the window. The image of loss substituted for the rush-around. A logic of destination had governed that rush – "I have to *get* there" effacing where I am. Loring believes that this logic impoverishes sensation in urban life – an impoverishment replaced, at least at Fifth Avenue and 57th Street, by a string of quieted, but not necessarily feelingful selves.

Read de Certeau again (p. 122). See the photographs. The child, the acrobatic man, the embracing old men, seem to be attempting to make solemn, image-struck space and frenzied, "euphoric" space into a ludic environment. Theirs perhaps is an extreme of affect for the recipient of late capitalist sign and image.

# Notes on Contributors

**Roland Barthes** (1915–80) was considered by many to be a founder of French and modern semiotics, a master at tracking and penetrating everyday life, the most insistent of all that nothing is natural, that everything is discourse. Although he proclaimed his sadness that he never wrote fiction, he was regarded by many as the greatest writer in Europe, a novelist whose characters were intellectual and emotional categories. At the time of his accidental death, he was a professor at the Collège de France. Many of his occasional texts remain unpublished.

**Michel de Certeau** is a dominant figure in rectifying the formalist tendencies of semiotics. Historian, anthropologist, psychoanalytic theorist by training, he has integrated into semiotics the epistemology of historiography, the history of ideas and cultural anthropology. His field work includes research into occult and popular culture in Latin America. De Certeau is Directeur d'Études at the École des Hautes Études en Sciences Sociales, Paris, and Professor at University of California, San Diego. Recent books are *La Fable mystique* (Paris: Gallimard, 1982) and *L'Invention du quotidien* (Paris: 10/18 1980; forthcoming from the University of California Press as *The Practice of Everday Life*).

**Guido Crepax,** one of Italy's foremost cartoonists, created the famous strip and heroine Valentina. After Valentina he designed other women ("always women," say his friends – "an erotomaniac," say his critics): Terry, Bianca, Anita, O, Emanuelle, Justine. One of the founders of the Italian magazine *Linus,* he has designed school books, adventure books, the newspaper *Tempo Medico* and other popular formats. He is the author of *Charles Darwin, Francis Drake, The Man of Harlem* and *The Man of Pstov,* among other books.

**Daniel Dayan,** formerly research assistant to Roland Barthes, introduced the concept of film enunciation to the American public through a series of articles and lectures in the mid-1970s. A principal in the Hebrew University/ Annenberg School of Communications Media Event Project (see also under Elihu Katz), he followed Pope John-Paul II on his visits to Poland, Mexico, etc., "running the risk of becoming either a theological enterprise or a travel agency". His team of scholars/interviewers "wished his Holiness to stop for a while to allow us some writing and rest". Dayan is the author of *Western Graffiti* (Paris: Clancier-Guenaud, 1983) and is collaborating with Elihu Katz on a forthcoming book devoted to television ceremonies.

**Jacques Derrida** is perhaps best known for correcting a postulate of linguistics which subordinates all language to its spoken form and ties speech to the person, to the will to possess and the passion to assign a unitary structure, a profound meaning to the contradictory play of human appearances. Derrida is widely studied for his researches into the density and complexity of signifying substance – its irreducibility to simple meaning. His *Of Grammatology* (Baltimore, Md: Johns Hopkins University Press, 1974), as well as other works, constitute a corrective motif applied to the simplistic tendencies of semiotics. Derrida is Professeur d'art at the École des Hautes Études en Sciences Sociales in Paris, and co-founder of the Collège International de Philosophie.

**Edmundo Desnoes** is a novelist and specialist in the effect of First-World media on their consumers – First and Third World alike. From 1966 to 1969 he was an editor and communications specialist in the Comisión de Orientación Revolucionari in Havana, and thereafter until 1973 taught at the Escuela de Diseño Industrial e Informacional in Havana. In 1974 *Memories of Underdevelopment*, based on his novel and scripted by him, was selected by *The New York Times* as one of the ten best films of the year. He is the author of several books – written from a semiotic perspective – on the function of images in society.

**Umberto Eco** proceeds in his activities along three different paths: the rigorous academic work represented by such books as *Theory of Semiotics* (Bloomington, Ind.; Indiana University Press, 1976) and *Semiotics and the Philosophy of Language* (Bloomington, Ind., Indiana University Press, 1984); the narrative activity represented by *The Name of the Rose*; and an exploration of everday phenomena, semiotics applied to everyday life through articles in *L'Espresso* and other popular magazines. Eco is Professor of Semiotics at the University of Bologna and a frequent Visiting Professor at Columbia University.

**Michel Foucault** (1926–84) was a major critic of semiotics, expanding it to encompass not only the meanings of discourse but its actions as well. Whether he studied psychiatry, penology, philosophy or literature, Foucault developed methods for understanding masses of documents, entire discourses – thereby reasoning his way into the collective mind of the periods he studied. At the time of his death, studying early Christian sexual documents, he was attempting to understand what he called the genealogy of modern self. He was a professor at the Collège de France.

**Jean Franco,** a writer of mass culture, was, in 1984, an investigator in El Salvador and Nicaragua on behalf of the Faculty for Human Rights in El Salvador and Central America. Director of the Institute of Iberian and Latin American Studies at Columbia University, she is the author of *César Vallejo* (Cambridge: Cambridge University Press) and *The Modern Culture of Latin America* (Harmondsworth, Middx.: Penguin Books). She is founder and contributing editor of the journal *Tabloid.*

**Milton Glaser,** one of the foremost designers in the United States and Europe, is a specialist in the effects of signs on their consumers. He is responsible for the design of numerous publications including *L'Europeo, L'Express* and *Esquire.* His work ranges from magazine and book design and illustration to the redesign of supermarket chains, restaurants and educational play parks. His most recent personal book is *The Conversation* with Jean-Michel Folon (New York: Crown, 1984).

**Wlad Godzich** is a theoretician attempting to articulate the imperceptible links between the semiotic revolution, or mutation, and the culture at large. In his writing and many interviews, he is seeking to insure that, as semiotics constitutes itself, it does not become overburdened with conceptions and notions borrowed from its own past and from its predecessors. Godzich is Professor of Comparative Literature at the Université de Montréal, editor of *The Yale Critics* (Minneapolis, Minn.: University of Minnesota Press, 1983) and author of the forthcoming *Essay in Prosaics.*

**A. J. Greimas** is regarded as one of the most rigorous theoreticians of semiotics, a specialist in constituting semiotics on a scientific basis. Accompanying his researches into narrative grammar are analyses of a diverse group of social phenomena from urbanism to juridical discourse to ethnic literature. He is Directeur d'Études at the École des Hautes Études en Sciences Sociales, a member of the semio-linguistic research group. His many books include *Maupassant* (Paris: Seuil, 1976) and *Sémiotique* (Paris: Hachette, 1979, translated and published by Indiana University Press at Bloomington, 1983) – his dictionary of the key words of semiotics.

**Geoffrey Hartman,** a distinguished historian of criticism, has tried in his writing to talk about the historical, affective milieu from which texts arise and to which they contribute. In such books as *Criticism in the Wilderness* (New Haven, Conn.: Yale University Press), he has sought to bridge the considerable gap between continental and Anglo-American modes of criticism. He is Chairman of Comparative Literature at Yale University. His latest book is *Saving the Text* (Baltimore, Md: Johns Hopkins Press, 1981).

**Vjačeslav Vsevolodovič Ivanov** is a leader in the Moscow-Tartu school of semiotics, which is rooted in the Russian tradition of formal and structural studies, and which applies structural method to myth and ritual, literature and culture as a whole. Ivanov is Director of the Section on Structural Typology of the Institute of Slavic and Balkan Studies, Soviet Academy of Sciences, Moscow. He is a specialist in Indo-European and Slavic linguistics, poetics and mythology. Recent publications, still untranslated, include *Essays on the History of Semiotics in the USSR* (1976) and *Indo-European and the Indo-Europeans* (with T. Gamkrelidze, 1984).

**Roman Jakobson** (1896–1982) was one of the founders of the Moscow and Prague Linguistic Circles and a dominant figure in twentieth-century linguistics, poetics and semiotics. Throughout his long career he emphasized the ties between sound and meaning and the necessity of studying the poetic function of language, a function by no means limited to poetry, but expressed as well in slogans, jingles, children's rhymes, etc. Over 300 of Jakobson's articles and monographs are included in the 17-volume edition of his *Selected Writings* (1962–84). His most recent books are *Dialogues* (with Krystyna Pomorska, 1982), *Russian and Slavic Grammar: Studies, 1931–1981* (1984) and *Verbal Art, Verbal Sign, Verbal Time* (1984).

**Fredric Jameson** is a specialist in the use of semiotics to recast Marxist theory as an instrument capable of understanding today's late capitalism in relation to current discourses such as literature, film, television, architecture and semiotics itself. Jameson teaches in the Literature and History of Consciousness programme at the University of California, Santa Cruz. His recent books include *Fables of Aggression* (Berkeley, Calif.: University of California, 1979) and *The Political Unconscious* (Ithaca: Cornell University Press, 1981).

**Elihu Katz** has for several years been welding semiotics with sociology, literally following contemporary media events from the Pope's visit to Poland to Sadat's arrival in Jerusalem. Collaborating with Daniel Dayan, Katz has been using interview as well as direct analysis to reveal the Event as narrative and as mechanism for the governance of populations. Apart from his well-known sociological contributions, Katz is the author with Dayan of a forthcoming case book and theory of media events. He is Professor of Sociology and Communications at the Hebrew University of Jerusalem and at the Annenberg School of Communications, University of Southern California.

**Matthew Klein** is a leading photographer of still lifes – specializing in food – and of people. He uses semiotics to construct images, which have appeared on the covers of *Time, Esquire, Saturday Review, Psychology Today, New York* magazine, *Discover* and others. He taught photography from 1969 to 1979 at the Parsons School of Design in New York.

**Jan Kott** is internationally known as a leading scholar of theatrical signs. He remarks that from his early years he was under the spell of Russian formalism – later, the semiotics of Roland Barthes and Mikhail Bakhtin. He is a retired Professor of English and Comparative Literature at the State University of New York at Stony Brook. At present he lectures in Europe. In English he is the author of *Shakespeare Our Contemporary* (New York: Doubleday). His latest book is *The Theater of Essence and other Essays* (Evanston, IU.: Northwestern University Press, 1984).

**Julia Kristeva** is associated with the maturation of semiotics from its language-dependent, systematizing origins to its newer concern with the speaking agent's body and unconscious revealed through extreme states of artistry and psychosis. A practising psychoanalyst in Paris, Kristeva has recently specialized in the topic of narcissism and abjection. Her many books include *Powers of Horror* (New York: Columbia University Press, 1982) and *Desire in Language* (Oxford: Basil Blackwell, 1981). She teaches at the University of Paris VII.

**Jacques Lacan** (1901–81) critiqued Saussurian semiotics which takes the sign as its object but cannot seize in its entirety the signifier – whose workings, said Lacan, exceed the consciousness of sign users. The largest quantity of Lacan's texts – including the texts presented in this volume – are transcriptions of the spoken lectures that Lacan called his Seminars. In his slow and deliberate speech, Lacan offered himself in the process of making theory, speaking intentionally to be difficult. "What I say is dedicated to the unconscious." He also announced, on French television: "what is enunciated well is conceived clearly – clearly means that it makes its way", it is "bought" by a public – but at the price of stupidity. Lacan's texts are, of course, available in French through Seuil and in English through W. W. Norton. His controversial affiliations, and disaffections, are widely known.

**Louis Marin** perhaps more than any scholar developed methods for tracking the narrator-encunciator in discourses seemingly as diverse as painting, historio-graphy, autobiography, fabulation, evangelical writing, narrative fiction and urbanism. His many books, most untranslated, include *Le Récit est un piège* (Paris: Minuit, 1978) and *Sémiotique de la passion* (Paris: Aubier Montaigne, 1971). Marin teaches at the École des Hautes Études en Sciences Sociales in the History and Theory of Art Circle.

**Susan Meiselas** experienced war for the first time during the Nicaraguan revolution. Her photographic coverage of this warfare was published in Europe, Asia, the USA and Latin America in such magazines and newspapers as *The New York Times, Epoca, Time, Geo* and *The Sunday Times* (London). She received the Robert Capa Gold Medal for this work in 1979. Her photographic books include *Carnival Strippers* (New York: Farrar, Straus & Giroux, 1976) and *Nicaragua* (New York: Pantheon, 1981).

**Christian Metz** has for twenty years been a major force – widely discussed – in the application of semiotic theory to film and image studies. His classic film-books include *Langage et cinéma* (Paris: Larousse, 1971; published in English as *Language and Cinema*, The Hague: Mouton, 1974) and *Essais sur la signification au cinéma* (Paris: Klincksieck, 1971; vol. 1 published in English as *Film Language*, Oxford: Oxford University Press, 1974). In 1979 he turned his attention to the analysis of wit and jokes, broadening semiotics to include psychoanalytic theory. Metz lectures internationally and teaches at the École des Hautes Études en Sciences Sociales in the Interdisciplinary Centre for Sociology, Anthropology and Semiology.

**Robert Scholes** founded the semiotic programme at Brown University, Rhode Island, at a time in the 1970s when semiotics was an intruder in America. Now a department, Semiotics has for a number of years been inserting sign-sentitive men and women into the American superstructure in professions such as law, advertising and journalism. Scholes' recent books are *Semiotics and Interpretation* (New Haven, Conn.: Yale University Press) and *Textual Power* (New Haven, Conn.: Yale University Press). He is chairman of the English Department at Brown University.

**Thomas Sebeok** is a leader in promoting the development of an American version of semiotics that is able to play a part in United States cultural and governmental life. A specialist in zoosemiotics, linguistics, mythology and folklore, he is responsible for the many semiotic publications of Indiana University Press, as well as Mouton's many semiotic undertakings. Sebeok's recent books include *The Play of Musement* (Bloomington, Ind.: University of Indiana Press, 1981) and editorship (with Umberto Eco) of *The Sign of Three* (Bloomington, Ind.: University of Indiana Press, 1983).

**Ronald Weintraub** was owner and president of Flexnit Company when he wrote the article in this volume. As an entrepreneur of a medium-sized company, he was open to new marketing approaches and thus reached out to semiotics. Flexnit was sold to Consolidated Foods Corporation and in 1984 Weintraub served as president of Bali Company into which Flexnit was merged. He is now a consultant to Consolidated Foods and a private investor.

# Acknowledgements

All the articles in this volume are original contributions destined for this anthology or appear here in English translation for the first time – a single exception being an article retranslated from the French for this volume. The editor thanks the following, who have granted permission to reproduce copyright material or have shown special courtesy to this large and complex undertaking:

Mobil Oil Company/Steve Gold Productions (for courtesy in supplying frames from "The Misunderstood Elephant: A Fable For Now", pp. xxiv, xxv, xxvi).

Chris Harris/Gamma-Liaison (Ronald Reagan, p. xxix).

Douglas Kirkland/Sygma (Christie Brinkley, p. xxx).

The New York Times/Bill Cunningham ("In Fashion. . ." article, p. xxxii).

UPI/Bettmann (President Reagan and Donald Duck, p. xli).

Umberto Eco (for his generosity in contributing both original writings and re-editing prior work as follows: "Strategies of Lying", p. 3, translated by John Shepley and Barbara Spackman; "Casablanca, or the Clichés Are Having a Ball", p. 35, translated by John Shepley from "Casablanca, o la rinascita degli dei", in Umberto Eco, Dalla periferia del'impero, Milan, Bompiani, 1977; "How Culture Conditions the Colours We See", p. 157; "Producing Signs", p. 176; "A Portrait of the Elder as a Young Pliny: How to Build Fame", p. 289; and "Towards a New Middle Ages", p. 488, translated by John Shepley and Barbara Spackman from "Verso un Nuovo Medioevo", in Eco, Dalla periferia dell'impero, revised for this volume by the author).

AP/Wide World (Richard Nixon, pp. 9, 10).

Edmundo Desnoes (for his generosity in contributing the original commission of "Will you ever shave your beard?", p. 12, as well as the other original commissions contributed to this volume, "The Death System", p. 39, and "Cuba Made Me So", p. 384).

The John and Mary R. Markle Foundation for their generous assistance to "Electronic Ceremonies", p. 16.

BBC Copyright Photographs (Royal Family, p. 18, Royal Child, fig. 2, p. 19, Royal Couple "Just Married", p. 20, whistle-blower, p. 21, BBC TV interviewer, p. 27).

Patrick Ward/Telegraph Sunday Magazine-Woodfin Camp (balloon vendor, fig. 3, p. 19).

Leif Skoogfors/Woodfin Camp (Union Jack faces, fig. 5, p. 21, crowd with periscopes, p. 23, Pseudo-Royal Couple, p. 31).

AP/Wide World (Trafalgar Square fountain dancers, p. 22; wedding dress, p. 30).

Kim Sayer/Impact-Woodfin Camp (crowd, p. 24).

Playboy France (Roland Barthes, "The Shape I'm In", p. 33, translated by Matthew Ward and Richard Howard from March 1980 interview).

Susan Meiselas (for the amplitude of her original contributions to the "Portfolio on Central America", pp. 43–53).

Franco Maria Ricci (Roland Barthes, "I Hear and I Obey. . .", p. 54, translated by Matthew Ward and Richard Howard from "J'écoute et j'obéis . . .", L'Histoire d'O, Milan, 1975).

Grove Press (Guido Crepax, 'From the Story of O', captions translated by Richard Miller, p. 56, from L'Histoire d'O).

Hermann (Roland Barthes, "Reading Brillat-Savarin", p. 61, translated by Matthew Ward and Richard Howard from "Lecture de Brillat-Savarin", introduction to Brillat-Savarin: Physiologie du goût, Paris, 1975).

Jan Kott (for his generosity in contributing the original essay, "The Infarct", p. 76, and Michael Kott and Ann Murphy for their translation).

Routledge & Kegan Paul (Roland Barthes, "Textual Analysis of a Tale of Poe", p. 84, retranslated by Matthew Ward and Richard Howard from the original "Analyse textuelle d'un conte d'Edgar Poe", in Sémiotique narrative et textuelle, ed. C. Chabrol, Paris, Larousse, 1973, appearing in a different translation in Untying the Text, ed. R. Young, London, Routledge & Kegan Paul, 1981).

Le Nouvel Observateur (Roland Barthes, "Day by Day with Roland Barthes", p. 98, translated by Richard Howard from "La chronique de Roland Barthes", Le Nouvel Observateur, Paris, 18 December 1978–1 April 1979; Roland Barthes, "How to Spend a Week in Paris: 8–14 October 1979", p. 118, translated by Matthew Ward and Richard Howard from Le Nouvel Observateur, n. 778).

Michel de Certeau (for his generosity in contributing the following:"Practices of Space", p. 122, translated by Richard Miller and Edward Schneider from "Marches dans la ville", in de Certeau, L'Invention du quotidien, 1. Arts de faire, Paris, 10/18, 1980, transformed by the author for this volume and including the original contribution, "Passers-By", p. 131, translated by Richard Miller; "The

Jabbering of Social Life", p. 146, translated by Richard Miller and Edward Schneider from "Croire/Faire Croire", in de Certeau, *L'invention du quotidien*; "What We Do When We Believe", p. 192, translated by Richard Miller from "Croire: une pratique de la différence", Documents de Travail, Centro Internazionale di Semiotica e di Linguistica, n. 106, settembre 1981; "The Indian Long March", p. 404, translated by Richard Miller from "La longue marche indienne", *Le Monde Diplomatique*.

The World Trade Center, New York (for courtesy in supplying the promotional cover illustrated on p. 123).

Richard Kalvar/Magnum (for the amplitude of his original photographic contributions, p. 125, figs. 2 and 3, p. 126, fig. 8, p. 134, p. 135, p. 145).

Raymond Depardon/Magnum (fig. 5, p. 132, fig. 7, p. 134, fig. 10, p. 138, fig. 11, p. 140).

Gilles Peress/Magnum (fig. 6, p. 133).

La Quinzaine littéraire (Roland Barthes, "Barthes to the Third Power", p. 189, translated by Matthew Ward and Richard Howard from "Barthes puissance trois", La Quinzaine littéraire, Paris, 1–15 March 1975).

Richard Miller and Edward Schneider (for translating Roman Jakobson, "Dear Claude, Cher Maître", p. 184). And for permission to reproduce masks, Editions Skira, Geneva, and the Museum of Anthropology, University of British Columbia, Vancouver, and Johsel Namkung.

Éditions du Seuil and Jacques-Alain Miller (Jacques Lacan, "Sign, Symbol, Imaginary", p. 203, translated by Stuart Schneiderman from "Radiophonie", Paris, *Scilicet* 2/3, 1970 and *Le Séminaire II: Le moi dans la théorie de Freud et dans la technique de la psychanalyse*, ed. J.-A. Miller, Paris, 1978).

Vjačeslav Vsevolodovič Ivanov ("Eisenstein's Montage of Hieroglyphic Signs", p. 221, a fragment from the unpublished manuscript entitled *Eisenstein and Modern Semiotics*, translated by Stephen Rudy).

The Department of Film of the Museum of Modern Art, New York, and Eileen Bowser (for lending the Museum's rare print of *October* to enable the illustrations to appear on pp. 227–32).

Jacques Derrida/The University of Chicago Press ("To Speculate – on 'Freud'", p. 236, translated by Alan Bass from "Spéculer – Sur 'Freud'", in Derrida, *La Carte Postale*, Paris, Aubier-Flammarion, 1980).

Christian Metz (for his generosity in contributing the original "Instant Self-Contradiction", p. 259, a chapter from his forthcoming book on jokes and wit – with an original ending written for this anthology, translated by Richard Miller and Edward Schneider).

Louis Marin (for his generosity in contributing "Writing History with the Sun King: the Traps of Narrative", translated by Richard Miller and Edward Schneider from *Le récit est un piège*, Paris, Minuit, 1978, with an original introduction written for this anthology by the author; also for contributing "The 'Aesop' Fable-Animal", translated by Richard Miller and Edward Schneider.

Roman Jakobson (who, when he lived, provided "Supraconscious Turgenev", p. 303, translated by Stephen Rudy from "Zaumnyj Turgenev", in Jakobson, *Selected Writings*, vol. III: "Poetry of Grammar and Grammar of Poetry", The Hague, Mouton, 1981).

A. J. Greimas (for permitting the transcription of his 1976 seminar for the graduate students of the Columbia University Romance Languages Department, "The Love-Life of the Hippopotamus", p. 341, translated by Richard Miller and Edward Schneider).

The New York Institute for the Humanities/Richard Sennett and Patrick Merla (for contributing the 20 November, 1980 Michel Foucault James Lecture, "Sexuality and Solitude", p. 365).

Wlad Godzich ("The Semiotics of Semiotics", p. 421, copyright © Wlad Godzich 1985).

*The New York Times* ("What's the Real Message of 'Casablanca'? Or of a Rose?", pp. 424–5).

Peter Angelo Simon (Mr Universe photographs, p. 506).

# Index